The Making of
Contemporary Africa

Third Edition

The Making of Contemporary Africa

The Development of African Society since 1800

Bill Freund

LYNNE
RIENNER
PUBLISHERS

BOULDER

First published in the United States of America in 2016 by
Lynne Rienner Publishers, Inc.
1800 30th Street, Boulder, Colorado 80301
www.rienner.com

First published in the United Kingdom by
Palgrave, an imprint of Macmillan Publishers Limited,
4 Crinan Street, London N1 9XW

Library of Congress Cataloging-in-Publication Data
Names: Freund, Bill, author.
Title: The making of contemporary Africa : the development of African
    society since 1800 / by Bill Freund.
Description: 3rd edition. | Boulder, Colorado : Lynne Rienner Publishers, Inc., 2016. |
    Includes bibliographical references and index.
Identifiers: LCCN 2016017142 | ISBN 9781626375765 (pbk.: alk. paper)
Subjects: LCSH: Africa—History—19th century. | Africa—History—20th
    century. | Africa—Economic conditions. | Africa—Social conditions. |
    Economic development—Africa—History. | Social change—Africa—History.
Classification: LCC DT28.F73 2016 | DDC 960/.23—dc23
LC record available at https://lccn.loc.gov/2016017142

Printed and bound in Hong Kong. This book is printed on paper suitable for recycling
and made from fully managed and sustained forest sources. Logging, pulping, and
manufacturing processes are expected to conform to the environmental regulations
of the country of origin.

Printed in China

Contents

List of Illustrations and Tables

Figures

Maps

Tables

List of Abbreviations

This list includes abbreviations used in the Notes to Chapters and the Annotated Bibliography. It does not include abbreviations used in the main text which are defined at the first mention.

AA	–	African Affairs
AB	–	Africana Bulletin
AEHR	–	African Economic History Review
AHS	–	African Historical Studies
BIFAN	–	Bulletin de l'Institut Fondamentale d'Afrique Noire
CEA	–	Cahiers d'études africaines
CJAS	–	Canadian Journal of African Studies
CSSH	–	Comparative Studies in Society and History
EAPH	–	East African Publishing House
EHA	–	Etudes d'histoire africaine.
EHR	–	Economic History Review
HJ	–	Historical Journal
HWJ	–	History Workshop Journal
IJAHS	–	International Journal of African Historical Studies
IRSH	–	International Review of Social History
JAH	–	Journal of African History
JAS	–	Journal of the African Society
JBS	–	Journal of British Studies
JDS	–	Journal of Development Studies
JHSN	–	Journal of the Historical Society of Nigeria
JICH	–	Journal of Imperial and Commonwealth History
JMAS	–	Journal of Modern African Studies
JSAS	–	Journal of South African Studies
KHR	–	Kenya Historical Review
MERIP	–	Middle East Research and Information Project
RH	–	Rhodesian History
RLIJ	–	Rhodes-Livingstone Institute Journal
ROAPE	–	Review of African Political Economy
SS	–	Science and Society
THSG	–	Transactions of the Historical Society of Ghana

Acknowledgements

The chief debt I owe for this third edition of *The Making of Contemporary Africa* is to the hospitality of Trinity College, Cambridge, which provided me with a very convenient, comfortable and carefree base to update my readings and my understandings of the history of the African continent in the final term of 2014. At Trinity, I was always grateful for the company and observations of John Lonsdale, who will I hope like this new version of a book he clearly enjoyed long ago in its first incarnation. As the Dutch say, *Lang zal hij leven!* Long may he live! I also have to thank Tim Gibbs as my entrée to Trinity although his last days there before heading off to University College, London just coincided with my first. As chapter readers for the new material, I made use of two friends, David Moore and Luise White, and I am grateful for their patience. Others will find that I have used their ideas picked up in their books, articles, talks and conversations. The literature relevant to this book has increased so dramatically that I also would like to excuse myself to those authors whose works I did not locate. I also must thank the anonymous readers of the manuscript that Palgrave Macmillan selected. This book has enjoyed a life of over thirty years which delights me, and I hope this edition will attract a new generation of readers.

The manuscript of this book was completed early in 2016 and inevitably contemporary history keeps becoming more contemporary, so readers in future will find some material outdated. Hopefully though, ideas have a longer shelf-life!

1

Africanist History and the History of Africa

Africans have been conceptualising their lives and social relationships historically since the advent of agriculture and stockherding gave importance to
questions of origin, genealogy and property long centuries ago. As state
mechanisms and social contradictions evolved in many parts of the continent, historical interpretation became increasingly formalised in the hands of
specialists. Informal traditions frequently survived in a masked form reflecting
subversive interpretations and societal conflicts. The issues that mattered to
such historians, the lineage of kings, the point of origins of peoples, the coming
of an ecological disaster or a political defeat, stemmed from prevailing material and social conditions. Although presented as objective truth, the tales of
praise-singers, diviners and court officials were actually ideological in purpose.
They represented the appropriation of social knowledge by particular groups
for particular ends.

In much of Africa historical knowledge was conveyed purely by word of
mouth in poetic, musical and dramatic settings. However, in some regions,
such as the Ethiopian highlands, the East African coast and the West African
savannah, the spread of literacy created the possibility of written history as well.
The chronicles of Ethiopian monks and Timbuktu scholars were not simply
royal commission work: they expressed the outlook of the class of men who
wrote them, a class whose worldview was closely linked to specific traditions of
Christian and Islamic knowledge.

However valuable these forms of knowledge transmission were, it is also
important to keep in mind that they hardly represent a simple objective truth
that can be accepted as such. They must be seen as discourses coming from
particular contexts and repeating them is insufficient if, as in this sort of
book, one is trying to look beyond that context. The distinguished historian
of Asante, Tom McCaskie, writes that 'plainly and surely, historical work and
other forms of scholarship about Africa should be about the recuperation and
explication of African views of African pasts and presents'.[1] However, having
done the recuperation, on what basis, we have to ask, do we do the explication?
McCaskie himself has written very astutely about recent Ghanaian politics, it
should be pointed out, without any methodological innovations that mark the
recuperation out from conventional practice.

Let us take the example of slavery in Madagascar based on the work of two recent studies by anthropologists. On the west coast of Madagascar, Sakalava kings once ruled. It is possible for possessed individuals to recall these kings and their families as *trombas*, who come back from the dead, make various demands, receive favours and gifts and interact with one another. However, as Michael Lambek writes, 'Sakalava history is not identical to the history of the Sakalava, neither to what happened in the past nor to what Sakalava represent as having happened, though it is shaped by both of those.'[2] Documentation reveals that among the Sakalava, rulers embraced and discarded Islam in a way that does not appear in these enthralling tales of reincarnations. Moreover, the real power of the Sakalava kings of Boina derived from their delivery of slaves both inland and to Europeans. A surviving document, for instance, shows the alliance established between such a king and a slave trader from New York City in the eighteenth century. Tsiminato lit fires along the coast to attract the ship to his harbour. Lambek says that the history emerging from *tromba* activity should be called historicity; it has a real cultural import and validity for Malagasy people but there is far more for historians to do than capture this historicity for outsiders. Another anthropologist, Sandra Evers, working in an area on the far south end of the great central plateau of this huge island, was surprised to find absolutely no discussion of slavery and emancipation amongst villagers she studied. However, her informants distinguished between the settlers who had proper tombs and lineages and others who were in some respects pariahs. The deeper she dug into stories, however, the more she came to realise that the respectable settlers were themselves the descendants of slaves from a slightly earlier time who had a certain success in legitimising their origins and hiding what was not desirable to recall. These writers give one a sense of the challenge facing those who try to make sense of stories of 'tradition' without losing respect for the kind of purposeful validity that they do have. Nobody has done more to promote the study of oral tradition in Africa than Jan Vansina. Yet on considering the rubber atrocities of the Congo Free State period in an area where he was collecting tradition, Vansina writes that: 'No account of those events appeared in the [Kuba] dynastic traditions. The rulers who had benefited from the system were not about to commit this to official memory.'[3] Whether indigenous or foreign, black or white, male or female, historians of Africa are inevitably outsiders who struggle with varying kinds of material to tell the story that they think is important.

With the conquest and partition of Africa by the European powers and its forcible incorporation into a world system of exchange based on capitalist production, the possibility of an autonomous development of intellectual activity in Africa was cut off as surely as the guillotine severs a head from a body. The praise-singers continued to chant, but what they had to say ceased to have the same relevance. The colonial masters of Africa took a keen interest in the territories they ruled, of course. They were as concerned as any African king had been to appropriate knowledge about Africa for the purpose of effective administration and the promotion of capitalist enterprise. Much of this knowledge was historical; quantities of historical material were amassed and collected in colonial archives and libraries. However, the colonial period produced very little in the way of overtly historical publications. The dominant colonial science was anthropology. From the time of Sir Harry Johnston, writing in 1899, it was a full half-century before a European again wrote a general history of Africa. What most interested Europeans in Africa was themselves: a history of trade and diplomacy, invasion and conquest, heavily infused with assumptions about racial superiority that buttressed colonial domination. For the period following conquest, colonial writing focused on the progress of administrative structures, transport networks and business enterprise in a heroic spirit. Yet it was in the colonial context that for the first time 'Africa' as an entity from the Cape to Cairo, from the coastal lagoons of the West to the Horn of the East, could be conceived. Attached to this concept there could be as well specialists, continental experts, 'Africanists'.

There are certain exceptions to this generalisation that deserve notice. First, in some parts of Africa, notably South Africa, imperialism brought in its wake large and internally complex settler communities, sections of which began to produce their own histories. The intellectual thrust of Afrikaner nationalism in South Africa was marked first by the publication of an anti-imperialist history of the country in the Afrikaans language. Jan Christiaan Smuts epitomised the antagonisms between the settlers of the South African Republic and the major imperialist power, Britain, in a famous pamphlet on the eve of the Boer War, *A Century of Wrong*. This historiography gave little consideration to the African masses of the country; its subject was the settler community.

As an African working class in the South African cities became stronger, more developed and a potential threat to the state and to capital, historical conceptualisation bifurcated along two lines of analysis. One increasingly posed racial conflict as a central theme, celebrating a racially defined society and re-expressing imperial oppression largely in terms of foreigners meddling with the appropriate racial ground rules of the 'South African way of life'. This line continued to take as its subject the 'white' community. The other, or liberal school, generally pro-imperialist, developed the new themes of 'racial conflict and co-operation' and 'race relations' in propounding more enlightened means of managing the black masses of South Africa. Within these limits a relatively richly documented and lively historical literature arose before World War II.

Secondly, in those parts of Africa where the indigenous elite shared in some of the fruits of colonialism and were sufficiently self-conscious as a class to seek an historical view of their own, local histories and traditions were collected, sometimes with great assiduousness, and published locally. They reflected the outlook of their authors, often championing the interests of a particular pre-colonial state, ethnic entity or important family of chiefs, and were generally under the heavy influence of a Christian mission education. A famous, early and relatively accessible example is the Rev. Samuel Johnson's *History of the Yorubas*, written in Nigeria before the turn of the twentieth century. Another would be *Bassekabaka ba Buganda*, The *Kabakas* of Buganda, by the Ugandan Sir Apolo Kagwa who served as the chief minister of this indirect ruler, the *kabaka*, in the early twentieth century. In many parts of Africa such histories came virtually to displace earlier oral traditions in popular knowledge. Perhaps it would be accurate to call them indigenous; however, in later phases to imagine that Africans have by virtue of their Africanness an indigenous mindset is incredible: inevitably influences from many places are part of their way of thinking and they do not necessarily stand out in their historical approaches.

One of these influences came from a particular part of the West. Intellectuals of African origin, both West Indian and North American, became fascinated by their ancestral continent, whose rescue from obloquy and oblivion in the eyes of their enemies ranked high on their own programme of national liberation. Like the colonial writers, they conceived of Africa as a whole, but their outlook was pan-African and closely tied to their own nationalist reaction to American and West Indian society. Unlike the colonial writers, they stressed an historical perspective, romanticising a grandiose African past and condemning its colonial present. A distinguished scholarly and sometimes stirring example in this category is *The World and Africa* by W. E. B. DuBois, an American who chose to spend his final years of a long life in independent Ghana.

In the 1940s all this changed rapidly. Under the impact of wartime pressures and a deteriorating living standard, African labour insurgency and peasant movements seriously challenged colonial strategies. Given a global perspective of growing Soviet power and more developed anti-imperialist movements in much of Asia, the West was under pressure and on the defensive. As a result, Britain, France and then Belgium moved towards restructuring colonial relationships and devolving political authority within Africa. The 'new nations' of Africa were conceived.

Within the West itself there were strong motives for creating a framework in which African history could be studied and taught. One was the practical requirement of developing history departments in the universities founded in Africa during the late colonial period. Another was the need for a better comprehension of an insurgent Africa. Most important, though, was engagement in struggle on the ideological plane in order to capture it for a new synthesis, a new form of collaboration between Western political and economic interests on the one hand and the dominant class within the new Africa on the other hand. One important part of this synthesis was the fleshing out of 'Africanist' history, which set the stage for a distinct disciplinary study of the history of Africa in libraries everywhere in the world.

In Britain much of this development took place in the School of Oriental and African Studies in London, which Lord Curzon had once described in the planning stage as 'part of the necessary furniture of empire'. The first African history conference in Britain took place there in 1953 as the West African colonies were moving towards self-government. In the USA, academic knowledge of Africa was sparse and African studies centres were created: the first at Northwestern University with Carnegie money in 1948; the second at Boston University in 1953 with Ford money. Others soon followed and attracted scholars from the old colonial powers. In France the first professorships in African history were funded in 1960, the same year as French West and French Equatorial Africa were dismantled and accorded independence. Such institutions could be the base, not merely of historians of Africa, but of 'Africanists' who interpreted

'Africa' both to the West and to the African intelligentsia itself. As the introduction to the published papers of an important conference in 1961 began:

> Every self-conscious nation looks back upon its past to revive former glories, to discover its origins, to relate its history to that of other parts of the world and to arrive at a knowledge of the development of its political, social, economic and other systems.[4]

What is a self-conscious nation? What are its glories? What relations to the rest of the world are relevant? All of these questions tended to be side-stepped in Africanist writing.

In general the new synthesis aimed at flattering nationalist sensibilities. Again and again, 'Africans' were programmatically placed to the fore without the issue ever being raised of which Africans or why. An overwhelmingly foreign group of scholars felt confident that they could express the 'African point of view'. The new writing was heavily dependent on material already available through colonial amateur history writing, travelogues, local histories, ethnographies and collected traditions, but it received a new ideological impetus through its central tenet: that Africans had a history. This could be pitted repeatedly against the racist and anti-historical synthesis of the colonial point of view which reflected, as it had created, 'common wisdom' about Africa in the West. Each subject in the history of Africa was reinterpreted (to borrow the words of Terence Ranger) in terms of 'African activity, African adaptation, African choice, African initiative', whether it was the slave trade, peasant cash crop economies, the formation of states or religious change: 'a straight line of initiative from human evolution at Olduvai to the modern period'.[5]

The Africanists' most indisputable achievements lay in the study of pre-colonial Africa. Here there was a welter of unsubstantiated but densely woven preconceptions in existing sources on the primacy of foreign contacts and foreign invaders which have gradually been sifted out and corrected in the name of an Afrocentric approach. Moreover, there has been a tremendous advance in the accumulation of evidence and information. Indeed, for many Africanists, despite their frequent insistence that they were addressing relevant current issues, pre-colonial history *was* African history.

This approach contained fundamental limitations. The most significant was the reification or foregrounding of *method*, defined as the technical collection and sifting of data, as opposed to *content*. This has created a

> mystique of method, conceived as the application of ever more refined techniques to ever larger quantities of facts, which is one of the means by which the social sciences – including history – cover up their theoretical impoverishment and contradictions.[6]

Secondly, the writing of much pre-colonial African history has been dependent on uncritical borrowings from the sophisticated and insightful writings in social and cultural anthropology, a field that developed with colonial domination of non-Western peoples. Anthropologists, focusing on small communities over a limited period, usually dealt with their subject peoples as residents of a 'timeless present' abstracted from history. The 'timeless present' could be extended back into the past at will and highlighted as the essentialist core of social relations whatever the twentieth century might be bringing in its wake. At the same time, anthropologists frequently underplayed or neglected material factors in the lives of their 'tribe'. Many (not all) Africanists sold a view of Africa as at bottom tribal, changeless and *essentially* unified in a spiritualised entity that defied rational penetration. Such social phenomena as slavery in Africa were thus assessed as timelessly 'African', rather than in terms of real historical categories.[7]

For Africanists the economy was a factor in society to be discussed (if it received much attention at all) separately from political or social developments. Analysis consisted of a history of trade at the expense of production, domination, sexual relations and other, more fundamental, aspects. Trade was ideologically cast as the bringer of good news and progressive change from long distances, the outside agent that made African history possible.

The essentialist cast of Africanist history was strongly enhanced by the influence of Islamic Orientalism. Orientalism combined a learned scholastic appreciation of the Islamic classics with a tradition of contempt for the people of the modern Middle East and an assumption that the categories of Islamic thought overruled any need for historical investigation of social and material change. The dead hand of the Islamicists, and their successful self-marketing to the needs of Western power politics, was dissected brilliantly by Edward Said:

> None of the innumerable Orientalist texts on Islam, including their summa, the Cambridge History of Islam, can prepare their readers for what has taken place since 1948 in Egypt, Palestine, Iraq, Syria, Lebanon or the Yemens. When the dogmas about Islam cannot serve, even for the most Panglossian Orientalist, there is recourse to an Orientalized social science jargon, to such marketable abstractions as elites, political stability, modernization and institutional wisdom, all stamped with the cachet of Oriental wisdom.[8]

The annexation of many parts of African history by the learned but self-contained, arid discourse of Islamicists with their assumption of a timeless Islamic 'civilisation' that can never really alter but only flourish or decay has had a crippling effect on serious historical study.

If Africanist history focused on an idea, it was that of state formation. It glorified state power in African empires of the past whose 'scale' steadfastly 'expanded'. These were held out self-consciously as worthy and relevant predecessors of contemporary African states replete with 'lessons' for the current ruling strata.[9] This idealist and moralist strain has in fact been fundamental to the Africanist synthesis.

More recent African history, the subject of most of this book, has also been touched by the magic wand of 'African initiative'. The subject and content of imperialism was discreetly abandoned to survivors from the older colonial school, a small academic establishment that continued to thrive, if not to grow, in the former colonial countries. Modern Africa was almost entirely interpreted in the light of the nationalist movements that came to power around 1960. Thus there is now a substantial literature on 'primary' anti-colonial resistance movements, focusing on religious and military aspects or on leadership and pointing to the more 'modern' secondary resistance that would bring about independence. The colonial period itself is usually cast in terms of a rags-to-riches saga for the African petty bourgeoisie that it engendered, the self-styled 'educated elite'. Book after book built up to the happy ending: national independence.

This very brief summary does not do justice to many variations and does not attempt to qualify the work of individuals. Africanists include men and women of profound learning. Some have drunk deeply from the Africanist well while others have remained relatively sober. Certain broad variants can be pointed out. In the USA the substitution of method for ideas has, until recently, been especially marked while the 'African initiative' message is often flashed in neon. The situation in Britain has been more complex, partly because British Africanists have perforce been less insulated from changes in the African universities and current events in Africa generally, but then colonial residues are also more significant there. In France it was difficult for long to conduct any serious examination of the colonial period in the universities, while history has been much less influential in the spectrum of African studies (truer yet for other European countries).

Within Africa itself the distinctive outlook of African historians can to some extent be delineated. Nigerians, notably the so-called Ibadan School, have until recently been overwhelmingly orientated to the study of administration, pre-colonial and colonial, and to their own class antecedents, reflecting their self-confidence as Africa's foremost bourgeoisie. In programmatic statements, they have laid especial weight on purging Nigerian history from what is still seen as too great an emphasis on foreigners. Yet African historians, including Nigerians, have always stressed material forces in history more than their mentors, as witness the work of Professors K. O. Dike or B. A. Ogot, the pioneer academic historians of British West and East Africa respectively.

West African history in general experienced a slightly earlier development than elsewhere along these lines. In East and Central Africa the shakier situation of the new ruling classes (although, once independence was achieved, far more stable politically in fact) and the potential for social revolution demanded a more protest-orientated and radical history with greater emphasis on the twentieth century. The tides of Africanist history swept at the cliffs of South Africa, but never have succeeded in establishing dominance. Typical Africanist monographs on protest and resistance, biographies of pre-colonial chiefs and an elevation of Africans as a blanket category to what Leonard Thompson (the doyen of South African liberal historians by the 1960s) called the 'forgotten factor' in southern African history, all made headway. However, it was patently impossible to explain South Africa in terms of African initiative or other Africanist techniques; too many fundamental questions were conveniently shelved thereby.

Is it true then that an 'Africanist is a specialist whom we employ to get the better of Africans?'[10] Not entirely. African history is a more complex and contradictory terrain than a simple conspiracy theory allows for. In the context in which it arose, African history (and African studies) had a radical edge to it. The founder of African studies in the USA, the cultural anthropologist Melville Herskovits, had first spent many years defending the existence and dignity of surviving aspects of African culture among New World Blacks within an intensely racist general milieu. His work, and that of many other Africanists, raised the issues of African pride, integrity and regeneration. At present this defence, with its attendant faith in what Herskovits called 'cultural tenacity', may seem romantic or even reactionary, but it cannot be dismissed as such in the context in which it arose historically. Two seminal British Africanists, Thomas Hodgkin and Basil Davidson, came to their African work from Left political commitments and an engagement in anti-colonial struggle, what Hodgkin himself called 'the radical anti-colonial tradition'.[11] Terence Ranger, nurtured in the growing environment of social history in Britain influenced by the political shift after 1945 and disgusted with what he saw of white society when he went to Southern Rhodesia to teach history, had a huge influence on British academic studies of African history and ended up as an Oxford professor.

In the 1978 synthesis, *African History*, produced by the most influential historians of Africa in the USA (Philip Curtin, Steven Feierman, Leonard Thompson and Jan Vansina), the virtues of the discipline were uncritically celebrated. The introduction began by assuring us that 'African history has come of age'! From the vantage point of the new century, however, this seems to have been a premature judgement. In fact, coming of age has hastened the destruction of the synthesis. During the 1970s the new wisdom of 'African initiative' came under increasingly effective attack, notably from Africans themselves. An examination of some relevant collections based on key conferences, *The Historian in Tropical Africa*, published in 1964, *Emerging Themes in African History*, published in 1968 and *African Studies since 1945*, published in 1976, shows an initial self-confidence, a progression of divergent views and ultimately, in the final volume, an acute sense of crisis in the field.[12]

In the middle volume, the editor, Terence Ranger, while sustaining the basic Africanist hypotheses, prophetically referred to a potential enemy who had not yet made his appearance, the 'radical pessimist'. In the mid-1960s radicals still generally followed the anti-colonial tradition of Hodgkin and Davidson, supported a nationalist line and were relatively optimistic about developments in the newly independent African states. A remarkable exception was the West Indian psychiatrist, Frantz Fanon, who saw a little of life in independent West Africa while in the service of Algeria. The result was his blistering attack on the new order in *The Wretched of the Earth*. However, it was quite some time before this was translated into historical writing.

By the end of the decade, though, dissent began to show its head in a number of directions. One of the few economic historians of Africa, C. C. Wrigley, wrote an important article criticising Africanist history for going to the extreme of celebrating the slave trade for strengthening and expanding the scale and bureaucratic sophistication of African kingdoms as part of a celebration of a long-time line of upward progress. In the radical academic atmosphere of Dar es Salaam (Tanzania) at roughly the same time, political economist John Saul wrote an important consideration of Tanzanian history writing which attacked the positivism and class bias of East African historiography. In 1973 a Kenyan historian, William Ochieng, in a controversial article, openly wondered about the celebration of the past, in particular of politically salient Kenyan tribal entities projected backward into time, so characteristic of Africanist scholarship. He proposed that historians concentrate rather on investigating the roots of underdevelopment and the oppressed conditions of the masses.[13]

The causes of dissent lay fundamentally not in the internal dialogue of scholars, but in the genuine contradictions and instability of the 'neo-colonial' social and political relations that dominate Africa. The obvious calamities which plagued African states were poverty and dependence, but underlying them were the gradual decay of the colonial economies in many areas and the increasing difficulties experienced by the ruling strata in holding the line and effectively controlling their own populations. The intensifying struggle for independence in the Portuguese colonies, which involved relatively concrete socialist goals and fighting on class as much, or more than, on national lines, highlighted related but unresolved issues everywhere on the continent. In this context, celebrating African achievement began to appear patronising, undercutting its own anti-racialist claims, as well as irrelevant.

The stage was now set for the 'radical pessimists' to enter the scene and they brought with them a powerful set of tools from elsewhere, conceptions of the 'development of underdevelopment' as part of the world process of capital accumulation which had been posed among radical South Americans and the North American Marxists Baran and Sweezy and were welded into a strong polemic by Andre Gunder Frank. Samir Amin, an Egyptian economist based in Senegal, began to bring this line of thought to African subjects and to reinterpret African history with reference to the roots of dependence and underdevelopment. In 1972 the Guyanese Walter Rodney, himself one of the most critical and far-ranging of Africanists, published *How Europe Underdeveloped Africa*. Although, as the title indicates, Rodney's polemic was continental (and by implication, radical) and he betrayed much of the influence of the earlier idealist and romantic Afro-American nationalist understanding of Africa, his book represented a powerful and effective break with the positivism of the Africanists.

During the 1970s the historiography of South Africa was rapidly transformed. At first the origins of reconsideration among writers on South Africa lay in the patent failure of liberal analysis to reflect adequately the realities of the apparently invincible apartheid state. To see capitalist development as steadily undermining the racial order, to advocate publicity for the 'African point of view' in the interests of managing better 'race relations', the stock-in-trade of South African liberals of the day, was transparently unconvincing. At the same time the failure of nationalist movements along the lines of those elsewhere on the continent to topple the regime brought a corresponding lack of nerve to Africanist interpretations of history. Historians began to penetrate the ideology of *apartheid* to search for social and economic structures and ultimately for a better comprehension of the logic of capital accumulation in South Africa.

These tendencies were intensified in the wake of renewed labour insurgency from 1971, the collapse of Portuguese colonialism in 1974 and the urban risings associated with the Johannesburg township of Soweto in 1976. A growing number of young historians (among others) searched for understanding in diverse currents: radical British social history, Marxist structuralism associated with the theoreticians Louis Althusser and Nicos Poulantzas, and labour history as well as neo-Marxist concepts of under-development. The most influential within an extensive new wave of writing have been self-consciously Marxist authors. If South Africa at the end of the 1960s appeared at the dead end of African history writing, twenty years on it appeared to be at the cutting edge.

In France the impact of underdevelopmentalism was at first felt in social sciences rather than in history. However, one major historian, Catherine Coquery-Vidrovitch, collaborated closely with Amin and directed research to bear upon the economic structures of colonial West Africa. She and other French historians have also felt the impact of the important French school of economic anthropologists who have revived the materialist analysis of pre-capitalist social formations first proposed by Marx. Some of these, notably Emmanuel Terray on this basis, began the re-examination of major themes of pre-colonial African history by questioning the nature of the dominant mode of production in African societies. There are clear indications also, from Kenya, Tanzania, Nigeria, Senegal and elsewhere, that the new generation of African intellectuals is no longer content to have ancient 'civilisations' glorified and African initiatives, of whatever stripe and regardless of content, vacuously applauded. Terence Ranger himself noted the 'widespread feeling of artificiality and distance from real issues' in Africa about Africanist history.[14]

As Marxist analysis of Africa deepened, the underdevelopmentalist hypothesis itself came under attack. The complete assimilation of African social conditions into those of Asia and Latin America as part of a deliberately, almost conspiratorially, underdeveloped 'Third World' failed to explain the immense range of variety in its patterns of economic and social life. It also obscured specific and concrete historical developments in particular areas while illuminating some widespread patterns. The affinities between underdevelopmentalism as an historical catch-all explanation and radical (but bourgeois) nationalism were numerous. In much of the writing on underdevelopment, internal social contradictions were passed over or treated superficially, while actual relations of production were subordinated to the problem of 'unequal exchange'.

There had long been a Marxist tradition of writing on Africa, stemming from the European Communist parties. Its strength lay in a resolute anti-colonialism, an interest in economic structures and an emphasis on protest and labour activity. However, it was unable and unwilling to challenge Africanist verities when couched in nationalist phraseology; and it was inept at conceptualising class relations and social change in Africa widely divergent from the European model with which writers in this tradition were familiar. After the 1920s Marxist writing was itself dominated by a crude positivism, despite the example of Marx himself, which prevented it from convincingly cutting through the Africanist paradigm. In the words of Raymond Williams:

Marxism, as then commonly understood, was weak in just the decisive area where practical criticism was strong: in its capacity to give precise and detailed and reasonably adequate accounts of actual consciousness: not just a scheme or a generalization but actual works, full of rich and significant and specific experience.[15]

From around 1970, a variety of currents from throughout the world, including the impact of Maoism, the revitalisation of Trotskyism and other directions of Marxist thought, made a revival possible. Marxist analysis suffered, however, after 1990, from the discrediting of the old Soviet Union, and its strengths tended to be labelled all too easily as part of a forgettable international politics. Even more problematic is the declining interest in economic history which was a great strength of African historiography in earlier phases where it was pursued.

If we look for trends from the late twentieth and early twenty-first centuries, it seems more possible to say now that African history has come of age. The number of scholars actively producing relevant work has greatly increased, their best work is inevitably more nuanced and also more detailed as professionalisation sets in. In the USA, a fascination with Africa has altered the teaching of African history from a specialist niche, enhanced through the lens of American racial politics, to a surprisingly popular and widespread area of interest taught in several hundred institutions by research-orientated scholars. A key early figure in the making of African historiography in the USA, Philip Curtin, himself initially a specialist on the slave trade and the West Indies, had an important influence in pursuing an Atlantic and trans-Atlantic way of looking at African history. Of course there is a significance in linking, as the Orientalists have done, trends within, north of and south of, the Sahara. Indian Ocean studies represent yet another spatial take on Africa and all of these links taking Africa at times out of Africa have legitimacy. In Europe, historical research on Africa is far more unusual as a topic for teaching and academic specialisation but there is a parallel interest in development studies, African politics and the like which forms an equivalent fount of new work. Where once large subjects were frequently a kind of gaping hole in modern knowledge, there are now apt to be several serious studies that vie for attention in taking them up. If anything the problem now is one of too many heads poring over very particular questions with too little thinking about the big picture. This is what has been lost, perhaps, compared to earlier African historiography.

The travails of African institutional life have not been good for African intellectuals participating actively from African centres, but many historians of Africa from varied bases in many countries have become more and more significant in the overall picture from wherever they can find an institutional perch. It would be very hard to take them aside and identify them as having a distinctive and recognisable single African perspective. However, certain countries, notably South Africa and Nigeria, do now have their own academic world of universities, journals and internal intellectual discussion on a notable scale.

This book, therefore, does not start with the old arguments about Africa having or lacking a history, with hypotheses about 'enlargement of scale' or balance sheets of good and bad in 'contact' with the West. It tries to adhere to the new critical tendencies emerging in Africa and elsewhere. The central themes which dominate the modern history of Africa are the penetration of capital with its relationship to political and economic imperialism and the resultant transformation of class and class struggles. The limits of transformation, the network of social forces other than class, are also fundamental. Chapters 12–14 try to consider the increasing divergence in the political fortunes of Africa based on contingent developments that are now themselves key layers on which society is being constructed. The final chapter in particular considers the dramatic social and cultural changes of the years since colonial rule came to an end. The ideas expressed there continue to try to speak to an early programmatic statement by Basil Davidson, of attempting to present 'the essential unity of the people of Africa with the peoples of the rest of the world' in a materialist context.

Notes

1. Tom McCaskie, 'Telling the Tale of Osei Bonsu', *Africa*, 84(3) (2014), 3.
2. Michael Lambek, *The Weight of the Past; Living with History in Mahajanga, Madagascar* (Palgrave Macmillan, 2002), p. 13.
3. Adam Hochschild, *King Leopold's Ghost* (Houghton Mifflin, 1998), cited on p. 300.
4. Jan Vansina, Raymond Mauny and Louis-Vincent Thomas, *The Historian in Tropical Africa* (Oxford University Press, 1964).
5. Bonaventure Swai, 'Antinomies of Local Initiative in African Historiography', Historical Association of Tanzania, pamphlet 12 (1979).
6. Henry Bernstein and Jacques Depelchin, 'The Object of African History: a Materialist Perspective', *History in Africa,* V (1978), VI (1979).
7. Frederick Cooper made this point in a review article on African slavery, *JAH,* XX (1979). New directions in anthropology there have certainly been. Anthropology was deeply afflicted by the attack on Eurocentricity discussed below which forced it to discredit its forefather. Today's anthropology, and anthropology has in its new form become a much larger field of teaching and knowledge in the USA while having largely disappeared within African scholarly circles, is too diffuse to characterise easily. As the field diversifies, it loses coherence but the excellent tradition of fieldwork continues to give it interest.
8. Edward Said, *Orientalism* (Random House, 1978), p. 109. Of course it is important to remember that getting rid of Orientalism only solves one problem of bias.
9. See, for instance, Ivor Wilks, *Asante in the Nineteenth Century* (Cambridge University Press, 1975). This was a remarkable recovery, of course, of material on what was indeed a major West African kingdom, and it told a plausible story.
10. Christopher Fyfe, ed., *African Studies since 1945* (Longman, 1976), p. 4.
11. Ibid., p. 11.
12. Vansina *et al.*; Fyfe; T. R. Ranger, (ed.), *Emerging Themes in African History*, (Heinemann, 1968).
13. C. C. Wrigley, 'Historicism in Africa: Slavery and State Formation', *AA,* LXX (279) (1970); John Saul, 'Nationalism, Socialism and Tanzanian History', in Peter Gutkind and Peter Waterman, *Africa: a Radical Reader* (Heinemann, 1977); William Ochieng, 'Undercivilization in Black Africa', *KHR,* II (1973).
14. Cited in Fyfe, p. 17.
15. Raymond Williams, *Problems in Materialism and Culture* (New Left Books, 1980), pp. 18–19.

2
Material and Cultural Development in Africa before the Nineteenth Century

'Accept the chief, fear him. May he also fear you.'
DANIEL BIEBUYCK AND KAHOMBO MATEENE, EDS, *THE MWINDO
EPIC* (UNIVERSITY OF CALIFORNIA PRESS, 1969)

Colonialists and nationalists, radicals included, have generally accepted the historical centrality of race and an identity of race, language and culture which defines the
history of Africa as a history of black people. Of course, at a practical level, most
Africans living south of the Sahara are and have been black, so the connection seems
obvious and demonstrable. Yet race, to the limited extent that it has a scientific
classificatory value at all, is purely a biological term that can only express relationships between physical characteristics. The Sahara, which has become increasingly
itself a terrain of study, never blocked human movement and was clearly at one
time, perhaps 3000 years ago, very much less of a desert. The only reason why
Africa north of the Sahara is not included in this volume is that it requires so
much additional text and knowledge that an essentially arbitrary decision has been
made in this regard. However, islands including the several island nations closest
to Africa, and the giant island of Madagascar, are covered even though most were
not settled by mainlanders. Africa is a continent, not a racial category.

Race has nothing whatsoever to do with culture or any cultural traits such
as language. Semitic languages, for example, have for many, many centuries
been spoken in Asia and Africa both by people whom we might call 'white' and
others whom we might call 'black'. Our world is so race conscious, with racial
divisions such a powerful force for antagonisms and oppression, that this fairly
obvious point is difficult to keep in mind. If the notion of a black or African
people has a justification today, it is as the result of a contemporary sensibility
and a consciousness formed within the capitalist world economy that has been
gathering strength during the past five centuries. To apply such a framework
to the more distant past, which this chapter examines, makes no sense.

Stripped of racial determinism, African history quickly loses the unity
which common prejudices, positive and negative, assume for it. There is no

foreordained African cultural oneness that has been convincingly defined that suggests otherwise. The broadest themes of African history mostly reflect continent-wide developments precisely because they are themes that belong to the basic stock of social and economic developments of mankind everywhere. The more detailed history, which belongs to another volume than this one, can best be treated on a region-by-region basis. African regions were not watertight compartments isolated from one another.

Trade goods, ideas and popular migrations long ago moved in ways which historians can reconstruct only very hazily. They were not limited by the Sahara Desert nor the oceans that surround Africa. Such interconnections, however, are not a sufficient basis for unity in our analysis. What must strike any student of Africa is, in fact, the immense variety among its peoples, cultures and institutions. Movement is something African peoples do, both now and in the distant past, as a consequence of varied pressures and because of the attractions of new resources.

Closely associated with Western racial stereotypes is the assumption in common wisdom of the historic backwardness of Africa. At one time this backwardness was defined largely morally, in terms of decadent and barbaric customs. In the commodity-laden world of the twenty-first century the term is used in general to refer to economic backwardness. Africanist historiography has placed an obsessive emphasis on reversing this perspective through haphaz-ardly celebrating the African achievement, often creating an implausibly ideal-ised and romanticised old Africa. Where does the truth actually lie?

It is undeniably the case that, in technological terms, no part of sub-Saharan Africa in recent centuries has been among the most advanced regions of our planet. Human developments, both social and technical, have proceeded most unevenly. This is true not only between continents but within Africa itself. The most developed regions in the sense of the development of complex organisational and economic forms, the West African savannahs and forests, the middle Nile valley and the Ethiopian highlands, have been the scene of class-based societies that show many parallels with the Middle East, India, China and medieval or early modern Europe. In other regions material advance has proceeded more slowly.

Only from the coarsest perspective of power politics, however, can history be reduced to a horse race. Even while accepting the centrality of material progress as an historical force, one people deserve as much respect, consideration and study as the next. Studies of the few surviving hunters and gatherers, the most technologically 'primitive' Africans, suggest that their human qualities, their ideological perspectives and their forms of aesthetic expression such as music and drawing, were in no whit 'inferior' to industrial civilisation.

Moreover, it is quite wrong to assume that Africans organised stable 'civi-lisations' or 'cultures' that suited their needs and then stagnated. The more recent centuries that precede the colonial occupation of Africa witnessed dynamic change rather than cycles of stagnation and decay, although these too can of course be found in Africa, as elsewhere. Two epochal events in the history of Africa, the Mfecane in the far south, which resulted in the first known wave of state formation in what is today South Africa, and the Islamic holy wars (jihads) which transformed society and culture in the central savannah of West Africa, both took place in the first quarter of the nineteenth century. This was late enough to allow for virtually first-hand European descriptions, but neither event has been explained very successfully through European influence or cause although this may have had an indirect impact.

Both processes represented major new developments of internal contradictions and forces. This dynamic, if increasingly influenced in the nineteenth century by the commercial expansion of Europe, was still clearly active until decisively cut off by conquest, largely in the final quarter of that century. Even then, intense external influences had to work through internal social processes and structure. The following two chapters will consider these influences; this one, in somewhat artificial isolation, is particularly concerned to recapture some facets of internal dynamism.

Hunters, gatherers and cultivators

For most of mankind's long history on the African continent, as elsewhere in the world, man was a hunter who gradually learnt more and more about his natural environment while refining his stone and bone tools. If the earliest bones of humanoids seem to be the leftover meals of predators, after the capacity to make fire was acquired in later epochs it was the predators' bones that have been found in human-inhabited caves. Along with man, the hunter, lived woman, the gatherer, and it was she who secured most of the food consumed as well as succouring the offspring. She acquired a knowledge of botanical lore that matched man's awareness of the animal world. The tropical grasslands that cover much of Africa were an attractive environment for foraging populations. This may help to explain why our species seems to have evolved in eastern Africa originally and why foraging communities persisted in many parts of the continent long after knowledge of agriculture was widespread. Even into the twentieth century a few such communities survived in a variety of natural environments. Most were the descendants of agricultural peoples, so far as we can ascertain from their languages and customs, but there are examples – notably the Hadza who lived in north-central Tanzania and the so-called San of the Kalahari Desert of southern Africa – who may well be descendants of ancient foraging communities.[1]

Studies of surviving hunters and gatherers, combined with physical remains uncovered by archaeologists, help to recreate a little of the life of ancient Africa. To the extent that environment limits their way of life, it has been argued that such a transposition is quite legitimate. The !Kung San of the Kalahari Desert in Namibia a couple of generations ago were organised into small bands, numbering up to several dozen people. Band membership was informal, shifting and based on little more than personal preference within the ecological limits. There was no systematic institutionalised leadership among them apart from what natural ability threw up; relations between men and women were relatively egalitarian. The evidence of cave paintings and travellers' accounts suggest that the !Kung San and similar peoples have long been accomplished artists and musicians who have found extensive and impressive forms for articulating their emotions. They had a remarkable command of knowledge over the flora and fauna of the Kalahari ecosystem.

The most remarkable facet of Richard Lee's important 1979 study of the !Kung San was his convincing refutations of the usual clichés about the short, nasty and brutish life of savages. For a small population (and the !Kung San were very careful to practise a system of long child-spacing), foraging provides a relatively secure and leisured life. Lee's subjects contained a larger elderly population than was typical in agricultural Africa and producing adults were able to support a substantial number of 'pensioners' and children. The !Kung San understood agricultural techniques from neighbouring populations perfectly well but they had no reason or desire to adopt them; they had adapted to a semi-arid environment. Not far away, Damara speakers seem to be one-time farmers who turned back to hunting and gathering in response to movement into dry parts of Namibia. This was adaptation, not regression, as Europeans used to write. Indeed, historians find a serious problem in explaining why Africans ever did turn to agriculture.

For this, several explanations can be offered, however inconclusively. One lies in the systematic emergence of that unique type of hunting which allows for a large stationary population – hunting for fish. The archaeologist J. E. G. Sutton has, in fact, suggested that a large section of the African savannahs between the Sahara and the forests, together with a swathe of East Africa, experienced an important transitional 'Aquatic Age' which allowed new skills and populations to build up. At the same time, it is possible that Africans began to acquire domesticated animals, especially cattle. Cattle-keeping allows for much larger populations than foraging, but it is also much more susceptible to the problems of climate and, particularly, drought or irregular rainfall. It is the irregularity of rainfall which to this day sets the parameters of the possible for agriculturalists in much of Africa.

A third consideration, not necessarily separated from the first two, revolves around the impact of more long-term climatic changes on foragers, in particular in the region of the Sahara Desert which crosses the African continent from the Atlantic to the Red Sea. It has frequently been asserted that the Sahara became notably drier starting 5000–6000 years ago, pushing out a numerous population who could not adapt to the change without moving. Much African agricultural innovation apparently occurred during this period and in regions not too far removed from the desert, involving more intense concentrations of population.

It is much easier to imagine how, rather than why, agricultural knowledge developed and it may be guessed that much of the advance was pioneered by women. Foraging populations became aware of the nutritional value of particular wild crops, especially grains, mastered the art of preparing and cooking them and took to camping on sites where they were plentiful. Observation led to experimentation in planting seeds; gathering began to give way to systematic sowing and harvesting of crops as populations expanded. Such at least is a logically schematic reconstruction of what happened, not one based on direct knowledge.

The classic African savannah grains are millet and sorghum, but other grains were developed where suitable, just as different varieties of millet and sorghum, appropriate to particular soils or rainfall belts, were developed. In the Ethiopian highlands, teff, a kind of grass, became the staple. In the western portion of West Africa, perhaps beginning in the marshlands known as the Interior Delta of the Niger River in present-day Mali, a type of rice was widely cultivated. East Africans may have initiated the planting of ensete, a root crop related to the banana. This would have disposed them to accept the banana, believed to have been introduced at a later date from Asia. Root crops enabled agriculturalists to penetrate the forests. The yam was the most significant, although the native oil palm of West Africa also provided a multi-faceted fundamental asset. In forest and savannah regions cultivators learnt to balance grain or root staples with vegetable crops such as the cowpea which perhaps was first cultivated in northern Nigeria.

Irregular rainfall, poor soil and relatively light population densities all encouraged the persistence of so-called slash-and-burn techniques which gave the soil a long time to recover from usage and reflected a satisfactory response to ecological possibilities. Yet in certain regions denser populations developed intensive techniques such as stall-feeding cattle, hill terracing, manuring of fields and irrigation. In grain-growing zones, the perfection of storage facilities was crucial to provide for the hungry season.

Some writers have claimed that after agriculture the greatest innovation of early Africa was the production and working of iron. Iron was first smelted in western Asia, the technique spread slowly to Egypt and then was taken up with amazing rapidity throughout Africa in the centuries immediately before and after Christ. Iron hoes allowed for much more efficient agricultural exploitation, although in many regions iron was too rare to be used in this way and farmers continued to make do with wooden digging sticks until very recently.[2]

Agriculture transformed social and cultural life in Africa. It allowed for vastly greater population densities and for the consistent production of a surplus beyond immediate consumption needs. Social organisation took on new complexities, the most fundamental being the intensified concern with property rights over resources. Whereas surviving foraging bands emphasise natural phenomena like the sun, moon and stars in their religious beliefs, agriculturalists devised earth cults and ritualised their ancestors, claiming that descent entitled them to possess the land they worked. Ancestor worship is closely linked to social ideas based on kinship networks. Lineage groups tracing a common origin from a real or legendary ancestor became the fundamental building blocks of social organisation. A conventional term for a social or political group defined in genealogical terms is tribe, a word that goes back to Roman lineage terminology. In principle, there is nothing wrong with its appropriate application to African conditions, but in practice the word has been abused so systematically that it is preferable to avoid using it. 'Tribe', in the African context, has become a kind of second-class term for ethnic group, especially where so-called traditional ethnic rivalries are assumed to be the natural basis for modern political life. It is then applied backwards sloppily with historical reference to states or language groupings as in the so-called Asante or Yoruba 'tribes' with their unchanging tribal identifier cultures.

A primordial unchanging character is far from the shifting and conflicting realities of lineage-based African communities. Lineage formation was as much or more ideological as it was a true reflection of literal prevailing social pattern. In reality lineages expanded through absorbing unrelated individuals such as captives or migrants who were incorporated through devices that anthropologists call 'fictive' kinship. And of course they innovated and borrowed culture traits they liked.

Within lineage groups, inequality could and did develop. Elders, the closest living men to the all-powerful ancestors, secured control of aspects of production and the distribution of foodstuffs for consumption. The head of the household was able to exploit the labour of junior members. Eventually juniors might succeed as heads, but they could not all do so and this was a major reason for internal tensions and the hiving off of new households.

Equally important, if not more so, was the potential for exploiting both the labour and the reproductive capacity of women, which alone made possible the growth of the household and the lineage. The desirability of control over women for elders encouraged polygamy as social ideal and reality. Marriages largely represented alliances between male lineage heads in which women were redistributed. Oyewumi states flatly that 'in Oyo-Yoruba society, marriage was essentially a relationship between lineages' (p. 51). Some writers, notably Signe Arnfred, have gone so far as to propose that the conventional relations between men and women were so different from what Westerners find familiar that it is distorting to use the word marriage at all to describe the bonds that existed.

The condition of women in lineage societies varied considerably, however. In some places women retained a large proportion, if not all, of the product of their labour while evolving situations which enabled them to function independently of a husband's household. In many places, some women could become heads of household and effectively marry other women who would bear children for the household. In other areas, women had the entire burden of bringing up children added to agricultural labour and were exploited harshly and, as we shall see, most slaves and pawns in African societies were women. Where the absence of the tsetse fly allowed for the keeping of cattle, the beasts were largely and often exclusively the province of men. In his memoirs, President Museveni of Uganda refers to his family cows as effectively his sisters. It has also been argued that women's rights were greater in those societies that reckoned descent through the mother (matrilineal) rather than the father (patrilineal), but this is at the least variable.[3]

Polygamy aimed at garnering more workers could more politely be defined as building up the productive capacity of a larger unit. Yet women in polygamous households had the capacity to organise amongst themselves and to become important themselves as time went on and they accumulated children and valuable social relationships. They had their own distinctive organisations with their own hierarchies and responsibilities. In West Africa, women often controlled markets and at least short-distance trade, while individuals became powerful and wealthy.

Lineage-based households were not geographically static. Migrations over great distances are attested as historical events in many regions, particularly within Bantu-speaking Africa. Migration is a response to changing environmental or social conditions; it may largely have represented a means of seizing upon new opportunities or a reaction to the scourge of drought. In the region of modern Angola, the Imbangala appear in Portuguese records as migrants who terrorised their neighbours probably as a predatory response to the commercial lure of the Portuguese slave trade. This was the basis for their 'tribe'. Nineteenth-century migrants in an adjoining area, the Chokwe, responded to new post-slaving international trade possibilities by migration, raiding and absorption of surrounding populations who could participate in Chokwe commercial operations.

Marriage, migration and expansion could bring about both friendly and hostile links between lineage societies. In addition, and from a very early date, they established networks of inter-regional trade. The two classic items of early African trade were iron and salt. Both could be found very widely but some natural sources were much richer than others and encouraged the emergence of long-distance trading networks. Dried fish as a preservable source of protein was another standard early trade good. Apart from iron, metals worked in early Africa included tin, gold and copper. Some of the technology involved in their processing is likely to have been derived from iron smelting and smithing. The resultant artefacts were highly prized but scarce, luxury goods par excellence. Mining developed on an important scale in many areas. It was largely alluvial or shallow open-pit work which agriculturalists could pursue in the course of the dry season, but sometimes surprisingly deep and ingenious in construction. Craft production, such as bead and basketwork, carving and pottery, sometimes became the speciality of particular villages who found a wide regional clientele.

Lineage organisation has shown a remarkable strength, adaptability and staying power in Africa as in farming villages throughout the world, but it rarely existed as the only community form. Other social linkages that cross cut lineages were virtually universal and extremely varied. The most straightforward were village assemblies and associations that could embrace villagers of different lineages. Disputes between villages could sometimes be settled by cult authorities who enjoyed a wide prestige; their protection often helped to further trade over long distances. Boys (and sometimes girls) were initiated into community-linked age sets that included representatives of different lineages. Age-set affiliation united generations over substantial territorial zones. In addition there existed other forms of societies which were not necessarily generational. West African title and secret societies, for instance, initiated a minority of the community, practised secret rituals and could adjudicate disputes. All such non-lineage organisations sprang out of the interaction of lineages and related to the contradictions and tensions that arose within them. Their emergence reflected the growing scale and complexity of agricultural communities which expanded through migration, peaceful interchanges and conquest.

The formation of states

At some point such contradictions led further to the development of the state. The origins of the African state have been disputed extensively by historians. Into the 1960s it was commonly held that Africans had a common pattern of 'divine kingship' which had diffused as an idea, perhaps from Egypt. Few hold such views any more for there is increasing evidence that states arose from internal forces prevailing in various parts of the continent. For, after all, if these forces were not called to bear, what sense would it have made for people to accept an alien concept? The ideology of royalty in Africa typically contained an important dimension of reciprocity, of mutual obligation between the subject and his ruler. The ruler protected his people and brought them prosperity through good harvests, varied rituals and his healing touch. There was also usually a sacral power that aligned the ruler to a chief of less monarchic days of yore or who overwhelmed the community with his miraculous powers. A ruler had to be seen to be a generous giver who could play host to the needy. This is not, however, to suggest that the relationship thus evoked was simply reciprocal. Reciprocity hid systematic appropriation of the goods produced by cultivators and had the potential thus to generate the reproduction of a ruling class.

The historical materialist concept of the state, as envisioned in the work of Friedrich Engels, lay here. Such a class could achieve success in containing some controls over the production and reproduction of society as a whole through the imposition of a state apparatus and state ideology. The internal logic is impeccable but the reality is clearly more complicated. In particular, African states often seem to have exerted little control over the production of cultivators. They continued to co-exist with lineage organisations, the two apparently articulating only through the collection of tribute from villagers.

One of the first contemporary Marxists to re-examine the question of the state, Catherine Coquery-Vidrovitch, suggested in a provocative article at the end of the 1960s that Africa was the seat of an original 'African' mode of production in which the kings, or ruling classes, were sustained largely through their control over long-distance trade in luxury goods. The principal problem

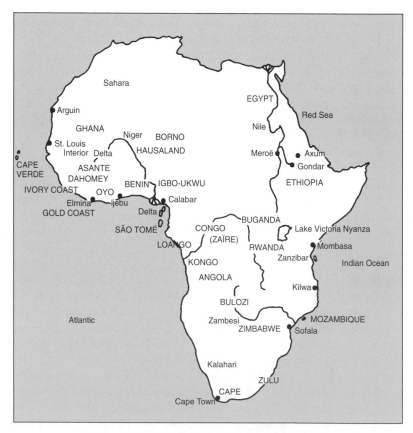

Map 1   Pre-colonial Africa: Places and Peoples

with such a formulation is that it fails to explain why the mass of cultivators should accept such a state in their midst. Wealth, however, could lead to the amassing of warriors who could impose control and fend off rivals even without much systematic extraction of labour. Control over trade does seem to be an important aspect of the origins of the state in many but not all parts of Africa. In most cases traders were not highly taxed, as they could find alternative routes for their goods rather than pass through the domains of an overtly greedy ruler.

The capture of individuals through warfare and raids could enlarge the lineage unit. It also allowed, particularly in the first generation of captives, for a large, dependent force that could be used either in battle to sustain the power of a particular household or as labour to support a homestead that might evolve into a court. In much of the West African savannah, royalty particularly prized their stables and cavalries which only a wealthy minority could maintain. Horse ownership allowed for sustained raiding and warfare. Even when, as would generally have been the case, captives were only a small proportion of the total population, they would have formed the forces required to allow states to collect tribute from villages of free cultivators.[4]

A distinct institution very prevalent in West Africa is usually known as pawnage. Pawns were obliged to work for an employer to repay a debt of their own or of somebody who had the power over them to engage in this transaction. In many situations, to repay the debt was almost impossible. Pawning enabled a wealthy or powerful individual to obtain more wives and could be used as a systematic means of exploitation although it also could represent a long-term trading and amicable relationship between household heads too. Occasionally pawns ended up on slave ships to the Americas but usually this ambiguous status was distinct from slavery.

One problem which bedevils much of the literature on the state in Africa is that authors of all persuasions tend to accept the arbitrary definitions of colonially minted social anthropology which propounded a rigid distinction between states and 'tribes without rulers' or 'stateless societies' in the interest of easing colonial administrative problems. The existence of a state was often assumed to equate to the presence of a big 'chief' and in other respects the state was confused with the tribe. African states were conventionally distinguished from lineage-based communities as 'tribes with rulers'. Yet in practice, almost by definition, the state comprised a mix of ethnic and linguistic groups, not the emanation of one.

The state needs to be assessed more broadly and historically in terms of the development of a ruling class and wide-ranging state apparatus rather than the mere presence of a monarch or leader. In most areas this was no doubt the product of a long process rather than an overnight change. Only at a late stage in this process could states effectively establish a national culture or entirely transcend earlier forms of social organisation and legitimacy. A state as developed as Asante was marked by rituals intended to knit citizens together. It is also true that Asante's relationship with conquered and aligned polities in a 'confederacy', as it is usually termed by modern historians, did not follow European diplomatic norms.

The cross-cutting institutions that existed in communities without kings also existed in state-like structures, often without any European parallel at all. Jean

Bazin has recovered the history of a part of the contemporary state of Mali where, in addition to those who can be translated as 'kings', there were also men, *tarawure*, whom he translates as 'women kings', who had certain political powers (but without the right to summon warriors) that appear to emanate from a previous political history but which they long retained. Oyeronke Oyewumi, herself scion of a royal house in an important Yoruba town, claims that Europeans often wrongly translated the names of rulers as referring exclusively to males where in fact powerful rulers of this type were likely often to have been women, as Yoruba names were not generally gender specific.

Much of the history of African states that can be reconstructed revolves around tensions between royal and lineage principles. Rulers were concerned to establish their own lineages in a special situation or to create a super-lineage basis for their own authority. Their 'divinity' was a means of distinguishing themselves from the human, the normal social chains that tied ordinary men and women to one another. They attempted to appoint their own men to tribute-collecting offices in order to supersede the control of lineage heads; here lay the seeds of a royal bureaucracy. In some cases, they were quite successful.

The *obas* of Benin ruled an area in south-central Nigeria which was an old-established state when first encountered by the Portuguese in the late fifteenth century. In Benin, lineage organisation had become attenuated and of limited importance. Villages paid tribute to office-holders who owed their power to the *oba*. The court sponsored a large amount of artisanal activity and commerce, providing the focus for a well-ordered capital city with several tens of thousands of inhabitants. The religion of Benin orientated people towards a hegemonic national, court-centred structure of belief. The state had become an inherent part of Bini political culture and it is not surprising that it survived until the British conquest of 1897. However, other states did not have this solidity and Benin is at one end of the spectrum. Thus it is usually better to understand state authority as emanating from a bright centre of force gradually dimming on the margins rather than to exist equally throughout a territory enclosed by boundaries that a contemporary historian may draw on a map.

Some major African states

The Ethiopian highlands were probably among the earliest centres of African state formation. The first Ethiopian state that can be identified was Axum, with its capital in the province of Tigre near to the Eritrean border. Axum controlled the port of Adulis in modern-day Eritrea on the Red Sea and traded with the Mediterranean world in the Roman era almost 2000 years ago. Archaeological evidence suggests Adulis thrived particularly a bit later based on links with the Byzantine Empire in Constantinople and down through the Indian Ocean to Persia and India until the rise of Islam, after which there is little evidence left to find. The minting of coins in Axum attests to the importance of commerce.

In the fourth century the Axumite rulers accepted Christianity. They retained links to the Coptic Egyptian church which also bore a strong monastic culture combined with what seem like elements of Jewish custom. The church links seem crucial in the adopting of a distinctive Ethiopian written script. For a time, Axum ruled across the Red Sea in southern Arabia. A new state culture, identified with Axumite kingship, spread through much of the highlands. This is often mistakenly identified with Ethiopia as a whole where in fact there were different, interpenetrating cultural and linguistic traditions linked to states in the central and southern highlands whose history is much less known. A state based further south in the highlands where the local language was Amharinya arose in the thirteenth century and succeeded in conquering both the old Tigrinya-speaking region further north, where Axum had been located, and other regions. This state, explicitly laying claim to the heritage of Christian Axum, was the expression of an expanding land-owning class that was thriving in the fourteenth and fifteenth centuries.

A succession of states going back at least as far in time centred in the valley of the middle Nile and particularly the region where the Blue and White Niles meet, far enough south of the Sahara for rain-fed agriculture to flourish away from the river while irrigation provided rich harvests adjoining its banks. Meroë, as the Greeks called it, was a prosperous centre even before the rise of Axum. The physical remnants of Meroë suggest a culture that borrowed much both from the Greeks and the Egyptians, while creating a distinctive synthesis. Meroë's successor states adopted Christianity as the court faith. While a Christian Abyssinian state thrived in the Ethiopian highlands, Christianity was replaced, apparently peacefully, by Islam as the state cult on the middle Nile and, by contrast with Egypt but as elsewhere in Mediterranean Africa, Christianity died out. In the sixteenth century the kingdom of Sennar reunited a large area which gradually became Islamised. As in Ethiopia the mass of peasantry in Sennar paid heavy taxes to subsidise their rulers' households. This was the one region of sub-Saharan Africa where literacy was effectively put to the uses of tax collecting. A large, literate merchant class made its home in numerous towns and played a crucial role in deepening Islamic cultural influence in what is today the Republic of Sudan. Far to the west of the Nile, an important state arose around the foot of Djebel Marra in Darfur in the sixteenth century, probably with predecessors, allowing the Fur rulers to command the varied population of this large region. Yet historians believe that the cultural influences here lay rather more to the west, in the lands that separated Darfur from the Niger rather than the Nile.

The formation of states in the savannahs of West Africa may also go back some 2000 years. The first to which written outside sources refer was Ghana, old at the time of the earliest Arabic reference in the tenth century. What we know of Ghana comes primarily from Arab travellers who were interested in its commerce, especially in gold. The gold trade seems to have had its beginnings following the establishment of Islam in North Africa. These sources, like those for other early West African courts, provide little information on aspects of West African society of less commercial significance. The apparent location of the core of Ghana in arid southern Mauritania, more or less on the far northern edge of cultivation, points to Ghana's crucial position controlling the 'port' from which gold could be carried north over the desert by caravan (although it is true that population concentrations may go back further to the time when the precipitation here was more generous). There is scattered early evidence of other very old states in the Senegambian region, further to the south-west and on the middle

Niger, which had commercial links to the north but were not really desert-side. Joloff dominated the Senegal valley long before the arrival of Europeans and pockets, at least, of Islam were already present in what is today Senegal.

Above the inner delta of the Niger lies the picturesque town of Jenne. Susan and Roderick McIntosh, excavating an ancient site nearby, have pioneered the study of pre-Islamic society in the western savannah at a nearby site. Other archaeologists have more recently examined a large mound near the town of Gao where the Niger bends and begins to wind its way south. This town too was pre-Islamic with limited evidence only of long-distance trade at first. Before the eleventh century, the presence of trade is indicated by glass, copper and beads, but with no indication of any royal power or of the existence of Islam.[5] However, from the eleventh century trade goods are strikingly more numerous. Archaeologist Mamadou Cissé believes that old Gao contained two settlements, one royal and one commercial, and that a ruler with a suitably sized palace moved to Gao in the eleventh century as trade suddenly took off, perhaps because the Almoravid dynasty that ruled from Mauritania to Spain succeeded the image-hating Ibadites of the Algerian oases as the main commercial sponsors. In the fifteenth century, Arabic sources begin to refer to a strong state called Borno, south-west of Lake Chad in what is today northern Nigeria. There is a connection between Borno and Kanem, an even earlier state near the desert edge in modern Chad. Here trade routes would have led north into present-day Libya or towards Egypt. If Kanem's location suggests a trading entrepôt function, this southward shift in the centre of gravity reveals a deepening control by a dominant class over a population of cultivators.

From the sixteenth century, the most economically dynamic region in the entire savannah was the Hausaland plain west of Borno. Here a high water table and numerous river valleys that permitted year-round irrigated cultivation provided the basis for an exceptionally dense population which established a thick network of walled settlements and extensive specialised commodity production, particularly of textiles and leather goods. In this region the economic foundation for the division of labour and production of a substantial surplus was surer than in lands further west where the gold-trade states of Mali and Songhay in their time succeeded Ghana.

It was the trans-Saharan trade which introduced Islam to West Africa by the tenth century at the latest. In time West African traders, like their North African colleagues, found the faith a firm bond along the chain of commercial routes and towns where business transactions, above all credit, depended on personal trust and affiliations. Islam brought literacy, as had Christianity even earlier in north-eastern Africa, and with literacy came in time a stratum of clerics whose surviving chronicles help us to recreate the history of the savannah region. Rulers also turned to Islam as an additional source for re-enforcing their own prestige and power. It bound them to distant centres with which they sought good relations while creating a new role for themselves as protectors of a universal faith. In most of the West African savannah before the nineteenth century, however, the peasantry remained deeply involved in earlier rituals and wore Islamic garb lightly if at all.

Some of the pastoral peoples of both desert and savannah took Islam to themselves with more passion. Certain pastoral lineages became specialists in Islamic learning and increasingly committed to the wider propagation of Islam and its establishment as the juridical basis of the state. Such lineages among the Moors of Mauritania, the Tuareg of the middle Sahara and the savannah Fulbe, who appear through linguistic evidence to have originated in the present-day republic of Senegal and ranged eastwards to Nigeria and beyond, interacted easily with one another and were the crucial factor in initiating jihads from the late seventeenth century onward. The idea of reform, of wiping out pagan accretions and returning to a pure faith is a powerful one in Islam, not least in Africa.

Without literacy, as is the case in the forest regions of West Africa, the history of state formation is far more difficult to retrace. It has already been pointed out that the Benin state had reached a high level of maturity by the end of the fifteenth century. The wonderful bronze work unearthed in various parts of southern Nigeria and dated even earlier can be associated with a substantial social surplus and a leisured class. The sculpture found in compounds in Ile Ife can be dated by the radiocarbon method to as far back as the twelfth century. One set of finds, just to the east of the Niger River at Igbo-Ukwu, contained a treasury of finely worked objects. We still have no idea as to the specific political or sociological context of these spectacularly beautiful handicrafts which specialists have dated variously to between the ninth and fourteenth centuries. It is clear from these many traces and surviving objects that there is a history involving state formation from at least the first millennium AD about which we know very little, beyond oral traditions.

The production of gold did not automatically bring about the creation of states directly based on mining activity. It has been suggested by Emmanuel Terray that gold production, involving control over slaves and thus linking up to slave raiding and trading, was fundamental to the authority of the ruling class of warriors among Akan-speaking peoples. This was a shift: in the first centuries of the trade, the source lay not far from the headwaters of the Niger and the Senegal rivers in present-day Guinea and Mali but then refocused to Ghana and, marginally, the Ivory Coast. It may have connected to the widespread presence of so-called Dioula or Diola traders who functioned as a kind of caste, even penetrating forest regions and sometimes establishing states with Islamic allegiance.

Yet in both cases, most of the gold produced came from dry-season, spare-time labour from ordinary free households. Of all the states in the region the most powerful was the confederacy under the Asantehene, the ruler of Asante, but this belongs to a rather later period. During the eighteenth century the Asantehenes succeeded in obtaining tribute from a large part of today's Ghana. With the decline of gold mining the commerce of Asante expanded to take in the sale of slaves and the purchase of guns, cloth and manufactured goods on the coast and the export of kola nuts to the savannah. The gold trade was obviously a stimulus to commercial development very generally.

Elsewhere in Africa it is possible to identify a number of major state clusters. The vast majority of the population in the southern half of the continent speak closely related languages, grouped together by linguists under the name Bantu. Bantu languages are believed to have a common origin in a dialect of the widespread Niger-Congo family of West African languages spoken in the Nigerian-Cameroun borderlands some 2000–3000 years ago. The similarity of Bantu languages suggests a dramatic process of migration, cultural adaptation or both. Various ingenious efforts to explain the spread of Bantu, notably involving the use of iron, have been made but none are entirely satisfactory. It may be surmised, though, given the absence of ancient archaeological evidence, that the establishment of well-peopled agricultural communities preceded the Christian era by centuries, but not millennia, in eastern, southern and south-central Africa.

At some stage a process of state formation involving the mixture of pastoralist and agricultural peoples began in the region of the East African Great Lakes. The best-studied states are Buganda and Rwanda. Buganda's heartland lay on the fertile and very well-watered plains north-west of Lake Victoria Nyanza. In the eighteenth and nineteenth centuries Buganda's *kabaka* extended his authority over a vast territory in modern Uganda, effacing some of the power of the earlier kingdom of Bunyoro to the west. This was coupled with flourishing trade and handicraft production and increasingly successful efforts by royalty to bypass the prerogatives of Ganda lineages. Parallel to this, Rwanda, to the south-west of Buganda, covering most of the territory of the contemporary republic of that name, was comparable in size and population to Buganda. Here wealth was more sharply indicated by the keeping of cattle and status as well. The physical differences between the cattle-keeping Tutsi and the agricultural Hutu – never considered then as a distinct ethnic group – would suggest to Europeans the presence of two different stocks or 'races' of people. Yet both speak the same language and their appearances may in fact reflect different diets. Even the supposed difference in appearance today is considered unsystematic and questionable. The royal lineage stood at the head of the great Tutsi cattle-keeping lineages. These collected tribute through clientage relations with poorer herdsmen and farmers. Cattle-keeping was reified as the essential part of the national culture; actually there were also wealthy Hutu households who themselves controlled the surplus labour and product of the poor while cattle-less Tutsi were dependent on the households of the great to gain access to the means of production. In neighbouring Burundi, the *mwami*, or ruler, was considered apart from and separate to the Tutsi. Blood brotherships between individuals, clan linkages and ritual performances often cut across the Hutu/Tutsi division. Thickly populated Rwanda was a crowded land; the poorest cultivators were forced to hire themselves out as day labourers.

Another belt of states came to stretch across much of the southern savannahs south of the equatorial forest of Middle Africa. South of the mouth of the river Congo lay the Kongo kingdom from whence the river had derived the name. When the Portuguese first arrived in the late fifteenth century it had already existed for at least several generations. Another node of political centralisation lay far inland in a basin particularly favoured by salt and iron deposits for the development of long-distance trade. This may have been a basic reason for the rise of the Luba kings in present-day Katanga province in the Democratic Republic of the Congo. Other states of the southern savannah of the Democratic Republic of the Congo, Zambia and Angola, associated their founding legends with the Luba.

This is true as well for the upper Zambesi floodplain region of western Zambia unified as the Lozi state – Bulozi – in the nineteenth century. Bulozi occupied a suitable zone for cattle-keeping where control over the flood waters by a class that could command the labour of many workers profoundly affected the quality of life. Such control came from a strong nineteenth-century monarchy. Canal construction and corvée labour gave the Bulozi state a direct interest in production and required a high intake of exploitable captives from the surrounding region.

Other states flourished in various parts of southern and eastern Africa. People ancestral to modern-day Shona speakers in Zimbabwe, another early source of gold deposits, created the massive and enigmatic stone ruins which have given their name to the modern state. In the far south of Africa, however, there appears to be little precedent for the great state-forming events of the early nineteenth century. Ecological pressures may have been responsible for the intensification of rivalries between small chiefdoms in the region between the Drakensberg mountains and the Indian Ocean. The most successful contender, Shaka, used an exceptionally aggressive and predatory army, which he developed through distorting the age-grade system so as to force an entire generation of warriors to fight for him while the women of the nation worked to produce the food to support them. This forged the Zulu state where, before, Zulu had just meant the members of one average-sized lineage group.

Following the creation of the Zulu state, yet other armies, desperate to re-acquire cattle stolen by the Zulu, exploded through the interior grasslands of modern South Africa and far beyond, creating new political formations in Zimbabwe, Malawi, Mozambique, Zambia and Tanzania, often in highland areas good for the raising of healthy cattle. The Zulu word '*Mfecane*', meaning 'crushing' or 'breaking', is often used by historians to refer to this often brutal historical era, after the writing of John Omer-Cooper who popularised the term. The pressures causing these movements must be considered to include the impact of Europeans, as well people of mixed origins in the interior of South Africa, and are more complicated than is captured by the idea of a single process so some historians today are discontented with the *Mfecane* idea.

A striking feature of African states and peoples was how little they looked to the oceans surrounding their continent. Men went out past the Atlantic breakwaters in West Africa to fish and established canoe networks along the lagoons that fringe the ocean, but they did not sail the seas. One exception was the Indian Ocean east coast, so favourably situated with prevailing winds for transit during the monsoons. The antiquity of the trade along the coast, attracted by products such as ivory and ostrich feathers, can be attested from a navigator's handbook that survives from Egypt in the first century after Christ. We continue to await the discovery of the site of the most southerly trading town mentioned therein, the mysterious Rhapta. Archaeological evidence goes back only to the beginnings of the Islamic era. An eighth-century site known as Shange, in the Lamu archipelago on the northern part of the Kenya coast, revealed an island agglomeration of huts and a simply made mosque. There is reason to believe that much of the trade at this time was with the ports of Persia. However, thereafter trade to Arabia and India became more significant and a cultural complex developed in the archipelago spread south all the way to contemporary Mozambique and the Comoro islands. Trading ports, most typically located just off the coast on islands, formed an important part of the commerce of the East. Of the rulers of the stone-built coastal cities that we know about the most powerful were those of Kilwa in modern Tanzania who controlled caravans bringing gold dust from the interior mines of Zimbabwe, a gold trade that no doubt built on earlier commercial networks. Neither the Kilwa rulers there nor their compatriots north or south ever appear to have ruled states of any continental compass.

Class societies orientated to commodity production and overseas trade, while assimilating the Islamic faith that arrived with the dhows from across the Indian Ocean, had taken root in these entrepôt states before Vasco da Gama first laid eyes on them in 1498; Kilwa minted its own coins. A common denominator of coastal culture was the Bantu language rich in Arabic borrowings spoken in the towns and on the islands – Swahili. Swahili culture is identifiable to students as the creation of traders from outside Africa with local people, notably local women whom they married. Despite the gold trade, coastal society had for many centuries only a very modest impact despite commercial contacts until modern times on even the immediate hinterland where people speaking languages closely related to Swahili continued to defend earlier cultural forms and reject Islam. This is true as well for the gold mining communities in Zimbabwe and even further south at the site we call Mapungubwe, just south of the Limpopo River within the borders of South Africa, now usually dated to the thirteenth century. The great Red Island off the east coast of Africa was never colonised from the mainland. Linguistic evidence shows that a core population came, perhaps in several waves, to Madagascar from south-east Asia, probably involving contact with the East African coast, in the early first millennium AD but with so far little uncovered material remains.

The state and class society

Africa provides fascinating examples of areas which produced substantial surpluses, organised trade, consumed and exchanged luxury goods and witnessed extensive social inequalities without the development of centralised state mechanisms. The Igbo country of south-eastern Nigeria is a major case in point. The Igbo and other 'stateless' Africans were hardly at a more primitive material state than their king-ridden neighbours and they represented as such a large proportion of sub-Saharan Africans in the nineteenth century and before. Igbo villages have been described by historians and anthropologists as democratic communities where each household head was capable through individual effort of earning coveted titles, position and wealth. However, Igbo communities did not lack for inequality, slavery and forms of social oppression. Title societies functioned as agencies of the richest and most powerful and so contained an incipient form of class rule. The imaginative recreation of Igbo society by such novelists as Buchi Emecheta and Chinua Achebe spotlights the intensity of contradictions and conflicts within superficially undifferentiated African communities. These went on not only beneath the façade of political events; they lay at the heart of social change and material developments that marked the history of Africa. So schematic approaches such as the Marxist idea of distinct modes of production have at best a preliminary and limited value in understanding pre-colonial societies, and exaggerating the importance of state formation as a stage of human progress can be problematic.

The Igbo notwithstanding, state formation very broadly appears to have intensified the articulation of class relationships in Africa. Class societies formed most unequivocally and consciously in parts of Africa where state forms developed most intensively. There is little question that the Hausaland plain had by the nineteenth century witnessed a remarkable convergence here. A clearly demarcated minority enjoyed leisure and consumed surplus without working with its hands. Its legitimacy was linked to close association with the state and the state in turn with the defence and propagation of the Muslim faith. Despite the extent of commoditised production and commerce, the important class of rich merchants relied on the protection and patronage of the state; they aspired to no autonomous political role. The Hausa language distinguished between free and slave, rich and poor, office-holder and commoner while the proverbial wisdom of the Hausa is rich in its consideration of these:

Mai abu shi ne da bara. (There is no rich man without clients.)

Abokin sarki, sarkin ne. (The friend of the ruler is a ruler.)

Dan halas ake zargi, bawa sai sanda. (The free man needs only a reproach; the slave must be beaten.)

The Hausa stressed above all the contradiction between two groups, the office-holding, horse-riding heads of great households whose existence defined the state – the *masu sarauta* – and the common folk – the *talakawa*. Throughout Hausa community life, among women's organisations, in villages and trade guilds, the standard names for the hierarchy of principal office-holders, chief, treasurer and so on were repeated. Such a structure lent linguistic legitimacy to the architecture of subordination. In fact the picture was greatly complicated by the other distinctions – the varying degrees of slavery, the situation of strata living off the surplus unproductively without being office-holders (for instance the Islamic teachers), and stratification within the household, the trade guild and between the sexes and surviving lineage linkages – which all require much deeper elucidation than can be done in these pages. Slaves, for instance, were used extensively as soldiers and were not exploited in ways that marked off their labour from that of free men and women. In West African societies further to the south, debt pawnage created another category of people: not really free or enslaved.

Class consciousness was generally masked by an established discourse of clientage and reciprocity and by local and religious identities. To an outsider, this suggests superficially a world of organic community and wholeness that seems now to have been lost both in the West and in Africa. This is an illusion. The task of historians is both to understand the ideology and to uncover the unfolding richness of the cultural and social contradictions that typified change in Africa as elsewhere.

Figure 2.1   *Pre-capitalist ruling classes*: the Timbo *almamy* and his retinue
(Futa Djallon, Guinea)

Notes

1. The hunting and gathering peoples whom Europeans called Bushmen and Khoi Khoi pastoralists called San actually had no generic name for themselves. San has recently become the preferred scholarly term.
2. Since the 1970s, as archaeological knowledge has increased, the sequence for the spread of iron use has been thrown into confusion. The complexity of smelting technology implies diffusion from one or certainly only a small number of centres of invention but, although many would argue to the contrary, there is no evidence that iron was not first smelted somewhere in Africa without techniques borrowed from elsewhere. The spread in Africa was both early and fast.
3. Scholarship with a feminist orientation should eventually allow for generalisations on a securer base. At present, though, feminists have opened up the question in forms which have invited intense ideologically determined disagreements which make a synthetic treatment difficult. It should be made clear that the issue of female subordination cannot be linked directly to the form of inheritance characteristic in particular societies. Many African societies determined inheritance through females and are considered matrilineal rather than patrilineal or double-descent form. However, this could simply hand power and wealth to maternal uncles not to fathers. Nor does double descent imply especially sexually egalitarian communities.
4. Such evidence as the existence of a slave trade across both the Sahara and the Red Sea attested for many centuries confirms that slavery long pre-dated the Atlantic slave trade at least in some areas of Africa, although doubtless on a relatively modest scale.
5. It is possible that early Muslim traders came to Gao but were Ibadite, a sect, strong in present-day Algeria very hostile to all image making.

3

The European Intrusion in the Era of Merchant Capital

Peace prevailing in these four kingdoms, one cannot hope for many captives.
LOUIS CHARBONNEAU, SEVENTEENTH-CENTURY TRAVELLER TO SENEGAL
(AUTHOR'S TRANSLATION), IN BOUBACAR BARRY, *LE ROYAUME DE WAALO*, PP. 155–6

We depend entirely on selling slaves and palm-oil for our subsistence, suppose then the slave trade done away with, the consumption of palm-oil in England to stop, the crop to fail, or that the English ships did not come to Bonny, what are we to do? We must starve, as it is contrary to our religion to cultivate the ground.
SECRETARY TO ANNA PEPPLE, BONNY HOUSE HEAD, 1839,
IN THOMAS HODGKIN, ED., *NIGERIAN PERSPECTIVES*, P. 304

Between the fifteenth and eighteenth centuries European traders, missionaries and soldiers arrived in sub-Saharan Africa establishing economic and, to a much lesser extent, political relationships that would lead ultimately to the colonial expansion of an industrialised, capitalist society. Before the impact of the Industrial Revolution in the late eighteenth century the dominant form of capital in Europe was merchant capital, capital originating from individuals or companies of traders. At its most sophisticated, long-distance commerce could begin to call on joint-stock companies, chartered ventures protected through royal monopoly and early insurance firms. The colonial slave plantation was the great innovation of this pioneering phase of capitalism. But merchant capital's ability to transform productive relations was limited. This was to depend on the gradual development of a world market, its tentacles stretching to every continent including Africa.

The most notorious aspect of this early contact period was the trade in men and women which brought millions of Africans across the Atlantic to the plantations of the New World. During this era Europeans in Africa did not establish territorially significant colonies outside the Cape of Good Hope. So what was the significance, scale and impact of their intrusion? Can we trace clearly features of this period which fatally hooked Africa into a relationship of 'underdevelopment' or 'dependence' on an emerging capitalist world order, as has frequently been claimed? Where does the slave trade fit in to this?

In order to pursue a more systematic account of Africa in the nineteenth and twentieth centuries we must first consider these questions with reference to an earlier period. It is convenient to divide the long phase of early European contact into two chronological eras. For two centuries, from the mid-fifteenth to the mid-seventeenth, the Portuguese were overwhelmingly the most important European presence in Africa. Their pre-eminence deteriorated rapidly in the second quarter of the seventeenth century giving way to the Dutch, French and British in particular. From then on the slave trade came to dominate European interest in Africa, which was not the case earlier.

The Portuguese epoch

Portuguese ambitions during the first two centuries of contact with Africa were diffuse. One was indeed to secure manpower to exploit in Brazil and the island colonies, but the Portuguese state and Portuguese merchants were equally interested in the spice trade, in precious metals, particularly gold, and in forging strategic alliances aimed against Mameluk Egypt and then the Ottoman Empire. By the early sixteenth century these interests began to mesh into a structure of strategic and economic considerations of world dimensions and complexity. Portuguese imperialism was not a consequence of the particularly advanced state of the Portuguese economy. The manufacturing sector in Portugal was weak. Much of the early wealth of the Portuguese ports originated rather from the trans-shipment trade between the North and Mediterranean Seas, and most of what the Portuguese had to sell in Africa originated from other parts of Europe. This gave a particularly sharp edge to the Portuguese search for gold and silver which could be used to buy other commodities.

The lack of desirable items for sale posed a dilemma to the Portuguese (and later other Europeans) in the Asian trade opened up by Vasco da Gama's fleet sailing around the Cape of Good Hope into the Indian Ocean. Europeans had little to sell Asians in exchange for the silks and cottons, tea, porcelain and spices of the East. Their greatest strength still lay not in superior techniques of manufacture but in their advanced weaponry and sailing skills. As a result there was a very strong element of force in the character of Portuguese commercial intrusion. This was the essential context for Portuguese involvement on the East African coast of what is today Kenya and Tanzania and in Ethiopia as part of a broader Indian Ocean strategy. The Swahili coast towns were either forced into submission or accepted alliances with Portugal. Occasional attempts to convert ruling houses to Catholicism invariably failed miserably and in general the Portuguese contented themselves with collecting tribute and imposing a close strategic watch on the ocean by means of strong forts, of which the most impressive was Fort Jesus in Mombasa (Kenya) which still stands. There is little to suggest that internal social or economic relationships changed notably during the era of Portuguese dominance.

Strategic considerations also informed the relationship established between the Portuguese and Ethiopia. From early in the fifteenth century there was speculation in Europe concerning the project of an anti-Egyptian and/or anti-Turkish alliance with the highland Christian kingdom about which a few held vague but increasing knowledge. This interest was reciprocated by several Ethiopian rulers whose relations with Egypt were sometimes poor and who were impressed by what they began to learn of European military technology. By the fifteenth century the Islamic world was feeling the growing pressure of expansionism fuelled by European merchant capital but put forth as part of a crusade to push back Islam. This, it has been suggested, gave to the politics of the Horn of Africa a Christian versus Islamic cast that had been a very minor element in previous centuries. In the early sixteenth century an Islamic religious teacher serving in the walled gateway town of Harar on the edge of the Ethiopian plateau, named Ahmad ibn Ibrahim or Ahmed Grañ, 'the Left Handed', organised a successful holy war through the plateau. He was assisted by Ottoman weaponry, the first intrusion of firearms into the region. However, before an Islamic Ethiopia could be consolidated, a Portuguese fleet cruising the Red Sea in pursuit of Turks made contact with refugees from the Christian kingdom. Vasco da Gama's grandson and several hundred Portuguese soldiers were despatched. They proved crucial in turning the tide against Ahmed Grañ, who was killed in battle with a new Christian ruler in 1543.

Thereafter, for almost a century, the Portuguese maintained some presence in Ethiopia. This took the form primarily of several generations of determined Jesuits who wished to win the Ethiopians away from heresy and became embroiled in the factional politics of the Ethiopian ruling class. They succeeded in converting one emperor, Susenyos, whose thirty-year rule was weakened partly as a result of the hostility this engendered among clerics and notables. His successor, Fasilidas, expelled the Portuguese so in Ethiopia the Portuguese intrusion was followed (much as in Japan during the same years) by a policy of exclusion and elimination of European influence. During the sixteenth and seventeenth centuries European artisans had made their way to Ethiopia and enjoyed considerable prestige, one surviving consequence being the construction of the castle-palaces of Gondar, but these techniques were not widely diffused and did not lead to significant long-term economic change. With the decline of Portuguese (and Ottoman) sea power in the Indian Ocean, European interest in Ethiopia and East African coast faded until the nineteenth century.

Nothing in Africa fascinated the Portuguese more than the prospect of gold. Everywhere they went they enquired after it. In two regions this developed into a strong, permanent interest. One was on the stretch of the West African coast that became known to Europeans as the Gold Coast. Here the Portuguese erected a great medieval fort at Elmina in 1481. To Elmina came caravans that diverted gold from older trade routes established throughout West Africa. During the sixteenth century this trade was a jewel in the Portuguese crown, a source of as much as one-fifth of its income in good years. The Portuguese rarely interfered in local politics and, so far as is known, hardly attempted to control gold production. From the beginning of the seventeenth century the Elmina officials suffered from the competition of private European traders who could offer African merchants better prices for higher quality goods. By the time the Dutch threw the Portuguese out of Elmina in 1637 its gold trade was in a state of decline.

The other gold-bearing region of Africa of which the Portuguese became aware was the plateau zone of south-central Africa now known as Zimbabwe.

As soon as they reached the East African coast the Portuguese ascertained that this gold was exported to Asia via Sofala, a port on the coast of modern Mozambique under the control of the city of Kilwa. Sofala was quickly seized and an attempt was made to redirect the trade to Mozambique island where the Portuguese built their fort and town in 1507. This tactic proved unsuccessful and, for reasons that are not entirely clear, the gold trade quickly dried up. It has been suggested that the gold supplies were in any case petering out at this time. Mozambique was retained in part as a stopping point to the East.

Moreover, the Portuguese persisted. They found a highway to the interior in the form of the Zambesi River which they followed inland, establishing forts and trading settlements in strategic locations. During the sixteenth century Portuguese soldiers and priests established themselves in market centres and became a factor in internecine politics in the plateau region south of the Zambesi valley. They may have been partially responsible for the collapse of the Rozvi state, then dominant on the Zimbabwean highveld. Commercially their intrusion was a complete failure. The amount of wealth that could be drawn from scattered alluvial pockets of gold mined by women during the dry season was very limited and the prospect of rich trade that lured the Portuguese into the interior never materialised. In 1693 a revived state on the plateau under the Changamire dynasty smashed the last remnants of Portuguese military force in the area.

However, the Portuguese remained in the lower Zambesi valley. Here the Crown granted land to Portuguese women in an unusual tenure arrangement that established property rights for the course of three lives heritable through the female line. The intention was to create a class of Portuguese landowners. The *prazos* were much too large to function as estates. Their owners survived primarily as traders and tribute gatherers who amassed considerable retinues of slaves but exerted a generally rather tenuous authority with some tribute rights over the free population of *colonos*. Some *prazeros* gained a kind of acceptance as chiefs, and by the eighteenth century the large majority were predominantly of African and Indian origin. This transformation has been described as an 'Africanisation'. Although the Portuguese state could exert little authority over them, the *prazeros* clung to a cultural identification with Portugal and with Roman Catholicism that reflected their continuing business as middlemen-traders caught up in ocean commerce. During the eighteenth century they turned to the burgeoning ivory trade to build their fortunes.

The only region other than Zambesia where Portuguese involvement had some lasting significance lay across the continent where the savannah that stretches south of the Congo basin reaches the Atlantic. Here the Portuguese encountered the one powerful African state that fronted the sea coast in the fifteenth century where savannah and forest meet – the kingdom of Kongo. Impressed by the state of order and control and the more open terrain which made possible physical penetration into the interior, the first Portuguese quickly established an alliance with the Kongo state. The Kongo rulers, particularly the early sixteenth century monarch usually known by his Portuguese name of Dom Afonso I (Mbemba-a-Nzinga), were in their turn immensely impressed by the material paraphernalia of Portuguese culture and attempted to secure aid for the introduction of techniques of all kinds into their state. Instead, they got priests. Dom Afonso, his successors and the Kongo ruling class in general accepted baptism and a veneer of Catholic practice diffused widely while the Catholic Church, in Rome as well as in Portugal, came to accept the Kongo as a nominal, if backsliding, Catholic state to which it had certain commitments. Over the centuries many priests were sent out who did in turn succeed in training Kongo priests. Historian John Thornton believes, however, that most Kongo believers were more interested in salvation against the forces of witchcraft rather than overcoming sin to get to heaven's gates. This aspect aside, Kongo was a grave disappointment to the Portuguese. It proved very remote from the Indian Ocean trade and lacked any precious minerals. Even before the death of Dom Afonso I, Kongo became a state that exported slaves. According to the testimony of the king himself, this initially had a very destructive impact, including, it may be imagined, on his own authority.

Therefore Kongo is often taken as the classic model of an African state whose autonomous development was destroyed and power laid waste by European commercial influence and the slave trade in particular. But the case is not entirely convincing. Kongo remained a strong state for almost two centuries after its 'discovery' by the Portuguese and its power was eventually broken through the revolt of a major provincial lord. After initial devastations the slave trade was largely redirected outside the kingdom's borders to raiding and trading networks deeper in the interior. Recent research has tended to refute the earlier stereotype of slavery-caused depopulation in Kongo.[1] There was one notable change, however; this was in agricultural production. The cultivation of African grains and root crops gave way relatively early to American cassava (manioc) and maize, crops which spread far inland but at first had no parallel in scale of adaptation elsewhere in Africa.[2] Cassava can be grown in poorer soil and with less labour than practically any other crop; it thrives where other plants will not take root. This may have freed women from agricultural labour and perhaps allowed populations to build up that might otherwise have diminished. However, the evidence for this is only indirect.

The Kongo kings failed in their efforts to spread new craft techniques among their subjects. Instead, the ruling class became enthusiastic consumers of imported textiles and other goods. Although several priests produced written KiKongo in dictionary form, no written culture emerged. Thus the Kongo ruling class came to depend on the consumption of goods available only through import from Europe in exchange for the sale of gathered natural products or human labour-power in the form of slaves. After their initial attempts the Portuguese did not do much to spread manufacturing techniques to the region. This was, of course, their policy towards other potential rivals, European as well. The dominant economic philosophy of European society at the time, mercantilism – the ideology of merchant capitalism – emphasised commercial secrecy and monopoly.

Yet rivals persevered and were able to copy and ultimately to innovate. Kongo society, for reasons that related to its own internal dynamic, remained relatively impervious to innovations that could not be fitted readily into the existing mode of production. The resulting interrelationship has been considered one of unequal exchange or dependence by those writers searching to find early roots of underdevelopment. This is a very simplified way of describing a complex of class and commercial interconnections engendered through contact, but it is significant that those commanding means of coercion in the Kongo preferred (they could not be forced) to sell people or products of the bush rather than to intensify the application of forces of production.

South of the Kongo state the Portuguese presence intruded markedly in the area that became known after the title of a local ruler: Angola. Angola was a particularly early focus for the slave trade and the one place other than the Zambesi valley where the Portuguese tried consistently to sustain a territorial empire in the course of wars in the seventeenth century. They eventually undermined the power of those Mbundu-speaking rulers nearest the coast, but others further inland continued to control, and indeed to fatten upon, the slaving operations. Mulattos or culturally 'Portugalised' African armed traders known as *pombeiros* served as the vital intermediaries.

The Atlantic slave trade

The Portuguese had an effective base for the penetration of Kongo and Angola in the island colony of São Tomé. During the first generation or two of contact it was here that most slaves were sent and here that a sugar plantation economy arose. Among famous names who partly learnt their trade in these waters was the Italian Christopher Columbus, discoverer of America, who took a keen interest in the slave trade and owned an African slave.

Another group of islands, much further north, served as a parallel base. These were the arid Cape Verdes, unsuitable for plantation agriculture but the site of a cotton textile industry used for the varied trade, including one in slaves, pursued by Portuguese settlers along the West African coast from modern Senegal to Liberia. Cape Verdeans included a bigger component of immigrants from Portugal and they, like their São Tomé compatriots, played a crucial role in providing personnel, as well as food and clothing, to man the commercial networks on the mainland as well as housing prominent slave traders. The complex of the Cape Verdes and the nearest African shores south of the Gambia River, including the island-flecked coast of present-day Guiné-Bissau, was already the site of a substantial range of exchanges by the middle of the sixteenth century. This included a quite large and growing slave trade that serviced the Americas, albeit part of a more complicated trade circuit where the Portuguese bought local cloth and leather to sell further down the coast, imported North African horses to sell locally and looked for hides and skins, ivory and other natural products of the region to buy.

São Tomé proved to be only one in a chain of land-exhausting sugar plantation centres which the slave trade serviced. In economic terms the organisation and evolution of the sugar plantation, demanding large inputs of firmly controlled, hard-worked human labour, determined the history of the trade. The first European-run sugar plantations were in Crusader Cyprus. The focus then moved westwards through the Mediterranean to Sicily and southern Portugal, then to the Atlantic islands of Madeira and São Tomé. São Tomé at the end of the fifteenth century was the earliest slave plantation colony to rely overwhelmingly on African labour. From the Atlantic islands the focus of sugar production then shifted to the tropical colonies of the New World whose vast lands required settlers to be exploited effectively. It was Portuguese initiative which created the important original plantation nucleus in north-east Brazil.

The very weakness of Portuguese power, political and economic, was ironically a factor in the spread of the plantation. During the 1630s the Dutch temporarily succeeded in conquering part of Brazil and, in so doing, mastered the art of sugar milling. They introduced the system into the Caribbean region and seized upon the growing importance of the Portuguese slave trade in providing a vast coerced workforce. To this end they captured and held for a time the Angolan capital of Luanda, although during this period they failed themselves to export large numbers of slaves. In 1654 a Brazilian force under Salvador da Sá, representing a revival of Portuguese power, threw the Dutch out of Angola.

By this time, under Dutch inspiration, the sugar plantations had begun to spread through the Lesser Antilles and later extended to the larger British island of Jamaica, with the French island colony of St. Domingue (Haiti) the greatest eighteenth-century exploiter of African slave labour. The merchant fleets of France, and especially industrialising Britain, overtook the Dutch to become the major slaving powers of the eighteenth century. The Portuguese, too, expanded their slave trade and remained the third most important agent while most of the other European powers, as well as Brazil and New England, were active participants.The cruelties of the slave trade have long been associated with unimaginably great profits and tainted wealth. In truth, the slave trade was immensely profitable for European merchants during the seventeenth century in that the price of goods bought in Europe for sale to Africa was very low compared with the money value of slaves sold in the Caribbean. The business was a risky one, though, subject to European wars, piracies, shipwrecks, slave resistance and disease. Throughout the slaving period voyages could be extremely remunerative, but during the eighteenth century, despite the insatiable demands of the plantations which were prepared to pay ever higher prices, profits on average appear to have diminished as African traders improved their bargaining power in this repellent business.

The slave trade was a factor in the accumulation of capital which helped to fuel the Industrial Revolution. The causal link cannot be traced directly for the trade itself (and Euro-African commerce in general) was just one element in a great complex of economic activities: the plantations, their exports, their consumption of foodstuffs and textiles from Europe, North America (and, on a small scale, Africa) and the general development of shipping, to name only the most obvious. Slaving played its part in laying the foundations of capitalism within this broader structure made possible by the expansion of world commerce. At its height the slave trade overtook or entirely replaced other forms of commerce between Europe and Africa. Regions such as the Swahili coast and Ethiopia which appeared to be less likely major slave exporters were neglected, although a slave trade arose in the late eighteenth century from Kilwa and the off-shore island of Zanzibar to service the plantations founded by the French on the fertile, previously uninhabited, islands of Mauritius and Réunion in the Indian Ocean. An increasingly important source of slaves too was the coast of Madagascar where European pirates and their locally generated offspring often held sway. The gold export trade of Elmina virtually disappeared in the eighteenth century as the Gold Coast too became a major slave exporter. The Senegambian region, briefly an important source of slaves but from the seventeenth century of declining salience in this sense, and in time largely transformed into an exporter of gum Arabic (a natural product of acacia bush) was an exception, as was the extreme south of Africa where a colony of settlement developed under Dutch rule, into which the slaves were imported. (This will be considered separately towards the end of this chapter.)

However, it is generally fitting to treat the period of contact from the mid-seventeenth to the early nineteenth century as the era of the slave trade. The Europeans did not introduce the slave trade to sub-Saharan Africa. The very first slaves purchased by the Portuguese at Arguin, on the desert shores of modern Mauritania, came from the diversion of caravans which carried a not inconsiderable ancient slave trade across the desert. Moreover the Portuguese, through their contact with Morocco, were quite aware of some of the commercial potential, slave trade included, on the far side of the desert. At Elmina the Portuguese at first bought gold through the sale of Angolan slaves to African merchants. While the treatment and use of slaves in Africa was very different from the commercially orientated plantations of the New World, nevertheless Africans were sometimes being seized violently, captured and made available for exchange purposes as commodities. But the Atlantic slave trade did increase enormously the amount of slaving in Africa.

In recent years there has been considerable effort given to trying to quantify the scale of the slave trade. Philip Curtin inaugurated this tendency with his 'census', published in 1969, which estimated that between eight and nine million slaves were despatched from Africa to the Americas. Subsequent studies have raised these figures by some twenty-five to fifty per cent to include those who died before reaching the African coast or on the coast waiting to be sold.[3] It is virtually impossible to gauge the social significance of the slave trade in quantitative terms. Our knowledge of the historical demography of Africa is, and will probably remain, virtually nil. It is often assumed that such a huge number of people lost to Africa must have had a severe effect on the population, but there is little hard evidence to back such a claim. After all a larger number of Europeans, some 20 million, crossed the Atlantic to settle voluntarily in the New World in a single generation before World War I with, it is usually argued, a generally beneficial effect on the economies of the countries left behind. Slaves were despatched from Africa over a period of almost four centuries (although mainly from 1750 to 1850) from an entire continent. Some of the most heavily slaved areas, such as the hinterland of the Niger Delta, are today among the most densely populated parts of Africa, while thinly peopled districts, once thought to have been denuded of people under the slave trade, are ecologically relatively unattractive and presumably were underpopulated in the past. The impact of such crucial factors as the preponderance of males among the slaves exported is another unquantifiable feature. It has sometimes been suggested that the spread of new American crops, especially cassava, neatly countered the demographic impact of the losses, but this seems unlikely as a generalisation because of their limited adaptation outside a zone radiating from Angola and Kongo. The qualitative loss of slaves to Africa is even harder to measure. It may best be imagined in terms of land not cleared, settlements not established, cultivation becoming cruder or more laborious but, like any other counter-factual view of history as it might have been, this cannot be assumed to have been the case. What is more sure is that the increase in insecurity and violence brought by slaving affected the quality of life.

For Africa the trade involved the import of new commodities as much as the export of human beings. In exchange for slaves Africans accepted from Europeans a wide range of goods, the most important being Indian and European textiles. These and a range of others, notably metalware and salt, replaced domestically produced goods that were highly valued, traded for centuries and scarce in many regions. From Ijebu in Yoruba-speaking country, Benin and the Ivory Coast, African-woven textiles were purchased for sale to the Gold Coast. Where inter-African trade had existed European merchants attempted to participate and control. Contrary to later stereotype only a moderate amount of alcohol was sold to Africans; it became par excellence a ruling class token of hospitality and prestige. Guns and ammunition became increasingly significant trade items as their quality improved. At first, primitive European muskets had been valued largely for their symbolic fright value. They were often depicted on decorative plaques in Benin but there, as elsewhere, were probably used in fighting only occasionally. In the eighteenth century, however, the sale of guns belonged to the brutal cycle through which the slaves were produced for the market. A noteworthy item in the trade was the cowrie shell of the Indian Ocean, brought in from the seventeenth century probably as replacement for local shell currencies that had already existed in parts of West Africa. A number of other durable trade items such as bolts of cloth and brass manillas became widely diffused bases for exchange. The slave trade thus gave a fillip to a vast expansion in the exchange economy and the role of commodities in African life. The geographic scale of slaving at its height was astounding; by the end of the eighteenth century slaves were coming for sale on the coast from such remote regions as the Hausa states and the centre of south-central Africa in the later Katanga province of the Democratic Republic of the Congo.

Europeans rarely ventured far from the coast in pursuit of slaves at this time, less so than the Portuguese had done earlier on. In some regions they established forts for which they paid a rent to the local authorities who saw them as guarantees for the steadfastness of the trade rather than as threats to local sovereignty. The Gold Coast numbered some two dozen on a 200-mile coastline where the savannah interrupted the West African forest and swept down to the sea, creating relatively healthier conditions for foreigners to the tropics. Off-shore islands were often ideal trade bases. In other regions, such as the Loango coast of modern-day Gabon and the Congo Republic, or the Niger Delta, Europeans generally spent the nights on their ships and hulks were moored just off the coast. The forts contained barracks to hold the slaves and small garrisons but were generally ineffectual at repelling assaults by sea and changed hands often. African rulers sometimes tried to establish permanent alliances with particular European companies or states, but usually were anxious to permit as much competition as possible in the interest of favourable exchange rates.

The trade was thus an African trade until it reached the coast. Only very rarely were Europeans directly involved in procuring slaves, and that largely in Angola. Particularly in savannah regions, long-distance caravans brought slaves from hundreds of miles in the interior. In forest regions such as the modern Ivory Coast 'stateless' communities passed on slaves like a baton in a relay aimed at the sea. Slaves generally appear to have been sold several times before reaching the point of shipment.

Powerful ruling classes were never so foolish as to sell their own manpower in significant numbers. There is evidence of important states eventually weakening and collapsing due to the trade but others for long periods did surprisingly well. Slaves – from, say, Asante – were generally procured either through tribute or through raiding expeditions on the frontiers. This seems to hold as well for Kongo, Benin and Dahomey. The Kongo kingdom remained strong until the seventeenth century when it disintegrated into what had been provincial centres, and the others survived the end of the trade. Some slaves were debtors, prisoners or the victims of famine or made available as a form of tribute, but the majority were obtained through violence: wars, raids and kidnapping. It was the small-scale societies unable to resist either systematic or random violence of this kind that suffered the most and were obliged, in order to survive coherently, to retreat to remote and defensible locales. If active slave-trading elites in upper Guinea were challenged by slaves' resistance (such as the Hubbu movement in the Futa Djallon) that brought about independence, this degenerated in time, according to Boubacar Barry, to raiding caravans and new layers of slaving-induced violence. In the African savannah, the Bandiagara massif in Mali, the Jos Plateau and the mountains that mark the Nigerian-Cameroun border, communities established sites for survival. Marsh country near the coast of what is today Guiné-Bissau and the hills and thornveld behind the East African coast held others which also resisted the spread of Islam in what we could call a form of cultural resistance.

A peculiar consequence of the efforts of the 'African initiative' school to promote the historic grandeur of African kingdoms has been a consistent attempt to play down the transparently enormous importance of slaving for the forest states of West Africa: Oyo, Dahomey, Benin, Asante and others. Undoubtedly major wars between these states continued to have political rationales; their foreign policies cannot be reduced to manhunts. Victims, though, were systematically sold as slaves and all such states engaged in bloody and deliberate raiding which, when successful, provided booty that justified the participation of the soldiers. When occasionally Europeans were in a position to foment armed violence they were not averse to doing so. Major wars invariably resulted in the arrival of large numbers of captives on the coast. At the same time, other states such as Kaabu in the hinterland of the upper Guinea coast actually shifted their vital centres so as to participate more profitably in the trade. The rise of Kaabu and the collapse of Mali, both dominated by Malinke speakers, may reflect the shift from gold to slave trading and indeed the expansion of the extant slave trade per se. Barry believes also that the break-up of Joloff further north and the rise of new warrior (*tyeddo*) states amongst Wolof speakers in present-day Senegal also had much to do with the appeal of participation in the slave trade.

The most successful societies retained many slaves. For domestic purposes African households preferred to absorb women; the Atlantic trade demanded mostly male labour. Often male slaves in Africa were used as soldiers, and thus as sustainers of class or state power, a practice that intensified under the slave trade. The armies of bravoes that typified nineteenth-century Yoruba states and the class of *tyeddo* warriors, or royal slaves, that served the rulers of the Senegambia were partly created by the trade. In some areas, notoriously in Dahomey, women were also used as warriors, perhaps reflecting the population imbalances caused by the slave trade.

So-called stateless societies sometimes found effective ways of participating in the trade too. Existing institutions could be altered to streamline involvement without actually establishing kings on thrones. For instance, the Igbo-speaking country behind the Niger Delta was a major source of slaves. Much of the trade down to the delta ports was organised through the Aro society, operating under the protection of a sacred oracle who could both demand slaves in notional human sacrifice and protect a long-distance marketing system that traversed often warring village communities. Another group, particularly associated with the Nike region, became the armed procurers of the slaves in alliance with Aro. It is not surprising that twentieth-century anthropologists in Igbo-land described 'democratically' ordered communities of autonomous households that nonetheless placed great value on wealth, contained secret societies with extensive punitive powers and held slaves and other dependents.

The commercial opportunities of slaving sometimes encouraged remarkable migrations and social and ideological changes to accommodate new material opportunities. In the Angola hinterland a new people, known as the Imbangala, formed out of bands attracted to slave hunting and trading. Predatory and terroristic in their seventeenth-century heyday, the Imbangala defied the norms of kinship, absorbed huge numbers of unrelated recruits and attracted Mbundu households of the area into alliance. The slave trade largely created the Imbangala as a corporate entity.

All along the African coast there arose intermediary strata whose way of life centred on negotiation between European and African traders. These children of the slave trade formed what may be described loosely as a class of compradores by analogy with those powerful Chinese merchants who controlled the contemporary trade at the Chinese ports between Europe and the Celestial Kingdom. Sometimes they were Europeans, particularly Portuguese, who had become half-absorbed into African society. More often they were the descendants of Europeans and their 'country' wives, perfectly situated to mediate exchange relations between different modes of production. Speaking European languages, most often a form of Portuguese, and adhering at least nominally to Christianity, they could communicate perfectly with whites. Their African background similarly equipped them to function among those with whom they had been brought up. Such communities arose all the way from Angola north to Saint Louis, the principal French settlement at the mouth of the Senegal River. There was some seizing of local political power by European-descended compradore dynasties like the Coker and Roberts families of the 'Southern Rivers' region of the present-day Sierra Leone coast. But purely African compradores were more successful at this. Such were the house heads of Calabar in the Niger Delta who transformed the elder-dominated lineage inheritance system to establish 'houses' organised to absorb large numbers of slaves and to sell others. Within the houses power was often unstable and trading slaves sometimes seized power. In Calabar wealth brought political authority.

At the economic heart of compradore relationships lay ties of credit. The trust system of the Guinea Coast was essential to the functioning of a trade where the captain of the ship did not have a local bureau to administer his business, to hold on to his unsold goods or to collect slaves in advance for him. Corresponding to trust was the comey, through which Europeans paid a 'customs' duty to African political authorities so as to be able to proceed with their affairs. Comey and trust relationships formed a class of considerable wealth and sophistication whose most successful members often sent their children to Europe for schooling and who were most tightly committed to, and dependent upon, the trade with the West. They generally commanded numerous slaves to minister to their household needs, to protect their masters and to engage in productive activity. Some, for example, had large farms manned by slaves which produced foodstuffs for the slave voyages.

Thus a major consequence of the slave trade was the creation of a class that depended for its existence on Euro-African commerce. According to Stephen Ellis, 'There were so many petty rulers in Madagascar's north-west who were descended from pirates especially on Sainte-Marie and around the shores of Antongil Bay, that their offspring formed a dynasty known in Malagasy as the Zamanalata (children of the mulattos)' (Ellis, 2007, pp. 446–7).[4] More broadly, in many parts of Africa those who could command force and appropriate surplus developed a general orientation towards the hunting and sale of people, rather than the systematic production of goods for sale through agriculture or crafts, as a means of acquiring desirable commodities. The slave trade did not introduce predatory ruling classes to Africa, who indeed could be found in areas relatively untouched by it, but intensified internal slavery, violence and what the radical West Indian historian Walter Rodney aptly called 'social oppression' without any corresponding development of the forces of production. From a class perspective, this was its principal significance to the African continent.

The foundations of South Africa

It was at the height of the slave trade that a different, directly colonial, form of European penetration crystallised at the southern tip of Africa. Ships en route from Europe to Asia and back had taken to calling at Table Bay to purchase fresh meat from the resident Khoi Khoi pastoralists and to make extended stops for repairs or convalescence. In 1652 the Dutch East India Company established a permanent base at Cape Town to regularise this contact as a useful staging point in its Asian commerce.

Within five years the Company began to permit individuals to retire from its service and to settle permanently at the Cape. Relatively few settlers emigrated to South Africa, but those who did flourished and by the end of the eighteenth century they numbered approximately 25,000. The Company hoped they would perform a useful service on its behalf by providing agricultural produce for passing ships and the garrison stationed at Cape Town. In fact the settlers quickly discovered that their best prospects were first in the cattle and sheep trade with the Khoi Khoi and then in founding their own herds and ranging far into the interior with them.

Pastoral competition led to quarrels over trade and raids for stock, bloodshed and colonial expansion. While the Company was uneasy at spreading its resources and expenses further into Africa, it lent occasional support to the *veeboeren*, the cattle farmers, and gradually annexed more and more territory. The *veeboeren* themselves organised fighting commandos who often effectively dislodged Khoi Khoi populations in raids. Gradually the Khoi Khoi, devastated by epidemics, were pushed far to the east or north of the Cape or pressed into clientage relationships with the *veeboeren* who appropriated most of their stock. Without the stock, Khoi social organisation dissolved.

Nearer to the Cape something like a plantation economy developed. Land was granted in freehold to farmers who cultivated European grains such as wheat and created vineyards. The Dutch East India Company imported slaves from Mozambique, Madagascar and Asia. In contrast with the classic plantation colonies of the Caribbean, the dominant economic element at the Cape was the passing ship trade and its purchases of liquor and animal products. Even the slaves, who came slightly to outnumber the free colonists, were used in large numbers as artisans and hired servants, particularly in Cape Town itself, the 'Tavern of the Seas'. The Company aspired to initiate an export-orientated agriculture but the Cape produced no tropical luxuries nor staples to sell.

Through the seventeenth and eighteenth centuries the Cape settlers, a mélange of Dutch, French, Scandinavians and Germans, evolved an African (or Afrikaner) society of their own with a distinctive dialect that moved away from standard Dutch. They ranged from a few wealthy individuals owning large numbers of slaves and controlling exclusive contracts for provisioning the Company to landless discharged soldiers. It was upon this settler community that Dutch rule depended and operated, however much metropolitan officials might fulminate against the impoverished and undeveloped character of the colony and the troublesome inhabitants from an imperial point of view. At the lowest level of authority the Afrikaners commanded effective political, military and judicial power. They in turn depended on the imperial economy to sell their produce and on imperial arms for the possibilities of further expansion.

The racism that accompanied European imperial expansion in the age of plantation slavery prevailed at the Cape as a concomitant of the high level of social stratification and the realities of conquest and slavery. However, class society at the Cape was less racially determined than the typical Caribbean plantation colony. The crucial relationships of domination were those between slave owner and slave, master and servant. Intermarriage and concubinage were very common, particularly between poorer whites and Asian slave women, and legal distinctions were made over status (freedom versus 'unfreedom') rather than race. Many of the offspring of mixed unions were accepted into the Afrikaner community. The small stratum of 'free blacks' held a shadowy and insignificant social position. Spreading over 100,000 square miles by the opening of the nineteenth century, the Cape was mainland Africa's first real colony apart from enclaves on the shores of North Africa. In time it was to witness the most intense form of capitalist exploitation and development on the continent, but this was in long years to come.

The age of merchant capital

At the beginning of this chapter it was suggested that during this era the foundation for a world economy was laid. In the fifteenth and sixteenth centuries Africa's participation was limited and intermittent. But with the development of the slave trade the significance of Africa as a source of labour and as part of the great global commercial network grew markedly. A crucial difference between merchant and industrialised capital is that the former generally depends on interconnections between existing productive and social systems, and the profits which can be obtained through mastering the interstices between them, while the latter derives from an actual transformation in a productive system as a whole. Merchant capital characterised and dominated world enterprise before the Industrial Revolution of the late eighteenth century. During this period corresponding productive changes occurred only to a limited extent, especially in Africa. Only at the Cape did a socio-economic system form that was in any way comparable with the intensification of unfree labour exploitation that merchant capital engendered in some parts of the world, notably the slave plantations of the Americas. Where European penetration of Africa went deepest, in the Kongo kingdom, along parts of the upper Guinea coast, in Angola and Mozambique, it did so by adapting to the existing political and social ideologies and relationships.

A consistent materialist analysis of the period suggests that while ruling classes in Africa sharpened their predatory character and orientation to trade in imported manufactures, it is not really satisfactory to see Africa as simply 'dependent' on the West as a 'periphery' within a neatly articulated world economic structure. Within African societies, surplus-appropriating classes and strata in non-class societies actually reinforced their own positions through their command of trade objects and the violence accompanying the slave trade. In the merchant capital era European commerce could not, and in general did not even try to, conquer African peoples and reorient African societies forcefully. Thus 'dependency' could develop only as part of the logic of the needs of dominant strata and classes in Africa. It is important to remember this point when examining the history of the greater part of the nineteenth century, as the next chapter will show.

Notes

1. In fact there was apparently significant depopulation only in the nineteenth century. This is argued in John Thornton, 'Demography and History of the Kingdom of the Kongo, 1550–1750', *JAH*, XVIII (1977).
2. From the nineteenth century, however, these crops became far more prevalent and often assumed the status of staples in many distant regions. They were very widely cultivated on a secondary basis earlier as a result of their introduction by the Portuguese.
3. In fact, taking the last qualification into consideration, many estimates of the slave trade from the 1960s or earlier (for instance, those of K. O. Dike) are not far from the mark. However, the old figures contemporary abolitionists liked to draw on were usually very exaggerated.
4. See Stephen Ellis, 'Tom and Toakafo; The Betsimisaraka Kingdom and State Formation in Madagascar, 1715–50', *JAH*, 48(3) (2007), 439–55.

4
The Era of Legitimate Commerce, 1800–70

Even the merchants themselves, finding that the quantity of goods thus sent for sale into the interior had a sensible influence in curtailing their own store trade, by preventing in great measure the resort of the Ashantees [sic] to the coast, were obliged to yield to the current and to carry on their business principally by means of agents employed in the same manner ... All was now cheerful bustle and activity. There was not a nook or corner of the land where some enterprising trade had not led him. Every village had its festoons of Manchester cottons and China silks, hung up upon the walls of the houses or round the trees in the marketplace, to attract the attention and excite the cupidity of the villagers.

BRODIE CRUICKSHANK, *EIGHTEEN YEARS ON THE GOLD COAST OF AFRICA* (HURST AND BLACKETT, 1853), II, PP. 323

Abolition and legitimate commerce

In the final quarter of the eighteenth century the movement for the abolition of the Atlantic slave trade gathered force in Britain, the premier European slaving nation, and culminated in a ban from 1807. The British then pressured other nations to sign anti-slave trade treaties. In 1833 slavery in the British plantation colonies was entirely abolished, to be followed in time by the French, Scandinavian and Dutch colonies, the South American republics, the United States (in the course of its Civil War), Spanish Cuba and finally, in 1888, the empire of Brazil.

There is substantial controversy among historians over the causes of the abolition movement and its relationship to broader trends within the world economy and capitalist society.[1] In the floodtide of colonialism the freeing of the slaves was frequently and fatuously underlined as the ultimate paternalist symbol of European moral superiority and goodwill; abolition helped to justify colonial conquest. One man at first, the West Indian historian Eric Williams, attacked this view. In his famous study, *Capitalism and Slavery*, he tried both to delineate the relationship of the slave system to the process of capital accumulation which made the Industrial Revolution possible and to demonstrate that its abolition had equally sound economic causes, particularly the

Map 2 Nineteenth-century Africa

declining profitability of sugar plantations on the British West Indian islands and the rivalry with free labour production interests elsewhere. Britain thus turned against slavery because it was expensive, not because it was immoral. Today Williams' work appears powerful in outline but too narrowly economic in focus. There is no question that the importance to British colonial trade of the sugar isles, particularly those that were worn out, was declining from the late eighteenth century, but Williams had no justification for assuming that the continuation of the slave plantations would actually have been unprofitable. Cotton plantations in the southern USA continued to prosper throughout the slave era past the middle of the nineteenth century. Fertile virgin lands for the expansion of British-grown sugar cane beckoned in newly conquered Mauritius, Guyana and Trinidad at the very time of abolition. The trade itself continued to be profitable, if less consistently so than a century earlier.

Moreover it is impossible to reduce the anti-slavery movement to narrow economic foundations alone. In France, for example, the debate on the future of the slave trade and slavery was an integral part of the radicalising process of the Revolution. France abolished slavery before Britain, although this liberation was reversed later by Napoleon. The fervour and moral emphasis of British 'humanitarianism' had the support of some self-interested investors in free labour but cross cut specific interest group politics.

Abolitionism was part of an ideological transformation in Western thought that in turn reflected the growing dominance of the capitalist mode of production and the capitalist conception of labour. For the capitalist, who finally came into his own with the British Industrial Revolution of the later eighteenth century, the ideal worker is one who has been torn from the land, lacks any claim on the landlord or employer beyond his wage and is obliged to sell his or her labour on the market. Slavery ties down capital and immobilises labour; it stands in the way of genuine free enterprise as a form of labour monopoly. That passionate insistence on liberty which gave to the great bourgeois revolutionary movements in the USA, France and elsewhere a cast of social radicalism could not tolerate the idea of institutional slavery. As a result, to a certain extent, the short-term interests of the slave owners in the colonies could be and were pushed aside by the broader demands of capitalism.

Practical critics of slavery also appreciated the possibility that slave disaffection and revolts could in time lead to outright rebellion. In the richest of all the West Indian colonies, the French half of Hispaniola now known as the Republic of Haiti, such a generalised slave revolution did take place in 1791, leading to the extinction both of French authority and of the entire plantation system. The Haitian revolution and the fundamentally backward nature of slave systems were the frequently repeated themes of colonial abolitionist reformers in the early nineteenth century. Use of escaped slaves as soldiers in the American War of Independence, in the Civil War and in the intermediate years in the long wars of independence on the mainland of Central and South America worked strongly towards emancipation in one form or another. Their arguments frequently pointed at the future not only of the plantation colonies but also of the African continent where slaving seemed to limit, if not to stifle, all other forms of commerce and industry. How could this situation be reversed so as to transform the continent into a hive of industrious activity for the benefit of European commerce?

Out of this problematic came the slogan of 'legitimate commerce' which could oust the horrors of the slave trade to the benefit of all parties; an ideology which dominated the intensifying European penetration of nineteenth-century Africa, the creed of explorers and missionaries as well as traders. While the Industrial Revolution in Europe gained breadth and complexity, the demand for new products for industrial processes and consumption increased and some of these could be found readily in Africa: beeswax, wild rubber, ivory and, above all, the vegetable oils derived from palm, palm kernel and groundnuts. All of these were relatively peripheral to the industrial needs of Europeans, yet they provided the basis of what has often been described as a commercial revolution due to the enormous increase in Afro-European trade.

Palm oil began to be exported from West Africa long before the start of the nineteenth century. The trade arose initially from the provisioning of slave vessels. The real stimulus for its massive expansion (150 tons average per annum in the 1790s, 3000 tons in 1819, 8000 tons in 1829, 25,000 tons in the mid-1850s, all from the Bight of Biafra),[2] came from the British demand for oil

Figure 4.1 *Merchant capital*: hide and skin merchant with his goods, Kano (Nigerian savannah)

used in soap, candles and industrial lubrication. Groundnut exports also aimed at producing oils took off in the late 1830s in Senegambia. After several years France became the principal consumer.

In the era of legitimate commerce what Africa imported was perhaps more vital than what she exported. During the nineteenth century Europe shipped to Africa enormously increased quantities of goods: alcoholic beverages, arms and, above all, cloth, whose European price fell precipitately to the advantage of African producers of oils and other products. 'The quantity of cotton goods (measured by the yard) exported from the United Kingdom to West Africa increased thirty times in the short period between 1816–20 and 1846–50.'[3] It was moreover industrialising Britain that secured the lion's share of nineteenth-century commerce. At first glance it does indeed seem that the good coin of legitimate trade succeeded in driving out the bad coin of slaving. A closer look suggests that this assumption misses the fundamental link between the two.

First, it must be pointed out that the Atlantic slave trade did not simply end as a result of British abolition. For as long as the market was good in Cuba and Brazil slaves continued to be shipped over the ocean in amazingly high numbers. It has been suggested that the years after 1807 actually brought record numbers of slaves to the New World. Only when slaves could no longer be marketed in the plantation economies there did the trade finally peter out and this is generally equated with the decade of the 1860s in West Africa. It should be noted, however, that in certain areas such as the Gold Coast the slave trade had practically died out decades earlier.

Yet this important qualification is only a chronological revision. Other issues might occasion more surprise. For instance, the new forms of commerce proved relatively compatible with slave trading. In a number of regions, notably the

Niger Delta and Dahomey, both trades flourished simultaneously during much of the second quarter of the nineteenth century. The commercial mechanisms created by the slave trade (credit, units of exchange, commission systems) continued.

Even when slaves were no longer exported, the impact of legitimate commerce was to increase slaving and the holding of slaves *within* Africa. The demand for new articles for sale to international markets was indeed a spur to intensified commodity production in Africa but, given African social conditions and the slaving heritage, there was no reason for this to lead to free labour production. Much of the newly applied labour was the task of dependants: women, clients, youths but, above all, slaves. Male labour, no longer transportable overseas, continued to be seized in raids by the predatory forces the trade had engendered, but now was available relatively cheaply for local use. Another expanded category of work for slaves was the porterage of enhanced quantities of goods.

Domestic slavery could be nicely fitted in to the expansion in oil products. Thus 'In 1841, McGregor Laird, a British traveller, visited a woman of Aboh [Abo in Igbo country], who had over 200 slaves whom she used for the production of palm oil, yams and maize.'[4] In the West African savannah, caravans from deep in the interior had brought slaves to the coast. Now enterprising traders took their domestics and slaves down with them to the vicinity of the sea and had them grow groundnuts. This was the origin of the so-called 'strange farmers' of the Gambia valley and migrant *navétanes* of Senegal. In Dahomey there are reports of actual plantations where palm oil was produced by the slaves of the king and perhaps other officials and merchants. There may have been similarly systematic cultivation (and certainly collection) of kola nuts in Asante for sale northward to the Sokoto caliphate region.

The expansion of slaving was very marked in the eastern half of Africa during the nineteenth century. During this era the *prazeros* of the Zambesi valley sold off large numbers of subject African *colonos* unable to flee their bands of armed retainers. Many of the slaves ended up on the sugar islands of the Indian Ocean. It was only after 1800 that most of the East African interior was 'opened up' by the expansion of trade in slaves and ivory. Some of the slaves were sold to Arabia and other parts of the Islamic world outside Africa, but many were retained in the great new commercial entrepôt of Zanzibar where there emerged a class of Arab plantation owners specialising in the production of cloves who required a massive importation of labour from the mainland.

Thus the main change between the eighteenth and nineteenth centuries was not so much the difference between slave labour and free but simply the quantitative intensification and significance of commerce. Increasingly improved weaponry arrived in Africa and assisted the expansion of hunting both animals and people and made warfare more murderous. Firearms made access to European traders of vital importance to African rulers if they hoped to keep up with their neighbours and rivals. They highlighted the growing dependence of African ruling classes and others, such as lineage elders who could appropriate surplus, on trade goods that were entering the continent on all sides. The slave trade prepared the way for the triumph of 'legitimate trade'; it may have been a necessary precedent for the smooth West African ascendancy of the latter. At the same time, despite prevailing philosophy in Europe, the intensification of commodity exchange required not the proliferation of 'free' labour but of slavery and other direct forms of labour coercion such as pawnage under African social conditions.

Class and trade in coastal West Africa

Ancient African state formation is often slightly shakily ascribed to long-distance trade. One reason for this may lie in an unthinking extrapolation from the nineteenth and twentieth centuries. For the nineteenth century there can be little doubt of the great significance of the penetration of the world market in Africa, although it was not always the existing ruling class that secured the greatest benefit from it.

The compradore acquired an unprecedented importance in this era. It was in West Africa, where commerce expanded so markedly from such a strong historic base, that he came most fully into his own. On the Gold Coast he was apt to be an active Methodist layman, anxious to educate his sons as far as possible, including if possible schooling in Britain, and eager to participate in the recreation of many aspects of respectable European society on the Guinea Coast. Such an individual was James Bannerman, the 'great man of Accra, wealthy, liberally educated and a gentleman.'[5] The gum trade in St Louis and the groundnut trade in Gorée island spawned an equivalent class that looked to France for its cultural reference point. Charles Heddle, the wealthiest West African coastal merchant of the second half of the nineteenth century, came from a Gorée background, settled in Sierra Leone where he amassed landed property, and spent his final days in nouveau riche retirement with a pretty young wife on the French Riviera. The Senegal coast was also the domain of the often entrepreneurial ladies of mixed backgrounds called *signares*. The opening of the Banque du Sénégal was aimed at benefiting from their custom.

The slave trade had depended on the trust or commission system whereby Africans were granted goods as capital to procure slaves between the visits of the European ships. Legitimate commerce required a great expansion of trust with credit made available to African traders on a considerable scale. Yet the sometimes grand lifestyle of the coastal merchant was rarely matched by capital resources; he was ultimately dependent for lines of credit on a small number of merchant firms: Brazilian in Angola, Bordeaux-based in the Senegambia, Liverpool-orientated in the Niger Delta and the Gold Coast. Control over small armies of slaves enabled him to provide for personal needs and further his business. To only a limited extent did the compradores turn their slaves to systematic plantation cultivation for commercial sale, although examples do exist. Never do they seem to have effectuated any transformation in local productive forces.[6]

Little bourgeois fish in a vast non-capitalist sea, they lacked the social wherewithal to initiate capitalist production and the essential accompanying state framework. This had the effect of increasing their dependence on European state power; if a crisis raised the necessity of transformation, they had to seek sustenance from one or another European state. Their struggle was one for recognition as the foremost agents of European commercial, political and cultural penetration.

An important section of compradores consisted of new strata issuing directly from the activities of the anti-slave trade movement. In 1787 the Province of Freedom was established under British authority on the Atlantic peninsula known as Sierra Leone, an African home for Maroons who had escaped into the interior from the slave plantations of Jamaica, Black Loyalists who had come from the USA to Canada during the American Revolution and migrants from Britain itself, where slavery was already illegal. The British philanthropists first organised the Sierra Leone Company to further commerce and free labour. Their overbearing conduct, together with poor administration, led to sharp conflict and Sierra Leone had a turbulent history before the British state assumed power in 1808. Under Crown Colony status Sierra Leone throve and its population grew as 're-captives' were released from liberated slave vessels and brought to the capital of Freetown where the anti-slavery squadron and court was headquartered.

The Sierra Leoneans, or Creoles, rapidly welded together a distinctive colonial culture characterised by the Krio dialect they spoke. Some Creoles, of re-captive origin, were Muslim, but the majority were Christian Protestants, and Christianity became their most distinguishing cultural feature, much as it served for the *trekboers* of South Africa. Within a generation the Creoles had produced their first ministers of the gospel; within two their first doctors and lawyers. Early British hopes for Sierra Leone as an agricultural export colony soon died. The wealthy Creoles of Freetown were often landlords, but above all merchants who established trading networks deep in the interior. Many of them returned to their places of origin in other parts of Africa, particularly present-day southern Nigeria, and here they occupied a major role in the spread of commerce, Christianity and European customs. The Yoruba called the Sierra Leone returnees 'Saro' and the Saro formed a decisive wedge of Western cultural influence and commercial innovation among them.

In Lagos the Saro met with another distinctive group, the Amaro or Brazilians. In Brazil, particularly Bahia, it was not uncommon for African slaves to acquire their freedom within their own lifetime and a few began to return to West Africa in the early nineteenth century. The most influential and historically significant were associated with the kingdom of Dahomey, where some were themselves important slave traders while the trade survived. Others engaged in 'legitimate' trans-Atlantic commerce as Africans continued to be good customers for the sugar-cured tobacco of Bahia. Amaro remained as Catholic as the Saro were Protestant and were less often merchants than artisans, skilled craftsmen in the new techniques demanded in the growing West African ports. Significant as the compradores were, they must be measured with other new classes that expanded: artisans, wage labourers, for which a regular pool began to exist in the Gold Coast by mid-century, and soldiers who were prepared to fight for pay in cash. The *tirailleurs* or sharpshooters of French Senegal were the most famous example, raised on a regular basis by the 1850s.

Several hundred miles down the Windward Coast from Sierra Leone, a parallel community was founded under the auspices of the American Colonization

Society which sought to establish a home for free American blacks. This was Liberia, whose capital, Monrovia, named for the American President Monroe, was established in 1822. Other settlements were amalgamated into the unified republic of Liberia which became a sovereign state in 1847. The USA had no interest in assuming here the authority that Britain did in Sierra Leone. There were West Indian immigrants and re-captives in Liberia, but the dominant settler element was the 'Americo-Liberian' population, immigrants from the USA impelled to Africa by the growing harshness towards free blacks in the republic. Although the Liberians recognised no foreign authority they also evolved a colonial middleman society expanding among hostile 'natives'. On the coast below Monrovia lived the Kru people. They were, par excellence, the sailors of West Africa and as such formed another key layer in the overall expansion of capitalist commercial interests.

The relationship of these trends to the jihad movement of the deep West African interior was not straightforward. As we shall see below, Islam can help drive a great trading state such as Zanzibar and the ambitious imperial thrust of Muhammad Ali in Egypt with more than a veneer of Western influence. The *navétane* migrants to the coast who sold groundnuts were certainly Muslim. Jean-Loup Amselle has highlighted the diffusion of long-distance trading communities that were also becoming more orthodox in their Islam in this period. Plenty of Muslims in Yoruba country were sold across the Atlantic during the wars of the early-to-middle nineteenth century.

Earlier though, in the first major jihad episode in the late seventeenth century in the Senegal valley, the Muslim enthusiasts were hostile to the slave trade and indeed to doing business with Europeans. This phase ended in defeat. In the mid-nineteenth century, as the French expanded inland, some jihadists such as Shehu Amadu who conquered Segu in the Niger valley and imposed a stricter form of religion, deliberately shifted inland to evade their influence. From Amadu's new capital of Hamdullahi, a new state was formed that did not encourage trade with the seagoing infidels. However, Umar Tall created a reform movement that in the 1850s would intensify commercial relationships in the region in overthrowing the Masina state Shehu Amadu had created. The Islamic principle of avoiding monarchy as a decadent idea propounded by their enemies remained a feature of the so-called Lebou republic of Cape Vert where Dakar would emerge as a town, in the Futa Djallon plateau of modern Guinea as well as in the theoretical logic of the caliphate of Sokoto. A common set of values tended to win out through the growing popularity of Islamic brotherhoods such as the Tijaniyya and especially the home-grown Muridiyya that accepted forms of monarchy and would also come to preach a quietist reaction to imperialism as it later expanded dramatically in Senegal.

Nineteenth-century East Africa

On the eastern side of Africa the mixture of intensified commerce, slaving and the import of firearms was more explosive than in West Africa because the slave trade had been so much less significant earlier. With the exception of the Zambesi valley and its ancient gold trade, links between coast and interior south of the Horn of Africa had been fragmentary. In the eighteenth century long-distance trade in ivory and slaves as a symbiotic commercial complex spread north of the Zambesi. By the end of the century great caravans began to criss-cross what is today mainland Tanzania from the Indian Ocean shores to Lake Tanganyika and beyond. The Nyamwezi people of the Tabora region, a pioneer trading town, specialised as caravan leaders and porters. Commercial networks extended through the corridor between Lakes Tanganyika and Malawi, into the copper mining district of present-day Katanga province, Democratic Republic of Congo, and north to the interlacustrine states, notably Buganda.

The country around Lake Malawi suffered intensely from slave raids as the junction point between the coastal trade and the explosive force of the *Mfecane* chiefdoms with their southern origins. Banditti with guns succeeded in establishing new power foci, the nuclei of states, at places where trade could bring an accumulation of wealth and command over the means of destruction. Msiri, a Nyamwezi from western Tanzania, established such a centre in Katanga. Further north around the headwaters of the rivers feeding into the Congo lay the headquarters of the great Zanzibar trader and marauder, Tippu Tip. Within Nyamwezi country itself, astride the principal route from the ocean to Lake Tanganyika, Mirambo was the most famous nineteenth-century power broker. Several Arabised Muslim states in formation flickered around Lake Malawi. However brutal the process of state-building noted by early European travellers as they approached the new domains being carved out by the great traders, they generally remarked on the prosperous and orderly conditions prevailing near the capitals where the new power was fitfully being born.

The Nyamwezi at least partly acquired their identity as a people from their characteristic commercial role. Traders from their region began to reach the coast around the opening of the nineteenth century and, by mid-century, the

Figure 4.2   *Merchant capital*: ivory caravan on march to the coast (mainland Tanzania)

economy of north-central Tanganyika depended upon porterage wage labour and other side effects of trade. If the slave and ivory business devastated some regions, it brought prosperity to others in the form of expanding markets for crops and cattle and generalised surplus accumulation. Access to trading routes and to firearms brought about great imbalances in power between regions and peoples. From the mid-nineteenth century the feared Maasai pastoralists lost their grip on the plains of central Kenya while the Kamba people, who traded extensively with the coast, became stronger, as did the Kikuyu agricul-turalists south of Mount Kenya. Charles Ambler has rightly pointed out that these ethnic or tribal categories were not necessarily in place in the nineteenth century; in fact, the development of new commercial niches may have helped them to begin to congeal.

Quite unlike any other contemporary East African state, however, was the island sultanate of Zanzibar. The impact of firearms and the caravan trade gave Zanzibar, an important slave trade centre at the opening of the nineteenth century, a special attraction to the rulers of Oman in Arabia who had estab-lished suzerainty over the old coastal ports with the collapse of Portuguese authority. In 1840 Seyyid Said (ruled 1804–56) moved his capital to Zanzibar island where a city of stone-built mansions, entered through great carved wooden doors, sprang up. Seyyid Said established excellent relations with the naval masters of the Indian Ocean, the British; it was under their aegis that his commercial empire prospered in close relation to the commerce of British India. It was largely to India that Zanzibari grown cloves were shipped. The lush, well-watered island proved to be an exceptionally well-favoured growing spot for this rare spice tree and by the middle of the nineteenth century Zanzibar had become its major world producer. Clove trees (and, to a lesser extent, coconut palms) formed the agricultural basis of a plantation economy which attracted a community of Arab and Arabised merchants into land ownership while depending on the finance of Indian capitalists. From Zanzibar's mainland port of Bagamoyo, caravans, fitted out by Indian merchants and often led by the dependants and sons of Zanzibari planters, headed inland. True Zanzibari authority did not extend beyond a very limited coastal zone but, as far west as the lakes, the Sultan retained esteem as protector of long-distance commerce.

The clove and coconut plantations of Zanzibar, partly equipped through staple food-producing estates on the mainland coast, responded to a process of intense commercialisation that led to total transformation in relations of production, an extreme example in Africa of the impact of nineteenth-century commerce. Yet the planters and (increasingly, Indian) merchants of Zanzibar did not have the makings of a capitalist class. Older, pre-capitalist values, empha-sising an integrating Muslim culture and paternalistic clientage relationships, inhibited the emergence of a full-blown, wage labour-dependent, capitalist society on Zanzibar. The Zanzibar state was also slow to develop the adminis-trative and military apparatus which might have given it more strength to fend off the pressure from European imperialism that built up dramatically. Both in the Great Lakes region north of Buganda and further north on the coast, in the Benadir of modern Somalia, travellers under the auspices of Zanzibar brushed against counterparts from another and far more politically ambitious Islamic state, Egypt. The attempt by the Egyptian Muhammad Ali (ruled effectively 1807–48) and his successors to forge a powerful regime, in good part through African expansion, is one of the epic stories of the nineteenth-century history of the continent. Muhammad Ali's most forceful economic and military measures frightened Europeans who felt their commercial position in the Near East threatened and pressed him at knifepoint to compromise. Yet the process of commercial penetration and state aggrandisement begun by Muhammad Ali continued until the bankruptcy of Egypt on the eve of the scramble for Africa.

Military expansion proved inherent in the logic of the state Muhammad Ali established. Under Muhammad Ali Egyptian armies succeeded in seizing control of the middle Nile valley and the adjacent Red Sea coast. Later Kordofan, far to the west of the river, was added. A somewhat expanded version of this territory is the modern Republic of Sudan. The search for slaves, who fed into the Cairo luxury market, the state army and workforce of the expanding cotton fields of the delta, formed a major facet of the Sudanese conquest. On the frontiers, armed merchants, the 'Khartoumers', led countless expeditions searching for elephants and people to enslave.

The ambitious Cairo authorities looked, as well, at the region of the Horn, establishing several coastal bases and penetrating the Ethiopian plateau on a number of occasions. In 1875–6 the financially overextended Egyptians launched an ill-fated, three-pronged invasion of Ethiopia which failed disastrously. If the mercantile forces emanating ultimately from industrialising Europe were the motor pressing Egypt forward into Africa, the ambitions of the Egyptian state lacked a solid economic basis in empire or elsewhere. Instead, grandiose imperial dreams led to grandiose expenses that helped to bankrupt Muhammad Ali's successors.

The third African power to emerge in a kind of pre-partition of eastern Africa was the Ethiopian monarchy. In the mid-nineteenth century a nobleman-bandit named Kassa took the throne as Emperor Tewodros (Theodore) and essayed the recreation of a unified imperial power in the highlands with an unprecedented importation of firearms. Tewodros failed to control the strong centripetal tendencies that worked against monarchy in Ethiopia. His inept dealings with Europeans led to the imprisonment of missionaries and others at Meqdela (Magdala) fortress, their rescue by the British Napier expedition in 1868 which met with little resistance from Ethiopians, and the emperor's suicide.

However, Tewodros had successors who followed his efforts to base a new power in Ethiopia on firearms and a partly remodelled state apparatus. One was the great Northern lord, the Tigrean who took the throne name of Yohannis (John) IV and achieved wide acceptance in the northern and central highlands as emperor after his coronation in 1872. His principal rival was the ruler of Shewa, Sahle Silasse, and Sahle's heir, Minilik. Shewa was so well situated, on the one hand, for the firearms trade to the coast, and, on the other hand, for commerce with the south (from whence slaves, ivory and coffee could be procured), that in the long term it made a more effective pivot to the new empire that would in time share in the imperialist partition of Africa.

Up to a point, another major beneficiary of the new forces operating in Africa was the kingdom of Imerina, which acquired control of most of the island of Madagascar in the late eighteenth and early nineteenth centuries under its rulers Andrianampoinimerina ('my paddy fields stretch to the sea') and his successor Radama I, who used commerce to acquire guns. A major slaving power, Imerina agreed to cease participation in the maritime slave trade while continuing to raid on the island for its own purposes. It was not only slaves who were put to work for the kings and queens of Madagascar. Intensive labour requirements foisted on the mass of commoners led to the diffusion of irrigated rice paddies where suitable, and (for a time) to the development of an industrial base which could produce armaments as well as allow for a large standing army to be created. For a significant phase, the Imerina state opted to isolate itself from most contacts with Europe while trying to continue a partial economic modernisation. At its peak, the kingdom of Madagascar had diplomatic relations with a number of European powers and accepted Protestantism as the state religion. Yet fear of imperial conquest always prevented the development of a modern transport system, notably over the escarpment from the ports of the east coast to the royal capital of Antananarivo. Internal tensions inherent in its incomplete modernisation coupled with the declining ability of Malagasy rulers to balance the hungry ambitions of different European powers led to the state being seriously crippled in a war with the French in 1883–5 and finally to its conquest in 1896.

In the conditions of eastern Africa the characteristic results of the age of legitimate trade were both the expanding African empires of Zanzibar, Egypt and Ethiopia and the predatory new state creations of Mirambo, Tippu Tip and their like. Existing states experienced variable fates. Buganda was at first strengthened by the sweep of new commercial forces after 1850. The great powers of the *kabaka* could only be enhanced by the possibilities of firearms and the sale of ivory. Yet, it can be argued from hindsight, social forces within the ruling class were beginning to consider action aimed at freedom from royal control, based on new contacts with the outside. In Bulozi, on the Zambesi floodplain, the expansion of commerce in the second half of the nineteenth century enabled the *litunga* to strengthen and greatly expand slavery, allowing for state-based water control works that in turn formed the basis for a much more rigid and harshly articulated class society than any known before.

It might be expected that the well-established states of West Africa would be more likely to absorb the press of commerce to themselves with their ruling aristocracies and kings best fitted to take advantage of opportunities for new wealth. It has been claimed, for instance, that Asante handily enough adjusted the focus of its trade from slaves sent south to kola nuts sent north. No great new empires that can be linked closely to the changing economic developments paralleled the scale of Asante, Oyo or Benin. One major forest state, Oyo, collapsed in the 1820s as a result of internal revolt, slave risings and the pressure of the jihad in the north. Over the next seventy years various new political units arose in the territory of old Oyo and tried to seize its mantel, but none succeeded entirely. Ilorin accepted Islam and the leadership of Sokoto and became a centre for the diffusion of the new and influential religion, Ibadan became a huge agglomeration where power was shared between several houses while Ijebu had the strongest hold on the trade route to the lagoon port of

Lagos. The issue of access to Western arms, which largely meant access to Lagos, often determined the balance of power in the lengthy series of wars that raged through Yoruba-speaking lands. Each contender depended on Saros and other contacts in Lagos to procure arms.

The era of informal empire

The first seventy years of the nineteenth century witnessed significant, but still very limited, extension of actual European colonial power in Africa. It has been called the period of 'informal empire', particularly on the part of Britain, whose commercial ascendancy in the overseas trade of Africa became more and more marked. So long as trade expanded satisfactorily under existing conditions there was little reason for Western regimes to plan military expeditions and colonial adventures that cost money and were unlikely to yield immediate results of any profit.

On the east coast the British consul in Zanzibar watched discreetly over British interests and the general conduct of commerce. The abolition of the slave trade in Zanzibar in 1873 was due largely to British pressure. In the Egyptian empire European influence became ever more important: Europeans in the service of the government were among the highest civil and military officials in the conquered areas south of the Sahara. But before 1870 the different nationalities tended to cancel out one another's influence.

A parliamentary select committee in 1865 virtually called for the complete withdrawal of the British state from West Africa, following the demise of the Atlantic slave trade. This commission, however, which envisioned a continued role for traders and missionaries of compradore background, took place at a period of particularly striking downturn in the palm oil trade when there was good, if short-term, reason for commercial pessimism. Its recommendations were almost entirely ignored. In fact, throughout this period both Britain and France tended gradually to increase their stake in Africa. The era was one of exploration, so much of which consisted of probing for commercial and political information. In West Africa Europeans discovered the course of the Niger and made direct contact with the savannah states. By 1870 the sources of the Nile were known and the mountains and lakes of East Africa seen by Europeans. The one great mystery remaining was the character of the central equatorial basin and the course of the Congo, which Stanley would solve soon afterwards.

Colonial expansion consisted largely in the seizure of points here and there along the coast which appeared most appropriate for controlling long-distance commerce, often under the cover of suppressing the slave trade. Like wary wrestlers, agents of European states sought out pressure points that could be used to lay effective hold on the trade of the African interior. In addition to Sierra Leone the British established themselves at the mouth of the Gambia (Bathurst, founded 1816) and, in 1851, on Lagos island, ideally situated to tap the commerce of Dahomey and Yorubaland. British political influence rose steadily along the Gold Coast where the old forts were directly ruled by the state again from 1850, after a period of purely merchant control. In the Niger Delta British treaties allowed increasing intervention in the political and commercial affairs of treaty-signing states. This was the most productive palm oil export zone of all and British traders began to dream, once the course of the river was known, of the possibility of direct commerce with the interior. This was anathema to the whole middleman character of the Delta ruling class and their dependants, but, despite all their efforts, steam ships began to penetrate up the Niger (after the Baikie expedition of 1854) and then the Benue and to establish, towards the end of this period, permanent commercial relations with the southernmost jihad emirates yielding allegiance to Sokoto.

Equivalent French finger-holds were established at Grand Bassam and Assinie on the Ivory Coast and at Libreville in Gabon. More solid was the foundation in the 1850s of a territorially extensive colony in Senegal following the river from the coast. After the retrocession of St Louis, on an island at the mouth of the Senegal River, to the French by the British following Napoleon's defeat, Baron Roger became the soul of a French attempt to establish a slave-based plantation colony in the valley of the Senegal River, an attempt which proved premature historically. Moorish raids, the inability to control a labour force and inept administration led to the collapse of the plantations after several years. The Roger initiative indicates the depth of French commitment to Senegal and its historic use as a precedent in capitalist penetration for West Africa.

In the 1850s, under the energetic leadership of General Louis Faidherbe (governor 1854–61, 1863–5), the French pursued a deliberate policy of expansion as a means of building commercial prosperity. Cape Vert, on which was built the new town of Dakar, the Petite Côte (Little Coast) to the south and the kingdom of Waalo behind St Louis were annexed directly to the French Empire, which already had another base of territorial control on the African continent in Algeria on the Mediterranean. The French decisively beat the most energetic jihad leader of the region, al hajj Umar Tall, at the battle of Medina in 1858, and he turned back towards the east to found his new state. French power was applied systematically to prevent the formation of a hegemonic Islamic power in the Senegambian region. The cause of Islamic reform either shifted inland away from the intruders or cautiously began to look for a way to live with the new Christian power. By 1870, with greatly increased commercial interests and knowledge of Africa, with potential available armies of cheaply paid Africans, improved arms and awareness of how to cope with tropical health conditions, the conquest of Africa by Europeans, if not inevitable or predictable for the immediate future, was no longer impossible. However, at the time the dominant trend was the expansion of African-based powers anticipating the future partition – the Sokoto alliance of emirates, the new Yoruba powers, Ethiopia, Zanzibar, Egypt and the politically ambitious traders and caravan masters of East Africa. This striking phenomenon is masked by what was to befall later. Nor did it exclude the south.

South Africa in the age of the Great Trek

In the extreme south of Africa colonial expansion had already reached a significant stage before the nineteenth century. The expansion of the exchange economy and capitalist productive forces had generated a complex class society at the Cape. In 1806 the last Dutch government at Cape Town surrendered to a British army. The British had already occupied the Cape for several years previously (1795–1803), but were now determined, for strategic purposes, to retain the colony. Thus the Cape came to be situated within the context of a far more dynamic economic system than that of the Dutch. Within a very short time British merchants dominated commerce at the Cape.

The principal goal of the Cape's new rulers was to establish a basis for progressive prosperity on capitalist lines to the advantage of Britain. This involved finding a commodity for the world market which could be produced locally. At first Cape wine exports prospered, thanks to preferred admission without tariff payments into Britain, but they suffered from the gradual imposition of free-trade regulations on wine benefiting competitors. Only in the 1830s did the eastern Cape begin to export wool on a significant scale, beginning a twenty-year boom that at last made the colonial South African economy modestly viable, allowing for transport improvement and giving a capital value to pastoral land.

The government was anxious to eliminate slavery and establish a free labour market, yet social stability at the Cape rested on the position of landowning slaveholders who stood to lose most of their capital in the wake of slave emancipation. A succession of laws shifted back and forth between more and less coercive solutions to the problem of labour control (Hottentot Proclamation of 1809, Ordinance 50 of 1828, appointment of a Slave Protector, abolition of slavery of 1833), while the community of masters became mistrustful. Although fearful of consequent military involvements leading to unremunerative expenditure and unknown political engagements, the British army intervened with increasing decisiveness to secure proclaimed frontiers and push back the Xhosa in the east from the regions where *trekboers* had established farms. This was insufficient to solve the needs of the pastoral economy. Frontier districts became overpopulated in terms of the extensive mode of production while the state appeared to threaten the basis of farmers' control over labour, especially those too poor to procure workers through competitive wages.

Between 1795 and 1815 frontier farmers engaged in several rebellions against the Dutch and British colonial government. The last of these, the Slagters Nek rebellion, was the most easily quelled. Direct resistance to the British appeared hopeless. Instead, scouts began to explore the possibilities of a leap beyond the colonial frontier to the north. The *Mfecane*, clearing populations off fertile areas which could serve as corridors for armies and livestock, greatly increased prospects of success.

In 1834 the first parties of some 10,000 emigrants initiated the Great Trek from the colony, establishing themselves through much of what has become the Republic of South Africa. This is not to say that, despite the advantage of firearms, the trekkers instantly conquered all the Africans of the region, but they did succeed in winning several crucial military victories that allowed for the establishment of zones where they controlled land and a limited amount of local labour. Throughout this period, hunting, trading and transport-riding remained very important in the trekker economy, more so than farming and stockherding, especially north of the river Vaal. Only in the 1860s did the political centres there consolidate into one South African Republic (SAR). Even then, the most northerly section, the Zoutpansberg, had to be abandoned with the revival of a powerful Pedi state. South of the Vaal after 1852, the British acknowledged the independence of the Orange Free State: smaller, more compact and more commercially integrated with the Cape than the SAR.

In one area, Natal, the trekkers were pursued and beaten back by British expansion. The trek to Natal put the emigrants directly in conflict with the Zulu state. After the Zulu massacre of an advance party, the trekkers won revenge at the battle of Blood River in 1838. The British feared both regional destabilisation and rival oversea links that the trekkers might establish on their newly acquired sea coast. An imperial force defeated the trekkers of Natal in 1842 and the territory became a second British South African colony.

By mid-century South Africa was the scene of several colonial or colonially derived societies with somewhat different economic and social forces in ascendance, depending on the strength of capital penetration. British merchant capital in South Africa held the Cape as its base with its ports and nascent finance facilities. In 1853 a constitution vested powers of self-government in an assembly elected on the basis of a low property qualification and no racial discrimination. The patronage that white politicians and merchants established over landless black wageworkers and farmers laid the foundation of 'Cape liberalism'. In the eastern Cape a prosperous class of labour-employing, plough-using, market-orientated black peasantry responded strongly to the advance of the market and accepted white merchants and professional men as political representatives; the successful amongst them were still able to call on the labour of extended families, although poorer families were more likely to be producing simply in order to pay their tax and survive. Mission schools formed their leaders. From the 1850s the first African professional men returned to the Cape from Britain, contemporaries of an equivalent generation of West African coastal compradores. Cape society was the strongest of the colonial and colonially derived states in relation to its African neighbours and it had a moderate basis of agricultural prosperity in wool.

Towards the end of its heyday the Cape liberal outlook was expressed graphically by one of its leading spokesmen in the Cape, premier John X. Merriman:

> The Cape ministry are not, as you know, Solomons; but they do heartily oppose and detest Mr. Froude's and Lord Carnarvon's native policy. We are gradually educating the natives. We are introducing individual tenure of land and European implements. We have four thousand natives at work on our Railways. Gradually the power of the Chiefs is being broken up, and our laws introduced, and I hope this session to get a measure for the modified municipal government of locations. Lovedale has three hundred native boys and seventy girls, very many of whom pay for their own education ... They learn trades and ... may earn forty shillings a week as printers.[7]

Natal was a vastly weaker unit, particularly as measured against its Zulu neighbour to the north. In Natal, settlers (mainly from Britain) struggled to find a profitable basis for economic exploitation. Much land became tied up in-speculative ventures orientated in fact towards the collection of tribute or cash from African peasants, at least until a higher level of capitalisation could be achieved. In the 1850s it became apparent that there was a future for sugar plantations along the coast, but the settlers lacked the coercive power to obtain African labour under plantation conditions at low wages. They turned to indentured labourers from India, who began to arrive in 1860 and made the fortunes of the lowland sugar planters. The Natal system had no room for the ideal of a liberal society; a non-racial franchise existed on paper, but in practice the Natal vote from its creation in 1856 was a white vote. Natal controlled extensive and populous African 'locations', upon which pressure could be exerted to draw labour and cash, a system associated with Theophilus Shepstone, Secretary of Native Affairs (1845–76) and self-proclaimed Great White Chief of the Natal Zulu. The strongest chiefs could be a bulwark of strength against the Zulu monarchy looming north of the Tugela. The South African historian David Welsh has argued that if a model of segregation in later South African society existed it lay in Natal, a theme recently taken up by Mahmood Mamdani in *Citizen and Subject* looking for a historic model of rural colonial administration in Africa. The weakness of colonialism in Natal encouraged the cult of African 'tradition', sustaining a system of indirect rule through the chiefs and extracting small amounts of labour and goods from African farmers through the modest application of force that was systematically feasible.

The trekker states, and especially the South African Republic, were yet slower to acquire commercial coherence. The newcomers awarded themselves huge landed estates, but their control over local labour, now officially considered to be squatting on private property, was more nominal than real. African squatters provided little labour and less cash to landlords, who in turn found the establishment of commercial agriculture a difficult process. Among the trekkers acute distinctions between rich and poor developed fairly quickly. A small class of notables whose commercial linkages gave them command over labourers and firearms dominated trekker society.

Some of the extension of wage labour in the Cape represented immigration and proletarianisation. To this category belonged the less fortunate *Mfecane* refugees of the eastern Cape, or Mfengu, who remained farm labourers, together with Xhosa ruined by the takeover of land or the destruction of stock commanded by the prophetic movement known as the cattle killing, in 1857. This does not entirely explain the spread of migrant labour in southern Africa, however. Initially wage labour could be quite advantageous to the worker, Mfengu included, who might return home with shotgun and cattle and supply the bridewealth that would enable him to found a new homestead.

By the 1860s migrants were coming to the Cape in large numbers from as far as the Pedi state in the north of the claimed territory of the South African Republic and what is today southern Mozambique. While major African states such as Lesotho, the Zulu kingdom, the Pedi state and others retained political independence quite effectively, and were if anything a threat to their colonial neighbours, rather than the other way around, exchange relations connecting Africans into circuits that ultimately linked back through the Cape to Europe had achieved a remarkable importance even beyond colonial frontiers.

On a much smaller, but still significant, scale, capitalist forces encouraged new social relationships in Angola. The fishing fleets off the coast of southern Angola as well as the thriving coffee estates of Cazengo, inland from Luanda, depended heavily on slavery, which remained legal under the Portuguese flag until the 1870s. From the slave trade era a small class of local capitalists, of varying racial origin but including an important number of both mulattos and Africans, arose. Inland the rapid extension from mid-century of the ivory and then the rubber frontiers brought advantages to two trading peoples, the Chokwe of the northern interior, who absorbed vast numbers of slaves, and the Ovimbundu of the central highlands, intermediaries par excellence in 'legitimate commerce' between the Portuguese on the coast and the interior peoples. They forged an identity as trading peoples that may be readily compared with the Nyamwezi and Kamba on the eastern side of the continent.

Southern Africa provides the most complex and far-reaching examples of class formation and economic change brought about through the extension of trade in nineteenth-century Africa, an extension that reached widely indeed. Through the century African ruling classes expanded their interests in the acquisition of commodities they could not produce through a social order increasingly dependent on firearms and trade goods. Defence and exchange goods equally must have extended their significance for the mass of cultivators. However, there is little reason to think that this era brought about a correction to the direction of change and the abuses of the slave trade. To accept this is largely to accept the propaganda of the old 'humanitarian' imperialist lobbies. The magnetic attraction of commercial enterprise to Africans did not often lead to change in the social and technical relations of production. This seems characteristic of merchant capital, based as it is on the interstices between productive systems, in exchange. Nineteenth-century Europe was industrialising rapidly, but in its relations with Africa the form and impact of merchant capital remained little changed. By mid-century, cheap, industrially produced cotton goods from Europe were reaching so remote a region from the sea as the central savannah of West Africa in large quantities across the Sahara, but without clear consequences. In fact, this chapter has undoubtedly exaggerated such consequences by generalising from those zones where they were notably significant. Thus the real meaning of 'legitimate commerce' for the African continent lay in an intensification of social and economic processes already initiated in the slaving era.

Notes

1. This approach to abolition is influenced by the ideas of Frederick Cooper, who has himself used the work of David Brion Davis, *The Problem of Slavery in the Age of Revolution* (Cornell University Press, 1975).
2. The figures are from David Northrup, 'The Compatibility of the Slave and Legitimate Trades in the Bight of Biafra', *Journal of African History*, XVII (1976).
3. A. G. Hopkins, *Economic History of West Africa* (Longman, 1973), p. 128.
4. From Suzanne Miers and Martin Klein, eds, *Slavery and Colonial Rule in Africa* (Frank Cass, 1999).

5. Cited by Susan Kaplow, 'The Mudfish and the Crocodile: Underdevelopment of a West African Bourgeoisie', *Science and Society*, XLI (1977), p. 318.

6. See the case study by Agneta Pallinder-Law, 'Aborted Modernization in West Africa: The Case of Abeokuta', *Journal of African History*, XV (1974).

7. From Stanley Trapido, 'Merchants, Peasants and the Political and Ideological Structure of Liberalism at the Cape 1854–1910' in Shula Marks and Antony Atmore, eds, *Economy and Society in Pre-Industrial South Africa* (Longman, 1980), p. 254.

5
The Conquest of Africa

But as for us, our Lord is Allah, our Creator and Possessor. We take what our Prophet Muhammad (upon him be peace) brought to us.

ABD-AL-RAHMAN, CALIPH AT SOKOTO TO THE ROYAL NIGER COMPANY, ?1900, IN R. A. ADELEYE, *POWER AND DIPLOMACY IN NORTHERN NIGERIA* (LONGMAN, 1971), P. 335

If I were received by the Queen ... nobody would ever think of attacking me.

MOSHOESHOE OF LESOTHO, IN PETER SANDERS, *MOSHOESHOE, CHIEF OF THE SOTHO* (HEINEMANN, 1975), P. 318

One thing only has checked the development of these rich regions – native misrule.

A. F. MOCKLER-FERRYMAN, 'BRITISH NIGERIA', *JAS*, II (1902), P. 169

Imperialism: theory and practice

In the last chapter, we have suggested that through much of the nineteenth century a process of partition and incorporation into much larger units was going on in many parts of Africa. The participants included the Boer republics, Egypt, Zanzibar, Ethiopia, the Yoruba successor states and a changing variety of reforming Islamic commonwealths while outside of South Africa and south of the Sahara, European expansion was very limited. However, within the last quarter of the nineteenth century the slow process of European political penetration of the African continent gave way to a scramble for colonies that resulted in a partition of all the lands south of the Sahara apart from the Republic of Liberia and Ethiopia. How and why did this happen? To understand, this process has to be related to the contradictions within capitalist economy and society in Europe as well as events in Africa.

Indeed, arguably those contradictions have been too dominant in the debates. Twentieth-century discussion was shadowed by one long pamphlet, *Imperialism, the Highest Stage of Capitalism,* written during World War I by the future leading figure of the Russian Revolution, Vladimir Ilyich Lenin. As the title suggests, Lenin considered that capitalism had advanced in the late nineteenth century into a qualitatively distinct phase of development through the formation of national oligopolies, particularly in the heavy industries such as coal and steel and in the most rapidly industrialising countries like Germany and the USA. Many believed that concentration of economic power would lead in turn to an

internationally interlocked and pacifist-minded capitalist class, increasingly unin-
terested in war or aggressive competition. Lenin disagreed: the monopoly stage
did not bring about an end to capitalist competition. Rather it placed competition on a ruthless and gigantic scale in which the monopolies could harness the
apparatus of militarised states to enforce their demands. Finance, unable to find
profitable outlets for investment at home, required new overseas outlets in order
to survive which could be guaranteed only through the economic and political conquest of hitherto non-capitalist societies elsewhere in the world, a point
stressed by another socialist contemporary, Rosa Luxemburg. Lenin realised that
there was a wide range of economic advantages potentially accruing to expanding imperialist states in this era. It included the creation of privileged markets
through tariff barriers for national monopolies; the extension of trade and the
acquisition of raw materials such as rubber and tin for new industries.

He gave pride of place, however, to the imperative of investment outlets,
following in this respect the arguments of the English anti-imperialist social
reformer, John Hobson. One result was the partition and threatened re-partition
of the world by the great powers. Imperialists demanded armaments and pressed
national regimes in Europe on from crisis to crisis, leading ultimately to the
catastrophic World War One. Lenin's analysis was exaggeratedly compressed; he
aimed at fitting together all the principal phenomena of his time into one clear-cut
statement about imperialism. If he had a focus historically it was the question of
the causes of World War I. The partition of Africa was incidental to his treatment.

Anti-Marxist writers often attack Lenin (and by implication other Marxist
writers) for exaggerating or inventing the economic side of imperialism. It
is pointed out correctly that African trade never became crucial to European
industry and that investment by capitalist firms in Africa (apart from South
Africa) never developed very far. Lenin, it is claimed, ignored the non-economic
motives which imperialists both in Europe and on the spot in Africa considered
as justifying their own actions. Imperialism was not simply a state economic
strategy, as Lenin did realise; it became a climate of opinion, linked to militarism, racism and nationalism, that blanketed Europe like a dark cloud. Mass
right-wing movements emerged in the late nineteenth century professing
nationalism, racism and imperialism as a means of solving European problems.
State school systems and the press endlessly reiterated patriotic and militarist
rhetoric. For the German Empire the historian Hans-Ulrich Wehler has stressed
that the imperialist banner was one under which an otherwise divided and internally antagonistic bourgeoisie could potentially be united by political brokers.
In Britain, Joseph Chamberlain of Birmingham, a modern-minded progressive
businessman and iconic civic benefactor, was almost the arch-imperialist.

The new 'scientific' racism, built around a vulgarised interpretation of
Charles Darwin's theory of the survival of the fittest as the key mechanism in
human (and biological) evolution, suffused European culture. Acceptance of
supposed objectively defined 'races' as fundamental human categories became
common wisdom. Black 'Negroid' Africans were assigned virtually the lowest
place on the human pecking order, fit only for rule by their white 'Caucasian'
superiors. The white conquistadores of Africa viewed themselves as the posses-
sors of racially and culturally superior ideas and behaviour patterns – bearers of
a 'civilising mission' first and foremost – rather than economic exploiters.

However, all this does not so much refute Lenin's assessment as amplify and enrich it. Where Lenin erred was in his acceptance of Hobson's impressionistic and moralistic picture of capitalist decadence. From today's vantage point, it is clear that in 1915 capitalism was not on its last legs nor was it entering a 'final' stage. It would continue to enjoy periods of great vitality and unprecedented expansion. Lenin underscored the link between overseas investment and imperialism. Africa received little of this investment before World War I, but it can be argued that conquest was part of the necessary process of creating social and political conditions under which capitalist investment would ultimately pay off. This assumes fundamental continuities in capitalist development from the earlier era of so-called free competition. There was more than enough economic evidence pointing towards both Hobsonian decadence and Leninist catastrophism.[1] However, in trying to explain the conquest of Africa by the European powers, the evidence examined today suggests exactly the opposite, stressing the vitality and hunger for new spheres to appropriate by capital.

Yet the extension of the new commerce made apparent to interested Europeans the barriers ahead before new qualitative advances could be reached. Europeans had to contend with paying off networks of middlemen and helping to sustain ruling classes and merchants who skimmed off profits and increased the price of commodities. African states fought wars to increase their territory and command over labour, a tiresome impediment to commerce that often blocked important trade routes. Abolition of the slave trade had failed to bring about the attenuation of African slavery which was held to stultify economic initiative and to cause warfare and social instability. Thus African society badly needed reform in order for the ambitions of Western commerce to be realised. Governments were required which could smash the power of ruling classes, construct telegraph lines and railways, impose uniformly peaceful conditions and permit coastal traders direct access to free peasant producers.

Colonial advocates often spoke of the need to 'open up' Africa, to protect the roads into the interior and to circumvent the middlemen. The trade depression of the early 1870s made this vision of Africa an increasingly urgent one. As oil prices fell, creditors foreclosed on coastal merchants and steamship lines undercut shippers; tensions mounted in West Africa. Cowrie and other local currencies suffered from an intensifying devaluation compared with European coin. The result, to borrow A. G. Hopkins' phrase, was a destabilisation of political as well as economic and social relations. The ensuing political crises contained a logic of their own which invited military intervention in response to the clamour of both local and European commercial interests. In the countries which traded most with Africa –Britain, France and Germany – the chambers of commerce of such major business centres as Liverpool, Manchester, Lyon and Hamburg demanded the extension of direct control to growing parts of the world outside Europe.

Special conditions in South Africa made the urge for intervention uniquely compelling. From 1867 the discovery of minerals brought to the fore the question not merely of trade, but of capitalist production. The British Union Jack flew ever further in the southern African interior in response to capitalist demands for creating social conditions favourable to cheap and efficient large-scale mineral production. Once colonial rule was established production-related imperatives were increasingly crucial to the policy of the new regimes throughout the continent.

Late nineteenth-century imperial conquest can be related also to other aspects of what the American economic historian, David Landes, dubbed the Second Industrial Revolution in *Prometheus Unbound*. The capitalist quest for raw materials, of which a bigger range was needed in more quantity than ever, enhanced interest in the tropics. New technology immeasurably cheapened the cost of expansion and conquest in Africa. Medical discoveries enabled Europeans to live there far more safely, avoiding the sacrifice in lives so typical of early experimental attempts at colonisation. Precision arms, which in turn depended on advances in the European machine-tool industry, presented European-led armies with an enormous new advantage over Africans. When they took elementary tactical and strategic precautions, tightly formed 'squares' of troops so armed could easily mow down infantry or cavalry charges aimed at them from so far away that they were virtually invulnerable. It was significant too that the commercial expansion of the era of legitimate trade had as one by-product the rise of European-controlled armies of African troops prepared to fight for small wages and the prospect of loot. By the 1870s the so-called Hausa troops, ancestral to the West African Frontier Force and their French counterparts, the *tirailleurs sénégalais*, or Senegalese sharpshooters, were well in formation. They and other African forces spared European governments the expense and political complexities contingent on the despatch of European armies overseas.

The relative cheapness of expansion allowed European officers in Africa, avid for glory and promotions, room for considerable initiative and permitted the conquest of many regions whose commercial appeal was severely limited. The scramble thus proceeded with a speed and a geographic spread that went far beyond the boundaries which can be directly explained by crisis in existing trade relations. Yet the need to expand these relations provided a solid economic base for the diplomatic, political and strategic aspects of the scramble. This helps to elucidate one obviously central fact of the conquest. It was Britain and France, with their long-established vested interests in Africa, who although least affected by the global tendencies towards industrial monopolisation and capital concentration among the major Western powers, took the lion's share of Africa.[2] In addition it underscores a dimension which African nationalists have long pointed out: the Partition had a strong co-operative and collaborative side to it, symbolised by the handshake over new African boundaries at European conference tables. For all serious capitalist interests, occupation by some efficient colonial power, if one's own regime was not able to assume control, was better than none. In this regard it is noteworthy that, despite much fighting talk, no European state went to war with another during the scramble era over a favoured chunk of Africa.[3]

The build-up to conquest

During the 1870s several significant manoeuvres in West Africa projected colonial build-up. They occurred in just those zones where commercial relations with Europe were most developed. On the Gold Coast the forts controlled by the Dutch and the British (the Danes having sold out in 1850) were rationalised geographically by agreement in 1867. This introduced a period of uncertainty as old alliances, commercial and political, were called into question. Asante had preferred to establish links with the Dutch rather than the British and was especially concerned. When complete withdrawal by the Dutch began to be considered, the old dream of achieving hegemony over the coast seized the imagination of the Asante. Those westerly coastal states which most resented the sudden imposition of Dutch hegemony were instrumental in forming the Fante Confederation in 1868. In part the confederation aimed at meeting the threat of the Dutch and of Asante, but it represented as well the political aspirations of the compradore merchants and chiefs of the Gold Coast. They conceived of the confederation as the bare bones of a Western-type state that would promote English education, road construction and commerce with a unified legal code, military force and political representation beneficial to the Anglicised merchants of the coastal towns. Despite the name, a number of non-Fante communities belonged to the confederation.

The weakness of the compradore stratum, which failed to organise an efficient fighting force or systematic revenue collection, brought about the collapse of the confederation after several years. Yet it was also subverted by British hostility. The British, for the first time, preferred to cut out the compradores from any potential role as a national bourgeoisie and to deal directly with the chiefs. As the Fante Confederation collapsed, British political involvement on the Gold Coast increased. In 1871 the Dutch were bought out of the western forts. Asante threatened to restore its old hegemony over most of the coast. The British were not prepared to tolerate such a development and organised an invasion expedition. This resulted not only in a decisive British victory, but in profoundly destabilising the Asante state. Effective alliances were made with various previously subordinate rulers who now refused to support the Asantehene. Some had been enriched and strengthened by the new direction and volume of 'legitimate' trade over the past half-century. The sack of Kumasi in 1874 heralded the end of Asante power, cutting it off from the coast and depriving it of all its tributaries. Its authority now extended only some thirty to fifty miles from Kumasi. Shortly afterwards the Crown annexed the coastal territories as the Gold Coast Colony.

Some two years later the arrival of Colonel Brière de l'Isle as governor of the French colony of Senegal marked a radical new advance movement in the region where French commerce predominated. The French systematically developed a policy of transport and communications networking: the construction of a railway from St Louis to the new port of Dakar through Cayor (which was essential for the expansion of groundnut production and export), and of a telegraph line to Futa Toro in the interior valley of the Senegal River and, most ambitiously, the extension of the railway to the upper Niger. The French move into the interior followed the great trade routes along which slave caravans had made their way.

For Brière de l'Isle and his henchmen, African rulers were so many impediments to the extension of a commercially viable French empire. Their taxes and marauding armies prevented the realisation of a great potential surplus production from the peasantry directed to a French market and their rule stood in the way of the establishment of the necessary transport network. Lat Dyor, the Damel of Cayor, formerly dependent on the French for his power, at first agreed to the laying of the railway but then reneged as he came to realise that the old forms of social authority might not long survive its construction. Through the early 1880s he harassed the French forces with the guerrilla warfare that represented a major phase of the wars of conquest in Senegal.

By this time, however, expansion into the interior had proceeded apace. In 1883 the advanced military stood at Bamako on the Niger, poised to wage a major attack on the Tukulor empire founded by al hajj Umar that controlled most of the western half of the modern republic of Mali. French expansion had come under the virtually autonomous direction of military officers who conceived of an unlimited strategically orientated expansion all the way across West Africa to Lake Chad, linking through the Sahara with French Algeria. From a business standpoint there was little to recommend colonial expansion into ever more thinly peopled and barren regions. Indeed, as the advance columns were increasingly forced to live off the newly conquered, they became brutal and rapacious.

The third great region of commercial interest to Europe on the West African littoral, together with Senegambia and the Gold Coast, was the Niger Delta, the heartland of the palm oil trade. The Delta experienced an intense version of the pressures caused by the profits squeeze and new technological development in Europe. The arrival of the steamship allowed new firms entry into the area through buying cargo space and thus threatening old arrangements and trade-share agreements. It was a British entrepreneur, George Goldie, who, through fair means and foul, succeeded in amalgamating firms and eliminating rivals to create the United Africa Company in 1879. He was particularly concerned to drive out of the area new French arrivals. By 1884 the Delta trade had become a virtual monopoly with Goldie an increasing political as well as economic force.

Hundreds of miles further to the south lay the mouth of that other great river flowing into the Atlantic, the Congo. This region experienced a rapidly growing trade in palm oil, ivory and wild rubber which, by the late 1870s, was beginning to approach the value of the trade of the Niger Delta. Yet Europeans knew almost nothing of the interior beyond the barrier of river rapids not very far inland until Stanley descended the Congo from the east to reach the coast in 1875, successfully crossing central Africa from shore to shore. He revealed to the West the existence of a vast navigable river system through which the equatorial forest could be penetrated. The trade middlemen who controlled stretches of the water could be circumvented and subordinated. Here was a potentially wealthy no man's land to attract capitalist cupidity.

The British had dominated overseas trade of the Congo region but they were never to establish colonies here. Instead Leopold II, king of the Belgians, who had devoted his energies and fortune to a feverish world search for an appropriate colonial sphere to carve out and eventually transfer to the Belgian state, successfully made it the focus of his attention, thus ensuring the European continent's first industrialised country its long-term place in the sun. The initial indifference of the Belgian bourgeoisie, coupled with the presumed jealousy of the British, stimulated the king to try a complex con trick. In 1876 he formed an International Association supposedly dedicated to opening up the Congo Basin to the benefits of free trade for all. Aware of the importance of British benevolence, or at least neutrality, he won or bought to his side the services of many figures on the British imperial scene, including Stanley himself and the British missionaries already active in the Lower Congo. Seeing through Leopold's schemes, but unwilling to advance into the interior, the British government chose to support Portugal's shadowy rival claims to the area. Portuguese expansion in Africa was pursued fitfully and with more or less success through the nineteenth century. The very economic weakness of the Portuguese bourgeoisie, given its old ties to, and knowledge of, the African trade lent a particular practical weight to imperial expansion, creating a sphere of commercial monopoly. Britain was inclined to favour the claims of this backward state because British commercial influence was strong in Portugal. However, for those Britons who took the promise of a commercialised Congo seriously, the extension of Portuguese control, with its tolerance of slaving and its protectionist customs barriers, was entirely unwelcome. Within the interested sectors of the British bourgeoisie, Leopold could count on support as an alternative to Portugal. Leopold had as well to consider the French factor. An Italian in the French service, de Brazza, had travelled overland to the Congo from the French trading posts in contemporary Gabon (*Libreville* or Freetown) to the site of modern Brazzaville, and the treaties he signed, particularly the 'Makoko treaty' with a Teke ruler, were ratified by the French Chamber of Deputies in 1882. As Leopold realised, this placed the question of a political partition directly to the fore and his Association was now reconstituted as a framework for the 'Congo Free State'. With the advancing claims of France, Leopold and Portugal, the characteristic pattern of the scramble began to emerge.

The next major crisis began in Egypt in 1882. The 'Urabi movement, which overthrew the Egyptian ministry and was linked to riots against Westerners in Alexandria, the city Muhammad Ali had created as a site for commercial development to the Mediterranean, was a classic response to one of the most important destabilising consequences of the great depression. Egypt's cotton production, its strategic location vis-à-vis both the eastern Mediterranean and the Suez Canal and the general scale of Western business interests involved, made its future a matter of great concern to the European countries. It was Britain who moved in alone to establish effective control over Egypt, a control which would bring great economic and strategic advantages although the policy of sole intervention was not at first intended. As a result the other European states were encouraged to make moves on the chessboard that would counter the new British advantage. So long as the British state was committed to some balance of powers arrangement in Europe, concessions were in order.

Egyptian intrusion in north-eastern Africa meant that the collapse of the Egyptian state had direct ramifications elsewhere. Parallel to the 'Urabi movement was the Mahdiyya movement in the Nilotic Sudan. From 1881 this movement of Islamic revival under a new prophet, or Mahdi, whose coming it was said Muhammad had predicted, aimed at the elimination of Egyptian control and swept from victory to victory leading to the fall of Khartoum and the beheading of the Egyptian commander, the Englishman Charles Gordon, in 1885. For more than a decade the new Muslim commonwealth encountered no serious threat from any Western state. The British contented themselves with controlling effectively the desert approach to Egypt.

Further south, along the Red Sea coast, they were disposed to accept the new imperialist claims of Italy in place of Egypt. Italy, like Portugal, seemed too weak to challenge British military or commercial interests. The real goal of Italian policy was domination over the highlands of Ethiopia and the first stage involved intrigue and arms sales to the most powerful Ethiopian provincial lords. It was with British complaisance also that in 1890 Italy established the colony of Somalia on the Benadir coast. If Italian intrusion into north-east Africa was not unwelcome to the British, there was a growing disquiet, still not leading to any definite policy, over potential European rivals' intrusion into the valley of the Nile and its sources.

In 1884, Germany, a far more significant European power than Italy, suddenly entered the colonial scene. German capitalism had made giant strides forward and by the 1880s was becoming a more serious commercial and industrial rival to Britain than France. German business interests in various parts of Africa were growing rapidly, although nowhere predominant, and from the late 1860s the chambers of commerce of the major coastal ports began to demand colonies. In the past the German chancellor Bismarck had always found such demands pointless and unappealing. Then towards 1884 he suddenly changed his mind. The Egyptian crisis appeared to create particularly favourable circumstances for the proclamation of colonies from the point of view of international rivalries. Political considerations seemed to make it advisable to do a favour for the German commercial ports and manufacturing interests. Moreover there is considerable evidence that Bismarck, once a great proponent of free trade, had gradually come to the conclusion that Germany required the protected markets and raw materials which colonial barriers could create. Very discreetly he lent approval to several expeditions that set out for Africa to make treaties and hoist the flag. Within a few months the foundations were laid for the establishment of four German colonies in Africa – Togo, Cameroun, South-West Africa and East Africa (Tanganyika).

At this juncture Bismarck hosted a grand conference in Berlin which in 1884 considered the outstanding issues concerning Africa from the point of view of the main European regimes involved. The German move became a kind of model for the proclamation of protectorates and colonies that all the powers could recognise. To Portugal's discomfiture, Leopold's Free State won control over a vast region in Central Africa, while French claims north of the Congo River were recognised. The Rivers Congo and Niger were declared zones of free trade. Goldie's position on the latter ensured who would turn this to benefit. Scholars have disputed which of the events of the late 1870s and early 1880s actually set off the scramble for Africa, but nobody would deny that by the time the Berlin Conference broke off it was well under way.

The partition of Africa

The French conquered most of the territory of West Africa, establishing control over the interior savannah, the Sahara and three new coastal colonies: Guinea, the Ivory Coast and Dahomey. British West African policy, perhaps in response, also became more aggressive. French occupation deprived British stations on the Gambia and in Sierra Leone of an economically significant hinterland, but this mistake was not repeated further to the east. Goldie's company received a royal charter and proclaimed a protectorate over much of the Niger Delta while the British state assumed control over the remainder. The coastal middlemen were forced into dependence upon the renamed and chartered Royal Niger Company. Attempts by the most prominent, Ja Ja (a former Brass slave who created his own state in Opobo), to organise palm oil shipment direct to Europe in league with some of the Company's rivals, led to his seizure by treachery, and deportation in 1887. Company treaties gave a legal cover to further penetration within the Sokoto caliphate and the French agreed to accept a demarcation line which granted to the British what became Northern Nigeria. Commercial interests were equally concerned to establish a viable economic hinterland for the British coastal port of Lagos. To this end the British engaged in a 'race for the Niger' to push back the French and preserve most of the Yoruba states as a British sphere of influence. In 1893 the Lagos regime provoked war with the most commercially effective Yoruba middlemen state, Ijebu, whose power was quickly smashed, an adventure that followed hard upon the French expedition to nearby Dahomey. As a result the British were able to secure as a colony the most populous region of West Africa, Nigeria. Simultaneously, pressure from Gold Coast commercial interests to destroy and annex Asante was becoming

Figure 5.1 *Imperialist conquest*: Asante, 1896. The perspective of a 'master race'

Figure 5.2   *Imperialist conquest*: Asante, 1896. A 'sketch from life' showing the Asantehene, his mother and the Ansah brothers of Kumasi

intense. It was the more attended by the state as the prospect of French moves in the area became likely. In 1896 the British found an excuse for war, Asante was conquered and the Gold Coast acquired a suitable hinterland.

Perhaps more surprising, given the relative weakness of developed economic interests, was the growing British commitment to intervention inland from the east coast of Africa. Two regions particularly fixated propagandist attention and ultimately became British colonies – Buganda on the shores of Lake Victoria and the lands west and south of Lake Malawi. In both cases Christian missionary penetration had begun in the 1870s and missionaries established strong lobbies to advocate new political arrangements that would further commerce with Europe and allow their own proselytising work to go ahead. In the powerful kingdom of Buganda, political competition took a unique form. Ambitious strata in the ruling class turned to the rival claims of Islam, Protestantism and Catholicism in their struggles against the throne and with each other. Buganda's purportedly strategic position on the headwaters of the White Nile may also have provoked intervention. In 1887 the British-sponsored International British East Africa Company established itself in Buganda and set up posts on the route inland. In 1890 Germany recognised a northern border for its new East African colony which acknowledged a British sphere of control in what became Kenya and Uganda.

Around Lake Malawi Scottish missionaries had established bases from the late 1870s among populations that had suffered raids from the *Mfecane*-derived Ngoni chiefs and from new, expanding state formations drawn into the commerce in ivory and slaves with the east coast. The Portuguese controlled access to the sea via the Zambesi River. The missionaries saw them as a blight on Protestant commercial and religious influence. But it was only through the influence and money of Cecil Rhodes' British South Africa Company that the British government finally asserted control over the region after 1890, pushing aside Portuguese claims.

Through the 1890s control over the upper Nile became the great question of the partition for European rivals. Leopold was extremely anxious to push the borders of the Free State to a navigable section of the river. The French organised advances towards the Nile east from Lake Chad and west from the Red Sea with the partial collusion of Minilik, the Ethiopian emperor. It was this threat to the waters and the rear of Egypt that finally led to a gradual organised British advance against the Mahdist state. By the time the Marchand expedition planted a French flag at Fashoda in 1898, it was confronted with a large British army that had destroyed the strength of the Mahdists at Omdurman next to Khartoum and was constructing a railway and telegraph system that efficiently linked the upper Nile to Egypt. The French were forced to withdraw while Leopold had to be satisfied with the lease of a small portion of land on the river. The British then controlled the entire Nile valley, apart from the source of the Blue Nile in Ethiopia.

The Ethiopian situation was unique. This was the only sub-Saharan state which succeeded in maintaining sovereign independence throughout the scramble. Indeed, Ethiopian expansion southwards leads one to the conclusion that Minilik was himself a major participant in the imperialist advance. Even before he secured the throne of the whole country, Minilik had been most energetic in procuring modern arms from the French and, ironically enough, the Italians. Through the 1890s Italian determination to subdue Ethiopia became increasingly clear and the British had effectively recognised their pretensions in the region. However, by 1896 Minilik was able to summon an army of perhaps 100,000 men with guns to meet an Italian military advance from coastal Eritrea. The Italians lacked seasoned local troops and made foolish tactical errors; the result was a spectacular victory for Minilik at the battle of Adwa. The Italian parliament was not prepared to continue the war and the ministry fell while Minilik agreed to recognise Italian control over Eritrea, thus blocking his own advance to the sea. On this basis, and as a result of delicately balanced diplomatic strategies, the Ethiopian state was able to survive.

The greatest prize for European capitalism in all Africa was the southern section of the continent. The discovery of mineral deposits of great wealth in the South African interior represented a potentially strong asset to Britain but created complex problems of transport, supplies, organisation and, above all, labour control, which required an appropriate state apparatus to be solved to the satisfaction of capital. The expansion of diamond mining at Kimberley from 1867, attracting a vast array of fortune-seekers of all races who descended on the dry countryside north of the Orange River, immediately engendered a piecemeal imperial response. The British engineered land claims to justify the proclamation of Griqualand West, a territory that enclosed the diamond fields. In 1868 the kingdom of Lesotho (Basutoland) was incorporated into the Cape Colony for fear that the Orange Free State, which had just defeated it in war, might annex it.

Then piecemeal schemes gave way to grander dreams of amalgamation and control. These were particularly associated with Sir Theophilus Shepstone, the Natal Secretary of Native Affairs. The continued independence of the last

Figure 5.3   *Colonial society*: diamond workers in iron 'mittens' being examined for stolen gems, Kimberley (South Africa)

strong African kingdoms of southern Africa, such as the Zulu state, prevented the satisfaction of expanding demands for labour. Shepstone felt that it was time for a reckoning with these states. Yet war with Zululand was beyond the capacities of Natal, while the South African Republic was unable to challenge the Pedi state within its claimed borders, the Zulu, or the Ndebele north of the Limpopo. For Shepstone and other would-be enlightened British labour managers, the marginal market economy of the Boer republics, concerned only to procure farm workers, militated even more than Natal's weakness against any efficient regional system.

Shepstone's influence on the Governor, Sir Bartle Frere, and the Colonial Secretary, Lord Carnarvon, helped bring about British intervention and annexation of the South African Republic in 1877. In the next years the dominant aspect of British policy lay in the subjugation of African states. The Pedi of the northern Transvaal were finally beaten and brought under control. War was provoked with the Zulu. The Zulu won a famous victory at Isandhlwana in 1879, but the British were determined to pursue their object and finally crushed Zulu resistance, exiling the king, Cetewayo. Zululand was broken up into thirteen separate chiefdoms, the strongest of which were controlled by notorious labour recruitment agents. Following a brief restoration of Cetewayo under conditions that led to a civil war, a second abolition of the monarchy and the proclamation of a British protectorate followed in 1881. Yet confederation failed. In 1881 the Boers north of the Vaal rose in rebellion and defeated a British force at Majuba. This, and the expense of the African wars, strengthened the hand of the Little Englanders in the British Liberal Party who had been dubious of the extravagant forward policy pursued by Carnarvon. W. E. Gladstone, who made successful political capital of the issue, returned to power in Britain and restored the South African Republic to independence on condition of a somewhat ambiguous British veto over its foreign affairs.

The policy of retrocession was profoundly undercut by the discovery of gold within the territory of the South African Republic in 1886. If Kimberley destabilised the South African status quo, the imperatives demanded by the rise of the new city of Johannesburg, on the ridge of white water, the Witwatersrand, were shattering. The sheer scale of gold discovered was spectacular by any standard; an impressive Gold Rush ensued rapidly. As geologists and engineers set to work it became increasingly clear, moreover, that seams of gold, not very rich but extremely reliable, stretched enormous, deep-level distances, seams which could form the basis of a gigantic, long-term industry requiring both vast numbers of workers and much capital investment.

As surely as though an earthquake had shifted the angle of the terrain, the centre of gravity in the political economy of southern Africa moved towards the Republic and the Rand. Within a few years Johannesburg had overtaken Cape Town as the largest city in the region. The Cape Colony, together with its weaker sister, Natal, could no longer serve as effective imperial instruments. The annexation of the Tswana chiefdoms west of the Republic and the establishment of the domain of the British South Africa Company north of the Limpopo in 1890 apparently hemmed in the Transvaal from three sides, but this was not necessarily sufficient to destroy its autonomous development. Men of talent and ambition from the Cape and Natal re-directed their interests and orientation to servicing the mining economy. The 'Cape Dutch' intelligentsia which had begun to emerge, perceiving the increasing contradiction between the republics and British imperialism, began to articulate an Afrikaner nationalism that crossed the existing frontiers and posed itself as an alternative to the imperial system.

President Paul Kruger was determined to use the rapidly growing revenues of the South African Republic to break away from the British stranglehold. Yet he, himself a participant in the Great Trek as a child, was also the prisoner of a social system which was not easily transformed towards meeting the requirements of capitalist mining. The Randlords objected to the tariff rates of the Netherlands railway company that connected the Rand to the Portuguese port at Lourenço Marques in Mozambique, the nearest outlet to the sea. They objected to the high charges of Eduard Lippert, the concessionaire who controlled the dynamite monopoly. They objected to the state dependence on liquor revenues which resulted in an intoxicated and inefficient labour force. Most crucially they objected to the incompetence of the republican state in procuring the huge, cheap and disciplined African labour force they required. For the Boer notables who controlled the *Volksraad*, or parliament, the creation of the requisite giant labour procurement system was not only beyond their technical capabilities, it also militated against what control they had over their farm workers. It was not that the Transvaal state was opposed to the gold mines. Kruger was only one notable who had made a small fortune through subsequent land specula- tion while a few, such as Louis Botha, the future South African premier, were turning their hand to 'progressive' farming to feed the urban population. The changes were slow in coming, however, too slow for those Randlords poised to make huge investments in the new deep levels of the gold field.

Cecil Rhodes, who had cornered the Kimberley diamond fields, was a crucial actor in the shift in imperial strategy towards confrontation in the Transvaal. Rhodes, as premier of the Cape, had stood for a policy of collaboration between Boer and Briton. His confidence in the course of events and the future of the Cape was shaken by his own rather unsuccessful financial interventions on the Rand, where he failed to capitalise on the deep-level discoveries. In 1890 his British South Africa Company sent the Pioneer Column into the lands of Lobengula, the Ndebele ruler north of the Republic, where they established 'Southern Rhodesia' stretching to Victoria Falls and the Zambesi river and then quickly extended control over a further vast swathe of Central Africa as far as Leopold's Congo, making of Rhodes the only European capitalist to have an African colony actually named for him. Rhodesia was meant to be the setting of a 'Second Rand', but Rhodes' advisors were misinformed; his Rhodesian adventures were anything but a boon to his pocket-book.

It was Rhodes, in collusion with Alfred Beit of the great deep-level firm of Wernher, Beit & Co. and the secret support of the British government, who hatched the conspiracy to take over the Transvaal. As a propaganda ruse, the British were inclined to defend the claims of the immigrant *uitlanders* to the vote in the South African Republic. Not surprisingly, faced with such a flood of new immigrants, the Boers had enacted tough laws to make the acquisition of citizenship a lengthy business. Rhodes and his henchmen hoped that the *uitlanders* of Johannesburg would rise in revolt if a small party of armed men crossed the frontier raising the British standard. This they failed to do. The Jameson Raid of 1895–6, launched from Bechuanaland, was a fiasco.

The raid eliminated Rhodes as a major factor in South African politics, but the British government, now dominated by Colonial Secretary Joseph Chamberlain, was determined to gain its object. The new high commissioner in Cape Town, Sir Alfred Milner, was a hawk anxious to smash the republics. A crescendo of increasing demands, followed by the stationing of troops along the border, finally led to the outbreak of war in 1899. The Anglo-Boer War was Britain's greatest imperial war fought on African soil. At enormous expense, some 300,000 armed men were required to subdue the Boers. The sheer weight of numbers turned around the initial advances of the republican commandos, and by mid-1900 the Boer capitals of Bloemfontein and Pretoria were conquered. The Boers, however, then determined on a strategy of guerrilla warfare which exhausted British efforts at control. In order to destroy the commandos, their families were rounded up into concentration camps, fields were burnt, homesteads looted and destroyed and a blockhouse sweep system inaugurated. Perhaps ten per cent of the Afrikaners in the republics, particularly children, died as a result of these policies.[4] It took until May 1902 and the Treaty of Vereeniging to bring the fighting commandos to a negotiated settlement which extinguished the independence of the republics. This gigantic war effort was the greatest and most costly episode of the scramble. With Britain's victory the City of London could rest assured of its position with respect to control over world gold supply and Milner could get on with the task of reconstruction to provide a political and social basis for mining production after the peace.

By 1902 Africa was partitioned. There continued to be talk of re-partition, particularly with regard to King Leopold's dubious Free State and the rich territories 'wasted' on the Portuguese, but these plans came to nothing. In the end, in 1918, the most energetic proponent of re-partition, Germany, found itself eliminated from the board as a result of World War I.

Resistance, collaboration and contradiction in African society

Samori Toure was able to take all the traditional resources of the African leader, adapt them to his needs and even occasionally transform them to meet some new requirements. He bowed to the social and technical customs of his background, but at the same time he had an instinctive feeling for terrain and a rapidity of reflex.[5]

In West Africa Samori was the greatest of all military resisters, not only because of his personal skills and his willingness to adopt extraordinarily mobile guerrilla tactics, but because he was not a 'traditional' ruler but a forger of empire with new weaponry and support, a man of the nineteenth century much like Mirambo or Tippu Tip. Through the 1880s and 1890s he fought the French in the lands between eastern Guinea, southern Mali and the northern half of the Ivory Coast as older political units collapsed. His admiring biographer, the French historian Yves Person, devoted a magisterial three-volume study to his career which nevertheless concludes that his 'Dyula' empire was doomed through its technical backwardness compared with the European powers that determined to crush him.

No historian of Africa disputes this technical inferiority and its importance in the defeat and conquest of African states, but it is often forgotten that technical inferiority was embedded in a social context that could not easily be altered from within. The threat of conquest brought out to the full the contradictions within African states which were a contributing cause of their conquest. In practice conquest only sometimes constituted a sudden overwhelming threat to African sovereignty. More typically, it was a process. The intensification of commercial relationships created conditions whereby access to trade goods had become the top political priority. After initial treaties and commercial arrangements, it was that much more difficult for African states to resist the next stage of penetration or effective control.

Only very fitfully or late in the day, if ever, did African ruling strata acquire a sense of 'Africanness', a view of a shared common confrontation against the force of powerful new enemies. Rulers and ruling classes alternated so deftly (and at times desperately) between strategies of collaboration and resistance that it is difficult to classify them along a sharp divide between the two except where circumstances clearly offered them little choice. They generally perceived the scramble in terms of their own specific class or personal interests, much as ruling classes anywhere, as well as in terms of older strategic and diplomatic objectives. There are certain examples of rulers who called for a common front of action. In the 1840s Moshweshwe, the creator of Lesotho, negotiated with other southern African kings, proposing an anti-European alliance. Minilik, the conqueror of Adwa, at one point proposed an alliance to the Khalifa, the successor to the Mahdi in the Sudan. Yet both these men, like Samori himself, pursued collaborative strategies as well. Moshweshwe often worked with the British and, at yet another point in his career, tried to organise an alliance against them with the highveld Boers. Samori was by no means always prepared to hurl defiance to the French and, towards the end of his career, rejected an alliance with Asante and sought actively for a British protectorate. Minilik's policies included deals with Italians and Frenchmen at various stages.

Where ruling classes were divided, the situation was most complicated. Buganda is a classic example. The very successes of the kingdom in the nineteenth century had thrown up ambitious men who were restive under the grip of the *kabaka*. Unable, as upstarts, to take a position on the basis of the old lineage structure of an earlier historical phase, they were very strongly drawn to the economic potential of expanding trade connections and the ideological attraction of new religions introduced by Muslim traders and Christian missionaries. Mutesa, the greatest nineteenth-century *kabaka*, was for a time inclined to become a Muslim, but he held back for fear of the threat to the basis of his own power that such a conversion might bring. From 1884 his successor Mwanga, alternately favoured, and then turned against, Islam, Catholicism and Protestantism, while around each religious banner congregated a committed sector of the ruling class. The British intervention, which ultimately dethroned Mwanga and replaced him with an infant and a regency, enshrined a balance of these factions under an Anglican ascendancy. Only when it was too late did Mwanga take up guerrilla warfare and make common cause with his great former rival and fellow refugee, Kabarega of Bunyoro.

In the Yoruba states of the Lagos hinterland the British had to engage in only one major military operation, that against Ijebu Ode in 1893. After the power of Ijebu was smashed, the other Yoruba states were willing to conclude agreements with the British that gave considerable social power to the ruling classes, particularly those who were involved in the Lagos trade. Lagos merchants came from, and traded with, virtually every Yoruba state which thus acquired vital firearms. The basis of economic and military power had already tilted powerfully towards reliance on these networks. Under these circumstances, if 'resistance' meant upholding the fundamental material interests of a class, collaboration itself became a logical, if discreet, form of 'resistance'.

Nor were African societies especially cohesive in the shadow of conquest. The impact of intensified commercial penetration under more favourable exchange terms through the middle years of the century created a variety of different new interests already undercutting the authority of the state in many regions. The economic basis of the Asante Confederacy, for instance, gradually altered with the decline of the slave trade and the rise of 'legitimate' commodity trade to the coast, upsetting the balance of control over many of the Asante tributary states. Every large state preyed on and raided its small neighbours who were often prepared to welcome European influence and power. Oppressed classes within the state also did not invariably support their rulers when given a choice. Philip Igbafe has noted that, following the conquest of Benin, plans by the *oba* and his court to organise resistance in the countryside were cut short abruptly by the British threat to emancipate all the slaves.

In South Africa the defeat of the republican Boers, who presented the strongest single challenge to imperialism, was in large measure due to their inability to garner any significant African support. Their commandos were hemmed in by Swazi and Zulu to the south-east, Tswana to the west and Pedi to the north-east, decisively limiting their scope of action. They fought for a particular way of life that depended on control, even if slacker than what was to follow, over African labour and land, that militated against establishing solid alliances with Africans. Even among the Boers a considerable number fought with the British. These were drawn disproportionately from among the underprivileged non-landholding *bywoner* class with nothing to gain from the notables' struggles.

In order for African states to have resisted conquest effectively, they would have required to put up not merely a very substantial military effort, but to move towards an economic and social transformation, the creation of a milieu for the reproduction of technology that could have met the depredation of the Europeans on their own terms. Samori and Minilik were able to procure weaponry, obtain training for many of their troops in its use and even organise simple repair work on materiel. Yet even they could not compete with the precision-arms factories of Europe. Moshweshwe, a particularly far-sighted individual, remarked in his wars with the Free State that what even the Boers, let alone the British, could potentially command was economic power and infrastructure, the capacity to supply and feed troops with which the social structure of his kingdom could not compete. One place where attempts to create a new productive system were relatively sustained and impressive was the Imerina kingdom that dominated nineteenth-century Madagascar. Imerina rulers encouraged Christianity and the spread of literacy. A few Malagasy acquired technical training and the state made use of occasional resident Europeans to establish the beginnings of a military-orientated manufacturing sector just as had Peter the Great's Russia or Muhammad Ali's Egypt. Yet such efforts were resented in many quarters and pushed aside during 'traditionalist' reigns. Attempts by the monarchy to extract more surplus from the masses and create a new basis of ideological support for the state met with powerful resistance. A first war with the French in 1883–5 led to peasant and slave risings that undercut the strength of the monarchy to resist the final onslaught a decade later.

Some African states were not prepared even to contemplate the necessity of such a transformation. The Sokoto caliphate, probably Africa's most populous country in the late nineteenth century, was a prime example. There was little 'collaboration' in Sokoto and its emirates until the actual conquest, but the resistance to Lugard's occupying armies was pitifully inadequate. When the British took Kano they seized large amounts of modern arms that no soldier had ever been taught how to use. Each emirate that fought did so separately with mounted cavalry attempting to charge squares of men armed with repeating rifles. When Sokoto was taken, the last caliph, Attahiru, escaped to the east, requesting in writing to the British that he be allowed to make his way towards Mecca in peace. At the battle of Burmi in 1903 he and his fellow refugees, men who 'knew how to die when facing the enemy',[6] were annihilated, but only British determination to prevent the flight occasioned their fierce resistance. It is especially remarkable that states such as Asante and Benin, with such long direct and indirect experience of Europeans, were so technically unprepared to cope with the intensified pressure of the scramble.

Yet the survival of independence might conceivably have been more feasible were the European powers not so determined to extinguish it. In all of Asia, only one state, Japan, witnessed an effective transformation under a section of its ruling class that made it rather quickly an industrialising, capitalist society. At the same time other states – Persia, Afghanistan, China and Siam – remained independent as a result of balancing the rivalries between potential occupying powers. A parallel case can be made for Ethiopia. Minilik did not transform Ethiopian society root and branch. He concentrated on building up military strength, purchasing armaments through the expansion of the Ethiopian state into the central and southern highlands, where resources could be plundered and loyal soldiers rewarded with grants of land. This enabled him to confront one of the weakest potential conquerors, Italy, with Africa's largest army, 100,000 men, considerably more than the Transvaal and Free State Boers ever assembled. After victory in battle Minilik benefited enormously from the reluctance of the Italian government to pursue the war further. He could with excellent effect play off one foreign power against the other, while gradually taming the autonomy of the provincial lords and creating the beginnings of a national bureaucracy. The transformation of Ethiopia was a very slow process; strong elements of older social relations, what revolutionaries called 'feudalism', were still evident at the time of the overthrow of the monarchy in 1974. Nor was imperial rule a pleasant experience for the mass of peasants, who bore its expenses and whose exploitation made possible some transformation, or the diverse peoples of Ethiopia who were forced to accept a Christian Amharinya ascendancy in the first stages of 'nation-building'. Even for Ethiopia there was no question of using independence to renounce change and pursue purely 'indigenous' historic patterns of development; it had to live within a world which was rapidly moving ahead. This dilemma would have faced other African states had they retained independence. Imperialist domination marked more than a phase in the history of Africa. It was the precondition for the emergence of African society as it now exists. Indeed, Africa as a meaningful concept owes itself primarily to the predatory instincts of the new conquerors and then, with time, to the opposition that they engendered.

The most interesting resistance struggles were not really those fought by African states to retain their sovereignty. More historically resonant were those popular risings against the imposition of colonial control which represented a reaction to new and oppressive demands on the masses that began to call up new kinds of leadership. Some, like the Herero war in South-West Africa in 1905–6 and the Bambatha rebellion among the Zulu in Natal soon afterwards, were sad affairs because they were largely a desperate response to extreme provocation by colonial and settler authorities. The Chimurenga risings of Zimbabwe and the Maji Maji fighting that swept southern Tanzania had a more forceful and original thrust while not without their complexities. They form part of the social and political dialectic of the colonial era which the next chapter begins to investigate.

Notes

1. For good critiques of Lenin see V. G. Kiernan, *Marxism and Imperialism* (St Martins, 1975), Anthony Brewer, *Marxist Theories of Imperialism: A Critical Survey* (Routledge & Kegan Paul, 1980) and Bill Warren, *Imperialism: Pioneer of Capitalism* (New Left Books, 1981).

2. Even more surprising was the expansion of Portugal, an extremely backward capitalist society, as a colonial power. W. G. Clarence-Smith has convincingly explained this in terms of the particular needs and background of the Portuguese bourgeoisie rather than, as had become traditional, despite economic rationality, in 'The Myth of Uneconomic Imperialism: The Portuguese in Angola', *Journal of African History*, V (1979).

3. For instance, during the Boer War, while popular sentiment in Germany and the USA was strongly pro-Boer, those forces that represented big money and political power strongly backed the British war effort.

4. And an equally high percentage of the many African refugees placed in camps.

5. Yves Person in Michael Crowder, ed., *West African Resistance* (Hutchinson, 1971), p. 114.

6. Quote from a British officer, cited in R. A. Adeleye, *Power and Diplomacy in Northern Nigeria, 1804–1906* (Longman, 1971), p. 310.

6

The Material Basis of Colonial Society, 1900–40

It is given to few men to think clearly on the Africa question. One of these few men is Sir George Goldie. He has said Africa should be divided up into that region which white men can colonize in the true sense of the word – a region so admirably represented by South Africa; then a region which white men can colonize to much the same extent as they can in India – the highlands of British Central Africa; and then that region which white men cannot colonize at all in the true sense of the word – West Africa. This is politically the Africa we must keep in our mind, remembering England wants markets as well as colonies; and so West Africa, the richest raw-material market in the world, is as much use to her as a colony and she can hold it easily by a garrison of Englishmen as a feeding ground for her manufacturing classes here at home.

MARY KINGSLEY IN THE LIBERIA BULLETIN, NO. 14 (1899), P. 48.

If I had only one brother,
He would go to Senegal, he would go to the Gambia
He would bring me back an undergarment cloth
A loincloth decorated with pearls which hangs to the ground
You, going to Senegal,
You are a hero like Jala Maxan
But the one who has not gone to cultivate the peanuts of Thiès Diakane
He can mend his own trousers.

A POPULAR SONG IN PARTS OF MALI DURING THE 1920S FROM FRANÇOIS MANCHUELLE, *WILLING MIGRANTS; SONINKE LABOR DIASPORAS, 1997* (OHIO UNIVERSITY PRESS AND JAMES CURREY, 1997), P. 171.

The imperial conquest of Africa was undertaken to tap African resources in order to help resolve the economic problems of Europe. Yet the circumstances of the conquest brought the colonial rulers to grips with a basic contradiction: only a long, intensive process could create conditions within Africa that could bring about substantial opportunities for investment, sales and profits. Beneath the surface of colonial political and administrative policy lay the unfolding process of capital penetration, a process that was far from reaching full fruition in the colonial era.

Anti-colonial writing tends to view the conquest and foreign rule of Africa as systematic plunder. While naked robbery plays a role in capitalist development, the remarkable feature of capitalism, which if ignored obviates the point of distinguishing it as a system or mode of production, is its ability to feed upon itself and to expand directly through the production process. Slavery, by contrast, is a system which has almost invariably required endless fresh inputs of labour from raids and conquests of other societies and other modes of production, off which it lives parasitically; it is not self-sustaining. Capitalism began, according to Marx, with an initiatory process: the primitive (i.e. original) accumulation of resources and labour. It comes into being 'dripping from head to foot, from every pore, with blood and dirt' through 'the expropriation of the mass of the people by a few usurpers'.[1] However, once an expropriated population, divorced from the means of production, is available for the 'free' sale of its labour to the highest bidder (which, since the owners of capital have probably been able to erect a suitably efficacious state apparatus, is not likely to be an impressive offer), expropriation becomes a daily part of the work process, not merely plunder of the people's resources. It is then no longer an expropriation but a systematic appropriation.

Colonial rule, generally speaking, began with an act of political expropriation, with the use or threat of force, to extract surplus from Africa in the form of either direct labour or the product of labour which could then be commoditised. The state acted as a tribute-taker rather than an organising agency for capitalist producers as in a developed capitalist society. This was indeed plunder pure and simple, but it could not yield any great wealth. Capitalism demanded the further development of commodity production and the circulation of goods from which firms in the metropolitan countries could benefit. Where possible, colonialism was about pressing forward the social and economic conditions that could lead to capitalist production in Africa itself. The tribute-taking stage had some significance throughout the period covered in this chapter, but was particularly important before World War I. In certain parts of Africa, particularly those with a long history of slave and 'legitimate' trade, commodity production was already well advanced at the time of conquest and now took off far beyond the level for which forced labour or crop plantings could have allowed. South Africa was the one place where capitalist production became generalised during this period and, for this reason, it is discussed below in Chapter 8.

Yet elsewhere the remarkable feature was the limited impact of capitalism in transforming economy and society at the root. In an important study, Anne Phillips rightly sees this as the 'enigma' of colonialism. Pre-capitalist social forms, showing extraordinary flexibility and powers of adaptation, survived to a remarkable extent. One reason was the resistance to transformation, to the appropriation or elimination of material, social and cultural values, by a resilient population of cultivators. The task taken on by capital, that of mastering an entire continent, demanded time, personnel and capital investment that two generations of colonialism did not have in sufficient quantity. This was so precisely because the slave trade, and even the far more extensive 'legitimate' trade, had not evoked the irrevocable dependency upon the West that the dependency school of writers have claimed. The high tide of colonialism in Africa came between the two world wars, an era when capitalist trade growth internationally was fitful and often problematic.

The result was the dual economy of 'tradition' and 'modernity'. Another way to frame this is to speak of the articulation of different modes of production in which Western-based capitalism becomes increasingly dominant. This takes into consideration the important additional factor of power. Such structural formulations help somewhat to describe social change, but are at such a high level of abstraction as to prevent the observation of a myriad of interconnections, of transitional forms, class relationships and human adaptations that make up the thread of twentieth-century African social history (and the next two chapters).

At the heart of the economic task of the colonial state lay the problem of labour. To open Africa to effective capital penetration, the most central issue which underlay all others, and which to some extent explains the need for conquest itself, was to prize open the labour resources of the continent, to redirect them functionally, socially and geographically in order to create a surplus from which capital could benefit. Even the basic requirement of improved transport, road and railway construction, was ultimately related to the urgency for releasing human labour used in porterage or managing beasts of burden to other forms of productive labour. Coupled with this was the objective of attacking local manufacturers to substitute a taste for imported commodities and to re-orient established trade routes and sometimes entire populations to the coast-interior trajectories. Much of the surplus production of Africans had passed through the hands of the dominant elements within Africa: women's surplus into the hands of men, youth's surplus into the hands of elders and, in many areas, the surplus production of the peasantry into the hands of ruling classes and merchants. The conquest enabled this to be made available to the benefit of Western business and the sustenance of the colonial administration.

The era of force and the chartered companies

The first two decades of the twentieth century have some unity in African history as the era of force, a period of raw and brutal intrusion by the developing colonial state into the lives of Africans. The use of force must be stressed first in the establishment of colonial domination politically. If the 1880s and 1890s were par excellence the era of wars against powerful African kingdoms: Buganda and Bunyoro; Asante and Dahomey; Benin and Ijebu; the realms of Samori and the Khalifa, successor to the Mahdi; the formative states of the Hehe and Ngoni; of Kazembe and Lobengula and the Merina, then the period up to World War I was one of smaller-scale operations against people without regular armies and structured states. Such peoples rarely surrendered to colonial authority without a fight and required to be conquered one by one, often only to reject authority repeatedly. Innumerable expeditions were sent through the forests, hills and broken country of central and south-eastern Nigeria, western Kenya, the Nuba Hills and southern savannah of the Sudan and the dense forests of the south-western Ivory Coast to name a few. When the people could not fight they fled, so colonial forces tended to adopt a scorched earth policy, stealing stock, destroying crops and burning huts, to bring them to their heels. It cannot be said that force was new to African history, but in the course of establishing colonial control a new purpose can be discerned. Such expeditions had as their goal not only recognition of a flag of sovereignty, but the systematic payment of tribute in the form of taxes and labour. They were as much economic as political in character. By 1914, when World War I broke out, colonial expeditions had generally accomplished their goals, but the war itself had led to renewed resistance, notably in French territory, where authorities demanded the 'blood tax' of young men for the army in 'pacified' areas. The most difficult Africans to conquer were pastoralists, particularly in desert country. The Italians effectively established their rule in the northern part of Somalia only in the late 1920s, while it took until the early 1930s for the French to break the resistance of Saharan peoples between Mauritania and northern Chad. Throughout Africa, but particularly in such regions, colonial administration had a strongly military cast in the earlier phases.

The economic system of early colonialism in Africa rested on compulsion in most regions. In virtually every territory the 1900s and 1910s were the most intense phase of forced taxation, forced cultivation and forced labour. It was only through the widespread use of forced labour that the characteristic essential requirements of the colonial system could at first be met. Men were needed everywhere to construct and maintain roads and railroads. Until a transport network could be developed, wherever animal power could not be utilised, porters were required on an immense scale to bear commodities in and out. Conditions in African construction camps were appalling. A notorious case (and a late one) was the line of rail that linked the French side of Stanley Pool on the Congo River to the sea, the Congo-Océan, which was completed in 1930. Some 20,000 conscript workers lost their lives as it made its course through the forests.

Nowhere in Africa was the regime of force so raw and dramatic as in the Congo Free State of Leopold II. King though he was, Leopold ran the Free State like a capitalist of the robber-baron era. The Leopoldine system had its roots in the king's pursuit of quick profits to create a capital base needed for large-scale investment, especially in transport. The forests of the Congo basin were rich in rubber. Companies, in some of which the king had shares, had exclusive rubber collection rights to large tracts of land, and rubber found a buoyant market in the West as the use of bicycles and then automobiles developed. It was rubber which, from the middle 1890s, made the Free State pay.

The king handed out most of the forest zone to concession companies, keeping a large zone, the *domaine de la couronne*, as his personal fiefdom. The companies enjoyed administrative as well as political power and their agents had orders to force the Congolese to bring in as much rubber as possible for a minimal price. Collection on the scale demanded required people to travel far from their homes, to work under sometimes dangerous conditions and to neglect normal domestic obligations. It was enforced through mass terror: armed expeditions, the use of hostages, especially women and children, mutilations and killings. Resistance evoked countless brutal expeditions and the flight of Africans away from the rivers of the Congo system to less ecologically favourable areas. The consequent devastation and depopulation are impossible to tabulate but are still thought to have approached a genocidal scale and probably outdid in horrors anything ever perpetrated by the slave trade. The era of 'red rubber' will always be associated with Joseph Conrad's great novella, *The Heart of Darkness*, which linked the Congo Free State terror to the 'horror of it' – the hideous, unacceptable face of European civilisation. Conrad was associated with a group of reformers who exposed conditions in the Congo in the early years of the twentieth century. Their writings excited the self-interested concern of those non-Belgian Europeans who realised that Leopold had duped them in selling the world on the free-trade character of his 'International Association' in 1884–5.

As a result, for fear of foreign intervention, the Belgian state took over the Congo in 1908, an object long intended by Leopold. The Free State regime was not changed substantially at first. Forest exhaustion and the flooding of the market with cheaper, high-quality South-East Asian plantation rubber cut into and eliminated the rubber-gathering system in time. With the reduction or abolition of compulsion, the rubber receipts fell. What really transformed the Central African economy, however, was the fruition of Leopold's real work: the establishment of the transport system that permitted the export of large quantities of minerals from the interior, which by 1914 formed the basis of the economy of the Belgian Congo.

The ruthless application of force gave way to a particularly effective, concentrated system of exploitation, admired by Belgium's fellow colonial powers and attracting investment funds from the biggest Belgian monopolies, of which one, the industrial-financial consortium of the Société Générale, controlled half the commoditised economy of the interwar Congo. A complex and occasionally changing system of regional zones subdivided the Congo for economic purposes into areas that produced particular cash crops, migrant labour or food crops for the mines and towns. Forced cotton cultivation, to the benefit of the Belgian textile companies, was widespread in savannah regions from the 1930s. The mineral wealth of the Congo furthered new investments and helped finance a river-rail network of great length. The size of the wage-labour force passed 500,000 before 1930, the highest total in tropical Africa. Not without justice, the Congo system has been described as an edifice resting on three pillars: business, the Catholic Church (the Catholic party usually controlled the colonial ministry) and the state, institutionally associated and intermeshed.

Elsewhere in the African forest zone conditions at first resembled those in Leopold's realm. Rubber regimes operating in much the same way dominated south of the Congo frontier in parts of Portuguese Angola, across the river in French territory and into southern German Cameroun. The French system was, if anything, even more brutal, and it survived into the late 1920s, despite the poor prices earned by wild rubber on the international market.

When the Belgian state assumed control of the Congo in 1908, concessions companies lost their administrative authority. Belgium was following a pattern noticeable in most of the African colonies. In many parts of Africa the crude commercial motives for conquest had brought the grant of charters to private firms for all administrative and economic authority. They then did the dirty work of subjugating the territory. Bismarck originally favoured this system in all four German colonies. The French granted most of French Equatorial Africa to concessions companies at first. More than half of Mozambique was chartered by the Portuguese. Kenya and Uganda were initially administered by the International British East Africa Company and the Rhodesias by the British South Africa Company, while the Royal Niger Company at first represented British rule in eastern Nigeria.

Such a system proved unworkable on the whole and many of the charters (such as the Imperial British East Africa Company in British East Africa and that of the Deutsch Ost-Afrika Gesellschaft in German East Africa) were quickly withdrawn. The companies were unable to function profitably while maintaining and extending an administration. European governments were not initially delighted to assume the running costs of African territories that might bring trouble with home legislatures, but by 1900 or soon after it was understood that there was no practical alternative. The concession system survived in French Equatorial Africa until the 1920s; the British South Africa Company was dismantled as a political operation as late as 1924, to the profit of its shareholders. Only in Mozambique, where the concessionaires were foreigners who held the Portuguese state to the full term of original agreements, did company rule persist in one section until 1942.[2]

Mines

For Western capital, especially big finance capital, by far the most attractive prospect held out by the conquest of Africa was its mineral resources. In the pre-World War I era, stock market booms and speculative rushes centred around a mythical second Witwatersrand in Southern Rhodesia, then the gold fields of the Gold Coast and finally the tin deposits of the Jos Plateau and environs in Northern Nigeria. However, the greatest mineral development in tropical Africa during the interwar years came in the Belgian Congo. Leopold II had pressed his agents to extend the Katanga province of the Congo in a deep salient that pushed like a great dagger into the Rhodesian reserve of Cecil Rhodes' British South Africa Company. Katanga was quickly ascertained to contain very rich copper deposits. Katanga copper was developed entirely by one company, the Union Minière du Haut-Katanga. UMHK, once divested of minority British interests, itself was controlled by the Société Générale, the largest Belgian financial and industrial trust.

The problem of obtaining labour in a sparsely peopled area, poor in water supply, in the southern savannahs of Africa was great. In the earliest phase of development the state coerced men, most of them 'freed' from slavery, to the mines. Later the UMHK experimented with a series of recruitment schemes that brought in migrant workers from hundreds of miles away in northern Katanga, Maniema Province and even the Trust Territory of Ruanda-Urundi carved from German East Africa for the Belgians after World War I. Partly because of the strong position of British recruitment agents, the copper mines then came to depend on the labour of British Central Africa – Nyasaland and especially Northern Rhodesia – as well as Portuguese Angola.

During the 1920s, however, technological development and geological research made it clear that an even greater copper supply could be exploited west of the frontier within Northern Rhodesia. The Northern Rhodesian Copperbelt went into full production in the middle and later 1930s. Two giant firms dominated it: the South African finance house of Anglo-American and (the genuinely British and American) Rhodesian Selection Trust. The British South Africa Company (BSAC) continued to enjoy huge royalty profits in its capacity as 'landlord' on the basis of concessions from Rhodes' time.

Labour from the British colonies now mainly stayed in Northern Rhodesia. UMHK turned largely in response to Congolese labour and consequently initiated a policy of labour stabilisation. Until the late 1920s the calculations of mining management everywhere in Africa assumed that the African labourer could be denied a family wage even at subsistence level. Brought in on a short-term contract basis, he was housed in a compound under conditions of extreme social control and deprivation while his family on the homestead were expected to look after themselves. UMHK continued to count on 'redundant' workers retiring to the bush, but they now encouraged mine-compound family life, engaged the Catholic Church to supply elementary education for the children and basic health care, and provided plots so that wives could cultivate food on a small scale. Skilled jobs reserved for immigrant European labour in other territories were done far more cheaply in Katanga by Africans, who were nevertheless much better paid than the unskilled mass of workers. Even before formal stabilisation policies were initiated, Africans had the option of settling in the shanties of the new city of Elisabethville, which allowed them a certain margin of freedom and enterprise. From the 1920s the appalling disease and accident rates on the Copperbelt fell rapidly. The poor conditions of rural life in south-central Africa on both sides of the frontier, Belgian and British, led to a flow of workers to the mining towns. In Northern Rhodesia this occurred well before the formal establishment of stabilisation policies.

In the 1920s other mining enterprises also flourished in the Belgian Congo, notably in the production of tin and industrial diamonds, of which south Kasai became the foremost world producer. Minerals dominated the Congo economy and led to its remarkable and close integration with all the biggest trusts of metropolitan Belgium on a scale beyond any comparison in Africa. UMHK relied on African peasant production from up the line of rail, especially Kasai Province, to feed the miners; this proved to be the cheapest system and was initiated through a massive forced cultivation and requisition system. From the 1930s Northern Rhodesian administration and economy too was suborned to copper production. Here, however, food came from European settler farmers and their workforces along the Rhodesian Railways line.

It is instructive to compare the Central African Copperbelt with the Northern Nigerian tin fields, which began to export on a substantial scale at about the same time as Katanga. Early tin production was in the hands of numerous small producing companies, of which most represented the financial interests of a range of inter-investing mining finance houses. The dominant power on the local scene, however, was the Niger Company, which had secured exclusive prospecting licences, partly through its close links with Lugard's new British regime, and transferred them to producing firms for handsome considerations. Like the BSAC it had 'landlord' rights, securing an income from royalties and rents. The Company also handled local financing and cash needs, supply provisions and transport of men, equipment and tin. It guaranteed a British Treasury loan for the construction of a railway, thus putting the burden on the state to procure forced labour to build it and exert its land right. Profits, as divided among many producing firms, were small. Mechanisation on the open-cast pits was at a low level, especially before the introduction of hydroelectric power in 1925. Production control largely took the form of forcing African miners to turn over ore to the European holders of exclusive leases, required for the export of tin from the ports. Only in the late 1920s did a large trust, Anglo-Oriental, which sought to corner the volatile world tin market, move in and assert control over half of total production. Based on control of access to mechanised equipment, its profits became quite handsome in the late 1930s once workers' wages had collapsed in the depression.

In the early phase of development there was much informal forced labour, arranged through the system of Native Authorities, colonial officialdom and mines managers. The managers wanted a system of intensive state-organised recruitment, both to assure their labour supply and to reduce its price, but the state could never make up its mind to back schemes along these lines. The highly commercialised peasantry of Northern Nigeria and poor men from over the borders in Cameroun, French West and Equatorial Africa, fleeing from taxes and conscription, threw up a huge labour force (approaching 40,000 averaged monthly on the eve of World War II) without compulsion. In Nigeria labour recruiters and skilled workmen were often African. The number of European employees was tiny in comparison with Central Africa and confined largely to management and petty stakeholders. Where mining operations held sway they invariably played a central role in the process of capital penetration in colonial Africa. In none of the cases described above did full-scale capitalist production relations come to prevail before World War II, however. A wage-labour force came to the mines through its need for cash, rather than through direct compulsion, but even where it was 'stabilised' men did not earn a family wage or one that allowed for social reproduction without the survival of the peasant household.[3] Workers had to go to the countryside and, in the case of commercialised Nigeria, the enormous trading sector that ultimately fed off peasant production, when their digging days were over. The mines, especially before 1940, did not so much proletarianise the peasantry as intensify the conditions through which the cash nexus and market demands penetrated the countryside.[4]

White settlers

In the absence of mineral prospects, colonialism and capitalism had to turn to agriculture and the African peasantry for the production of wealth. Before the beginning of the twentieth century, African producers had sold gathered and hunted products for the world market in large quantities, but only to a much lesser extent cultivated crops. At first the colonialists were gloomy about their prospects of doing so. Plans for agriculture were generally linked to plans for the settlement of planters from the metropole.

White settlement colonies and plantation agriculture had a lengthy and profitable history in other parts of the world. Settlers from the mother country were likely to retain a myriad of ties to it and they shared deeply internalised capitalist values that might radiate out to the conquered African population. Colonial governments had a natural sympathy for what seemed to them to be the most efficient, progressive, European-like production techniques which settlers were likely to initiate. Ideal colonial collaborators, settlers could share in the tasks of local administration, justice and defence, easing burdens of state. Rich settlers often had excellent connections at home, notably in Britain. In British Central and East Africa, moreover, settlers were often part of a spillover from South Africa, from where they emigrated willingly without special encouragement from the state.[5]

However, there also proved to be considerable negative aspects to settlers from the colonial point of view. They required large-scale infrastructural expenditures in the form of social services and economic assistance. Their total dependence on colonial political domination and their tiny numbers created among them an intense and uncompromising racism that outdid that of administrators or merchants and deeply antagonised Africans. Settlers rarely came to Africa intending to live from their own and their families' labour alone, although there were exceptions in the Portuguese and Italian colonies. Elsewhere they aspired to be capitalist farmers requiring vast outlays of land and the subordination of a great deal of cheap, initially coerced labour. In the production of most crops, unless economies of scale were of great weight, 'modern' settlers could not in fact compete economically with African peasants. They consequently required subsidies and price supports from the state that drained the colonial treasuries. This was so especially during the great depression.

Kenya is often seen as the classic 'white man's colony'. When originally conquered, the colonial budget had a large deficit and the British were anxious to find a way to make it pay quickly, especially after the expensive construction of the Uganda Railway from the Indian Ocean to Lake Victoria which passed through its heart. There appeared to be large tracts of vacant arable land in high, healthy country only sparsely inhabited by Maasai pastoralists and ideal for handing over to settlers. Appropriate and gigantic land grants became policy from 1903. The largest number of settlers were South African or connected with South Africa. Their viability depended on state authority to enforce their property rights and state expenditure to support their agricultural endeavours. In the Kenya highlands farmers could raise many temperate climate crops with which Europeans were familiar, but it took a generation of expensive experimentation to gauge the effects of local plant and animal diseases and, even then, Kenyan wheat, bacon or dairy products were not competitive on the world market. The middle and lower reaches of Kenyan commerce came into the hands not of white settlers but of immigrants from India. Largely to prevent Indian competition the settlers persuaded the British government to reserve large sections of central Kenya for whites only, creating the infamous 'white highlands' policy.

Figure 6.1   *Colonial agriculture*: white settler cultivation, Delamere estate at Njoro, Kenya Highlands

In order for the highlands to achieve any viability, settlers successfully demanded the stifling of any African enterprise that might affect their needs of cheap labour. In fine quality arabica coffee, the settlers found an apparently ideal export crop, but it could be grown just as well on a smaller scale by Africans and indeed already was south of the frontier in Tanganyika. Thus settler pressure imposed upon Kenya a policy of 'whites only' coffee-growing. In fact only a small proportion of the reserved 'white highlands' were effectively farmed, less than ten per cent on the eve of World War I and never over twenty per cent in the interwar era. Labour and especially land policies engendered by the settler system led quickly to organised and intense African opposition, even in circles that might have been expected to support colonial rule. So it is hardly surprising that for many officials in Britain the white settlers seemed to hang like a weight around the neck of colonial development in Kenya, both on political and economic grounds.

In a consideration of the most easterly part of Northern Rhodesia abutting Nyasaland, which the British intended to be a settler zone, settlerdom actually engendered ecological deterioration, at least from a human perspective. The Ngoni people of this region were herded onto a tiny, insufficient section of land and obliged to migrate for cash on unfavourable terms. The lower country in the valley of the Luangwa River was given over to wild animals as a game reserve, which in turn allowed trypanosomiasis (sleeping sickness) to spread like wildfire since it uses wild game as a carrier. This disease makes it impossible for domestic cattle to survive. The land alienated in large quantities in higher country around Fort Jameson was hardly used by settlers who had no convenient transport outlet and failed to establish a profitable basis for agriculture. As a result this land also reverted to bush, game brought trypanosomiasis and the cattle population was permanently decimated.

Small wonder then, when faced with such examples, that finance capital in the Belgian Congo, where it was dominant beyond any other African colony, allowed little scope for settlers and that by the 1920s the mines decided to rely on African farmers for their needs in foodstuffs. Despite their tiny numbers in

Africa before 1940 in numerous colonies, the settlers had acquired an important position as a pressure group and, in a few places, formal representation within the government. The state resisted the demands of Kenya settlers for political domination in the territory, but granted them innumerable favours. In one colony, Southern Rhodesia, the British South Africa Company administration gave way in 1924 to a settler-dominated local government under Crown Colony authority. The Company linkages combined with the proximity of South Africa to bring about the special circumstances there.

In certain parts of Africa corporate plantations run by European managers took shape. Some major examples were the Firestone rubber estate in Liberia, the Unilever palm oil properties in the western Belgian Congo and the Tanganyika sisal estates. Unilever effectively purchased palm oil tapped by peasants who were forced to sell to them at monopoly prices, thus paralleling the ground monopoly of the capitalist tin-mining firms in Nigeria. On the sisal estates migrant labour from poor parts of Tanganyika and Ruanda-Urundi did the work with a recruitment system much like that in the mines of southern Africa. Migrant labour combined with a strong element of direct coercion to produce the workforce on the northern Mozambique sugar plantations. This type of agriculture only partly fitted the settler pattern.

Lords and chiefs

Where they appeared as obvious alternatives to settlers in certain parts of Africa, the colonial regimes dreamt of transforming native aristocracies into capitalist farmers and improving landlords. Such aristocracies had often been able to command tribute, tax and labour from a dominated population in the past. In sub-Saharan Africa the potential for pursuing such a strategy lay largely within British domains, which included the most populous and stratified social formations in Africa as a whole. A classic case was the island of Zanzibar where the sultans presided over a class of Arab or Arabised landlords whose wealth derived from the slave-based production and export of cloves. The British, after proclaiming a protectorate in Zanzibar, were anxious that this high-value export crop should continue to flourish. They therefore buttressed the rights of landowning aristocrats and attempted to transform the freed slaves into a class of docile, proletarianised, agricultural labourers.

Another apparently propitious locale for the pursuit of such a goal was Buganda, where British conquest had been assisted by the scheming of ambitious chiefs who eagerly seized upon European religion, literacy and culture as tools in conspiring against the *kabaka*. The Uganda Agreement of 1900 apportioned much of Buganda to them in the form of large landholdings. Ultimately there were some 4000 such *mailo* estates. It was hoped that the landlords would persuade a peasantry, transformed into trusty tied labourers, to produce valuable export crops. Lord Lugard, the conqueror of northern Nigeria who had earned spurs in Uganda earlier, at first wished to turn the emirs and their officials into landowners there. As in Buganda, Northern Nigeria was an area where a ruling class had enjoyed control over a substantial surplus, but without any obvious commercial commodity sought after in Europe.

On the whole the strategy of working through an African aristocracy failed and was fairly swiftly abandoned. The basis of authority, political and economic, of the African ruling classes over the free peasantry was very different from that of improving European landlords and they were unable to enforce a transition to capitalist agriculture, particularly when it was coupled with the abolition of slavery. The Uganda Agreement initially appeared to be a great success as the Ganda peasantry began to grow cotton for export in appreciable quantities, with the *mailo* owners commanding various means of coercion and taking a share of the produce for their own benefit. However, as early as 1911 production began to stagnate and other areas of Uganda overtook Buganda as cotton producers. Social tensions within Buganda deepened, bringing with them administrative headaches. The colonial state began to turn against the landowners' prerogatives after World War I.

In northern Nigeria, policy was totally the reverse of what Lugard at first envisaged: land was declared to be state property and all private ownership was disallowed. The 'aristocracy' became a class of venal state functionaries. Only in Zanzibar, where the landowners held a monopoly over both land and clove trees, could the colonial regime keep faith with an African ruling class. Yet even there the landowners' appeal lay far more in their political hold than their economic efficiency as producers. For much of the colonial era they were hopelessly in debt to Indian merchants. Where conditions for class control were less propitious, on the old slave estates in the hinterland of Malindi (Kenya) or the Pangani river valley (Tanganyika), plantation agriculture did not long survive the end of slavery.

Abolition had a profoundly negative effect on the power of the old ruling classes which had so generally depended on unfree labour to sustain and fight for their great households. At first colonial regimes gingerly went about abolishing 'domestic' slavery. Ex-slaves formed a major part of the coerced labour force of mining areas and the 'villages de liberté' of French West Africa became notorious for French labour coercion of the liberated populations. For a long time slavery existed in practice almost everywhere despite its legal disappearance. German East Africa still had not yet taken the legal steps here before World War I broke out. Yet with time and state encouragement the developing cash nexus brought about a slackening or disappearance of the old bonds that held captives and outsiders to their dependent roles in households. Clientage continued, but it too came to function on a cash basis. The power of African ruling classes, where they existed, to command labour and production faded or disappeared. An interesting exception existed within an economy with little to export internationally on the Sahara edge where the slave population continued and continues to function very distinctively. In far more parts of Africa, slave origins only remained a social stain that was and is remembered.

Peasant production

The real motor force of capital penetration in colonial Africa, mining excluded, proved to be peasant-grown cash crops. Given the alternatives the African cultivator faced during the first half of the twentieth century, this was generally the most attractive. In comparison with settler agriculture the development of peasant commodity production required much less effort and social outlay from the colonial regimes. Peasants were actually more productive in per-acre use of the land.

There are two widely prevalent stereotypes concerning the cash crop phenomenon which are clearly incorrect: that peasants produced crops simply as rational 'economic men' responding to cash incentives like businessmen, and that they were or became an undifferentiated class or community of producers. Neither captures what happened in reality. The capacity of pre-colonial African cultivators to produce a surplus for storage or exchange and to adapt their lifestyle, including short- and long-term physical mobility, to take advantage of new opportunities or to avoid ecological catastrophe was very considerable, if variable, from place to place. Sometimes African producers responded with alacrity to new market opportunities after conquest. In Southern Rhodesia, for instance, despite the seizure of half the land by settlers, peasants produced most foodstuffs for the towns and mine camps until, in the 1920s, the settlers seriously began to turn to capitalist agriculture and to block peasant access to the market.

This peasant response has been characterised mechanically in terms of a 'vent for surplus': the new roads and railways (coupled with Pax Britannica, Germanica, Belgica and so on) yielded produce from hitherto idle peasants. Celebrating the virtues of the enterprising peasant had been the contribution of economic historians to the Africanist school. What actually occurred was more complex. Social and cultural, if not technical, aspects of the production and reproduction relationships changed substantively to allow for the cash crop phenomenon. The simplest way to explain these changes is in terms of capital penetration, the investiture of commodity relationships ever deeper within the necessary transactions of life. Extended families and communal work obligations gave way to more individual relationships, or at least became ever more nakedly conducted in cash terms. Often peasants initially produced cash crops in response to the regime of force and its tax demands.

Chiefs, notables and household heads pressed those under their control to produce. This gave way to production that operated more freely in terms of the market mechanism: producers sold to traders because they needed cash to survive. They could no longer withdraw from commercial interchange. A man's productive and reproductive capacity depended on marriage, marriage depended on bridewealth payments and bridewealth had to be produced in cash. In certain areas of West Africa, pawn debt relationships survived and even expanded during the 1930s as a means for creditors to acquire wives while short circuiting this system.

World War I was more of a landmark in the social and economic, rather than the political, history of Africa. The principal political consequence was a repartition of the colonies with the Germans eliminated from Africa. In three German territories (Cameroun, South-West Africa and Tanganyika) heavy fighting caused great hardship to the vast numbers of African soldiers and porters drafted into service. The French, moreover, pressed into service a large conscript force from Africa on the European front. South-West Africa passed to

South African rule. Cameroun and Togo were split between Britain and France with France gaining the bigger share. Britain acquired German East Africa, now renamed Tanganyika, apart from Ruanda-Urundi which went to Belgium and a small corner handed over to Portugal. In theory the ex-German territories were all under the trusteeship of the League of Nations, but this had very little practical effect; the smaller units were largely absorbed into bigger neighbouring colonies and all were run in the manner of the previously established systems of domination.

The sufferings of Africans during the war probably marked the last high point of the reign of crude force. During the interwar years a surplus was increasingly produced in Africa through the play of already powerful market forces. In the first years of the century the population probably declined, and in some places was devastated, in most of sub-Saharan Africa, apart from the already heavily commercialised zones of West and South Africa. With new social and economic conditions there was a trend towards an increase in population. This, of course, began to impose new kinds of pressure on peasant reproduction as land became scarcer, but it is also an important reminder that the intensified cash nexus brought both opportunity and oppression. The lure of money suggested, by no means unrealistically, that the client, the slave, the youth, the woman, had some chance to earn his or her freedom. Depending on family circumstances and the terms of trade, the household head could aspire to be a petty commodity producer.

Every African peasant community ever studied has shown striking differentiation among households between the (relatively) rich and the poor. Yet the remarkable feature reproduced in so much of the continent was the failure of class lines based on production to cohere firmly among the peasantry. The successful producer did not long remain a 'kulak'; he generally used his success to buy his way out of production entirely, not to buy more land or equipment. He invested in lorries or in town property that could bring in rents. In some regions he (although not all were men) bought ploughs and oxen and rented them at a profit, in others he took to moneylending.

What so sharply characterised the colonial era in Africa was the continued dominance of merchant capital, acting now entirely in harness to financially consolidated, cartelised and concentrated industrial capital in Europe. Calling into being this massive outpouring of peasant surplus, capital did not thrust towards the immediate dissolution of existing productive forms, but instead intensified the web of traders' and middlemen's activities on an unprecedented scale.

The human links in this dense chain of traders and middlemen were very often foreigners. The colonial economies attracted commercial pioneers from throughout the world: Greeks in the eastern half of Africa, Jews in southern Africa, Lebanese in West Africa and Indians everywhere, particularly in East Africa. With their strong kin networks, extending through the caste system (in the case of Hindus), the Indians rapidly developed trading systems which played the central role in the commercialisation of rural Uganda, Kenya, Tanganyika and, to a lesser extent, Nyasaland, Mozambique, Madagascar and other territories. In West Africa, African traders, middlemen and purchasers of crops were also very significant, despite Lebanese competition. Here there was an Asian-like bazaar economy where a multitude of household goods were traded.

Most of the profits creamed from the surplus of peasant production, however, accrued to a small number of monopoly firms who generally controlled the credit of the smaller traders. The economy of French West Africa was dominated by the *Compagnie Française de l'Afrique Orientale* (CFAO) and the *Société Commerciale de l'Ouest Africain* (SCOA) in particular. The third powerful firm there was the Anglo-Dutch house of Unilever which based its finances on control of palm oil sales and soap manufacturing. Unilever absorbed the Niger Company and its smaller rivals, previously amalgamated into Lever Brothers, and had the lion's share in the economy of British West Africa as a general trading firm, as well as an important share in the French colonies.[6] Colonial banking was also controlled by a small number of firms. Until the mid-1920s it was monopolised in the Gold Coast and Nigeria by the Bank of British West Africa, integrated with the shipping monopoly of Elder Dempster. In British East Africa commercial houses often represented Indian-based imperial firms.

The conditions under which the peasant household and these oligopolies established relations varied enormously. In fact those areas in West Africa where a high level of commoditisation had preceded conquest were also very important cash crop areas. There and elsewhere cash cropping relied on the articulation of a great network of labour migration. Such variables can best be understood through surveying the export crop zones. Only to a very limited extent did the African colonies export basic foodstuffs to the world market. The cash crops were largely discretionary items of consumption such as coffee, tea and cocoa or industrial crops such as oil-bearing nuts and kernels, cotton and sisal.

Therefore a major consideration in their acceptance by Africans was the extent to which they cut into food production. The ideal cash crops were what the French called 'rich' crops – tree crops that allowed for continued self-consumed staple production with a relatively limited input of labour. Cocoa was an ideal example and a remunerative one. At the opposite end of the scale was cotton, which interfered with food crop agriculture and offered the peasantry pitifully low prices for a large amount of labour time. Because most of the colonising powers were anxious to control a supply of cheap cotton for their respective textile industries its cultivation was often pressed, but state compulsion was in general essential throughout this era for its systematic development. However in certain regions and when better prices prevailed, cotton did take off as a large-scale export.

The cocoa export production of West Africa makes a striking contrast. In what was the Gold Coast it is said that a labourer brought back the first pods from the plantations on the Spanish island of Fernando Póo (now called Bioko) in the Gulf of Guinea. Its cultivation was furthered by the Basel Missionary Trading Company, which successfully combined the Gospel with business, as well as by coastal middlemen merchants who knew the prices and potential value of the crop in Europe. From the 1890s enterprising cocoa tree cultivators often travelled deep into lightly settled forest country and obtained

Figure 6.2   *Colonial agriculture*: cocoa production in a rich peasant household, Gold Coast

land cheaply from communities there. At first they could count on the labour of subordinated household members, youths and women and perhaps also slaves for the initial hard work of clearing. In western Nigeria twenty years later the labour of slaves and pawns, who were engaged to work for a household head to fulfil a debt, appears to have been fundamental to the original cocoa plantings.

In all Africa the southern Gold Coast and western Nigeria were the most commercialised zones before conquest. In part this reflected the development of internal productive forces, but clearly it must also be related to the intensity of commercial contact with Europe from the days of the slave trade. Neither colony collected head- or poll-taxes as in most of Africa; revenue sufficient to balance the colonial budget could be derived from customs income alone – in Nigeria mainly from spirits imports. Thus commerce in cocoa, already preceded by the trade in rubber, timber and palm oil in the nineteenth century, was not originally or merely a response to taxation. By World War I the Gold Coast was becoming the main world producer of cocoa.

Gold Coast cocoa production depended upon tens, then hundreds, of thousands of migrant workers who obtained a share of the crop for their labour. Through the 1920s, as cocoa farming spread further east in Nigeria and north in the Gold Coast, migrants still hoped to acquire cocoa plots of their own eventually. This became less and less possible and their situation became more marginal as time went on. Within the cocoa tree owning population there was a concentration in the hands of bigger producers. Beyond the zone of cocoa farming there developed rural communities devoted to producing foodstuffs in which the cocoa plots were now deficient. Fewer yams were grown and more people ate cassava, a protein-poor but relatively easy-to-grow root crop, as their staple. Cocoa trees also flourished west of the Gold Coast border in the Ivory Coast and here too migrant labour was a crucial component in the economy.

The great export crop of the West African savannah was groundnuts, an annual growth long cultivated and consumed by Africans. It was less soil destructive and less demanding than cotton and could be intercropped with grains. One great centre of groundnut production was northern Nigeria. Groundnut cultivation for export was largely induced through both administrative and economic pressures by the local merchants and ruling class whose agents demanded cash taxes and bought crop advances. The sudden surge in groundnut sales that followed the completion of the railway to Kano in 1912, plus a major drought, led to a severe famine. As a result groundnut production fell off for some years, only to rise again in the 1920s.

The other great groundnut-growing zone was in Senegal and Gambia. Here, much as in the southern Gold Coast, the historical conditions included a background of commercial production and transport aimed at overseas sales. Groundnuts were cultivated with such intensity as to affect foodstuff production and, under French auspices, Senegal became a major importer of Asian rice and therefore sub-Saharan Africa's first food-deficient territory. Much of the expansion of groundnut production related to the control over a great labour pool of youthful adepts by Islamic orders, particularly the Senegalese-originated Murids. To work for a holy man was among the highest obligations enjoined by the Muridiyya. The *shaykhs* could order new settlers in a community to produce groundnuts and make over the harvest for a period of some years before granting the land to them. The most intense groundnut production in Senegal occurred in the Murid 'new territories' opened up by the French-built railway on land previously limited to pastoral activity. In other parts of Senegal groundnut production relied upon the labour of seasonal migrants from the French Sudan and Guinea – the *navétanes* (or strange farmers, as the Gambians called them). Across Africa in Buganda there was a new spurt in cotton production during the 1920s, linked to the use of massive migrant labour from Ruanda-Urundi and intensifying commercial pressures and inducements. This went hand in hand with a diminution in the legal power of the *mailo* landowners, for here smallholders directed the advance. Elsewhere in Uganda cotton production was associated originally with pressures from administratively appointed chiefs who garnered the lion's share of the profits.

The greatest cotton zone in Africa, however, was just south of the Sudanese capital of Khartoum, in the land between the Blue and White Niles called the Gezira. The 'Gezira scheme' relied on a special agreement between the British state and a corporate consortium which shared the profits. The state erected a series of waterworks and irrigation facilities upon which the peasantry depended. Within the Gezira, under the umbrella of state coercion, a class of moneylenders and rich farmers pressed the poor to produce cotton while a bottom layer of migrants from northern Nigeria and other parts of Islamic West Africa supported the heaviest burden of exploitation. Elsewhere in the Sudan religious orders organised the growing of cotton in circumstances not dissimilar to Senegal.

Most of the examples considered above cannot be comprehended entirely on the basis of pressures affecting the local household. The question of whether cash cropping helped or hurt African women is a difficult one to answer. A recent attempt with regard to cocoa in the Gold Coast was equivocal, suggesting that it did open up opportunities at times but also could lead to dangerous risks and to exploitation. It is true that the labour of youths, women and other dependants within the household was crucial for the efflorescence of cocoa in south-central Cameroun or coffee on the slopes of Mount Kilimanjaro in Tanganyika. Elsewhere, as indeed with mining and settler agriculture, 'peasant' export agriculture depended fundamentally on migrant labour. Labour migration came to involve millions in every section of the continent. Workers circulated within the more commercially developed colonies such as Nigeria, Kenya and the Belgian Congo. Elsewhere they crossed borders to where they could find the source of cash they needed.

Labour migration developed at the intersection of two powerful tendencies. On the one hand, it initially offered to the migrant the possibility of returning home having achieved a particular target in cash, whether under compulsory or voluntary circumstances; youths could escape from exploitation by elders and grasping chiefs and win money to be used in arranging a marriage. On the other hand it appealed enormously to capitalists of all sorts who were able to procure a wage force without paying for long-term subsistence costs or family support; all they needed to offer was a wage to cover the immediate survival needs of the individual worker while on the job together with a cash sum to be introduced into the rural household. Under these circumstances the social obstacles that obstructed the introduction of capitalist production could be profitably evaded. The extent to which labour migration disrupted (or actually assisted) the viability of household production varied enormously, not the least on the specific conditions of each individual. Whether or not agricultural labour was women's work was an important factor. Cattle-owning communities where the migrant worked to buy stock seem also to have been able to sustain a higher rate of migration. Workers became experts at knowing the conditions in different distant labour markets and the fortunate could sometimes accumulate cash to begin a little business or acquire land. Others, however, were trapped in a cycle of stagnation and decline where the viability of rural communities became affected, notably in southern Africa.

Many colonies became informally divided into 'rich' export-producing zones and 'underdeveloped' reservoirs of migrant labour. Apart from Nigeria, where the north absorbed much of its own wage-labour force, the West African savannah away from the coast was such a reservoir for the southern forest belt. Rural Northern Rhodesia and Nyasaland, southern Mozambique and Ruanda-Urundi, were others. In those colonies and, above all, in and immediately around South Africa where the demands of capital for labour were truly voracious, peasant production suffered most drastically and African lands were virtually synonymous with migrant zones. Parts of Kenya and especially Southern Rhodesia and South-West Africa also approached such conditions.

It has been suggested earlier that capital penetration in Africa through the nineteenth century had a real but fairly limited impact. The colonial era, however, marked a watershed. Dramatic evidence came with the onset of the great depression. Obliged by the tax system and by their own dependence on cash, Africans in many regions responded to catastrophic declines in the price of produce by growing more, not less, cash crops. They could no longer simply withdraw from the market when prices were poor. The regimes in settler colonies such as Northern Rhodesia and Kenya actually turned increasingly to the encouragement of African production as the peasants so clearly best sustained the new harsh conditions of the international market. The depression also revealed that migrant labour could no longer be summoned or dismissed at will; Africans were not always able or did not choose to leave town and return to the bush as jobs became scarce. A process of proletarianisation had begun which helped to sustain the first serious waves of strikes by workers in the late 1930s (Copperbelt strike of 1935; Thiès, Senegal railway strike of 1938; Mombasa dock strike of 1939) as more prosperous conditions returned and portended a new era.

The colonial state

Colonial administration was shaped to the needs of the material conditions of the African colonies as seen from the metropolis. Initially after the conquest the administrations had a strongly military character. Individual officers had enormous discretionary powers and were often eccentrics and adventurers. In time the systems became increasingly bureaucratised with larger and more specialised services emanating from the colonial capitals. Yet in the countryside a small number of all-purpose local administrators, those the French called the *rois de la brousse* (kings of the bush), still retained a great deal of authority, especially in assessing politically the balance of social forces. The British referred directly to a 'political' service at the local level.

From the pages above it should be clear that the state intervened crucially and repeatedly to promote capitalist enterprise through policies regarding labour, taxation, land and business; this after all was its main purpose in Africa, where it cannot be said to have stemmed from the interplay of local forces. The state never simply represented the interests of a firm, however. It mediated between the needs of a variety of metropolitan interests, occasionally conflicting. This is where it differed from the chartered companies that often had done the dirty work of conquest.

More surprisingly, the colonial state often acted to limit or even to block capital penetration in the course of dissolving existing social relationships. This was largely for reasons of expediency. Resting on a small military presence, which was small because home treasuries had limited patience with expenditures on African adventures, local interest groups had to be appeased and balanced against one another. Social conflicts had to be avoided when possible. Indeed, the state often acted as a brake for capital through conservative policies meant to shore up existing African institutions which seemed to form an essential prop of the system as a whole. At the same time, as the era of force began to fade in most regions, military regimen began to give way to bourgeois normality and the rule of law; this also began to limit the sway of colonial despotism.

The colonialists saw themselves as paternalist, bureaucratic dictators, yet they relied on creating a class of African intermediaries who could effectively

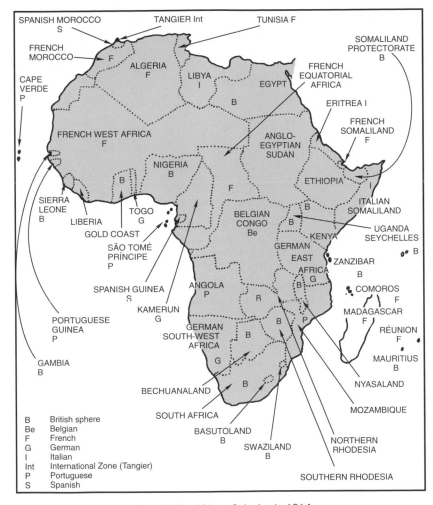

Map 3 The African Colonies in 1914

intervene in the daily lives of Africans. This meant, in the countryside, the recognition (or creation) of the colonial chiefs whose primary function was to collect taxes and to preserve administrative control. Sometimes chiefs were members of old royal families carefully selected for their subservience and at first frequently removed when they failed to serve their purpose. Sometimes they had no traditional legitimacy at all, occasionally having been interpreters or even servants to the first generation of Western conquerors. The latter were particularly to be found in regions where no hierarchical political authority had previously existed.

Traditional legitimacy was often irrelevant so long as patrimonial ties in society continued to be salient. Upstarts in such areas as south-eastern Nigeria (the 'warrant chiefs') and northern Uganda proved very effective at exerting their authority and incidentally used their administrative situations to form the lynchpins of a new class. However, the British in particular were often convinced that, when possible, it was worthwhile to establish the appearance of a 'traditional' government as a means of securing effective overall control, particularly where the very low level of economic development did not disrupt the superficial workings of such 'traditions'. Indeed social science research of the period, largely under the rubric of anthropology, was directed to finding the real chiefs, the 'legitimate' older forms of social and cultural authority, in the service of fine-tuning colonial domination.

This policy is generally known as 'indirect rule' and is particularly associated with Lord Lugard and northern Nigeria, in part because of the ideologically efficacious propaganda of Lugard and his wife Flora Shaw, an imperialist publicist. Under indirect rule the British claimed to interfere as little as possible with the regime of the emirs whose 'native authorities' were buttressed by 'native treasuries'. Thus Africans could advance along 'their own lines'. In reality, while the emirs could use their positions to extort substantial incomes, their freedom to rule was very circumscribed. The original ruling emirs were almost all deposed while their allegiance to Sokoto was largely nullified. In one emirate, Daura, the pre-Sokoto jihad ruling family was 'restored' to the throne as a prospective lesson to other notables. The treasuries went largely to the sustenance of the indirect rule bureaucracy and emirs, although the very biggest also supported public works, thus subsidising the colonial administration as a whole in which the 'native authorities' had absolutely no authority. Undoubtedly, though, they were as a result able to become crucial in the maintenance of colonial power and in the conduct of political intrigues within the context of colonial northern Nigeria.

The indirect rule model was copied elsewhere. Lugard, after unifying northern and southern Nigeria, used it to reintroduce the monarchy to Benin in 1916. In the 1920s the Asantehene was restored to the Golden Stool in the Gold Coast while a strange, deeply resented attempt was made to resuscitate the Oyo Empire after a century of eclipse in Yoruba country, Nigeria. Other classic locales for indirect rule were Swaziland and Basutoland in southern Africa, Barotseland in Northern Rhodesia and Buganda in Uganda. The first three were migrant labour reserve zones, a condition that went well with the depredations of 'traditional' authority reinforcing its own controls while acting in the colonial economic interests.

In contrast the continental European powers tended from an early date to humble the prerogatives of most local aristocracies. Their relative disinterest in indirect rule partly reflects the extent to which so many of the strongest and most coherent nineteenth-century African states lay in the areas of commercial importance that the British managed to reserve for themselves. Yet the French and the Belgians too made an effort to utilise the old ruling strata when it seemed advantageous and the difference in colonial policies on this score is sometimes overdrawn.

Colonial success in making use of African authorities in this manner varied, often with the particular social and political circumstances of the territory involved. The authorities could not bother with very small political units and jumbled them together, creating rivalries and hostilities that would persist from one generation to the next. In most African societies, power was exerted through a variety of institutions such as title and secret societies, through the recognition of leadership from migrant or antecedent communities, through the acceptance of sacral power, and, as feminists have pointed out frequently, through the recognition of separate community and leadership amongst women. This too was very inconvenient for colonial bureaucrats. Sometimes it meant that there was a dearth of understanding and efficacy; sometimes secretly older forms continued to exist. Undoubtedly in some areas the mass of people were caught up sufficiently in apparently traditional systems that continued to maintain real patrimonial force locally so as to blunt effectively the development of an anti-colonial consciousness. As Thomas Spear aptly put it, 'for tradition to be deployed successfully in support of colonial rule, it had to resonate with colonial values and historical consciousness'.[7] It is also interesting to note that when gold was discovered in an African rural location in western Kenya in 1930 called Kakamega, it looked briefly as though the whole informal rule apparatus would be eliminated in the district when there was real money to be made. When it was clearer that the gold prospects were limited and exports, briefly the number one commodity sold internationally from Kenya, would flatten out and then dwindle fairly quickly, nothing was done.

The French colonies were as despotically ruled as any, but they contained the anomaly of the *quatre communes*, the four towns of Senegal – Dakar, Saint Louis, Gorée and Rufisque – where all locally born residents had the legal rights of French citizenship from 1871 and were represented in the French Chamber of Deputies. A small number of Africans outside the communes, through the administrative evaluation of a variety of criteria, could obtain a similar status. Such representation existed also for the Portuguese colonies in the Portuguese parliament under the republic (1910–26). A system of individual juridical assimilation was also created. This eventually covered perhaps one per cent of the Angolan population with a smaller proportion in Guiné or Mozambique. The legal rights of Africans in the French and Portuguese systems (including the existence of a free press) were at times significant, but varied depending on the vagaries of metropolitan democracy. Such democratic rights as existed diminished under Vichy France (1940–4) and in Portugal after the overthrow of the republican regime in 1926.

Nevertheless African intermediaries of the old compradore type were deliberately rejected by the colonial powers as principal bearers of intruding capitalist values, political or economic. In the economic sphere they were outdistanced by Indians, Lebanese and other immigrants who carried little political weight while the framework of indirect rule was deliberately designed to exclude them. The 'native authorities' system aroused the anger of any Africans of weight excluded from them, notably among the trading and clerical class of coastal British West Africa. Now thoroughly subordinated economically to the monopoly firms, but increasing in numbers and sophistication, this class found limited outlet for development or accumulation in a system dominated by the concept of indirect rule. In West Africa a few representatives of this class became elected members of legislative councils and municipal officials, but their powers were purely advisory. Yet all the other potential agents of a new society – accumulating peasants, white settlers, old ruling classes – also presented problems as much as opportunities for capital, a situation the next chapter explores.

Table 6.1.   Expansion of export cash crops from tropical Africa in '000 tons

	1895	1905	1920	1928	1934	1938	1941
Coffee							
Angola					16.4[a]		
Belgian Congo					17[b]		
Ivory Coast					1.3[c]	10.1[d]	28
Kenya			3.5[e]	7.9[f]		17.7[g]	
Tanganyika		1.1[h]		6[i]	14.8	13.7	
Uganda			0.2[j]			12.6[k]	
Cotton							
Belgian Congo (fibre)			0.02[l]	9.6[m]		42	
French Equatorial Africa				0.8[n]	5[o]	9[p]	
French West Africa				4.2[q]		3.9[r]	
Nigeria		1.9[s]		6[t]	4.6[u]	8.3[v]	
Uganda		0.2[w]		36[x]		80[y]	
Cocoa							
Cameroun			2.5		21[z]	31	
Gold Coast	0.01	5	125	225	230	263	
Ivory Coast			2.5[aa]	16[bb]	26[cc]	55[dd]	
Nigeria		3.9[ee]		45[ff]	63[gg]	96[hh]	
Togo					8.6[ii]		
Bananas							
Cameroun						17[jj]	
French Guinea			0.1	4.0[kk]	22[ll]	53	
Groundnuts							
Gambia		58[mm]		75[nn]		50[oo]	
Nigeria			41[pp]	109[qq]	189[rr]	250[ss]	
Senegal		220		410[tt]	520[uu]	601[vv] (French West Africa)	
Palm Kernels							
Belgian Congo						85	
Cameroun						36	
Dahomey						52	
French Equatorial Africa						13	
Ivory Coast						36	
Nigeria	121[ww]	174[xx]		255[yy]	275[zz]	334[aaa]	
Sierra Leone						78	
Togo						13	
Palm Oil							
Belgian Congo						66	
Cameroun						8.9	
Dahomey						16.6	
Nigeria	54		78	125		122	139
Sisal							
Kenya			5[bbb]	15[ccc]		31[ddd]	
Tanganyika		21[eee]		18[fff]	73	107	

(Continued)

Table 6.1.   Expansion of export cash crops from tropical Africa in '000 tons (*Continued*)

	1895	**1905**	**1920**	**1928**	**1934**	**1938**	**1941**
Tobacco							
Southern Rhodesia			1.6[ggg]	9.6[hhh]		9.2[iii]	

[a] 1934–8 average	[u] 1930–4 average	[pp] 1915–19 average
[b] 1934–8 average	[v] 1935–9 average, [w] 1905–6	[qq] 1925–9 average
[c] 1932	[x] 1925–6	[rr] 1930–4 average
[d] 1937	[y] 1937–8	[ss] 1935–9 average
[e] 1920–2 average	[z] 1935	[tt] 1924–8 average
[f] 1927–9 average	[aa] 1922	[uu] 1930
[g] 1936–8 average	[bb] 1929	[vv] 1936–8 average
[h] 1913	[cc] 1932	[ww] 1900–4 average
[i] 1925	[dd] 1939	[xx] 1910–14 average
[j] 1923–5 average	[ee] 1913	[yy] 1925–9 average
[k] 1936–8 average	[ff] 1925–9 average	[zz] 1930–4 average
[l] 1917	[gg] 1930–4 average	[aaa] 1935–9 average
[m] 1929	[hh] 1935–9 average	[bbb] 1920–2 average
[n] 1929	[ii] 1934–8 average	[ccc] 1927–9 average
[o] 1933	[jj] 1936	[ddd] 1936–8 average
[p] 1938–9	[kk] 1929	[eee] 1913
[q] 1929	[ll] 1933	[fff] 1925
[r] 1939	[mm] 1910	[ggg] 1922
[s] 1910–14 average	[nn] 1930	[hhh] 1927
[t] 1925–9 average	[oo] 1936	[iii] 1939.

Source: Official figures from varied sources.

Notes

1. Karl Marx, *Das Capital*, I, chs 31–2.
2. The weakness of Portuguese capitalism meant that national interests were unable to compete very effectively within Portuguese colonies in many spheres and that different regions of the colonies were never integrated into one coherent economic unit. British interests predominated in the plantation sector of the Zambesi valley of Mozambique while South African and Rhodesian interests affected the entire colony. Belgian capital, according to W. G. Clarence-Smith, predominated in the economy of northern Angola.
3. With the exception of a small minority of skilled workers, European or South African whites in southern Africa, Africans from the coast in West Africa.
4. The size of the mines work force in cases discussed (1937): UMHK mines, Belgian Congo, 8166 averaged monthly; Northern Rhodesia mines, 19,304; Nigerian tin mines, 36,142.
5. Europeans in tropical Africa in 1935–6; the largest settler communities:
   1. Southern Rhodesia 55,419
   2. South West Africa 31,049
   3. Angola 30,000
   4. French West Africa 19,061
   5. Belgian Congo 18,680
   6. Kenya 17,997
   7. Mozambique 10,000
   8. Northern Rhodesia 9913

   Adapted and selected from figures in Lord Hailey, *An African Survey* (Oxford University Press, 2nd edn, 1945) as with fn 4., p. 109.
6. Confusingly the name United Africa Company was revived by Unilever for their Nigerian operations in the interwar years.
7. Thomas Spear, 'Indirect Rule, the Politics of New Traditionalism and the Limits of Invention in Tanzania' in Gregory Maddox and James Giblin, *In Search of a Nation: Histories of Authority and Dissidence in Tanzania* (James Currey, Kapsel and Ohio UP), 2004, p. 71.

7

Culture, Class and Social Change in Colonial Africa, 1900–40

The white man had indeed brought a lunatic religion, but he had also built a trading store and for the first time palm-oil and kernel became things of great price, and much money flowed into Umuofia.
CHINUA ACHEBE, *THINGS FALL APART* (FAWCETT CREST, 1967 PRINTING), P. 162

Immediately white men came justice vanished.
TESTIMONY OF A CHIEF IN OKIGWI DIVISION, NIGERIA, AS REPORTED IN A. E. AFIGBO, *THE WARRANT CHIEFS* (LONGMAN, 1972), P. 283

Class relations in colonial Africa

Did colonial conquest mean the dominance of capitalism in Africa? Theoretically the development of capitalism may tend towards the increasing dominance of two antagonistic classes: the capital-holding and investing bourgeoisie and the landless and resourceless working class or proletariat. However, the operative word here is 'tend'. Even in the most advanced capitalist society at present, the picture is far from being so simple. Technological needs create new strata who are part-managerial, part-worker in outlook and function; increasingly elaborate state mechanisms need manning. The classic division of capitalist/proletarian is in any event the historic product of centuries of economic change and class struggle in Europe. In Africa the classic tendency also began to take shape during the colonial period but, in accordance with the limited economic development of capitalism, achieved only a modest hold.

In Europe capitalist development had determined a process of growing privatisation of land rights with the dominance of capitalist social, legal and economic arrangements on the land. There was little of this in colonial Africa. Even where settler agriculture predominated, as in the highlands of pre-World War II Kenya, the 'landless' squatters continued to have extensive access to land and stock through the inability of the settler landlords to control the situation.

As we have seen, attempts to turn African aristocracies into progressive land-lords generally failed and private land tenure developed only very fitfully. In most of the continent, population densities were not high enough to prevent continued cultivators' access to basic resources. Where pressure on the land occurred it took the form of tilling increasingly less favourable soils or the decline in the amount of fallow time to which the land had exposure. Instead of straightforward capitalist farming, a bewildering and rich variety of transitional forms between pre-capitalist and capitalist social types arose, depending on a host of specific circumstances. Of uniform weight as a cause of change in rural life was the greatly increased role of cash transactions, infesting all the ceremonial rituals and essential interactions that marked the community. Social reciprocity linking large households and villages gave way before the smaller household and this in turn provoked greater emphasis on the need to secure money and to buy services and goods.

Some researchers have followed the lead of K. W. Post in taking the increasing subjection of a more individuated peasantry to the cash nexus and the economic demands (and political controls) of the state as part of an historic process of peasantisation in the colonial period. Such a process would require qualification for those parts of the continent where either a sharply articulated class structure had long existed (Hausaland or highland Ethiopia) or commodity exchange had become extremely important by the nineteenth century (the Niger Delta or southern Gold Coast). Lord Lugard, for instance, saw the British, in conquering northern Nigeria, as replacing an earlier ruling class through making demands upon the *talakawa*, the mass of poor commoners. 'Peasantisation' may also obscure the great variety of situations which came to prevail depending upon the sexual division of labour, prevalence of pastoralism, existence of a 'rich' cash crop and so on.

Peasantisation, for instance, could lead to both immiseration and modest prosperity. In the first generation of colonial rule the evidence of warfare, disease, famine and depopulation in much of sub-Saharan Africa suggested the predominance of the former. When crops brought in relatively good prices and the opening of transit routes enabled commodities to be bought and sold comparatively cheaply, the situation was reversed. Populations began to increase and living standards, from the point of view of commodity accumulation and circulation, to rise. The worst conditions never applied to some parts of Africa while the improvements characteristic of the 1920s never much assisted such backward regions as Portuguese Guinea. It would be wrong to overstress the development of distinct (and potentially antagonistic) classes among a socially isolated peasantry. The most prosperous peasant often moved out of agriculture entirely and learnt to exploit the system commercially. It was here, rather than in agriculture proper, that profits lay. In the richer coffee or cocoa zones the peasantry as a whole tended to aspire to petty proprietorship and the accumulating drive of the little capitalist. The scale of this drive, despite the absolute poverty of Africa compared with industrialised countries, was strong. As the more important zones of cash crop agriculture attracted large migrant labour forces, the aspirations of the successful local farmer passed on to those from other zones.

Where settlers or urban-based enterprise pushed against such possibilities being realised, peasantries were often most frustrated. Thus in southern Africa many rural zones were increasingly unable to permit the extended reproduction of peasant families. The population depended so heavily on cash flows from mines, farms and towns that they were no longer able to sustain themselves on the land, let alone export cash crops. Settler areas generally sharply demarcated 'white' and 'African' productive spheres; thus even here the extreme differentiation that followed was territorial and entire districts decayed.

The peasantry generally confronted two basic forces against whom it could strive directly: the colonial state with its agents and the merchant network. Thanks to the almost universal and inevitable use of African agency in both these spheres at ground level, such confrontation was often not perceived by peasants as being confrontation simply with 'colonialism', 'whites' or 'the state'. Indeed social and political conflict in rural Africa was frequently imbricated into older conflicts and cleavages.

This was especially so in supposedly traditional settings. No sooner had the British restored the Asantehene to his throne in Kumasi in 1935 and the rejoicings of the Asante nation died down, than conflicts began to break out within the framework of the indirect rule system. Cocoa wealth and the end of slavery with other forms of pre-capitalist dependence made it impossible to reorder smoothly the old hierarchies. Some of the chiefs were soon in sharp conflict with the 'young men' or commoners. Some provincial notables were advantaged through the restoration of the Golden Stool, others resented the new framework through which they were obliged to operate and agitated for separation from Asante. The Asantehene had to find a way to promote the interests of his richest subjects, the large farmers and cocoa-brokers, without losing the esteem of the masses.

There were some close parallels in Buganda. The depredations of the *mailo* lords evoked intense antagonism expressed in the name of those lineage chiefs whose humbler claims had been ignored in the Uganda Agreement. The Ganda commoners often supported this agitation, having little more affection for the principal agency of the new ruling class, the *Lukiiko*, or legislature, than the eighteenth-century English artisans held for their corrupt House of Commons. They preferred to defend the prerogatives of the *kabaka*, now transformed in memory into a stern but just champion of the poor. It does not take too searching a light to see an acute class conflict operating through the veil of constitutional and cultural forms.

Retention of land rights and the strength of merchant, as opposed to industrial, relations within colonial Africa, meant that the rise of a large wage-labour force did not entirely proletarianise, or divorce from the land, the workers. Instead the cash nexus, together with pressure from the colonial state, threw up an immense migrant population while constantly pressing men (and, far more slowly, women) into the towns to lead a marginal life searching for patrons and work.

Conditions in the towns outside the colonial centres (which lacked decent housing or sanitation and the most basic amenities), not to speak of rigidly controlled mining compounds, were stark: the worker had to rely on maintaining home contacts if possible. This helps to explain the close links which often

bound him or her to more thriving kin and neighbours who could offer lodg-
ing or an employment opening in the town and/or access to land and services
in the country. It is sometimes rather too crudely stressed that this meant that
Africa developed no real working class. In fact, workers, even those not entirely
committed to life on a payroll, could and did resist capital and fought it when
they felt that it was necessary to their interests. However, the form of struggle tended to reflect their continued attachment to the land. It seems typical
of early working-class history in colonial Africa that labourers shirked, evaded
discipline or control and deserted rather than strike or establish formal industrial organisations. Yet such resistance could be most effective. According to the
Rhodesian Chamber of Mines in 1905:

> [F]rom the majority of natives of the town to obtain a good day's work is
> an impossibility. By a system of passive resistance they are able to defeat the
> objects of a master who deserves value for his money.[1]

However, the relationship of worker to peasant was close and responses to
rural conditions had the greatest significance for the urban workplace or mine
camp and vice versa. The extension of wage labour was to have important
consequences, economic and social, for the rhythms of rural life. It was through
wage labour, particularly when cash cropping was not a feasible option, that
cash entered into the community to the benefit of the worker. Whereas cash
agriculture could sometimes be a means of maintaining existing social control
mechanisms, wage labour, especially if it benefited former slaves, youths or
women, tended to threaten them and destroy the patriarchal coherence of the
household, lineage or village. Without placing him in the position of a pure
proletarian, wage labour increasingly put the African worker in direct contact
with capital and created the conditions for new forms of class struggle throughout the continent.

On the higher rungs of the labour hierarchy, though, stood a growing
number of skilled workmen, generally paid far more than the unskilled and able
to support a family with their wage. The railwayman and the clerk are the most
important and widely distributed examples. The experienced clerk in Nigeria in
the 1920s made five, six or seven times the wage of the building worker. Skilled
workers often identified with some aspects of the colonial system to which their
skills seemed linked. These were often derived from a mission education and
they aspired to running small businesses while looking up to those Africans
at the top of their hierarchies at work and outside. When they formed labour
organisations, their severance pay as a base for capital accumulation in trade or
land was generally a much more significant demand than the pension. Often
the clerk or artisan kept to his job for only a limited number of years while he
planned his entrée into the petty avenues of commerce. Where women played a
major role in trade he sometimes lent money to set up his wife or other female
relations with goods and connections. At the same time, vulnerable to the trade
cycle through dependence on wage labour and occupying a strategic position in
the colony, the skilled worker had the capacity to disrupt a whole territory with
a major strike and could display a strong labour consciousness.

What was barely discernible within colonial society was an African bour-geoisie. African businessmen there were, but largely in the sphere of circula-tion. Within the systems of production, whether in agriculture or in industry, pre-capitalist ownership of the means of production dominated or foreigners were essentially in control. Some historians stress that African businesses were overwhelmed by unfair competition from both European settlers and trading diasporas such as the Indians, with the complicity of the colonial state. It has often been noted that colonial banks were reluctant to make credit available to African concerns. Of course a few Africans, those who had the collateral that fitted the banks' requirements, did succeed in procuring loans.

The impermeability of African social and economic conditions to capitalist transformation, which can be celebrated or condemned, was perhaps as, or more, crucial than discrimination in blocking the formation of a capitalist entre-preneurial class. No native bourgeoisie seriously contested, however unequally, the conditions for capitalist accumulation in Africa with the great Western banks and industrial trusts. This contrasts sharply with conditions in much of colonial Asia, particularly British India, or in South Africa, which will be discussed in the next chapter. It is quite wrong, though, to assume that because no African bourgeoisie existed, there were not African surplus-consuming classes. They existed and grew in extent, without coming together as a unified class before 1940. Undeniably those who already commanded labour and resources were in the best position to improve upon their opportunities.

Chiefs were often the ideal and premier local opportunists with a punitive corrupt power enhanced by their chance to be the first to know what the colo-nial administration's plans were about, all the more so given the authoritarian, bureaucratised character of administration at the top. Scheming and acquisitive chiefs star equally in *Mister Johnson*, Joyce Cary's comedy on rural northern Nigerian colonial society, and in the Camerounian fiction of Mongo Beti and Ferdinand Oyono. In Iteso, a district of northern Uganda where cotton farming flourished from the 1920s on the basis of plough and oxen ownership, it was a small number of local notables, made into 'chiefs' by the British, who, accord-ing to the studies of Joan Vincent, formed the basis for a powerful new class.

It was more advantageous for such figures to draw in the masses as clients through the continued promotion of pre-capitalist forms of social association rather than to isolate themselves as innovative capitalist proprietors. Polygamy might give a man power over the labour of several healthy young women as well as pride in numerous offspring. The survival of extended kinship relations allowed for the establishment and spread of ties that provided both labour and commercial advantages. The capitalist 'miracle' of cocoa production in the Gold Coast did not destroy older concepts of property: matrilineal rights and obligations and traditional forms of loan were very effectively enforced by accu-mulators. In Western Nigeria also, cocoa did not lead to a rapid deterioration of lineage land rights. Individuals placed strategically within households could operate to their advantage through the claims of lineages.

An immense network of apparently independent traders, tied to the great firms through control of goods and credit, filled the markets of West Africa. Potentially hostile to their creditors and to capitalist firms, they had as well a deep commitment to working this bazaar economy engendered by the extension of merchant capital. In both commercial and state sectors, there was also an important, if strictly subordinated, component of African employees, particularly in West Africa. The United Africa Company component of Unilever and other trading firms employed considerable numbers of African agents. Their promotion was slow and they were usually under fairly direct supervision of an expatriate manager. Nonetheless many enterprising traders got their start in this way and used their connections with Western capital to good advantage, particularly given the difficulties they experienced in obtaining bank loans.

The state created a substantial class of subservient African bureaucrats whose certification depended on the acquisition of formal education. As we have seen, on the west coast from Senegal to Angola, African compradores had occupied very important positions in the administration of the nineteenth-century colonial enclaves. With the conquest of the interior these opportunities were sharply circumscribed as their ranks were hemmed in by new arrivals from Europe and formal or informal racial discrimination. Before the 1890s the leading African officials and traders of Lagos were likely to socialise at the governor's home on a familiar, collegial basis. By the early years of this century, however, they were only rarely invited to formal affairs as representatives of a class from which the new 'top brass' felt utterly distant. The occasional African continued to hold an important post. The Lagos Director of Education, Henry Carr (1863–1945), a man of more (Western) culture than most of his European colleagues, (and whose library eventually formed the cornerstone for the post-war University of Ibadan) was a paragon. Very conservative in his views, Carr despised the social atmosphere of African Lagos, especially its working class, as much as might any colonial official and considered himself to have the mind of an Englishman. Erudite and devout, Carr believed that the African needed above all 'a severer discipline'.[2] Yet his career and social life were invariably surrounded by racist restriction and occasionally unpleasant incidents. Men such as Carr were the most eminent of a growing class who formed associations, based on state service or a common schooling, that marked a growing territory-wide consciousness and a sense of belonging to a distinct interest group within the colonial sphere. In the 1920s the principal clerks and traders of Tanganyika organised an African Association, deliberately intended to represent 'the African' as opposed to Asians or Europeans. In French West Africa, association with the Ecole William Ponty as an elite-forming institution remained of the greatest significance to graduates and unified them despite origins and careers in territories that spread two thousand miles across West Africa.

Before 1940 such men did not easily come together with chiefs, especially given the efforts of British and other colonial administrators to exclude the educated from the 'Native Administrations', into a single class. The top levels of the African state employees saw this as a deliberate attempt to stymie their own ambitions. Tensions often ran high in the Gold Coast with its level of commercialisation and numerous educated men, despite the trade and family links between the two strata. The exclusion of European-trained lawyers from the 'native courts' was perhaps the most obvious symbol of this antagonism.

The 'educated elite', as they liked to call themselves, had as yet no systematic economic or political project. Their working lives were bound up in the commercial and administrative structures engendered by capitalism in its colonial guise and those structures generally bounded their imaginations and aspirations. However, this did not detract from their great importance as models, patrons and potential power brokers within African society. Because they were at best (and indirectly only) an incipient bourgeoisie, it is tempting for those inimical to class analysis to suggest that Africa thus had no classes in colonial times, its social contradictions confined to those between ruler and ruled. In fact, social cleavages reformed and intensified in the pressures of the developing colonial economy while new class struggles abounded in many guises.

Culture and social organisation

New cultural forms that arose in the colonial period betray in their tensions as in their creative spark the material forces at play underneath. In eastern and central Africa a pervasive phenomenon that spread from town to town was the *mbeni* or *beni* dance society. *Beni* dancers sprang from peoples for whom dance had been perhaps the supreme form of musical and aesthetic expression. Yet *beni* was par excellence the medium of new communities of urban and wage workers. The uniformed dances imitated military gear and hierarchy within the colonial armed and civilian establishments. Dancers could express at once a pride in mastering the new techniques of survival in the land while mocking and expunging colonial symbols. In Mombasa the gang leaders on the docks combined labour recruitment with leadership in *beni* troupes which could serve capitalist work rhythms. Yet it was the *beni* leadership which structured communications during the first African strike on the Northern Rhodesian Copperbelt in 1935. The social and organisational uses of dance were not confined to men, but engaged the emotions and energies of women equally. The strength of the dance lay precisely in its power to represent and symbolise social tensions and in the absence of a more political way of resolving them.

Dance was at once a form of cultural expression and social organisation. The dance societies were one among many new organisations that multiplied in work camps and towns, based on cultural linkages, economic interests and mutual aid. Football, which everywhere was taken up as the African male sport, spawned not only playing sides but sports clubs which transcended incipient class tensions while providing an outlet for leadership (and often possibilities for business) to the petty bourgeoisie. Another popular competition alive with ritual and competition that defined allegiances was boxing. In Accra, boxing matches by the sea were viewed as subversive by colonial officials who deliberately cut through the structures that had emerged by introducing European-type rules so that conflict and violence were acceptably controlled, while boxing was introduced along these lines as a model in certain elite schools. A study of football in Lourenço Marques suggests strong parallels. Reliance on charms and amulets, techniques aimed at disabling opponents, frequent outbreaks of violence and a playing style focusing on impressive dribbling patterns rather than goal scoring marked the play of teams from the city of shacks outside the city of cement. However, this in turn contrasted with the activities of a few teams identified with mulatto origins or the quest for assimilado status. Football at this stage represented an urban civilised aspiration but also an African character that did not follow the universal script.

Burial and lending societies and African-run churches proliferated. Perhaps most significant was the urban tribal or home-boy association which linked countrymen who had migrated to town from the same area. It was in the towns and under the inspiration of the patterns imposed by capital penetration that 'tribalism' and tribal feeling arose.

In the greater part of Africa lineage or other kinship affiliations had certainly been of the greatest importance in the way people conceived of social organisation. However, these were not closely associated with language, ethnicity or 'race' so as to forge a tribal identity. Conquests, absorptions and migration interspersed and intermingled Africans. Pre-colonial states were often identified with a ruling house defined in terms of lineage, but they were not nations in the sense of a specific culturally determined people.

Tribes are often conceptualised by Europeans as poor man's versions of their own nationalities and ethnicities. However, colonial tribes were not merely inventions of the conquerors. Their self-definition came out of the harshness and competitive character of economic conditions. The lucky migrant to the town could count on close kin to shelter him and to lend him access to a job or a niche in the petty marketing world. For every job there were competing work seekers who had other friends and relations pressing for an advantage. Most had to rely on wider cultural affinities, real or invented, for establishing an ability to survive. This encouraged ethnic brokers who were able to create advantageous niches in the accumulation process through their exploitation of the patronage they could exercise.

Abner Cohen, writing on the Hausa trading and butchering community of the Yoruba city of Ibadan in Nigeria, provided a classic description of ethnic solidarity in practice. The ethnic leaders there were at the same time religious brokers, patrons of trade and landlords, recognised as spokesmen by the local Yoruba establishment. The 'Hausa' of Ibadan were far from all being Hausa speakers at home, hundreds of miles to the north, but in the Ibadan situation, clustered around an occupational nexus, this is what made the most sense for them to claim to be. In one way the Ibadan Hausa were an atypical example. The Islamic Hausa community of this type clearly has far deeper historical roots; this is the ethnicity of long-distance traders in agricultural societies, reminiscent of Islamic trading communities in the West African savannah centuries ago.

The choice of ethnic boundaries varied enormously and could be differently defined from place to place. In East Africa there are excellent examples of 'tribes' arising from no historical roots at all. The congeries of Bantu-speaking peoples in eastern Kenya were dubbed the Bantu Kavirondo by the British for convenience. Later their leaders chose to call themselves Abaluhyia. In the Rift Valley and surrounds, largely pastoral Nilotic speakers began to be called Kalenjin instead of terms applied to a variety of smaller and more specific units only in the 1940s, a term that would in time have a sharp political salience.

The biggest 'tribe' in Tanganyika, the Sukuma, were until colonial times only the varied groups designated by the Nyamwezi as 'south'.

Capitalist firms and the state deliberately provoked such ethnic identifications, linked if possible to 'traditional authority' back home in the bush, in the interests of effective labour control and stable administrative patterns. Indirect rule lent itself exceedingly well to hard and fast ethnic definition, however artificial at first. Even when self-definition had firmer roots, such as among the Yoruba of Nigeria and Dahomey, the definitions became clear-cut and functional largely in the colonial context. In the nineteenth century 'Yoruba' meant someone from Oyo. Only during the colonial period was the language standardised in written form by Christian missionaries and made the basis for a timeless and clearly defined cultural oneness. The promotion of hard and fast identities tied in missionaries to the need for written texts to translate and advertise the Gospel. In this volume for convenience I talk of Shona people, or Shona-speaking people. The customs and language of the majority of Zimbabweans are closely related but written Shona was really only standardised as primary education expanded massively as late as the 1950s. Yet identities such as this tied in very well with the prestige associated with an identity recognised by colonial authorities and in line with what we might call colonial culture.

Zulus in South Africa are an interesting case study. Zulu was a clan name that became of great importance through the conquests of Dingiswayo and Shaka from the very late eighteenth century onwards. However, what we usually call the Zulu kings or rulers had both subordinate breakaways and enemies. The culturally identical chiefs recognised south of the Tugela River in Natal Colony and awarded locations by Shepstone were anything but loyal Zulu subjects. It seems to be really as colonial power waxed and the kingdom's power waned, as it became clearer that even property-owning black Christians were not going to be really accepted as citizens of the British colony, that Zulu became a word appropriate for hundreds of thousands of people who began to acquire an affection for their beaten royal house. It is true, though, that the standardisation of written isiZulu and cultural affinities (even if they had to be acquired) played a part as well.

Often tribal solidarity was situationally variable. People who identified themselves as being part of a common 'tribe' in a distant town split up into competitive groups that were equally considered to be 'tribes' closer to home, where they were more numerous. Whether or not you were 'Yoruba' in Ibadan required further clarification to be significant. Were you an Ibadan Yoruba or something else?

A changing faith

After ethnicity, religious activity has received by far the most interest of all forms of cultural expression in colonial Africa. The variety and cultural richness of African religious forms command attention while expressively infusing other facets of life.

In eastern, southern and central Africa a striking consequence of the defeat of African kingdoms was the reorganisation of resistance to conquest in the form of religious movements under the authority of oracles, prophets and doctors. The Maji Maji rebellion, which engaged a large part of the people of central and southern Tanganyika in 1906, originally focused on the healing and prophecy of a man named Kinjikitile. While it arose in an area that particularly suffered from German demands for cotton deliveries, it nevertheless required a particular local spark, a particular ideology of cultural reference. In some parts of Tanganyika, Maji Maji failed to catch on because chiefs viewed it as a threat to their authority. In other areas chiefs modified and controlled it to make sure that any successes against the Germans would be theirs.

At almost the same time as Maji Maji threatened German rule in East Africa the British faced a rising in Sokoto province in northern Nigeria. People gathered around the settlement of Satiru and threatened the authority of the state in the name of an original, egalitarian and just Islamic community that represented a peasant interpretation of the jihad tradition of Usuman dan Fodio.[3] They fought (and with utmost severity, were crushed) just as much or more against the Sultan of Sokoto as against the British; in fact their movement and challenge to authority antedated the British conquest.

As colonial domination became an irreversible reality, religious movements lost their political character and began to interrelate more closely with colonialism. On the eve of World War I the cult of Mumbo arose on the eastern shores of Lake Victoria in Kenya. Mumbo particularly affected the Gusii-speaking people although it seems not to have originated with them. Mumbo first appeared to its followers in the guise of a giant snake come from the lake to repair the damages in the cultural fabric of rural life. It first attracted serious attention when the British briefly evacuated the border town of Kisii, fearing German invasion in 1914. Mumbo prophesied the more or less violent disappearance of Europeans and the colonial apparatus through supernatural means and a future good life of leisure and plenty without labour. The empty town was looted and burnt and on their return the British investigated the cult members as potential subversives. However, if anti-colonial in form, Mumbo was quietist in content. God, not man, would cleanse the world of injustice. In Mumbo's visions, Christian and material ideas occupied an important place. Mumbo attacked 'traditional' customs like circumcision, challenged elder and male authority and was particularly hostile to chiefs. It was in no real sense a simple return to the old ways, but rather a synthetic movement subsuming both criticism and admiration of changing values.

Much the same could be said of the crusade against witches led by Mwana Lesa (the son of God) who roamed through eastern Northern Rhodesia and Katanga Province of the Belgian Congo in the early 1920s. Mwana Lesa sniffed out evil in the form of witches and arranged for mass killings of the accused before the British government caught up with him and had him executed in 1925. A number of writers have suggested that witchcraft accusations intensified in the early twentieth century in response to social tensions and differentiation within the community. While previously they were part of a more integrated cultural and social system and often under effective control of the chiefs, witchcraft accusations now occurred in the context of sudden enthusiastic eradication movements that could for a short time promise to rid the community of evil. Rarely did they lack for Christian symbolism or borrowings.

It was in the wake of the failure of great movements against early colonial authority like the Chimurenga (Southern Rhodesia) or Maji Maji and prophetic cults that the Christian missionaries followed, gathering up unprecedented mass support. Witchcraft presented a challenge to colonial authorities. Few Africans had shown much interest in Christianity before conquest. Ardent African converts of the nineteenth century were to be found largely in the colonial enclaves of the West African coast and in South Africa. It was a striking feature of the Americo-Liberian settlers and particularly the Sierra Leonians that they emphasised Christian credentials as part of their validation within the capitalist commercial nexus and in association with their trading ventures, much as Afro-Portuguese commercial communities in an earlier era. Only in a few spots (Buganda, Madagascar) had nineteenth-century social changes paved the way for early mission success in attracting important networks of people.

Conquest brought a quickening tempo to mission activities and in some areas mass conversions by the 1920s. Some of this may be comprehended as part of a desire by Africans to succeed in, and be accepted as part of, the new regime. In all the colonies where schools were common the missionaries completely dominated the new formal education and insisted on conversion as part of the price of schooling. So an ardent Christian faith became a part of the cultural baggage of many African accumulators. And Christian performativity became itself a mark of respect and honour. Missions were often of great significance in the acceptance of new commodities, commerce and crops and the source of technical and artisanal skills through their establishment of schools. They were par excellence the vehicle for capitalist values in much of the continent. As Stephen Ellis has put it in the case of Liberia: 'Children attended school primarily to learn the speech and manners of a burgher, in which patterns of consumption and clothing played an important part.'[4]

There was a certain degree of irony to this. The missionaries were typically products of declining classes and regions in the West, such as small-town southern Germany or the North American Great Plains in the era of fascism, populism and rural radicalism. For them, taking up the mission vocation was often a reaction, through personal sacrifice and commitment, against the new industrialised, concentrated capitalism at home. Missionaries tried to spread the values of an earlier capitalism – Western family structure, individualist orientation and the self-justifying work ethic. The Catholic missions of Belgian and Portuguese Africa worked particularly closely with the state. This was far less true in French territory, although the French usually insisted that missionaries be French nationals. The British colonies permitted the activities of a great variety of mission groups who competed vigorously for African souls. It was not unusual for missionaries to fight the settler interest where this was a factor, which enormously increased respect for them among Africans. Even then, with rare exceptions, they did not oppose the essence of the colonial system: segregation, land alienation and migrant labour. Few if any missionaries challenged the political and economic imperatives of colonial domination, as opposed to specific policies, and they usually accepted the racist aspect of it fairly easily.

Becoming a Christian was more than a political choice; it was also a cultural one. Before 1940 a peasant Christianity sustained by semi-literate cultivators, who could not seriously have aspired en masse to clerical jobs or professions, had come into being in certain parts of Africa. The significance of this, the atrophying of older religious values, may be related to the broader changes in material life considered above in which the new faith promoted greater conviction.

For a minority of African Christians the mission-derived churches were not wholly satisfying. Independent churches split off, partly provoked by the racial exclusivity of the mission churches and the domineering attitude of many missionaries. In addition African accumulators used the new sects as a means of satisfying their ambitions for leadership and making business. Some independent churches were completely conventional in doctrine, others allowed or encouraged customs that the mission churches frowned upon. Polygamy is the most important example. No mission tolerated polygamous marriage, yet material conditions coupled with older beliefs to encourage the urge for a successful man to take additional wives. The most notorious struggle along these lines came in Kenya in the 1920s when the Scots missionaries among the Kikuyu tried to force the abandonment of female circumcision. Most other missions tolerated the practice and encouraged it to take place in mission clinics or hospitals, but not the Scots. In Kikuyu society female circumcision was considered a gauge of a woman's modesty and had thus become indirectly a key symbol of male power. There ensued a strong reaction leading to large-scale schism within the mission church.

In a typology put forth by the Swedish missionary-sociologist, Bengt Sundkler, such independent churches could be called Ethiopian. Another group he labelled Zionist (deriving from an American sect that focused in Zion City, Illinois, with an early influence in South Africa) because it appeared to represent a yearning for emotional and social connections that the mission churches failed to make. Sundkler felt that the Land Act of 1913 and the impact of the policies of segregation helped to spread the independent churches in South Africa.

Figure 7.1 *Colonial society*: missionaries and staff, Nanzela, Barotseland, Northern Rhodesia

In the Zionist churches a central place was reserved for the ecstatic personal experience: messianic beliefs in a better world to come on earth through supernatural means were often fundamental. Faith healing and witch cleansing were also part of Zionist practice. In the Zionist churches it is possible to see both continuity with ancient religious forms, no longer accepted as valid without some Christian context being provided, and a response to social dislocation and deprivation.

Simon Kimbangu, who in 1921 in the lower Belgian Congo began to preach that he was the son of God, able to work miraculous cures, was the most famous Zionist prophet of all. The Catholic influence in the Congo was such as to convince the authorities to seize and detain Kimbangu, who lived as a prisoner in Elisabethville for thirty years until his death. Horrified and fascinated by him, missionaries began to produce a vast descriptive literature on his life and teaching. After his departure from the scene Kimbangu's followers converted a huge proportion of the Kongo-speaking peoples of the lower river valley to the new church, which itself frequently splintered.

The extreme Belgian reaction to Kimbangu belonged to an almost universal colonial assumption that active African religious initiatives were inherently sinister and subversive. Africanist scholars of recent times gave independent churches an enormous scholarly press, assuming that they were in some sense proto-nationalist, prefiguring fully political forms of protest in colonial Africa, like all manifestations of African 'initiative'. The truth is nearly the reverse. Few independent churches functioned as anti-colonial wellsprings. They were indeed a response to colonial conditions, not in the politics of protest but in the ideology of displacement. Healing and issues of psychic as well as physical health were very important to Christian belief and even much more so in the breakaway churches. Much religious practice can be understood as an ideological alternative to an historical outlook. It aims to cross cut any notion of the contradictions and historical discontinuities that mark social development with a message of timeless truth. Religion thus serves as a means of acceptance and creative adaptation. The apocalyptic predictions so characteristic of the Zionist churches were part of their failure to imagine a rational transformation of social conditions through struggle. Visions of the hereafter replaced assessments of the present. This is by no means to denigrate the importance of sects as social phenomena, understood for what they were. In some colonies they absorbed the energies of a large proportion of the population and undoubtedly their study sheds great light on changing social values.

Like Christianity, Islam has been subsumed under the anti-colonial protest heading, not entirely helpfully. Certainly in strongly Muslim parts of Africa rulers tried, with varying success, to organise resistance to conquest in the name of the true faith. Samori, although not a real jihadist, played the card at times. A dramatic example, and not that of a dynasty, was Sayyid Muhammad Abdile Hassan, the Somali teacher and poet who harried the British in their Somaliland enclave with great success for twenty years until his natural death. From the Muslim point of view, however, the decisive issue was the establishment of a society that upheld Islamic precepts and supported religion, an ideology open to varying interpretations. In Senegal the jihads persisted through the nineteenth century and continued to be aimed at the Wolof kings and their retinues. The French may have been infidels, but they were also the source of trade goods and arms; they succeeded where the shaykhs failed in destroying the authority of the 'pagan' rulers. So long as they did not interfere with religious practice, Christian rulers could be obeyed.

Islam is a religion of traders and townsmen. Capital penetration brought an augmentation of market life that encouraged Muslim values while typically Muslim crafts and trades flourished. The Murid phenomenon in Senegal was discussed from the economic perspective in the last chapter. Ahmadu Bamba, founder of the order, was at first mistrusted by the French and exiled to Gabon. However, he was permitted eventually to return to Senegal and became a decisive figure in the new social and economic system. In Senegal when the old ruling class was deposed it was the brotherhoods and the shaykhs leading them who captured the convictions of the peasantry. On the other side of the Sudanic belt, the posthumous son of the Mahdi (who in time became a knight of the British Empire) had his followers cultivate cotton with similar results to the religious leadership in Senegal. In some respects Islam became cement in the colonial order. Colonial regimes generally took good care to restrain missionary zeal and keep a low Christian profile in heavily Islamic areas.

Yet Muslims could pose as cultural counterweights to the prospect of mere imitation of the colonial master. Islam was apparently a dignified and respectable social garb; Muslims built up their own schools and promoted their international language of discourse, Arabic. Within Islam, every conceivable type of reaction to colonialism and capitalism could be and was expressed. In Muslim northern Nigeria rich merchants effectively usurped the place of the ruling families as principal patrons of religion. In West Africa particularly, Islam spread rapidly under the colonial aegis, adapting itself to new social forms and economic relationships. By 1940 over half the peoples of West Africa were Muslim and Islam acquired a depth impressive compared to the syncretic world that had prevailed for centuries. In Tanganyika the figure was more like one-third, with much smaller proportions elsewhere in eastern Africa, apart from the older Islamic predominance in parts of the Horn and the middle Nile Valley.

The modalities of resistance

Much of what has been written about colonial African resistance reflected the desires of nationalists to discover a tradition of resistance to colonialism or white rule that provides an historical platform for the political leadership that took power with the end of the colonial era. In most of Africa the display of force by the colonialists had been overwhelming and quite effective. Pride in the fighting spirit of one's parents or grandparents did not mean that one forgot their defeats and the terrible repression that often followed. Resistance existed, of course, but it was rarely to do with either race or sovereignty in the sense that would suit the fancies of later nationalists. Rather it resulted from crises in the material life of Africans and was related to class and other social cleavages within African societies.

Two of the best-known African revolts of the early twentieth century, those of the Herero in German South-West Africa in 1905–6 and the Bambatha in Natal (South Africa) shortly afterwards, must be considered as revolts of despair, however heroic. The German regime sought an excuse to dispossess the Herero of their herds and lands. They 'succeeded' beyond intentions – most of the Herero were driven into the desert and died, causing a severe labour shortage. Shula Marks, Bambatha's historian, described that event as a 'reluctant rebellion', largely provoked by the Natal authorities with their intensifying land, cash and labour demands. Chimurenga, now enshrined as the nationalist rising of the Shona people of Zimbabwe in 1896–7, similarly was brought about not through conflict over national sovereignty but through resistance to the increasing economic demands of incoming settlers and the British South Africa Company in Mashonaland. Maji Maji, as we have seen, began in response to the German regime of forced cotton plantings. Of course, none of these can be reduced to purely economistic actions; they all developed particular spiritual and ideological forms that were inspirational and convinced a variety of peoples to lend support.

There was nothing to compare with any of these revolts after World War I. For a generation military resistance to European rule was of marginal significance. Yet there was resistance to the state. Through much of the central provinces of French Equatorial Africa (Ubangi-Shari and Moyen Congo) a serious armed rebellion spread during 1928–9 in response to the collapse in rubber prices and the French demands for forced labour under particularly brutal circumstances on the Congo-Océan railway. Economic decline equally provoked disturbances in the central Belgian Congo, the Pende rising, in 1931 when cultivators resisted the demands of Unilever to whom they were forced to sell their palm oil and for whom they had to provide labour. Between 1924 and 1931 the Baya war took place in Ubangi-Shari. Despite the name, it unified resisters who were classified as speaking different languages and belonging to different tribes. Tax collection set it off. In the vision of the leader, Karinou, the whites would be forced to do the work of the blacks as the world turned upside down following victory.

Struggles of this kind (like Bambatha or Maji Maji) held no interest for the rising African elite. Why should they sustain resistance to the spread and intensification of the colonial economy on which their existence depended? When the elite spoke out they tended to remain narrowly class based in their demands and too deeply rooted in the colonial structure to question the colonial order very profoundly. Attempts at class alliance with the African masses were rare and came unstuck fairly quickly; indeed elite organisations generally did not enjoy long lives and frequently collapsed when the state applied hostile pressure.

The African petty bourgeoisie of the Gold Coast were relatively articulate and able to conduct their own case. Before World War I their most significant organisation was the Aborigines' Rights Protection Society, founded in 1897. It engaged the government over proposals to alienate forest land to the Crown which potentially threatened African property rights to the advantage of British gold-mining concessionaires. The colonial government withdrew its legislation, but despite this success the ARPS continued to sit on a very narrow social base and became attenuated in time. After the war a pan-territorial organisation, the National Congress of British West Africa (NCBWA), was briefly of greater weight. The Congress agitated for those issues that most concerned the Gold Coast elite – improved education, especially at the higher levels, and promotion of Africans within the civil service.

During this period the rhetoric of Pan-Africanism – the regeneration of a united continent, the need for Africans to rise through their own effort – gained currency within the West African elite. Pan-Africanism, including its visionary strain that followed the agitation of the Jamaican Marcus Garvey, was a creation of black America, where Garvey, who preached a return to Africa and a black people's capitalism, achieved a great mass following through the 1920s. In West Africa Garvey's economic ideas appealed particularly to those on the margins of capitalist enterprise, resentful of the handful of big Western commercial firms and ground down by the war and the severe business crisis of 1920–2. This provided a stimulus for regional or even continental political visions. It was not carried to the point of political anti-colonialism, however.

Nor did this would-be ruling class establish a political practice that could link up to mass agitation. This is remarkable because after World War I a wave of political and economic struggles swept West Africa. On the Gold Coast skilled workers began to unionise and strike. In Sierra Leone riots provoked by inflation took an anti-Lebanese cast in 1919. Porto Novo, capital of French Dahomey, experienced a comparable riot in 1922, while early union activity and strike action hit the crisis-ridden groundnut economy of Senegal.

The political implications convinced the British authorities to institute elective representation in coastal West African municipal bodies and legislative councils. Sir Gordon Guggisberg, governor of the Gold Coast from 1919 to 1927, while a champion of indirect rule, conciliated the professional men of the towns through the promise of better opportunities in the civil service (a promise never kept), infrastructural investment by the state and the creation of a particularly lavish and elitist secondary school for Africans, Achimota College, which was seen as the seed from which local higher education could grow. Reform and the return of better times silenced the elite. The NCBWA virtually died of inactivity by the middle of the decade.

In the Senegal communes, where Africans had the right to elect a member of the French Chamber of Deputies, a class alliance based on African unity did occur. In 1914 Blaise Diagne, a civil servant who had spent most of his career in the West Indies, became the first African to run for deputy, pulling against the big Bordeaux firms that had previously controlled the seat. Diagne attracted the vote of poorer Africans and established an alliance with the Muslim orders; he helped to arrange for Ahmadu Bamba's return from exile. But Diagne did not establish a base for challenging the French system; indeed he backed conscription of the *Armée Noire* during World War I in return for a government pledge to retain the rights of the four communes. By the end of the war he was invariably put forward as an international spokesman defending the merits of French colonialism to the world, having made his peace with French firms in Senegal. Behind Diagne lay an electoral machine through which mass support could be garnered for an elite, using the state to carve out a small niche in the colonial economy in return for petty privileges and patronage.

The nearest British equivalent was Herbert Macauley, piano tuner, chess aficionado and tribune of the Lagosian masses. For Macauley the equivalent to Diagne's alliances with the shaykhs was involvement in the intrigue-ridden competition for control of the old Lagos ruling house. He also led the long fight against the raising of the water rate. He was not consistently even anti-colonial, but was extraordinarily effective at uniting Lagosians.

In general the French system was more liberal than the British in promoting Africans within the colonial administration. It was harsher though in dealings with African businessmen. The commercial elite in Dahomey, although relatively timid politically, was crushed by state policy in the 1920s. Perhaps because its aspirations were so narrowly administrative, the elite stratum in French West Africa always emphasised the call for greater opportunities for African individuals within the French system.

The deterioration in commodity prices on the eve of the depression brought a new wave of confrontations. In eastern Nigeria Igbo women started by refusing to register as taxpayers, attacked the canteens of the monopolies as well as government buildings, and defied state authority in a series of riots, the 'Women's War' of 1929. Thirty-two were killed in the town of Opobo. Hit hard by the deteriorating terms of trade, they were responding to rumours of new taxes and the possible elimination of the warrant chiefs who were exclusively male. Eventually the warrant chief system was abolished and elders were systematically recognised as office-holders in Igboland.

Equally dramatic and significant were the Gold Coast cocoa boycotts of 1930 and 1938. The great depression particularly threatened the interests of the more prosperous cocoa farmers who had gone heavily into debt during good times and were entirely dependent upon sales of cocoa. The first cocoa hold-up centred around their efforts to hold back production and force better prices from the buying firms, a venerable commercial tactic on the Guinea coast. The boycotters won support from many chiefs and, for a time, a broad cross-section of farmers. However, they had ranged against them other factions, particularly the cocoa brokers who depended directly on the firms and needed quick sales. The poorer cocoa farmers and especially the landless labourers depended on what cash they could earn and also opposed or quickly abandoned the boycott which failed by the end of 1930.

Seven years later a more effective boycott was organised. This time, in organising a new monopoly Cocoa Pool, the firms were directly challenging the brokers' power as well so the Gold Coast petty bourgeoisie had more capacity for unity. Moreover the price of cocoa was again falling, but had recovered from the worst phase of the depression. The Pool had to be abandoned formally after months of boycott and in response the state began to plan active intervention in the organisation of cocoa marketing, a process which became of great importance after World War II and will be discussed below in Chapter 9. The class alliance of the boycotts were sustained only briefly, but they were a more weighty harbinger of the forces to be called into play in the 1940s than the promotional demands of coastal civil servants and lawyers' associations such as the NCBWA.

Thuku and Chilembwe

On the other side of Africa new types of regional and tribal associations formed in Kenya from the end of World War I. Most interesting was the East African Association (EAA), an inter-tribal group in Nairobi led by a telephonist named Harry Thuku. With the economic downturn of 1920 Kenya Africans were hit by wage cuts, settler plans for an extended pass system on the South African model and a substantially increased tax to force out labour. Despite similarities to West African agitation of the period, the activities of the EAA posed a greater threat since potentially they could tie into revolt against the entire labour system. Thuku found an audience both in Nairobi and in the countryside. His movement rapidly became political in character and took on these mass economic issues. To the horror of the settlers and the regime in the midst of Kenya's 'plural society', Thuku began to work with an Indian lawyer who had been struggling against settler attacks on the Indian community. Following what was claimed to be a demagogic speech in rural Kikuyuland, Thuku was arrested and his movement suppressed. The 'Thuku troubles' melted away and the tax increase was cancelled, although land and labour issues continued to be pressed by other organisations. When released, Thuku transformed himself into a conservative capitalist farmer, but he was more closely the forerunner of a type of political leadership to come than any other East African. Even the final apotheosis resembled Kenyatta's career once independence was won.

What Thuku hoped to achieve in 1920–1 is not entirely certain; it does not seem likely that the EAA had the capacity to develop into a revolutionary organisation. The one attempt at revolution in the British colonies was idiosyncratic and to this day wrapped in some mystery, but it is a story all the more worth telling. When World War I broke out John Chilembwe was an independent missionary in Nyasaland, theoretically backed by black American Baptist support, but in practice largely self-sufficient. Chilembwe was a cash crop farmer and petty businessman. Pictures survive displaying the elegant and constricted Edwardian clothes in which Chilembwe dressed himself and his family. His Providence Industrial Mission Church was a grand new brick structure, one of the largest edifices in Central Africa. He was an orthodox Baptist preacher; there is no indication of any Zionist yearnings on his part and the photo album suggests a family modelling themselves on the European mission plan, a perfect aspiring African in miniature.

As a boy Chilembwe had been the protégé of a very rare missionary, Joseph Booth, whose social radicalism was intolerable both to the colonial state and the mission societies. Booth was always associated with the notorious slogan 'Africa for the Africans'. In his search for religious sponsorship he established contact with black American Baptists. He went to America, taking the youthful Chilembwe with him. Chilembwe spent three years in Virginia at a training centre before returning to Nyasaland. (Booth eventually joined the Jehovah's Witnesses, settled in Cape Town and lost touch with Chilembwe.)

In the final months of 1914 Chilembwe planned in secret a rising against British rule in Nyasaland. Exactly why is not clear. We do know that he came into ever sharper conflict with a large neighbouring settler estate, whose manager, William Jervis Livingstone, a relative of the great Scots missionary David Livingstone, had forbidden Chilembwe's people to build a church on his property. Some of Chilembwe's supporters were estate workers from over the border in Portuguese Mozambique where conditions were yet more oppressive. However, Chilembwe had also acquired a chain of fellow conspirators among Nyasalanders of his own class. It is clear that Chilembwe hoped to profit from the war; this helps to explain his timing. His motives are harder to read. One published but unreliable account suggests that he simply wanted to make a witness and turn martyr – 'to strike a blow and die'. It may be that he had more concrete plans to gain control of Nyasaland and work out some modus vivendi with the Germans to whom he sent a message.

In January 1915 the rising took the form of attacks on several estate owners and managers, missions and arms depots. Livingstone was killed. Chilembwe preached a sermon in the grand church the next morning, Livingstone's severed head near the pulpit, calling for resignation and courage according to the most reliable witness. None of the co-ordinated parallel risings elsewhere took place and the government reasserted itself within a couple of days. Chilembwe was killed in flight across the border. The rising had no successor.

One discussion of the Chilembwe rising has suggested that the place of the minister and fellow conspirators of his own class has been totally misconstrued and exaggerated.[5] What was significant was an armed rebellion of plantation labourers, abused by Livingstone and his men, who were well aware of resistance to the state still going on across the frontiers in Portuguese Mozambique. It was they who spontaneously killed Livingstone, and Chilembwe's conspiracy represented only a confused and half-hearted response to their workers' militancy. This interpretation has the great advantage of accounting for the otherwise remarkable willingness of Chilembwe and his friends to take on the British Empire.

The elites of colonial Africa (and most of the time, the masses) did not resist in this way. This was not only because the odds were apparently hopeless. It was also because colonialism was a phenomenon of overwhelming complexity that contained attractive as well as repellent features for Africans. No writer has expressed this better than the Nigerian novelist Chinua Achebe, in *Things Fall Apart*. Umuofia, the village of the book, is from the beginning not the harmonious bucolic community of the romantic nationalist's imagination. It is rife with contradictions and tensions. The rich heads of households who dominate the youths, women and slaves and determine the community's fate are the sources of injustice and hardship for many. Conquest evokes in Umuofia a process of disaggregation that strains and sunders the web of familial relationships, using an already existing potential for social dissidence: 'The white man ... has put a knife on the things that held us together and we have fallen apart.'[6]

Achebe shows many of the finer aspects of Igbo village life; he produces an elegy to Okonkwo, the hard-working, pious and successful household head and the way that he is humiliated and killed by the coming of colonialism and Christianity. Yet Okonkwo is also an arrogant bully. Achebe portrays equally the brutality of many Igbo customs, typified in Okonkwo's murder of a captive boy he has adopted into his household when the boy is demanded in sacrifice by the gods. This above all nauseates Okonkwo's own son who leaves the homestead and ultimately becomes a Christian minister. Achebe suggests the terror and cultural ruthlessness of the colonial impact, but also its liberating and stimulating effect, a heady brew not so different from that served to the masses by early capitalism in the lands of its origins.

Notes

1. Cited in Charles van Onselen, 'Worker Consciousness in Black Miners', in Robin Cohen, Peter Gutkind and Phyllis Brazier, eds, *Peasants and Proletarians* (Hutchinson, 1979).
2. Patrick Cole, *Modern and Traditional Élites in the Politics of Lagos* (Cambridge University Press, 1975), p. 106.
3. Satiru casts a long shadow. A century later, the vastly more widespread Boko Haram movement has some of the same inflections.
4. Stephen Ellis, *The Mask of Anarchy: The Destruction of Liberia and the Religious Dimension of an African Civil War* (Hurst, 1999).
5. Suggested by J. McCracken in Leroy Vail and Landeg White, *Capitalism and Colonialism in Mozambique* (Heinemann, 1980), p. 177.
6. Chinua Achebe, *Things Fall Apart* (Fawcett Crest, 1969 printing), p. 152.

8

Industrialisation and South African Society, 1900–48

There are others again, and these are found among the advanced class of Europeans, who maintain that the solution of the problem will be found in segregation. They say: 'Segregate the native so as to enable him to develop according to his own lines.' But this policy cannot be successfully carried out today when the interests of both races are so interwoven, when there is no land in South Africa which is not occupied by Europeans, and when the industries of the country cannot be developed without native labour... To my mind, between this policy and that of repression there is no difference.

R. V. SELOPE THEMA (1922), IN GWENDOLEN CARTER AND THOMAS KARRIS, *From Protest to Challenge*, I (HOOVER INSTITUTION PRESS, 1972), P. 213

While the rest of sub-Saharan Africa witnessed the expansion of merchant capital in relation to a commodity-producing peasantry, South Africa went through the early stages of an industrial revolution. Fundamental economic changes clustered around the expansion of mining whose needs had spurred the imperial thrust into the South African interior. Colonial conquest intensified dependence on the world market, but brought wide-ranging economic growth and ultimately a variegated industrial development. South Africa is one country whose history suggests that there is little truth to the assertion by dependency theory radicals that imperial conquest and economic 'dependence' necessarily leads to national poverty, the 'development of underdevelopment' or indeed any determinate set of social and political arrangements. Instead, it is to the particular social and political forces within South Africa that we must look for an understanding of the form taken by South African capitalist development. South Africa can obviously be differentiated from the remainder of colonial Africa by the depth, size and antiquity of its population of European origins, but the presence of a white minority does not necessarily answer any questions; it poses new ones. In the first half of the twentieth century class struggles were intense in South Africa and class lines were not so easily definable as race lines.

The 'white' population at the beginning of the century consisted of a widely differentiated community, ranging from the Randlords down through rich commercial farmers, state employees and independent professionals and tradesmen to skilled and unskilled workers. The Boer War precipitated a rapid expulsion of poorer whites from the land to the towns, where their rural skills were useless and they formed a potentially explosive element in the population. The skilled workers attracted from Europe to the mining sites and new cities held a seemingly stronger position but were subject to the vagaries of the trade cycle and, if miners, the dangers and discomforts of underground work.[1] Conflict with capital went raw and deep on their part.

At the start of the century Africans still often related to capitalist forces as peasant-pastoralists exchanging a surplus when available or working for wages when the cash could be usefully ploughed back again into the household. Such relations were common elsewhere in Africa, if particularly intense in the south. For capitalist penetration to move forward, the subjection of African labour on a much grander, cheaper and more violent scale was necessary and this set the stage for the application of pressures and the waging of struggles. In the Cape the labour of 'coloured', or mixed race people, the bulk of the old colonial proletariat, formed a continuum with that of Africans and whites. In Natal and, to some extent, the newly conquered Transvaal, the children of Asian immigrants began to compete effectively against merchants of British extraction while a larger number, introduced as indentured labourers, shifted into the working class too. Workers of both sexes and all races and colours jostled into South Africa's towns and cities seeking a wage. How, with what sort of ideology and under what political arrangements could capitalist forces control them? The answer emerged only after a generation of conflict.

Nor was capital itself a socially undifferentiated whole. The Randlords (not themselves always in cheerful agreement) confronted the fears and conflicting labour needs of other types of employers, notably the farmers, who could not compete with the payrolls and social control mechanisms that the mines were able to afford in order to hold down a workforce. From World War I on, the interests of manufacturing industry, in need of a different and differently controlled labour force than gold mining, also became a significant force. Both manufacturers and farmers held a local financial, and thus a political, base. In time, both became skilled at using the apparatus of the South African state to advance their interests; they were in effect a 'national bourgeoisie' of a kind unique in scale in Africa. The mining interest, particularly after World War I, is also more and more difficult to characterise simply as 'imperialist'. The establishment of some kind of working arrangement, the alliance, in Stanley Trapido's phrase in the title of an often cited article, of 'gold and maize', came together with the fight of labour against capital to form the essentials in the historical development of twentieth-century South Africa. Those who emerged on top did so through the creation of a racial order that ran right through South African society until recently, an order far more systematic and more profitable than the equivocal racism of the nineteenth century and earlier, although ultimately it proved to be a larger and larger problem that became unsustainable. What must be stressed is that this order emerged from intense and continuing struggle, not a pre-ordained consequence of different races co-habiting the same land.

Reconstruction and Union

The conclusion of the Anglo-Boer War set the stage for the social, political and economic reconstruction of South Africa after 1902. Far from solving the mines' problems, the war had made their situation particularly difficult through the disruption of supplies and the dispersal of the labour force. Central to the social programme of Lord Milner, the British High Commissioner, was the reconstruction, on a sound, efficient basis, of gold mining.

The first years of the new century were difficult ones for the Randlords as they passed through a period of low returns, little investment interest and severe labour shortages. In 1904 the British government agreed to permit the entry into the Transvaal of a large migrant labour force from northern China. The culturally isolated and miserably paid Chinese workers were crucial in restoring profitability to the mines. White workers viewed them as a threat and demanded their repatriation from Africa, which took place after 1908. By this time, however, South African blacks were prepared to enter the mines in larger numbers and for lower wages than before the war. Yet it took almost a decade for South Africa to regain its pre-eminence among world gold producers.

Wartime propaganda had frequently stressed the role of imperial Britain as the guardian of the native peoples of South Africa against the Boer republics. In practice, Milner was careful to retain all the racist elements of Transvaal custom and constitution, refusing to alter the racially determined local franchise. The colour bar was part of his own plans for the South African future. Under Milner's inspiration the South African Native Affairs (Lagden) Commission, dominated by men close to the mining interest, deliberated and made its final report in 1905. The Commission proposed reconceptualising the position of Africans in the country in terms of segregation by race, land and especially political representation. It was a member of Milner's brain trust, the so-called Kindergarten, Lionel Curtis, who in practice first systematically applied the word 'segregation' to the South African context.

Segregation represented the fruition of 'native policy' in British Natal and, increasingly, in the Cape Colony as well. The movement had been towards reducing the black franchise and squeezing the African producer to churn out a workforce too cowed to press forward its demands. This was the intended upshot of the Glen Grey Act of 1894 concerning land tenure in Cape locations, introduced into the legislature by Cecil Rhodes during his years as premier. Now a Union-wide 'native policy', operating above the petty interest of particular parties, was wanted.

For Transvaal Afrikaners the Milner regime became a byword for repression and enforced Anglicisation. Milner strongly favoured the large-scale immigration into South Africa of British artisans and capitalist farmers so as to deprive Afrikaners of their franchise majority. This tied in very well with the needs of mines and towns for more efficient and mechanised agriculture. In this Milner had only very modest success, as the number of immigrants at a time of relative economic stagnation in South Africa was small. But his policies helped ensure the rapid revitalisation of Afrikaner national sentiment, enflamed with bitterness about wartime death, deportations and the concentration camps.

From the time he entered Johannesburg Milner's plans included the ultimate union of all the British colonies in South Africa. The restoration of self-government to the old electorate in the Transvaal and the Orange River Colony (as the Free State had been renamed), the re-enfranchisement of Cape rebels and increasingly acrimonious bickerings over railway and customs policy made the need for union more urgent. In 1906 the weakest of the colonies, Natal, was faced with a serious Zulu rebellion generally known by the name of Bambatha, the chief who led one phase of it. It was a response to intensive land and tax pressures and the gross insensitivity of the Natal regime. Among those who fought the colonial forces were many who had worked in the urban economy and many Christian converts. Bambatha was surrounded and killed and the rebellion suppressed with the loss of several thousand lives. Brutal deeds, such as the final massacre at Mome Gorge, revealed the very hard core behind the paternalist façade that normally governed 'race relations' in the colony. For observers from outside the province it highlighted Natal's weakness and incompetence at dealing with Africans.

The Kindergarten proposed the negotiations for a unified South Africa, but they were taken up by local politicians who stood ultimately for a compromise between varied South African interests and the British Empire. In the Transvaal the willingness of the Liberal ministry to grant self-government in 1906 had brought into office Het Volk led by the defeated generals, Jan Christiaan Smuts and Louis Botha. Oranje Unie held an even stronger position in the Orange River Colony under another Boer War military figure, James Barry Munnik Hertzog. Hertzog's movement was considerably more militant on certain nationalist issues, especially language in education, but had no coherent ideological or class basis to challenge the imperialist system. Also crucial were representatives of the pre-war political order, John X. Merriman, premier of the Cape and opponent of Milnerism, and ex-president Steyn of the Orange Free State.

Union was achieved in 1910. One provision of the new constitution was especially noteworthy: the retention in each province of the franchise as it stood. Thus Africans and other non-whites could vote in the Cape according to the existing property qualifications, but were forbidden to sit in the Union Parliament, while in the other provinces they were entirely disenfranchised. This provision practically killed the mid-Victorian political conception as applied to the Cape of incorporating the black middle class as junior partners in the political system. The Union Constitution paved the road for a strictly racially defined participation, rather than non-racial liberalism, as the politics to accompany the growth of South African capitalism.

Classic liberal judgement tended paradoxically to see at once Britain's willingness to re-enfranchise its old enemies as magnanimous and its abandonment of any pretence at championing African interests in South Africa as a sell-out, an unfortunate lapse of conscience. Yet for British imperial interests as a whole, and for finance and mining capital in particular, Union was above all a brilliant political achievement that could begin to put down those barriers to capitalist development in South Africa that had been so prominent. It was to people of the black middle class that the arrangements leading towards Union did indeed seem like a betrayal on the part of Britain and what remained of the Cape liberal establishment. Their deputations, associations and protests were ignored in the horse-trading atmosphere of negotiation.

At the same time the economic foundations of the African petty bourgeoisie were collapsing about them. The rinderpest stock disaster of 1897 and consequent serious animal epidemics and the ravages of the war were mileposts in the overall deterioration of African agricultural production in the reserves which had been excluded from settler expropriation. Erosion, ecological decline and 'overpopulation' fed into a growing pattern of indebtedness and immiseration. Instead of emulating the African progressive farmer of yore, youth looked to labour migration for its survival. The political irrelevance of the Christian African leadership accompanied the decline of merchant capital which in an earlier period had depended upon local alliances with this class. The mine labour tout replaced the shopkeeper (sometimes the same person) as the most important white man in the location.

In the first decade of the twentieth century there was some compensation in increasing land purchases outside the reserves by African land societies, often composed of ex-wage workers, and in the relatively favourable position of half-shareholders and other squatters who farmed commercially on white-owned land. However, these avenues began to be closed off with the passage of the 1913 Land Act by the Union Parliament. The Land Act confirmed the emphasis on segregation envisioned under Milnerism. Land ownership was divided strictly on racial lines, with the Native Reserves constituting barely seven per cent of the total area of South Africa albeit scheduled for expansion. Squatting was outlawed and although it continued in some form until well after World War II, it did so under increasingly unfavourable and unstable circumstances. The new system was underpinned politically by the Native Affairs Act of 1920 which enshrined chiefs and tribal authorities, now no longer capable of resistance to state authority, as the intermediaries between the state and the mass of Africans.

In struggling against these catastrophes African politicians from the entire country succeeded in establishing a national forum: the Native (later African) National Congress, originally founded in 1912. Congress was an impressive step forward in its national constitution, but had severe limitations as an effective force. It had little taste for mass organisation or, indeed, representation. Political inclinations of the petty bourgeois leadership remained moderate and defensive of existing rights. At first, even opinions about segregation were divided, since much of the leadership sought to cling to its established modest rung on the ladder. Above all, there was no strategy aimed at power or capable of presenting an alternative consistent road of national development. Much the same could be said of the African People's Organisation (APO), dominated by Dr A. Abdurrahman, representing the Coloured people in the Cape. The APO, like Congress, was most comfortable doing deals with white patrons, a policy with increasingly shrinking rewards.

The Indian community of Natal and Transvaal appears at first sight to represent a militant contrast, particularly under the leadership of the young Mohandas Gandhi who helped to lead the Indian struggle until his departure from South Africa on the eve of World War I. Gandhi led a remarkably dogged fight against the imposition of poll tax and several other noxious ordinances by the Transvaal government before Union. While his movement achieved some success, culminating in the Gandhi-Smuts agreement, it fell far short of achieving basic social or political rights, avoided any movement towards co-operation with other oppressed South Africans and led ultimately into a pattern of dependence on the intervention of the top Indian merchant stratum nationally and the Indian government internationally for the negotiation of specific narrow redress of grievances.

An era of confrontation

From Union until his death in 1919, Louis Botha was prime minister. Jan Smuts, already a dominant figure under Botha, then succeeded him in office. Having played a major role in the British war cabinet during World War I, Smuts conceived of South Africa playing a sub-imperial part as Britain's junior sibling throughout southern, central and eastern Africa. With this policy never far from his mind the Union government actively fought the Germans in Tanganyika and South-West Africa during the war and South Africa was permitted to administer the latter territory as a League of Nations mandate afterwards. Union policy consisted of initiatives designed to encourage the penetration of South African settlers and capital. Smuts also favoured the emergence of British settler communities in the territories stretching from Kenya down to Southern Rhodesia that would look to Pretoria for leadership. He sought unsuccessfully to annex much of Mozambique and Southern Rhodesia, the latter being frustrated in a 1923 referendum when the Southern Rhodesian settlers voted instead for a separate status of self-governing colony. Smuts was a highly articulate ideologue of compromise between imperial interests, mining capital and a moderate white South African nationalism. There was little in fact to differentiate his South African Party (SAP) from an apparently more 'British' Unionist Party.

With World War I and the rapid boom and slump that followed, however, the Smuts government faced increasingly intense challenges. The war brought unprecedented numbers of rural South Africans, black and white, to the cities in an era when South African secondary industry began to develop in isolation from Europe. By the end of the decade the South African population was one-quarter urbanised. The war boom was followed by a sharp economic decline in demand that hit manufacturing severely. Pressures on the working class appeared intolerable.

The gold mines, still the heart of the economy, experienced particular problems. With lowered profit margins, capitalists needed vast sums to develop new mines on the Far East Rand and new forms of labour organisation and discipline to introduce cheaper production methods. In the circumstances the Smuts government had to take up the cudgels to defend business interests. This set the stage for a phase of confrontation between the white workers, who formed approximately one-eighth of the mines labour force, and capital, quite openly backed by the Smuts regime.

Confrontation had been brewing for some time. Among the immigrant British workmen were many who had picked up syndicalist, socialist and trade unionist ideas before coming to South Africa. Particularly after Union, the cockpit that was the Rand became a perfect site for the expression of radical ideas. Afrikaner miners, newly arrived in the harsh urban milieu, were far from immune to such influences. White workers feared being pushed down to the living standard of the mass of African miners. In the Milner era a small mines manager, Frederick Creswell, achieved fame through his experiment with running gold mining operations entirely on a white labour basis. The experiment proved an economic failure and Creswell resurfaced as a leader of the South African Labour Party which was organised after the grant of responsible government to the Transvaal. For Creswell and others on the Labour Right the issue was above all to firm up a colour bar and to direct a politics that aimed at protecting white labour against black and local, South African-based, business against the dictates of mining capital. An unsuccessful attempt by workers to seize control of some mines in 1913 led to management recognition of a white mineworkers' union. The following year Labour won the largest number of seats in the Transvaal legislature.

There is reason to believe that African miners were deeply impressed by the 1913 strike. By this time a few socialists within the white labour movement had come to see the importance of organising the mass of unskilled workers and helped initiate radical ideology among some of the most receptive Africans on the Rand. An extensive history of African insurgency and labour resistance unstructured by any trade union culminated in the great mineworkers' strike in early 1920, which at its height brought out more than 70,000 Africans for a week. The strikers showed impressive discipline and control and it took a violent suppression with attacks on African compounds to smash it. It was of great significance that among the African demands was a call for raises and re-grading that would have challenged the existing colour bar, and of even greater significance that white labour felt deeply threatened and refused to support the strike in any way. The 1920 strike marked a watershed of different forms of resistance to capital and the state by white and black which took quite separate courses.

As slump conditions hit in 1920 the mine owners felt it was the time to break the strength of white labour. The miners were frightened; their response was similar to that of 1913 but on a bigger scale: the Rand Revolt of 1922. Workers' councils seized power in many public installations of the Rand and openly threatened the authority of the state. Smuts responded with a full military onslaught that led to over 200 deaths. With the Rand Revolt finished, the mine owners were able to reduce the size and payroll of the white workforce and to reorganise the labour process so as to enhance profits substantially.

Among Africans resistance shifted from the mines to other enterprises and other parts of the country. For the first time the ANC disposed itself to support ordinary workers and protested the violence and victimisation that followed the 1920 miners' strike and other outbreaks. One largely successful African strike occurred among the Cape Town dockers in 1919, greatly enhancing the prestige of the leader, Clements Kadalie. Kadalie was a mission-educated Nyasalander of chiefly origin with a home background and outlook not very different from that of the Congress leadership, but through chance and astuteness he rose to prominence on the tide of labour militancy. Kadalie became the spearhead of the Industrial and Commercial Workers' Union (ICU) which eclipsed Congress in size and importance among African organisations of the 1920s. The ICU had an amorphous quality which defies easy categorisation. It had some of the characteristics of a trade union, but acquired much of its strength in rural areas and almost invariably shrank from industrial action or even struggle for recognition from companies. It also had some of the characteristics of a political party and frequently placed its demands in the context of general protest at the oppression of Africans in South Africa. However, it lacked a clear ideological content or political programme to give it coherence. Kadalie and other leaders were like Congressmen in favouring alliances with influential and apparently sympathetic whites of various stripes.

The ICU was at first infiltrated by the small number of white labour radicals who increasingly despaired of the possibility of opening up the existing labour movement to African workers. If most white workers feared the potential of black working class organisation as a threat to their jobs and living standards, these few went forward from the white labour struggle of the period leading up to the Rand Revolt towards seeing a non-racial labour movement, and eventually a movement for the liberation of black labour, as fundamental. In 1921 most of them re-organised as the South African Communist Party (CPSA). In the mid-1920s, after considerable internal struggle, the CP moved towards concentrating on black membership and organisation. Some of the early African and Coloured CP militants entered both ICU and ANC. In the ICU, Kadalie's political views wavered, but he came increasingly under the influence of anti-Communist liberals and social democrats, especially after he travelled to Europe in 1926. Afterwards the Communists were expelled from the ICU. At the end of the 1920s Kadalie removed himself to the town of East London and the ICU virtually disintegrated due to regional and factional disputes and the mismanagement of the organisation, and in the wake of popular disinterest as its militant rhetoric failed to acquire content.

Pact and Fusion

Smuts' government was challenged by the emergent Afrikaner nationalist movement which took political form under General Hertzog's leadership. Hertzog broke with Smuts and Botha to form his own party in 1913. Milner's army of British migrants had failed to materialise. Indeed, as the skilled immigrant population aged, left Africa or died, the voting population became more and more Afrikaans speaking. In 1915 de la Rey, Beyers and other Boer War veteran leaders attempted to stage a rising in collaboration with the Germans in South-West Africa. Hertzog steered clear of open involvement and capitalised on opposition to the post-rising suppression. The emphasis in Nationalist Party politics on the language question reflected the domination of rural ministers and school teachers, but Hertzog also gained ground from the increasingly patent identification of the regime with the Randlords. The suppression of the Rand Revolt was coupled with Smuts' spectacularly bloody actions against an unarmed religious sect of Africans, the Israelites, at Bulhoek in 1921 and in 1922 against a small section of the Nama people in South-West Africa, given to South Africa by the League of Nations to hold in trust, known as the Bondelswarts. Both were glaring examples of the government's incapacity to deal with fundamental opposition. Nor did the Nationalists favour Smuts' expansionist plans in Africa which threatened to drown Afrikaners in a profitable sea of black labour coerced and dominated by imperial Britain.[2]

As Hertzog's party gained strength the Unionist opposition, with their Milnerite heritage, joined Smuts and his SAP in 1919. Hertzog astutely moved in turn towards an alliance with the Labour Party which could carry urban seats that eluded Nationalist appeal. Indeed, he made friendly overtures to the ICU and attacked repressive features of the African policy of the government. In 1924 Smuts was thrown out of office and the Pact government took power, with Hertzog as prime minister and minority support from the Labour Party.

Certainly at first sight Labour and the Nationalists appear to represent very different strata than Smuts' SAP. However, the evidence suggests the timorousness of the Pact's challenge to either the British connection (politically) or the Randlords (economically). Yet its existence highlights growing elements in South African society whose practice ensured a different political, economic or social development from any we have examined elsewhere in Africa at this time. The petty bourgeoisie, manufacturers, 'new' or employed middle class and so-called 'aristocratic' and supervisory labour used the Pact to forge a place for their own interests in the South African sun. In defining themselves racially (or, in the case of Afrikaners, even more narrowly) they contested control over the surplus; they eschewed questioning the basic character of capital accumulation within the Union. The Pact created the political conditions for a resolution to the disputes of gold and maize (or, in Hertzog's terms, the two leadership streams of Briton and Afrikaner) through the more rigid application of racial segregation.

The Pact claimed to defend the interests both of white labour and of the national economy as a whole. The rapid growth of industry during World War I had been a response to local consumer needs and wartime conditions. The mining interest was partly sympathetic to protection for industry because of its own needs for cheap, regular supplies for its workers and for the urban population in general, but it opposed state intervention to create a manufacturing sector that would compete for labour and re-orient the direction of the economy. Even under Smuts, however, the government had moved to create the Reserve Bank in 1920 and the Electricity Supply Commission (ESCOM), the national electric supply company, in 1923. Under the Pact a battle was successfully waged for the establishment of the Iron and Steel Corporation (ISCOR), the state steel monopoly. In the teeth of mining opposition, tariffs on imported manufactures were raised and, most significantly, the mines began to be taxed more stiffly in order to benefit other sectors of the economy. At this stage it was still agriculture rather than industry which profited, on the whole. A state support system for agricultural produce was put into motion.

The state did not interfere with the employment of cheap black labour by secondary industry or the mines, but within the state sector of the economy increasing numbers of jobs were made available for unskilled white workers, notably in ISCOR and on the railways, while a statutory colour bar was enshrined on the books for various categories of jobs. The struggle to obtain equal language rights for Afrikaans enabled more Afrikaners to enter the civil service.

The mines came to appreciate, or at least to accept, much of the logic of this re-orientation. By the 1930s, forty per cent of share capital in the mines was locally owned, as opposed to fifteen per cent at the time of Union. Sir Ernest Oppenheimer's Anglo-American Corporation had become the dominant force in both diamonds (DeBeers) and gold. Oppenheimer and DeBeers took a more broad-ranging view of South African capitalist development than had the old Randlords of Rhodes' time. They themselves would invest heavily in South African industry. If elsewhere in Africa colonial mining appeared to stand in the way of the emergence of any other form of economic orientation, in South Africa it was effectively harnessed as the motor force of a wide-ranging capital accumulation process.

With the growth of industry and economic decline of the African reserves the number of urban Africans increased substantially and began to include an ever larger proportion of women and children. This went totally against the grain of the segregation ideology. In 1923 the Smuts government had institutionalised the establishment of 'native locations' based on strict segregation in South African cities in the Native Urban Areas Act although at first the funds to make such a system operational were not available. There was little to differentiate the policies of Smuts and Hertzog on the use of segregation as a fundamental tool of white domination, although Hertzog was more systematic. In 1925 Hertzog introduced legislation to increase the territory available for Africans in the country as part of a final solution to the land question. In return for this he sought an end to the Cape African vote and the establishment of a special Native Council system instead that would act as a buffer between the state and African opinion. In the 1920s discussion in Parliament proceeded while legislation was passed piecemeal: for instance, the Immorality legislation aimed at sexual relations between whites and Africans outside marriage and the whites-only franchise for women which at a stroke reduced by half the impact of the Cape African vote.

The late 1920s brought a remarkable decline in African militancy. The ICU became weak and localised; the ANC too was virtually moribund. For a brief period the ANC president, James Gumede, had taken a radical, if eclectic, line and strongly supported a policy of working with the energetic but tiny CPSA but the Right ousted him in 1930 and, under his conservative successor Pixley Seme, the ANC reached the nadir of its influence. From 1929 the severity of the great depression evoked a new wave of labour militancy in part demonstrating Communist Party influence. The Party had adopted the so-called Black Republic thesis which stressed the African destiny of the country and this appealed to a new generation of black radicals and inspired intense struggles on the Rand and in Durban. These in turn met the tough tactics of Oswald Pirow, Hertzog's Minister of Justice. Moscow-inspired self-inflicted purges also helped to weaken the party which lapsed into virtual irrelevance in the 1930s.

The growing intensity of the depression threatened the social basis of the Pact. Pact policies had not gone far enough to change substantially the situation of its supporters. Conditions in agriculture deteriorated drastically and migrants to town met little but unemployment and short wages. Hertzog's reluctance to break with the British connection entirely and to establish a Republic made his Nationalist followers increasingly restive, while the base of the allied Labour Party shrank. It lost support in the 1929 election and thereafter split. Fearing a continued slide in his political fortunes, in 1933 Hertzog fused his party with Smuts' SAP to form the United Party, effectively a party of national unity, to meet the emergency conditions of the depression and to get South Africa off the gold standard. Many of the Cape Nationalist politicians, however, refused to accept Fusion and the following year formed a Purified Nationalist Party under the leadership of Revd Daniel François Malan.

Fusion provided the ideal basis for carrying through the legislation on Africans to which Hertzog had deferred in the 1920s. The agricultural interests had never liked the extent to which African land reserves were preserved, but in the new regime they were less consequential and the segregation impetus could now be taken up in more prosperous times with widespread backing from the white electorate. In 1936 the Native Bills, while slightly augmenting the scale of the African reserves (to thirteen per cent of the land area of the Union), put an end to the Cape African franchise and instead created a small representation in Parliament elected exclusively by Africans (with only white representatives) and the Native Representative Council (NRC), which exerted no power but were supposed to reflect African opinion. At the same time the pass laws and other controls over the influx of Africans into towns were extended to reinforce the segregation system. There was little dissent to the bills; only a few Cape liberals still beholden to an older tradition opposed them in the House of Assembly.

By this time African opinion was more aware of how segregation hit against their interests. A new body, the All-African Convention, attempted to rally protest against the bills. In the end, however, most of the small educated leadership core were willing to fight for seats on the NRCs and to attempt to work within the new system.

How did segregation operate? During the course of the interwar period it was more and more systematically introduced into both social and economic spheres. Schools and churches were almost uniformly divided by race. Whites were treated in separate health systems, welfare organisations and penal institutions. In the cities sanitary needs and custom were used to justify urban residential segregation, while the rights of Africans to own and improve property, varying from one municipality to another, were in general very limited. Health conditions in the towns were usually neglected and terrible. Ideas about racial purity and the evils of miscegenation, now made illicit outside marriage, became widespread. A fourfold system of job discrimination, white/Coloured/Indian/African became standard. All this cemented the growing self-consciousness of whites as part of a racially defined South African people.

Capitalists found that in return for tolerating better conditions and wages for a minority of white workers, it was possible to collude with the state in organising controls that kept black workers poor and unable to defend their own interests. Pass laws made it difficult for black workers to find employment where and when they liked and put them under the constant, if irregular, discipline of the police. The reserve system was ever more successful in supplying very cheap labour to the farmer in particular. The system of social controls as a whole (the exploitation colour bar), as Frederick Johnstone has argued, determined the 'ultra-exploitation' of black workers far more than the rather limited number of jobs withheld entirely from them by statute following the legislation of the Pact era (the job colour bar):

> And nonwhite workers have suffered far more from the exploitation colour bars of the employers than from the job colour bar of the white workers, and their grievances have always centred not around the job colour bar and their more productive employment in the prevailing system of production, but around the forced labour system and their ultra-exploitable position in, and ultra-exploitation by, that system of production.[3]

The dilemma for capital came when times were slow and white workers had to be employed in large numbers for relatively good wages. Then business was tempted to agitate for at least a weakening of segregation. Under Fusion, however, this pressure was for a time reduced. Whites could move into supervisory positions and their children, increasingly better educated, could jump up into a higher slot in the job market. The white worker, once terrified at being ground between capital and cheap black labour, could then find in segregation a viable and apparently stable form of survival. Fusion, however, proved to lead to a period of more than just stability; the contradictions in Hertzog's segregation system actually widened in the context of economic recovery.

The crisis of the 1940s

Fusion was linked to placing South Africa, the capitalist world's main source of gold at a time of economic collapse and dislocation, off the gold standard. From the mid-1930s, as the price of gold soared, it fuelled an unprecedented boom in South African industry which with few breaks continued through World War II and beyond. It was the pressures people experienced as a result that evoked a new era of challenge to the capital accumulation process in South Africa. At first the boom made segregation more feasible, but then it threatened to dismantle it.

Table 8.1. Percentage of total population urbanised

	1911	**1946**
White	53.0%	75.6%
Asian	52.8%	72.8%
Coloured	50.4%	62.5%
African	13.0%	24.3%
All races	25.9%	39.3%

Source: *The Statistical Year Book of the Republic of South Africa, 1964.*

With the depression the mines were able to begin recruiting a larger and larger proportion of their labour force from the High Commission territories – Bechuanaland, Basutoland and Swaziland. These three protectorates had been left out of the Union deliberately by the British imperial government which thereby retained a special handle on South African affairs. Now their economy, once based on the export of agricultural produce to South Africa, was transformed into that of rural slums dependent on the remittances of migrant workers. Nyasaland also began to function as a major source of mines labour. For black South Africans the 1930s marked the beginning of the end of the viability of the reserves. Hundreds of thousands streamed to the cities, increasingly women as well, seeking work in manufacturing which began to displace mining for a central position in the economy. Industrial employment increased by more than sixty per cent between 1933 and 1939 and more than fifty per cent again between 1939 and 1945. Nearly two million Africans were living in South African cities by 1945.[4] The urban locations strained at the seams from the mass of new workers and shanty towns emerged despite attempts to limit entry into urban areas.

The situation was intensified by the entry of South Africa into World War II in 1939. In wartime conditions it was impossible to police the bounds of segregation that had been laid so carefully through interwar legislation. Smuts, again prime minister after Hertzog's unsuccessful opposition to South African entry in the war, was in any case more of a pragmatist. Strikes broke out frequently, especially on the Rand, and the government labour department moved towards unofficial negotiations with the illegal African trade unions. For part of the war years pass laws were virtually suspended and African wages rose after a long period of decline and stagnation.

Boom and war reignited African militancy. A new generation of labour activists such as the Durban docker Zulu Phungula stood for the rights of the African proletariat within the urban areas, where alone they could now subsist. The African Communist J. B. Marks began to organise effectively among miners. In 1940 Alfred Xuma, influenced by his time in New Deal America and his American wife, embarked on his decade-long presidency of the ANC which began to consider the possibility of mass mobilisation and the espousal of mass issues, thus moving away from the traditional defensive policies of the past. On the Rand, conditions in the shanty towns and inflation inspired a large, militant squatters' movement. Among Coloureds and Indians also the old leadership of negotiation and defence of existing privileges was discredited and radicals took the initiative.

However, these tendencies did not all come together readily. Within the ANC an 'Africanist' tendency emerged associated especially with Anton Lembede, a self-taught intellectual originally much under the influence of Afrikaner populist nationalism. Lembede and the Africanists were in favour of a growing mass involvement in the ANC while bitterly opposing socialist influence in the form of the Communist Party with which other ANC leaders co-operated; yet others were active as Communists but hardly involved in the ANC.

By 1945 conditions in South Africa appeared to be undermining the basis for the segregation ideology. Smuts made a famous intervention in 1942 declaring that segregation was effectively dead – but he meant that there was the need to streamline and rename segregation so that it would fit his grand plans for a South Africa transformed through heavy industry. During the war years, a series of important commissions were created spelling out the potential steps in this transformation. For instance, the Fagan Commission broke with tradition and supported the permanent place of black family life in the city but proposed the creation of 'native villages' where such families would live without getting in the way of whites. Indifferent to the interests of small farmers and business- men while giving mining its due, Smuts pursued the creation of large parastatal corporations that could build up big industries – steel, chemicals, fertilizer, shipbuilding – which could be organized so as to mimic the labour practices on the mines more readily and find a market in settler Africa. At the same time, it was crucial for Smuts to smash the initiatives of African militancy that had developed all the more forcefully precisely because relative labour scarcity gave such economic force to their efforts. In this context can be seen the suppression of the African Mineworkers Union strike in 1946 which had broken out under Communist leadership. The NRC representatives were so outraged by the subsequent arrogance of the government that they boycotted further proceed- ings, breaking down the Hertzog system of native representation.

Thus the last phase of the United Party government had a contradictory character. Repression was mixed with promises of liberalisation. Attempts to give the Indians a vote while restricting their economic activities, and the proposals of the Smit (1942) and Fagan (1946–8) Commissions to register African trade unions – but only in secondary industry and not in the mines – and extend urban rights of Africans belong to this phase. Smuts, now in his seventies, failed to capture the imagination of white South Africans sufficiently to support this vision under his leadership. He ended his political career with a second crucial defeat in 1948 which brought Malan and the Purified Afrikaner Nationalists to power.

Notes

1. Mineworkers were often more inured to the conditions of mine work as opposed to certifiably skilled workers.
2. Hertzog continued, however, to pursue Smuts' aggressive policies towards Mozambique.
3. Frederick A. Johnstone, *Class, Race and Gold* (Routledge & Kegan Paul, 1976), p. 214.
4. D. Hobart Houghton, *The South African Economy* (Oxford University Press, 1967), p. 188.

9

The Decolonisation Of Africa, 1940–60

We have been informed of your good activities. Many of our recent recruits praise you very much for equipment, guidance, help and your wife's welcome. But there is something else you should bear in mind and that is (1) You are still teaching under Beecher's Report; (2) We have been informed that our enemy Bildad Giticha lunches with you in your house and that you have been dressing his wounds helping him to recover; (3) You can not serve two masters.

LETTER FROM MAU MAU FIGHTERS TO SCHOOLTEACHER KARARI NJAMA, IN DONALD BARNETT AND KARARI NJAMA, *MAU MAU FROM WITHIN* (MONTHLY REVIEW PRESS, 1966), P. 141

One must render me this justice that during the five months the strike lasted, I did not write a single article on the question and that if I dealt with it at times in my speeches, I did so voluntarily, in measured terms. Although I affirmed the legitimacy of the principles supported by the strikers ... I advocated a compromise solution as the only one possible under the circumstances. The event proved us right.

LEOPOLD SÉDAR SENGHOR ON THE 1947 RAILWAY WORKERS' STRIKE IN FRENCH WEST AFRICA, CITED IN J. SURET-CANALE, 'THE FRENCH WEST AFRICAN RAILWAY WORKERS' STRIKE, 1947–48', IN PETER GUTKIND, ROBIN COHEN AND JEAN COPANS, EDS, *AFRICAN LABOR HISTORY* (SAGE, 1978), P. 145

A magical word meant to exorcise ethnic quarrels and antagonisms – and as such very precious in contemporary Africa – 'nation' is a fetish-word as well aimed at abolishing class differences.

A. TOURÉ, 'PAYSANS ET FONCTIONNAIRES DEVANT LA CULTURE ET L'ÉTAT', IN Y. A. FAURÉ ET J. F. MÉDARD, EDS, *ÉTAT ET BOURGEOISIE EN COTE D'IVOIRE*, (KARTHALA, 1982), P. 242 (AUTHOR'S TRANSLATION.)

Table 9.1.   Pre-war and post-war population of the largest African cities, c. 1955
(1000 persons)

Ibadan, Nigeria	387 (1931)	459 (1952)
Addis Ababa, Ethiopia	150 (1939)	431 (1956)
Lagos, Nigeria	126 (1931)	312 (1956)
Léopoldville, Congo	36 (1938)	300 (1955)
Dakar, Senegal	93 (1936)	231 (1955)
Nairobi, Kenya	65 (1939)	210 (1956)
Luanda, Angola	40 (1934)	190 (1955)
Tananarive, Madagascar	127 (1936)	190 (1955)
Salisbury, S. Rhodesia	33 (1936)	168 (1956)
Accra, Gold Coast	70 (1931)	165 (1954)
Kano, Nigeria	89 (1931)	130 (1952)
Abidjan, Ivory Coast	10 (1931)	128 (1955)
Douala, Cameroun	28 (1931)	119 (1956)
Omdurman, Sudan	111 (1938)	116 (1956)
Resident in cities with populations of 100,000+	901000	3,149000

Source: Extracted and selected from Marvin Miracle, *Maize in Tropical Africa* (University of Wisconsin Press, 1966), pp. 34–5.

The second colonial occupation

Two related watersheds divide the twentieth-century history of Africa: the great depression and World War II. Neither had African causes; the second was fought only tangentially in tropical Africa. Both, however, brought about fundamental shifts in the world political economy that deeply touched material life and ultimately initiated far-reaching social, political and economic change. For the colonial regimes the depression was a time of stagnation and retrenchment. The limits imposed by the kind of capitalist development being pursued in Africa became very apparent. If that development was to go further, social and economic investments were necessary. Although this was increasingly obvious to the more forward-thinking colonial administrators by the 1930s, funds for new ends were rarely available.

As world trade gradually recovered, political crises in Europe and Asia quickly unfolded leading towards the giant confrontations of World War II. If the depression had marked an era of retrenchment in Africa, the war was the reverse: a forcing house of quick change and intense pressure. For war-orientated fascist Italy, this pressure on the colonies began well back in the 1930s. Eritrea was turned into a forward base for the conquest of Ethiopia. New investments brought in a large Italian settler community and rapid urban growth. After the conquest Ethiopia was set upon by the Italians who proceeded to pour money into infrastructure without precedent. Such pressures became generalised in Africa by 1941. Britain relied heavily on African raw materials. The Belgian government, exiled from its homeland after 1940 but still in command in Léopoldville, and the Free French, who by 1942 effectively took over the sub-Saharan African colonies from Vichy officials, were even more dependent on Africa as a base. African troops were requisitioned for fighting in Asia and the Mediterranean as in World War I, but now the effect of a total imperial war economy was far more intensive. Forced labour was revived in many spheres of the colonial economy, administrations pushed forward both cash crop and foodstuff production as much as their means allowed while imported goods became scarce or unobtainable. The result, in Kenya and Tanganyika, in northern Nigeria and French West Africa, was massive food shortages and famine conditions. Africans responded with immigration to the towns, where imposed isolation from Europe was creating new job opportunities. It was the war which witnessed the beginning of a wave of entrants to urban areas that has not ceased even now. In the cities conditions for poor migrants were deplorable. Food was short, housing unavailable and sanitation terrible. While employment chances existed for wage earners, the worker was met with rocketing inflation that exerted its own radical autonomous pressure on living conditions.

The war dramatically exposed the poverty of Africans to Europe. Dependent colonies with limited infrastructures and populations producing little beyond their barest needs could offer limited assistance to the mother countries. In this context, and this was particularly noticeable in British thinking, what once had been the idea of isolated reformers fast became generalised. Africa needed a 'new deal', to begin as quickly as possible, both for its own good and, more importantly, for the good of Europe. Catherine Coquery-Vidrovitch, writing about the depression in French West Africa, and John Lonsdale and Anthony Low writing on British East Africa, have noted independently the significance of this transformation. The last two have referred to the post-war years as those of a 'second colonial occupation'.

Behind the second occupation were some entirely new considerations, such as the encouragement of secondary industry or the corresponding attempts to create a small, relatively well-paid and conservative urban working class. Other aspects though were really an extension and an intensification of earlier forms of capital penetration. Thus development plans continued to lay great stress on transport infrastructure connected to the evacuation of export crops. The railway lines were now supplemented by feeder roads and even tarmac highways on which ran imported lorries and vans. Large sums of money were poured into improving existing routes or artificially constructing new ones. A striking example is the Vridi Canal, which cut across from the open Atlantic to the West African lagoon network, opening up Abidjan as a sea port for the Ivory Coast. It was a major example of the work of FIDES, the French *Fonds des Investissements Economiques et Sociales*, which were intended to co-ordinate development finance.

Cash crops remained an inherent part of economic expansion. After years of war the world was prepared to buy unprecedented amounts of agricultural commodities and to pay unprecedented sums for them. Colonial coffers filled to heights unimagined in the 1930s. The colonial bureaucracies also swelled, and increasingly their characteristic and most numerous members were technical specialists, particularly in agriculture. Until the 1930s the colonial regimes intervened relatively little in peasant agriculture; they preferred simply to squeeze producers. Now grandiose schemes for irrigation and community development were planned. Agricultural experts trained assistants as a task force to coerce peasants into producing according to what were assumed to be superior techniques based on European models. Agricultural ordinances with penal sanctions were passed with alacrity.

Effective new inputs into peasant agriculture were limited but not insignificant. Ploughs, tractors and particularly chemical fertilisers played an increasingly significant part in expanding production, while frequently exhausting the soil and marking the intensification of social distinctions within the rural population. Greatest of all post-war agricultural experiments was the Tanganyika Groundnut Scheme. In the mid-1940s there was a world shortage of edible oils and India, the principal exporter of groundnuts, was unable to make up for the scheduled needs. So, with the advice of Unilever, the British government embarked on a scheme for turning large sections of Tanganyika into a mechanised groundnut producer. There was little planning and the local colonial administration was scarcely consulted. As a result virtually every choice regarding soil, machines, labour and land was wrong. Old tanks were unconvincingly transformed into agricultural machinery. At the beginning of the 1950s the Groundnut Scheme was wound up, a disastrous failure to which the British government had dedicated tens of millions of pounds. The French equivalent was the *Office du Niger* irrigation scheme, which had begun a generation earlier. This was tied into the earlier dream of creating in West Africa a vast reservoir of cheap cotton for the French textile industry to rival Egyptian and Sudanese cotton. The settler schemes attached and the forced labour involved never produced the requisite cotton which suffered from very poor prices. In the end, resident peasants grew other crops and, just as earlier in Northern Nigeria, a different section of the same colony (French Soudan) did become a successful cotton export zone with favourable prices and appropriate state support. In these years authorities see-sawed between bureaucratic imperatives and a growing push for consultation. Rarely, in fact, were grand mechanised schemes based on naïve faith in scientific models very successful. Even when colonial experts had important advice to give, their lack of connection to African cultivators negated the effect. The real backbone of what increase in productive wealth could be found in agriculture lay in the roads stretching deeper into new country, and the excellent post-war produce prices, both of which stimulated most of the old, and created new, cash-cropping zones.

In effectively isolating Africa from Europe, the war spurred on the first significant wave of industrialisation orientated to local markets, producing either the small range of mass consumption goods such as soap powder, matches, beer and cigarettes, or goods designed for the affluent local bourgeoisies, especially where important populations of European or Asian origin resided. Salisbury and Nairobi, Dakar and Léopoldville, Accra and Lagos, Asmara and Addis Ababa were the main centres of industrial growth. Much of the new industry was related either to export processing or import substitution and involved the dominant export-import houses. The profile of their interests changed rapidly as the 'second colonial occupation' shifted the import cargoes increasingly from basic industrial consumer goods to machinery and capital goods. The import, marketing and servicing of automobiles became big business. Firms such as the United Africa Company withdrew from produce storage in small market canteen centres to concentrate on establishing retail department stores in the major cities. This shift in business interests dovetailed with colonial policy which sought at once to preserve the prosperity of the oligopolies and the security of the peasant base of society by eliminating or streamlining middlemen operations.

In the post-war era co-operative societies expanded their base widely. The co-operatives received state assistance in recognition for functioning as mediators between the small producer and the European firms. The largest in all Africa, the Victoria Federation of Co-operative Unions, organised the marketing of the booming cotton expansion of northern Tanganyika. It was specifically directed at pressing Asian middlemen buyers out of business and, under the façade of co-operative principles, was effectively dominated by the richest and most ambitious Africans of the area. Wealthy farmer-transporter-moneylenders were just as prominent in the cocoa producing co-operatives of western Nigeria and the Gold Coast. In French Africa a somewhat parallel system, the *Sociétés Indigènes de Prévoyance*, had an earlier origin and were historically tied to both the forced cultivation tradition and the French need to establish collaborative linkages with chiefs and big men in rural areas.

Together with co-operatives the other major new, related institution was the marketing board. These boards were formulated in response to depression conditions and fears of producer antagonism against middlemen, or even the expatriate firms, as manifested in the great cocoa holdup in the pre-war Gold Coast. They set seasonal prices for particular export crops on a territorial basis and controlled the licensing of buying agents with whom producers could deal. Initially justified as a means of stabilising peasant income, in practice they withheld large sums for the benefit of the state. In theory these were to be used for development purposes, but the British particularly made use of them to back their currency by placing the balance in Britain. Marketing boards, like co-operatives, were intended as a means of direct state accumulation from the agricultural production process.

The other side of post-war colonial planning was the new emphasis on social welfare. The war revealed the inadequacies, from the point of view of colonial needs, of an ill-housed, badly fed, illiterate population. The new stage of economic development towards which colonial regimes were preparing required a more qualified, stable working class. Considerable emphasis began to be laid on medicine, including rural and preventative medicine, which, for the first time, had some effect on the health of the masses in many areas. In most colonies a dramatic growth of primary education and state support for it began after the war. By this time school expansion was widely popular in Africa and a conveniently common ground of state and mass ambitions. The spread of schools, even though not effectively universal anywhere before 1960 (and admittedly still seen with suspicion in Muslim communities), was a powerful force in integrating African youth into wider colony-wide political and social networks.

A remarkable aspect of this spectrum of reforms was its conception and direction in a political void; it represented a programme by and for bureaucrats. Some major administrative decisions seemed remarkably deluded. The British pressed forward with a problematic model of colonial federation, of which one controversial feature lay in the inclusion of a major new white settler initiative. During the war consensus developed in Britain about the overriding need for large, amalgamated economic units that could be the arenas of effective new levels of capital penetration in Africa. Of these the most significant was the proposed federation of British Central Africa – the Rhodesias and Nyasaland. As profits from Northern Rhodesian copper mining mounted, bringing to the Copperbelt a rapid increase in immigrant British and South African whites, uniting the Rhodesias became a very attractive proposition both to Rhodesian settler interests and to the copper companies. The growing emphasis on industrial markets and services in Southern Rhodesian capitalism strengthened this trend. When in 1948 Afrikaner Nationalists came to power in the South African general election, the British government at first feared an anti-British orientation in Pretoria and sought to buttress Salisbury as an alternative pole.

The Labour government in England was afraid to be seen openly pressing for settler domination in all Central Africa and pursued an incongruous policy of calling for massive new British immigration to the Rhodesias while claiming to champion African rights in the territories. It was apparently Whitehall insistence that led to the inclusion of impoverished Nyasaland in overall federal planning. After years of negotiation, amalgamation of the Rhodesias was rejected in favour of federation, which preserved the internal administrative systems of each territory intact. The Conservative government which came to power in 1951 pressed ahead and two years later established the Central African Federation, which indeed proceeded to attract both new white settlers and substantial British investment capital. With its spurious propaganda about racial partnership, federation never had better than passive African mass support and was feared and hated by the politically conscious. It was the partnership between the horse and his rider, in the phrase of Lord Malvern, Southern Rhodesia's long-time premier. In attempting to foist an administrative fiat, the British were placing their heads in a hornets' nest.

Despite parallel economic thinking on the subject the British East African territories of Kenya, Uganda, Tanganyika and Zanzibar were never federated. Kenya settlers sought federation only on terms that would be highly favourable to their political interests, while the colonial officials of Tanganyika and Uganda actually opposed it. As a result, what emerged were the East African common services which eschewed political unification but created a general venue for regional capital development that was almost as attractive to business as the arrangement in Central Africa. The Kenya highlands and Nairobi prospered as the local metropole for this zone.

In Uganda there was the additional problem of how to amalgamate 'indirectly' ruled Buganda into the wider territory. By the early 1950s Britain was committed to a unitary administration for Uganda and so evoked a political crisis of intensifying dimensions. The other model paragon of indirect rule, northern Nigeria, faced a similar dilemma. During the war, economic considerations led to the determination of a federal but unitary development for Nigeria, pitting one interest which had favoured the emirates together with other artificially preserved or invented monarchies and the imperative, now potentially triumphant, representing the central bureaucracy. As in Uganda the fruits would prove bitter.

The question of settler power connected closely to that of federation in British East and Central Africa. During the war settlers held a particularly

Table 9.2.   The growth in the European settler population

	1935/36	1953
Southern Rhodesia	55,419	160,000
Angola	30,000	78,826 ('50)
Belgian Congo	18,680	76,764 ('52)
French West Africa	19,061	62,236*
Northern Rhodesia	9913	50,000
South-West Africa	31,049	49,612 ('51)
Mozambique	10,000	48,813 ('50)
Kenya	17,977	42,200

*Includes 'assimilated' Africans.

Source: Selected from census figures in Lord Hailey, An African Survey (Oxford University Press, 1957 edn), p. 144 (1945 edn, p. 109)

strategic position to which metropolitan authorities were indebted. After the war ended their numbers grew fast in much of Africa while economic conditions greatly favoured their prosperity. The 'second colonial occupation', in conjunction with excellent demand for tropical produce, created possibilities for a small bourgeoisie in most territories and European colonists had the education, techniques and connections with officialdom to fill that role. It was in the late 1940s that the 'white highlands' of Kenya finally became the scene of capital-intensive and very lucrative agriculture, while African squatters were increasingly evicted and pushed out to the Kikuyu Reserve. The tobacco boom fuelled a big push in capitalist agriculture in Southern Rhodesia. The white population of the Belgian Congo more than tripled in fifteen years after the war while a doubling of the Portuguese in the decade of the 1940s alone finally appeared to fulfil the vain dreams of earlier eras for Angola and Mozambique. Wherever they settled Europeans served their own interests best by a rigid group identity and a racism increasingly shorn of old-fashioned paternalism. Nothing roused and united Africans more than their advances. The settler thrust, as much in its economic as its political manifestations, was another main ingredient in the tensions and transformations of the era.

The new colonialists gave overwhelming emphasis to social and especially economic change. Political change was envisioned only rather gingerly, in step with the most liberal colonial thought of the pre-war era. Within the oppressive, racist ideology characteristic of the old colonial rhetoric a more idealistic old coin had occasionally been polished and brought down from the attic for international inspection. In the case of the British the message was that Africans could eventually, in the remote future, follow in the footsteps of their white brethren in colonies of settlement and obtain self-governing institutions within the Commonwealth. The most one could say for its application before 1939 was the presence of legislative councils in nearly all the colonies. Only the all-white legislature in Southern Rhodesia had any real weight, however. In West Africa these councils contained African members, a few of whom were elected on a limited urban property franchise. The French, in contrast, occasionally professed a belief in assimilation, (ideally) the total economic and political integration of the colonies into France with their inhabitants receiving the normal political and legal rights of other French citizens. Here a taste existed in the form of the deputy elected to the French Chamber by the voters of the four communes of Senegal and in the personal achievement by several thousand African individuals of French citizenship rights through a stiff bureaucratic procedure.

The war saw greatly renewed propaganda along both these lines. In fact the new thinking in London and Paris involved reforms that represented concessions to precisely those demands made by elite African organisations before the war. In British West Africa the territorial coverage of the legislative councils was extended to include the entire colonies, while in the Gold Coast the franchise was extended. Reforms were proposed in local government to give a large stake in them to the educated and restless. Economic grievances were attended to by the encouragement of industry, the marketing boards and co-operatives, while the social side received the response of substantially increased state involvement in education and health. Immediately after the war planning for a university in the Gold Coast, and, shortly after, one in Nigeria, appeared to be concessions to reach the acme of the coastal elite's dreams. Within the administration the hiring of Africans for high-level positions and the dismantling of the social colour bar were considered. Outside West Africa reforms were less bold. However, here too there was educational expansion and a beginning of legislative representation. The latter started with the appointment of Eliud Mathu as the first African member of the Kenya Legislative Council in 1944.

French reforms were more dramatic and were more dramatically inaugurated at the Brazzaville Conference in 1942 by General Charles de Gaulle after the adherence of the regime in Equatorial Africa to the cause of anti-Nazi, pro-British Free France. After the war constitutional meetings led to the establishment of a pan-imperial representative French Union and the admission of elected African deputies from all territories to the French Chamber of Deputies. The electoral franchise was limited and a special electoral college was designed to appease the French settlers in Africa. Admission of Africans to the highest echelons of the colonial service, municipal self-government and rapid educational expansion were also planned in the French model while the franchise was extended by stages.

The abolition of forced labour in 1946 was the most solid token of a new stage being reached in French Africa. In contrast, there was no equivalent reform in the Belgian and Portuguese systems during the decade following the war. What characterised both these systems was their different relationship to the 'second colonial occupation'. In the Congo the intensification of capital penetration really went back to the 1920s and had proceeded smoothly without political or administrative concessions to Africans. So why not continue in the same mould? Portugal was too backward to advance on this front until after 1960 when it faced the stark challenge of wars for liberation in the colonies. In the quantitatively more significant cases of France and Britain political reform was closely linked to what were seen as the necessary social bases for the new planned level of capitalist development. Both powers appreciated the importance of some kind of new basis for collaboration with Africans.

Social confrontation and class struggles

The political reforms of the new colonialism were based, at least initially, on an estimate of the social forces of the pre-war era. They were profoundly behind the times.

The greatly altered international political sphere provided a wider setting of pressures that worked to provoke change. The destruction of liberal political institutions by fascist regimes in Europe, together with the new prestige and power of the Soviet Union following its decisive role in the defeat of fascism, left the social groundwork of capitalism in Europe very weak after 1945. Reforms to secure political and social democracy were considered essential in this climate and such considerations were particularly acute in the colonies. The war virtually swept away European colonialism in Asia. There the West faced the stark choice of anti-capitalist regimes, of which a most important one came to power in China in 1950, or compromise with nationalist-minded bourgeoisies, as in India. Perceptions of Africa were necessarily clouded by the far more advanced Asian colonial crisis.

The greatest Western power had almost no stake in maintaining colonial rule. American policy was committed to containing the advance of socialism through establishing ties with nationalists in the colonies who could be won over to the American view of the world. This was a strategy closely related to the desire of American business to establish a stronger position in the trade and material resources of African and other colonies dominated by European industry. American wartime propaganda was often sharply anti-colonial. Later the imperative need for good relations with European allies blunted the thrust, but the general lines of pressure remained constant.

Within Africa the situation differed in 1945 from what it had been a decade earlier. Indeed the economic and social initiatives of the colonial authorities themselves helped to make early political reforms inadequate. Economic pressures had thrown up a rapidly growing wage-labour force and swelled the population of the cities. The boom in commodities that followed led both to rising expectations and to differentiation between the less and more fortunate that fuelled the grievances. Consequently the 1940s were an era of unprecedented labour organisation and labour insurgency. There were instances of worker action and strikes within the colonial African economy as far back as the late nineteenth century and an important wave of labour unrest struck many African administrations after World War I. The next significant crest followed the return to prosperity in the late 1930s when continuing depression-rate wages brought about several important strikes, notably on the Mombasa docks and the Northern Rhodesian Copperbelt. Britain began to turn to a policy of fostering legal trade unions, permitted also by the French during the Popular Front government of 1936–8. This merely foreshadowed the labour unrest that gathered strength in the last couple of years of the war.

There was virtually no African colony without a major strike phase. The workers who were most able to organise and make their demands stick were those in the public sector, particularly in transport and communications – railway workers, dockers, telegraphists and postal workers. Major and briefly crippling strikes affected the docks of Lourenço Marques in Mozambique and Matadi in the Congo. Those in Lagos (1945) and in Dar es Salaam (1947) successfully spread inland along the lines of rail in Nigeria and Tanganyika to become general strikes. In 1947 the railway workers of French West Africa struck for an unbelievable four months, largely on the issue of racist pay differentials. Union organisations of indeterminate character and explosive force mushroomed.

The colonial authorities were anxious to prevent labour from turning overtly to political issues that could challenge the basis of exploitation as a whole. They responded to strikes not only with repression (notably severe in the Portuguese colonies and in the wartime Belgian Congo), but with a positive programme of non-political, colonially directed unionism, to which end labour departments were organised. The British government despatched conservative British trade unionists, by agreement with the Trades Union Congress, to spearhead the effort. The result was a formal union structure that came to resemble the Western collective bargaining model. The leadership that emerged from the African unions typically (not always) consisted of outsiders who belonged by training to the clerical stratum or above, organising with the mentality of would-be bureaucrats on the make or petty entrepreneurs. Thus, in Nigeria union secretaries would often serve several unions at once and were in effect professional self-made go-betweens. Yet this business unionism strategy had only limited success before the mid-1950s. Even the most co-operative union officials could not always effectively control mass action, although they failed to give it revolutionary political leadership. Moreover they often retained political ambitions personally. The likelihood of labour unrest dominated colonial fears throughout this period.

Peasant unrest was much less focused and less strategic but it potentially involved much larger numbers. Three not unrelated issues gripped rural Africa: reaction to intensifying cash pressure and class differentiation; the apprehensions caused by settler prosperity and expansion; and the resistance to agricultural improvements imposed by force. All three in conjunction typified British Central and East Africa. Opposition to agricultural ordinances was coupled with a refusal to pay taxes and hostility to the regime of the chiefs. In Tanganyika the most massive rural resistance movement occurred in Lake Province. The peasantry rallied against the attempt to impose what was called 'multi-racial' government, the association of Indians and Europeans, an infinitesimal minority, in the organs of local government. Non-co-operation and sabotage effectively brought provincial administration to a halt. Other social conflicts of the time in Tanganyika show different facets of rural protest: tax resistance among the Pare; anti-chief struggles among the Shambaa; the fight against land alienation to settlers in a land consolidation programme aimed at agricultural efficiency in Meru; development legislation aimed at pastoralists affecting Maasai speakers. These conflicts went back to the war years and intensified to reach a peak in the late 1950s, when the British were hardly able to collect any tax in Tanganyika. During the 1950s anti-chief and anti-agricultural ordinance crises swept the new Central African Federation of the Rhodesias and Nyasaland as well.

In West Africa the classic agriculture-related political issue revolved around the bureaucracy's efforts to stamp out swollen shoot disease among cocoa trees.

The government remedy was to destroy all infected shoots and cut down whole areas in order to isolate the disease. Farmers realised this was ineffective and that they could at least get some profit from a poor harvest which was better than none at all. (Indeed, swollen shoot is no longer treated according to the prescriptions of the period.) The resultant conflict was acute and resulted in a deep alienation of cocoa farmers, especially in the Gold Coast, from the colonial state.

Pride of place in any discussion of peasant resistance to colonialism in this era must go to three great armed risings: one in Madagascar in 1947–8; one in central Kenya in 1952–5, usually called 'Mau Mau', and one in Cameroun which began in 1955. All are usually placed in the context of the movement for independence as a form of political nationalism. But more attention should be given to their social context and the material pressures that the African peasantry was feeling. In Kenya and Cameroun the uprisings' links to urban communities and to the labour movement were significant.

In Cameroun the rising took place under the auspices (and, in part, control) of a political party, the *Union des Populations du Cameroun* (UPC) with some systematic involvement of radicalised, educated Camerounians. The nationalist politicians and the educated population generally had a far more tangential role in the other two. All three took place in colonies with aggressive and militantly racist settlers. Cameroun's post-war political history had begun with a vicious attack on Africans by the settlers of the port city of Douala. In Madagascar a major geographic focus of rebellion was the plantation sector of the eastern coastal lowlands. In Kenya, Mau Mau sought the recovery of land proclaimed for white ownership only. Many fighters were evicted squatters who had found a cold welcome in the increasingly cash-orientated, commoditised, crowded Kikuyu Reserve. Mau Mau was in part a fight against the growing intrusion of capitalism into Kenyan agriculture. The guerrillas struck above all at the new class of Kikuyu accumulators. They called themselves the Land Freedom (or Land and Freedom) Army.

In Kenya the Land Freedom Army held a secret parliament in the recesses of the remote Aberdare Mountains and called for the emergence of a united African nation in Kenya. Yet a decisive weakness of Mau Mau was its failure to gain much active support among non-Kikuyu. In Madagascar some of the military commanders appear to have been men of considerable political ability; there was a strong element of continuity with peasant movements that had fought in the nineteenth century against the exactions of the autocratic Imerina kingdom. However, in contrast to Kenya the political leadership was afraid to tamper with the village elites and made compromises with them on a pragmatic basis. The violent repression of the rising also involved the persecution of those France suspected of disloyalty. Jacques Mananjara, already a distinguished poet and member of the French parliament, was stripped of his office and sentenced to life imprisonment at hard labour. He was pardoned a decade later. In Cameroun several areas (in turn) took up arms, but as in Kenya no national basis for the fighting was found by the UPC. The leadership deliberately restricted their political demands to two minima: formal independence from France and the unification of French with British Cameroun, thus uniting the old German colony. These were two demands which, eventually and ironically, the French were prepared to grant once the UPC was effectively beaten. All three rebellions occurred almost independently of the sympathy of the outside world and this was ultimately a major source of weakness. They never developed the global analysis or linkages which might have brought them more success.

Only with an understanding of this background of urban and rural mass protest and the new colonial context does the post-war expansion of nationalist mass movements – incredible compared with those of earlier times – begin to be explicable. The ideology of nationalism, apart from becoming more insistent, did not change much from that developed by the petty bourgeoisie before the war. Until 1940, however, this class had never succeeded in winning mass support (only rarely had it been sought), nor had it established viable political organisations. After 1945 it could call upon both the need of the colonial regimes for some new sort of association with Africans and the enormous possibilities opened up by proletarianisation, labour struggles and rural discontent. Between these two forces a vacuum had been created.

The classic case in the British colonies was the Gold Coast. The liberalised constitution of 1946 paved the way for the creation of the United Gold Coast Convention to fight elections. It was led by the old coastal elite based on pre-war alignments who favoured heightened agitation and an eventual development towards independence. The UGCC, however, stood aloof from social issues and continued all too obviously to represent the interests of the most privileged strata. In 1947 the leadership called on the services of a man who had made a name as an organiser for black causes in Britain, the American-educated Kwame Nkrumah.

Nkrumah set the pace for Gold Coast, and indeed African, nationalism. He had a magnificent sense of personal style, spoke powerfully and was a tireless organiser. It was his politics which brought nationalism to the people. He evoked a political imagery and an appeal to the underdog that attracted a nucleus of dedicated militants, frequently from among the unemployed urban school-leavers and ex-servicemen, the new 'urban crowd' of African cities. He made alliances with market women and labour unions. Opposing swollen shoot policy and agitating about cocoa prices, he penetrated the countryside. He effectively established a network that covered much of the Gold Coast, cross cutting language and religious boundaries. When the UGCC, increasingly uncomfortable with his politics, tried to get rid of him, Nkrumah successfully established his own Convention People's Party (CPP) in 1949.

Nkrumah may be taken as the model radical nationalist. However, the limits to his populist politics need to be considered simultaneously. At the heart of CPP affairs lay an ambitious core of businessmen and functionaries, less established than the UGCC stalwarts but with similar aims and ambitions. The CPP is sometimes considered a 'mass' party, but it rested heavily on networks of elite-dominated home-boy associations and the patronage of community notables. It in no way contradicted or compromised the social basis of Gold Coast merchant capital. Nkrumah-style politics could not accommodate a class-based orientation. Instead he emphasised national 'unity', a programme that apparently offered something to all classes but rested heavily on an aspirant bourgeoisie of outsiders to establish a firmer position in the colonial economy, above all through winning control over the bureaucratic machinery of the colonial state. 'Seek ye first', said Nkrumah, 'the political kingdom'. The other side of the emphasis upon unity was the necessity to balance rival power brokers who based their influence on ethnicity, religion or region and prevent their mutual antagonisms from getting out of control.

Much of Nkrumah's language and emphases had already been polished abroad. By 1945 the number of Africans studying or working in Britain and France had increased significantly. There Pan-Africanism had been born from the element of race consciousness that flowed naturally from the situation of blacks in much of the Americas (classically articulated by Marcus Garvey in the interwar era), offering an ideal that was sufficiently vague to include potential support of bourgeois, workers and peasants. In England many of the major political figures of the nationalist era – Nkrumah, Hastings Banda of Nyasaland and Jomo Kenyatta of Kenya – worked together closely and found support within a small but articulate reforming stratum of metropolitan opinion. A second influence, perhaps as much rhetorical as real, came from the Communist Party whose agitational and organisational skills much impressed Nkrumah and others. Nkrumah took from the political Left, not only the Communists, his relatively early orientation towards state involvement in economic development, especially industrialisation.

After the Gold Coast became independent in 1957 under the name of Ghana (chosen from a favoured antique empire in African nationalist litanies) Nkrumah made it the haven for anti-colonial movements from all over the continent. As the focus of decolonisation shifted southward, a similar role was played by the Tanganyika regime (Tanzania from 1964) of Julius Nyerere, which was granted independence in 1961. Nkrumah and Nyerere were central figures articulating the inspiring rhetoric of radical nationalism. They espoused international non-alignment, African unity and the struggle against dependence and underdevelopment and their influence was everywhere infectious.

Nyerere's Tanganyika Africa National Union had a similar mix of petty bourgeois ambitions to the CPP, battening upon mass social and economic issues. Co-operative leaders, local notables, urban landlords and traders dominated its cells. An important role was played by single urban women, usually Muslim, who formed a formidable network. Yet most of the African political parties of the late 1940s and the 1950s were even less genuinely mass parties. The framework of ambitious local businessmen, rich farmers and labour union brokers was much more nakedly obvious and popular involvement largely passive in the Sierra Leone People's Party, the Uganda People's Congress or the National Congress of Nigeria and the Cameroons. They too, however, could occasionally galvanise protest around particular issues and effectively present themselves to the British as potential power brokers.

In Paris the parallel cultural nationalism of *Négritude* emerged from similar influences. It was particularly associated with the Senegalese poet and teacher, Léopold Sédar Senghor. Yet the political organisations developed after the introduction of elections were largely not nationalist at all; they accepted the broad framework of assimilation proposed in various forms by liberalised French imperialism. Here the radical impulse was at first weak. It gained more strength in a new wave of politicisation in the 1950s, reacting upon the renewed vitality of French capitalism applied to Africa.

In recent years historians have also been eager to recapture something far more intangible than political struggle and the conflicts and frustrations that were spelt out through conflict. They have focused on the emergence of what seemed at the time 'modern' in the growing towns, modernity that was participatory, engaged in symbolic hardware and decor and began the romance with consumer products. Culturally there were major changes which would only become more important with time. Just before the war typically, radio broadcasting began in African cities, such as Dakar in 1939. Commercial films, including Westerns which demonstrated overt and morally signposted physical conflict in a way that appealed to the hearts of African men, became available and won growing audiences. Traditional physical competition gave way to football. Football teams might have strong local support bases but these were usually not older ethnic identifiers. Rather they represented new kinds of cleavages competing for new resources that chimed with news of epochal contests in distant Europe. Popular music and dance also arrived. In Dakar, local musicians discovered Latin American rhythms. In Dar es Salaam, men and women began to dance together as couples in the Western manner. Commercial photography was a medium Africans admired and took upon themselves as a form of expression. All of this fed into a sense of the 'modern' which, as Jim Ferguson has so eloquently captured for Northern Rhodesia where copper created an unheard-of consumerist prosperity, seemed a tangible model at least for the rapidly growing urban public. Tapping into international networking was seductive, neither inculcating Africans with sober European habits nor promoting political subversion, but stirring the beginnings of a new kind of cultural milieu that would have a growing influence on social change and indeed politics.

The political setting

In 1945 it was hardly the intention of the colonial regimes to get out of Africa in the foreseeable future. However, they were already committed to the new United Nations Organisation (UNO) system established by the victorious anti-fascist Allies. The terms of the UNO charter contained an affirmation of the right to popular self-determination which could be applied to the world outside Europe. The very establishment of the UNO already brought certain African questions to the fore. The world organisation had vested rights in the old League of Nations mandates over the ex-German colonies. These continued to be administered by Britain, France, Belgium and South Africa, but the new format refused to allow the amalgamation of smaller territories into the neighbouring colonies and established a commitment to eventual independence, although pressure for speed towards that goal was at first minimal. Additionally there was the problem of the colonies of defeated Italy: Libya, Somalia and Eritrea. Wrangling over their future continued for many years between the Great Powers. Libya was eventually conceded independence in 1951, the fourth internationally recognised sovereign African state after Ethiopia, Liberia and Egypt.

For the two colonies in the Horn of Africa various solutions were proposed. A British mandate over a unified Somali-speaking territory to include British Somaliland Protectorate and a part of eastern Ethiopia was one possibility. This idea confronted the ambitions of Haile Selassie who sought to end the isolation of Ethiopia from the sea which he felt had been crucial in its seizure by Italy. The strategic value of Ethiopia to the West, due to its proximity to Middle Eastern oil reserves, was substantial and there was a predisposition, especially by the USA, to go some way towards accommodating Ethiopian state claims. As a result the eastern frontier of Ethiopia was left where it had been and Italian Somaliland reverted to Italian control, but with the international guarantee of sovereign independence in ten years. Eritrea was granted autonomy within Ethiopia, which proceeded to receive in return an increasing American military involvement, including the grant of Kagnew air force base in Eritrea. Eritrean autonomy lasted only ten years, from 1952 to 1962. Then the Eritrean assembly, surrounded by troops, was forced at gunpoint to accept integration into Ethiopia as an ordinary province.

A second internationally determined decolonisation decision concerned the Anglo-Egyptian Sudan. The Sudan was to all intents and purposes a British colony, particularly after the White Flag Rebellion of 1923 convinced the British to try and close it to Egyptian nationalist influence. Yet Egypt had residual treaty rights in the Sudan, as well as an enormous cultural influence among the Arabic-speaking intelligentsia of the Nile Valley. So long as Egypt was a monarchy, the formal, if ineffectual, position of its government was that the Sudan must eventually revert to the kingdom of Egypt. But after the overthrow of King Farouk in 1952 the Naguib government (Naguib himself being half-Sudanese in origin) took a far more accommodating stance and established accords with the principal Sudanese political factions. Britain was prepared to proceed with a rapid transition to independence in the Sudan which actually took place in 1956.

This was only a decade after the war ended. Yet within another ten years most of Africa had also become independent. From a distance this seems like a single direct process. Observed more closely, it was a contradictory period marked by distinct if short-lived stages and, at the time, apparently conflicting policies on the part of the colonial powers. Thus it seems best to consider the sequence of developments in Africa by establishing four separate, regionally focused narratives in looking at the decolonisation of British West Africa, British Central and East Africa, the French-run territories and finally, the Belgian Congo where the Belgian withdrawal provoked the most dramatic events in the entire era.

Independence for British West Africa

For British West Africa the key territory was the Gold Coast, whose decolonisation we have already begun to examine. The reforms of the first post-war constitution in 1946 were meagre, but they initiated unintentionally a timetable whose logic was eagerly seized by nationalists. Once the possibility of self-government within the colonial system had been conceded, pressing the issue towards greater speed and resolution was a viable and extremely attractive tactic.

In the immediate aftermath of the war the Gold Coast at first largely evaded the labour agitation typical of most colonies. Yet social tensions ran high. In 1948 a demonstration of ex-servicemen outside Christianborg Castle, the seat of government in Accra, was fired upon by government troops. This was the signal for days of rioting in which the property of foreign companies, including the principal United Africa Company outlet in Accra, was looted. In the countryside the swollen shoot agitation turned cocoa farmers against the state. The high point of militancy was the general strike of January 1950. It was initiated neither by Nkrumah nor the CPP, but fell into their laps as the ideal pressure point against the colonial regime which began to fear that, if collaboration with Nkrumah was not established, a far more serious threat to capital in the Gold Coast might ultimately emerge. Nkrumah and most of his closest associates were then, or soon would be, in prison, which gave them the aura of heroes and martyrs: 'Prison Graduates'.

By the time of the strike the Coussey Commission had already prepared a condemnation of administrative policies with regard to the 1948 violence, and important concessions were under consideration. In 1951 a new constitution proposed direct elections for the entire territory and ministerial responsibility to the successful party. The CPP gained a substantial majority of seats and Nkrumah agreed to call off Positive Action and serve as Leader of Government Business. His release from jail was the archetypal nationalist triumph, a model that politicians elsewhere, with Nkrumah's warm encouragement, sought to emulate.

For six years Nkrumah functioned as a colonial premier, establishing close relations with the British governor, Sir Charles Arden-Clarke. This transitional period was crucial for underpinning the continuity which typified the transition to independence as the state machinery was gradually handed over to Africans. Africans were promoted rapidly in the civil service and began to acquire control over more and more patronage and funds. The CPP government carried out the established colonial development schemes, with a particular emphasis on education which was sure to gain popular approbation.

Not surprisingly the CPP machinery became increasingly closely identified with the state and evoked opposition from strata that had felt left out of Nkrumah's coalition. The CPP had mushroomed so fast that many local power brokers had simply been left standing in amazement at the beginning of the 1950s. Opposition began to crystallise around regional discontents aligned to Nkrumah's old UGCC opponents. Nkrumah won a second election victory in 1954, impressively but not overwhelmingly. As hostility to him spread in the cocoa-growing Asante region, the British obliged him to call a final election in 1956 before proceeding to the grant of independence. Asante was a typical product of the indirect rule system, under which 'traditional' authorities had clustered a nexus of influence and patronage that was being undermined by the ascendancy of centralised initiative implied in the plans for decolonisation. The relatively high level of wealth provided by cocoa gave weight to the local power elite; in equivalently governed areas that had only meagre resources, no such effective opposition movements arose. The anti-Nkrumah forces did succeed in weakening the CPP in Asante tremendously, but their alliance on a national scale was motley and could offer no effective alternative to the vitality of the CPP and its now unshakeable association with a programme for immediate independence. Thus the CPP won some 72 out of 104 seats in the 1956 election and Nkrumah led the Gold Coast to independence as the new state of Ghana in 1957.

Why were the British authorities prepared to work with Nkrumah and concede major constitutional reforms? Privately, colonial officials remained convinced that they alone could render the 'second colonial occupation' effective and profitable. They could presumably have exerted enough force to suppress nationalism in the colony for another generation. Yet there was a sense that the handwriting was on the wall, whatever the economic imperatives. The die was cast by 1951 and decolonisation began to look like a European scramble out of Africa, reversing the rapid conquest of sixty to seventy years earlier. From the point of view of London, there was no strategic or economic logic to justify digging in, a reverse of the processes of the late nineteenth century.

One of the most significant aspects of the Gold Coast experience was the absence of overt challenge to the interests of Western security or business interests in the transition years after Nkrumah entered the government. The commodity boom was still in full swing and generated optimism that the economic underpinnings of at least the more substantial colonies were firm enough to withstand political readjustment. In the event the lessons established in the Gold Coast were quickly applied elsewhere. In 1951 Sierra Leone held its first colony-wide legislative elections, while regional assemblies on a wide franchise were placed in operation in Nigeria.

Decolonisation in Nigeria displayed fundamental structural similarities to, but also important differences from, the Gold Coast. The broad social issues were very similar. Shortly following the end of hostilities in Europe government workers in Nigeria staged a remarkably effective general strike. The labour movement showed militancy and intensifying politicisation, despite attempts by the state to impose a business union system, and problems posed by its own fragmentation. Labour agitation was coupled with the emergence of a volatile urban crowd, open to radical and nationalist activism. The first major post-war political party, the National Congress of Nigeria and the Cameroons (NCNC), bore a strong resemblance to the CPP. Its leader, Nnamdi Azikiwe, was a journalist who, like Nkrumah, had received much of his education in the USA. He established ties with the labour movement, fed off popular agitation and inherited the mantle of the more populist strand of pre-war Lagos politics as typified by Herbert Macauley.

What made Nigeria different was particularly its incomparably greater size and population, in which the capital, Lagos, carried much less weight than Accra. Nigeria had been a united colony economically, but the administration of different areas, particularly north and south, had been entirely distinct. It contained the most highly developed stratum of bourgeois entrepreneurs in Africa, notably merchants and professional men, and they advanced their fortunes very markedly in the post-war years. However, they generally operated local or, at most, regional networks and their relative strength as a class was coupled with intense internal rivalries as they jockeyed for positions in the new national arena created by the process of decolonisation. The problem posed by

Asante within the Gold Coast was magnified enormously in Nigeria. Powerful local notables had the means and the will to prevent being upstaged from the centre. This was most markedly true of the north, where the old ruling class and a merchant stratum had profited from the indirect rule system.

The NCNC had radical elements, some of them loosely associated as 'Zikists', but their influence was always tempered by the strength of the Nigerian bourgeoisie. The last major instance of an NCNC appeal to class concerns was its protest campaign after striking demonstrators were murdered by colonial troops at the government coal mine in Enugu in Eastern Nigeria in 1949. By 1950 the Zikists were mostly purged from the party largely dominated by business interests. While Nkrumah came from a small, out-of-the-way corner of the Gold Coast with little political influence, Azikiwe was an Igbo from eastern Nigeria. Tribal boundaries had become particularly politically salient in Nigeria and the Igbo were a 'tribe' which dominated one of the three regions demographically. In the 1920s they had accepted Christianity and schooling on an immense scale, often as tickets out of their impoverished homeland, the most densely populated section of tropical Africa. From the 1920s Igbo artisans and clerks spread throughout Nigeria and by 1945 were increasingly prominent as well among the new generation of university graduates and ambitious businessmen.

The NCNC was never wholly Igbo in composition, but it evoked hostility from others who used ethnic solidarity as a vehicle of political and economic competition. In the west, much of the Yoruba elite rejected the NCNC and established the rival Action Group whose leader, Obafemi Awolowo, advocated decolonisation towards a rather weak federal Nigeria. Other Yoruba continued to function within the NCNC and, as a result, control of the west was hotly contested through the 1950s. The greatest Yoruba town, Ibadan, continued to back the NCNC under the impress of the patronage system established by its 'boss', Adegoke Adelabu. Adelabu was a flamboyant and corrupt politician, fundamentally demogogic in that his vague populism was devoid of any serious social critique. He was the quintessential Nigerian politician whose following was built on a use of bread and circuses for the masses and manipulation of the petty bourgeois aspirations that stemmed from the strength of the vast bazaar network and myriad of small producers.

In the north two major parties developed – the Northern People's Congress (NPC) and the Northern Elements' Progressive Union (NEPU). The NPC was the agency of the strong men of the emirates. At its most effective it represented an attempt to modernise the power base of the administrative hierarchies by coalescing rival groups from different emirates, while according some patronage to the commoner merchants on the one hand and the non-emirate and often non-Islamic minority of the Middle Belt and the hill country on the other, symbolically creating 'One North'. Its leader was Ahmadu Bello, a previously unsuccessful aspirant to the sultanate of Sokoto, often known by his Sokoto title of Sardauna.

NEPU was considerably more radical, taking on itself the grievances of younger disaffected northern officials and well-to-do commoners. It had a nationalist outlook and its populism was often cast in classic Islamic terminology. It shared both the NPC's fears of southern domination and its demands for the 'northernisation', rather than the 'Nigerianisation', of the civil service. NEPU's strength was obscured in elections thanks to the strength of the administrative and commercial networks the NPC could call into play, as well as coercion in which British officialdom played an important hand.

By 1945, whereas the British in Lagos envisioned a gradual process of devolution in Nigeria that would reconcile elements from the entire territory, their counterparts in the north strengthened and indeed partly created the provincial chauvinism that typified the NPC in particular. There is little evidence to suggest that the British as a whole sought to weaken potential Nigerian unity; for good economic reasons, quite the contrary. However, those whose careers were bound to the north were in good part responsible for the increasingly acrimonious, chauvinist and squalid form that Nigerian politics took.

By 1951 it was clear that Britain would grant Nigeria independence in coming years. Thereafter, political life as defined by the parties and the incipient ruling class focused around the quarrel for present and future spoils. In 1954 a constitution was devised which gave substantial financial powers to the three regional governments. This fundamentally entrenched on a regional basis the three political parties, although the Action Group actually lost control of the west for a time. The coming of independence then required some form of agreement between the parties. In 1959 the NPC finally agreed to independence based on a strongly federal constitution. Nigeria's first government in 1960 was a coalition between the NCNC and the NPC with an NPC premier, Sir Abubakar Tafawa Balewa.

In Sierra Leone the most dramatic social conflicts lay in the peasant revolts of the mid-1950s aimed at authoritarian and venal chiefs. These ultimately reasserted themselves under the patronage of the Sierra Leone People's Party led by Milton Margai. Margai and his machine brought Sierra Leone to independence in 1961 while the principal opposition leader, Siaka Stevens, whose party had a strong hold on wage workers, foundered in jail. The last British colony in West Africa was the Gambia. By the early 1960s Britain was determined to relinquish its administrative position in Africa and the Gambia was granted independence in 1965, however unlikely it was that this mini-state with a population only equal to that of Luxembourg could function as an effective sovereign entity.

The end of British rule in East and Central Africa

The British authorities saw the problem of devolution in the major colonies of East and Central Africa rather differently from that in West Africa or the Sudan. With the exception of Uganda, which presented its own special problems as we shall see, the African bourgeoisie was very much less developed and, in colonial terms, very much less fit to administer the infrastructure it would inherit on independence. Devolution of any effective power to Africans was considered to lie a generation off even at the beginning of the 1950s. At the same time the British were anxious to balance concessions to Africans with support for the white settlers who remained the bulk of the local bourgeoisie. In the economic circumstances of the late 1940s settler agriculture began to boom while in-migration of Europeans increased steadily.

Thus the official British goal was to try to establish a balance between black and white in the interests of regionally based capital development. We have already mentioned one aspect of this, the politics of federation, applied only to a limited extent in East Africa but established as the basis for a potential new dominion in Central Africa in 1953. Another aspect was generally called 'multi-racialism' which established separate, racially defined electorates. The white and Asian minorities were given vastly greater representation within this system than their numbers warranted, but nominated Africans were also now admitted to the assemblies. Only from the late 1950s did any of the plural racial systems set into motion actually allow Africans to vote.

In reality the compromise sought by Whitehall was an impossible one. Settlers were intransigent and unwilling to take any steps that challenged their hegemony in a 'white man's country'. Even where, as in Tanganyika, truculent settlers were not really a serious political force, the state held out for the 'multi-racial' society in a way no class of Africans found acceptable. The timid advances in African representation meant little or nothing to an increasingly radicalised populace.

African nationalism in East and Central Africa had a much sharper radical edge than in West Africa. The weakness of the bourgeois component may explain this in part. The cause, though, lay more in the escalation of post-war capitalist development, felt by peasants and workers with unprecedented force and identified locally not merely with the distant 'government' but with the racially defined minorities: white settlers, Asian businessmen and, in Zanzibar, 'Arab' planters.

Post-war Kenya experienced a quickening of tension from the end of the war. The labour movement burgeoned out of control, leading to general strikes in Mombasa in 1947 and in Nairobi in 1950. Chege Kibachia organised a politically orientated general workers' union that appeared for a time to herald the birth of class-based politics. Sharpening rural differentiation, especially on the Kikuyu Reserve, led to increasing anger and frustration on the part of the poor who linked up to the urban crowd in Nairobi and the radical wing of the union there. The old agitational politics of the Kenya African Union seemed tame and inadequate in these harsh times. The only one of the established leadership to keep in effective touch with the new radical trend was Jomo Kenyatta, a brilliant orator and organiser who returned to Kenya in 1946 after fifteen years abroad, mainly in Britain, as a worker, student, political agitator and man of many parts.

Many of the young radicals were Kikuyu who had been initiated in the 1940 age set. They were thus known as the '40 Group'. By the end of the 1940s mass oathing had been initiated by those who were determined to see the status quo in Kenya overturned in any way possible. Oathing evoked the loyalties of Kikuyu peasants in what became a largely Kikuyu movement; it may have alienated Africans for whom it was not a traditional practice. Violence erupted with assassinations of those who, both in Nairobi and Kikuyuland, were felt to be the lackeys of the regime and traitors. In 1952 the governor proclaimed a state of emergency while fighters took to the hills, initiating the Mau Mau rising. Mau Mau took essentially three years and some severe measures indeed to control. Large numbers of Kikuyu were herded into detention villages or imprisoned while the Kikuyu population of Nairobi was mostly expelled and replaced by other Kenyans. The radical wing of the labour movement was also quashed. Kenyatta himself was considered by most of officialdom as the mastermind of Mau Mau. This seems unlikely to be the case although he was much too shrewd a politician entirely to disavow sympathy for the struggle, let alone the causes, of the Land Freedom Army.

The British denounced Mau Mau as a psychological aberration, a retreat into 'darkness and death' by savages with their veneer of civilised behaviour removed. Yet Mau Mau caused British policy to shift towards reform. The crucial element was the Swynnerton Plan, a programme of land consolidation which aimed at securing political stability in Kikuyuland through the creation of a capitalist, small farming class. Closely linked to the Plan was the abrogation of the ban on growing coffee by Africans, a ban which had long been enforced in order to preserve a profitable settler monopoly. Under this aegis African coffee production grew rapidly, and a minority of rich peasants began to grow further with it. They came to establish links with the very small but also expanding class of professionally educated Africans, few of whom had any sympathy for the form or the radical potential of Mau Mau.

A great weakness of the Land Freedom Army had been its relative failure to provoke sustained support from non-Kikuyu apart from immediately neighbouring groups. The other Africans in fact benefited from the suspicion that fell on all Kikuyu during the 1950s. Politicians from the Luo-speaking people near Lake Victoria and other newly self-conscious 'tribes' began to make themselves heard. A major figure of the new era was Tom Mboya, a Luo who became the leader of the reconstituted Nairobi labour movement. Mboya managed to retain his nationalist credentials while establishing a new trade union base with strong American affiliations. He was aided by the interest of British and other firms in Nairobi's growing industrial sector in creating a relatively small, better-paid, stabilised labour force. Mboya and others established the Kenya African National Union (KANU) in 1960, the first political party among Africans to function throughout Kenya.

KANU demanded an end to the white highlands, African majority rule and Kenyatta's release from detention with an eventual commitment to independence. This proved sufficient as a programme to hold its various factions together and overcome the challenge of a rival party that based itself on the jealousies of the smaller 'tribes'. KANU's effectiveness as a machine and the rapidly growing maturity of the African bourgeoisie led to British concessions, with a devolution process initiated in 1961 that brought independence in 1963. The white highlands were made available to Africans by purchase, but part of the independence package enshrined private property in Kenya. The purchase by the state of settler land was guaranteed by a British loan whose repayment ensured capitalist stability as state policy. From the time of his release Kenyatta, despite his long imprisonment and advanced years, quickly assumed effective control of KANU and became Kenya's first president.

Kenya's southern neighbour, Tanganyika, had already attained independence in 1961, the first of this bloc of countries in East Africa. The Tanganyika African National Union (TANU) has been described as a classic example of an African 'mass' political party. Its most notable accomplishment was the effective weld-ing together of the petty bourgeoisie on a territory-wide basis, cutting through religious and language boundaries. Its leader, Julius Nyerere, was remarkable for his modest habits, personal integrity and moralist's social vision. TANU's struggle was fundamentally against the attempt to foist 'multi-racialism' on Tanganyika. It was conducted on strictly reformist lines, but assisted by the long shadow of Mau Mau, the intensity of rural conflicts and the particular strength of the Tanganyika labour union movement which had organised more than forty per cent of wage labourers. The collapse of British authority in Lake Province was a major precipitating factor in the turnaround of 1958, which brought TANU participation in elections, Nyerere's entry into the government and then independence.

Just out to sea from the Tanganyikan mainland lay the British protectorate of Zanzibar. Britain faced no settler question here but tensions escalated in the 1950s between one nationalist movement that represented the Sultan and the landlord interest, generally qualified as Arab, and another which saw itself as African and wanted the end of landlord power. It was not coherently socialist or class based, though; indeed it took a much less bold attitude towards the British regime than its rival. A third party, with its strength on the sister island of Pemba where the population was more intermingled and small landowners dominant, held the balance of strength. At first ethnic politics covered up the intensity of class conflict on the plantation island.

Ironically it was within the Zanzibar Nationalist Party, the more national-ist but less African party, that a class-conscious Left, with real strength among the important docker community and other wage workers, formed. This group coupled with some elements in the 'African' Afro-Shirazi Party (ASP) to radicalise Zanzibar politics. The Sultan's party took the reins of power in an independent Zanzibar at the end of 1963. In little over a month a violent coup overthrew the new regime and it looked as though a revolutionary government might emerge. At this point Tanganyika intervened. Zanzibar was incorporated into the new united republic known as Tanzania, with local power in the main going to former ASP stalwarts.

The nationalist struggle in Northern Rhodesia and Nyasaland was first and foremost a struggle against the Central African Federation. Anti-federal agita-tion, based on apprehensions about the introduction of the Rhodesian system into the territories further north, was widespread in the late 1940s. However, the British Conservative Party government decided to go through with federa-tion. At first, opposition melted away surprisingly. Federation meant retaining the extant administrative system in each territory and thus forbade new land alienations to whites in Nyasaland and Northern Rhodesia. The growing labour movement on the Copperbelt received important concessions in 1955 after a successful African strike significantly increased wages although virtually leav-ing the racial colour bar in mine work intact. In these circumstances the small organisations of the local African elites proved incompetent at carrying through their opposition.

However, after several years the growing sophistication of new protest asso-ciations, the intensity of anti-chief, anti-agricultural ordinance agitation and fears of a more effective Rhodesian domination after the constitutional revision of 1960 brought a mounting wave of agitation, culminating in the proclamation of a state of emergency in Nyasaland in 1959. Britain had been anxious to make federation work as a viable financial unit, but this seemed increasingly unfeasible. To the enormous anger of federal premier Sir Roy Welensky, Harold Macmillan dropped the issue of movement to dominion status and organised instead a policy of greater African representation within the Northern legislatures. Hastings Banda, a Nyasaland doctor who had lived in the USA, Britain and then the Gold Coast for more than thirty years before being brought back by the various factions of the Nyasaland African Congress, was now released from jail and agreed to co-operate with colonial authority. In Nyasaland the right of secession from the federation was granted in 1962; Northern Rhodesia followed suit a year later. By 1964 they were independent states under the names of Malawi and Zambia.

The decolonisation of Uganda presented problems for the British as severe as anywhere although not quite of the same nature. There was no settler question. As elsewhere in East Africa the large Asian immigrant minority had prospered in the post-war era and, in Uganda, it appropriated the lion's share of the opportunities available for a local bourgeoisie. Therefore anti-Asian feeling was more politically significant than elsewhere, as witness the boycott of Indian-owned shops in 1959–60. The British were far less committed to the Asian than to a European settler bourgeoisie, however. The real dilemma they faced in Uganda was what to do with the Buganda protectorate. Buganda had been administered separately from the rest of the territory with only tangential representation on the Legislative Council. Its distinctive role might be compared to Asante in the Gold Coast, but Buganda occupied a yet more pivotal place in the wealth, population and position of its educated stratum in Uganda. Uganda without Buganda was unimaginable to British administrators. Yet the Buganda elite were completely hostile to closer relations with the rest of the territory. The peasantry were deeply involved in social and economic agitation but tended to see the future in terms of a restoration of the full rights of a sovereign *kabaka* who could mend the evils of the day.

In 1952 Sir Andrew Cohen, the British Colonial Office's master mind of decolonisation, came to Kampala as governor to press Buganda into an arrangement. Crisis ensued and the *kabaka* was exiled for two years. The solutions later found were quite superficial. Only in 1962 did the Kabaka Yekka party, dominant in Buganda, agree to a patchwork compromise which brought Uganda to independence. By this point, Apollo Milton Obote's Uganda People's Congress had achieved majority support elsewhere in the territory. It included what politically conscious radicals there were, but basically was a federation of rural notables. This militated against any challenge to the status quo other than anti-Indian agitation (which could benefit the aspirant African trader or cotton ginner). Thus Obote's new regime rested on especially insecure foundations, despite the presence of the most sophisticated African bourgeoisie in any of these territories and the weakness of political radicalism.

The Kenya independence bargain and the break-up of the Central African Federation were the finale in this second wave of British decolonisation. There remained several minor colonies of which the British were now anxious to dispose. These were the so-called High Commission territories, Basutoland, Swaziland and Bechuanaland, within the sphere of South Africa, all of which were handed independence by 1968, and the Indian Ocean island territories of Mauritius and the Seychelles which became national states as well.

Decolonisation in French Africa

The French colonial practice stressed the development of assimilation as a policy. Demands for secession or full national independence outside this framework were treated as treasonable and suppressed. It was the demand for independence which made the UPC completely unacceptable in Cameroun. Nevertheless the French constitution of 1946 allowed for the establishment of political parties which affiliated to the parties of the French political spectrum in order to fight elections for the French parliament. Only in two areas of French West Africa did viable 'mass' parties appear quickly – Senegal and the Ivory Coast. The scene of the most intense social agitation of the late 1940s, they also felt the major brunt of capitalist development in the first post-war years. In Senegal Léopold Sédar Senghor had returned in 1946 from Paris to found the *Bloc Démocratique Sénégalais* (BDS). He upstaged the older generation of politicians from the four communes through alliances with the shaykhs of the Islamic orders.

The Ivory Coast witnessed a more radical upheaval. The league of Africans who represented the most progressive wing of the new politicians in French-speaking Africa, the *Rassemblement Démocratique Africaine* (RDA), established an effective branch there, the *Parti Démocratique du Côte d'Ivoire* (PDCI). The PDCI capitalised on urban and rural discontent but won as well the adherence of a significant group of prosperous, labour-employing cocoa planters. The leader, Félix Houphouët-Boigny, was a particularly successful planter and chief. His class was locked in struggle with French agricultural settlers who, through the war years, monopolised access to forced labourers on their estates. Forced labour affected not only the mass of Ivory Coast peasants, but also nascent capitalists on the land. The PDCI rose to strength on the prestige won from the abolition of forced labour in 1946 and the subsequent rise of a prosperous African cocoa-growing sector.

The RDA worked in alliance with the French Communist Party. It did not agitate strongly for independence, but with the onset of the Cold War the administration was determined to root out Reds from the colonies. From 1948 the PDCI suffered from an intense administrative persecution, although it retained a remarkable amount of support. In 1951 Houphouët-Boigny came to terms with a visiting cabinet minister, François Mitterrand, then the leader of a small fragment of moderate socialists in the French chamber. He broke with the Communists and affiliated to Mitterrand's faction. Most of the RDA then joined this or other non-Communist blocs in the chamber. The radical element in PDCI politics was dropped and the French administration began to patronise Houphouët-Boigny. Thus the PDCI, like the BDS in Senegal, grew into an effective electoral machine, but hardly a revolutionary force.

The political organisations in other parts of Equatorial and West Africa were weak and narrowly patron-based at this time. However, the situation changed in the 1950s as French capitalism began to enter into a long wave of growth and confidence that swept many new corners of the colonies. It was within the context of renewed French investment in Africa that a new group of mass parties emerged, notably Sawaba (Freedom) in Niger, the *Parti Démocratique du Guinée* (PDG) in Guinea and the *Union Soudanaise* in the Sudan. Sekou Touré, leader of the PDG, the Guinean section of the RDA, came from the trade union movement, if not from the ranks of the manual workers. In Guinea a sharp PDG-led struggle was directed against the old aristocracy of the impoverished Futa Djallon, where an attenuated form of slavery survived and much of the population depended on migrants' wages for their livelihood. Muslim traders formed a crucial link in the network of associations that held together the *Union Soudanaise*. Both parties gave unprecedented scope to demands for independence.

French colonialism experienced its most serious reverses not in sub-Saharan Africa but in Indo-China and, later, North Africa. The French Republic reluctantly granted independence to Vietnam, Morocco and Tunisia and became locked into an intensifying struggle over Algeria. The Algerian war was, in fact, the main cause of the coup that overthrew the Fourth Republic in France in 1958 and established General Charles de Gaulle in power. De Gaulle, reflecting on this, may have wondered at the good sense of the British in organising an orderly retreat from their colonies so well. He was put in power to carry on the French Empire, but reconsiderations began quickly.

A plebiscite was organised to determine the support of the colonies for continued association within the French Union. One major African politician, Sekou Touré, was unwilling to accept the humiliating demand of rejecting the independence option.[1] Guinea alone in Africa voted *non* in 1958 and De Gaulle proceeded to order a spiteful withdrawal not just of French authority but of technical personnel and movable infrastructure. It was expected that Guinea would quickly collapse into chaos. However, it survived and managed to get its services functioning while interesting other powers in its fate. The chorus of *oui*s could not endure a successful Guinea. There was increasing opposition at the UNO to France on its policies in Togo and Cameroun, the two trust territories it controlled. Armed resistance in Cameroun, if much less damaging than in Algeria, was threatening to French prestige. De Gaulle reversed his policies entirely and announced plans for independence to come in all of the black African colonies in 1960.

Thus the two trust territories, Madagascar and the two federations of West and Equatorial Africa were transformed into fifteen nominally sovereign states. It remains to assess the French role in the break-up of West and Equatorial Africa. It appears likely that a strong element of divide and rule attached to the motivations behind the dissolution of the two federations. The decisive development was the *loi-cadre* of 1956 which had created territorial assemblies while virtually universalising the franchise. It was the *loi-cadre* which provided the steam for separate territorial movements to seek nationhood. Houphouët-Boigny, whose influence in Paris had become very great, adamantly opposed any diminution in his powerful position, particularly given the position of the

Ivory Coast as the wealthiest French territory, and wanted no federation. In contrast, Senghor favoured some kind of federal union but his solution, the Mali Federation, embraced only the French Sudan and Senegal by the time of independence and tensions between them brought the federation to a quick end, Sudan choosing to retain the name of Mali.

French decolonisation was far less genuinely a retreat from Africa than its British equivalent. In part it was a nominal change of sovereignty that did not much affect basic French interests. On achieving independence, the new nations signed agreements with France on foreign aid and defence that reinforced French cultural and economic predominance and left the French army as a guarantor of the new regimes. Close personal ties bound the new African political leadership with top figures from French politics, while annual summits of 'Francophone' countries were used to harmonise views. The Africanisation of the state services took place far more slowly and decorously than in ex-British Africa.

The Congo crisis

As De Gaulle mulled through new options an even more dramatic policy turnaround took place in the Belgian Congo. Through the first post-war decade the Congo economy boomed. As the wage-labour force passed the 1,000,000 mark in the mid-1950s it was more than twice the size of any other in Africa between the Sahara and the Limpopo. The high level of capital penetration built on the advanced character of Belgian business involvement going back to the 1920s. A new element in the situation, though, was the dramatic urban growth, rapid even by African standards, that followed from the ever-wider gap between the harsh life of the peasantry and the possibilities that beckoned in the towns.

During the boom years the Belgians never seriously considered political reform. In the mid-1950s, however, their thinking began to alter, perhaps in the wake of influence from more powerful Western countries, perhaps as a reflection of pressures for modernisation within Belgian capitalism as the Congo boom gave way to stagnation. In 1952 the Catholic party, which had almost invariably controlled the colonial ministry and the governor-generalship of the Congo, was for once thrown out of office and this proved to be the first impetus of rather timid reforms that built up in the 1950s. Secular education was introduced and the first Congolese permitted to go to Belgian universities. In 1957 a university was actually established in Léopoldville. The market economy was allowed more scope in rural areas, permitting the growth of a cash crop peasantry and a class of petty shopkeepers, especially in the Bas-Congo province between Léopoldville and the Atlantic. Political liberalisation led to the foundation of African urban associations and journals. In 1957 municipal elections were held in the biggest cities. Two years earlier Professor van Bilsen, associated with the Institut Solvay, an influential think-tank for Belgian capitalism, had predicted the independence of the Congo within thirty years. Once unthinkable, this marked a decisive break in colonial planning.

The municipal elections introduced the first party political groupings among urban Africans. They revealed bitter cleavages on ethnic lines, typically between people from the vicinity of the town and those, often long orientated to migration, who had acquired greater skills, from further away. In the Katanga capital of Elisabethville there was tension between the Luba from Kasai Province and local Katanga people, and in Luluabourg between Luba and Lulua. In Léopoldville the Kongo speakers were ranged against people from up-river. Little of this reflected any genuine cultural or even historical differentiation; it was a question of politics along the lines of protective association, combined with the ambitions of the rising bourgeoisie, whom the Belgians quaintly called *evolués*, trying to establish a clientele. The increasingly charged atmosphere in Léopoldville, where employment opportunities were diminishing in the late 1950s, led to serious riots in January 1959, attacks on property and substantial violence. To the surprise of the world, within a fortnight King Baudouin announced that Belgium would bring the Congo speedily to full independence.

In less than eighteen months independence had indeed come to pass. What explains the rapid shift? A major element, however hidden in official explanation, may lie in Belgian conviction that rapid decolonisation would be meaningless decolonisation, that the transition to increased African participation in directing the system might best happen under the rubric of a nominal independence. However, the Belgians were certainly feeling under pressure due to decolonisation in neighbouring territories such as the Sudan, Uganda and, in 1960, French Equatorial Africa.

The apparently awesome administrative and economic structure of the Congo was characterised by an equally great rigidity and as such proved remarkably vulnerable to pressure from below once a momentum had been established. In 1959–60 Belgian authority, especially in rural areas, began to crumble rapidly and the defensive posture of uncertain bureaucrats led to an intensifying weakness and disorder. Collapse of local authority was often coupled with the crudest form of manipulation. It is likely too that the Belgian elite was itself deeply divided and unable to pursue a coherent policy.

The leap of the Congolese petty bourgeoisie to the realisation of its dreams was thus an extremely rapid one, especially in the less developed parts of the colony. The immaturity of this class showed itself in two striking tendencies. First, it was slow to create an ideology that could resolve its own ambitions into a general nationalist posture to win wide popular support. Congo politicians tended to be exceptionally supine and reactionary as a whole. A minority, however, were open to a more radical critique of colonialism and the colonial formulae for decolonisation than virtually any equivalent group in sub-Saharan Africa. Secondly, by 1960 the throng of politicians trying to establish themselves in each provincial centre of this vast country were unable to solder together true national political networks.

The situation might be clarified by a look at the developments in the three nodal points of Léopoldville, Elisabethville and Stanleyville. In the capital and its hinterland the dominant party was the *Association des Bakongos* (ABAKO), led by Joseph Kasavubu. ABAKO reflected the relative sophistication and wealth of the Kongo elite while containing a strong populist element. It looked not much unlike the 'mass' parties of West Africa. However, it contained a parochial outlook focused on Kongo unity with aspirations in the direction of a restoration of the ancient Kongo kingdom, including parts of Angola and the French Congo. Therefore it was potentially secessionist. In Elisabethville the *Confédération des Associations Tribales du Katanga* (CONAKAT) and its partners fed on the anti-Luba fears of various Katanga groupings who resented the copper centre's most effective migrants. The large resident European population looked askance at the gradual liberalisation of the Congo system and began to dream of a secession that might take in the eastern part of the colony. CONAKAT's leader, the venal and brutal Moïse Tshombe, established a close alliance with them and plotted the potential break-up of the Congo. In sharp contrast, Stanleyville, the third major centre of the country and capital of Orientale Province, was a hodgepodge of heterogeneous Africans. The politics of ethnic competition were much less sharp there and the dominant figure to emerge in the late 1950s was Patrice Lumumba, a radical nationalist committed to Congo unity, and his *Mouvement National Congolais* (MNC).

As 1960 advanced the MNC gained ground and Lumumba established a range of useful if tenuous alliances, although sustaining little support from either Elisabethville or Léopoldville. The MNC won the largest number of seats in the one election held before independence and Lumumba became prime minister with Kasavubu as president. The various parties, despite their intense rivalry, were able, as in Uganda, to agree sufficiently for the presentation of a common position in the round table which brought independence in July. Lumumba seemed sure to become the dominant national politician. He had no coherent social outlook; indeed occasionally he took an obsequiously pro-colonial line. At other times, however, he expressed a deep awareness of the sufferings of the Congolese under Belgian rule and possessed the quality of unpredictability which made him highly suspicious in Western eyes. He was capable of a sharp quick development in ways inimical to Belgian interests. This was typified by his famous speech on Independence Day. Enraged by the text of the king of the Belgians, which celebrated the colonial past and had the temerity to extol the virtues of Leopold II himself, Lumumba issued an eloquent diatribe on the racism, oppression and exploitation suffered by Africans under the Belgian yoke (while still expressing hopes for Belgian aid!). The king and the Belgian premier, also present, were insulted and Belgian opinion in high places made up its mind that Lumumba was a madman who had to be eliminated soon.

Within a fortnight they found an excuse. The army mutinied, stung by the attitude of its Belgian commanders (General Janssens was justly famous for writing prominently in the main barracks, 'Before Independence = After Independence') and indifferent to the squabbles of the new parties. Belgium responded by sending in paratroopers without Congolese government request. Shortly thereafter, Tshombe proclaimed the independence of Katanga while an equivalent figure, Albert Kalondji, produced his own secessionist declaration in Kasai. Lumumba disposed of no force to deal with the situation. Instead he appealed to the UNO for assistance. The secretary-general, Dag Hammarskjöld, saw UNO intervention as a means for the organisation to establish itself as an effective world peace-keeping force and dispatched a multinational army. The Western powers made sure, however, that the UNO concerned itself with the

establishment of a more 'rational' government in Léopoldville before organising any intervention in Katanga that might negatively affect the mining interests of the UMHK.

In September Lumumba was arrested by Joseph Mobutu, his former press
secretary who had been despatched into the service to create the beginnings
of a loyal army. Subject to a rather mild detention he began to consider closer
links with the Soviet Union and the Soviet bloc, one solution that the West
was unprepared to tolerate. A new army mutiny called for his release. It was
suppressed but the bickering cliques of politicians in Léopoldville began to
fear that Lumumba was becoming the focus of support in mounting popular
discontent. The wealth of the Congo ensured that they and their friends were
now moving, with a rapidity unprecedented in Africa, into control of substantial fortunes in an atmosphere of unbridled corruption and contempt for the
people. At this juncture Lumumba arranged an escape. It was a failure. Unable
to reach his home province of Orientale still under the administration of his
associate Antoine Gizenga, he was returned to Léopoldville. Soon after he
was flown secretly to Elisabethville and murdered on Tshombe's orders early
in 1961.

The Lumumbists still held Orientale, but Gizenga agreed to negotiate with
the politicians and, after long rounds of talks, was eventually imprisoned. The
Binza clique dominated affairs in the capital while complex intrigues surrounded
the lengthy attempts to find a basis for agreement with Tshombe. Only in
1963, after Hammarskjöld too had come to a mysterious end over its airspace,
was Katanga finally reintegrated into the Congo. By this time US influence,
which sought the integration of Katanga into a reunified 'Katangalised' Congo
in which American interests could vie effectively with those of Belgium and
Europe generally, was in the ascendant.

The Congo decolonisation exercise was now apparently complete. However,
the new ruling class was especially blatant in its ostentation and especially
unconvincing in its nationalist pretensions. For the masses the confused events
of 1959–61 had brought about a real withdrawal of state authority together
with a longing for a genuine 'second independence'. By 1963 cadres associated
with the MNC and related groups were already filtering into the countryside
to organise independent Africa's first major revolutionary confrontation. The
rural rebellions of the mid-1960s, however, belong more properly to the next
chapter's discussions.

Decolonisation was as quick a phase in African history as the scramble of the
late nineteenth century, and at least as complex an historical process. Its causes
lay partly outside Africa also, in the changing force-field of world affairs as well
as the structural alterations in the needs of capital which now showed substantially less interest in the initial extractive processes that had characterised the
African colonial systems in their heyday.

In part, independence negotiations set the stage, as they were meant to do,
for a new alliance between an emergent indigenous ruling class and Western
business. This new ruling class was a creature of colonialism but it had its own
trajectory of development based on the unleashing of capitalist forces since at
least the start of the century. Yet the European retreat, if not whole-hearted and

largely strategic, was genuinely a retreat. The immense wave of popular resist-ance to the state in the 1940s and 1950s had made African colonies potentially ever more difficult to administer. It was this groundswell which transformed the ineffectual little nationalist societies of the pre-war years into dynamic political agencies contending for state power. Caught between the pressures that the West continued to exert in Africa, political and economic, the popular expecta-tions on whose back they had ridden and the need to fulfil their own ambitions, they would have their chance to show their mettle.

Notes

1. Bakary Djibo of Sawaba in Niger tried the same but he was effectively eliminated from power with French connivance. Niger voted *oui*.

10

Tropical Africa, 1960–80: Class, State and the Problem of Development

In our revolution, we believe that we have broken the chain of a consumer economy based on imports, and we are free to decide our destiny. And in order to realize the interests of the Somali people, their achievement of a better life, the full development of their potentialities, and the fulfilment of their aspirations, we solemnly declare Somalia to be a socialist state.

SIYAAD BARRE, 1970 SPEECH CITED IN AHMED SAMATAR, *SOCIALIST SOMALIA* (ZED PRESS), P. I

Neo-colonial myths and realities

The attainment of independence inaugurated an uncertain and increasingly crisis-ridden period of transition in Africa. Colonialism largely destroyed the fundamental rhythm of pre-capitalist social and economic life without fully advancing a new, self-sustained process of accumulation. The commoditisation of agriculture had been pivotal to the processes of capitalism in colonial Africa. After 1960 continued growth along these lines faltered, while varying in extent from country to country and crop to crop. With the 1970s export-orientated agriculture (and the entire agricultural economy) entered into sharp decline in most countries. While circulation of goods and even productive activity had become dependent on industrial processes, the independent African states lacked the finance, infrastructure and skills needed in order to reproduce an industrial society. Secondary industrial growth actually occurred quite rapidly, particularly through the 1960s, but from a very low base and with a high reliance on imported capital goods, spare parts, raw materials, know-how and technology. Intended to further the prospects of national economic independence, industrialisation necessarily deepened dependence on international trade.

Kwame Nkrumah, the Ghanaian president who deserves pride of place among African nationalists for his early insistence on the importance of industrial development and economic independence, was responsible more than any other individual for popularising 'neo-colonialism' as the source of independent Africa's troubles and the gap between promise and performance of the new states. The 'neo-colonial' idea is pithily captured in the Swahili phrase, *uhuru wa bendera*, 'flag independence'. The existence of neo-colonialism, which can most simply be defined as the continuation of practices of domination after independence by the old colonial powers, is incontrovertible. The independence bargain invariably contained guarantees for the property rights of Western business enterprise and strategic or military arrangements that ensured continuity for a time at least on the most basic imperial desiderata.

Direct intervention in political affairs through the operations of foreign troops and intelligence agencies was common in the wake of the Congo crisis of the early 1960s. Western involvement in Kwame Nkrumah's overthrow was a response to his increasing alignment with the Soviet Union in the mid-1960s. President Apollo Milton Obote of Uganda's tough line on South Africa and Rhodesia, together with his reluctance to continue allowing Israeli military aid to the southern Sudanese rebels via Uganda helped to bring about his downfall in 1971. In contrast, the long-time president of oil-rich Gabon, Léon Mba, owed his survival from the wrath of his own people to French paratroop intervention in timely fashion. French interventions, typically masterminded by Jacques Foccart under the long-lasting Gaullist continuation of what is now commonly called Françafrique politics, became notorious. American and Soviet policy made costly use of the nationalist antagonisms of the peoples of the Horn of Africa for strategic advantage in what was seen in both Washington and Moscow as the back door to the Middle East.

Figure 10.1   *In the wake of independence*: Emperor Haile Selassie, Jomo Kenyatta and Idi Amin meet in Kenya

Foreign corporations, especially the transnational giants, continued to seek and obtain advantages in pursuit of their profits, marketing and supply needs in Africa at the same time. African economic development continued to depend on their technology, trading strategies and expertise. Where nationalisations occurred, like those in the copper mines of Zaïre and Zambia, they were inevitably followed by lucrative management and technology transfer arrangements as well as financially advantageous compensation payments. Where African states became partners in ventures with transnationals, a strategy of product development, sales and labour control could often be worked out whereby 'Africanisation' could suit the transnational firms' interests. None the less this represented a retreat, albeit in a sophisticated form, back to a trading company mode and an older tradition of economic involvement more than a qualitative shift. Trading companies, such as Unilever's United Africa Company, proceeded even before independence to speed up their exit from the produce business and to concentrate on more technologically and industrially sophisticated operations where they could long continue to hold the upper hand.

Nkrumah's panacea for evading the dilemma lay in Pan-Africanism, the establishment of a union government that could pool together the resources of many capital-poor lands. Undoubtedly the autonomous development potential of many of Africa's smaller or less populous states is meagre under any circumstances and co-operation on many issues between neighbour states welcome. Yet political unity guarantees no solutions. If a unified state contained more people, more skills and more capital, it would have correspondingly more tasks to accomplish as well, more infrastructure to create, more poverty to fight. Impoverished territories developed under colonialism along similar lines do not have potentially complementary economies in the short term.

The larger African political units and pan-state entities concentrated development narrowly and oppressively in one or a small number of centres, intensifying contradictions between town and country. The classic example was the ill-fated East African Community, initially hailed particularly by President Nyerere of Tanzania as the herald of African unity. The common services worked heavily to the advantage of one partner, Kenya, and to the development of the Nairobi area as an industrial and service centre. Ultimately tensions broke up the Community in 1977. At first, the Tanzanian economy did well from the decline and collapse of 'unity', particularly its industrial sector.[1]

In practice, despite the lip service paid to it, Pan-Africanism has had to face the entrenched interests of state apparatuses throughout the continent. In the wake of the Congo crisis the Organisation for African Unity (OAU) was born in 1963. While it played a useful arbiter's role in certain international conflicts, in general it functioned as a kind of trade union for the existing constellation of continental regimes, more a bulwark against change than a force pointing towards effective united action. The successor African Union today struggles to do more but has very limited finances of its own.

In a world of giant trade and finance oligopolies, the weakest capitalist fish fare poorly in the competitive sea. The African bourgeoisie were, and are, little fish indeed. It is hardly surprising, when we appraise ourselves of their weaknesses, to see them ensnared in the plots and plans of European trade ministries, 'aid' planners or the World Bank minions. Simultaneously, however, these very weaknesses inhibit their ability to work efficiently in the interests of international finance and industry. 'Neo-colonial' Africa as it became *cannot* be mistaken for the ideal demanded and striven for by transnational corporations; its utility to them declined as administrations became more unstable, arbitrary and corrupt with basic economic services frequently disrupted. To the extent that capital takes the development of Africa seriously, the regime of a thug like Idi Amin Dada in Uganda (1971–9), once the colonial 'pearl' of East Africa, was an economic disaster. If we take 'imperialism' to mean the policies of the Western states and firms in Africa, imperialism is certainly going to oppose the struggles of workers or peasants that threaten capital, and during the Cold War was prepared to undermine states that were friendly with its enemies. However, imperialism does not profit from, and use of the term cannot explain, many crucial aspects of what is usually termed 'underdevelopment' in Africa and other parts of the world.

The serious investigator of such issues has to consider as well the failure of those who manage African states to preside over economic development, *however* this ambiguous phrase is politically and socially defined. Most writing on 'underdevelopment' falls short of resting upon a serious appraisal of class forces. In fact, in the 'right-wing' countries, there appears to be a capitalism without capitalists, especially in the smaller and most dependent cases. In their 'left-wing' counterparts, significant in this period, socialist struggles were pursued without a working-class base, either in formal organisational terms or more broadly in terms of popular support. Development without either a strong capitalist class or a politicised and mobilised proletariat presents a fundamental quandary, one that has proved largely beyond the abilities of African states to solve. One answer that contemporary literature proposes is the presence of an autonomous 'developmental state' with powerful agencies that can either cut through interest groups with their special concerns or work with them effectively; as will be discussed later, Africa has not got far in mounting such formations.

Dependency theory also has assumed that capitalism is rather more monolithic and less contradictory than it actually is, reducing it almost to a conspiracy. Were it possible, under politically friendly auspices, 'imperialism' acting as a united force would like nothing better than the rapid development of productive forces in Africa for reasons both of political stability and of profit. Not that it does act so rationally or in unison. To comprehend why Africa's situation is what it is, a consideration of internal social forces is fundamental and lies at the heart of this chapter.

The ruling class in contemporary Africa

What is Africa's ruling class? A satisfactory answer to this question has eluded most analyses. The commonest is to describe it as a petty bourgeoisie, a phrase which has been used in these pages. This is, however, a somewhat vacuous and negative definition. The term has been used for a heterogeneous group who control and consume surplus that they do not labour to produce, without actually participating in industrial management or commanding huge financial resources. It is very generally agreed that the dominant class in tropical Africa cannot be big capital, because it is not really represented internally.

In most countries the ruling class also exhibits relatively little continuity with the old pre-colonial ruling elements. In contrast to Asia or Latin America, landowning has not been a major aspect of economic and political dominance. During the colonial period in many areas monarchical governments were preserved and utilised. As we have seen, the classes that profited from these systems had generally collected tribute and slaves rather than possessing the land in hereditary ownership. Nor did they effectively crystallise into a land-owning class during the colonial period; their authority did not allow for it and the profits were probably not especially encouraging. Where the nationalist movements were more radical, the chiefs and the other instruments of indirect rule were a magnet for mass antagonisms. In such countries as Guinea, Mali and Tanzania the chiefdoms were abolished on the assumption of independence. In other cases, people clung to older forms as a defence against unwelcome change. Conflicts involving surviving pre-colonial forms ran deep and shaped political forces.

Barotseland's pre-independence conflict with the United National Independence Party (UNIP) in Northern Rhodesia was characteristic. Under the indirect rule system the *litunga* was the nexus of clientship networks under the patronage of the British, and Barotseland served as a mines labour reservoir, particularly for South Africa. UNIP's anti-South African, anti-Rhodesian perspective was, in this context, an economic threat and bitterly opposed by the hierarchy. Barotseland appeared ready at one point to secede and make common cause with Tshombe's Katanga and Rhodesia. However, the *litunga* himself lacked full influence over educated Lozi who repudiated him and opted for UNIP and Zambian independence. In independent Zambia Barotseland lost its separate autonomous status entirely.

The parallel situation in Uganda provoked a far deeper crisis. Whereas Barotseland was a relatively remote and backward region holding less than one-tenth of the population of Zambia, Buganda held the capital, the richest parts of the country and one-fifth of Uganda's people. No national party succeeded in gaining a real purchase on Buganda and Apollo Milton Obote, leader of the Uganda People's Congress, had to accept a coalition with the Kabaka Yekka party, pledged to the maintenance of Buganda sovereignty, to lead Uganda to independence. The *kabaka* became President of Uganda. This compromise proved very fragile. In 1966 the breakdown in relations between the Ugandan state and Buganda culminated in violence, the storming of the *kabaka*'s palace and his exile from the country.

Elsewhere in East Africa independence brought about the collapse of traditional ruling classes both in Rwanda and in Zanzibar. In both cases the colonial era had lent to the character of class rule a strong racist odour; as a result, popular vengeance and racial massacres seized both countries. What were defined as the old ruling classes, Tutsi in Rwanda and Arab in Zanzibar, were considered often first and foremost as racially superior minorities. In Rwanda the circles around the king were influenced by Lumumba and embraced Third

World nationalism briefly; as a result the Belgians colluded against them. In Zanzibar an independent regime barely survived a few months when overtaken by revolution. The only surviving ex-colonial monarchies in 1980 were those in Swaziland and Lesotho (where the king's power is nominal). In Botswana, the first president and dominant political figure, Seretse Khama (died 1980), was also the paramount chief of the most important section of the Tswana. It is hardly coincidental that all of these survivals occurred under the shadow of the Republic of South Africa and its Bantustan system. The most weighty indirect rule system of all, that in northern Nigeria, never experienced revolution. Yet the power of the emirs of the north has markedly declined with every major twist in the fortunes of the state. At the same time the Mai Tatsine movement in the 1980s and the Boko Haram movement in the new millennium were popular and violent Islamic risings that rejected the old social order.

The African ruling class are thus neither aristocrats nor planters. Even when they obtain revenues from commercial farming, as notably in Kenya or the Ivory Coast, they were attached by an umbilical cord to the state bureaucracy. Indeed it is not unreasonable to suggest that the new ruling class comprises first and foremost those who took over from, or Africanised, the colonial state hierarchy. Following popular usage in Tanzania, the German radical scholar on development, Michaela von Freyhold referred to them simply as 'nizers'. Others have attempted working definitions to encompass all the activities of the 'nizers' – auxiliary bourgeoisie, bureaucratic bourgeoisie – none of them entirely satisfactory. None, at least, successfully conveys the relationship of this class with others in society as well as its internal ambiguities.

Perhaps the most straightforward if limited way of looking at African state officials is as the agents of Western capital, in power to execute its demands much as colonial officialdom once was. Evidence for this type of function is particularly satisfying for the least changed countries in Africa, where decolonisation was unproblematic and largely manipulated from Europe. However, in most nations there is strong evidence as well to suggest that state agencies were and are used by Africans to obtain advantages for their own class interests. General Olusegun Obasanjo, military head of state in Nigeria from 1976 to 1979 and then elected president from 1999 to 2007, referred in a memorable phrase to 'gatekeepers', the class of Nigerians who in effect hold state office for the sake of charging a toll on foreign enterprise seeking to do business in Nigeria. The gatekeepers function as *rentiers* – essentially parasitic – battening themselves on the thrust of Western finance capital like barnacles to a whale.

Yet the parasitism has a tendency to turn itself into a more 'conventional' form of capitalist accumulation. Under conditions less hectic than those in oil-boom Nigeria the state has also been manipulated, it is argued, in the interests of a burgeoning local bourgeoisie no more parasitic or discreditable than its colleagues elsewhere in the world. African capitalists, precisely because of their competitive weaknesses, necessarily lean heavily on state connections and power to establish their place in the sun in the shadow of the giant foreign corporations. In a substantial debate in the late 1970s such writers as Nicola Swainson and Colin Leys furthered Kenya as the ideal example for spotlighting the trend. After independence Kenya did not entirely turn its back on the colonial heritage of white settlerdom. Capitalist private land tenure was pressed ahead while the old white highlands became non-racial, agro-business highlands. This was the fruition of 'land consolidation'. African accumulators therefore held a solid base in capitalist agriculture and could move under the effective political umbrella of the Kenya African National Union, the nationalist political party which pressed forth with African capitalism while retaining substantial popular backing in the country. Defenders of this thesis see the Kenyan bourgeoisie advancing in strength through the increasingly efficient use of state power. Should this picture be accepted as the basic pattern, it would have important consequences theoretically. It would suggest that countries such as Kenya ought to be seen primarily as developing capitalist states with the indigenous ruling class, its foreign allies notwithstanding, in fundamental contradiction to the masses rather than cogs in the wheel of an undifferentiated 'neo-colonialism' or 'imperialism' represented locally merely by a thin stratum of 'elites', agents or stooges.

It can be objected that the continuing backwardness and dependence of the African bourgeoisie is obscured by such a portrait. African capitalists undoubtedly command little of the finance, technology or industrial base that presses forward accumulation within the capitalist world at large. The policies of the Nigerian state since 1960, the home of probably the wealthiest and most sophisticated class of African entrepreneurs, did everything to advantage those entrepreneurs with favourable treatment in contract awards, financial assistance, tariff legislation and 'Nigerianisation' legislation designed to place the hands of local capitalists on the driving wheel of the economy. Yet Nigerian business remained dominated by money-lending, contracting, rack-renting, importing and the establishment of 'gatekeeper' relationships with foreign enterprise, building on compradore traditions that go back to the slave trade. Only a small amount of Nigerian capital is concentrated in industry; Nigerian company directors and shareholders are often sleeping partners in enterprises operated with a logic beyond their effective control.

The Ivory Coast was sometimes depicted as the French-speaking equivalent of Nigeria or Kenya. Yet studies that focus on it tended to stress the colonial continuities and the extreme nature of Ivory Coast dependency.[2] Through the 1960s and even much of the 1970s the Ivory Coast economy boomed, largely through rising volumes of cash crops produced by both African cultivators and European-managed (largely corporate) plantations. As dirt roads cut swathes through the forest to establish new tree farms and fields, the virgin timber was hauled off for export. Economic growth was closely linked to continued French influence – special trade arrangements offering the Ivory Coast a secure market in return for consuming over-priced French exports and acceptance of the CFA franc as currency totally convertible with the French franc. In twenty years of independence the European population of the Ivory Coast tripled, from 20,000 to 60,000. In addition an even larger Lebanese community resided there. This seems to present the *portrait nonpareil* of dependence and the 'development of underdevelopment' in Africa.

Paradigm of dependence though it may be, however, the Ivory Coast regime was financially associated with most significant foreign investment and production ventures and the state endowed a small wealthy class of Ivorian entrepreneurs. The heart of the Ivory Coast phenomenon was the high level of collaboration obtained between the local and international (largely French) bourgeoisie. To a large extent the oppressed in Ivorian society (but also some-times the entrepreneurs) were migrants from other ex-French territories who form a majority of the wage-employed population. The Ivory Coast became a magnet for migrants, first of all agricultural workers but then employees in every field of endeavour, from Mali, Burkina Faso and Benin particularly, many of whom prospered. Indeed some individuals were appointed to the highest offices by President Houphouët-Boigny. Ivorians at all social levels became as prosperous as any tropical Africans and productive forces developed further there than elsewhere in West Africa. The system appeared for long to be as self-sustaining as that of its neighbours. Dependence cannot thus be said to have brought about instability or impoverishment particularly in the Ivory Coast when compared with equivalent states.

Whatever their specific relationship to foreign enterprise, African accumula-tors in every bureaucracy have used their offices, connections and qualifications to further their personal advancement and feather their own nests. At the same time the state service contains a significant technocratic element, reproducing itself through education and envisioning itself as a permanent salariat. For this stratum anti-colonial nationalism developed into an ideology of patriotism that sometimes supported and sometimes struggled with the private sector 'national' bourgeoisie. The technocrats were not would-be capitalists, but nor were they simply selfless servants of the people. They acceded to a standard of living enor-mously more affluent than that of the mass of the population, measured both in terms of private consumption and socialised benefits and entitlements. Within the general African sea of poverty lie considerable islands of welfareism, in which access to subsidised housing, free health care, schooling and other amenities has been apportioned according to civil service rank. In defence of the island, tech-nocrat and compradore, gatekeeper and national bourgeois unite. Technocrats are then potentially also in a position of confrontation with workers and peasants.

Class, party and state

The relationship of those who wield state power in Africa to the West and other foreign forces has perhaps been given more attention by scholars than their crucial relationship to the mass of Africans. In the 1960s the political parties which had apparently brought Africa to independence were the main focus of such analysis as existed. Most of these parties are no longer in power or in exist-ence. Even where they have continued to survive they have become imbricated within the machinery of the state. Party militants of the late colonial period tended everywhere to be local businessmen, chiefs and civil servants who on independence sought to transform their activism into commercially advanta-geous linkages, often with success. The 'mass' party of populist mythology was impressive at stadium rallies and demonstrations called from the top but usually had little depth.

A common feature of the African political party was its all-purpose appeal. The party invariably claimed to represent the 'Africans', but never admitted to speaking for the interests of specific classes. A vaguely articulated 'African socialism' rejected the possibility of a class analysis of African society and tried speciously to reconcile the aspirations of the ambitious few with the needs of the majority. A socialist or communist party actually building upon the movement of the oppressed in society emerged almost nowhere.

However one can also err in overly cynical formulations about the emerging African states. During the period on which this chapter focuses, there was an idealism about social change, about what Africans could gain: from the point of view of the increasingly present Western consumerism to the potential of nationalist articulation on the global stage. Most African governments believed in, promoted and gave some institutional reality to this vision. This idealism, this vision of the modern, is the more striking when viewed from a later perspective. More recently scholars have explored the considerable extent to which the vision of an African version of modernity inflected this period and captured imaginations. This can interestingly be done in the apparently corrupted and degenerate atmosphere of the Congo, renamed Zaïre, as well as the relatively cohesive environment of Tanzania where this sense of the royal road to progress was especially strong and long-lasting.

Zaïre was the site of the emergence from nothing of a large system of standardised secondary and higher education which still knits this huge and diverse country together more than anything else. The nationalist projections of the Mobutu regime in Zaïre correlated with the emergence of an infectious music and dance culture that epitomised freedom for many. The Mobutu years are associated with the rise of a formidable music industry which adapted African folk rhythm and Latino beats that highlighted the good life in Kinshasa *la belle*, the former Léopoldville. Mobutu favoured especially the superstar Franco and many of the artists appreciated the favours coming their way from powerful men. Staging the 1974 Mohammed Ali–George Foreman boxing match in Kinshasa – the 'rumble in the jungle' – was for this kind of regime a coup of coups, an international black event that perhaps compensated for the failures of material developmental projects like the steel mill and the planned car assembly plant. Nationalist sentiments were coupled with enthusiasm for the consumerist delights of London, Paris and Brussels.

In austere Tanzania, there was more of a conflict between the desirable consumerist world reflected in film and internationally generated entertainment available in the cities and the calls for a self-sacrificing socialism. However, at the same time, the state did what it could to promote culture and performances in drama and music that fitted the imagination of the state and ruling party. Andrew Ivaska captures this tension very well: the modernism favoured by the state was austere and vigorously nationalistic with Nyerere exemplifying ideals of honesty, hard work and modesty; the modernism favoured by its arch-beneficiaries was full of the African equivalent of wine, women and song even though the salaries of the bureaucrats in Tanzania remained relatively low.

Indeed the emergence of more independent women in the cities was a very difficult challenge in this regard and seen as most threatening to the desired moral order. The newspapers fed off agonised discussions of wigs, miniskirts and the foibles of popular musicians. Sugar daddies in cars became stock figures while mission ideals of gender relations failed to hold. At the same time, the state struggled to establish laws that were workable and visibly 'modern' in relation to marriage and the rights of women.[3] Another way to look at this bifurcation is to point to the contrast between the colonial and post-colonial states. The former was increasingly interested in politically neutral technological change which it defined as its basis for legitimacy with the fading of racist premises about human nature. The latter at first inherited this trajectory but inevitably also combined it with political ambitions that increasingly militated against Western-style modernist culture and developmental ideas.

Thus once in power the ruling parties anxiously moved towards the creation of the one-party state, often expressed as the logical outcome of the African political genius, coupled with a more or less ruthless attempt to destroy autonomous organisations. Working-class organisations suffered here particularly and notably at the hands of the more radical nationalists as in Ghana and Tanzania. In Nkrumah's Ghana, where the unions had played such a vital role in the assumption of power by the Convention People's Party independence brought about confrontation, the takeover of the union leadership by Pan-Africanist party men notorious for their corruption, and a general strike of the workers in 1961. The strike was broken, but it cost Nkrumah the support of the working class. In Nyerere's Tanzania a parallel conflict marked the relationship between the Tanganyika African National Union and the Tanganyika Federation of Labour, abolished in 1964 and replaced by a federation totally dependent on state patronage. In Tanzania the state was quick to insist that truculent workers were privileged 'aristocrats of labour', whose seemingly low earnings none the less represented an exploitation of peasant production and the even poorer rural population.

Yet the legitimacy of the state required its continued presentation in populist form. Both in Ghana and in Tanzania (but equally in such relatively 'right-wing' states as Nigeria and Kenya) attempts to smash or to subordinate the unions were initially coupled with a genuine rise in the workers' real wage. The state sought to make itself the workers' patron: in return for obedience the populace was to be rewarded with increased and improved amenities, particularly in the spheres of health and education. The CPP regime in Ghana made unprecedented efforts by West African standards to put state resources into public welfare. During the 1950s conditions in world trade were sufficiently favourable as to allow for massive expenditures on health and particularly educational facilities. It was as provider of amenities, above all, that the independence regimes sought legitimacy from their own populations. However, in Ghana, the falling prices for cocoa and stagnation in the mineral sector meant that material support for workers became unsustainable.

Among the former British colonies Tanzania took a social vision the furthest. Social improvement was coupled with economic development as national goals under state auspices. This was the brunt of President Nyerere's eloquent Arusha Declaration of 1967 which introduced what were then considered to be sweeping nationalisation measures (always with generous compensation to foreign owners), coupled in 1971 with the Leadership, or *Mwongozo* Code, prescribing good conduct for the bureaucracy. In Tanzania the regime talked in terms of African socialism or later the Tanzanian road to socialism, but the Tanzanian case reveals an outlook that is essentially populist. The language and practice of Tanzanian 'socialism' has been sufficiently ambiguous, however, to allow for the flourishing of a radical political consciousness able to exert pressure on the state. It was imitated during the Obote period in Uganda, in Kenneth Kaunda's Zambia and elsewhere. Following Nyerere's example, these turned into one-party states, an evolution that was legislated in most countries. Nyerere took the view that internal divisions in a country were dangerous and would only strengthen the potential for politics to degenerate into ethnic feuding. In Tanzania, individuals could run for office within the TANU rubric and the system Nyerere created not merely endured but has continued to win office (up to 2015 at least) despite the return of multi-partyism after his retirement.

A striking feature of ruling bureaucracies in tropical Africa lies in the extent to which recruitment is based largely on educational qualifications. Only the military in grabbing power bypass the formalised hierarchy which still adheres closely to late colonial norms enshrined in the secondary schools or universities of the continent. The heart of the African educational system, itself in good part still dependent upon European aid and models, is, as much as before independence, the mastery of English or French. This has a functional character; bureaucratic structures built around English or French language usage do hold the national entities together, but the emphasis on European language study reinforces the imitativeness and cultural dependence of the African intelligentsia and its institutions. For this reason, securing the best and most elite education

Figure 10.2   Mwalimu, 'The Teacher'. Julius Nyerere, President of Tanganyika and then Tanzania 1960–85

possible for one's children is the virtually obsessive goal of middle-class Africans. Education also serves the purpose of building a myth of social mobility. The poor cultivator, worker or craftsman is encouraged to press his children at all costs into a giant lottery from which a few, with ability and luck, will eventually draw 'deserved' success. The state, in its technocratic aspect, also intends that mass education will bring about the acquisition of patriotic values, state loyalty and useful habits. However, this is only fitfully why the African masses have pressed forward with enthusiasm for more schools.

Generally only secondarily involved in production, the African state managers engage to place themselves where they have the best strategic access to the most cash and goods in circulation. Thus they can be the ultimate patrons in a patrimonial society network on a national scale. If the state intrudes as a gate-keeper for the multinationals, it does so as well for the mass of Africans in the humbler pursuit of basic goods and services. A study of life in Lisala, a town in provincial Zaïre as it then was, graphically illustrated the point. From beer to salaries, schooling to foodstuffs, access to the individual in the state apparatus who has the power to permit the circuit of goods to proceed to the next stage was vital as patterns inherited from colonial times faded away.[4] In such an economy mass consciousness tends to be geared towards admiration for the big man, however grudgingly, at least so long as there is some payoff for the client within the patrimonial relationship. Some of the most convincing studies of popular culture demonstrate a continuing admiration for the holders of wealth and power together with the intense significance of the cash nexus.[5]

Patronage, populism, relations with Western political and economic managers, these are the hallmarks and the strengths of the African ruling strata. In accounting for their weaknesses, we must also reckon with the severe potential for disunity that has made the establishment of national cohesion in the majority of states problematic. Internal divisions and weaknesses within the ruling elements have been striking.

The most well-known example from the first generation of independence is the most populous African country, Nigeria. The federal structure of independent Nigeria in 1960 reflected the economic and political development of the country under colonial rule. Rival elites, based in each of three regions, were unable to establish working alliances within a national framework and the political institutions of the First Republic quickly broke down. From the farcical general election of 1964 little remained of parliamentary democracy or stability as crisis intensified. A general strike in 1964 unified the urban working class temporarily but failed to give rise to a coherent political movement that could cut through the impasse. Early in 1966 a military conspiracy brought about the assassination of the federal prime minister and the premiers of the northern and western regions. The army chief of staff, General Ironsi, was able to assert control for a while. Attempts under Ironsi to destroy federalism were feared by the regionally based elites, particularly in the north, who saw the new unitary regime as an agent of eastern, or Igbo, domination.

At different times the elites of each region appeared to contemplate secession seriously. In the end it was the eastern region, in the wake of the murder of Ironsi in a counter-coup and the massacres of easterners in northern cities, which actually broke away and proclaimed itself the Republic of Biafra. Biafra eventually got support from a motley collection of allies – Tanzania and Zambia, much of the Catholic Church, France and the Ivory Coast, South Africa and Portugal. Britain backed Nigeria in the light of its considerable economic interests as did the Soviet Union, generally inimical to movements against national unity. It took three years of heavy fighting, from 1967 to 1970, until Biafra was effectively besieged by the Nigerian army and the last representative of its government surrendered after terrible losses.

Geographically the largest African country at the time of independence, Sudan has equally experienced civil war conditions for most of its existence since. An army mutiny on the eve of independence in 1955 began a cycle of violence in the southern part of the country, where the British had long excluded northern Arab influence and deeply anti-Islamic missionary attitudes prevailed. The budding elite of the south (which held something over one-quarter of the Sudanese population) saw no future for itself in a broader national circuit that looked north and east to the Arab world and had little interest in, or time for, its problems. Only in 1972 did General Nimeiri succeed in negotiating an agreement with the south to end the fighting, abandoning the purely forceful methods of previous Sudanese regimes, a solution which Nimeiri himself revoked after a decade leading to renewed violent conflict in the early 1980s. Eventually South Sudan would become an independent country in 2011.[6] A third and wide-ranging civil war long engulfed the huge territory of Chad which lies between Sudan and Nigeria. As in other instances, no clear-cut ideology marked the protagonists apart from their international affiliations. The extremely weak local (and regionally divided) ruling strata have never succeeded since independence in establishing a unified national authority.

The problems of African regimes have not only been regional or secessionist. In many states the weak hold of the politicians very early gave way to military coups that swept them from power. Coups were particularly frequent during the middle and late 1960s. If, broadly speaking, they can be explained in terms of the weakness of class and state, part of a crisis in the establishment of state legitimacy, the particular factors bringing them about have varied so notably as to defy common assessment. Some, like that led by Idi Amin in Uganda, have been under the aegis of the head of the armed forces. Others, like that which toppled the Margai regime in Sierra Leone (1967), were led by non-commissioned officers in the so-called sergeant's coup. The Ghana coup that overthrew Kwame Nkrumah in 1966 was notoriously hatched by right-wing, naively pro-Western policemen and army officers. That in nearby Dahomey (1972) reflected a populist, anti-corruption, rather left-wing bent. The first coup was in Togo by a tiny, newly formed army, manned by only a couple of hundred individuals. In Sierra Leone, the 1967 coup quickly resulted in a trade unionist active in the diamond industry and electoral winner, Siaka Stevens, being released from prison and allowed to take office. The soldiers' rule presented no long-term real solution to the problems of state legitimacy and authority in Africa although a few individuals, such as Matthieu Kérékou in Dahomey (renamed the Popular Republic of Benin), his neighbour Etienne Eyadema in Togo or Mobutu Sese Soko in Zaïre, became in effect long surviving non-elected politicians, sometimes with patrimonial party machines organised to certify their entrenchment in office. Generally speaking it can be said that there was little institutional capacity, little civil society, that stood in the way of such events or could stop them.

It also quickly became salient that ethnic division was a growing factor in political crises. As we have tried earlier to emphasise, this was not usually a question of some kind of renewal of pre-colonial political formations at war with one another. Indeed pre-colonial formations rarely had an ethnic definition apart from affective ties that might bind leading individuals and families to one another. Ethnicity was, however, crucial in how African colonies were governed and administered given the indirect rule format. Ambiguities of belonging were replaced with hard and fast definitions which could classify the whole population in bureaucratically legible terms.

The nature of the post-colonial state with its centrality for access to wealth on the one hand, and its political construction through clientage networks on the other, made ethnic identity and ethnic alliance of critical importance. John Lonsdale, early in writing about ethnicity, has made an important distinction between moral and political ethnicity. The former binds Africans together in relationships of trust and respect which often circumvent the formal rules of institutional games. This can be the basis for businesses and for social and culturally valuable institutions. One might think here of the ethnic associations that promote schools and other useful institutions back in home towns sustained by a leadership with clout and resources. However, there is almost inevitably the other side of the coin, where ethnic networks mapped out a vicious contest for power in the centre. The Nigerian political scientist Peter Ekeh framed the issue earlier in terms of two 'publics' on somewhat similar lines. This current of thought, and here we could add the ideas of Basil Davidson, that pioneer of writing on African history and politics, is inevitably critical of national political forms that lack any patriotic commitment or deep belief in the eyes of either the masses or their leaders with consequently little potential for forming nation-states in the classic definitional mode of that term. If we return briefly to the Nigerian civil war, it is obvious that the regional division of the country whereby locals saw citizens from outside their area as foreigners, the large population resident in each of the main divisions plus the growing importance of the oil industry as wells opened in the south-east, all lent themselves to ethnic competition taking the form of a war of secession in a particular conjuncture. However, ethnicity rarely followed the lines of attempted secession. More prosaically the desire to gain access to the resources of the centre, perhaps in likely or unlikely alliances, was more critical.

In the late 1970s coups became rather less frequent; the search for stabler political bases in Africa continued. The examples of Tanzania and Kenya, whose one-party states allowed individuals to contest legislative elections vigorously (although not to question fundamental state policies or to form organised tendencies within the parties) were much admired. Ghana tried to restore civilian rule in 1969–72 and again in 1979–81. After thirteen years of military rule, civilian politicians took power in Nigeria in 1979 on the basis of a complex constitution that owed much to the US model of checks and balances with allowances made for strong centres of regional power in nineteen states. In Senegal Léopold Sédar Senghor retired to his French villa in 1980 and a liberalisation allowed for the legalisation of opposition parties.

Not surprisingly these states contained perhaps the most sophisticated bourgeoisies in Africa from the point of view of their historical antiquity, their scope of economic interests or their cultural self-confidence; all were eager to legitimate a typically West African sort of class society through political means. From the perspective of the early 1980s, military rule seemed most characteristic of the smaller Francophone territories. The most brutal and lawless military regime, that of Amin in Uganda, was overthrown by a Tanzanian military expedition in 1979 after Amin arbitrarily annexed a corner of Tanzania. Shortly afterwards his equally murderous colleagues, Jean Bédel Bokassa (Emperor Bokassa I) in the Central African Republic and Macias Nguema in Equatorial

Map 4   Independent Africa, 1982

1. Western Sahara is administered by Morocco and disputed by an independence movement in control of much of the territory.
2. Ethiopia administered Eritrea contested by a strong independence movement.
3. Namibia was administered by South Africa and disputed by an independence movement.
4. Réunion is a French department.
5. The Comoros are partially independent, partially French ruled.

Guinea, the tiny ex-Spanish colony, were also eliminated, with the respective connivance of French and Spanish agents.

At first sight it might seem that a certain stabilisation of regimes was becoming more characteristic of Africa. Right-wing mercenaries from the era of Tshombe and the first Congo crisis were increasingly stopped in their tracks and disappeared from the scene, the OAU established an international presence with some credibility, Africans generally began to assume more and more effective control over the state machinery as the Africanisation schemes in each country gained ground. In reality, however, the growing class confidence of the African state hierarchy began to be undermined through intensified challenge from below in the context of a changing political economy.

Notes

1. The international blockade of Rhodesia during the Ian Smith era caused parallel benefits, as well as hardships, in Zambia.
2. This is no longer the case. See Y.-A. Fauré and J.-F. Médard, *Etat et bourgeoisie en Côte d'Ivoire* (Editions Karthala, 1982).
3. The newer literature on the conflicts over what was modern tend to focus heavily on an urban context. However Tanzania was overwhelmingly, 90%+, a rural country in 1961 and the overall population still remains predominantly rural today. For the incomprehension and often destructive nature of the imposition of state policy on rural people with little say from a largely culturalist perspective, see Dorothy Hodgson, *Once Intrepid Warriors: Gender, Ethnicity and the Cultural Politics of Maasai Development* (Indiana University Press, 2001) and T. O. Beidelman, *The Culture of Colonialism: The Colonial Subjection of Ukaguru* (Indiana University Press, 2001). By extension, the obvious appeal of indirect rule for colonial regimes becomes clearer by retrospection.
4. Michael Schatzberg, *Politics and Class in Zaïre* (Africana, 1980).
5. G. S. Darah, 'Ig'ho Sh'ema Sua: A Note on Capitalist Ideology in Urhobo Oral Literature', *Theory and Practice* (Ibadan) 2 (1977), and studies of popular literature in Yoruba by Karin Barber.
6. Sudan was the largest country in Africa. Even the new Republic of South Sudan can hardly be described as small.

11
Southern Africa: The Liberation Struggles

I won't be a member of the Communist Party that seeks to use the apartheid colonial state, that seeks to use the latter's institutions, as an alternative to organs of people's power.

THEO MOLAPA, 'LETTER OF RESIGNATION', *THE AFRICAN COMMUNIST* (135) 1993, P. 19

The Nationalist Party victory and its implications in South Africa

World War II was a time of social and economic pressures in South Africa just as it was further north. It spurred an intensified industrial growth that gave to secondary industry an unprecedented importance in national life. The proportion of Africans increased greatly among factory workers and the flood of new migrants to the cities, responding to job opportunities, swamped the existing locations allocated for Africans. As Chapter 8 suggested this gave to African workers a new bargaining power that took the form of strikes and squatter movements, particularly in the Johannesburg area.

The response of the state was equivocal. Within the Smuts government there were liberals who favoured social, economic and even political reforms that would incorporate the industrialised African into capitalist South African society. Eloquent spokesmen for this point of view, who represented a small but growing climate of opinion in the educated middle class, began to insist that this was inevitable. The reserves' economic viability had declined enormously and large developmental expenditures would have been required to recreate conditions whereby Africans would voluntarily want to reproduce a workforce there. Conservatives, however, including Smuts himself, cleaved to segregation. Yet the force that captured the imagination of more whites lay in the opposition to him.

When Hertzog abandoned the Pact and formed the United Party with Smuts in 1933, most of his Cape following, led by Malan, seceded and regrouped after the next election as the Purified Nationalists. A particular strength of the Cape Nationalists was their association with an ambitious class of entrepreneurs who stood behind the emerging Sanlam-Saambou building society/insurance complex and needed state patronage to expand. The Broederbond, a small Nationalist organisation of great importance in the 1930s and 1940s, had a particularly strong business orientation and spearheaded the movement towards Afrikaner economic 'self-help'. Hertzog's own son Albert was the central figure in a parallel drive to turn the unionised white workers into Afrikaner nationalists, especially on the mining belt around the Rand.

At first Malan suffered from having to meet the competition of rival groups which were directly under the influence of European fascism and more orientated to the notion of an authoritarian, corporatist state and a generalised white race identity. These groups gained impetus when Smuts brought South Africa into World War II on the British side and Hertzog resigned from the cabinet. Only when the defeat of Germany became imminent and the divided new organisations sympathetic to Germany failed to make headway was Malan's triumph against them assured.

The Nationalists won the 1948 election in the Transvaal, where they reversed Smuts' long-time dominance in the countryside and secured an important base in working-class constituencies in the outer Rand. Transvaal farmers had been hard hit by the growth of industry which threatened their ability to control cheap black agricultural labour as well as the low support prices of the Smuts government on maize. The urban workers reacted against the weakness and corruption of the old British leadership of the mineworkers' union and the decay of the Labour Party. A third and equally important element was popular reaction to the waverings of the Smuts regime on segregation; the Nationalists appeared to stand firm on the need to repair the dikes that had been damaged by the economic and social strains of the war years. The massive 1946 black mineworkers' strike, despite its brutal suppression, characteristically frightened whites, particularly the least skilled.

The Malan government actually had no substantial policy on race other than had been developed previously under Smuts or Hertzog. Apartheid, the new key word which was to become so notorious, was more or less an Afrikaans – and national – sounding term for segregation. The most original aspect of Nationalist ideology was rather its use of the state to advance the place of Afrikaners in the South African capital accumulation process through ethnic solidarity and, in so doing, to replace class cleavages with an outlook of ethnic cohesion. The ideology of Afrikanerdom, however, strongly encouraged as well the intensification of a racially defined social order as a logical extension of its worldview. Under state patronage Afrikaners rose in the ranks of an expanding bureaucracy while the Afrikaans medium universities grew rapidly and trained the youth. Useful connections helped Afrikaner capitalists such as Anton Rupert of Rembrandt Tobacco to find their place in the sun. The general prosperity of South African capitalism, coupled with the maintenance of segregation, built up loyalty to the party. The 1948 electoral victory depended on the constitutional overloading of seats to benefit farmers, but thereafter the nationalists moved from strength to strength in subsequent elections, reaching majority support among whites nationwide by the end of the 1950s. Nationalist politicians were concerned to stay in power. To this category belongs the admission to the Senate of representatives from South-West Africa and the successful fight to eliminate from the Cape franchise, Coloured people, who voted overwhelmingly for the opposition as had once been done to Africans.

This was the principal systemic and intended result of apartheid. Earlier paternalist patterns of administration were marginalised. Plans that had been under discussion to legalise segregated African trade unions in consumer goods industry, to give a racially bounded vote to Indians, to install a national health system and to procure more secure tenure for Africans in the cities, were shelved.[1] This meant that henceforth South African economic growth would have to accommodate an ever-more rigidly defined segregation mechanism. It must be emphasised that this did not, as some of the liberals of the 1940s feared, hobble the economy; harsh labour controls and poor wages made for high profits in many sectors. Plans that began to see the day under Smuts for recharging South African industrialisation so as to focus around giant state-controlled corporations promoting heavy industry, notably iron and steel and chemicals – including the manufacture of petroleum – as well as exploration of the potential of nuclear power, were all carried through with enthusiasm.

New legislation was adopted to close loopholes and in general to make a racial system more inflexible. Intermarriage and indeed, sexual intercourse between whites and 'non-whites' was made illegal by the Immorality Act while all South Africans were forced to carry (or possess in the case of whites) identification labelling them according to race. Arguably the most significant piece of Nationalist legislation was the Group Areas Act of 1950 (consolidated in 1957) which led to the ever more formalised segregation of racial groups in urban areas and formed part of a process that involved moving around Africans, Coloureds and Indians on a big scale over the next twenty years. The Act and related policies served many interests; it was indirectly a great boon to property speculators and, in striking at Indian merchants, seemed to assist white shopkeepers handsomely.

The state now carried out some of the plans envisioned for urban development. Instead of a national health system, facilities were created on a strictly segregated basis for black residents of cities, such as the formidable Baragwanath Hospital on the outskirts of Johannesburg, to match the health systems of the mines. The training of black nurses expanded and a medical school for 'non-whites' was created. The scale of primary schools for African children expanded dramatically. Mission schools were taken over and closed down with few exceptions, to be replaced by government-controlled institutions.

Vast new black townships were organised so that they could be patrolled and, if necessary, cut off in the case of insurrection. At first stable family life was to be encouraged through the housing allocation system in municipalities. Through the destruction of shanty towns and massive construction of new housing, urban segregation policy hit at the squatters' movement and attempted to draw a line on black migrations from the farms and reserves to the city. The biggest new urban centre for Africans was the South Western Township of Johannesburg – Soweto. Older neighbourhoods, largely slums, that had circumvented racial lines, such as Korten in Port Elizabeth, District 6 in Cape Town or Sophiatown in Johannesburg, were destroyed.

The state also intensified the pass system, incorporated into the larger framework of influx control. All Africans had to carry a police-endorsed pass showing that they were employed or in transit at all times in 'white' areas. Before the war legal pressure on Africans had mostly consisted of poll tax administration; now Africans were jailed and harassed primarily as pass offenders. This marked the end of pressures to induce male labour to the cities with the new emphasis instead on penning as many Africans as possible into the reserves. Only now were women consequently forced to carry endorsed passes. By making it hard for Africans to live permanently in the towns the state benefited white farmers who needed a tied labour force. Government aid to agriculture spearheaded the development of a prosperous agro-business sector and enabled capitalist farmers to eliminate the last pockets of rural squatting by Africans. By the 1980s South Africa, despite its limited fertile land mass, was a net agricultural exporter on this basis.

Hendrik Verwoerd, appointed Minister of Native Affairs in 1950, was the most consistent and ruthlessly coherent architect of the renewed 'positive' segregation, increasingly called separate development, and his influence increased when Malan retired in 1954 and the Transvaal wing of the party came to the fore with Johannes Strijdom as the new premier. Perhaps in response to the rapid evolution of decolonisation to the north, for him a serious threat as actually it had been for Smuts, apartheid was transformed from a slogan into a system. All future development for the 'Bantu', as the state began to refer to the natives, was to be focused in the reserves and on thoroughly segregated institutions. The powers of chiefs were increased as government agents. It was an ironic sign of the times that the Zulu paramountcy, once so feared by whites and deliberately smashed by British imperialism, was restored in 1952. The Bantu Education Act provided for a completely separate and pedagogically distinct educational system for Africans, leading logically in 1959 to the establishment of separate institutions of higher education in the homelands, as the reserves were now called. The Strijdom government had promoted the research of the Tomlinson Commission which stressed that the economic viability of these homelands would require very substantial investment. These recommendations were rejected as extravagant and unnecessary but, with Verwoerd and his successors, this route was engaged with growing emphasis.

Living conditions for Africans in the Union were abysmal in the 1950s. Industrial growth was slower and more uneven than during the previous decade, while material possibilities in the homelands for anything beyond a resting space between jobs for prospective household heads diminished. Under Nationalist auspices life in the cities was insecure and degrading. The vast new housing schemes were badly overcrowded, poorly provided with amenities and linked to a demoralising bureaucratic surveillance where the paternalist element (where white supervisors actually lived in the townships) faded. Alcoholism and other facets of social despair were especially rife. Violent crime associated with *tsotsis*, delinquent youth, developed on a rampant scale.

It might be expected that African resistance could capitalise on the prevalence of such harsh conditions of life. This was true only to a limited extent, however. In 1949, for instance, Zulu workers took out their frustrations on the Indian population in Durban race riots that cost dozens of lives while the police intervened only at a late stage. Hundreds of thousands of Africans turned to the consolation of independent churches, often as followers of one or another prophet, in what was almost invariably a rejection of political conceptualisation of their lives. Political organisations failed to come up with programmes and, more crucially, association and action that could counter the pressures felt by black South Africans.

The major African organisation during the 1950s was the revitalised African National Congress (ANC). On the one hand, A. B. Xuma, under the influence of his American wife and knowledge of the New Deal, promoted civil rights and welfare state ideas injected into the ramshackle older structures during the previous decade; a Women's League was created. At the same time in 1949, under the influence of the Youth League Africanists who were eventually instrumental in removing Xuma, the ANC adopted the Programme of Action, which appeared to promise militant resistance to state oppression. The ANC moved as well towards alliances that extended its scope. After the Durban riots the pact with the Indian National Congresses of the Transvaal and Natal was reaffirmed (the Doctors' Pact) and links were also forged with Coloured leaders who before 1948 had been partly exempt from aspects of the segregation system.

The Communist Party, which had enjoyed a revival from the time of the war and succeeded in electing 'non-European' representatives to Parliament and the Cape Assembly, was outlawed in 1950. Reforming illegally as the South African Communist Party, it now sought to find common ground with Congress and its African members became prominent within it. The alliance system led ultimately to the Congress of the People, held in 1955 at Kliptown, which adopted the Freedom Charter as a defiant alternative to the Union constitution. The Charter committed the ANC and other constituent parts to a somewhat vague socialist formulation, advocating nationalisation of some leading sectors of the economy, redistribution of land and democratic representation. The alliance form of the Congress, representing as it did discrete 'peoples' racially defined (except for the primarily white Congress of Democrats), showed the extent to which the ideology of segregation had come to permeate even the strongest opposition to the system that existed at this time.

Part of the Youth League, in fact, was deeply hostile to the participation of non-Africans in ANC affairs and even the rather general commitment of the Charter to social democracy. It rejected the shift carried through by Oliver Tambo, Nelson Mandela, Walter Sisulu and others of its leaders. Decrying Communist influence and egged on by virulently anti-Communist white liberals, it moved towards a more overtly oppositionist stance within Congress. This 'Africanist' tendency reflected as well a discontent with the political practice and elite leadership of the ANC. During the early 1950s the ANC devoted its efforts to the Defiance Campaign, a passive resistance drive influenced by the Gandhian model of civil disobedience. It participated in pass burnings and defied signs marking off racially exclusive amenities in public facilities. Thousands of defiers were arrested but the campaign eventually petered out without result. The Kliptown Congress was also followed by many arrests and a treason trial that lasted for five years. The courts, applying formal legal criteria, did not sustain state charges of treason but they forced the ANC and its allies to devote energy and time to courtroom activity that took the movement away from mass action.

Yet an intensification of militancy was on the agenda in the late 1950s. Influx control, imposition of unpopular chiefs, regulations and removals of Africans from 'white' areas led to serious rural unrest in a number of districts. Early in 1959 violence broke out in Pretoria and in Cato Manor, Durban. The Africanists were anxious to capitalise on this unrest and, late in 1958, they broke away from Congress to form the Pan-African Congress (PAC). Committed to action, the PAC had no actual new strategy to hand. When the ANC declared a renewed pass-burning campaign the PAC countered with one aimed at an earlier date in March 1960. In two places, Sharpeville outside Vereeniging in the Transvaal and Langa, a Cape Town township, police-inspired violence broke out. Sixty-nine Africans died when the police fired into an unarmed, fleeing crowd at Sharpeville, an event publicised throughout the world which revealed the hard core of the South African system while suggesting its potential fragility.

In the wake of Sharpeville the grip of the state appeared to loosen. Pass inspections were suspended, a stay-at-home brought cities, especially Cape Town, to a halt, riots broke out in a number of places and an African demonstration took 30,000 black marchers through the streets of the centre of Cape Town. International financial confidence in South Africa suddenly plummeted, hitting the regime where it most hurt and threatening the basis of South African consumer society as stock and property values fell and investment funds were withdrawn. It appeared that the day of reckoning was at hand.

However, neither the ANC nor the PAC was capable of taking up the initiative. Instead the government, led since 1958 by Verwoerd following the death of Strydom, succeeded in gaining the upper hand so effectively that the pundits who had expected the imminent collapse of the South African system after Sharpeville, with equally limited prophetic talent, would speak of it lasting forever a decade later. It is, however, essential to examine those elements of policy carried through by Verwoerd and his successor, B. J. Vorster, which brought about what their friends considered a new lease of life and their enemies an unprecedented period of silence and oppression.

A major element of Verwoerd's strategy was repression. The ANC and PAC were banned in 1960 and obliged to go underground, a step for which they had laid few plans. They both opted for a policy of armed struggle based on sabotage that would lead ultimately to guerrilla warfare. This failed to bring about, as hoped, an effective wave of popular risings. In 1964 much of the internal leadership of the ANC and Congress movement was surprised and arrested at a farmhouse in Rivonia on the periphery of Johannesburg. Most were found guilty and sentenced to long jail terms. Nelson Mandela, the most important active underground ANC leader, had been arrested earlier and was linked to the Rivonia defendants. His opposite number in the PAC, Robert Sobukwe, like Mandela was imprisoned for many years. The Rivonia trials brought effective ANC and PAC activity to an end while the ANC-linked South African Congress of Trade Unions was also virtually stifled.

The state had fared poorly in securing convictions from the Treason Trials. Now legislation itself was altered to give the police a freer hand. Ninety-day detentions without legal process were instituted and made renewable. Reports of torture and suspicious deaths of prisoners spread. Within the townships a strong network of informers served intelligence purposes. The liberation movements found it difficult to operate effectively from exile. The PAC proved especially vulnerable to splits and internal dissensions. Its one-time anti-Communism gave way to a nominal Maoism. The Congress Alliance held up better but also could not seriously challenge Pretoria in the middle and late 1960s.

Verwoerd determined to extend his separate development orientation to a level never previously envisioned, establishing homeland governments, encouraging their autonomous development, introducing elections and ultimately leading them to independence and separate citizenship. This, at least, was the picture to be planted abroad: South Africa too was prepared to 'decolonise'. By 1963 elections were prepared in the Transkei. On the strength of the large number of state 'nominated' seats, Kaiser Matanzima, a relative of Mandela who championed separate development, became the first prime minister of a Bantustan.

South African retention of effective power through its officials in the Bantustans, its overwhelming economic influence and security arrangements gave to this initiative an element of farce. However, unlikely candidates as were the Bantustans for any meaningful independent existence, their expanding bureaucracies provided jobs for new strata of educated Africans tied to the system in a new way and a basis of accumulation for a small number of Africans with access to loans and political influence. Repression, too, could be indigenised through developing homeland police and army personnel. On the fringe of the Bantustans, border industry growth centres were planned as a means of freeing capital from some of the restraints that influx control imposed on industrial expansion elsewhere and to take advantage of virtually captive and particularly cheap labour. They never employed the numbers hoped for but the biggest of these centres attracted all the big companies and became considerable.

In the cities politicians proclaimed that the day when the tide would turn and the population would start to become proportionately more white and less African was around the corner. Influx control was applied with new rigour, sometimes to the discomfiture of business. The police hounded Africans to prove their right to live in town. From the late 1960s special relocation centres began to be created in the homelands for 'redundant' Africans – poorly planned dumping grounds in inhospitable spots that were meant to intensify the dependence of African labour even further and to cut the links of community in urban areas. While Soweto and other townships experienced massive overcrowding, the state (and municipal bodies) stopped building family houses and imitated the mining companies by expanding the construction of single men's (and a few women's) hostels inhabited by people from poor rural settings with little education.

The intensification of apartheid accompanied a period of highly profitable industrial expansion in the cities of South Africa. Crucial to recovery from the crisis of 1960 were loans from foreign banks and sympathetic assistance from foreign industrialists. British, American, European and Japanese industrial investors led the 1960s boom, sinking more funds into South African industry and the Johannesburg stock exchange than the rest of the continent put together; strong protectionist legislation protected profits. A striking feature of the South African economy was the dominance in the economy of a handful or less of big national companies in each branch and the remarkable rise of one particular corporation, Anglo-American (Anglos), which by the 1960s was an international giant that dominated the burgeoning stock exchange. Anglos expanded from South African gold mining into every facet of the South African industrial economy, at the same time investing in mining and other interests elsewhere in Africa and beyond.

Apart from certain specialised areas such as coal-to-oil technology, energetically pursued by the state for security reasons, and mining machinery, secondary industry exported little and required inputs of foreign investment to expand and modernise. It based itself also on the rather lavish use of cheap coal as an energy source, an eventually serious deficiency when coal ceased to be cheap. Manufactured goods found a market mainly in South Africa's weak neighbours, Botswana, Lesotho and Swaziland, in the Central African Federation and Mozambique. From 1957, in fact, this African trade tended proportionately to decline in significance. As imports of manufactures declined and capital goods imports rose, South Africa had become a typical import-substitution economy comparable broadly to the major Latin American economies.

The realities of the boom forced the Nationalist regime to consider itself increasingly as the agency for capital in South Africa rather than merely as promoter of a sectional Afrikaner interest. In 1960 Verwoerd organised a referendum for white voters only, which, by a small margin, emboldened him to proclaim South Africa a Republic. He then withdrew the South African application for retention of membership in the Commonwealth. For the first time English-speakers were introduced into the cabinet (1961) and the Nationalists began to abandon notions of Afrikaner apartheid for a generalised identity of white supremacy through 'separate development'. The maturity of Afrikaner capitalism was celebrated in 1964 by the establishment of a major Afrikaner-run mining finance house, Federale Mynbou, with Anglos' blessing. The long boom fathered an economy of affluence among the whites, allowing even the working-class children of former poor whites to enjoy a modest standard of comfort at home and to identify with the international American-derived culture of consumerism which tended to efface older values.

With each election the fortunes of the United Party (UP) fell lower. It never succeeded in presenting a coherent alternative to the Nationalists once it ceased being the party of government. Within the UP the split between those who wanted a liberalisation of apartheid and those who stood merely for the ethnic British interest (opposing, for instance, the Bantustan policy as a potential security risk offering blacks too big a concession) grew. A small Liberal Party broke off after the 1953 elections. It had considerable influence among African nationalists, but little vote appeal to whites. The following election in 1958 so demoralised UP liberals that eleven of their MPs resigned to form the Progressive Party. Only one, Helen Suzman, was successful in the next and subsequent elections through the 1960s. With African and then Coloured representation removed entirely from Parliament, she was frequently alone in questioning aspects of government policy and pinpointing contradictory and inhumane aspects of separate development.

The Progressives survived in good part through the backing of Anglos' head, Harry Oppenheimer, whose companies owned much of the English-language press which was used to propagandise the need for change, for adjustment to developments elsewhere in Africa, for flexibility and liberalisation in state policies. However, the limits to Progressive liberalism in the 1960s must also be stressed: they opposed black trade unions and universal suffrage and, unlike the Liberals, did not object to legislation that forbade them to have black members. Were it not for the Anglos connection and the sympathy of liberals abroad, the Progressives would have been insignificant.

The armed struggle in southern Africa

The real challenge to South Africa in the 1960s appeared to come not from any internal source, but from an increasingly unfavourable external situation. Sharpeville came as a jolt as much to Western business and political circles as to those in South Africa. The military, economic, intelligence and political links between South Africa and the West were strong, but for the first time it became transparent that South Africa could be a liability in Cold War strategies. Both the Macmillan government in Britain and the new Kennedy administration that took office in Washington tended to regard a suitably anti-Communist African nationalism as the best possible bet in the changing circumstances in Africa towards 1960. Failure by Pretoria to accommodate the South African system with political reform was worrisome. Harold Macmillan, who had found white settlerdom tiresome and retrograde even when a Colonial Office official before the war, pointedly chose Parliament in Cape Town, rather than Nairobi or even Salisbury, to make his 'winds of change' speech in 1960.

By then, the winds had begun to waft towards the South African periphery. Britain agreed to dismantle the Central African Federation and to promote the two non-settler units, the future republics of Malawi and Zambia, towards independence. The High Commission territories, which as late as the 1950s Pretoria still dreamt of annexing, were destined for a similar fate. Basutoland and Bechuanaland were granted independence as Lesotho and Botswana in 1965, to be followed by Swaziland in 1968. Small and impoverished, they posed no challenge to South African power. Malawi, which like the ex-High Commission territories had been developed essentially as a labour reserve, even moved to establish closer ties with South Africa. However, their existence placed the legitimacy of African nationalism on the political agenda while they were able to use widening trade and aid links with Europe and America to expand their ability to function autonomously.

Far more serious as a threat to Pretoria was the spread of insurgency under the aegis of national liberation movements stretching across the length of southern Africa. South Africa became deeply involved in trying to prop up regimes far weaker than her own while staving off armed opposition from her borders. Under B. J. Vorster, Verwoerd's successor after his assassination in 1966, an outward policy as he called it was coupled with growing emphasis and expenditure on the military.

The first territory in southern Africa to face an open insurgency was Angola. The Portuguese state, by virtue of its economic weakness and political rigidity, was completely unable to forge the compromises with African nationalism that its peers in Europe were doing during the 1950s. With independence, former Portuguese colonies would undoubtedly break most links with metropolitan trade and industry. Thus Portuguese colonial policy in the 1950s went directly against the wider current. Portugal pressed forward with intensified emigration from Europe, including settlement schemes with attendant land alienation. The position of the mulattos and *assimilados* deteriorated while the colour bar became more blatant. Opposition groups that emerged, notably in Angola, were ruthlessly suppressed to nip rebellion in the bud. Yet Angolans were naturally aware of events north of their frontier in the Congo and elsewhere. They began to consider a resort to arms against the Salazar regime.

Few local observers were surprised when a threefold insurrection broke out in 1961. The first phase, Maria's War, took the form of a popular rising in the northern district of Uige. Resistance to the collection of cotton and the chiliastic teaching of local prophetic movements make for descriptions reminiscent of the days of Maji Maji in Tanganyika. The second phase came in the capital, Luanda, where raids were mounted on police stations and government installations, kamikaze actions that were doomed to failure and invited mob action from white crowds. The third and most serious rising took place in the far north-west among Kongo-speaking Angolans who were experiencing a big rural settler influx coupled with deteriorating prices for their coffee. The Kongo rising was essentially an uncontrolled peasant rebellion of wide and terrible force. Some two hundred Portuguese civilians were killed as well as mulattos, *assimilados*, contract plantation workers from the south and even militants from rival organisations to the *Uniaõ das Populações de Angola* (UPA), which had gained support in this area. However, the UPA had little control over what was going on. Although the Portuguese were forced to beat a retreat from a wide zone, no revolutionary organisation or activity emerged in the midst of this chaos. After some months the Portuguese army returned to sweep up most of the area amidst scenes of vengeful violence, while a huge proportion of the population fled to the now independent Congo.

Thereafter, for thirteen years, the Portuguese army was obliged to fight a shooting war in Angola. The anti-Portuguese movement, however, was badly divided. Two dominant tendencies emerged. The UPA, later known as the *Frente Nacional de Libertaçaõ de Angola* (FNLA) after absorbing smaller groupings, was led by Holden Roberto, who had grown up in Belgian territory and emerged from the rival faction quarrels in Kongo regional politics. Hostile to those he did not consider 'African' and firmly in the Western camp (he was on the payroll of the US Central Intelligence Agency from 1961), he depended on a small cohort of Kongo-speaking followers and, increasingly, on the support of a succession of Kinshasa (Léopoldville) governments, particularly that of Mobutu after 1965, into whose family he married. The FNLA counted on the support of the large Angolan Kongo community in Kinshasa, could mount raids across the frontier and maintained an armed maquis that neither noticeably expanded nor contracted over the years in the hilly country north of Luanda.

Roberto always rejected unified action with the *Movimento Popular de Libertaçaõ de Angola* (MPLA), which included some of the most educated black Angolans and had its following in Luanda and its hinterland and other urban communities. The MPLA had strong fraternal links with the anti-fascist Left within Portugal and accepted a markedly socialist orientation. Portuguese Communists were crucial to the dramatic prison escape in 1962 of the poet Agostinho Neto. On arrival in Africa Neto became head of the MPLA. Far from its natural urban social base and surrounded by the debilitating atmosphere of Kinshasa, the MPLA deteriorated in morale, entered into opportunist alliances with a bevy of local exiles and appeared on its way to extinction when the Massamba-Débat regime came to power in Brazzaville in 1964, allowing it to resurface in a more sympathetic environment. MPLA militants had been murdered by Roberto's people during the rising of 1960, were prevented by force from entering Angola that way, and consequently felt bitterly towards the FNLA and its Western backers.

The MPLA had a chance to engage in armed struggle against the Portuguese after Zambia achieved independence in 1964. In 1966 guerrilla warfare began in eastern Angola and had considerable success in this thinly peopled region remote from centres of wealth. From 1970, friction grew between elements among the fighters and the leadership in exile. A major breakaway under Daniel Chipenda virtually grounded MPLA guerrilla activity beyond the fringe of the Zambian frontier by the beginning of 1974. FNLA efforts to open up a new front in the east also culminated in a breakaway movement under the direction of Jonas Savimbi, *União Nacional para a Independencia Total de Angola* (UNITA). On the whole guerrilla successes were then quite limited and did not approach threatening the major economic activities and political bases of Portuguese power. However, the struggle forced the Portuguese to spend vast sums of money militarising Angola and made the stakes of their commitment high.

Across the sub-continent Portugal faced a more formidable military foe in the *Frente de Libertaçaõ de Moçambique* (FRELIMO), the Mozambique liberation movement. FRELIMO may instructively be compared with the armed groups in Angola. It enjoyed in Tanzania a rear base less debilitating and manipulative than Zaïre-Congo. Although the Makonde people played a somewhat equivalent frontier role to the Kongo they had much less influence in Tanzania than the Kongo in Zaïre, and they could not shape the course of events in FRELIMO. South of the border, where FRELIMO initiated guerrilla activity in 1964, was a thickly settled zone of peasant agriculture, in contrast to the almost empty savannah of eastern, and the refugee-denuded forests of northern, Angola. Here FRELIMO could form an effective base and initiate programmes of production and social services sufficiently developed to allow them even to export small quantities of cash crops and to construct the skeleton of a future national society. The FRELIMO leader, Eduardo Mondlane, was remarkably effective at retaining the support of ideologically diverse elements and thus reducing rival groups outside FRELIMO to the status of non-entities.

Nevertheless, chauvinist and opportunist elements as well as Portuguese infiltrators did emerge into greater prominence. They, operating in collusion with the Portuguese, have been blamed for the assassination in 1969 of Mondlane in Dar es Salaam. This provoked an open crisis in FRELIMO, but the FRELIMO Left, among whom Samora Machel emerged as principal spokesman, was triumphant. Their opponents discredited themselves through negotiations with Portugal and the fighters remained faithful to an effectively purged movement.

FRELIMO had little success in assaulting towns, the remaining centres of Portuguese strength in the north, but they were able to expand their zone of operations continuously. In 1968, they succeeded in establishing a new front in Tete Province in the north-west. Within a couple of years they had effectively crossed the Zambesi and began to render inoperable the Beira railway which was vital to Rhodesia. They also raised tremendously the cost of constructing the giant Cabora Bassa dam on the Zambesi. Cabora Bassa, financed by European and South African capital, was meant to feed the Rand with electricity. It was only a new and powerful symbol of the intense symbiosis of Mozambique with South Africa (and Rhodesia). Mozambique supplied labour on a huge scale for the gold mines of the Rand and handled much of South Africa's international trade; these were in fact the dominant features of its colonial economy. The FRELIMO guerrilla movement, gradually expanding southwards, threatened not only the Portuguese treasury but Portuguese political power and with it, South Africa.

The other Portuguese mainland colony lay on the Guinea coast of West Africa, but it deserves mention here because it too was the scene of a major guerrilla struggle. By the end of the 1960s the *Partido Africano da Independencia da Guiné e Cabo Verde* (PAIGC) controlled a large part of the territory and people of Portuguese Guinea (now Guiné-Bissau) and held down a sizeable army. The gifted PAIGC leader, the Cape Verdean Amilcar Cabral (assassinated by a Portuguese bomb in 1972), co-ordinated his international solidarity activities with FRELIMO and MPLA.

Some Portuguese officials understood the need for reform. Thus assimilado status was formally abolished and steps taken to reduce the element of force in the labour system. Much of the reform programme, though, was cosmetic or half-hearted; it could not make profound changes that undercut the basis of colonial exploitation. Perhaps the most noteworthy shift was the opening of Angola in particular to much freer investment opportunities by non-Portuguese and thus giving other countries a bigger stake in a Portuguese victory. This helped to create some prosperity in the colonial economy but, ironically, at the same time it strengthened those elements in Portugal who sought to re-orient Portuguese capitalism from a colonial to a European and Common Market direction. As the few dominant Portuguese monopolies became more competitive, their commitment to Africa lessened.

A third zone of fighting in southern Africa opened up in Rhodesia. With the collapse of the Central African Federation the Rhodesian whites rejected those managers of settler domination whose reform plans since the 1940s had closely paralleled the Smuts liberals of the South African scene. The newly triumphant Rhodesian Front Party was as determined as the Nationalist Party in South Africa to stop the rot (the crucial moment was probably the quashed move to abolish racial restrictions on land ownership) and to draw a line on concessions that threatened white rule. Under Confederation the Front had already rallied support around the idea of a Rhodesian declaration of independence. The Unilateral Declaration of Independence (UDI) was proclaimed in 1965 with Ian Smith as independent Rhodesia's first and only prime minister, once it was clear that the British government under Harold Wilson of the Labour Party had absolutely no intention of stopping the move by force. Britain instead opted for a policy of sanctions, a policy that could achieve little without the co-operation of Portugal and South Africa. Indeed, it was sanctions in particular that brought South Africa together with her neighbours to attempt jointly to put out the brushfires of revolt. However, as with the Portuguese colonies, Rhodesia attracted the enmity of an international solidarity movement with a strong United Nations Organisation (UNO) presence.

At first Smith had in his favour a measure of prosperity brought about through the rapid development of heavily protected industry and a significant flow of South African investment. Rhodesia attracted a stream of Western immigrants and adventurers. Weakness and disunity on the part of Rhodesia Africans was, however, the strongest card in his hand for a long time. In 1963 the nationalist movement, dominated by Joshua Nkomo's Zimbabwe African People's Union (ZAPU), split. Organisationally inept, it had lacked any clear strategic or ideological orientation. It never had come to grips with the special problem posed by white settlers in Rhodesia, relying entirely on a decolonisation formula that would 'transfer' power to blacks from on high in Britain. The new group, called Zimbabwe African National Union (ZANU), was led by Revd Ndabaningi Sithole. Sithole and Nkomo were soon under arrest and both parties banned. ZANU was fortunate in the doggedness and perhaps ruthlessness of its exiled leader, Robert Mugabe, who came under the influence of Mondlane and Nyerere and helped to formulate a more militant kind of politics. Both ZANU and ZAPU felt forced to turn to armed struggle and from 1966 chronic raids were conducted across the Zambesi to engage Rhodesian security forces. The UDI regime could manage the Zambesi front. Rhodesia's real problems began when FRELIMO moved into Tete Province in 1968 and then proceeded to cross the Zambesi and to politicise the Shona peasantry in Mozambique. FRELIMO offered ZANU an excellent base of operations and fighting in eastern Rhodesia began in earnest. As ZANU activities became more effective they took on the character of a peasant insurrection liberating many areas 'by night'.

A final insurgency had by then begun in South-West Africa. The South West African People's Organisation (SWAPO), with a strong base in the northern part of the country, committed itself to guerrilla activity in 1966. The fighting was often sporadic but SWAPO had an unshakeable base among the Ovambo, who constituted almost half the population and a majority of the working class of South-West Africa. This was, moreover, an insurgency in a territory where South Africa claimed direct control and it required an ever-mounting military involvement by the South African state. South Africa sent as well materiel, troops and police to fight in Rhodesia and it co-operated closely with the Portuguese. Yet all these wars could not be won by an unholy southern alliance; the cost of holding the ring grew constantly and not least was the fear of international isolation.

In the 1950s it was South Africa that had spurned any diplomatic contact with the African nationalist movements elsewhere on the continent while fretfully advising the colonial powers against decolonisation. Only well after Sharpeville was it realised that this had been a serious miscalculation. Condemnation of apartheid became a pillar of the foreign policy of all African states, even if honoured more rhetorically than practically. The assistance of independent African states was helpful to the rising guerrilla movements of the south. South Africa tried to counter this with an outward policy of 'dialogue', beginning with the most dependent labour-exporting states, Malawi and Lesotho. In the late 1960s Pretoria began to court a whole phalanx of right-wing African countries – Mauritius, Madagascar (Malagasy Republic), Gabon, the Ivory Coast, Zaïre, Liberia, Ghana, the Central African Republic. Reactionary African regimes had little stomach for a confrontation with the South. Western advice lay in the direction of compromise while the South African state seemed internally invulnerable. Vorster realised that the Rhodesian situation was intractable so long as the Smith regime rode high and corresponded secretly with President Kaunda of Zambia in the hopes of finding some formula of compromise that could bring to power in Salisbury a docile black government.

Thus the internal strengths of the South African regime, which appeared so manifest in the late 1960s, drifted into an increasingly complicated and far less favourable situation in southern Africa as a whole. The 1970s saw the complacency of Pretoria disappear as blows to its hegemony began to reach their target.

The challenges of the 1970s and 1980s

As the 1960s came to an end, the state appeared to be in remarkable control of the situation. In reality, the boom paved the way for a new wave of struggle in the 1970s that coalesced with the problems South Africa confronted along the northern frontiers. In 1969 a community of workers with a long history of militancy, the dock workers of Durban, went out on strike. The workforce was expelled from Durban and summarily replaced by a completely new body of men from the impoverished homelands. Despite its failure, the strike kindled a modest spark of labour revival that would develop further. The real turning of the tide occurred in late 1971 when virtually the whole labour force of South-West Africa came out, returning to Ovamboland, and demanded the end to the entire degrading migrant contract system. After weeks of pressure, the state was forced to intervene and offer some compromises to the workers. Through 1972 and 1973 strikes spread, notably in Natal and the Transvaal. The bitterness of workers coincided with a significant downturn in the South African economy; the long boom was over and prospects for economic growth evaporated. From the strikes emerged a new, unaffiliated labour movement which threatened to take openly political forms.

The expansion of Bantu Education had evoked the growth of an enlarged student body that began to challenge the university authorities and state hegemony. Breaking with the predominantly white liberal National Union of South African Students (NUSAS), African university students attempted to build a new unity of the oppressed in adopting the word 'black' for themselves and thus forging links with Indian and Coloured comrades. In South African parlance, 'African' implies indigeneity, the assumption of a nationality with pre-colonial roots; 'black' was promoted as an identity based on resistance to oppression within industrial South Africa that crossed cultural barriers. From the student movement grew a larger Black Consciousness movement that established outreach programmes through urban black communities. At a lower level, high school attendance expanded dramatically. The gap between the promise of a secondary education and the prospect of poorly paid drudge work, in the footsteps of the students' parents, was glaring.

At first the emphasis on blackness allowed for a measure of government tolerance in accordance with separate development philosophy. From 1973, however, Black Consciousness leaders and organisations began to be repressed as they challenged state hegemony. They had struck roots, more informal and vague than organisational, in the black townships and particularly among black schoolboys and girls. In 1976 Soweto exploded with demonstrations that began with the government attempt to impose Afrikaans on a par with English as instructional language for African secondary school students. The state responded with all the firepower at its command, but despite the deaths of hundreds the marches and demonstrations continued for months and spread to all parts of the country, involving Coloured as well as African crowds on a large scale, an unprecedented phenomenon in South Africa.

Figure 11.1 Soweto schoolchildren teargassed, South Africa 1976

The 1976 insurgency clearly had another indirect and external cause. It was inspired by the collapse of Portuguese power in Africa. In the early 1970s Portugal was strained to its limits. Inflation, labour migration to France, draft evasion and mounting military budgets led to a coup in April 1974 that finally finished off the Estado Novo moulded by Antonio Salazar. While other European countries had solved their colonial issues satisfactorily from the political point of view through various forms of decolonisation procedures, in Portugal the African wars led to the collapse of the state itself. After a short period the Armed Forces Movement, itself influenced by the ideas of the African liberation organisations, seized power and put in office men sympathetic to independence for the colonies. Thus in 1975 FRELIMO triumphed in Mozambique and began the difficult struggle to re-orientate colonial economic, political and cultural life.

The situation in Angola was more complex. The West was determined to prevent the MPLA from enjoying a similar accession to power, despite its success in re-establishing strong bases of support in urban Angola. Savimbi's UNITA and Roberto's FNLA formed an alliance, drew on undercover American aid and forged ties with South Africa, which in turn was very eager to put paid to Angola-based SWAPO guerrilla activities. As Portuguese power waned in 1975, the South African army marched north in force with UNITA while FNLA proceeded from the other direction to the capital. By November the South Africans were hardly 100 miles from Luanda while FNLA guns bombarded the northern suburbs. The MPLA, which had by then proclaimed independence, was largely saved through the intervention of a contingent of Cuban troops. Gradually the MPLA and its Cuban friends drove the rival right-wing nationalist groups beyond the borders. Well before this Pretoria had ordered its troops to retreat in good order. The results for the South Africans were bad. All possibilities of dialogue with African states were at an end. Instead of hoped-for credit at helping to install Savimbi and Roberto in power, South Africa had now to face the victory of an uncompromised MPLA enjoying the friendliest relations with Cuba and the Soviet Union.

Mozambican independence allowed ZANU to expand its activities in Rhodesia. Despite Rhodesia carrying the war into Mozambique on a big, damaging scale, the days of UDI were numbered. In 1978 Ian Smith felt obliged to set up an internal settlement and to allow Bishop Abel Muzorewa to take office as prime minister of 'Zimbabwe-Rhodesia'. Muzorewa had become a national political figure by standing up and denouncing the Smith regime before the British-sponsored Pearce Commission in 1972 but he did not pursue any real efforts to break settler power and he continued the war. In the following year the situation for Rhodesia was so poor that Muzorewa and Smith accepted British-run negotiations for a referendum, to which South Africa, hoping for a Muzorewa victory, acquiesced. ZANU and ZAPU had by then, under intense pressure from the 'Frontline States' – Zambia, Mozambique, Angola, Tanzania and Botswana – agreed to a formal alliance. The Patriotic Front, as it was called, was initially reluctant to participate in a referendum under an unpurged Rhodesian administration. However, they could not get support for a refusal to co-operate with Western plans. The more conservative Frontliners feared a growing radicalisation of the Zimbabwe struggle. Zambia and Mozambique, particularly, suffered the consequences of the fighting so severely that they exerted pressure to get the consent of the Patriotic Front to the referendum. In the event, ZANU won a strong victory in the election and Mugabe became prime minister of an independent Zimbabwe in April 1980. This was the end of South Africa's last really dependable ally in Africa.

The combined result of labour militancy (which, with ups and downs, developed qualitatively and quantitatively), the dramatic Soweto rising which forever ended the myth of the African masses' acquiescence in Pretoria's policies and the collapse, first of Portugal and then of Rhodesia, placed the South African regime in a state of mounting disarray. Nor was the economy as buoyant as in the past. It became more difficult to get foreign loans and investment to meet the restructuring needs of the 1970s. The independence of Mozambique in particular affected South Africa's dependence on ultra-cheap foreign labour. The gold mines felt obliged to raise wages very substantially in order to attract South African black workers. Labour militancy also forced wages to rise in industry and, unlike the gold mines, industrial firms could not avoid the squeeze on profits through favourable world prices.

Superficially the government enjoyed an unprecedented parliamentary majority with the collapse and dissolution of the old United Party. However, the leadership was torn by feuds and afraid of change that would threaten its political base. The Nationalists (and indeed even the Broederbond) were divided between *verkramp* and *verlig*, conservative and reforming factions, and the direction of change, seen as essential after Soweto, was equally under dispute. In this atmosphere Vorster fell from office in 1978, to be replaced by the Cape *verlig*, P. W. Botha.

Some of the direction of reform pointed back to the United Party commissions of the early 1940s. African trade unions were allowed to register for the first time in South African history in 1979. Urban Africans received for the first time in a generation the right to hold houses on long leases. In the middle 1980s, the pass laws controlling the movement of Africans within South Africa were scrapped and the Immorality and Mixed Marriages Act abolished. The state moved towards encouraging black homeownership and business rights in townships. The tightly regulated apartheid system was being modified and riddled with increasingly obvious contradictions.

By this time also, from 1983, a new Constitution was created which assembled Houses of Parliament for Coloureds and Indians and would bring them into the South African cabinet. But the state was not prepared to accept the logic of incorporating the entire citizenry into the South African polity. Increasing favours were showered on to the Bantustans and their leaders who were becoming simultaneously less reliable. On the one hand, the reforms were intended to create a stable, capitalist consumer society. On the other, National Party politicians were not prepared to preside over their own exit from power; they also feared that democratisation would initiate a social and economic revolution.

In exile, the ANC revived from the late 1970s under an increasingly revolutionary ethos with the SACP influential and the guerrilla movement, Umkhonto we Sizwe, the focus of organisation and propaganda. Umkhonto

(MK) mounted a few very public sabotage attacks. It secured significant military support from the Soviet Union which hoped that South Africa might join Cuba and Vietnam as strategically well-placed states as allies. Against this Pretoria launched the so-called 'total onslaught'. In particular, those neighbouring states that harboured guerrillas and ANC activity were targeted for destruction. An intensified occupation of the northern section of South-West Africa, into which white conscripts were sent in large numbers, drove SWAPO activists largely into exile. South Africans took a widening role in sustaining Jonas Savimbi's UNITA movement and participated actively in the Angolan civil war. When the Samora Machel government in Mozambique gave facilities and encouragement to the ANC, the South Africans took over an insurgent exile movement that had been previously financed by the Rhodesians, called RENAMO.

FRELIMO had come to power determined to construct a new society in Mozambique with revolutionary fervour. However, revolutionary fervour on the part of urban-based bureaucrats and militants did not necessarily win over the massive peasantry scattered over the vast national territory. Dreams of a rapid transition to an urbanised, industrialised modern society were matched by few realities on the ground beyond an impressive new infrastructure of social services. Government projects and settler farms were nationalised and run by the state without the expertise or equipment for efficient management; the surrounding peasantry resented being turned into proletarians rather than having a land reform divide up fertile land amongst themselves. In many areas, ethnic and cultural resentments were fuelled by the dismissal of chiefs as colonial stooges, and by campaigns against polygamy and African medicine. As a result, RENAMO raids found local support while deeds of terror were carried out in areas loyal to FRELIMO. After 1980 conditions in Mozambique deteriorated dramatically and rapidly; the economy and social services collapsed and FRELIMO lost control of large areas of the countryside. When COMECON, the Communist equivalent of the Common Market, refused to accept Mozambique as a full member, the writing was on the wall: the East was not prepared to go far enough to save socialist Mozambique from her enemies.

By 1984, Mozambique was prepared to sign the Nkomati Accord with South Africa. With this important turning point, MK was unceremoniously turned out of Mozambique. However, the South Africans kept up the pressure. The war continued and evidence suggests continuing and substantial South African aid to RENAMO. In 1986, Samora Machel was killed in a mysterious plane crash just over the South African frontier. In Angola, a stalemate was reached. South African intervention peaked at the siege/battle of Cuito Canavale (1987–8). Committed Cuban intervention, coupled with the declining capacity of South African aircraft and a loss of nerve in being prepared to sacrifice the lives of conscripts, led to South African withdrawal. The potential for further 'total onslaught' seemed lost. This, together with the far more internationally dramatic decline of the Soviet Union, where powerful voices began to call for the abandonment of aid to this kind of conflict, brought together the possibility of negotiations over the fate of South-West Africa which brought the UNO into play.

In some respects, the South Africans saw these negotiations as a dress rehearsal for their own domestic drama. In return for Soviet and Cuban withdrawal from Angola, from which the ANC pulled out (as it did from Zambia as a military force), the South Africans agreed to allow the UNO to preside over a free election for an independent Namibia which duly came about in 1990. Sam Nujoma's SWAPO formed the government but quickly shed any revolutionary or socialist pretensions. Namibia accepted a constitution negotiated with minority parties and agreed to a framework to which the Western powers and South Africa could hardly object. As a small, thinly peopled republic dependent on mineral exports and very much within a South African economic orbit, the new Namibia resembled its pacific neighbour, Botswana. To a very large extent, South Africa's total strategy policy had been a success.

The real challenge to South Africa, however, came not from military invasion but from within. Within a year of the proclamation of the tricameral constitution, the townships were again aflame. The township risings of the middle 1980s occurred on a much wider scale than anything previously known. Whereas the forces of order had been able before to counter youth action by rallying covertly workers afraid of losing jobs and uncommitted to urban life, now a rapidly growing and demonstrably more disciplined trade union movement was being mobilized against the state. Civic organisations, sometimes under the control of the unions, sometimes taken over by insurgent youth groups, sometimes neither, were able virtually to oust state control in the townships. State efforts at reform through commercialising township social and economic relations (growing differentiation, economic rents and service charges, growing power to black authorities willing to co-operate with the state) backfired dramatically and created a groundswell of support, and perhaps more importantly a belief in the possibility of a different future, by the majority of once dispirited township dwellers. As the economy stagnated, the state found it had only limited capacity to purchase approval. Waves of revolt spread to previously untouched corners of the country, although they still remained predominantly urban.

In the 1980s state-inspired assassination and terror like that in Latin American dictatorships became a significant feature of South African political life. However, the government was unwilling and unable to abandon reform. Botha appeared at times to favour a Napoleonic regime, placing himself above parties on a platform that would allow him to 'cross the Rubicon'. But, despite the revenues and power at his disposal, he was reluctant to do more than get his toes wet. A first tentative series of moves leading to significant political negotiation began in the mid-1980s when it was clear that tricameralism had failed. A committee of Commonwealth politicians – the Eminent Persons Group – was drawn in as potential power brokers, although a crucial part of the political establishment could not face the music at this point and torpedoed negotiations with a series of cross-border raids.

There was really no retreat from this path for long, however. On the one hand, the ANC, both in the form of its top exile leadership and in the increasingly significant imprisoned leader Nelson Mandela, well before the Rubicon speech was moving towards a negotiations mode that would fall far short of demanding the dismantling of South African capitalism or even its corresponding social institutions. On the other, many links began to build up, both between the external and internal opposition (the loosely organised United Democratic Front and the Congress of South African Trade Unions, which had largely evaded repression) and with such forces as the powerful businessmen and key cultural figures who met with the ANC in Lusaka and elsewhere. In the end, it was not P. W. Botha, but F. W. de Klerk, who succeeded him as state president in 1989, who was prepared to take the unprecedented step of unbanning the ANC and the SACP, freeing key political prisoners and undertaking the abolition of all the laws that had signalled the foundation of apartheid. Internal instability and violence coupled with increasing isolation through sanctions and disinvestment from the main Western partner countries, devastating given the extent to which South Africa was a trading nation. This anteing up of the odds went together with the emergence of dedicated anti-apartheid movements increasingly influential in many countries.

The end of apartheid

Mandela was released early in February 1990 and thereafter embarked on four years of negotiation in an interim political period whose late phase was marked by political co-responsibility. De Klerk virtually abolished the chief apartheid institutions singlehandedly and made the running at first. However, in terms of a new settlement, he had no clear strategy and relied too much on the support of African allies or at least fellow enemies of the ANC, notably Chief Mangosuthu Buthelezi, the one leader of a homeland whose patrimonial system enjoyed wide public support in rural Kwa Zulu. Tensions and manoeuvres on both sides (the notorious 'Third Force' which emerged with state backing was a major part of this) brought about unprecedented levels of violence. De Klerk failed to realise until too late that there was no road back; the West would not allow him to abandon the ANC, which in turn limited the muscle power of the security state to intervene.

In any case, the strength of the ANC lay not in its arms nor in its guerrilla efforts, which had largely failed, but in its acceptance by virtually all Africans (apart from the Natal Zulu constituency of Buthelezi and his Inkatha Freedom Party (IFP)) as their champion. The ANC, however, was unable to force the situation into a revolutionary capsule. It was obliged to accept that change would come according to the pace permitted under law and, in effect, that it would at most be able to preside over a capitalist South Africa where civil society would, at least at first, be much as it had always been. Thus the establishment of a new rights-based constitution was critical. However, the ANC was able to win the major concession of something approaching straightforward majority rule.[2] In return, the ANC agreed to the four provinces being replaced by nine with considerably enhanced powers and the creation of all kinds of representative mechanisms, which seemed to assure some representation (and patronage) for all those with any kind of constituency who were prepared to co-operate. The context was one of deteriorating economic conditions and an overhanging threat of renewed, accelerated violence.

To the surprise of international opinion, in circumstances where the range of choice had seemed to narrow for countries all over the world, this stalemate proved to be the foundation of a compromise which led to quite peaceful elections in 1994. A key stumbling block had been removed with the easy overthrow of the most truculent of Bantustan leaders, Lucas Mangope of Bophuthatswana, and the pitiful failure of efforts to rescue him on the part of the white far Right. Both these menaces to a pacific solution suddenly evaporated. In the election, characterised by very high turnouts, the ANC won well over sixty per cent of the vote. However, this in turn depended on its overwhelming support amongst African voters outside of Kwa Zulu Natal, as the province was now known. Most white, Indian and Coloured voters all turned to the National Party as their principal bulwark while Kwa Zulu Natal gave just over fifty per cent of the vote to the IFP, according to disputed results.

The 'new South Africa' was presided over by Mandela, a man of great charm and stature who made an impressive advertisement for the political transformation that had taken place. South Africa, freed of sanctions and international opprobrium, began to experience moderate but real economic growth and also was able to develop relations with the rest of Africa on a new basis. However, the problematic character of transition has to be underlined. It became obvious that the great problem that lay ahead was to find some way of reconciling the differences, cultural, social and economic, between a core population used to living according to the ways of wealthy nations formed by European settlers and their descendants and a much larger periphery, whose poverty was conditioned by the decay of the institutions of the past and massive levels of unemployment. The core was less and less white, but that did not necessarily solve the problem. Social forces tended to lead towards the decay of middle-class institutions and prerogatives (although not necessarily those of the rich) to the at best slight advantage of the far more numerous poor. As a result, the ANC did not endear itself to the middle class, beset by very high crime rates and swingeing taxes, as its constituency of the poor protested against the inevitable shortfall in promises of 'delivery'. While sustaining the constitutional instruments adopted in 1994, the party, still far stronger than any opposition force, has increasingly lost coherence as it tries to reconcile different forces – international business interests, a network of relatively dependent new multimillionaire capitalists, the trade unions, the allied but partially distinct Communist Party and the mass of poor voters, especially in the former Bantustans who ensure the big voting turnout.

The Mandela years were inevitably marked by the gradual institutional transformation towards the creation of common institutions. Perhaps the most impressive achievement under Mandela was the success in nipping in the bud a potential coup amongst top white military officers and stabilising the new regime. The second ANC president, Thabo Mbeki (1999–2008) presided over a minerals boom. Mbeki promoted affirmative action heavily but coupled this with the adoption of Western business models that actually made some key state agencies more efficient than in the past. His authoritarian manners were resented and he was ousted in 2008 by his former vice-president Jacob Zuma. Zuma, indecisive on policy issues, presided over a party that continued to win elections, apart from in the Western Cape Province where blacks were not in a majority of the population, and has become associated with a subsidence into clientelist networking politics as the economy again moved into a phase of slow growth.

The ANC government found it easiest to use state machinery and mechanisms to promote the interests of a fast-growing black middle class through systematic affirmative action measures and the pervasive spread of patronage. Black school and university attendance expanded very rapidly. A few great fortunes were created by the most strategically placed but the new middle class struggled to meet the consumerist pot at the end of the rainbow and was often encumbered with severe debts. It cannot be said that a systematic welfare state was created but the ANC government once it got started did construct hundreds of thousands of small secure houses on the urban peripheries. Pensions were made automatic and became for many poor people the basic source of income for families. State employment expanded substantially. However poor management affects the quality of education and health and local government is often incompetent and dominated by political rivalries and splits. Big contracts have encouraged the rise of increased corrupt practice. The accumulation model established in earlier decades moreover is no longer dynamic.

In the years before the political transformation, massive unemployment began to become a serious feature of social existence. Only about sixty per cent of South African adults of working age are employed compared to eighty per cent or more in developed countries while peasant agriculture is virtually insignificant and the so-called informal sector, deprived of roots in an active peasantry, quite small. The continued effective power of the big companies in the different spheres of consumer life tends to stifle small business competition. This couples with the continued salience of crime, especially violent crime, which expanded dramatically in the struggle years and thereafter continued at high levels afterwards, and the weakness of family life whereby most children are born out of wedlock and raised largely in one-parent households. The AIDS pandemic which peaked in the first decade of the twenty-first century, caused almost entirely through sexual contact, affected a larger absolute number of victims than in any other country in the world. While the prevalence of the disease has diminished somewhat and it has declined very largely as a source of mortality, it remains true that South Africa has the largest percentage of sufferers as well, barring a few other southern African neighbours. The usually very rational Mbeki fought against the conventional diagnoses of AIDS for reasons that are disputed and large numbers of deaths ensued until he was finally overruled by the party and a more humane national policy supplying drug treatment to control the infection was instituted.

Finally, South Africa is at present the seat of a myriad of local protest movements, sometimes leading to violent confrontation with authorities. There is much literature debating its importance, pointing to the inheritance of a successful protest tradition, the ineptitude of local government or developmental planning and the aura of beautiful horizons held out as the future by the ruling party compared to the reality of standing on the outside of an affluent consumerist world with limited social mobility. However there is little evidence that these movements are leading to a new national politics within the ANC or against it. If the trade union movement is no longer a solid phalanx of support for the government, workers still engage in major strikes continually, sometimes winning gains beyond the inflation rate. The 2013 Marikana platinum mine strike is notorious; it led to more than thirty deaths, including those of several policemen.

What might be said is that the model of development of the old regime has decayed without any clear replacement. Agriculture has shed labour massively and is now primarily dependent on contract labour. Mining also uses massive amounts of contract labour and employs fewer workers than it did; South African gold has lost its dominant position in the world and South Africa does not attract the attention of prospectors as in its heyday. Manufacturing too employs fewer workers and the most successful companies are now part of global networks, not national ones, and are often owned by foreigners. The potential prosperity held out to graduates is rarely available to the less-skilled majority – less skilled according to the economic norms of today. The combination of democratic governance and socio-economic continuity in the structures governing civil society and perpetuating high levels of inequality does not augur well for nation-building.

The emphasis that this book places on political economy hopefully justifies the presence earlier of a special chapter on South Africa where an accumulation and development trajectory, if not entirely unique on the continent, is certainly so remarkable as to require a lot of special treatment. For much of the twentieth century, Mahmood Mamdani's often-cited view criticising an analysis of South African history as exceptional to the continent seems questionable. However, since 1990 there is more and more to commend itself to his perspective as economic growth has become more incoherent. It will surely be increasingly easy to integrate South Africa once again into a broader African historiography. As we shall see, the economic revival of many countries in Africa after 2000 allows it to be once again possible to see it as a continent that is going somewhere; in fact South African economic growth is sluggish compared to many other African countries; Nigeria may well surpass it in economic size in coming years. The growing importance of clientelism and corruption in high places within the ANC and the state, not a good augury for so-called governance, has however meant a growing resemblance to governance elsewhere in Africa. South African business has expanded massively, especially throughout the southern half of the continent; it has meant the presence of thousands of South African business personnel and a major stake notably in the service sectors catering to the more affluent, and in mining. South Africa has also become a Mecca for large numbers of natives of other African countries, ranging from the Somali shop owner networks dotting rural areas and poor townships throughout the country and contract workers from Mozambique in agriculture and construction to Zimbabwean post-graduate students and the large numbers from everywhere occupying professional jobs. They have been from time to time (notably in 2015) victims of violent attacks reminiscent of the so-called race riots of 1949 in Durban. Nevertheless the level of integration into Africa has intensified.

Thabo Mbeki, who tried to revive what is now called the African Union under the presidency at the moment of writing of one of his closest collaborators, the one-time Mrs. Nkosazana Zuma, and was also interested in reviving the moribund international Non-Aligned Movement, clearly saw himself as the first African president able to alight in a conflict-ridden country from his own presidential plane and pull some African weight in favour of a solution. His long-time diplomatic background propelled him into a sense of continental self-consciousness. Jacob Zuma has rather promoted South African membership in BRICS, a would-be league of emerging international political players also including Brazil, Russia, India and China, that has seemed to some as heralding the dawn of a new international economic order – still probably a vision rather than a reality apart from the case of China. However, Zuma too is happy to engage in African conciliation and peace resolution initiatives with equal success at least to Mbeki.

Although rarely noted, a bottom-line phenomenon, especially in the context of the bad press Africa tends to receive in the West, is the striking political stability in southern Africa since the end of apartheid. Except for the little landlocked kingdoms of Lesotho and Swaziland, the former zone of liberation struggles is in fact administered entirely by the successful liberation movements that have stabilised themselves and kept in power. Even in Lesotho and Swaziland, South Africa has blocked efforts at coups in the former case and been a force for the continuation of the grossly patrimonial monarchy in the latter. Namibian society has exhibited considerable continuities with the past while attempting to forge a more independent path from South Africa. Its social structure is quite similar to South Africa and SWAPO, the ruling party, achieved an eighty per cent majority in the fair 2014 elections, much more successful yet than is the ANC itself. In its neighbour Botswana, a nurtured partnership between the Anglos diamond mining interest and the state has been the bedrock of a stability which makes the pula a stronger currency than the South African rand and a per capita income measured as higher than that of South Africa. Again, however, it is more questionable whether the social structure has changed in character very much from the past from the point of view of less-educated Batswana in the villages.

In the one-time Portuguese colonies of Mozambique and Angola, not only is Portuguese very much the official national language but in prosperous conditions tens of thousands of ethnic Portuguese have come back, no doubt mostly temporarily, to settle. In both cases, the dominant liberation movements felt constrained to introduce contested elections and a deal ended the civil war tragedies of the early independence years but the losing opposition parties were not admitted to any governing partnership. Thus UNITA in Angola resumed its armed struggle for a time until the leader, Jonas Savimbi, was killed in 2002. In Mozambique RENAMO continues to attract electoral support in the central part of the country and retains some support and more restiveness, excluded from the spoils of government. The booming oil prices of the 2003–13 years enormously benefitted Angola which became one of the richest countries in Africa although once again this wealth did not translate itself into much improvement in the life of the poor, a large part of the population of which is now gathered into the shanty towns in Luanda and other cities because of the war. Luanda is an extreme example of the juxtaposition of deprivation and luxury. Two features noted by observers are the extensive presence of Chinese trading partners, active notably in construction activities (although the largest foreign investor is Brazil) and the impressive role of SONANGOL, the state oil company which is Africa's largest and most successful corporation between the Sahara and the Limpopo. SONANGOL has its tentacles in many economic activities, invests back in Portugal and elsewhere and has a good reputation in international management circles. Mozambique, when peace finally came, was a desperately poor country heavily dependent on aid where non-governmental organisation (NGO) senior employees were better off than government ministers. With time, this changed. South African money created a huge aluminium refinery in Maputo, extensive natural gas resources were discovered off the coast in the north and coal deposits around Tete, now a boom town, are beginning to be exploited.

The only southern African case where one can speak of real crisis, and a crisis attracting much attention internationally, has been in Zimbabwe. The Lancaster House deal of 1980 which secured an end to the armed struggle gave way to a period of apparent stability and even harmony. Here was a society where guerrillas had been keen on popular music described by Thomas Turino as replete with 'references to machine guns and ancestors set to a church hymn'.[3] The emigration of two-thirds of the white population left considerable numbers of farms for redistribution and a sudden availability of jobs and homes on offer to the growing number of black civil servants. The economy fluctuated with the price of agricultural commodities and the state of the harvest and was reasonably stable if not very dynamic. The election alliance between ZANU and ZAPU was retained as the Patriotic Front (PF) and virtually all opposition subsided. Whites had no political outlet after 1990 when they lost their quota of reserved parliamentary seats and remained weakly integrated into the new dispensation rather as in South Africa later. An attempt to revive ZAPU and contest with ZANU was met with harsh repression in Matabeleland, some of it at the hands of a battalion trained by North Koreans. The trade union movement was also suppressed and shut down albeit allowed to reopen as a government agency. There was also virtually no critical voice in the media.

For a time, ZANU-PF was well able to garner developmental enthusiasm. Zimbabwe became a darling of the NGOs and aid agencies. It ranked highest in the entire world in the proportion of the budget reserved for education. Above all, it was important due to its position on the 'front line' of the wars for and against South Africa, a model of apparent harmony and stability, holding up an example of a successful transition to independence that did not leave the white businessmen and farmers bereft.

However, with the end of the South African struggle, this advantageous situation disappeared. Zimbabwean industry was swamped by South African competition and the West lost interest in tolerating protectionist economic policies dating from the UDI years, an ever-growing civil service as graduates multiplied and a perennial budget deficit. Zimbabwe was more than ripe for what a further chapter will focus on – structural adjustment – and its home-grown attempt in this direction – called ESAP – proved unsuccessful while emboldening those who disliked ZANU-PF. Unsurprisingly workers in the towns and cities were increasingly restive and the union movement revived, becoming a source for the first time in decades of significant opposition to the state. With the plausible hope of ensnaring the urban vote, this became the core of the Movement for Democratic Change (MDC) which had the support of human rights NGOs based on Western aid as well as the representatives of big farm interests particularly. In Matabeleland where ZAPU had once been strong there were also reserves of hostility to the strong-arm measures of ZANU-PF. In Zambia on the other side of the Zambesi, Kenneth Kaunda had been forced to accept multi-party elections and this nationalist stalwart was voted out of office while his successor, Frederick Chiluba, came out of the trade unions but was prepared to tell the unions to 'die a little' for Zambia and sign on for proposals that were part of the new governance and structural adjustment packages being imposed throughout Africa. Could not Zimbabwe be rescued from its out-of-date liberation mentality too?

In the late 1990s, it seemed as though Robert Mugabe was facing an insoluble dilemma. On the one hand stood the restive masses, including a veterans' movement that first demanded pensions, the payment of which seriously undercut the value of the Zimbabwe dollar and undermined state budget planning. On the other, his favoured new constitution was defeated by the electorate in 1997. The British, whose vague promises of financial assistance to pay for more transfer of agricultural land for redistribution had fallen into abeyance, now made it clear that these promises no longer fitted the international situation and would not be honoured, certainly on any scale. And the MDC appeared to be a strong candidate to oust Mugabe in the 2000 election, the first where the ruling party would face real opposition.

Interestingly Mugabe, like the other liberation party leaders, survived. If this election and subsequent ones were conducted in dubious ways with much violence and intimidation, he also unleashed the veterans and their supporters so that most of the land in private hands was taken away from owners by force. The hard men (and sometimes women) in his party and a greedy military command came increasingly to the fore and disrupted the relatively well-run bureaucracy from placing any brakes on party power. In 2008, Mugabe's support base was so weak that he was forced to concede a parliamentary loss and opt for a coalition government but the MDC itself was too incoherent and organisationally disunited to promote its own interests and its power base fell away with the party going down subsequently to defeat and splits. For Mugabe, this was a victory for the essential core of the liberation trajectory; ZANU-PF did not accept whites (or the smaller number of other non-blacks) as real Zimbabweans or indeed generally as members and fast-track land reform, brushing aside any court rulings, represented a renewal of the spirit of liberation.

Zimbabwe survived economically on the basis of new sources of platinum, gold and diamonds discovered and developed and a reluctant deal with the biggest platinum producer but the developed core of economy and society was fragmented if not destroyed and hurt further by the pariah status of the government in the West. Much of the redistributed land went to peasant farm families, industrious and as commercially active as was possible but the state did not have the ability to nest these farmers in a broader developmental strategy with inputs and necessary supports. By 2010 Zambia had a higher GNP per capita than Zimbabwe, the spectacular collapse in value of the local currency led to its extinction, social services barely limped along and the remittances from hundreds of thousands of Zimbabweans were crucial to keeping things going. It was, to put it mildly, no longer a darling of aid donors in the West.

The largest single emigrant community was now in South Africa with varying degrees of permanence. Mbeki, who appears to have been urged to be the 'point man', using basketball terminology, for Britain and its friends in eliminating Mugabe, refused to play this role even while undoubtedly preferring a less noisy neighbour than was the case. Zuma had been less compliant, with a nationalist consensus in Africa supporting ZANU-PF until the 2013 election; this seemed to be as acceptable as was possible and any conflict then tended to subside as the opposition to Mugabe lost credibility. South Africa here too has been important in stabilising the continued political power of the liberation movements of the region, even while Zimbabwe was the scene of the playing out of the tensions that lay behind the scenes.

Notes

1. Such plans found a close equivalent north of the Limpopo in Southern Rhodesia, where British constitutional influence was still very important.
2. This was probably the chief issue in any case for Mandela. The exceptions to majority rule initially in 1994 were the ANC's willingness to enter a Government of National Unity with any party obtaining more than ten per cent of the vote and making the head of any party with twenty per cent of the vote a deputy president, and the arrangements for amalgamating local government districts on a parity rather than one-person one-vote basis during the first few years.
3. Thomas Turino, *Nationalists, Cosmopolitans and Popular Music in Zimbabwe* (University of Chicago Press, 2000), p. 218.

12
Structural Adjustment Kicks In

People talk about capitalism as one mode of development and communism or socialism as another mode, but at least they're both on the move, using different paths. They have something in common, namely a certain level of social integrity, a certain national character, a demand for accountability. All of which is missing in most of the third world. But without it, your capitalism or your socialism, or whatever it is, isn't going to work.

FLIGHT-LIEUTENANT JERRY RAWLINGS OF GHANA, AS QUOTED IN INTERVIEW,
THE GUARDIAN (NEW YORK), 28 APRIL 1982

Intensifying contradictions in the 1970s

This chapter focuses on the context for the increasingly hard times that most of Africa experienced in the last quarter of the twentieth century. In fact, much of Latin America and the Middle East shared this experience by and large.

For the mass of Africans the oppressors have been identified again and again in the course of demonstrations, riots and revolts, as the agents of the state. For worker and cultivator they constitute an ambitious class of private accumulators eager to subject the population to collective state appropriation. The bureaucracy is so corrupt, so committed to procedural and managerial practices of limited productive value despite its ideology of development, that its incessant growth can only be felt as a hated burden by the peasantry in particular, whose commodity sales sustain the state in many cases. Nonetheless there is a considerable measure of ambiguity here as the consumer society is so closely linked to access to the capital city, national institutions and the state apparatuses themselves.

In the rhetoric of radical anti-colonialism that informed the African regimes of the left, little attention was given to this basic contradiction between state and society. If Nkrumah's Ghana is taken as an example it demonstrates with particular clarity that contradiction and the alienation of the masses from the regime. Nkrumah himself was full of majestic dreams of a new Africa which took incoherent, but sometimes visually impressive, shape in the industrial harbour and factory centre of Tema, the great Akosombo dam bridging the

Volta and an impressive expansion of social services. All this rested on the cocoa economy, which the state milked despite increasing strain as the world price for the commodity collapsed in the early 1960s.

There was no real political or social basis for revolution within the populist Convention People's Party whose cadres, once tasting power, sought the good life through their new positions. When they encountered opposition, including that of the working class, they crushed it, creating a personality cult around Nkrumah, dubbed the *Osagyefo* or Redeemer. The social relations at the heart of the production of cocoa, foodstuffs and petty commodities in Ghana could not be transformed by administrative fiat into functioning within state farms as Nkrumah desired. When producer prices fell, even the expanded services and new industries the state offered decayed. His turn left from 1961 onwards occurred in a social and political vacuum. When the Pan-Africanist dreamer was toppled in a coup in 1966, there was little reaction. Nkrumah's closest contemporaries, Sékou Touré of Guinea, Modibo Keita of Mali (also overthrown in a coup of 1968) and on the other side of Africa, Nyerere, Obote and Kaunda, ran into similar difficulties.

After independence, peasant resistance first emerged on a spectacular scale in the Congo, overwhelmed by risings that swept more than half of its immense territory between 1964 and 1968. Demands for a 'second', real independence were expressed with most clarity in the Kwilu region of the western Congo, where Pierre Mulele, an articulate leader who had absorbed Maoist ideas of a peoples' rising along with radical nationalism, was the foremost spokesman. Mulelism as a formal ideology used an often mechanical Marxist language, but it contained the crucial advance of speaking in plausible terms to African peasants. In the east and north the *simba*, teenage soldiers fighting in the hopes that magic medicine could fend off the effects of bullets, evoke memories of Maji Maji half a century earlier. They were the first of several equivalent forces to emerge in the next half-century. All the harsh efforts at control by Bula Matari, the colonial state, the disillusionment of independence under the nouveaux riches whose rise rapidly followed upon the elimination of Patrice Lumumba, now found its cultural antithesis. Only at length and with the use of European mercenaries did the new regime of Mobutu, once Lumumba's press secretary and now the USA's main man in Kinshasa, regain control of the situation.

At the same time, across the River Congo one of the most blatantly dependent and reactionary of the ex-French regimes, that of the defrocked *abbé*, Fulbert Youlou, in the Brazzaville Congo, was overthrown after a combination of strikes, student demonstrations and urban struggle. This brought a notably more radical regime to power. The Brazzaville revolution of 1964, if less spectacular than the great risings in the Léopoldville Congo, beginning in that year also, formed a model for later mass revolts in Africa. Popular forces threw out Youlou but found no real political outlet. Radical army men stepped in to create a relatively left-wing regime that none the less failed to come to grips with the fundamental issues that had alienated people from the state. Events in the Congo were repeated in Sudan in 1968, where the trade union-based Communist Party (the only significant CP in tropical Africa) played a particularly active role until its destruction by Nimeiri, and in 1972 in the Malagasy Republic.

During the late 1970s populist urban risings built up renewed momentum in West Africa – the coup associated with Flight Lieutenant Jerry Rawlings in Ghana in 1979 which overthrew the military regime of Colonel Acheampong, the bloody end of a century of True Whig Party rule and Americo-Liberian oligarchy in Liberia shortly thereafter and a revolution in Gambia in 1981 only suppressed through the intervention of Senegalese forces. This sweep of events indicated the disgust of large sectors of the people, including the most organised among the workers and the least co-opted among the educated, for the putrefying condition of the state apparatus, inept at devising any strategy to relieve popular miseries. Yet they all relied on no clear ideological trend or party organisation; they were great cries of anguish to which elements from the military most sympathetic to the sufferings of the population responded by seizing power. Men such as Nigeria's Brigadier Murtala Muhammad (head of state from 1975 until his death in an unsuccessful coup attempt in 1976) offered honesty, a high moral code and ruthless purges as understandable but insufficient answers to mounting structural problems.[1]

The most awesome political convulsion of the 1970s was the Ethiopian Revolution of 1974, which put paid both to the half-century political career of Haile Selassie and the imperial monarchy. In his last years Haile Selassie had presided over feudal and capitalist elements uncomfortably juxtaposed. The abolition of feudal dues in 1973 removed an important pillar of support for the monarchy. While the emperor relied increasingly on educated courtiers, the great feudal aristocracy lost power and influence. They could no longer present a bulwark against social currents reacting to the spread of capitalism. In the countryside estate-based export agriculture was beginning to throw peasants off the land in parts of the cash crop-producing south. In the cities secondary industry and a proletariat were at last developing. The educated bureaucrats created by the regime only felt frustrated and alienated by the corrupt feudal crust. They were not ready to back the state.

In 1973 drought convulsed much of Ethiopia while the inept imperial regime simply pretended it did not exist. Starvation and misery stalked the land while grain was sold abroad to pay for oil, industrial and luxury imports. A February army mutiny over stinking food in an isolated desert outpost was the first blow in the 'creeping coup' that led by September to the deposition of the emperor and the proclamation of sweeping changes, notably comprehensive land reform. Social forces long hidden in Ethiopia were now at liberty to develop: trade unions, the radical students' movement, ethnic and religious minorities' organisations. Over this presided a heterogeneous amalgam from the military, the Derg.

The Derg is an excellent example of the remarkable strategic position and political ineptitude of the military and bureaucratic Left in Africa. Originally its slogan was the bland and inoffensive 'Ethiopia First'. It effectively accepted peasant land takeovers and the elimination of feudal and royalist elements from the Ethiopian state system, but it had nothing to offer on the increasingly burning 'national question'. Revolution had heartened the various ethnic, regional and religious entities that had gained consciousness as the victims of state oppression. Part of the Derg was prepared to consider a negotiated settlement especially with the nationalists of Eritrea, but in the end the dominant faction under Lt.-Col. Mengistu Haile Mariam stood by Greater Ethiopia and the fighting went on. Additionally in 1976 Mengistu led the suppression of the insurgent students and workers belonging to the Ethiopian Peoples Revolutionary Party which had begun an ill-conceived armed campaign. He then turned against their fellows in the Meison movement who had until then always collaborated with the military.

In 1977 Mengistu found his armies being pushed inland by Somali insurgents in the east while the radicalised Eritrean Peoples Liberation Front (EPLF), increasingly the strongest element within the Eritrean movement, succeeded for a time in seizing virtually every Eritrean town, confining the Ethiopians to a couple of strongholds. Only the support of Soviet and Cuban troops enabled him to survive and carry on what increasingly looked like an imperial war. The radical social character of many of the insurgencies in Ethiopia – Eritrean, Somali, Tigre, Oromo – was directly aimed at what was seen as the continuing centralising Amhara state even though Mengistu, himself of humble origin, began to open up opportunities within the state to those outside the old establishment. Mengistu was unable to consolidate a political movement outside the army or to develop an economic strategy.

Central to the onset of the Ethiopian upheaval was the great drought, the crisis in Ethiopian agriculture and the drastic decline in trade due to the rapid rise in the price of imported oil. Therefore the fall of the Ethiopian regime was just one tremor in a continent-wide earthquake. From 1973 economic conditions in most of tropical Africa deteriorated markedly as demand for exports to the industrialised states fell while the price of imports, especially of oil, rocketed disastrously. African industrialisation and infrastructure had been built up, quite as much as American and European, on cheap oil and the change induced by the price rise was catastrophic. Stagnation in the world economy put the squeeze on backward, weak African productive systems.

As governments pressed peasantries to produce they met unprecedented resistance and the virtual collapse in many countries of the cash crop export structure. Peasants, short of a great inchoate upheaval as the Congo had known in the 1960s, were unlikely to crystallise an effective political protest but they were able to 'strike' with devastating effect by ceasing to produce the desired commodities and to concentrate instead on food crop production which fetched better prices in the towns and was less effectively subject to state control. This in turn brought home the crisis that had generally caught up with African agriculture – its failure to compete on the world market or even to produce sufficient surplus to feed the continually growing towns. From the end of colonial rule on, African agricultural production grew more slowly than the overall population particularly where local markets did not grow substantially.

The 1973 drought struck the entire sub-desert belt of West Africa. Herds and populations had grown in part thanks to new wells which now ran dry. Moving southwards pastoralists antagonised cultivators and were forced to sell herds. Large refugee populations built up in the main administrative centres such as the capital of Mauritania, Nouakchott, and the capital of Niger, Niamey, where food relief was given out. Military coups swept out the regimes in Mauritania and Niger. In Senegal the drought led the peasantry to refuse to grow groundnuts. They were openly supported by the Murid shaykhs. Nor did conditions change with the improved weather. By 1980 Senegalese groundnut exports had fallen to pre-World War II levels and could no longer keep pace with the bills for imported oil alone. The roster of African countries increasingly unable to feed themselves – oil-rich Nigeria, 'socialist' Tanzania, 'revolutionary' Angola, 'neo-colonial' Zaïre are just a few – was long and depressing.

Where possible, African states (and by implication, Western businesses) turned to minerals for export earnings. Most countries in the western and more mineralised half of the continent had come to depend on minerals by the late 1970s for most of their export income. Nigeria was the greatest success story here as Africa's premier oil exporter. Oil exports allowed the Nigerian economy and state revenues to expand spectacularly in an apparently costless way, without qualitative social change. Production is extremely capital intensive and requires few workers while the state derives an enormous rent for allowing the transnational oil oligopolies to extract Nigerian natural resources.[2] This largesse can then be distributed along well-established lines of patronage and used to reinforce the existing social order. This apparently perfect success formula for the Nigerian surplus-absorbing class, however, brought its problems – severe inflation, the extension of unproductive services in an imbalanced way, the pressure on agriculture unable to compete with food imports and the consequent proletarianisation of peasants by the hundred thousand. Within the cities all clambered to get their little share of the available goods. In the words of the novelist Felix Iyayi, 'everywhere life was one heated and confused argument, leading nowhere'.[3] State expenditures began to skyrocket to absorb revenues. There were many less spectacular mineral exporters who none the less were also in a stronger position to avoid challenges to the state through selling goods produced by only a tiny fraction of workers: Guinea, the world's largest holder of bauxite reserves, phosphate-selling Togo, oil and manganese-exporting Gabon, uranium-rich Niger, to name but a few.

Crisis after 1980

In the 1970s, the state of African economies was decidedly mixed. Many countries were suffering from a decline in the value of the agricultural commodities that they sold to the world while many of the post-colonial elected governments had given way to military regimes or degenerated into corrupt dictatorial systems. However, for those countries, most notably Nigeria but also Angola, the Congo Republic and Gabon and later Cameroun, the dramatic hike in oil prices after 1973 provided windfall incomes. Moreover, the price of some mineral products such as phosphates and uranium continued to hold good. The Niger Sahara yielded uranium deposits for the French nuclear industry while unprecedented diamond discoveries on the edge of the Kalahari in Botswana became DeBeers' main money spinner; both states, which had seemed hopelessly poor at independence, profited considerably. Aid conditions were not unfavourable. Talk of a new international order in trade relationships found prominent and respectable support.

Before 1980, few African states were significantly in debt. From the end of the 1970s however, the situation deteriorated very substantially. The 1980s were marked by a decline in production and income per capita in most African countries, a declining share in world trade participation and an impending sense of crisis. At the material heart of this lay rising African debt. Recycled petrodollars had begun to flow into the wealthiest and most bankable countries such as Zaïre and the Ivory Coast. After 1980, changes in the financial regimes in America and Europe suddenly saw these debts mount, measured in hard currency, as Western banks called them in seeking greater liquidity. The prices of virtually all of Africa's export commodities deteriorated quite sharply in comparison to imported manufactured and capital goods. Once it had looked relatively plausible to evaluate international commercial relationships in terms of national exploitation: rich countries sought cheap raw materials for their industries and working populations in return for little. Now it increasingly appeared that the poor countries of Africa were simply left out of the picture, forced to accept less and less for commodities that the world could manage without.

Aid that came with strings gave way to loans on harder terms. Africa had learnt to gain something from the competition for favours between different donors and from Western fears of 'losing' another chunk of territory to Communism. In the 1980s, the West increasingly ceased to bother with this kind of competition, while a crisis-laden Soviet Union dropped out of the race and a booming but inward-looking People's Republic of China lost interest. Aid consolidated. At the start of the 1980s, the Bretton Woods institutions – the World Bank and International Monetary Fund (or IFIs) – increasingly took charge of the whole aid game barring humanitarian relief, not so much in sourcing aid but in giving the go-ahead to aid projects and certifying the worth of recipient countries. Squeezed to the limit, every African country was forced to proceed through what were generally termed 'structural adjustment programmes' (SAPs), engineered by the Bank.

The World Bank itself had undergone a dramatic transformation. It had already shifted its international interests to developing countries and was employing a growing army of relevant experts. While the Bank had previously supported industrialisation efforts and assumed the leading role of the state in developing nations, it now returned to precepts that had marked orthodox economic policy in the long ago days before the great depression. For the bankers, the villains in Africa were the governments of the continent. These were now defined as fundamentally parasitic, 'rent-seeking', corrupt, wasteful and living beyond their means. Thus, even the welfare functions they had undertaken were unaffordable, if worthy, endeavours. The Bank went rural; it was committed to agrarian reform and development as the key to further progress in Africa. The African states were said to be subject to 'urban bias'; they squeezed rural producers to advantage unproductive urban dwellers who were ballooning in numbers as well as in their ability to cause political trouble.

The IFIs now insisted that Africans must learn the lesson that intensifying economic links with the world economy was an unmitigated blessing, as though the dependency school had never existed. If this meant abandoning support for unviable secondary industry in order to concentrate on sectors of the economy where African countries held a so-called comparative advantage in terms of trade, i.e. in the sale of primary agricultural and extractive products, so much the better. Even where more generous counsels prevailed, this kind of wisdom was ensconced. Thus the Lomé Convention of 1975 – renewed at intervals thereafter – guaranteeing entry to Europe of African agricultural products (which did not compete with home-grown ones) offered little incentive to structural change in Africa. Alternative sources of aid, such as the Scandinavian countries, were no longer prepared to support African efforts to find a different road to development. If these precepts were pressed on Africa sincerely and were little different than the new economic wisdom being taught to everyone, even in Western countries, it was just possible to detect an element of sly satisfaction and revenge against the spirit of charged African nationalism lurking under these cool prescriptions. The Lagos Plan of Action, adopted by the Organisation of African Unity (OAU) just before the World Bank released its report, *Accelerated Development in Sub-Saharan Africa*, in 1981, reiterated once again what African intellectuals themselves thought important: the imperative of industrialisation; the need for countries on the continent to co-operate closely and develop in tandem; the requirement for Western participation in some kind of new order that would open windows of opportunity to African producers. This line of argument was simply swept aside.

In the context of the debt crisis where African countries such as Ghana, Mozambique or Tanzania were starved of foreign goods, pressure to adopt this development approach as the only possible means of restarting the economy became apparent sooner or later. This was an even more striking development perhaps in those lands such as the Ivory Coast, Kenya or Malawi which had been the darlings of the Right, had experienced significant economic growth through following the precepts of an earlier orthodoxy, and which were now the more precipitately plunged into crisis, precisely because they had been entrusted with generous loans and had prospered on the basis of promoting cash crop production whose international purchasing power was now fading. Where the equivalent SAP programmes instituted painful shock medicine in countries such as Britain or Malaysia, in Africa they became indefinite, renewed in phases as the need for credits and loan from overseas piled up.

The heart of the theory behind structural adjustment was financial, summarised in breezy catchphrases of the age such as 'getting prices right' or 'market clearing prices'. Inconvertible African currencies that could buy little and were illicitly traded for small sums on street corners were to be replaced with readily available convertible money at whatever exchange rate the market could bear and import controls were to be removed. Beyond this, governments were pressured to reduce spending of all sorts, to privatise or sell state assets, especially those with monopoly control over economic activities, to cut the numbers of civil servants and aim at balancing the budget. State farms, state commercial monopolies and other such activities were to be disbanded. Unproductive industries were to be denied support.

Of particular importance was insistence on the removal of market controls over African farming; marketing boards were, if not disbanded, deprived of their monopoly authority to purchase particular crops. On the assumption that the prices which had been offered producers were consistently low and exploitative, this, it was hoped, would lead to a new resurgence in African agriculture. If colonial planning had placed considerable emphasis in its day on food security in the countryside, this was now to be abandoned or minimised in favour of letting market prices alone regulate production and distribution.

Structural adjustment in Ghana and Uganda

Could structural adjustment work in practice? Perhaps the best places to test this hypothesis are Ghana and Uganda. Ghana after 1981 and Uganda after 1986 were the scene of popular new governments that came to power by force and seemed to represent a new brush sweeping the scene. In both cases, by contrast with most of Africa, economic growth rates were high, approximately five per cent or more in Ghana through the decade of the 1980s and even higher in Uganda by the middle 1990s. Paradoxically, the central figures of these regimes, Jerry Rawlings and Yoweri Museveni, were at first identified as heroes of the radical left.[4] The first was the gallant air force officer unprepared to sit aside and tolerate the continued decay of Ghana whilst Museveni, a youthful intellectual unwilling to accept the results of the post-Amin election in 1980, took to the countryside and eventually marched triumphantly into Kampala after years of popular insurrection in the Luwero Triangle of northern Buganda. The president, Obote once again, was overweening and corrupt and proved unable to bring the predatory state of Idi Amin under control; indeed, it is often argued that the post-Amin Obote years were worse than those under Amin in terms of abuses against human rights. Both Rawlings and Museveni could be identified particularly with hostility to the residue of indirect rule, the governance of chiefs and so-called traditional authorities upholding ethnic claims in the countryside. Both were astute strategists who seemed to bear comparison in stature not unfavourably with their predecessors, Nkrumah and Nyerere, in the previous generation. Both championed and based themselves on new institutions of apparently direct democracy in the countryside and supported the cause of poor producers. Both, however, after short stints in power, decided to accept the logic of the SAPs and became energetic champions of measures designed to promote them as thoroughly as possible.

Evaluating the two governments requires taking a number of issues into consideration. There were certainly real benefits in the financial reforms instituted. If currencies such as the Ghanaian cedi and the Ugandan shilling were now worth very little, at least they were completely and conveniently convertible. The goods flowed back into shops and what people earned was now worth something. Higher salaries chasing non-existing goods had at any event become valueless.

Most observers also find a genuine shift in returns to agricultural producers. In Ghana, while cocoa producers had been earning as little as a quarter of the value of their crop, their returns rose now to approximately half the value. Ghana also benefited from a major innovation, new cocoa strains that permitted trees to thrive on previously exhausted land. In Uganda, while the coffee marketing board continued to have a significant role in processing, it no longer controlled buying and this advantaged many growers. Both Ghana and Uganda found areas in the economy to privatise. The most profitable gold mine in Ghana, Ashanti Gold Fields, was sold to foreign interests and refurbished, becoming once again a major source of foreign exchange. In Uganda, the Asians expelled under Idi Amin had their property restituted and their numbers started to increase again significantly in the 1990s. The Madhvanis, for instance, rehabilitated the sugar estates around Jinja and sugar again became a prosperous concern in Uganda. In Uganda, particularly, the good public image created by adherence to the SAP itself not only attracted continuous flows of aid: a small tourist industry developed and some international organisations moved their operations from Nairobi, beset by crime and physical dangers, to Kampala, rendered safe by Museveni's demilitarisation of Ugandan society. At least some aspects of physical infrastructure were renewed or reconstructed.

The limits to SAP success need to be signalled as well, however. First, the meaner, leaner state demanded by aid donors meant that the welfare provisions on which the state's legitimacy historically depended was not only not restored but in some respects fell back further. Privatised education, social welfare and health care are not only extremely inequitable and unlikely to create adequate coverage, they also place key decisions about policy in the hands of foreign donors, the so-called non-governmental organisations or NGOs, and their local partners. NGOs have their origins effectively in charities. However, in the structural adjustment environment they became aid and development theorists. Collapsing national systems were to some extent replaced by NGO projects. NGOs became sources for original and innovative interventions but there was never any intention of long-term commitment. Fashions for aid projects changed and what became an increasingly professionalised world depended on the ideas of the donors with money, often in fact sourced from the foreign governments that had supposedly withdrawn from the picture. Foreign-based NGOs spawned local NGOs which operated as intermediaries between donors and recipients and occupied an important economic niche, especially in poorer countries. Uganda, for example, was before 2000 probably the African country most seriously affected by the AIDS epidemic but it had no capacity to establish and finance even a basic national health policy; NGOs stepped into this gap as best they could.

Second, important elements of the economy are not really restored by means of SAPs. Secondary industry, for instance, cannot really be revived according to the dictates of the SAP. It might be more instructive to turn here momentarily to Zimbabwe, because of the relatively important weight of industry in the Zimbabwean economy. When Zimbabwe adopted the ESAP, its own version of structural adjustment, after 1990, it opened its gates wide to foreign industrial competition. Zimbabwean industry was completely unable to adapt and by the mid-1990s major companies were closing down and a significant deindustrialisation of the economy ensued. The end of international sanctions against South Africa in particular proved to be an unfortunate coincidence for Zimbabwean industrialists.

Third, both Ghana and Uganda were countries whose economies had regressed very substantially in the post-colonial period. The gains that were achieved under SAPs were impressive but they started from very low points on the graph. Thus in Ghana, production figures achieved in the middle 1990s were only on a level or somewhat higher than those of twenty years earlier. This was quite a different proposition from one that could assert a whole new trajectory of growth. If Uganda became a favourite of aid donors, it is important to signal that the state budget continued to depend heavily on aid, despite an aura of self-reliance.

Finally, even when they were most successful, it was a success that at best tended to restore the colonial structures of the economy. Dreams of pan-African co-operation, industrialisation that could sustain the rapid growth of African cities and even the most basic of development desiderata – increased productivity and skill levels – were set aside in this mind-frame. Africa has massive needs for social and physical infrastructure which can only hope to benefit investors indirectly and in the long term, however judiciously constructed. There is little scope for such investment on a hard money basis. Given the strength of feeling of the class that had come to power within the African state, denationalisation of state enterprise and renewed entry of foreign owners and investors represented a dramatic historic reversal. Yet only a limited range of conventional investments interested foreigners (for instance, almost nothing in Ghana outside the mining sector). Even the warmest defenders of structural adjustment could not claim to find much sign of new investment flowing into these model countries. The World Bank began to have a strong stake in continuing their viability so liquid resources continued to be made available to them but they cannot be said to be paying back the accumulated debts that initiated the crisis in the first place. Some debt forgiveness to well-behaved structural adjustment pupils, however, took place with time.

If we turn from Ghana and Uganda to elsewhere, the record of the SAPs in promoting African development is more consistently unsuccessful. Zambia was a nearly test case for them, associated with the electoral defeat of Kenneth Kaunda in 1991 and his replacement by Frederick Chiluba in a fair multi-party election. In Zambia, the basis of the colonial and post-colonial economy was copper. While problems of mismanagement in the nationalised copper mines were significant, they coincided with a drastically reduced price of world copper. President Kaunda had alienated the miners and Chiluba was the political heir of Simon Kapwewe, once a United National Independence Party (UNIP) stalwart who turned against Kaunda; Chiluba benefited from the disillusionment in consequence. As elsewhere, currency reform did allow for goods to flow into Zambia again but at prices that few could pay. There was no fundamental basis in production that could power the restoration of the Zambian economy. Chiluba counselled Zambians to 'die a little' and they did. In Malawi, the government was pressurised to abandon the colonial habit of storing foodstocks as counter to market dominance; the result in a famine was dearth and unnecessary deaths. For donors at the time, corruption was a far more exciting issue than whether poor Malawians lived or died.

The growing reliance in development discourse on the 'informal sector', the economy unregulated by the state and able to absorb an apparently unlimited amount of human labour, is problematic. It often seems to make a virtue of necessity; the breakdown of the formal wage-granting part of the economy forces people to survive through small-scale production, commerce and activities not sanctioned by the state. It is true that there are windows of opportunity in this sector. In much of Africa, it is only here that women, no longer able to function within the mechanisms of the large patriarchal family, and far less likely than men to find waged labour, are able to survive. None the less, 'survive' is all most denizens of the informal sector can do. Only a few accumulate within this sector successfully and then according to networks which are understudied and not well understood. Certainly it is likely that those with state connections, past or present, are still apt to be the best placed, whether in dealing with actual economic structures functioning autonomously of the purview of the state or in terms of advantageous arrangements with foreigners. In Zaïre, where the 'second economy' was so powerful and obvious, the state appeared to be a parasite that lived off a burgeoning, highly commercialised and unregulated world. The decline of the state promoted this development rather than the prototypical fantasy of a mean, lean capitalist state that delivers the goods.

Indeed privatisation operates in a very different context in Africa from the European model that its ideological sponsors have had in mind. In Africa, 'rent-seeking bureaucrats' were hardly just a useful fiction and reform aimed at weeding them out made sense, but to a large extent it was precisely these individuals who were able to arrange reform to suit themselves. Thus, in the once radical epigone state of Guiné-Bissau, Rosemary Galli and Jocelyn Jones considered that this class was able to use new ideological currents to stake out for itself profitable areas for its activities, effectively on a monopoly basis. For Galli and Jones, the economic history of radically different stages in the terms of development was a history of renegotiated relations between the domestic class of officials and the international donor bureaucracy. Galli has pointed particularly to the activities of the *ponteiros*, 'merchants and concessionaires who have direct ties to the state class' who have been the principal beneficiaries of the liberalisation of the economy. In the evocatively named *Tropical Gangsters*, Robert Klitgaard paints a similar picture from the perspective of a reforming World Bank-linked advisor in Equatorial Guinea. The growing importance of Western NGOs required local partners and it was this class which fulfilled this need the best. The hunger for Western currency pressed educated Africans into the service of whatever activities were negotiable in this sense.

Klitgaard has put much energy into the small states of West Africa. In the unusual case of Equatorial Guinea, large oil reserves created a special advantageous situation. However the Gambia essentially lives off smuggling as has in the past Togo while Guiné-Bissau, the former Portuguese colony, has a notorious reputation as a way station in the drug trade. Jean-François Bayart has argued for the importance of illicit and blackmailed commerce as being a considerable part of Africa's insertion into globalised economic circuits while Kate Meagher has written that:

> A close empirical examination of African clandestine economies (or informal cross-border trade, aka 'smuggling') reveals that they have always involved a variety of elements, ranging from responses to economic distortions through indigenous entrepreneurship to criminalization, depending on which countries or regions one is looking at, and when. In some countries, such as Nigeria, clandestine trade has weakened industrialization efforts and undermined the formal economy; in others, such as Benin or the Gambia which derive significant state revenue from operating as local import hubs, clandestine trade is central to the organization of the formal economy. In still other countries, such as Sierra Leone or the Democratic Republic of the Congo (DRC), clandestine economies are bound up with rebels and rogue military forces that ravage the state and society, while in contrasting cases, like Senegal or Somaliland, such trade has actually contributed to economic revival and processes of state formation.[5]

In Senegal, the protected little world of consumer goods industries, dating back to late colonial times and largely owned by French businessmen, collapsed in good part because influential Senegalese, notably associated with the Muridiyya religious order, were primarily interested in imports and free entrance of industrial goods into the country.

Neo-liberal structural adjustment theory altered considerably the model presented earlier of neo-colonialism. In a general way, the particular and sometimes clashing interests of the USA, France and Britain as well as the Soviet Union were now modified by the IFI insistence on rules of behaviour which contained, as we shall see, a regulatory framework for political conduct that would legitimate African states in a way acceptable to the West, in particular and in common. However, from the start, it is essential to realise that these lofty ideals were always compromised to meet realities, realities in which shrewd African leaders were often able to get their way as has, for instance, Museveni. One could certainly assess the policies towards Africa of any particular major state, but for our purposes it seems at least crucial to point out the continued critical involvement of France in African affairs. Françafrique, as the linking agencies and personalities between France and its former colonies (plus occasional other entities such as the old French-speaking Belgian colonies) is called remained a force through to the end of the twentieth century, particularly in the lifetime of the Gaullist Jacques Foccart (1913–97). Foccart could act very ruthlessly against what he saw as traitors to the alliance system but also established close and complex relations with the occasional trusted ally, notably his contemporary President Félix Houphouët-Boigny of the Ivory Coast. In the former French colonies there were French military bases, aid programmes were dominated by France and key resources (for instance oil in Gabon and the Brazzaville Congo) controlled by French companies. The African currencies were interchangeable with French francs and many French businesses continued to operate profitably while ruling elites looked to France for leadership. Deviations, of which there were many, were punished with coups and military interventions. For France, the world of French speech (*Francophonie*) and the dependable links of Françafrique were critical in defining its search for continued status as a great power, more than was the case for any other post-colonial Western state. Thus the French looked unhappily at the efforts of the oil rich Libyan government of Colonel Gaddafi to disperse money to win support from West and Central African states and woo them out of this enchanted circle. As we shall see, these kinds of ties brought phases of stability for some territories for a long period but also provoked crises and proved difficult to sustain.

Given the emphasis in liberal ideology on pushing back the role of the African state, it is tempting indeed to understand a range of serious political crises in the last years of the twentieth century and onwards as a hollowing out of state capacity. However, this would be an oversimplification. The assault of structural adjustment on the state at most aided in rubbing festering wounds with older histories and the crises themselves, by no means universal, are individuated events that are not easy to assimilate into a single pattern. The following chapter, however, tries to discuss the most flagrant and salient and suggest some ways of analysing them.

Notes

1. There is something deeper at stake in the political ferment in Ghana following the second Jerry Rawlings coup which ended civilian rule in 1981.
2. In time, a Nigerian oil company was set up that took an interest in the production companies as an investor.
3. F. Iyayi, *Violence* (Longman, 1979), p. 65.
4. By contrast, a third figure, superficially equivalent, was the young soldier Thomas Sankara, who became prime minister of Upper Volta in a military regime in 1983 and, after struggles that led to his imprisonment, was freed and proclaimed president shortly thereafter. He was a classic example of the radical egalitarian nationalist with strong emotional affinities to liberation movements in Africa and elsewhere, a distaste for the perquisites and measured life of the African bureaucracy, and a romantic longing to stand outside existing social forces. A long-distance runner and lover of the guitar, he was certainly filled with joie de vivre. By contrast with either Museveni or Rawlings, however, he compromised less and less with the forces of international order and was assassinated by a close associate in 1987. From the French perspective, his growing association with Libya would have been a particular problem. His stature in Francophone Africa can be equated with that of Cabral, Nkrumah or Nyerere. He was the last major figure cast in this mould to date. His successor, often associated with his murder, Blaise Compaore, another soldier, became a key figure in the region over many years until he was overthrown in a popular rising in 2014.
5. Kate Meagher, 'Smuggling Ideologies from Criminalisation to Hybrid Governance in African Clandestine Economies', *African Affairs* 113 (453) (2011), p. 498. Meagher correctly stresses that these practices are far from having disappeared in better times.

13

Democracies, Dictatorships and Disasters: Africa into the Twenty-First Century

In the 1990s the very limited successes of structural adjustment, at least in terms that Africans experienced, led to a change in tack. International pressures focused on so-called 'governance', not merely a more limited sort of state that would be purged of 'rent-seeking' and tower above clientelist networking, but one that could also effectively manage a stable, modern capitalist society. African governments were pressured to permit a freeing up of the media, especially the print media, to institute a plausible system of contested elections and to limit the office term of the incumbent president. A respectful pupil could then expect the necessary flow of aid and resources to open up.

One dramatic point here was the speech of French President François Mitterrand at La Baule in 1990. Difficult as it was for the French socialists to challenge the covert agents of French power in Africa associated with Gaullism, the poor economic circumstances gave Mitterrand some slack and he insisted on the need for consultation and opening up the political arena to all parties in the former French colonies. In Francophone countries, the institution of a national conference (*Conférence des forces vives*) in Benin that established an electoral process which unseated Mathieu Kérékou, the once Marxist military dictator, in 1991, was a key catalyst. The institution of civilian rule, opposition parties and a lively press was particularly marked in such countries as Mali, Niger and Madagascar with their very limited experiences of formal democracy. This, however, was the positive side of a contradictory situation. If the networks that had offered something to at least some Africans dried up, the state was in danger of hollowing out, of offering so little that it could in fact become less stable and, under circumstances we will consider a bit later, fall prey to violent forces deriving from outside.

There was also a secondary contradiction which became increasingly salient in the early years of the twenty-first century and tilted the political situation in another direction: the West (indeed perhaps the East as well) desired stability in Africa. If that was the goal, growing tolerance towards African leaders who could manipulate the political situation, perhaps flying in the face of 'good governance', was also increasingly a factor. The Cold War faded in importance as the 1980s wore on but in 2001, the successful attack on the USA by Islamic militants who destroyed the twin towers of the World Trade Center in Manhattan and a section of the Pentagon, with more loss of life than the Japanese had inflicted at Pearl Harbour seventy years earlier, led to a new international polarisation. The 'war on terror', which of course is not a conventional war on definable state forms, cast its shadow on relevant parts of Africa, notably the bombing with large loss of life of the American embassies in Dar es Salaam and Nairobi, and dramatically affected Western relations with the predominantly Muslim countries of West Africa, the Horn of Africa and Sudan. Indeed Islamic networks also, if secondarily, became active in support of what they understood as resistance and the attempt to create a new global moral order by fighting back in Africa. This inevitably distorted the developmental model emanating from the IFIs and their supporters. The view that development can go together smoothly with so-called securitisation is not very convincing. Islam in Africa itself experienced substantial change but that will be left to a further discussion that looks at religion more generally.

An interesting case study here is the republic of Chad. In the very heart of Africa, Chad is a large country, much of its population Muslim, that has abutted on regions beset by violence, notably the southern and western Sudan. It has had a strategic importance for France which intervened more than once in its restive politics. The initial government, run by more educated southerners, was unable to impose itself on the Saharan peoples who effectively overturned the state and control it, by contrast with Mali and Niger, the neighbours to the west where this kind of scenario is desired by some but is not really capable of realisation. At the close of the millennium, it became clear that Chad had considerable reserves in oil. In response, the West insisted that the country agree to a bundle of structural adjustment guarantees in return for the construction of a pipeline. With the spike in oil prices, unprecedented wealth flowed to the government in Ndjamena but Chad is hardly a model of civil society autonomy and democratic governance, although its educated strata have significantly expanded. Instead Chad repaid its debts with the oil money and has succeeded in building up its armed forces. In various crisis situations today Chadian soldiers are prominent (for instance in the neighbouring Central African Republic) in serving with African Union forces and appearing as a force for stability in central Africa. Chad's neighbour, through where the pipeline flows, is Cameroun. Paul Biya, the second president of Cameroun, was still in power as of 2015 at past the age of 80. While Cameroun has passed through electoral processes, it is hardly a secret that it is no model of good governance-style democracy. However, located where it is on the pivot of the western coast of Africa, Cameroun is apparently stable and stability counts for a lot whatever the lofty pronouncements about form of government.

There is a third and final perspective although it will be far more central to the last, subsequent, chapter. Intensified internationalism of economic structures and chains and the ease of cultural interchange and multiple new influences, which we somewhat imprecisely call globalisation, also became a continued presence. However, globalisation has not meant that African countries should be seen as blurring into one another. If similar social and economic trends affect most or all, the particular pieces of the jigsaw puzzle turn out differently in different cases. African countries half a century after independence are discovering their own distinct trajectories, are however not yet really strong enough to influence one another very strongly, and they are in fact diverging increasingly from one another as a result.

Yet it is important to recognise that Africans have over and over again showed a strong preference for democracy and an opposition to dictatorships. Once sterile and robbed of vitality, African regimes have been overthrown from time to time. From the bloody overthrow of Moussa Traore, dictator of Mali in the March Revolution of 1991, to that of Blaise Compaore, long-time ruler of Burkina Faso in 2014, the urban crowd has been at times able to express itself and push out the apparently unmoveable object in power. Students played a key part in Mali. The established churches (for instance in Malawi and in Kenya) and the trade unions, whose influence can be underestimated, played some role in projecting a sense of a discontented civil society in need of democratic institutions. However, here too a counterweight needs to be laid down. Poorly motivated and deracinated youths can be won over to the most implausible offers of liberation as we shall see in our assessment of the collapsing regimes of Liberia and Sierra Leone. Moreover democratic forms can be pushed in the direction of offering 'choiceless' choices, in the words of the Malawian political scientist Thandika Mkandawire, where the inchoate longings of ordinary people for a government that speaks to them are bottled up securely.

The shaky Big Three

This chapter means to consider situations of intense crisis and violence in very recent African history but it might be useful first to sketch some features of three particularly important African countries in the decades around the turn of the twenty-first century: Kenya, Nigeria and the Ivory Coast, which are the sites of short- and long-term problems that exemplify some of the issues sketched above.

Kenya, where the economy depends on tourists from the West, on the export of fresh flowers, tea and coffee, swung around fairly early, if reluctantly, to multi-party elections. The second president, Daniel arap Moi, had his political roots in the late colonial regional opposition in any event. His successors Mwai Kibaki, a stalwart of the old Kikuyu elite, and Jomo's son Uhuru Kenyatta, have succeeded one another in regular elections since 1992 which have also involved party shifts in contradistinction to a number of brutal assassinations in earlier decades that ended the life of key Kenyan politicians such as Tom Mboya. Two dominant facts, as Susanne Mueller has pointed out, go together in surveying this situation. The first is the continued high level of centralisation in power and the second is the intense ethnicised rivalry for spoils and influence. An electoral system ensures that no single ethnic group can control such a system because none has anything like an absolute majority; instead shifting alliances dominate. The dark side of such a system is that manipulation, given high levels of politicians' impunity and corruption, can be coupled with violence aimed at winning the zero-sum game in particular localities.

When the British left Kenya, they had imposed on much of the White Highlands a land settlement aimed at encouraging independent family farms (rather at the expense of poorer families, however). These farms came with title deeds but in fact the Kikuyu households that were the chief beneficiaries organised inheritance, succession and sale in their own way that did not follow British rules. In the renewed democracy of Kenya, and notably with the election of 2007, the state conspired in effect to drive unwanted Kikuyu out of the southern Rift Valley and place Kalenjin, former Moi supporters, in. The game for the centre trumped any orderly drive for capitalist transformation in this fertile, commercially important area which had been relatively empty of people due to internecine violence at the time colonialism established itself.

The Kalenjin were themselves an interesting case. Nobody spoke of Kalenjin people at all until the 1940s except for scholarly linguists. Different groupings were recognised, sometimes rivals and sometimes co-operating with one another. In the late colonial period, the Kalenjin came together and Moi moulded networks amongst them into a potent and lucrative machine. However, in terms of the neo-colonial economy, they were otherwise losers. As Peter Kangwanja points out, this sense of winners and losers and the violent reaction of resentment by the latter has come to play a key role in African countries where only a few are rich and access to power by force if need be is attractive as a way to become less poor. Political rivalries also spread to towns, including Nairobi itself, where 'minorities' were driven out of some poor neighbourhoods. This in turn did provoke a reaction on the part of the growing and maturing Kenyan middle class of whom significant numbers began to look for an alternative kind of practice. The constitution of 2010 has not brought to power innocents who did not participate in this violent game but it may represent the start of a settlement that could stabilise Kenya.

The stability of Kenya is important to the West where it is clearly seen as a kind of frontier against an uncertain Muslim world. If Islam is very much a minority faith in Kenya, of no great consequence for its Establishment, Kenya has been inveigled into military intervention in its neighbour Somalia. The Kenyan army and police, whatever mayhem they have caused to democratic protestors, have shown limited capacity to stop murderous incursions – and indeed Kenya has itself a significant Somali ethnic minority and considerable economic ties that cross the borders.

This same mix of violent reactions from below while a centre has held, more or less, also typified Nigeria once it escaped from the Biafra War episode. Several episodes of state formation left open opportunities to more and more groups of ambitious men (and occasionally women) to share the possibilities created by Nigerian oil wealth. By 2015 there were thirty-six states, all of them entitled to some largesse while the centre continued to control the oil-derived purse strings. Nigeria also was able to design and promote a new central capital city, Abuja, more controllable and more organised than the older colonial and pre-colonial cities of the country although its well-financed centre was shadowed by some impoverished peripheral settlements. Massive and legendary corruption fed into growing private wealth held by individuals. Democratisation permitted an array of publications and newspapers exposing the schemes of competitive accumulators.

However here too there is a dark side, or perhaps various dark sides. Again the anger and frustration of outsiders has been important. Nigeria experiences student movements that have descended into vicious secret societies and crime waves with vigilante organisations turning bad. The low point politically was reached under the administration of Sani Abacha, who seized power in a military coup in 1992 from the structural adjustment-orientated Ibrahim Babangida who was on the verge of instituting civil elections and thus a loss of army control, but Abacha died of a heart attack in 1998. Not only immensely corrupt, Abacha also reacted to opposition with a ferocity unknown before. He will always be associated with the judicial murder of the poet-activist from the oil rich Niger Delta, Ken Saro-Wiwa, as well as with the death in prison of his foremost political opponent, the wealthy businessman and newspaper magnate Chief Mahmood Abiola. With the sudden death of Abacha, however, Nigerian democracy returned for its thus far longest stage. As in Kenya, retaining a central state where revenues were controllable and ratifying power through an electoral process began to be a national characteristic, if still less assured. However, the national state in Nigeria enshrines ethnicity via citizenship in a particular state of origin and encourages the use of ethnic identity as a means of trying for a better life. At its worst, it tolerates and perhaps more than tolerates criminality and the use of force, especially if it does not directly challenge state power which withdraws from some kinds of organisations and confrontations.

Saro-Wiwa's activism connected to the particular problems of the Niger Delta. While the state certainly diverted resources to a local elite there, not much of this money found its way more widely in a particularly corrupt conjuncture and many people suffered from severe environmental deterioration due to the careless, poorly policed activities of the oil companies. The form of politics understood locally was ethnic and Saro-Wiwa spoke for a small ethnic group, the 'Ogoni', largely a post-colonial creation as a bounded group, that sat on some of this ruined but cash-producing soil.[1] The Ogoni movement was harshly suppressed. However the Delta continued to be plagued by criminal gangs, responsible for murders and kidnappings, and capable of setting out to sea to rob platforms off the coast. On land, too, illicit mining spread, giving way in time to the government's licensing of exploration and drilling space to ambitious local entrepreneurs.

The one-time Northern Nigerian region also remained a source of violent conflict. As has been suggested already, sectors with a purchase on mass Islam turned against the apparently corrupted world of emirs, Islamic courts and secularised wealth in the old Muslim towns. In other cities such as Kaduna, once the regional capital created by Lugard and the former tin-mining centre of Jos, militant Muslims and Christians engaged in serious violent confrontations disrupting what had often been tolerant and even easy-going interrelationships. Toward 2010, Muslims, very aware through global communications networks of developments in the Middle East and preaching a new and purified Islam, came together as Boko Haram. Nigerian state agencies were hard pressed to combat this extremely violent movement that came to control key centres in remoter areas, frequently kidnapped or bullied young women in particular to be used as suicide bombers and caused havoc, primarily in the north-eastern part of the country. As with the Delta resistance, while the Nigerian state was hardly likely to fall apart or collapse, its practices did not allow for the apparent consensual order that one might have expected from a diet of electoral alliances and systematic vote counts to determine those in power.

Within Francophone West Africa, the Ivory Coast was by far the economic success story, presided over by France's key ally, President Houphouët-Boigny, in the first two independence decades. Under this regime, the economy was diversified to export, for instance, cotton and pineapples, and a moderate light industrial base was created. Houphouët-Boigny, hardly Africa's harshest dictator, deftly balanced a typical ethnic and regionally based patronage network where individuals strongly identified with their group of origin as collectively evolved in the colonial period but with a welcome to foreigners who ranged from Lebanese businessmen and French professionals to Ghanaian traders and a multitude of farmers renting land according to diverse agrarian property systems in the more commercialised parts of the country. The largest number came from Upper Volta, now Burkina Faso, which had in fact been administered together with the Ivory Coast for a considerable phase under French rule. Their status in the country, however, remained fluid and ambiguous legally; the scale of foreign immigration into the Ivory Coast was completely beyond that of any other part of the former French West Africa. The Nigerian move of capital city was paralleled by Houphouët-Boigny who chose his home town of Yamoussoukro. However, this was an uncharacteristic failure; the life of the state proceeded and proceeds in the cosmopolitan city of Abidjan on the coast.

After 1980, however, virtually every facet of this growth system, still very largely based on agricultural exports, was shaken by poor prices that drove gross national product down by more than one-third and hollowed out the system decisively. Houphouët-Boigny died in 1993 and his political system, which was no longer able to deliver for the population on remotely the same scale, began to collapse. The reaction to this took the form of an intensified national conflict between the largely Muslim north and the largely Christian south. His successor, Henri Konan Bédié, initiated the concept of *ivoirité*, which found a base materially in the issue of identity cards. At its core was the rivalry with his slick former World Bank executive opponent, Alassane Ouattara, who could be excluded from power on the basis of his Upper Volta ancestry and his employment by the Upper Volta government at times, albeit that he was also a Houphouët-Boigny favourite. The institution of *ivoirité* had a rapid and strong effect on identity formation in the country. Northern fears of exclusion led to Bédié's overthrow by a general, Robert Guéï, from outside the south-central core. The sense of a new popular culture based on reaction to economic decline and a desire to exclude the North swept Abidjan and its hinterland. Guéï was himself overthrown in 2000 (and murdered with his wife in 2002) in the first stage of a popular rising that engaged the urban youth, especially, whose hero was the historian Laurent Gbagbo who had earned his spurs defying Houphouët-Boigny years before. Madame Gbagbo signified the cultural break as an influential supporter of militant Pentecostalism. Gbagbo supporters saw the Ivory Coast in terms of the mass culture of the capital city and the south, largely rejecting the old, more balanced, notion of the country.

The Ivory Coast in this sense exhibits a cultural turn that was true in Nigeria and influential there too but far less so in the development of Kenyan politics. However, like Kenya, the willingness of politicians to play the ethnic card in the most murderous and dangerous ways proved compelling and they had their eyes on the whole prize.

Gbagbo, although he had some northern allies, was quite unable to control the situation in the northern half of the country and civil war ensued with a division that remained in place until the agreement to hold an election in 2010. Gbagbo antagonised the French, for whom this country had remained so central to the whole Françafrique set-up, and this reached a climax when an airstrike resulted in the death of several French soldiers in the north responsible for keeping the truce since 2004. In response the French destroyed the whole national air force and Gbagbo became a national hero of resistance to France. Yet, as the 2010 count revealed, only with the exclusion of some northern districts could Gbagbo claim a victory and, when he attempted to do this, the army (in which the north was very well-represented) moved to seize Abidjan and finally to take Gbagbo prisoner in the presidential palace. At last it was Ouattara, to the satisfaction of France and no doubt the IFIs, who acceded to power early in 2011. What kind of stabilisation of the situation the Ivory Coast might witness remains to be seen.

It might be worth very briefly considering, however, the two model 1990s structural adjustment regimes considered in the previous chapter as well as some others. Jerry Rawlings had seized power in Ghana but ran successfully for president against opposition in 1992 and 1996. He ceded power to his former vice-president in 2000 and since then Ghana has followed the routine of good governance with ruling parties changing in office. This is not true for Museveni in Uganda whose foibles will be explored further in this chapter. However, the Francophone match for stability in West Africa could be said to be Senegal. When Abdoulaye Wade refused to abandon the idea of a third term in office in 2012, a large-scale popular movement finally forced him to reconsider. This underscores once again the dislike of the African street for dictators and corrupt machine politicians that has surfaced repeatedly. A third model republic thus far of democratic succession in West Africa has been Benin. Here the one-time radical military ruler, Matthieu Kérékou – 'the Chameleon' – was returned to office in a contested election and became president again from 1996 to 2006.[2] These examples, together with the overall picture given of southern African political life, belie the 'dark ages' imagery that behind the scenes is so popular in the West; the reality is complex. These are examples, instead, of working democracies according to the IFI criteria.

Collapsed states

There are also a few examples that fit the stereotypical view of Africa as the home of failed states. While it is argued that this is not particularly typical or caused by the machinations of neo-liberal policies alone, in some circumstances the post-colonial state structure has proven so hollow or irrelevant that this is not incorrect to see collapse as a way of looking at matters.

One key weakness of certain states has been the general prevalence of extreme centralisation of power. In most of the developed world, it is not inaccurate to draw a map defining a certain territory and consider that what lies within those boundaries constitutes the writ of a state. However, in Africa this is rarely the case. Power emanates from the centre and with it the capacity to construct and maintain physical infrastructure and provide social infrastructure. As one casts a gaze further and further from that centre, this power weakens and the presence of the state is weak. Few African states have the wherewithal to patrol extensive waters or to control the air in regions that are remote or inhabited by few people. Thus border regions have a life of their own and often an economy of their own based on the uneven market prices on offer within different political entities.

States also find difficulty in maintaining effective command over large-scale arid regions inhabited only by pastoralist communities. The impoverished Sahelian states have little to offer to their Saharan territories in the way of services or desirable facilities and desert people tend to be restive in accepting the authority of distant sedentary states. Yet the Sahara is far from being the romantic site of an older European imagination. Borders hard to plug in combine with the effective penetration of modern vehicles to breathe life into oasis settlements that burgeon and attract ever larger cosmopolitan populations – merchants, pastoralists, travellers and migrants.

A further condition that attracts secession movements as we have already seen in the case of Biafra is the presence of some kind of major resource yielding hard money to a locally dominant group. An example already noted is the diamond resources of the interior of Angola which were milked by Jonas Savimbi of UNITA. Control over coltan mining in the Democratic Republic of the Congo, very valuable as cellphone usage mushroomed, fuelled conflicts in the east in this way. The presence of diamonds, oil or some other equivalent substance allows the possibility of a guerrilla movement sustaining itself and in some cases promoting the cause of some sort of territorial sovereignty breaking through colonial frontiers, although in fact secession has not very often been on the cards in Africa. Competing 'ethnicities' are far more inclined to form alliances and to strive to control the resources of the centre than to try to break away entirely.

When resources and space are available, there is less difficulty in attracting manpower to form an insurrection. As we shall argue systematically, the older social structures in Africa as adapted by colonial rulers are both attenuating and losing their cultural and emotional hold on the rapidly growing number of young people. Without opportunities to improve their livelihoods in terms of access to the emerging consumer societies, they become available to armed bands prepared to structure their lives and provide some kind of hope for a purposeful existence. These factors – a potential armed force of youths, a source of ready money, a difficult to assail geographical base and the absence of a civil society institutionally able to resist force – have come together to make border regions ungovernable at times and, in certain cases, to overwhelm state institutions entirely. Attempts to resist violent incursions on the part of roughly traditional vigilante groups, such as the Kamajor hunters in Sierra Leone, have enjoyed only a limited success in this kind of maelstrom.

A final element to add to the mix has been the involvement of determined outside forces, particularly at a local level. In the first cases to be examined, this can be seen in the way that Libyan propaganda and support excited a misbegotten Sierra Leonean would-be vanguard while Libya tried to contest with the West for influence in West Africa. The initial fighting in Liberia, taken up in the heavily forested south-east, probably relied on back-up from the Ivory Coast where Houphouët-Boigny resented bitterly the coup that had overthrown and killed his friend, President Tolbert.

Starting in 1992 a decade of complete disorder marked by extreme acts of violence swept through the small West African adjoining countries of Sierra Leone and Liberia. Initially both had been associated with the ascendancy of local elites with a particular history. In Liberia, it was a question of the Americo-Liberians, largely the descendants of former American freedmen who chose to come to Africa before the US Civil War. While they formed commercial and clientage relationships with the people of the Liberian interior, they promoted in their pseudo-democracy a culturally dominant façade of civilisation. This was also true of the Creoles of Sierra Leone, descended from other American and British freedmen together with those liberated by the British Navy from slave ships in the early nineteenth century. In the decolonisation era, however, the hegemony of these two groups frayed and then vanished.

William Tubman, the most dynamic Liberian president of the twentieth century, used revenues from vast Firestone rubber plantations and iron ore mines to begin a modernisation process that created a new kind of elite. The old patrimonial networks were outstripped and lost traction. In 1980 his successor William Tolbert was overthrown and murdered in a coup staged by Master Sergeant Samuel Doe. Doe's cruelty and crudeness were for a long time overlooked by American backers who had seen their old dominance in Liberia weaken for a time and felt that they could control Doe. Liberian society was changing. Stephen Ellis writes that

> Children attended school primarily to learn the speech and manners of a burgher, in which patterns of consumption and clothing played an important part. Positions of power and authority in 'traditional' society, dominated by chiefs who claimed to represent a pure tribal culture, were unattractive to members of a younger generation who found in education an alternative source of advancement. This considerably diminished the grip of chiefs and elders generally on rural society.[3]

In 1989 an invading force led by the adventurer Charles Taylor, an Americo-Liberian who had successfully escaped from a prison sentence in the USA, and with collusion from the Ivory Coast, created havoc in the thick forests of eastern Liberia under these circumstances. Taylor promoted unprecedented brutality. His forces included adolescents and children, both boys and girls, torn loose from weakened rural societies, and they probably engaged in ritual killing as well as creating frightening and striking imagery through paint and masks that mingled modern and ancient symbolism in a parody of some kind of lost

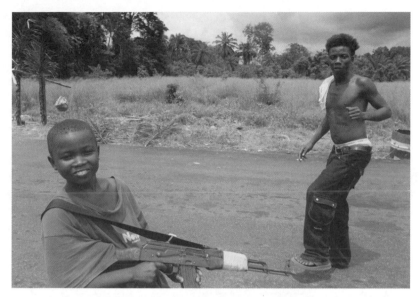

Figure 13.1   Child Soldiers in the Liberian Civil War. Reproduced with the kind permission of Greg Marinovich

spiritual order. In 1990 Taylor's forces took Monrovia and tortured and killed Doe brutally on camera. The old Liberian elite now turned against Taylor but were unable to figure out how to turn the situation around. One answer lay in a force of West African troops (ECOWAS) but when elections could be organised it was Taylor who won and remained in power between 1997 and 2003 when he in turn was overthrown by a guerrilla group and fled Liberia.

This devastating story was mirrored just to the north-west in Sierra Leone. The dominant political figure in Sierra Leone for a generation was Siaka Stevens, a trade unionist who got to know intimately the world of the artisanal diamond miners in the part of the country near Liberia and formed close ties with Lebanese merchants who bought the diamonds. The old corporate management of the diamond fields was wound up and the country came to depend, in the context of structural adjustment and poor national budgets, on these illegal links. Stevens retired in 1985 but his replacement, Joseph Momoh, was corrupt and weak. Indeed, a striking feature of the descent into hell of Sierra Leone was the corruption and indiscipline of its violent soldiery. The term *sobel* would gain currency for men who were soldiers in uniform by day and violent gangs of robbers supporting a rebel cause by night. Momoh was overthrown in 1992. At this point, the Revolutionary United Front invaded Sierra Leone from Liberia with the collusion of Taylor and resources from diamond digging that fuelled a situation where relatively limited numbers of fighters were able to silence and terrorise civil society. A first phase of bush warfare ended with ECOWAS intervention and an election in 1996. However the new president was overthrown within a year and a yet harsher phase ensued with perhaps the worst point being the reign of terror in the capital Freetown in 1999. Foday Sankoh, a paranoid, brutal ex-corporal who had spent years in jail was the equivalent of Doe or Taylor in Sierra Leone. If the Kamajor militias had been able to take on Sankoh for a time in some regions of the country, this second phase required a set of interventions, notably by ECOWAS, by the largely South African mercenary outfit of Executive Outcomes and finally by a British military force prepared to do more than just take defensive action. From 1998 the situation started to come under control and notably so after Sankoh's death and Taylor's elimination from power in Liberia in 2003.

Here too descriptions are striking of the hollowing out particularly of the structure of chiefs, secret societies and other forms of rural association that had long stabilised society in the Sierra Leone hinterland. Sankoh and some others had not merely the influence of Taylor but also exposure through the Green Book to the glorious nationalist and anti-Western ideology of Libya that came with some military materiel. Here too there were many child soldiers, perhaps one-third of them girls, enabled by the simplicity of deadly gun handling and removed from family and village controls. Swept away by supernatural imagery and with a way to apparent power opened through terror rather than mass support, they were fortunately also rather easily reintegrated into society later. However they were often the victims as well as the perpetrators of brutal mutilations, a hallmark of this decade of wars. This kind of warfare recalled the popular struggles in the Congo during the 1960s but politically it was yet less acute and largely inchoate. Yet it did have an edge to it, a feeling of the fight of the excluded and marginalised, however poor the quality of the leadership.

Turning to a second region away from the so-called Mano River states (a grouping that also tends to include the republic of Guinea) a second area of state collapse, or state overthrow better put, with a very different point of origin is to be denoted in central, ex-Belgian Africa. The small, if heavily populated, country of Rwanda had not ranked very high in interest for students of African society and politics after independence in 1960. As mentioned earlier, the once highly favoured Rwandan elite dubbed an ethnic group – the Tutsi – were essentially pushed aside and the monarchy abolished. Violent spates (1959, 1962) led to many Tutsi fleeing the country, especially to Uganda, once the destination of many migrant workers from Rwanda in the cotton and coffee industries. Young Tutsi in Uganda were poorly integrated while others, scattered in Western countries, often benefited from good education and work experience. When Museveni went to battle with Obote and his successors, young Tutsi were recruited and became crucial to the success of this guerrilla force. After his victory, however, Museveni struggled to find a place for them in a now very impoverished Uganda and he settled on supporting armed intervention in Rwanda.

Rwanda's chief foreign backer was no longer Belgium but France. It had the image of a land of well-ordered, industrious peasants held together by a revolution that had overthrown a class of feudalists in what were described as *jacqueries* as though the French Revolution had come alive again. Hutu memories of the demands for harvests and labour imposed in Belgian times by Tutsi chiefs were also not dead. Those Tutsi who remained in the country were largely excluded from government (although past social capital tended to make them on average more educationally successful and subsequently prosperous) and the population lived off the story that nothing could be worse to imagine than that they might return to power. For years, the insurrection in the north begun from Uganda did not get very far. However, in the early 1990s and with growing international pressure to establish a more plausible democracy plus declining aid budgets, Juvénal Habyarimana, the Rwandan leader, began to enter into negotiations about a reintegration of Tutsi into Rwanda. Returning home from Arusha, Tanzania, where the talks were being held, Habyarimana, himself a former military coup-leader who favoured a clique from his home region, was killed when his plane was shot down by still undetermined missile firers. Circles close to power in Rwanda, faced with the growing successes of the Rwandan Patriotic Front (RPF) in the north and very hostile to the possible change in power, spread, notably through the radio – Radio Mille Collines (A Thousand Hills) – a message of hatred and fear, urging local notables to organise the mass murder of Tutsi in the country.

Most commentators have accepted that this was in fact a genocide of Tutsi, although many Hutu individuals, descendants of cultivators who were married to Tutsi spouses or who clearly favoured the reforms bruited by Habyarimana, were also killed. The scale of these killings, in the hundreds of thousands, was overwhelming, yet it has to be said that the retreating Hutu state possessed neither gas chambers nor weapons of mass destruction; the dead were victims of assault by axe, machete and hammer, farm tools that were to hand. Well over 500,000 died including perhaps two-thirds of the resident Tutsi population. Far from the context of a failed state, the killings were impressively well organised at the behest of the old government. As the RPF advanced under the leadership of Paul Kagame into the heartland of the country, an even larger number of ordinary people panicked and fled, finding refuge over the border in Zaïre, notably in the huge refugee camp at Goma.

It cannot be said that foreigners had a special affection for the not especially harsh old regime on the whole, but resident French aid workers and military men attached to Rwanda were slow to grasp what was happening and covered the retreat of their people, the so-called *génocidaires*, out of the country. The relative indifference of the USA and other Western countries (by contrast to the situation thousands of miles away in Sierra Leone) was remarkable and caused enormous later anguish when the scale of the catastrophe was realised. It is perhaps unsurprising that books about this hitherto obscure land emanated from Paris by the dozen in the following decades, often reinterpreting its history in a way that properly questioned the ethnic determinism that had little bearing in reality, although it had become a dominant discourse in colonial times. The mass killings were at the behest of a state-linked network determined to stay in power, not the product of some kind of deep inexplicable hatred of the other.

There is far less angst about Rwanda's southern neighbour Burundi, also a densely populated, well-watered country once administered jointly within Ruanda-Urundi and with a similar social structure. In Burundi the elite were not attracted to Lumumba and did not take positions that frightened the Belgians. Prince Louis Rwagasore, the most impressive nationalist figure, died in an air crash in 1961. Thus independence saw the entrenchment of the equivalent Tutsi faction to the one that was toppled in Rwanda.[4] Tensions increased in response to events in Rwanda and in 1972 Burundi witnessed a smaller earlier genocide aimed at the Hutu elite, killing perhaps 100,000 people, a terrible event hardly noticed in the English-speaking world. It led to a refugee situation as well with major refugee camps in neighbouring Tanzania, where the Nyerere regime tended to identify with the 'commoner' Hutus and the post-1960 Rwanda government. Eventually and simultaneously with the Rwandan crisis, Burundi achieved, not without violence, assassinations and continued tensions, an easier passage to a tentatively more inclusive but still unstable society.

If events in Rwanda led to the destabilisation of Burundi, the impact on the other former Belgian colony, Zaïre, dwarfed this in scale. The Kagame government was understandably anxious about its enemies grouped together across the border in the midst of huge refugee camps that were only closed down with the inhabitants sent home many years later; for long, well-meant international aid kept these camps going. Armed forces began to rally and Kagame began to enter schemes about the future of what was to become the Democratic Republic of the Congo (DRC), as Zaïre was renamed. The immense Congo really deserved more than most, as we have seen in earlier discussions, the label of a failed state. During the 1990s as Mobutu aged, he presided over a complex game in which numerous rivals contested for potential support in a huge constituent assembly created to meet the pressure of foreign donors. Yet in reality aid budgets were cut as Mobutu, no longer a Cold War stalwart and no longer remembered as the successor to the unreliable Lumumba, presided over a steady decline and collapse of infrastructure and the economic wherewithal of a modern state. The crucial copper revenues from Katanga (as Shaba would be renamed) virtually disappeared. With its aura of rich natural resources, this was a rotten fruit ripe for the picking.

Most of the neighbours of the DRC would participate in a complex series of military manoeuvres accompanied by looting and questionable, reversible deals concerning mines and other resources. Angola, Zimbabwe and Uganda were all involved. However, the most critical intervention was on the part of Kagame who resurrected an ancient warrior from Che Guevara's time, Laurent-Desiré Kabila. A dramatic march from east to west under the headship of Kabila finally brought the Mobutu regime to an end in Kinshasa itself in 1997, a city which offered very few jobs but held millions of former refugees from previous fighting as well as most of the country's professionally trained citizens. In this instance, Kinshasa itself suffered from destructive riots by soldiers themselves where it had previously been spared. Other once neat colonial towns had gone back to semi-bush with inhabitants struggling to find means of survival.

Kabila, the victor in the capital, turned against the Rwandans when he found his dependence on them too unacceptable (and they lost the support of the USA when President Bill Clinton left office) but then lacked any other base of support. He was assassinated in 2001, probably by unpaid and unhappy youths of the sort we have depicted in the Mano River states, but his son Joseph, more adept at dealing with many foreign suitors, succeeded in establishing some order over time. Eventually a more effective government came to roost in Katanga, presided over by Moïse Katumbi, the son of a Greek Jewish businessman, and his African wife, and the mining industry gradually revived. Substantial military

Figure 13.2   A statue of Patrice Lumumba erected by Laurent Kabila, and an unfinished tower built during the Mobutu years, look down on Jean Pierre Bemba supporters as they make their way to a rally, Kinshasa, July 2006. This was a prelude to the Congolese election of 2006. © Guy Tillim. Courtesy of Stevenson, Cape Town and Johannesburg.

presence sponsored by the UN, including international forces, struggled to maintain and restore order on a more long-term footing.

The chief remaining problem of order lay in the east with its agricultural wealth and mineral resources far from Kinshasa. Here gold and coltan played the part of diamonds in Sierra Leone, and simultaneously in Angola prior to the death of Jonas Savimbi. New forms of accumulation fuelled the continued upsurges of violence as bands that began with some kind of ideological purpose simply carried on. In addition to the pro and anti-Rwandan forces, easily turned into mercenaries looting the neighbourhoods where they were found, local but old social quarrels not unlike those in Rwanda created antagonisms that led to recurring violence. The whole twisted history of the Congo is probably where the failed state story is most apt. Yet the extent to which national systems of thought, held together by the schools and churches, by cultural forms and a common identity, at least amongst the elite, linked to each other by cellphone networks, prevailing over any significant movement for secession, is also a remarkable feature of post-Mobutu Congolese society.

The final example of a failed African state must be Somalia. The post-colonial Somali state reached a kind of apogee when it made war on Ethiopia which it invaded in 1977 assuming that the Derg was in disarray. Siyad Barre, the military ruler, stood for the idea of unifying Somali speakers in not only what were the British and Italian colonies but also the Somali Coast Protectorate around Djibouti which France continued to rule, plus the Somali-speaking parts of Kenya and Ethiopia. In fact, Barre depended in this grandiose plan on Soviet-made weapons, but the Soviet Union was unprepared to back Somalia in a war with Ethiopia which it was also assisting and the military effort collapsed. From that time on, Barre's state weakened until he was driven from the country in 1991. Thereafter Somalia effectively split open with various clans maintaining their independence. An early American attempt at intervention was met with resistance and led to withdrawal.

This situation has never been entirely remedied. Eventually Mogadishu, the capital, fell under the control of what were called Islamic Courts in 2006 which had some prospect of returning a state authority to the entire territory, but the Americans panicked at the links which the Courts had with what were considered to be radical Muslims, number one enemies at this crucial point on the global map of the USA, and an intervention was arranged. Indeed, as we shall see in the following chapter, the nature of Somali Islam was changing. A stricter brand of Salafi Islam, Ittihad al Islami, was replacing religious practices linked to clan structures and Sufi brotherhoods; this is what gave life to the Courts. The core Islamists (Somalia is virtually an entirely Muslim country) turned themselves into el Shebab, carried on outside the coastal towns and continued to have some purchase on the southern countryside where fighting and occasional terrorist killings in Mogadishu, Nairobi and elsewhere take place. Troops from Ethiopia and Kenya were instrumental in recreating a weak kind of authority in Mogadishu. This use of African troops, largely funded from the West and with the Congo as the rather large-scale model, has become extensive in response to African crises. However, its authority is very limited and what was once British Somaliland broke away early and has an effectively independent government. One critical reason for intervention was an area of Somali enterprise which attracted world attention: attacks on international shipping passing the coast, with individuals and valuable liners held for ransom. This only stopped when ships began to be armed substantially. For a time this was a lucrative business for shadowy figures based in Dubai, Nairobi and elsewhere.

There have been waves of serious fighting in Somalia and phases where warlords used shortages of food to try to control people, and in so doing provoked much human misery. However, the theme that emerges so often from studies of the Congo, that people often manage to survive despite, and even because, a predatory state has eviscerated, that they find ways of prospering in adversity in fact, is far more developed in studies of Somalia. The Somali economy has become both more concentrated and diffuse. A massive Somali diaspora is to be found in dozens of countries and communications via telephone and through wire agencies has allowed a substantial development of commercial activity. A recent (2015) Wikipedia count suggested that there were perhaps one million expatriate Somalis with the most favoured countries of destination headed by Yemen, the USA, Canada, Britain and Sweden. There is not only a massive daily incursion of funds from outside into Somalia; a whole international system of communications with significant economic potential has emerged. Somalis have worked out common law formats that create impressive links of trust. Dubai is the site of several private airlines that fly just to Somalia. Somali traders dominate the trade in *qat*, a mild relaxant drug widely smoked throughout the Arabian peninsula, but also the meat market in Kenya. Astonishingly the collapse of a post-colonial state has created avenues of prosperity and accumulation and turned the Somali into an unprecedentedly cosmopolitan people.

For Western ideas of what makes a nation-state, a further paradox is the collapse of Somalia despite the ethnic 'community' of culturally like-minded Somalis who ought to hold it together. Under Barre, uniting all ethnic Somalis in and outside the country had been the glue to hold nationalism together. However, here as elsewhere, the difficulty of integrating pastoral and hunting peoples into a modern state form is the salient fact.[5] Clan loyalties that easily fragment or dissolve but reform again, and effective commercial linkages that cross national boundaries and ethnic silos, so far trump the nation-state idea.

Secessions

Frequently described as the most orderly and peaceful part of ex-Somalia, former British Somaliland has been consistently barred for many years from achieving international recognition as a state. The bad example of secession, the commitment to a sometime re-unified Somalia is too strong so far. However not very far away, in and around the Horn of Africa periphery, there are two late born internationally recognised African states. As previously mentioned, one consequence of the defeat of Mengistu and the collapse of the post-revolutionary government of Ethiopia in 1991 was the acceptance of Eritrean independence. This therefore was a product of the decision making of the new Ethiopian state brought into being by the Tigrayan People's Liberation Front (together with its allies). A striking feature of the Eritrean struggle, developed at its peak accompanied by a left discourse increasingly derived from those few Communist states completely independent from the Soviet Union and China, was the emphasis given to self-reliance. However, an independent Eritrea was just a small state, strategically situated but lacking in any obvious source of wealth and now bereft of any models, allies or sense of destiny. In 2001, following a brief period of political relaxation, the ruling party cracked down severely on dissent and thereafter maintained relative isolation and sole dispensation of power. Eritrea's foreign policy has been a changing mix of difficult to follow conspiracies focused on the broader region and jealous guarding of its independence, the latter leading to a border war in with Ethiopia between 1998 and 2000 that led to the loss of several not especially desirable frontier posts. Economically Eritrea benefits enormously from remittances; proportionately there are even more emigrant Eritreans than Somalis dating back to the war for independence but continuing clandestinely in the present situation. Perhaps one-third of Eritrean gross national product depends on remittances although resource exploitation has begun to improve the prospects of the state, at least after 2010.

More hapless thus far has been the equally internationally recognised independence of South Sudan, even though its borders with Sudan are not fully established. Sudanese independence was followed by decades of wars in the south. Under the British, the south was almost a *chasse gardée* administered quite separately in which the absence of Islam was a critical marker. At the same time, before World War II this was a region bereft of railways, of more than very limited cash crop production, without a city that could be a potential national capital. Britain considered linking it up to its East African domains instead. Once the site of substantial slave raiding in the nineteenth century, the southern Sudanese divided into clan and ethnic loyalties and of course the raided not infrequently became the raiders. They had proven tough subjects to conquer for the British. The later famous British anthropologist E. E. Evans-Pritchard had been sent out at the end of the 1920s to make sense for his government of the customs and political ideas of the Nuer speaking people, only then very recently under colonial authority. His anthropological classic *The Nuer* was published barely 25 years before the date of Sudanese independence in 1956.

The context for Southern independence was contingent indeed. The most impressive southern leader, who had been prepared for a period to serve in a Sudanese cabinet, John Garang, was expected to support some kind of federal solution in a proposed referendum to which Omar al-Bashir, the Sudanese leader, had agreed. However, he died in an air crash soon after the deal was done in 2005 and the rest of the local leadership, seizing on the huge potential of oil wells beginning to flow in the otherwise desperately poor south, came together sufficiently to steer towards a massive vote for independence in 2011. Al-Bashir, who had ties to Islamic militants not just locally but elsewhere in the Middle East, was a hate figure in the West, where he was portrayed as the mastermind of a racialised Arab conspiracy to dominate and persecute black Africans; there was hardly any Western support for holding Sudan together; in fact quite the opposite. As Alex de Waal, hardly a champion of the Southern cause, pointedly puts it:

> The SPLM [the Southern political movement that at times united Southern opposition to Sudanese rule] deftly manipulated American and European sentiment, developing the narrative of a Christian people oppressed by an Arab-Muslim government, in order to win international backing including a free pass on human rights and corruption issues, at least for a while.[6]

Indeed, while the future of the south lay in the balance, a crisis in western Sudan reached international attention simultaneously. Darfur, once a Muslim sultanate that had succeeded in retaining its independence from Muhammad Ali, then succumbed to a militarised jihad emanating from further west late in the nineteenth century and finally definitively became incorporated into Sudan only in 1916 when the last dynasty was overturned. Darfur, like the south, was poorly integrated into the Sudanese economy which focused on the very successful cotton export industry of the Gezira and the linkages to Egypt and Arabia. The political ties linking its elite (black and Islamic as are most central Sudanese) to their counterparts on the Nile have been complex, have changed over time and shifted from membership in Sudanese cabinets to a sense of exclusion and an appetite from the 1990s for secession. A particular dimension lay in the use by the state of pastoral peoples from the north of Darfur, anxious about population pressures and the desiccation of living conditions, as raiders and fighters in the south – the *Janjaweed* – to secure some control over this region. The potential conflict between farmers and pastoralists was fanned by the central government and sometimes given a racist spin in a part of Africa where a claim on Arab identity has been a historic marker of civility and status, albeit no religious issue was at stake whatsoever. This in turn erupted into international crisis when a variety of Western activists took up the Darfur cause – at least for a few years until Darfur resistance fragmented. However, thus far international recognition of an independent Darfur, or indeed a successful insurrection, seems far away. At the same time, however, South Sudan only achieved independence to collapse into anarchy and civil war with the new government exerting little or no control in many areas as power became contested between factions; the oil failed to flow and the new state was almost entirely propped up by Western aid.

Indeed the examples of Eritrea and South Sudan do not bode very well for future African breakaway movements albeit quite a few exist, occasionally with armed activity accompanying them. Two threads to take up in the Darfur/South Sudan narrative, however, should perhaps be underlined. The first was the growing hostility between Western establishments and militant Islam, which would have implications elsewhere, and the extent to which these regions, poorly integrated into national states, could slide from apparently domestic crises into ones involving neighbouring states. In the case of Darfur, the web of intrigue and at times invasion and open fighting involved close links going back to pre-colonial times with the republic of Chad to the west.

For a considerable time, South Sudan was also the site of a wandering army from Uganda receiving indifferent assistance from varying parties. The victory of Museveni in Uganda from 1986 was to some extent a victory for the most prosperous southern provinces with the best links beyond Lake Victoria and through Kenya and Tanzania to the broader main lines of economic development in East Africa. Northerners had to some extent made their way in the broader Ugandan context as soldiers and other low-skilled government employees. Idi Amin was a northerner as was Apollo Milton Obote. However, under Museveni the army was purged of northern elements by and large and the north was frozen out of state patronage, creating a sudden and enduring crisis of notable exclusion.

A remarkable response was a religious movement first headed by an Acholi woman, Alice Lenshina/Auma, the Lord's Resistance Army (LRA). This movement of religious purification with Christian roots marched under her leadership to Kampala as though Alice was a latter-day Joan of Arc, but it then collapsed with what used to be called a whiff of grapeshot. Lenshina ended up a refugee in Kenya where she died. But some of the LRA persisted and gained support as Museveni tended to treat the movement as an Acholi insurrection, a policy that led to increasing numbers of recruits continually joining the forces now led by Joseph Kony.[7] There are certainly parallels between Kony's forces and the rebel movements in Liberia/Sierra Leone at the same time. While southern Uganda recovered after 1986 from fifteen years of violent and arbitrary government, much of the north fell into a phase where kidnappings of youths, often held and reintegrated as LRA soldiers, multiplied. Atrocities highlighted a reign of terror, which began to drive a large minority of the population into towns that seemed safe. In Uganda, however, the rebels were never able to seize control of sizeable settlements. Probably more critical was the presence, as in other cases above, of men who had broken free from established social restraints prepared to fight for some kind of access to resources in depressed economic circumstances. With time the LRA lost any ideological or religious underpinnings of any consistency and was driven north into the Sudan and eventually even further west into the more lawless northern regions of the Central African Republic. One and another state was prepared to give it some support but very gradually the LRA declined in size and importance.

The politicised new trends in Islam, which will be explored further in the next chapter, ought also to be extended to an understanding of Saharan Africa. A group calling itself al Qaeda and affiliating to the Middle Eastern Muslim reformers challenging Western power elsewhere managed to hijack a Tuareg insurrection in what the rebels called Azawad in northern Mali and take control not merely of the desert regions but down to Gao, Timbuktu and the Niger river until foiled and driven back by the French, whose interventions exposed the very limited capacity of the Malian state but who struggle to find a political solution to integrate the Tuareg into Mali. To contextualise the Mali war of 2012–13 it is helpful to perceive the changing nature of the whole Saharan region. Far from being remote, the Sahara is crisscrossed with trails that allow for long-distance travel, various categories of migrants and refugees agglomerate in its towns, a number of which have become not just far more populous but also cosmopolitan. Once again the desert is a challenging but real site for complicated routes following human endeavours and ambitions, full of intrigues that mark the 'war on terror'.

The different sections of this chapter thus far have tried to establish some patterns in the tangled and increasingly varied history of Africa in the final quarter of the twentieth century. The impact of structural adjustment policies combined with existing and more deep-rooted trends to lead to quite different consequences in different regional and national settings. To understand this better, we need to devote far more space to social and cultural trends which are changing life in Africa substantially and will get the centre stage in the final following chapter. However, to conclude this chapter it is still necessary to stress that the broad global stage itself changed quite dramatically around the years 2000–3. Aid-dependent and struggling under the weight of irregularly but steadily declining cash flows from its colonially derived exports, Africa attracted commentators who began to focus on criminal activities such as the drug trade (by no means to disappear entirely); the African state seemed to evaporate in importance.

A tide comes in from the east

However, a linked range of circumstances began to create quite a new kind of context in the early years of the new millennium. Against so many economists' notions, natural products, particularly, but not only, mineral products, began to gain again in value, and it was industrial imports rather that became cheaper. Under these circumstances new mines were uncovered and developed, new oil fields exploited and state revenues increased substantially. Beneficiaries such as

Chad or Nigeria were able to repay their international debts and lose interest in the imprecations of the Bretton Woods institutions trying to set the tone for a Western-orientated reconstruction of Africa. In 2005 Angola broke off endless discussions with the IMF over debt repayment and conditionality; this was no longer a humiliating problem for the MPLA regime. Countries such as Tanzania and Zambia have introduced compulsory primary education and been able to pay for it, more or less. Under particular circumstances, some agricultural and even industrial enterprises began to flourish. The great major- ity of African countries benefited from remittances as emigrants established themselves in Europe, America and elsewhere including some African countries, notably South Africa. The whole tone of writing about African prospects altered dramatically. Now glowing if vague reports in financial journals consider the rapid rise of African billionaires, of a huge African middle class.

These circumstances are somewhat distorted. Most of the African billion- aires are North Africans or white South Africans and the huge middle class is generally made to enlist virtually everyone with regular employment if not too impoverished. Nor is the sustainability of this new prospect very clear as, for example, fracking in the USA leads to dramatically lowered oil prices and an abandonment of drilling plans in many areas. However the general direction is not wrong. The water has risen and the ships are again often afloat.

During the structural adjustment dominant phase, a counter-discourse emerged from heterodox development theorists. Their response to this discour- aging wave was to look to the East where a number of countries, notably Taiwan and Korea but to a lesser extent South-East Asian lands, were promoting rapid economic growth through successfully combining export and internal industri- alisation projects, through land reforms that stabilised a commercially minded peasantry and through getting prices 'wrong' on a few key products that could enter world markets very successfully with purposeful state intervention. This meant defying while playing the markets. Japan, in a sense the model for these countries, in fact insisted on writing its own story up because the World Bank tale seemed so remote from the truth.

As a result, certain African countries, not necessarily adjudged successes on the scorecard of democracy, began to look a bit different. Might they not have, for instance, key dedicated agencies that were above politics, that avoided mere rent-seeking and could acquire the capacity to structure a march into the future? The much respected new post-1991 Ethiopia, under the aegis for twenty years of former revolutionary Meles Zenawi who died in 2012, seemed to be the best case of all. In 1991 the Derg was chased from power. Although opposition to the Mengistu regime was complex, the key element was the armed struggle in Tigre, the northern province which had become somewhat marginalised in Ethiopian political life since the nineteenth century. While Mengistu had presided over the demise of Ethiopian feudalism, he had insisted on a system of state farms and blocked outright peasant ownership of land. This and the continued toll of drought made the success of a peasant insurrection possible. The new government, once in power, called for a new constitution of Ethiopian statehood based on ethnic self-determination and specifically reject- ing the Amhara character that had remained strong in the central government even after the fall of the monarchy. Eritrea, after thirty years of fighting, was permitted to go its own way as has been noted above. The turnaround from the terrible famines that accompanied the end of the empire and continued into the Mengistu era was certainly noteworthy. Ethiopia did seem to be on a consistent quest for industrial, agricultural and service activities that could fit into the globalising international markets and it experienced rapid economic growth. Addis Ababa's endless building boom and the construction of the new dam on the Blue Nile seemed markers in this time of growing self-confidence and dynamism.

Another candidate under the strict control of the RPF and President Paul Kagame was Rwanda. Booth and Golooba-Mutebi have taken the state-formed Tristar Company as a key government installation for promoting desirable investment relatively free from corrupt practices and committed to long-term developmental practice. As in Ethiopia, a new literature conveys a sense that substantial economic growth would paper over the cracks that could easily reappear. One assessment is that it is pre-eminently the foreign-born Tutsi youth who are the most detached from the old ways of the thickly populated countryside and apt to be the beneficiaries and the new entrepreneurs of Rwanda. In Ethiopia, it was a question of finding a way for the multi-ethnic, multi-religious country, based on imperial conquest and with its most desirable space for new economic activities in the periphery, to achieve some plausible national unity. Amhara dominance, especially of the old ruling class, faded but it is certainly not yet clear how sufficiently this process is working and certainly political opposition is hardly tolerated. In Rwanda, the reconciliation of Hutu and Tutsi is equally problematic and silence and repression are perhaps inevitably part of the picture.

A third interesting case was the presidency in Madagascar of Marc Ravalomanana, the yoghurt king and industrialist. Mauritian and Réunionnais islanders have been very successful in founding factories based on cheap Malagasy labour and Ravalomanana seemed to be the bearer of the values of the elite ready to bring Madagascar in as an imitator of the successful ASEAN states of the other, eastern end of the Indian Ocean. However, corrupt and incompetent as had previous regimes been, they were far better at speaking to poor Malagasy and at providing some kind of clientelist linkages albeit the radical phase of Malagasy nationalism was abandoned in the early 1990s – and Ravalomanana was overthrown in 2009. If the developmental state projects do achieve significant traction, however, we shall see more clear inequality within the success story lands as well as between different African countries.

It is not African dynamism that is originally the cause of this remarkable shift so much as the successful economic development of the Asian giant, China. To a lesser extent economic growth in India and surrounding countries, the rise of the Gulf States as a source of financial power and the emergence of Brazil as a significant international economic player assist this impact. However it is clearly China that is hungry for natural resources that it can exchange for its mass-produced articles of cheap consumption. China is capable of forging long-term deals with African states that involve provision of badly needed infrastructure that can kick-start other productive activities. It lacks the Western vision of a well-behaved Africa, however honoured in the breach. The Chinese broadly identify with African nationalism and with resentments against the former colonial powers; they are happy to assist Africans in moulding a genuinely post-colonial identity. Nor of course is China a democracy. The Chinese government, which often plays a key guiding role in Chinese investments, may desire stability in order for economic activities to go forward, but it doesn't have much interest in African state forms and Chinese intellectuals are just beginning to place Africa on their conceptual map. Chinese demand and that of other Asian countries has certainly been crucial in promoting the rise in value of African products.

With the advance of China and India, moreover, the problems of underdevelopment that so vexed the West in the second half of the twentieth century and were so salient to political intrigues and diplomacy, look less overwhelming on a global scale. Africa now stands out as the main needy area. Some would argue that in terms of basic issues, the distribution of free food, especially in disaster conditions, the diffusion of medical practices required for longer lifespans on average and even the availability of cheap clothing, either used clothing or clothing produced in Asia, are going to eliminate the characteristic features of extreme poverty even in Africa and perhaps through the agency of benign international structures.

The countryside alters

Africa today is no longer the Africa of Senghor and Mobutu, Nyerere or Nkrumah, of the Cold War and apartheid. The hunger that sat behind the drive for independence is played out and social antagonisms that always lurked in the background are now more and more obvious. The 'middle class' finds ways to protect and promote its interests and those of its kin while others feel excluded and marginalised. The ideal for much of this class is emigration, if possible to the West. Emigration, as witness the desperate numbers trying to cross the Mediterranean into southern Europe, is hardly confined to them however. It reflects material deprivation but also the start of cultural upheavals that power the ambitions and daring of young people no longer encased in the social structures of the past. It is not of course only emigration out of Africa, but emigration from rural areas which superficially transform only very slowly. Here a social, and in places even a demographic, hollowing out of the tribal Africa once beloved by romantically minded anthropologists and colonial cadres is underway.

The African continent is vast and mapping rural change an impossibly complex exercise. The rise of the NGOs and their command of publicity and the air waves has given an entirely exaggerated sense of rural disasters – famines, floods, desertification, hunger. However in some of the circumstances we have looked at above these were factors of real importance. The Ethiopian famine of the 1970s was an immediate cause of the end of the monarchy. Warlords in Somalia and elsewhere have made very effective use of famine to corral support and resources to their own ends.

With better times, it is hard to avoid the endlessly repeated insistence, in Western media at least, for the privatisation of land and an intensified farming, unburdened by parasitical governments, that can bring secure livings to African peasant families. As we have seen, one problem here is the failure to comprehend the equivalent needs in communities that are essentially pastoral. Peasants themselves require a great deal from an effective state to do more than just survive: subsidised inputs, disaster aids, sound advice, good and inexpensive transport connections maintained, are a list of the most obvious. Two patterns are however everywhere discernible. The first is the emergence of rural classes. A relative few are able to organise labour and provide crucial services; they are frequently the movers and shakers on the agrarian scene. The other is the growing interpenetration with, and dependence on, other sources of power and income such as involvement in commerce and transporting. For the successful, city jobs and professional qualifications are often coupled with agricultural enterprise. For the masses, survival means finding other supplementary sources of income within the family circle. This very likely means physical movement, migration. In Kenya, as noted, a model late colonial programme in land privatisation led to farmers being turned out and replaced by others on the right side politically. This kind of privatised land redistribution on a chaotic basis outside the law has been noted as well for Juba, the new capital of South Sudan where everything is for sale.[8]

There are new crops being cultivated. South African sugar firms grow elsewhere, notably in Mozambique and Malawi, not usually to produce edible sugar but to grow the plant as a source of biofuels. Some countries, notably Mauritius, Kenya and Ethiopia (and before the land invasions, Zimbabwe) have reached out to markets especially in Europe for fresh produce and flowers. However, it is largely big growers who can meet the required standards and specifications imposed by European retailers and these are very often foreign companies or members of the racial minorities of colonial times, who possess the business acumen, connections and capital to participate successfully. A shriller literature has made huge claims for capitalist 'land grabs' of immense dimensions with consequent potential for expelling peasants from their land and transforming the African countryside in a ruthless way. While a few countries such as Sudan, Mozambique and Ethiopia have seen land alienations with this kind of intention on a significant basis, here again there is much exaggeration. In many areas, though, it is however true that entrepreneurial-minded farmers do benefit from the growth of cities and the immense urban markets that have opened up within African countries in recent decades.

The need for security, however, remains overwhelmingly important for most African cultivators and the charms of privatisation are consequently very slow to appeal. The prominent, too, still often need to live in some harmony with poorer neighbours. In reality, inequities are masked by the formal continuation of rules of redistribution and inheritance that appear to be unchangeable parts of the scenery. However, as Africa urbanises and Africans leave the continent, the very tortured road to a more capitalist countryside integrated with world markets slowly resumes. The urban side of the picture of course needs stress too but that will be part of the further exploration of change in our final chapter.

The overall scene is one of increasing differentiation, of complicated crises resolved in various ways and of a gradual and uneven lurch out of ways associated with 'traditional' Africa. The ability of the West to shape African politics is uneven at best but the emergence of patterns of accumulation and power from African sources is still hard to discern. The end of history is definitely not in sight.

Notes

1. Ogoni identity emerged juxtaposed with better-known Eastern Nigerian identities: Igbo and, in the Delta, Ibibio, Efik and Ijaw late in the colonial era. As devolution progressed in the late 1950s it began to pick up traction but developed overwhelmingly as a post-colonial phenomenon of any political salience.
2. In 2015 Nigerians returned the 'reformed' former military dictator Muhammad Buhari to power. Hostility to dictators does not sum up African popular politics.
3. Stephen Ellis, *The Mask of Anarchy: The Destruction of Liberia and the Religious Dimension of an African Civil War* (Hurst, 1999), p. 217.
4. Interestingly Museveni came from the Hima, a similar social layer associated with cattle keeping, within Uganda. The one-time kingdom of Nkore also has never known a revolution of the sort experienced in Rwanda although it is true, too, that British rule did not operate in quite the same way, engendering antagonism as deep.
5. For the dilemmas of pastoral people in East Africa, the work of Dorothy Hodgson and Spear and Waller on the Maasai in Tanzania (see Chapters 6 and 7 in the bibliography) is a good introduction; a thoughtful article on this subject is Tor Benjaminsen et al., 'The Kilosa Killings; Political Conflict of a Farmer-Herder Conflict', *Development and Change,* 40(3), 424–45 (2009). This team believes that mediation can resolve conflicts peacefully but stresses the often negative consequences of political interventions at a higher level. The adaptation of Kalenjin speakers to agriculture in and around the Rift Valley in Kenya has been impressive but also has lain the stage for rival land claims and conflicts taken up by politicians. The situation in Mali is very well covered by Baz Lecocq as in the bibliography. Again a positive spin is provided in Mirjam de Bruijn and Han van Dijk, 'Changing Population Mobility in West Africa; Fulbe Pastoralists in Central and Southern Mali', *African Affairs*, 102(407) (2003), 285–307. The situation of San people in Botswana and their hostility to expulsion from a wilderness area designed for tourist interests has been taken up by many authors. One of the most unsuccessful land reform settlements in South Africa has been Riemvasmaak, designed for San people whose men served in the South African Defence Force. Well-known, too, is the conflict over the former Spanish Western Sahara occupied by Morocco. In fact, a large portion of Sahrawi pastoralists live in refugee status camps in the Algerian Sahara. However, there are also more positive situations. In Chad, the arrival of more pastoralists near to the lake and the capital has made them a reasonable source of inexpensive dairy products...but then in Chad desert-edge dwellers are politically dominant.
6. Alex de Waal, 'When Kleptocracy Becomes Insolvent', *African Affairs*, 110 (452) (2011), p. 354.
7. A somewhat parallel movement ended differently, with a mass suicide. The Bakiga leadership felt excluded and eliminated from any circuits of power after Museveni's victory. They had tended to back Idi Amin. See Richard Vokes, *Ghosts of Kamungu: Fertility, Secrecy and Exchange in the Great Lakes of East Africa* (James Currey and Fountain, 2009).
8. Gabriella McMichael, 'Rethinking Access to Land and Violence in Post-War Cities: Reflections from Juba, Southern Sudan', *Environment and Urbanization*, XXVI(2) (2014), 389–400. This phenomenon has also been witnessed in the much larger theatre of Nairobi.

14

A New Africa: Cultural and Social History Since Independence

Populations and cities

One way to introduce the subject of social and cultural change in Africa from the middle of the twentieth century on is to consider some live and very material statistics. In 1948, censuses in the Gold Coast and in Kenya both revealed populations in the four to six million range. Slightly earlier, Bechuanaland census gave a count of 296,310. Comparable counts to those in the Gold Coast and Kenya were found in Denmark, Switzerland, Venezuela and Cuba while Luxembourg had a population that was very similar to that of Bechuanaland at 290,222 and to British Guiana at 315,701. By contrast today the latest census or most recent estimate sets the proportionate population increases since then up to 2010 or later for Denmark at 37.1 per cent, Switzerland 68.1 per cent, Luxembourg 88.9 per cent, Cuba 103 per cent, Guyana (ex-British Guiana) 137 per cent and Venezuela 493 per cent. The increase in the USA population between the 1950 and 2010 censuses was 105 per cent.

Compare with Africa: Ghana (ex-Gold Coast) 488 per cent by 2010, Botswana (ex-Bechuanaland) 582 per cent and Kenya, with relatively little in-migration, a whopping 614 per cent.[1] It is true that African populations may well have fallen in the era before imperial conquest and in early colonial times before increases were systematically registered after World War I (earlier though in the Gold Coast). However, these are spectacular increases by comparison with any of the comparative countries except for Venezuela. While reductive conclusions are not helpful, it is difficult not to point to what this means in terms of required social and physical infrastructure, growing pressures on livelihoods dependent on the natural environment and the pressing need for employment far beyond what previously had existed. African living has become more competitive, requiring more innovation and change to avoid exclusion and indeed often, to survive. Indeed it can be argued that for much of Africa the problem is not that jobs have dried up but that they have failed to expand remotely in proportion to the population. The challenges for creating a working social and economic system with suitable infrastructure to meet people's needs are consequently huge. This is a stark way of understanding the challenges of development.

At the same time, the population of African cities has also grown spectacularly. Lagos, no longer the capital of Nigeria, is still its great economic hub and it may well hold more than ten million inhabitants. Kinshasa, whose great era of growth came in the course of the troubles of the early 1960s, has continued to expand if more gradually not very far behind Lagos. Moreover estimates for other cities that easily exceed three million are available for Kano and Ibadan, great regional centres in Nigeria with a pre-colonial past, and Luanda, the capital of Angola, a city that originated essentially in the slave trade era under Portuguese control. The adjoining complex of Johannesburg-Pretoria-Ekurhuleni in South Africa has additionally probably surpassed eight million inhabitants in size and Durban and Cape Town belong to the three million category. Not far behind are Abidjan, Khartoum and Addis Ababa and two to three dozen more African cities pass the million mark, mainly but not entirely national capitals.[2] These figures correctly suggest that the urban form and facilities evolved under colonial rule have been dramatically overtaken by current requirements.

The emergence of cities has been noted continually in this volume and the sense in which the bigger colonial towns were already sites where very mixed populations lived and where receptivity to social and cultural currents of startlingly new sorts were strikingly obvious by the interwar years. French scholars, with their specific interest in cities, notably Georges Balandier and Claude Meillassoux, were really pioneers in this regard and very much less concerned than their English language counterparts to stress links to the pre-colonial past or to rural systems of belief and association or to critique urbanisation as dysfunctional; they were interested in the emergence of something new even before the coming of independence. From the 1990s, some scholars added to this a particular interest in looking at forms such as music, sport and cinema using the rubric of leisure activity. However leisure seems to imply something extra or additional to the core businesses of production and reproduction. Here we would go much further to see the African city as very largely now the source of new ideas, new identities and new ideals as well as new problems. These are cities of consumption. If, as Fred Cooper stresses, governments in Africa are gatekeepers between foreign productive enterprise and the population, cities can also be said to be gatekeepers that structure this relationship.

A sharp line could probably be drawn half a century ago between the rural and the urban in Africa; now urban-derived trends, themselves connected to international circuits, penetrate the countryside through roads and across telephone links and it is the rural civilisation that is beginning to fade. If one looks not at macro-statistics but at the assemblages of trade goods in a busy border town such as Oshikango, Namibia near the frontier with wealthy Angola, the manufactures available are not especially likely to come from the old colonial powers. They have been made in Brazil, in Pakistan, in India as well, of course, as in China and represent a multi-polar commercial world that creates new tastes and replaces old solutions.[3] In addition, Africans add distinctive voices of their own to the mix. They volunteer to be part of what they see as a culture that is very different from the world of their own grandparents but one of which they want to take possession. Economic reality is a question of access to credit and connections; possession of particular kinds of consumer goods spells prestige and exudes the whiff of power.

Let us turn briefly to the capital city of Ghana, rapidly-growing Accra, a city whose more desirable new neighbourhoods are full of villas constructed by Ghanaians who have emigrated to Britain, North America and elsewhere, often professional people but who want a base in what they still see in some respect as home. These constitute consumer icons for a broader population. On this basis, the city sprawls along old and new roads out into the bush. In Accra also, according to an excellent monograph by Martin Verlet, there is a poor neighbourhood called Nima. Nima is close to some of Accra's oldest quarters that date back to the days of the slave trade and the antique forts, three of which still stand. Nima, however, is not exactly a community. It is a largely Muslim neighbourhood which has attracted a restless population of migrants from the north of the country and across the border in Mali and Burkina Faso. This kind of cash-seeking migration has roots in the nineteenth century, to the kola trade, the hiring of so-called Hausa soldiers and the opening of commercial, European-run gold mining, not to speak of labour in the cocoa fields.

Up to the 1970s in Nima there were jobs for poor residents but this became far less true afterwards. The so-called informal sector (unregistered, that is, by the state) grew substantially, it became more critical for women to work and the approved forms of family life tended to attenuate. Children are also off at work earning something for the family and schooling suffers. In a poor Muslim neighbourhood like this, the high road to university and professional status is very hard to ascend and the quality of the local schools suffers accordingly. New forms of stricter Islam spread and become a new social binding force. And the locals do not simply stay. For a great many, Nima now is a platform that makes further out-migration on to various Western countries by whatever means, often dangerous and adventurous, possible.[4]

A long way from Nima is the Zambian capital of Lusaka. Yet here Karen Hansen reports on some similar findings: the growing autonomy and effective prestige women need to apply to survive, physical mobility as people find their way back to the countryside and then, dissatisfied, return to the city as the boundaries between the two weaken. Women compete with one another, notably for men, but they also find crucial forms of co-operation and bonding. The Lusaka kitchen party is a salient and very common expression of this kind of union. Many marriages cross 'tribal' lines and there is considerable movement of foreigners into the neighbourhood. It used to be that UNIP, the original ruling party, had an ability to regulate disputes and provide services for loyal members but this has long since ceased to be the case.

These new economic trajectories are piecemeal and lack career structures. Petty commerce has expanded massively – and is no longer dominated as it was by men. Home production of garments for sale also has become more extensive but on a far more restrained scale given the competition with cheap imports against which customs regulations hardly apply, and used clothing from the West admitted as a charitable gift. However, while a poor or mixed African neighbourhood will certainly contain a multitude of spaces for commercial transactions, it has so far not been hospitable to much productive and particularly industrial activity.

Kate Meagher has considered the situation of shoes and clothing production in the eastern Nigerian city of Aba where in fact mass-orientated consumer goods began to be produced from the 1950s. Many of these goods do find their way for sale across the borders in several other West African countries. There is virtually no regulation: no registration with the state, no control over zoning, and rapid turnover of firms. However as the twenty-first century approached, despite a concentration of thousands of producers and some subsidiary trades, these businesses had failed to find much basis to either co-operate or expand and tend to remain essentially survivalist, just a world of 'poor producers', whereas big businesses do form in very different spaces of the Nigerian economy. For the poor, Meagher felt that social networking imposed obligations rather than credit or useful linkages; associative life is very weak. Indeed one dysfunctional phenomenon that she notes was the arrival of the vigilante Bakassi Boys who turned to crime and engaged in large-scale pogrom-like murders of northern Nigerians in 2001.[5]

Housing has become a more competitive issue in Lusaka. Whereas poor people could often access subsidised housing from the state, now they have increasingly to become tenants, which of course also allows others to accumulate on a small scale. The sale of houses is rare. The plight of urban women in Zambia in particular was captured by Ilsa Schuster when the urban economy in the country was stronger. Schuster noted that women with a modest education, literate but unable to compete for professional work, which she called a sub-elite, place crucial attention on rearing children but are often unable to form stable relationships with men who feel driven towards multiple sexual relationships. One particular difficulty women face is in formation. According to Schuster, schooling stresses a conventional Western feminine ideal which is simply unworkable in African situations. Here a rootless and somewhat pointless modernity is propagated in which reality can only cause intense disappointments.

Africa still suffers from health problems that have for now been set aside in many other parts of the world. Some countries still experience very low life expectancy and high infant mortality rates. In the 1990s, HIV infection took off in central Africa and had a devastating effect in some parts of West Africa, but especially to the east and the south. Death from AIDS threatened 10 per cent and more of the sexually active adults in East Africa or the Ivory Coast and much higher figures for South Africa and adjoining countries such as Swaziland and Botswana. Millions of Africans are now kept alive through a drug regime, but the sense of vulnerability and chance are inevitable.

Modernity and post-coloniality

Cultural history has become a lively sub-field within African historiography as it has in the study of other parts of the world, especially with regard to recent history. For this there are several reasons. First, writers who use culture as their key structural determinant in examining contemporary Africa are frequent and insightful where once they were a rarity. This is the lens through which they try to make sense of the contradictions and complexities we have started to illustrate. Second, a cultural lens gives us an opportunity to understand the contemporary African world in African eyes and in African terms. Third, while it is not always easy to measure cultural change there can be little doubt that African society is very different than it was at the end of the colonial era. For this reason, cultural analysis has itself to take on a historical dimension. The material changes can be registered but it is insufficient to understand both motivations and performance of African people in the real world. This is not to suggest that a book like this in any sense can be a substitute for 'African voice'; what it tries to do is suggest some key issues in generalising about and discussing African voice in the present era.

In planning this chapter, there was originally an intention to emphasise the idea of modernity: Africa does go modern or hopes to go modern, or, as James Ferguson so bleakly tells us in *Expectations of Modernity*, fails to modernise. However, the more thought that was given to this idea, the more there was scepticism that we could escape from a simple Weberian tradition/ modernity binary that did not explain enough. In the title of an article, Joost Fontein gives away the plaintive reason in a woman's quoted voice: *We Want to Belong to our Roots and We Want To Be Modern People.*[6] Stephan Miescher has explored the diary of a well-off Ghanaian man who accumulated eleven wives and seventeen children, albeit he essentially practised sex with one wife at any particular phase of time. At the same time he maintained this patrimonial presence in his domestic life, he was a keen reader of Soviet political materials, a great admirer of Nkrumah and a loyal elder in the Presbyterian Church. Just how modern was he? This story is typical of a number, admittedly from colonial times, in a volume where historians have considered the testimony of writings from largely elite Africans. If modernity should show a connection, if not an influence, with Western twentieth century modernist high culture, there is nothing there. Instead, these individuals generally display a remarkable mix of ideas and behaviours from African familial and economic life juxtaposed with borrowings from the norms of the coloniser, with a considerable amount of attention to the Gold Coast. To a Western reader, the striking feature is one of disjuncture although it is not clear even in the early twentieth century that this is how it felt to the people being described as one interrogates their own writings.[7]

From such private testimonies, one could turn, notably in West Africa, especially Nigeria and Ghana, to the rise of so-called market literature, booklets that exemplify approved and disapproved new ways of behaviour, especially in the unstable field of gender relations. The focus in this literature, much of it created and sold in the great Niger River market town of Onitsha, was on personal messages. Nationalist heroes such as Nnamdi Azikiwe were praised as the ultimate models of home-boy success replete with glamour and symbols of the good life as a reward for heroism. Romantic stories, as idealised as the European medieval romances of the troubadours and as remote from reality, fascinated large numbers of readers once literacy had become widespread.

In Northern Nigeria, an equivalent literature developed somewhat later in the Hausa language. Far more than Igbo or even Yoruba, Hausa has taken off as a standardised written and spoken language for several tens of millions of Nigerians and beyond Nigerian borders. Already committed to writing using Arabic letters in the nineteenth century, Hausa, transliterated into Roman script, benefited from its use in colonial schools and official documents and then post-colonial broadcasting and news production. By the 1980s, Hausa readers could uncover mirrors of their concerns in tales of 'love unrequited, love thwarted, love fulfilled, unemployment, poverty, criminality, violence, corruption, and the pressures of family and responsibility.'[8]

An alternative to modernism as a concept might be creolisation. A frequently cited observer who rejected the kind of cultural perspective that had long been typical amongst anthropologists and dubbed what he saw in a small northern Nigerian town as creolisation was Ulf Hannerz, writing in the late 1980s. By this he meant original cultural forms of mixed origins. Hannerz opened up a very interesting door and in these pages we shall try to explore what creolisation, with an African flavour and in fact very diverse and complex as a phenomenon, might actually mean, but it seems right to follow him in stressing the *viability* of creole forms: they work for significant numbers of Africans.

One of the forms creolisation takes is agglomerative. Kwame Gyekye, the Ghanaian philosopher, claims as follows:

> I might mention...that one of the most famous Ghanaian musical and verbal artists, Ephraim Amu (1895–1993) whose native language was Ewe, produced his most important and lasting musical pieces in the Akan language (undoubtedly the most widely spoken language in Ghana), which he had thoroughly mastered in his youth. One of the songs he wrote in the Akan language has, in fact, been elevated to the level of a national...anthem, appreciated and enjoyed by the entire state.[9]

The tentative growth of a national culture such as Gyekye favours is urban inevitably; he tries to be a somewhat beneficent policeman, finding some kind of middle way between modernity and tradition as he defines the terms. However not all new cultural forms can be taken for a new harmonious structure. New kinds of identities, ethnic, religious and otherwise, can equally be decisive in terms of state formation or subversion against the state. However in this chapter we are focusing on cultural phenomena themselves.

Creolisation implies the patching together into a plausible whole of elements from the colonial and pre-colonial into a new pattern or discourse. It seems a better approach than appropriating the vague term post-colonial stretching into the distant and unending future. Authors who use post-colonial tend to use it arbitrarily when it seems to fit and ignore it when it doesn't; it takes away from the creativity of what is emerging. There is also the implied half-politicised carryover of colonialism which marginalises African agency. Here it seems more important to stress that colonialism has to be seen both as genuinely an indelible part of formative experience, and thus as legitimate as anything else, but also as well and truly over, in part because the construction of some coherent new whole is still work in progress and hard to read legibly. Instead of post-colonial, it might be more useful to understand cultural trends as cosmopolitan – of a sort. This will be explored below as we consider a number of important cultural markers. Trends usually laid down to globalisation, another vague but perhaps more useful term, are powerful currents but these trends are not entirely arbitrary nor are they unidirectional. Indeed another way to read the situation might be *We Want to Reject and Forget about Colonialism and also We Want to be Modern People,* modern but often self-consciously black or self-consciously Christian or Muslim, people. These labels too are of course very different than the more or less generic, typically 'tribal' identifiers that hardened in colonial times, with earlier, over-whelmingly rural, roots.

An obvious area of investigation would be sport. In late colonial times, football took over almost everywhere as the pastime for African boys (and occasionally girls) albeit it emanated from towns and was copied from colonial employees and settlers from Europe. Football disciplined young men into something that connected to apparently great events occurring far away with uniforms and rules and a whole way of talking and thinking that seemed to spell modernity, calling for a new sort of conformity that brought respect. It was also an area which created some possibilities for accumulation, for players but also for those on the business side of the game. Support for the team in one's city or neighbourhood (possibly, as in other countries, with some other specific association) and for one's country was an important part of football culture.

However since independence African football has globalised: it has been incorporated far more intensely into a global game, where massive possibilities for money making are available to a few and dangled before the many at least as an ambition. Potential African stars are spotted, identified and whisked off to more high-powered training contexts and there are always a few who are extremely successful household names, especially remarkable in the cases where they come from the smaller countries such as Mali, Liberia or Togo. Many more big names are the children of African parents who moved to France, Britain and other countries. They represent a different history, but a related one about which a great many Africans know something. The arrival of television and video on a mass scale has meant that African audiences are able to watch and identify with international sport at this level and are drawn into what goes on in Europe as the defining criterion of success. The playing field is apparently level and experiencing the world outside Africa a massive aspiration. Dominant as is football, one should also mention the specialised discipline of long-distance running. At professional level, marked by the running of thousands in the big international marathons, most stars today are African, particularly Kenyan but also from Ethiopia and sometimes other countries, typically where a significant portion of the population live at high altitudes. Here again as wide audiences in Africa will know, boys and girls with potential are identified early, trained professionally and cast into an international limelight.

Lights and sound

Films began to arrive in Africa before World War II. Colonial authorities had fine intentions of using film (and also radio) to demonstrate the high calibre of Western civilisation but the message was often reinterpreted in subversive or simply autonomous ways. For a long time, Westerns from America held sway in the cinemas. Africans loved the fight scenes and the triumph of the hero. However, in post-colonial cinema the heroes started to come from elsewhere. So-called black exploitation films were brought from America, but their impact was small compared to the immensely wide diffusion of Indian cinema with its display of urban settings, wealth, colour and an equivalent face-off of good versus evil. To this was attached as well dance and music, for which the plot was often something of an excuse.

In so-called Bollywood productions (which have never appealed to mass audiences in the West), relations between men and women were stoked with desire but essentially kept demure and as such more comprehensible, easier to read as it were, than the complexities of Western gender norms and particularly the poignant portrayal of individual behaviour often set against those norms. The interventions of the gods and Indian supernatural forces were by no means a barrier to African comprehension. If Indian film casts at first had a predictable appeal in East Africa to audiences of Indian origin, these actors, by virtue of at least not being white, helped to extend this market dramatically in Africa.

Indian films were immensely popular in Nigeria, for instance, where the norms of the films certainly were taken into the realm of urban popular culture. Fascination with the cinema world contested often very successfully with the maintenance of older Muslim values in the North. However, there and elsewhere, one needs also to mark the equivalent popularity of kung fu action films from Hong Kong, another Asian point of origin. From the 1980s and 1990s, as economic circumstances deteriorated in Nigeria, the maintenance of cinemas became more and more untenable. This went together with the advent of video technology which allowed the filmic world to shift to the showing of videos, and here low budget Nigerian films could compete.

Nollywood was born in the 1990s. In studios on the mainland peninsula of Lagos, Nigerians themselves started to produce large numbers of videos which in turn were widely diffused in Africa and in the African diaspora. Western film, putting aside raw displays of action, heroism and watchable technological prowess, portrayed individuals in ways that did not fit the consciousness of many Africans. Nollywood by contrast created a moral universe where men and women, typically overwhelmingly driven by greed and power, fall into moral traps and use sinister forms of witchcraft to get what they want. 'Nigerian films...draw on themes of corruption and betrayal, naked desire for material goods unrestrained by loyalty or love'.[10] These jibed with magazines that put forward new daily life challenges and new values in print. In the videos, an anti-witchcraft morality combats evil successfully with forms of goodness that are rewarded with comfort, love and prosperity. Commentators see these films as influenced by the new styles of Christian belief which have become very potent as discussed below. Witchcraft is now taken quite outside the framework of pre-colonial political and social ideas moored to local community specificities and historic legitimacy to become a generalised force that obviously thrills and sways the viewers.

Some side issues of special salience can also be noted. The theme of childless women and their plight, in a context where child-bearing is defined as the chief source of satisfaction for women, is frequent in Nollywood. So is the portrayal of consumerist status symbols, particularly if associated with foreign black individuals offering the mirage of a dark-skinned Hollywood sprinkled with glamour. However people might like to gaze at the latest model expensive cars and large houses, there is not much excitement about individual actors. There is very little of a star system in Nollywood and the values exhibited by the actors also tend to transcend any sense of their individual magnetism. Moreover, by contrast to Indian cinema, there is very little comedy.

Politics is also a minor theme. At most, it is possible to find examples of films that expose dictatorship. In Nigeria, the Abacha years were seen as cruel and excessive in this sense and did get some attention as a theme, mainly from Yoruba film-makers who thought of themselves as victims in this period where the most prominent Yoruba politician, Chief Abiola, was imprisoned. However there is nothing like a general critique of political manners and a genuine voice of a counterweight civil society. Great power and wealth is more easily ascribed to occult forces than to some unusual violation of norms held by a general public. If cinema is no longer what it was, television of course remains in most countries a major opening to international, national and urban sport and to the weaving of stories that are grist to the same mill as the Nollywood studio productions, and it can be serviceable for displaying the videos.

African popular music is in some crucial respects different than the world of film and video. Here we enter into a realm of vast and varied popular intervention by Africans. International music, particularly popular as a form of entertainment in Europe, includes memorable African stars such as Angélique Kidjo from Benin, Baaba Maal from Senegal, Oliver Mtukudzi from Zimbabwe, Salif Keita from Mali and the late Cesaria Evora from the Cape Verde islands. The pioneer here was the South African Miriam Makeba who went into exile and linked up with the politically sophisticated American musician Harry Belafonte at the end of the 1950s, only to queer her pitch in the USA when she married the black nationalist ideologue Stokeley Carmichael. These are names with which to reckon, and with whom to identify, talented and successful genuine heroes to millions of Africans. There are many local stars as well but with very limited ways to access a fortune; most earn little. However, identity with individuals or groups comes as firmly as it does with football teams and is equally important to urban youth. Yet African popular music has for a long time borrowed extensively, adapted and indigenised foreign music starting with the ballads available on colonial radio programmes and the advent of Latin American dance rhythms (which had partially African origins) and through rock 'n' roll, West African highlife, reggae and on to rap and hip-hop. In Zimbabwe, using Thomas Mapfumo particularly as a model, Thomas Turino describes a new music which emerged mixing 'S[outh] A[frican] harmony and rhythms, rural Shona rhythms and texts, and influences from Congolese rumba'.[11] The rumba and indeed the South African music, of course, had other, more distant origins.

In colonial and early nationalist times, African music was generated especially effectively from nightclubs which acquired a legendary glamour, was associated with the sexual and other forms of prowess of the new leaders, but also sometimes celebrated new ruling ideals. Thus the lubricious world of Mobutu's Congo had a remarkable musical outpouring. In Ghana, Tanzania and Zimbabwe, liberation movements tried to project a cultural image of dedication and pursuit of the national dream and there was music to associate with their ascendancy. The Rhodesian Forces Requests radio show was imitated by ZANU-PF. When Julius Nyerere died, the Tanzanian air waves were flooded with musical memorials. However today there is little left of this kind of political celebration.

Rap and hip-hop with their emphasis on recitation tend to speak to the disinherited and alienated who are unwanted by the local and global establishment but crave some kind of recognition and respect (a word obsessively used) where daily humiliations by establishment-run institutions can be brushed aside. Many of the lyrics are vaguely political and speak to disinheritance and impotence in a world that makes no sense to the excluded, but its projections are relatively hopeful. Lyrics are easily developed in widely spoken languages, notably Kiswahili but others such as Asante Twi, Wolof or various West African pidgins as well. Here there is the excitement of participating in an international milieu largely defined as black and the opportunity to express the sexual longings of frustrated youth. There are occasional female voices to be heard as well but the music generally tries to speak to young men. Musicians celebrate the unattainable and berate the present. Only to a very limited extent do they celebrate older values; they are rather an insertion into a self-defined and projected sort of modernity.

Koen Stroeken refers to the knowing urban male Tanzanian as the iMbongo in *Bongo flava*, the hip hop of Dar es Salaam. Such a man despises Indians and 'Boers' and castigates government, big business and the West but – within limits. He is no revolutionary. Hip hop is an illusory but supportive state of mind. Popular song has, however, accompanied democracy movements or reflected badly on the dictators of the past. Fela Kuti was in the 1970s the star proprietor of a memorable Lagos nightclub, scion of a politically important Yoruba family and a real forerunner of the kind of political comment on power, cultural and political, that has typified generations of music makers. Fela was a kind of pioneer of these later musical genres as forms of expression albeit musical language has altered. More recently, entertainers proved a powerful force in 2011 in getting rid of Senegalese president, the elderly Abdoulaye Wade, who had designs on a third term in office and a son as his successor. Music is not a good medium for complex political or social assessments but it is powerful and access to it is after all very easy. The music is everywhere, at least in town, you need no money to hear it, and it is a binder that knits together local people.

Music and other cultural forms were noticeable in the formation of what Sasha Newell has called 'modernity bluff' and I would prefer to call pseudo-modernity in the southern Ivory Coast. Here cultural presentation came together with a political trajectory which we have considered in the last chapter. Even before the death of Houphouët-Boigny, youth gangs formed in Abidjan and the south. They sang and spoke in creolised argot, incomprehensible to foreigners, rather than grammatical French, held up a black American imagery as a counter to the respectable French association of the fraying Ivorian bourgeoisie, and ridiculed the hick northerners and those from the Ivory Coast's northern neighbours. This was a response to economic decline and the closing of opportunities with the Ivorian economic miracle well and truly finished. Madame Gbagbo, an iconic figure in the regime of her husband, was an enthusiastic Pentecostal Christian by stark contrast to Houphouët-Boigny's orthodox Catholicism which had notoriously culminated in the construction of the huge cathedral in his home town of Yamoussoukro in imitation of St. Peters in Rome.

Performativity was also very important in defining, creating a style, for this new southern Ivorian youth. Newell records an Ivorian survey in the 1990s reporting that 83 per cent of those questioned saw clothing style as important and 73 per cent as very important in life.[12] The diversity of ethnicity in the Ivory Coast where there were few pre-colonial states of any antiquity made ethnicity per se an impossible marker, but this battery of cultural weapons was enough to provoke tension, perhaps pointing to a new kind of smaller core state that rejected Houphouët-Boigny's cosmopolitan vision of the Ivory Coast where the colonial ethnic definitions had also more of a place. But this perspective proved too excluding: with the fall of Gbagbo after the 2012 election all this went into reverse as national ideology with still untold consequences. The results of populism are not necessarily admirable.

A new Christianity

Indeed morality and what it means in the quest for money, credit and new forms of prestige lies at the very heart of the issues that trouble contemporary Africans. It is hard to abandon the idea of membership in a family group or some kind of collectivity in favour of an unsure destiny as an individual. If these values wither, where to turn in a sea of potential wrong-doing? The Yoruba novelist, Amos Tutuola, in novels such as *My Life in the Bush of Ghosts* expressed the nightmare in his vivid, apparently naïve, tales of a life 'in the bush of ghosts', one of the first novels by an African to circulate in the West. How to find a path out of the bush? Weberian ideas of secularisation, disenchantment as Weber put it, won't do. Not surprisingly, dramatic new expressions of religious belief are key factors in the new Africa. There are some interesting parallels in these shifts within the two great world religions, Islam and Christianity, as they intensify their spread but also are the site of important cultural changes on the African continent.

It is possible to exaggerate the changes in Christian worship and organisation in Africa as too recent. A century ago, Africans accepted the discourse of Christianity but sometimes demanded control of congregation life by an African leadership, now of course hardly an issue, and introduced elements from familiar forms of sacral recognition and performance with varying degrees of acceptance. This was the start of an indigenisation project. There are long antecedents to the growth of new forms of ideas primarily within Protestantism. In the 1920s, for instance, an aggressive new enthusiastic gospel from America preached by the Faith Tabernacle Congregation, effectively promoting capitalist values, had an early run in the Gold Coast and somewhat parallel groupings, such as the Seventh Day Adventists in British Central Africa, began to be active. Faith healing, in a context where modern health practices were difficult or impractical to institute, powerfully reinforced a more emotional and anti-scientific Christianity. The chronicler of the Congregation, Adam Mohr, has also demonstrated the growing power of new ideas and practices even within the Presbyterian Church in Ghana which has lost much of its staid character. Even the Catholic Church experimented with African musical structure in the composition of the Missa Luba and other sacred musical pieces.

The establishment churches with their roots in colonial times or even earlier are still markers of social prestige and cultural formation; they remain important bulwarks of associative life and institutional stability in almost any African country. It is notable that from these churches – Catholic, Methodist, Anglican, etc. – have come the cases where churchmen have taken the part of civil society movements calling for a halt to dictatorial rule, postponement of elections, demands by presidents to run for a third term or more and the like, as has been noted for Malawi, Kenya and the Congo amongst other countries. However even here while the respectability and international associations of such church bodies help to give weight to their participation in protest, these are not protests that have taken on board cultural life and they have frequently gone back to quiescence when the state does not budge.

A particularly negative note has to be sounded on the Catholic Church in Rwanda. The church, which had once been instrumental in identifying a respectable Tutsi elite, shifted from the 1950s to support Hutu claims as the rightful majority population and, with this, the Hutu regime in power from 1960 on. The church has frequently and tellingly been implicated in criminal violence during the genocide and notably in sheltering Hutu criminals in making their escape from the country. Whole congregations taking refuge in large churches were murdered en masse. The result is that the post-1994 regime has turned sharply against the Catholics and embraced Pentecostal Protestantism. Interestingly the most unequivocally positive position in Rwanda was taken by the small Muslim community which rejected any part in the genocide and gained support as a result after the success in overthrowing the state.[13] The Catholic Church itself, however, has been far from immune to calls for more emphasis on healing and casting out the devil. Emmanuel Milingo became the centre of a cause célèbre when he was forced to resign as Archbishop of Lusaka in 1983 (and eventually stripped of his priestly office) because of his activities in exorcising evil ceremonially and later his enthusiastic embrace of the idea of a married priesthood. Africa has been a hotbed of opposition in the Anglican Church to the ordination of women and to the acceptance of homosexuality as a practice without sin.

Ruth Marshall, a very sympathetic observer of the new largely Pentecostal movements in Africa, has characterised mission Christianity as it worked itself out in the colonial period as thriving not so much because it provided a plausible belief system but due to what the anthropologists Jon and Jean Comaroff call 'working misunderstandings'. The missionaries provided and could be associated with desirable health and education systems, with forms of dress and appearance that signified dignity in a new context and promoted hygiene which actually fitted African ideal preferences. One could also add that, especially in the last generation of colonialism, missionaries created systems of respectful hierarchy amongst Africans and often championed the nationalist cause, notably in the case of Protestants in the Catholic Belgian Congo and in Portuguese colonies where the Catholic Church was effectively associated with colonial rule. This argument could be continued to assert that the new Pentecostal churches while taking some of this on board speak rather to African hearts.

How were they different? It is a classic proposition thanks to Max Weber to associate Protestantism and what he called the Protestant Ethic with capitalism through the institution of capitalist values. But this ethic in Africa was sharply deviant. Whereas Weber laid emphasis on thrift and modesty and the capacity for long-term planning, the new African Protestant Ethic, while usually taking up ideas such as marital fidelity (and in general rejecting borrowings from African mores of the past) is in large part about display and the celebration of worldly success in which God rewards the pious. In Pentecostalism there is little talk about the rich being forced to go through the eye of a needle to get to heaven or about the poor bearing up under their burdens and looking forward to a better afterlife. Yet it is Weberian in its emphasis on individual achievement and salvation rather than adherence to a pious community policed so as to promote virtuous communitarian values. This worldly success is able

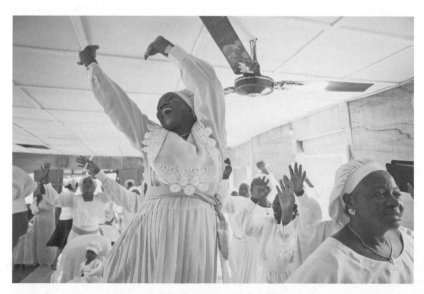

Figure 14.1   Worshippers at the Celestial Church, Lagos, Nigeria. Reproduced with the kind permission of Greg Marinovich

to defy and match the bad worldly success that can only be described as the work of the devil. Therefore Pentecostalism must be very public and performative; it cannot simply be a faith in the heart. Prayer and church attendance are a necessity. Music, notably gospel music, is a key practice and one that calls for active female participation. However there is a powerful belief with older roots in witchcraft manipulated by the devil and those under his spell which must be present as the antagonistic force against which faith fights. The struggle against witchcraft, together with the emphasis on faith healing which often comes first, takes one back in Christian history to early modern times and before in Europe and America.

There are few niceties of theology here. However, there is equally in general a promotion of monogamy and established rules of Christian morality as a code. Churches are also profoundly entrepreneurial. There are breakaways and there are an infinite number of entrepreneurs who arise to the Lord's call and found churches which multiply but also split. The international links are extraordinarily rich and multifold. The United States is a plentiful source of new preachers and evangelists, black and white. However Nigeria has become a real source of energy and religion doused business (as with music and film) with an array of Pentecostal ministers who in turn travel Africa with their message. The Congo is a lesser but significant source of church leaders.

On the one hand, generally speaking Pentecostal and post-Pentecostal leaders tend to steer clear of the state and talk about it very little. Faith and belief are a separate matter. They have great success in attracting major political figures. Not merely Madame Gbagbo but also Thabo Mbeki's wife Zanele in Pretoria had the reputation of being an enthusiastic Pentecostalist. Paul Kagame, president of Rwanda, has the most amiable relationship with his favourite American evangelist. Olusegun Obasanjo, the former Nigerian general and president, is a keen supporter of the movement. And the wealthy and successful, who rarely see themselves as creatures of the devil, are attracted to these cults of healing and the worship of success through faith. This is a remarkable reversal of the gospel of colonial times, which was aimed at creating a responsible and moral sub-elite that might gradually assume positions of leadership coupled with a dutiful, respectful, hard-working mass of parishioners, and it has swept Africa with its dynamism.

Islam in transition

Although there are also some important differences from Christianity, Islam has also altered very considerably in recent decades in Africa creating a fascinating parallel. Pentecostalism is unlike the independent churches of the colonial era that accepted various forms of older beliefs and customs. Similarly newer trends in Islam, usually called Salafist, reject 'innovation' and elements that seem like accretions denounced as ungodly compromises with local traditions. In West Africa, where Islam is so ancient, this involves a rejection of the brotherhoods such as the Qadiriyya and the Tijaniyya. In northern Nigeria, where the traces of indirect rule are still there to behold, the new Islam is hostile very often to the class of the *masu sarauta*, the emirs, their courts and their traditions as impure. The change is particularly dramatic in areas where Islam was worn very lightly, often away from the cities. Here women have started to seclude themselves, sobriety starts to be enforced and no doubt very old customs at variance with typical Muslim codes have fallen away. Fiona McLaughlin reports that Muslims in Senegal have evolved their praise songs so that dignitaries with roots in the historic past are no longer praised; instead it is Muslim brotherhoods – which survive better there – and social movements who are lauded.[14] A study of rural Ethiopia shows very similar tendencies. The tendency to worship at tombs of those considered saints and Sufi mysticism has fallen away while Salafism is strongly promoted by Saudi Arab media.

In 1952 a riot broke out in Kano because a cinema was planned for within the walled city. Muslims, however, have come to embrace technology and turn it into a tool. A key feature of current Islamic practice is the systematic use of technology to propagate ideas and promote belief. Just as with the new Christians, Islamic reformers reach out to international, indeed global, networks and their capacity to access radio and television, video, cellphones and computers creates the sense of a virtual community that seems desirable and progressive. Outsiders are uncomfortable with the apparent emphasis on covering women and taking them out of the public sphere. However scholars who have worked with them have found that there are an unprecedented number of women who are themselves actors, promoters of women's education along acceptable lines, who use veils as symbols of legitimacy and righteousness. In general this is a world that does not reject new technology but rather seeks to use it. It is another kind of thrust at modernity.

It would be unfair to discuss the Salafists as though they have things all their own way. For instance, amongst Yoruba speakers in Nigeria there is an Islamic movement which fits the older Yoruba ways of tolerating Muslims and Christians in the same community, even often in the same family. The Muridiyya brotherhood centred in Senegal has shown an adaptability, notably in establishing colonies throughout the world and promoting trade rather than agricultural production as was once true and it continues to thrive. It is still well able to direct the lives, material lives included, of its followers as it meshes with familial structures or replaces them. In one sense, new trends in Islam are very unlike what we have seen earlier for Christianity. They continue to propound the future glories of the Muslim community rather than validate individual trajectories; the individual finds respect and honour within those larger communal achievements.

Islam is also capable of radical reactions aimed at what it sees as its enemies. In the 1980s the yan Tatsine represented a populist, anti-authority mass movement of relatively poorly educated northern Nigerians alienated by the elite, lacking any secular radical alternative. It was eventually suppressed by force. Boko Haram formed in 2002 and demanded a sharp break with the Nigerian state and the old local elites. A violent wave of hostility against Christians was part of this trend in a context where Muslims and Christians have fought each other with many casualties in cities such as Kaduna and Jos, colonially founded towns that cannot be said to 'belong' to any ethnic or religious group and were once more peaceful. The name of this organisation in Hausa (there is a formal

Arabic name as well) baldly calls for a rejection of Western education. Here alienation from the consumerism and credit-orientated world promoted by the successful meets a tradition of popular rejection of decadent secular oppression going back to the great jihad wave of the early nineteenth century. Boko Haram kidnaps women, tries to turn them into Muslim housewives and has its main headquarters not in Hausaland but rather in north-eastern Nigeria, an ethnically mixed region where once the ancient state of Borno held sway nominally. Much of its core support gathers outside the cities, which must seem strange, and indeed 'haram' or forbidden to adepts with centres in relatively remote towns. It has been willing to turn to horrific levels of violence to create a sense of fear and terror in the Nigerian population very clearly aligned with al Qaeda and ISIL terrorism in the Middle East.

Boko Haram is truly indigenous even though it is happy to claim affiliation to al Qaeda and more recently the more potent ISIL and perhaps whatever group in the Middle East may be seen to be striking terror in Western hearts. However, after the Twin Towers attack of 2001, and here there is no comparison in Christianity, militant Muslims are a cause of suspicion and potential violent opposition to the USA and its friends and allies. Indeed we have already seen the complex play of forces in the Sahara which attract both sides and the interventions in Somalia to eliminate the el Shabaab ('the youth'), the group that originated with the Islamic Courts whose authority the Americans refused to accept in the capital Mogadishu in 2006. This group was run out of Mogadishu but through the assistance of African Union troops, notably non-Muslim Ethiopians and Kenyans, has been driven into pockets of the southern Somali countryside. There is certainly a potential for enhanced antagonism to the West and violent reprisals in other parts of Africa. Muslims often feel alienated and beleaguered in this context and will at least passively sometimes support militants even if they are themselves not part of their numbers. Yet it would be a mistake to dismiss them as enemies of modernity, a part of which empowers them, or cosmopolitanism. Different international links connect them to Cairo or Riyadh and even to the distant frontiers of Pakistan and Afghanistan.

Conclusion

One thread that ties together the constantly interrelating themes of this chapter is the extent to which Africa is becoming, largely via its cities, connected in diverse ways with a wider world, taking up influences from different points of origin, Africanising different trends as Africans move around, take pictures, make calls and communicate with one another and with the world beyond, searching for movement towards dignity and respect. These are the threads of globalisation that operate in Africa with an unprecedented intensity. African intellectuals still often like to call for some kind of African authenticity and uniqueness, often based on racial identity; the reality is that gatekeeper cities are knitting Africans together in chains that stretch through the world in different directions, certainly with the delights of advanced capitalism shedding a powerful attractive light but also with influences from elsewhere. Moreover Africans themselves are active participants and cultural studies will inevitably highlight original contributions that they themselves make, using their own presence and their own voices. And of course they travel to an unprecedented extent, bringing the experience of many different scenes to bear. In so doing, the dominant social and cultural patterns of colonial times, while not vanishing, have been transfigured and transformed. The neo-colonial decades are over, and what is to come will be gradually more and more dependent on different sorts of African agency. In this there is vice and virtue, comedy and tragedy in unfolding patterns still to be revealed.

Notes

1. For these figures, I have used censuses of the 1946–50 years for each country or territory, censuses for 2010–12 or estimates that are slightly more recent in the cases of Botswana, Luxembourg, Denmark, Venezuela and Cuba.
2. A table with these figures can be found in my *The African City: A History* (Cambridge University Press, 2007).
3. Gregor Dobler, 'Oshikango: The Dynamics of Growth and Regulation in a Namibian Boom Town', 115–33 JSAS, XXXV(1), 2010. See also André Chapatte, 'Chinese Products, Social Mobility and Material Modernity in Bougouni, A Small but Fast-Growing Administrative Town of Southwest Mali', *African Studies*, LXXIII, 1, 22–40, 2014, for transformation in a very distant small African town.
4. For the story of Nima, see Martin Verlet, *Grandir a Nima, Ghana: Les figures de travail dans dans un faubourg populaire d'Accra* (Karthala, 2005).
5. Kate Meagher, 'Social Capital, Social Liabilities and Political Capital; Social Networks and Informal Manufacturing in Nigeria', *African Affairs*, 105(421) (2006), 553–82.
6. Published in the *African Studies Quarterly*, X(4) (2009), 1–35. Fontein is not notably discussing change in the city.
7. There is nothing typical here as the subjects studied largely belong to the reasonably well-educated and then tiny elite and deeply personal reflections are eschewed, but nonetheless the collection is very revealing: Karin Barber, ed., *Africa's Hidden Histories: Everyday Literacy and the Making of Self* (Indiana University Press, 2006).
8. Graham Furniss in Barber, op. cit., p. 430.
9. Kwame Gyekye, *Tradition and Modernity: Philosophical Reflections on the African Experience* (Oxford UP, 1997), p. 93. African intellectuals are often equivocal and differ on the question of modernity. For other thinkers, see Achille Mbembe, the Camerounian post-modernist with his striking impressions of contemporary Africa, Paulin Houtoundji, the Béninois student of Althusser or James Gikandi the Kenyan literary critic (see his 'Reason, Modernity and the African Crisis', 135–57 in Jan-George Deutsch et al., eds., *African Modernities* (James Currey, 2007).
10. Brian Larkin, *Signal and Noise: Media Infrastructure and Urban Culture in Nigeria* (Duke University Press, 2008), p. 171.
11. Thomas Turino, *Nationalists, Cosmopolitans and Popular Music in Zimbabwe* (University of Chicago Press, 2000) p. 228.
12. Sasha Newell, *The Modernity Bluff: Crime, Consumption and Citizenship in Cote d'Ivoire* (University of Chicago Press, 2012), p. 196.
13. I am very grateful to Andrea Grant for her informative talk on this subject at the African Studies Centre, Cambridge in the Trinity Term, 2014.
14. Fiona McLaughlin, 'Islam and Popular Music in Senegal: The Emergence of a New Tradition', *Africa*, 67(4) (1997), 560–81.

Annotated Bibliography

CHAPTER 1. Africanist History and the History of Africa

The view that Africa itself is an intellectual construction that needs interrogation dominates the work of Valentin Mudimbe, *The Invention of Africa: Gnosis, Philosophy and the Idea of Knowledge* (Indiana University Press, 1988). For the standard older British Africanist analysis, see Roland Oliver and John Fage, *A Short History of Africa* (Penguin, 1st edn, 1962; 5th edn, 1975) and the multi-volume *Cambridge History of Africa*, edited by Oliver and Fage (Cambridge University Press, 1975–86). A more recent and refined contribution is John Iliffe, *Africans: The History of a Continent* (Cambridge University Press, 1995). The American style is epitomised in Curtin, Feierman, Thompson and Vansina, *African History* (Longman, 1978), although the last two authors were originally from South Africa and Belgium respectively. Africans, especially the doyen of African historical scholarship in French, the Burkinabe Joseph ki Zerbo, are largely responsible for the *UNESCO History of Africa* (UNESCO, 1985–1999); Paul Tiyambe Zeleza, *A Modern Economic History of Africa* (CODESRIA, 1993) is useful.

Pre-Africanist views that may be noted with profit are W. E. B. DuBois, *The World and Africa* (International Publishers, 1965), reflecting a specific Afro-American tradition and Samuel Johnson's *History of the Yorubas* (Routledge & Kegan Paul, 1966 reprint), a typical but distinguished example of the kind of written histories Africans were producing during the colonial period; or Apolo Kagwa, *The Customs of the Baganda* (Columbia University Press, 1934). For 'homespun historians', see Toyin Falola, *Yoruba Gurus: Indigenous Production of Knowledge in Africa* (Africa World Press, 1999) and Derek Peterson and Giacomo Macola, eds, *Recovering the Past: History Writing and Political Work in Modern Africa* (Ohio UP, 2009).

Consensus and criticism within the field can be better understood by a progressive examination of Vansina, Mauny and Thomas, Ranger and Fyfe, the three collections discussed in the text and cited in the notes. On method and oral tradition, see its foremost champion, Jan Vansina, *Oral Tradition* (Routledge & Kegan Paul, 1965) as well as the more nuanced and thoughtful *Oral Tradition as History* (James Currey, 1984). On the perspective of an African collector and analyst of traditions, see Mamadou Diawara, 'Les recherches en histoire orale menées par un authochtone', *CEA*, 97 (1985). Historiographic considerations discussed in the text make use of Michael Lambek, *The Weight of the Past: Living with History in Mahajanga, Madagascar* (Palgrave Macmillan,

2002) and Sandra Evers, *Constructing History, Culture and Inequality* (Brill, 2002). On official state history vs. popular memory in a very different setting, M. Anne Pitcher, 'Forgetting from Above and Memory from Below: Strategies of Legitimation and Struggle in Post-Socialist Mozambique', *Africa*, 76(1) (2006), reminds trained historians of an important but more familiar scenario.

A collection presenting a critical view of anthropology is Talal Asad, ed., *Anthropology and the Colonial Encounter* (Ithaca Press, 1973). A brilliant portrait of one of the most influential anthropologists of the colonial era was penned by Richard Brown: 'Passages in the Life of a White Anthropologist: Max Gluckman in Northern Rhodesia', *JAH*, XX (1979). The eminent anthropologists associated with the Rhodes-Livingstone Institute in Northern Rhodesia gradually shifted towards calling themselves sociologists as they committed themselves to studies of social change outside the rural setting.

Some of the earliest criticisms of Africanist history by Wrigley, Saul and Ochieng are cited in the text. The underdevelopmentalist hypothesis was raised in E. A. Alpers, 'Rethinking African Economic History' *KHR*, I (1973) and Samir Amin, 'Underdevelopment and Dependence in Black Africa – Origin and Contemporary Forms', *JMAS*, X (1972). See also Walter Rodney, *How Europe Underdeveloped Africa* (Bogle-L'Ouverture, 1972). For an early survey, Bogumil Jewsiewicki and David Newbury, eds, *African Historiographies* (Sage, 1986), present the picture as of the middle 1980s.

Arguably the finest work in the South African liberal tradition is C. W. DeKiewiet, *A History of South Africa: Social and Economic* (Oxford University Press, 1940). South Africa lends itself to national history writing more than most African countries. Some useful texts are Rodney Davenport and Christopher Saunders, *South Africa: A Modern History* (Palgrave Macmillan, 2000) and the new *Cambridge History of South Africa*, volume 1 edited by Carolyn Hamilton, Bernard Mbenga and Robert Ross (Cambridge University Press, 2010), and volume 2 by Ross, Anne Mager and Bill Nasson (Cambridge University Press, 2012). Among the landmarks of the new historiography of southern Africa were Charles van Onselen, *Chibaro* (Pluto Press, 1976) and *The Seed is Mine* (Hill & Wang, 1996) and Shula Marks and Anthony Atmore, eds, *Economy and Society in Pre-industrial South Africa* (Longman, 1980). Drawing on underdevelopmentalist and Marxist thought is the major collection by Neil Parsons and Robin Palmer, *The Roots of Rural Poverty in Central and Southern Africa* (Heinemann, 1977).

The colonial creation of today's African boundaries does not lend itself so well to national histories but there are some worth the reader's attention. Barring discussions of pre-1800 developments and post-colonial developments since publication, John Iliffe, *A History of Modern Tanzania* (Cambridge University Press, 1979) is surely a classic of its time but John McCracken, A *History of Malawi 1859–1966* (James Currey, Woodbridge and Boydell & Brewer, 2012), for which Iliffe is also a kind of model is itself excellent while Andrew Roberts, *A History of Zambia* (Heinemann 1976), is still serviceable. With the growing interest in the area of the Great Lakes, there are some good newer summaries: Jean-Pierre Chrétien, *The Great Lakes of Africa: Two Thousand Years of History* (Zone Books, 2003) and H. Lugan, *Histoire du Rwanda: de la préhistoire à nos jours* (Bartillat, 1997). Other newer national histories include Yénouyaba Madiéga et Oumarou Nao, *Burkina Faso: Cents ans d'histoire* (Karthala, 2003, a collection), Solofo Randrianja and Stephen Ellis, *Madagascar: A Short History* (Hurst, 2009), Bahru Zewde, *A History of Modern Ethiopia,* 2nd edn (Ohio University Press, 2002) and Marion Wallace, *A History of Namibia from the Beginning to 1990* (C. Hurst, 2011).

The decline of economic history as a part of African history is captured by a man who contributed so much to its study in A. G. Hopkins, 'The New Economic History of Africa', *JAH*, L (2009). For examples of ways in which postmodern thinking has been introduced into African studies, see E. S. Atieno Odhiambo and David Cohen, *Burying SM: The Politics of Knowledge and the Sociology of Power* (Heinemann, 1992), Achille Mbembe, 'Domaines de la nuit et autorité onorique dans les maquis du sud-Cameroun 1955–58', *JAH*, XXXI (1991) and *On the Postcolony* (University of California Press, 2001); James Ferguson, 'Mobile Workers, Modernist Narratives', *JSAS*, XVI (1990) and Kirk Hoppe, 'Whose Life is it Anyway? Issues of Representation in Life Narrative Texts of African Women', *IJAHS*, XXVI (1993).

CHAPTER 2. Material and Cultural Development in Africa before the Nineteenth Century

For those interested in Marx's scattered writings on pre-capitalist society, there are a number of editions, including one with a distinguished introduction by Maurice Godelier in French. A convenient English version was edited by Eric Hobsbawm, *Pre-capitalist Economic Formations* (International Publishers, 1964). The one Marxist classic on related material is Friedrich Engels' *The Origin of the Family, Private Property and the State* (Pathfinder Press, 1972). The serious student should also consult Lawrence Krader's edition of Marx's *Ethnological Notebooks* (Van Gorcum, 1974).

The modes of production debate touched on in this chapter was inaugurated in France in the 1960s. Many of the early articles are collected in *Sur le 'mode de production' asiatique,* introduced by Jean Suret-Canale (Éditions Sociales, 1974). Catherine Coquery-Vidrovitch's seminal article, 'Research on an African Mode of Production' is translated in Martin Klein and G. Wesley Johnson, eds, *Perspectives on the African Past* (Little, Brown, 1972). Claude Meillassoux has provided a provocative exposition of his concept of lineage society in *Maidens, Meal and Money* (Cambridge University Press, 1980). Studies specifically inspired by these issues include Marc Augé, *Pouvoirs de vie, pouvoirs de mort* (Flammarion, 1977); J. P. Olivier de Sardan, *Le Système de relations économiques et sociales chez les Wogo* (Musée de l'Homme, 1969); Pierre-Philippe Rey, *Colonialisme, néo-colonialisme et la transition au capitalisme* (Maspéro, 1971) and Eric Pollet and Grace Winter, 'L'organisation sociale du travail agricole des Soninke', *CEA*, VIII (1968). American considerations of the debate with some interesting case studies are edited by Donald Crummey and Charles Stewart, *Modes of Production in Africa* (Sage, 1981). An excellent case study is Jeff Guy's 'Analysing Pre-capitalist Societies in Southern Africa', *JSAS*, XIV (1987). On agrarian systems in Africa, Thomas Bassett and Donald Crummey, eds, *Land in*

African Agrarian Systems (University of Wisconsin Press, 1993) is a very useful recent collection. It can be supplemented with Andrew Smith, *Pastoralism in Africa* (Hurst, 1992) or John Galaty and Pierre Bonté, eds, *Herders, Warriors and Traders: Pastoralism in Africa* (Westview, 1991).

Meillassoux has also edited a wide-ranging and major collection on slavery in Africa, *The Anthropology of Slavery: The Womb of Iron and Gold* (Athlone Press, 1991). This and other work is critically surveyed by Frederick Cooper, 'The Problem of Slavery in African Studies', *JAH*, XIX (1979). On forms of slavery in Africa see also Paul Lovejoy, *Transformations in Slavery* (Cambridge University Press, 1983), Claire Robertson and Martin Klein, eds, *Women and Slavery in Africa* (University of Wisconsin Press, 1983) and Marion Johnson, 'The Slaves of Salaga', *JAH*, XXVII (1987). For a related form of structured dependency relations, see F. Adeniyi Orogo, '"Iwofa": An Historical Survey of the Yoruba Institution of Indenture,' *AEH*, 14 (1985) and Paul Lovejoy and Toyin Falola, eds, *Pawnship, Slavery and Colonialism in Africa* (Africa World Press, 2003).

Recent radical considerations of gender relations in Africa that look back to the past include Oyeronke Oyewumi, *The Invention of Women: Making an African Sense of Western Gender Discourses* (University of Minnesota Press, 1997); Ifi Amadiume, *Male Daughters, Female Husbands, Gender and Sex in an African Society* (Zed, 1987) and Signe Arnfred, *Sexuality and Gender Politics in Mozambique: Rethinking Gender in Africa* (James Currey and Nordiska Afrikainstitutet, 2011).

These pages can only touch on the vast literature of specialist interest on pre-colonial Africa. This selection is based on those works that cover major areas or have some wider import. For more detailed references, the multi-volume *Cambridge History of Africa* edited by Roland Oliver and John Fage is a good starting point. The *Cambridge Encyclopaedia of Archaeology* (Cambridge University Press, 1980) provides a convenient, brief overview, now somewhat dated. J. E. G. Sutton, 'The Aquatic Age in Africa', *JAH*, XV (1974) was a provocative discussion of one facet of the transition to agriculture in Africa. See also J. D. Fage and Roland Oliver, eds, *Papers in African Prehistory* (Cambridge University Press, 1970); J. R. Harlan et al., eds, *Origins of African Plant Domestication* (University of Chicago Press, 1976) and L. Krzyzaniak, 'New Light On Early Food Production in the Central Sudan', *JAH*, XIX (1978). Hunting and gathering communities in Africa are the subject of J. Woodburn, *Hunters and Gatherers: Material Culture of the Nomadic Hadza* (British Museum Trustees, 1970) and Richard Lee, *The !Kung San: Men, Women and Work in a Foraging Society* (Cambridge University Press, 1979). A salutary critique of how anthropologists have treated such societies is Edwin Wilmsen, *Land Filled with Flies* (University of Chicago Press, 1989). Mobility – the capacity in many parts of Africa for individuals and groups to move into new environmental niches and find new opportunities at considerable distances is highlighted in François Manchuelle, *Willing Migrants: Soninke Labor Diasporas* (Ohio University Press and James Currey, 1997), Sylvie Bredeloup, *Migrations d'aventures, terrains africains* (CTHS, 2014) and Michael Mortimore and William Adams, *Working the Sahel: Environment and Society in Northern Nigeria* (Routledge, 1999).

The West African past is surveyed in the compendium J. F. Ade Ajayi and Michael Crowder, *History of West Africa* (Columbia University Press, 1976). Some of the most interesting thinking on the ancient states of the upper Niger Basin was done by Polish scholars. These include Marian Malowist, 'Social and Economic Stability of the Western Sudan', *Past and Present*, XXXIII (1966, with a rejoinder by A. G. Hopkins, XXXVII, 1967); Michel Tymowski, 'Société sans état et sociétés à organisation étatique en Afrique noire', *AB* (Warsaw) 40 (1992) and 'Les domaines des princes du Songhay', *Annales*, XXV (1970). For later research and archaeological evidence, see Roderick McIntosh, *The Peoples of the Middle Niger: The Island of Gold* (Blackwell, 1988); M. Cissé et al., 'Excavations at Gao Saney: New Evidence for Settlement, Growth, Trade and Interaction on the Niger Bend in the lst Millenium CE', *JAA*, XI(1) (2013) and Shoichiro Takezawa and Mamadou Cissé, 'Discovery of the First Royal Palace at Gao and its Implications for the History of West Africa', *CEA*, 208, 52(4) (2012). For the Saharan world 1000 years ago, E. Ann McDougall, 'The View from Awdaghast: War, Trade and Social Change in the South Western Sahara from the Eighth to the Sixteenth Centuries', *JAH*, XXVI (1985) is interesting and, for a later period, taking the story of present-day Mali through the pre-colonial era to the twentieth century, Richard Roberts, *Warriors, Merchants and Slaves: The State and the Economy in the Middle Niger Valley 1700–1914* (Stanford University Press, 1987). For the female kings south of Segu, see Jean Bazin, 'Princes désarmés, corps dangereux; les "roi-femmes" de la région de Segu', *CEA*, XXVIII (1988) 111–12.

Three important books on territories further to the west are Jean Boulègue, *Les royaumes wolofs dans l'espace sénégambien (XVe–XVIIIe siècles)* (Karthala, 2013), Boubacar Barry, *Senegambia and the Atlantic Slave Trade* (Cambridge University Press, 1998) and Philip Curtin, *Economic Change in Pre-colonial Africa* (University of Wisconsin Press, 1975). James Searing, 'Aristocrats, Slaves and Peasants: Power and Dependency in the Wolof States 1700–1850', *IJAHS*, XXI (1988) is very useful. On the Mossi-Volta section of the savannah (Burkina Faso-Ghana), see Nehemiah Levtzion, *Muslims and Chiefs in West Africa* (Clarendon Press, 1968) and Michel Izard, *Introduction à l'histoire du royaume mossi* (Centre National des Recherches Scientifiques, 2 vols, 1970).

On the central savannah, H. F. C. Smith, 'The Beginnings of Hausa Society' in Jan Vansina, Raymond Mauny and L. V. Thomas, eds, *The Historian in Tropical Africa* (Oxford University Press, 1964) is still thought provoking. So is Nicole Échard, *L'Experience du passé; ethno-histoire de l'Ader haoussa* (Paris, 1972). The best introduction to the most famous jihad state is Murray Last, *The Sokoto Caliphate* (Longman, 1967). See also his 'Administration and Dissent in Hausaland', *Africa* XL (1970); Phil Burnham and Murray Last, 'From Pastoralist to Politician; The Problems of a Fulbe "Aristocracy"', *CEA* 133–5 XXXIV (1994), 313–57; Michael Mason, 'Captive and Client Labour and the Economy of Bida Emirate, 1857–1901', *JAH*, XIV (1973); and for one aspect of slavery in this region, Sean Stilwell, 'Power, Honour and Shame: The Ideology of Royal Slavery in the Sokoto Caliphate', *Africa* LXX (3) (2000). This could be compared with Toyin Falola, 'Power Relations and Social Interactions among Ibadan Slaves 1850–1900', *AEH* 16 (1987).

On post-jihad society in western West Africa, there are several stimulating articles: Youssouf Guèye, 'Essai sur les causes et les conséquences de la micro-propriété au Fouta Toro', *BIFAN, série B*, XIX (1957); Walter Rodney, 'Jihad and Social Revolution in Eighteenth Century Futa Djallon', *JHSN*, IV (1968); Roger Botte, 'Révolte, pouvoir, réligion; les Hubbu du Futa Djallon', *JAH*, XXIX (1988); Marion Johnson, 'The Economic Foundations of an Islamic Theocracy – the Case of Masina', *JAH*, XVII (1976), Richard Roberts, 'Production and Reproduction of Warrior States: Segu Bambara and Segu Tukolor', *IJAHS*, XIII (1980) and David Robinson, *The Holy War of Umar Tal* (Oxford UP, 1985).

Standard treatments of major states in the forest and adjacent West African forest include Ivor Wilks, *Asante in the Nineteenth Century* (Cambridge University Press, 1975), T. C. McCaskie, *State and Society in Pre-colonial Asante* (Cambridge University Press, 1995) and Robin Law, *The Oyo Empire, c. 1600–1836* (Clarendon Press, 1977). See also Kwame Arhin, 'Trade, Accumulation and the State in Asante in the Nineteenth Century', *Africa*, LX (1990), Joseph Nevadomsky, Natalie Lawson and Ken Hazlett, 'An Ethnographic and Space Syntax Analysis of Benin Kingdom Nobility Architecture', *African Archaeological Review*, XXXI, 2 (2014), and Simi Afonja, 'Changing Modes of Production and the Sexual Divisions of Labour among the Yoruba', *Signs*, VII (1981). Raymond Dumett, 'Precolonial Mining and the State in the Akan Region' considers the Terray thesis in George Dalton, ed., *Research in Economic Anthropology* (2) (1979). Terray's magnum opus is *Une histoire de royaume abron de Gyaman* (Karthala, 1995). On a similar theme for an area to the west, B. Marie Perinbam, 'Political Organization of Traditional Gold Mining: The Western Loby c. 1850–c. 1910, *JAH*, XXIX (1988) is a convincing study. On West African states generally there is an interesting if technologically determinist hypothesis in Jack Goody, *Technology, Tradition and the State* (Oxford University Press, 1971).

The most vigorous debate about forest societies centred on the state of Dahomey. Much of the discussion focused on a period when the Atlantic slave trade was already of great significance, yet it is relevant to this chapter. See the classics: Melville Herskovits, *Dahomey* (J. J. Augustin, 1938); Karl Polanyi, *Dahomey and the Slave Trade* (University of Washington Press, 1966), K. Moseley, 'The Political Economy of Dahomey' in George Dalton, ed., *Research in Economic Anthropology* (2) (1979) and Robin Law, *The Slave Coast of West Africa 1550–1750* (Clarendon Press, 1990). Another provocative study is by Robin Horton on state-formation and slavery, 'From Fishing-Village to City-State: A Social History of New Calabar' in Mary Douglas and Phyllis Kaberry, eds, *Man in Africa* (Tavistock, 1969).

The main lines of early Ethiopian highland history are traced in Taddesse Tamrat, *Church and State in Ethiopia 1270–1527* (Clarendon Press, 1972) and, for an even earlier period, David Phillipson, *Foundations of an African Civilisation; Aksum and the Northern Horn 1000 BC–AD 1300* (James Currey, 2012). See also Chiara Zazzaro, Enzo Cocca and Andrea Manzo, 'Towards a Chronology of the Eritrean Red Sea Port of Adulis (1st – early 7th Century AD)', *JAA,* XII(1), 2014. A distillation of scholarship in this area is found in

Donald Crummey, *Land and Society in the Christian Kingdom of Ethiopia from the 13th to the 20ᵗʰ Century* (James Currey, 2000). Another interesting account is Richard Caulk, 'Armies as Predators: Soldiers and Peasants in Ethiopia, c. 1850–1935', *IJAHS*, XI (1978). On the region of the modern Sudan, R. S. O'Fahey and J. L. Spaulding, *Kingdoms of the Sudan* (Methuen, 1974) on Sennar and Darfur; Anders Bjorkelo, *A Prelude to the Mahdiyya: Peasants and Traders in the Shendi Region 1821–88* (Cambridge University Press, 1988), Lidwein Kapteins, 'The Historiography of the Northern Sudan from 1500 to the Establishment of British Colonial Rule: A Critical Overview', *IJAHS*, XXII (1989) and R. S. O'Fahey, *The Darfur Sultanate, A History* (Hurst & Co., 2008), are all important.

A large swathe of African history is surveyed in the two-volume *History of Central Africa*, edited by David Birmingham and Phyllis Martin (Longman, 1983) which begins with material relevant to this chapter. For the early settlement of eastern and southern Africa and the often-debated questions it raises, see Derek Nurse and Gerard Philippson, *The Bantu Languages* (Routledge, 2003), Christopher Ehret, *An African Classical Age* (University of Virginia Press and David Philip, 1998) and Jan Vansina, *Paths in the Rainforest* (University of Wisconsin Press, 1990). The most useful monographs on the history of this area include Georges Balandier, *Daily Life in the Kingdom of the Kongo* (George Allen & Unwin, 1968); Joseph Miller, *Kings and Kinsmen* (Clarendon Press, 1976); Andrew Roberts, *History of the Bemba* (Longman, 1973), Mutumba Mainga, *Bulozi under the Luyana Kings* (Longman, 1973) and Thomas Reefe, *The Rainbow and the Kings: a History of the Luba Empire to 1891* (University of California Press, 1981). More concerned with social structure are John Thornton, *The Kingdom of the Kongo: Civil War and Transition 1641–1718* (University of Wisconsin Press, 1983) and W. G. Clarence-Smith, 'Slaves, Commoners and Landlords in Bulozi, 1875–1906', *JAH*, XX (1979). On the lands south of the Zambesi, turn to D. N. Beach, *The Shona and Zimbabwe 900–1850* (Africana, 1980).

The first essays in Shula Marks and Anthony Atmore, eds, *Economy and Society in Pre-Industrial South Africa* (Longman, 1980) consider pre-conquest South Africa. The standard history of the Mfecane, now subject to reinterpretation, is J. Omer-Cooper, *The Zulu Aftermath* (Longman, 1965). John Laband, *Ropes of Sand: The Rise and Fall of the Zulu Kingdom in the Nineteenth* Century (Jonathan Ball, 1995) is a readable introduction. For one Mfecane state, see J. Cobbing, 'Evolution of the Ndebele amabutho', *JAH*, XV (1974). For foraging and especially pastoral communities, Richard Elphick, *Kraal and Castle* (Yale University Press, 1977) is foundational. Studies of inter-lacustrine states are Semakula Kiwanuka, *A History of Buganda* (Longman, 1971), S. R. Karugire, *History of Nkore in Western Uganda to 1891* (Clarendon, 1971) and Richard Reid, *Political Power in Pre-Colonial Buganda; Economy, Society and Warfare in the Nineteeth Century* (James Currey, Fountain and Ohio University Press, 2002). Other treatments of East African states are Steven Feierman, *The Shambaa Kingdom* (University of Wisconsin Press, 1974) and R. G. Willis, *A State in the Making* (Indiana University Press, 1980). Rwanda has been assessed by many writers since the genocidal experience of 1994. See Catharine

Newbury, *The Cohesion of Oppression; Clientship and Ethnicity in Rwanda, 1860–1960* (Columbia University Press 1988), Jan Vansina, *Antecedents to Modern Rwanda: The Nyiginya Kingdom* (University of Wisconsin Press, 2004) and on the whole of the Great Lakes area from Buganda to Burundi, Jean-Pierre Chrétien, *The Great Lakes of Africa: Two Thousand Years of History* (Zone Books, 2003).

Some of the more successful attempts to recreate the history of peoples without state institutions have been made in East Africa. These include B. A. Ogot's pathbreaking *History of the Southern Luo* (East African Publishing House, henceforth EAPH, 1967); Godfrey Muriuki, *History of the Kikuyu 1500–1900* (Oxford University Press, 1974) and John Lamphear, *Traditional History of the Jie* (Oxford University Press, 1976). Descriptions of early trade within eastern, southern and south-central Africa are to be found in Richard Gray and David Birmingham, eds, *Precolonial African Trade* (Macmillan, 1970). The Swahili coast is re-examined perceptively in Thomas Spear, 'Early Swahili History Reconsidered', *IJAHS*, XXXIII(4) (2000). For Madagascar, see Gerald Berg, 'Riziculture and the Founding of the Monarchy in Imerina', *JAH*, XXII (1981) and Gwyn Campbell, *The Economic History of Imperial Madagascar 1750–1895*, Cambridge University Press, 2005, although both reach into the nineteenth century extensively.

CHAPTER 3. The European Intrusion in the Era of Merchant Capital

The slave trade has inspired a large literature, some of it concerned with quantitative data only. Basil Davidson, *Black Mother* (Little, Brown, 1961) is still a moving introduction; a survey is M. Craton, *Sinews of Empire* (Doubleday Anchor Books, 1974). Philip Curtin has drawn an effective, short picture based on the history of the sugar industry in his chapter in Ajayi and Crowder, *History of West Africa*, 1, already cited in the Chapter 2 section; Walter Rodney provided a strong, brief summary in a pamphlet published by the Historical Association of Tanzania in 1967 entitled *West Africa and the Atlantic Slave Trade*. Curtin's slave-counting exercise, *The Atlantic Slave Trade: A Census* (University of Wisconsin Press, 1969) is most valuable for its demonstration of the ebb and flow of the trade and the relative importance in it of different parts of Africa. Later research is collected in Henry Gemery and Jan Hogendorn, eds, *The Uncommon Market* (Academic Press, 1979) and J. E. Inikori, ed., *Forced Migration* (Hutchinson, 1981).

On chartered slave trade companies, see Abdoulaye Ly, *La compagnie du Sénégal* (Présence Africaine, 1958) and K. G. Davies, *The Royal African Company* (Longman, 1957). Other aspects of the trade are discussed in Walter Rodney, 'Gold and Slaves on the Gold Coast', *Transactions of the Historical Society of Ghana*, X (1969) and Marion Johnson, 'The Ounce in Eighteenth Century West African Trade', *JAH*, VI (1966). The new American crops introduced during this period are surveyed in William O. Jones, *Manioc in Africa* (Stanford University Press, 1959) and the first chapters of James McCann, *Maize and Grace; Africa's Encounter with a New World Crop 1500–1800* (Harvard UP, 2005). Michael Mason, 'Population Density and "Slave Raiding" – the Case of the Middle Belt', *JAH*, X (1969) and Jean-Pierre Warnier, 'Traite sans raids au Cameroun', CEA, 113 (1989), Walter Hawthorne, 'Nourishing a Stateless Society during the Slave Trade: The Rise of Balanta Paddy Rice Production in Guinea-Bissau', *JAH*, XLIII (2001) and Nicholas David, 'Patterns of Slavery, Prey-Predator Interfaces in and around the Mandara Mountains (Nigeria and Cameroun), *Africa*, 84 (3) (2014), are striking and surprising accounts of the local impacts of slaving on important source areas.

A large and important literature on the slave trade, slavery and the rise of industrial capitalism was born with Eric Williams's classic *Capitalism and Slavery*; this does not really belong to the sphere of African history, however. For a powerful modern account, Robin Blackburn, *The Making of New World Slavery from the Baroque to the Modern 1450–1800* (Verso, 1997) offers a sophisticated evaluation. The first step into this world is movingly considered by Marcus Rediker, *The Slave Ship: A Human History* (Viking Penguin, 2007). On the general impact of slaving in Africa see J. D. Fage, 'Slavery and the Slave Trade in the Context of West African History', *JAH*, X (1969), the important rejoinder by C. C. Wrigley, 'Historicism in Africa: Slavery and Slave Formation', *AA*, LXX (1971) and Walter Rodney, 'African Slavery and other Forms of Social Oppression on the Upper Guinea Coast in the Context of the Atlantic Slave Trade', *JAH*, VII (1966). For the early emergence of a middleman stratum see Peter Mark, 'The Evolution of "Portuguese" Identity; Luso-Africans on the Upper Guinea Coast from the 16th century to the early 19th century', *JAH*, XL (1999). An anti-dependency polemic is contributed by John Thornton, 'Precolonial African Industry and the Atlantic Trade 1500–1800', *AEH*, 16 (1987). The middleman world Mark identifies is given extensive coverage with a focus on women in Hilary Jones, *The Métis of Senegal: Urban Life and Politics in French West Africa* (Indiana UP, 2013) and for Mark's area at a later date, Philip Havik, 'From Pariahs to Patriots; Women Slavers in 19th century "Portuguese" Guinea', in Gwyn Campbell, Suzanne Miers and Joseph Miller, *Women and Slavery I* (Ohio University Press, 2007).

The history of Senegambia is extensively studied in Boulègue, Barry and Curtin as noted in the Chapter 2 section. In addition, Boubacar Barry, *Le Royaume de Waalo* (Maspero, 1972) and Abdoulaye Bathily, 'La traite atlantique des esclaves et ses effets sociaux et économiques en Afrique: le cas de Galam au XIXe siècle', *JAH*, XXVII (1986) are recommended. The region between the Gambia and present-day Liberia is the subject of two excellent studies: Walter Rodney, *A History of the Upper Guinea Coast, 1545–1800* (Clarendon Press, 1970) and Toby Green, *The Rise of the Trans-Atlantic Slave Trade in Western Africa, 1300–1589* (Cambridge University Press, 2012). For the Gold Coast, there is John Vogt, *Portuguese Rule on the Gold Coast* (University of Georgia Press, 1979), Kwame Daaku, *Trade and Politics on the Gold Coast, 1600–1720* (Clarendon Press, 1970) and Ray Kea, *Settlements, Trade and Politics in the Seventeenth-century Gold Coast* (John Hopkins Press, 1982). Most of the books cited above for the last chapter on the forest states of West Africa treat the slave trade. See, as well, A. F. C. Ryder, *Benin and the Europeans, 1485–1897* (Longman 1969); James Graham, 'Slave Trade, Depopulation and Human Sacrifice in Benin History', *CEA*, V (1965); P. Morton-Williams, 'The

Oyo Yoruba and the Atlantic Trade,' *JHSN*, III (1964); Kwame Arhin, 'The Financing of Ashanti Expansion, 1700–1820', *Africa*, XXXVII (1967) and Pierre Verger, *Trade Relations Between the Bight of Benin and Bahia 17th–19th Centuries* (Ibadan University Press, 1976). On the impact of the slave trade in the Niger Delta, important work is contained in E. J. Alagoa, 'Long Distance Trade and States in the Niger Delta', *JAH*, XI (1970); David Northrup, 'The Growth of Trade among the Igbo Before 1800', *JAH*, XIII (1972) and A. J. H. Latham, *Old Calabar, 1600–1891* (Clarendon Press, 1971).

For Angola, there is a massive study by Joseph Miller, *The Way of Death: Merchant Capitalism and the Angolan Slave Trade 1730–1830* (James Currey, 1988). See as well David Birmingham, *Trade and Conflict in Angola* (Clarendon Press, 1966) and Joseph Miller, 'Lineages, Ideology and the History of Slavery in Western Central Africa' in Paul Lovejoy, ed., *Ideologies of Slavery in Africa* (Sage, 1982). For the political shifts in an area which was a major source of slaves, Jan Vansina, 'Ambaya Society and the Slave Trade ca. 1760–1845', *JAH*, 46 (2005) and John Thornton and Andrea Mosteman, 'A Reinterpretation of the Kongo-Portuguese War according to New Documentary Evidence,' *JAH*, 51 (2010), are suggestive.

Older standard histories of Kongo are by Georges Balandier and W. G. L. Randles. John Thornton has returned repeatedly to the archives to develop further ideas such as those in 'Demography and History in the Kingdom of Kongo, 1550–1750', *JAH*, XVIII (1977) and 'Afro-Christian Syncretism in the Kingdom of Kongo, *JAH*, LIV (2013). For the region north of the River Zaïre, see Phyllis Martin, *The External Trade of the Loango Coast, 1576–1870* (Clarendon Press, 1972). For the Zambesi and the region to the north of it, the most important studies are: M. D. D. Newitt, *Portuguese Settlement on the Zambesi* (Longman, 1973); Allen Isaacman, *Mozambique: the Africanization of a European Institution* (University of Wisconsin Press, 1972) and Edward Alpers, *Ivory and Slaves in East Central Africa* (Heinemann, 1975).

On South Africa under the Dutch, Richard Elphick and Hermann Giliomee, eds, *The Shaping of South African Society, 1652–1840* (Maskew Miller Longman, 1989) and Nigel Worden, *Slavery in Dutch South Africa* (Cambridge University Press, 1985) examine this period. The first section of Hermann Giliomee, *The Afrikaners, The Story of a People* (C. Hurst, 2011), is an excellent later study more capacious than the title indicates. P. J. van der Merwe, *The Migrant Farmer in the History of the Cape Colony* (Ohio University Press, 1995), is a neglected social history classic.

CHAPTER 4. The Era of Legitimate Commerce, 1800–70

A general overview of the issues discussed in this chapter can be found in Martin Klein, 'Slavery, the Slave Trade and Legitimate Commerce in Late Nineteenth-Century Africa', *Études d'histoire africaine* 11 (1971). On the abolition of slavery and the slave trade the reader can still profit by consulting Eric Williams, *Capitalism and Slavery* (Capricorn, 1944), but empiricist critiques require consideration, notably Roger Anstey, *The Atlantic Slave Trade and British Abolition, 1760–1810* (Humanities Press, 1975) and Seymour Drescher,

Econocide (University of Pittsburgh Press, 1977). A major reinterpretation of the link between political conflict and abolition is Robin Blackburn, *The Overthrow of Colonial Slavery 1776–1848* (Verso, 1988).

Nineteenth-century West Africa is covered by numerous economic historians but, as with other areas, few works are limited exclusively to this period of history. One with its strongest pages on the nineteenth century is A. G. Hopkins, *Economic History of West Africa* (Longman, 1973). A very informative economic study is David Eltis and Lawrence Jennings, 'Trade Between Western Africa and the Atlantic World in the Pre-colonial Era', *American Historical Review*, XCIII (1988). Of note are the relevant chapters in Claude Meillassoux, ed., *The Development of Indigenous Trade and Markets in West Africa* (Oxford University Press, 1971) and the economic studies of Colin Newbury such as 'Trade and Authority in West Africa from 1850 to 1880' in Lewis Gann and Peter Duignan, eds, *Colonialism in Africa*, I (Cambridge University Press, 1969).

For this epoch in Senegambia, the reader should consult the relevant pages in Barry and Curtin's studies cited earlier (Chapter 2 section). Aspects of the impact of groundnut exports are discussed in Ken Swindell, 'Serawoolies, Tillibunkas and Strange Farmers: Development of Migrant Groundnut Farming along the Gambia River, 1848–95', *JAH*, XXI (1980) and George Brooks, 'Peanuts and Colonialism: Consequences of the Commercialization of Peanuts in West Africa, 1830–70', *JAH*, XVI (1975). For another commodity see James Webb, 'The Trade in Gum Arabic', *JAH*, XXVI (1985).

On Sierra Leone there is Leo Spitzer, *The Creoles of Sierra Leone* (University of Wisconsin Press, 1974) and Allen Howard and David Skinner, 'Network Building and Political Power in North-west Sierra Leone 1800–65', *Africa*, LIV (1985). Magdalene Davis, 'The Love of Liberty Brought Us Here', *ROAPE*, 31(1984) provides an analytical introduction to Liberia. For the Gold Coast in this period see Edward Reynolds, *Trade and Economic Change on the Gold Coast, 1807–74* (Longman, 1974). The Saros in Yoruba-speaking lands are the subject of Jean Herskovits Kopytoff, *A Preface to Modern Nigeria* (University of Wisconsin Press, 1965). The strengths and limitations of their position in Abeokuta, the greatest Saro centre inland from the coast, are analysed in Agneta Pallinder-Law, 'Aborted Modernization in West Africa? The Case of Abeokuta', *JAH*, XV (1974). On other political and economic aspects of nineteenth-century Yorubaland, the more significant titles would include: S. A. Akintoye, *Revolution and Power Politics in Yorubaland, 1840–83* (Longman, 1971); Bolanle Awe, 'Militarism and Economic Development in Nineteenth-Century Yoruba Country the Ibadan Example', *JAH*, XIV (1973); Babatunde Agiri, 'Slavery in Yoruba Society in the Nineteenth Century' in Paul Lovejoy, ed., *The Ideology of Slavery in Africa* (Sage, 1981); E. A. Ayandele, *The Missionary Impact on Modern Nigeria, 1842–1914* (Longman, 1966) and T. G. O. Gbadamosi, *The Growth of Islam among the Yoruba, 1841–1908* (Longman, 1978).

The Niger Delta region is examined in K. O. Dike, *Trade and Politics in the Niger Delta 1830–85* (Clarendon Press, 1956); G. I. Jones, *Trading States of the Oil Rivers* (Oxford University Press, 1963) and Obaro Ikime, *Merchant*

Prince of the Niger Delta (Heinemann, 1968). More recent are A. J. H. Latham, *Old Calabar 1600–1891* (Clarendon Press, 1973) and David Northrup, *Trade Without Rulers* (Clarendon Press, 1978). A. E. Afigbo, *Ropes of Sand: Studies in Igbo History and Culture* (University of Nigeria Press, 1981) also takes the story further. Political conflict engendered by the burgeoning palm oil trade elsewhere is highlighted in Robin Law, 'Politics of Commercial Transition; Factional Conflict in Dahomey in the Context of the Ebbing of the Atlantic Slave Trade', *JAH*, XXXVIII (1997).

A number of family and individual studies of the coastal compradore class exist. They include Raymond Dumett, 'John Sarbah the Elder and African Merchant Entrepreneurship in the Gold Coast in the Late Nineteenth Century', *JAH*, XIV (1973); A. G. Hopkins, 'Richard Beale Blaize, 1854–1904', *Tarikh*, I (1966); David Ross, 'The Career of Domingo Martinez in the Bight of Benin, 1853–64', *JAH*, VI (1965); and Margaret Priestley, *West African Trade and Coast Society* (Oxford University Press, 1969). A class perspective is suggested in Edward Reynolds, 'Rise and Fall of an African Merchant Class on the Gold Coast, 1830–70', *CEA*, X (1974) and developed in Susan Kaplow, 'The Mudfish and the Crocodile', *Science and Society*, XLI (1977). On women in coastal centres in Senegambia, see Hilary Jones, *The Métis of Senegal: Urban Life and Politics in French West Africa*, cited for the previous chapter.

The jihad movements, covered in the last chapter's bibliography, dominate the historiography of the savannah region of West Africa for the nineteenth century. However, for the empire-builder Samori, consult the three-volume history by Yves Person, *Samori, une révolution dyoula* (Institut Fondamentale de l'Afrique Noire, 1968–75). On the quest for a pure Muslim state in what is today the republic of Mali, see David Robinson, cited for the previous chapter, on Umar Tal. A summary of French colonial intentions during this era, exclusive of Senegal, was Bernard Schnapper, *La politique et le commerce français dans le golfe de Guinée de 1838 à 1871* (Mouton, 1961).

For East and Central Africa, this chapter relies on books covered in other chapter bibliographies, including work by John Iliffe, Andrew Roberts, D. A. Low and J. Forbes Munro. The nineteenth century looms large in Richard Gray and David Birmingham, eds, *Pre-colonial African Trade*, already cited (Chapter 2 section). Zanzibari history is surveyed in Abdul Sheriff, *Slaves, Spices and Ivory in Zanzibar* (James Currey, Ohio University Press, Heinemann & Tanzania Publishing House, 1987). There is an excellent study of the slave plantations on the Kenya coast and the island of Zanzibar by Frederick Cooper, *Plantation Slavery in Kenya and Zanzibar* (Yale University Press, 1977) and an interesting piece on the dislocations in East African women's lives: Marcia Wright, 'Women in Peril', *African Social Research*, XX (1975). The immediate interior away from the Indian Ocean coast is the subject of Thomas Herlihy's 'Ties that Bind: Palm Wine and Blood Brotherhood at the Kenya Coast during the Nineteenth Century', *IJAHS*, XVII (1984). On the Lake Malawi region, see Harry Langworthy, 'Central Malawi in the Nineteenth Century' in R. J. Macdonald, *From Nyasaland to Malawi* (EAPH, 1975) and Leroy Vail, 'Suggestions towards a Reinterpreted Tumbuka History' in B. Pachai, *The Early History of Malawi* (Longman, 1972). Tippu Tip's memoirs are available in Swahili and English: *Maisha ya Hamed bin Muhammad yaani Tippu Tip* (reprint of Edward Arnold edn, Nairobi, 1966). The cultural and economic world of the caravans is surveyed in Stephen Rockel, *Carriers of Culture: Labor on the Road in Nineteenth Century East Africa* (Heinemann, 2006). On the Zambesi valley in the nineteenth century, sources cited elsewhere in this bibliographical guide – Newitt, Isaacman, Vail and White, are the most helpful. For Angola there is in particular Clarence-Smith's *Slaves, Peasants and Capitalists in Southern Angola* (Cambridge University Press, 1979) and David Birmingham, 'The Coffee Barons of Cazengo', *JAH*, XIX (1978).

Davenport's general history is a passable detailed introduction to nineteenth-century South African events and provides a useful bibliography. The first volume of the *Cambridge History of South Africa* is more recent and proposes some newer themes. Timothy Keegan, *Colonial South Africa and the Making of the Racial Order* (University Press of Virginia, 1996) is a good introduction to this period. For the Shepstone system in Natal, see Jeff Guy, *Theophilus Shepstone and the Forging of Natal: African Autonomy and Settler Colonialism in the Making of Traditional Authority* (University of KwaZulu-Natal Press, 2013). Patrick Harries, 'Plantations, Passes and Proletarians: Labour and the Colonial State in Nineteenth Century Natal', *JSAS*, XIII (1987) is an important supplement. There is a major revisionist interpretation of the imperial factor: Anthony Atmore and Shula Marks, 'The Imperial Factor in South Africa in the Nineteenth Century: Towards a Reassessment', *JICH*, III (1974). Another still often cited approach is Colin Bundy, *Rise and Fall of the South African Peasantry* (University of California Press, 1979). An important corrective to Bundy is Jack Lewis, 'The Rise and Fall of the South African Peasantry: A Critique and a Reassessment,' *JSAS*, XI (1984) while Timothy Keegan demonstrates the limits of the peasant prosperity thesis in 'Trade, Accumulation and Impoverishment: Mercantile Capital and the Economic Transformation of Lesotho and the Conquered Territory.' *JSAS*, XII (1986). Another aspect is traced by Charles Ballard, 'Repercussions of Rinderpest: Cattle Plague and Peasant Decline in Colonial Natal', *IJAHS*, XIX (1986). An earlier disaster is the subject of J. B. Peires' eloquent *The Dead Will Arise; Nongqawuse and the Great Xhosa Cattle-Killing Movement of 1856–57* (Ravan Press, Indiana University Press & James Currey, 1989). For an original look at the confrontation of white settlement and black interests in the new economy see Keletso Atkins, *The Moon is Dead: Give Us Our Money!* (Heinemann & James Currey, 1994). On the emergent African entrepreneurial class, Norman Etherington, 'Mission Station Melting Pots as a Factor in the Rise of South African Black Nationalism', *IJAHS*, IX (1976) is interesting. The post-emancipation fate of the western Cape is discussed in Wayne Dooling, *Slavery, Emancipation and Colonial Rule in South Africa* (Ohio University Press, 2008) and Hermann Giliomee, 'Western Cape Farmers and the Beginnings of Afrikaner Nationalism 1870–1915', *JSAS*, XIV (1987). For the transition at Kimberley towards more revolutionary changes in South African society, there are two excellent monographs to consult: Robert Turrell, *Capital and Labour on the Kimberley Diamond Fields 1871–90* (Cambridge University Press, 1987) and William Worger, *South Africa's City of Diamonds; Mine Workers and Monopoly Capitalism in Kimberley 1867–95* (Yale University Press, 1987).

Another region with a fairly well-developed historiography for the nineteenth century is the Ethiopian plateau; it is, however, largely political and dynastic in character. This is the case with Sven Rubenson, *The Survival of Ethiopian Independence* (Heinemann, 1976); R. H. Kofi Darkwah, *Shewa, Menilek and the Ethiopian Empire, 1813–89* (Heinemann, 1975) and Zewde Gebre-Selassie, *Yohannis IV of Ethiopia* (Clarendon Press, 1975). Social and economic considerations have some purchase on Mordechai Abir, *Ethiopia: the Era of the Princes* (Longman, 1968); Donald Crummey, 'Initiatives and Objectives in Ethio-European Relations, 1827–62', *JAH*, XV (1974) and 'Tewodros as Reformer and Modernizer', *JAH*, X (1969). On the Horn of Africa in the legitimate trade era, Edward Alpers, 'Muqdisho in the Nineteenth Century', *JAH*, XXIV (1983) and Lee Casanelli, *The Shaping of Somali Society* (University of Pennsylvania Press, 1982) make a good beginning.

The standard work on Egyptian rule along the middle Nile is Richard Hill, *Egypt in the Sudan 1820–81* (Oxford University Press, 1959). Madagascar is the subject of the magisterial work of Françoise Raison-Jourde, *Le Bible et le pouvoir à Madagascar au XIXe siècle* (Karthala, 1991). She has also written important essays in *Les souverains de Madagascar* (Karthala, 1983).

CHAPTER 5. The Conquest of Africa

V. I. Lenin, *Imperialism: the Highest Stage of Capitalism* (International Publishers edn., 1939), and Nikolai Bukharin, *Imperialism and World Economy* (Merlin Press edn., 1971) remain compelling while John Hobson, *Imperialism: A Study* (originally published 1902) repays examination. This is also true of the work of other past partisan writers and thinkers such as Rosa Luxemburg. For critical assessments, the most significant used here are the excellent edited collection by Bob Sutcliffe and Roger Owen, *Studies in the Theory of Imperialism* (Longman, 1972); V. G. Kiernan, *Marxism and Imperialism* (St Martin's Press, 1975); Anthony Brewer, *Marxist Theories of Imperialism* (Routledge & Kegan Paul, 1980) and Bill Warren, *Imperialism: Pioneer of Capitalism* (New Left Books, 1981).

Important examples of the anti-economic (and anti-Marxist) school of imperialist historians are Ronald Robinson and John Gallagher, with Alice Denny, *Africa and the Victorians* (St Martin's Press, 1961) and David Fieldhouse, *Economics and Empire 1830–1914* (Weidenfeld & Nicolson, 1973). There is a balanced interpretation in George Sanderson, 'The European Partition of Africa: Coincidence or Conjuncture', in E. F. Penrose, ed., *European Imperialism and the Partition of Africa* (Cass, 1975) and a novel and important analysis in A. G. Hopkins, *An Economic History of West Africa*, already cited under Chapter 4. For a French equivalent to the anti-Marxist British school, see Henri Brunschwig, *French Colonialism 1871–1914: Myths and Realities* (Pall Mall, 1961). The diplomatic history of the scramble is surveyed in a broader context of European power politics in W. L. Langer, *European Alliances and Alignments, 1871–90* and *The Diplomacy of Imperialism, 1890–1902* (Alfred A. Knopf, 2nd edns., 1950 and 1951). For the material foundation of British imperialism, see Eric J. Hobsbawm, *Industry and Empire* (Weidenfeld & Nicolson, 1968) and

P. J. Cain and A. G. Hopkins, 'The Political Economy of British Expansion Overseas, 1750–1914', *EHR*, XXXIII, N.S. (1980). These two authors also produced a new general interpretation to try and combine the economic and non-economic schools in a two volume synthesis: *British Imperialism, Innovation and Expansion 1688–1914* and *Crisis and Deconstruction 1914–90* (Longman, 1993). The social context was explored in Bernard Semmel, *Imperialism and Social Reform* (Harvard University Press, 1960) and Richard Price, *An Imperial War and the British Working Class* (Routledge & Kegan Paul, 1972). A different side of imperialism is approached in John MacKenzie, *Imperialism and the Natural World* (Manchester University Press, 1990).

On France see C. M. Andrew and A. S. Kanya-Forstner, 'The French Colonial Party: Its Composition, Aims and Influence', *HJ*, XIV (1971) and John Laffey, 'The Roots of French Imperialism in the Nineteenth Century: The Case of Lyon', *French Historical Studies*, VI (1969/70). Colin Newbury has written several pieces on the impact of French protectionism such as 'The Protectionist Revival in French Colonial Trade: The Case of Senegal', *EHR*, N.S. XXI (1968). For a provocative and important reinterpretation, see Jacques Marseille, *Empire colonial et capitalisme français: histoire d'un divorce* (Albin Michel, 1984).

There is a large literature on the imperialism of the Second Reich. Major works include Fritz Ferdinand Müller, *Deutschland-Ostafrika-Zanzibar* (Rutten und Loening, 1959); Manfred Nussbaum, *Vom 'Kolonialenthusiasmus' zur Kolonialpolitik der Monopole* (Akadamieverlag, 1962) and Hans-Ulrich Wehler, *Bismarck und der Imperialismus* (Kiepenheuer und Witsch, 1969). Wehler's ideas are summarised in the Owen and Sutcliffe collection and criticised in Gifford and Louis by Henry Turner. Neal Ascherson, *The King Incorporated* (George Allen & Unwin, 1963) and Adam Hochschild, *King Leopold's Ghost*, Houghton Mifflin, NY, 1998, tell different aspects of the story of Leopold II. For the narrative of Portuguese expansion, see Eric Axelson, *Portugal and the Scramble for Africa* (Witwatersrand University Press, 1967) and R. J. Hammond, *Portugal and Africa, 1815–1910* (Stanford University Press, 1966), but also the significant revision, W. G. Clarence-Smith, 'The Myth of Uneconomic Imperialism: The Portuguese in Angola', *JSAS*, V (1979).

Issues relating to medicine and ideology are handled in Philip Curtin, *The Image of Afri*ca (University of Wisconsin Press, 1964) and the technological aspect of expansionism in Daniel Headrick, *The Tools of Empire* (Oxford University Press, 1981). There are rather flattering biographies of a number of the major African conquistadores such as Margery Perham, *Lugard* (Collins, 2 vols, 1956–60); J. E. Flint, *Sir George Goldie and the Making of Nigeria* (Clarendon Press, 1960) and Roland Oliver, *Sir Henry Johnston and the Scramble for Africa* (Chatto & Windus, 1964). On a major business figure within British imperialism, see John S. Galbraith, *Mackinnon and East Africa, 1878–95* (Cambridge University Press, 1972).

The conquest of West Africa is considered generally in John D. Hargreaves, *Prelude to the Partition of Africa* (Macmillan, 1963) and *West Africa Partitioned: The Loaded Pause* (University of Wisconsin Press, 1974); Obaro Ikime, *The Fall of Nigeria* (Heinemann, 1977) and Michael Crowder, ed., *West*

African Resistance (Hutchinson, 1971). There is a valuable set of volumes collecting primary source material in C. W. Newbury, *British Policy Towards West Africa: Select Documents* (Clarendon, 1965–71). The context of conquest in southern Nigeria is considered in: S. A. Akintoye, *Revolution and Power Politics in Yorubaland, 1840–1893*, cited under Chapter 4; Bolanle Awe, 'The End of an Experiment: The Collapse of the Ibadan Empire 1877–93', *JHSN*, III (1965); Walter Ofonagoro, *Trade and Imperialism in Southern Nigeria, 1881–1929* (Nok, 1979); S. J. S. Cookey, *King Ja Ja of the Niger Delta* (Nok, 1974) and A. E. Afigbo, 'Patterns of Igbo Resistance to British Conquest', *Tarikh*, IV (1973). A. G. Hopkins, 'Economic Imperialism in West Africa: Lagos 1880–92', *EHR*, N.S.,XXI (1968) is perceptive. The lands to the west of Lagos, including Dahomey, are the subject of C. W. Newbury, *The Western Slave Coast and its Rulers* (Clarendon Press, 1961). Toyin Falola has placed together the story of the best-known Nigerian resistance struggles in *Colonialism and Violence in Nigeria* (Indiana UP, 2009). A Béninois historian, Luc Garcia, has written *Le royaume Dahomé face à la pénétration coloniale* (Karthala, 1988). For northern Nigeria the main study of the conquest is Roland Adeleye, *Power and Diplomacy in Northern Nigeria, 1804–1906* (Longman, 1971). For the conquest of contemporary Ghana see Adu Boahen, 'Politics in Ghana, 1800–74' in Ajayi and Crowder, *History of West Africa*, II, cited already and Thomas Lewin, *Asante Before the British; the Prempean Years, 1875–1900* (Regents Press of Kansas, 1978). Some of the economic context emerges from Kwame Arhin, 'Ashanti Rubber Trade in the 1890s', *Africa*, XLII (1972) and Raymond Dumett, 'The Rubber Trade of the Gold Coast and Asante in the Nineteenth Century', *JAH*, XII (1971).

Considerations of the French intrusion in West Africa are in A. S. Kanya-Forstner, *The Conquest of the Western Sudan* (Cambridge University Press, 1969); Martin Klein, *Islam and Imperialism in Senegal* (Stanford University Press, 1968); Mamadou Diouf, *Le Kayoor au XIXe siècle; pouvoir ceddo et conquête coloniale* (Karthala, 1990); Jeanne-Marie Kambou-Ferrand, *Peuples voltaïques et conquête coloniale 1885–1915* (Harmattan, 1993) and Yehoshuah Rash, *Les premières années françaises du Damergou; des colonisateurs sans enthousiasme* (P. Geuthner, Paris, 1973). Klein, Diouf and Kambou-Ferrand focus on African initiatives as does Timothy Weiskel, *French Colonial Rule and the Baule Peoples.* (Clarendon Press, 1980). David Robinson's study of Umar Tall cited in the previous chapter introduces the Tukulor empire and its role in this area.

The study of imperialism in East Africa is less well developed. David Arnold, 'External Factors in the Partition of East Africa' read with A. J. Temu, 'Tanzanian Societies and Colonial Invasion, 1875–1907' in Martin Kaniki, ed., *Tanzania under Colonial Rule* (Longman, 1980) makes a serviceable introduction. The special circumstances of Buganda are discussed in D. A. Low, *Buganda in Modern History* (University of California Press, 1971); C. C. Wrigley, 'The Christian Revolution in Buganda', *CSSH*, II (1959) and John Rowe, 'The Purge of Christians at Mwanga's Court', *JAH*, V (1964). There is a survey of British involvement in Nyasaland in A. J. Hanna, *The Beginnings of Nyasaland and Northern Rhodesia 1858–95* (Clarendon Press, 1956). For north-east Africa, the struggle over Ethiopia is treated in Harold Marcus, *The*

Life and Times of Menelik II: Ethiopia, 1844–1913 (Clarendon Press, 1975) and Sven Rubenson, 'Adwa: The Resounding Protest' in Robert Rotberg and Ali Mazrui, eds, *Protest and Power in Black Africa* (Oxford University Press, New York, 1970). For the Islamic revolution in the Sudan, see P. M. Holt, *The Mahdist State in the Sudan 1881–1898* (Clarendon Press, 1958). The race to the Nile is covered in G. Sanderson, *England, Europe and the Upper Nile, 1882–1899* (Edinburgh University Press, 1965) and Marc Michel, *La mission Marchand* (Mouton, 1972). For the English-speaking reader, a clear introduction to the conquest of Madagascar is Phares Mutibwa, *The Malagasy and the Europeans: Madagascar's Foreign Relations, 1861–1895* (Longman, 1974). See also Steven Ellis, *The Rising of the Red Shawls* (Cambridge University Press, 1985) and Gwyn Campbell, 'An Industrial Experiment in Pre-colonial Africa: The Case of Imperial Madagascar', *JSAS*, XVII (1991).

On resistance to the European conquest of East Africa, studies include G. H. Mungeam, 'Masai and Kikuyu Responses to the Establishment of British Administration in the East Africa Protectorate', *JAH*, XI (1970), J. M. Lonsdale, 'The Politics of Conquest: The British in Kenya, 1894–1908', *HJ*, XX (1977), Edward Steinhart, *Conflict and Collaboration: Kingdoms of Western Uganda, 1890–1907* (Princeton University Press, 1977), Jonathon Glassman, *Feasts and Riot* (Heinemann, 1995), on the Abushiri rising in coastal German East Africa, and Jamie Monson, 'Relocating Maji Maji; The Politics of Alliance and Authority in the Southern Highlands of Tanzania 1890–1918', *JAH*, XXXIX, 1997, on another major resistance phase.

There is a large and controversial literature on various aspects of the conquest of South Africa. It is surveyed and assessed in Atmore and Marks, cited for the previous chapter and included in the E. Penrose collection on European imperialism. This analysis is extended in Marks and Stanley Trapido, 'Lord Milner and the South African State', *HWJ*, 8 (1979). Some of the process of revision is encapsulated in a series of writings on the Jameson Raid: G. A. Blainey, 'Lost Causes of the Jameson Raid', *EHR*, N.S. XVIII (1965); R. V. Kubicek, 'The Randlords in 1895: A Reassessment', *JBS*, II (1972) and R. Mendelsohn, 'Blainey and the Jameson Raid: The Debate Renewed', *JSAS*, VI (1980).

A classic study of the politics of confrontation between Britain and the South African Republic is J. S. Marais, *The Fall of Kruger's Republic* (Clarendon Press, 1961). One phase has received attention more recently in Peter Henshaw, 'The "Key to South Africa" in the 1890s: Delagoa Bay and the Origins of the South African War', *JSAS*, XXIV, 1998. Transvaal society is re-interpreted in Stanley Trapido's contribution to the Atmore and Marks book cited earlier, 'Reflections on Land, Office and Wealth in the South African Republic 1850–1900'. Norman Etherington has written a very important consideration of Confederation, 'Labour Supply and the Genesis of South African Confederation in the 1870s', *JAH*, XX (1979). On the Boer War itself, Peter Warwick, ed., *The South African War* (Longman, 1980) is a very useful resource. The perspective of dominated populations is explored in Bill Nasson, *Abraham Esau's War* (Cambridge University Press, 1991).

The intrusion of Rhodes' chartered company north of the Limpopo and the consequent conflict with Lobengula and the Ndebele state has often been recounted, for example in Philip Mason, *The Birth of a Dilemma* (Oxford University Press, 1958) and Stanlake Samkange, *The Origins of Rhodesia* (Heinemann, 1968). A more recent analysis more widely set is David Beach, *War and Politics in Zimbabwe 1840–1900* (Mambo Press, 1986) but see also Julian Cobbing, 'Lobengula, Jameson and the Occupation of Mashonaland', *RH*, IV (1973) and Ian Phimister, 'Rhodes, Rhodesia and the Rand', *JSAS*, I (1974). The situation in what was to become South-West Africa is analysed by Brigitte Lau, 'Conflict and Power in Nineteenth Century Namibia', *JAH*, XXVII (1986).

CHAPTER 6. The Material Basis of Colonial Society, 1900–40

A compendium of essays on colonial Africa in four volumes, most of which reflect the apologist viewpoint of the editors, is Lewis Gann and Peter Duignan, eds, *Colonialism in Africa* (Cambridge University Press, 1968–75). The fifth volume contains an important bibliography. Among regional and national studies some of the best come from the French tradition. Jean Suret-Canale, *French Colonialism in Africa, 1900–1945* (C. Hurst, 1971), is stronger on economic than social history. For a recent perspective, see Alice Conklin, *A Mission to Civilize, The Republican Idea of Empire in France and West Africa 1895–1930* (Stanford UP, 1997).

Catherine Coquery-Vidrovitch, *Le Congo au temps des grandes compagnies concessionaires, 1898–1930* (Mouton, 1972) is on French Equatorial Africa. An outstanding synthesis was achieved by Michel Merlier, *Le Congo de la colonisation belge à l'indépendance* (Maspéro, 1962). A number of authors have expanded on Merlier's vision in general articles, notably Jean-Philippe Peemans, 'Capital Accumulation in the Congo under Colonialism: The Role of the State' in the Gann and Duignan collection. By contrast the best single national history in English, John Iliffe's on Tanganyika, has a lot of social and economic analysis. A pathbreaking reinterpretation is made by Anne Phillips, *The Enigma of Colonialism: British Policy in West Africa* (James Currey, 1989). Another thoughtful set of critical ideas emerge in Fred Cooper, *Colonialism in Question* (University of California Press, 2005). The tripartite definition of African colonial development is adapted from a classic article by Samir Amin, 'Underdevelopment and Dependence in Black Africa: Origins and Contemporary Forms', *JMAS*, X (1972).

There is a solid historical literature in German, particularly on economic factors, dealing with the old German colonies. Of particular significance are: Helmuth Stoecker ed., *Kamerun unter Deutscher Herrschaft* (Deutscher Verlag der Wissenschaften VEB, 1960–8); Rainer Tetzlaff, *Koloniale Entwicklung und Ausbeutung* (Duncker und Humboldt, 1970); Karin Hausen, *Deutsche Kolonialherrschaft in Afrika: Wirtschaftsinteressen und Kolonialverwaltung in Kamerun vor 1914* (Atlantis Verlag, 1970); Albert Wirz, *Von Sklavenhandel zum Kolonialhandel* (Atlantis Verlag, 1972) and Helmut Bley, *South West Africa under German Rule, 1894–1914* (Northwestern University Press, 1971). More recent contributions include Peter Geschiere, 'European Planters, African Peasants and the Colonial State: Alternatives in the Mise en Valeur in Makaland,

South East Cameroun in the Antebellum Period', *AEH*, XII (1983), Wolfgang Werner, 'A Brief History of Land Dispossession in Namibia', *JSAS*, XIX (1993), and Juhani Koponen, *Development for Exploitation: German African Policies in Mainland Tanzania 1884–1914* (Tredekirja and Lit, Helsinki and Hamburg, Finnish Historical Society Studia Historica 44, 1994).

For Kenya, studies of the political economy are Richard Wolff, *The Economics of Colonialism* (Yale University Press, 1974) and on the East African region, Edward Brett, *Colonialism and Underdevelopment in East Africa: The Politics of Economic Change 1919–1939* (Heinemann, 1973). Bruce Berman, *Control and Crisis in Colonial Kenya: The Dialectic of Domination* (James Currey, Ohio University Press & Heinemann, 1990) and the essays in Berman and John Lonsdale, *Unhappy Valley* (James Currey, Ohio University Press & Heinemann, 1992–4, 2 volumes) are important further interpretations. On particular regions, J. Forbes Munro, *Colonial Rule and the Kamba* (Clarendon Press, 1975) and Charles Ambler, *Kenyan Communities in an Age of Imperialism* (Yale University Press, 1988) are good. On Uganda see Mahmood Mamdani, *Politics and Class Formation in Uganda* (Onyx Press, 1980) and Jan Jelmert Jorgensen, *Uganda, A Modern History* (St Martin's Press, 1981).

On British Central Africa of pioneering importance is Giovanni Arrighi, *The Political Economy of Rhodesia* (Mouton, 1967). An excellent synthesis has been written by Ian Phimister, *An Economic and Social History of Zimbabwe 1890–1948* (Longmans, 1988). The relevant pages in Andrew Roberts, *A History of Zambia*, make an introduction to colonial Northern Rhodesia. The relevant parts of John McCracken's new history of Malawi are the best guide now to its colonial history.

Reference has already been made to the Belgian Congo. However, a number of works on the period of the Congo Free State should be noted: Neal Ascherson's biography as previously noted for Chapter 5; Robert Harms, 'The End of Red Rubber: A Reassessment', *JAH*, XVI (1975); Roger Anstey, 'The Congo Rubber Atrocities', *AHS*, IV (1971); Mutwale-Muyimbwe, 'Les sources publiques de financement de l'Etat Indépendant du Congo, 1885–1907', *Cahiers du CEDAF*, V (1973). Rubber, however, was not everywhere a disaster for African people. It was an effective source of cash in parts of West Africa: see Emily Osborn, '"Rubber Fever", Commerce and French Colonial Rule in Upper Guinea 1890–1913', *JAH*, XLV, 2004. For Ruanda-Urundi, Belgian from 1918 onward and a key place for exploring the realities of indirect rule, two works are Catherine Newbury, *The Cohesion of Oppression: Clientship and Ethnicity in Rwanda 1860–1960* (Columbia University Press, 1988), a local study, and Joseph Gahama, *Le Burundi sous l'administration belge* (Harmattan, 1983).

On the political economy of Portuguese Africa see W. G. Clarence-Smith, *The Third Portuguese Empire* (Manchester University Press, 1985); Michel Cahen, 'Corporatisme et colonialisme au Mozambique', *CEA*, 92/93 (1984) and Malyn Newitt, *Portugal in Africa, the Last Hundred Years* (C. Hurst, 1981), with a good bibliography. A good case study is Otto Roesch, 'Migrant Labour and Forced Rice Production in Southern Mozambique: The Colonial Peasantry of the Lower Limpopo Valley', *JSAS*, XVII (1991). On the slave trade scandal contemporary with the Congo red rubber affair in Angola see James Duffy, *A Question of Slavery* (Harvard University Press, 1967). In Portuguese there is Armando Castro, *O Sistema Colonial Português em Africa* (ed. Caminho, 1978).

Overviews of the French mainland colonies have already been noted with reference to the first chapter. See also Sheldon Gellar, *Structural Changes and Political Dependency: Senegal 1885–1945* (Sage, 1976) and Christopher Gray and François Ngolet, 'Lamboréné, Okoumé and the Transformation of Labour along the Middle Ogoué (Gabon) 1870–1945', *JAH* (1999), XL, an area where coerced local labour gave way to use of migrants, especially from more populous Chad at the other end of French Equatorial Africa.

On a special topic Myron Echenberg, 'Les migrations militaires en Afrique Occidentale Française 1900–40', *CJAS*, XIV (1980) and Gregory Mann, *Native Sons, West African Veterans and France in the Twentieth Century* (Duke UP, 2006) look at the lives of conscripted black soldiers. African soldiers were, however, also found elsewhere and their lives, including those of wives and children, are explored in the Africanist studies in David Killingray and David Omissi, eds, *Guardians of Empire; The Armed Forces of the Colonial Powers c. 1700–1964* (Manchester UP, 1999) and in Timothy Parsons, *The African Rank-and-File; Social Implications of Colonial Military Service in the King's African Rifles, 1902–64* (Heinemann, James Currey, etc., 1999). Two extraordinary colonial travel volumes are Geoffrey Gorer, *Africa Dances* (Faber & Faber, 1935) and André Gide, *Voyage au Congo* (Gallimard, 1927).

There is a useful general history of West Africa in Michael Crowder, *West Africa under Colonial Rule* (Hutchinson, 1968). An overview on Nigeria by Gavin Williams in his edited book, *Nigeria: Economy and Society* (Rex Collings, 1976) may be supplemented by Robert Shenton, *The Development of Capitalism in Northern Nigeria* (James Currey, 1986) and Toyin Falola, *Colonialism and Violence in Nigeria*. On Ghana, Rhoda Howard attempted an underdevelopmentalist overview, *Colonialism and Underdevelopment in Ghana* (Croom Helm, 1978). See also Geoffrey Kay's book of readings, *The Political Economy of Colonialism in Ghana* (Cambridge University Press, 1972).

On colonial north-eastern Africa, works to consult include I. M. Lewis, *The Modern History of Somaliland* (Weidenfeld & Nicolson, 1965); Abdi Ismail Samatar, *The State and Rural Transformation in Northern Somalia 1884–1986* (University of Wisconsin Press, 1986); Peter Woodward, *Sudan 1898–1989* (Lester Crook, 1990); Irma Taddia, *L'Eritrea-Colonia 1890–1952: paesaggi, strutture, uomini del colonialismo* (Franco Angeli, 1986) and Alberto Sbacchi, *Ethiopia under Mussolini: Fascism and the Colonial Experience* (Zed Press, 1985).

The economic and social themes at the core of this chapter were advanced enormously by a seminal collection that bears on all aspects of agriculture, Robin Palmer and Neil Parsons, eds, *The Roots of Rural Poverty in Southern and Central Africa* (Heinemann, 1977). Martin Klein, *Peasants in Africa* (Sage, 1980) is a very useful collection as well as the more general volumes on agriculture and pastoralism cited for Chapter 2. Judith Heyer et al., *Rural Development in Africa* (St Martin's Press, 1981) considers colonial economic history.

The slow decline of slavery has attracted many authors, particularly more recently. A major study of the impact of the decline and abolition of slavery is Frederick Cooper, *From Slaves to Squatters* (Yale University Press, 1980), which deals with Zanzibar and the Kenya coast. Also on this theme are Denise Bouche, *Les villages de liberté en Afrique Occidentale Française, 1887–1910* (Mouton, 1968); Tim Weiskel, 'Labour in the Emergent Periphery: From Slavery to Migrant Labour among the Baule Peoples 1880–1925' in W. L. Goldfrank, ed., *The World System of Capitalism: Past and Present* (Sage, 1979) Philip Igbafe, 'Slavery and Emancipation in Benin 1897–1945', *JAH*, XVI (1975), Carolyn Brown, 'Testing the Boundaries of Marginality: Twentieth Century Slavery and Emancipation Struggles in Nkam, Northern Igboland 1920–9', *JAH*, XXXVII (1995) and Jan-Georg Deutsch, *Abolition Without Emancipation in German East Africa* (Ohio University Press, 2005). Kristin Mann, *Slavery and the Birth of an African City, Lagos 1760–1900* (Indiana University Press, 2007) and Ahmad Sikainga, *Slaves into Workers: Emancipation and Labor in Colonial Sudan* (University of Texas Press, 1996), combine studies of the persistence of slavery and its eventual fading with excellent histories of African cities after colonial conquest. There are also the collections – Suzanne Miers and Richard Roberts, eds, *The End of Slavery in Africa* (University of Wisconsin Press, 1988) and Suzanne Miers and Martin Klein, eds, *Slavery and Colonial Rule in Africa* (Frank Cass, 1999). For the parallel gradual decline of pawning, see Paul Lovejoy and Toyin Falola, eds., *Pawnship, Slavery and Colonialism in Africa* (Africa World Press, 2003). The use of unfree labour to build up cash crop production is highlighted in Salau Mohammed Beshir, 'Role of Slave Labour in Groundnut Production in Early Colonial Kano', *JAH*, LI (2010).

A pioneering study of colonial labour in Africa by a South African Communist in Moscow from the beginning of the 1930s has been reissued: Albert Nzula, *Forced Labour in Africa* (Zed Press, 1979). I have written a short general modern survey, *The African Worker* (Cambridge University Press, 1988). Aspects of labour history are taken up for Kenya in Sharon Stichter, *Migrant Labour in Kenya* (Longman, 1982); K. K. Janmohamed, 'African Labourers in Mombasa 1895–1940', in Bethwell Ogot, ed., *Hadith* (2), 1972, and Roger van Zwanenberg, *Colonial Capital and Labour in Kenya 1919–1939* (East African Literature Bureau, 1975). On Zimbabwe, Tsuneo Yoshikuni, 'Strike Action and Self-Help Associations: Zimbabwean Worker Protest and Culture after World War I,' *JSAS*, XV (1989) is significant. For an apparently prosaic but omnipresent part of colonial and post-colonial labour in Africa see a case study by Karen Hansen, 'Domestic Labour in Zambia', *JSAS*, XIII (1986).

The scattered history of labour in West Africa would include, in a developing literature, A. G. Hopkins, 'The Lagos Strike of 1897: an Exploration in Nigerian Labour History', *Past and Present*, XXXV (1968); Roger Thomas, 'Forced Labour in West Africa; the Case of the Northern Territories of the Gold Coast 1906–27', *JAH*, XIV (1973); Michael Mason, 'Working on the Railway: Forced Labour in Northern Nigeria, 1907–12' and Arnold Hughes and Robin Cohen, 'An Emerging Nigerian Working Class: The Lagos Experience 1897–1939', both in Robin Cohen, Jean Copans and Peter Gutkind, eds, *African Labor History* (Sage, 1978); Gilles Sautter, 'Le chemin de fer

Congo-Océan', *CFA*, VII (1967) and Ibrahim Abdullah, 'Liberty or Death: Working-Class Agitation and the Labour Question in Colonial Freetown 1938–39', *International Review of Social History*, 40 (1995). A general study of forced labour in French West Africa is achieved in Babacar Fall, *Le travail forcé en AOF* (Karthala, 1993).

On labour migration, see Samir Amin, ed., *Modern Migrations in West Africa* (Oxford University Press, 1974), and Sharon Stichter, *Migrant Labourers* (Cambridge University Press, 1988). Some case studies from different parts of the continent are: W. M. Freund, 'Labour Migration to the Northern Nigerian Tin Mines 1903–45', *JAH*, XXII (1981); Marvin Harris, 'Labour Migration among the Mozambique Thonga', *Africa*, XXIX (1959); J. P. Chrétien, 'Des sedentaires devenus migrants: motifs des départs des burundais et des rwandais vers l'Uganda', *Cultures et développement*, X (1978); F. E. Sanderson, 'Development of Labour Migration from Nyasaland 1891–1914', *JAH*, II (1961) and Segun Osoba, 'The Phenomenon of Labour Migration in the Era of British Colonial Rule', *JHSN*, IV (1969). A key controversy over proletarianisation is marked by the interchange between James Ferguson, 'Mobile Workers, Modernist Narratives,' *JSAS*, XVI (1990) cited for Chapter 1 and a response by Hugh Macmillan in *JSAS*, XIX (1993). On migration as opportunity, see Isaie Dougnon, *Travail du Blanc, travail du Noir* (Karthala, 2007), on the land-poor Dogon of Mali or François Manchuelle, *Willing Migrants: Soninke Labor Diaspora* (Ohio University Press and James Currey, 1997) who also has much to say on the Office du Niger project.

Quite unlike anything else are the finely observed and fiercely empiricist books of Polly Hill: *Migrant Cocoa Farmers of Southern Ghana* (1962); *Studies in the Rural Capitalism of West Africa* (1970); *Rural Hausa: a Village and a Setting* (1972) and *Population, Prosperity and Poverty in Kano 1900 and 1970* (1977), all published by Cambridge University Press. An excellent contrast to Hill's approach and area may be found in Jean-Marc Gastellu, *Riches paysans de Côte d'Ivoire* (Harmattan, 1989). Ken Swindell, *Farm Labour* (Cambridge University Press, 1985) repays much re-reading.

In the scholarship produced during the late colonial period, the Makerere school of writers on Ugandan agriculture had a special importance and remains valuable despite the now transparently too heavy celebration of the cash crop. A classic is C. C. Wrigley, *Crops and Wealth in Uganda* (Kampala, 1959). Two late works deriving from this school are H. W. West, ed., *The Transformation of Land Tenure in Buganda since 1896* (Afrika Studiecentrum, Leiden & Cambridge University Press, 1971) and Audrey Richards et al., *Subsistence to Commercial Farming in Present-Day Buganda* (Cambridge University Press, 1973).

Among a list of works of analytic merit on cash cropping in various parts of tropical Africa: Sara Berry, *Custom, Cocoa and Socioeconomic Change* (Clarendon Press, 1975); Yves Mersadier, 'La crise de l'arachide sénégalaise au début des années trente', *BIFAN*, série B (28), 1966; Osumaka Likaka, *Rural Society and Cotton in Colonial Zaire* (University of Wisconsin Press, 1997 – in the Belgian Congo, extensive cotton cultivation did not long survive the departure of the Belgians); Herman Pössinger, 'Interrelations between Social and Economic Change in Rural Africa: the Case of the Ovimbundu of Angola' in Franz-Wilhelm Heimer, ed., *Social Change in Angola* (Weltforum Verlag, 1973); Leslie Bessant and Elvis Muringai, 'Peasants, Businessmen and Moral Economy in the Chiwesha Reserve 1930–68', *JSAS*, XIX (1993); Tony Barnett, 'Production of Cotton and the Reproduction of Underdevelopment' in Ivar Oxaal, ed., *Beyond the Sociology of Development* (Routledge & Kegan Paul, 1975); John Tosh, 'Lango Agriculture during the Early Colonial Period: Land and Labour in a Cash-Crop Economy', *JAH*, XIX (1978) and E. S. Atieno-Odhiambo, 'The Rise and Decline of the Kenya Peasant' in P. Gutkind and P. Waterman, eds, *African Social Studies: A Radical Reader* (Heinemann, 1977). For a pastoral equivalent, see Abdi Samatar, 'Merchant Capital, International Livestock Trade and Pastoral Development in Somalia', *CJAS*, XXI (1987), Douglas Johnson, 'Political Economy in the Upper Nile: The Twentieth Century Expansion of the Pastoral Common Economy', *JAH*, XXX (1989) and Dorothy Hodgson, *Once Intrepid Warriors: Gender, Ethnicity and the Cultural Politics of Maasai Development* (Indiana UP, 2001).

On the economic role of white settlers, a standard work is M. P. K. Sorrenson, *Origins of White Settlement in Kenya* (Oxford University Press, 1968). Isaac Mazonde, 'Vorsters and Clarks; Alternative Models of European Farmer in the Tuli Block of Botswana', *JSAS*, XVII (1991) is perceptive. For the view from below there is Frank Furedi, 'Kikuyu Squatters in the Rift Valley 1918–29' in Bethwell Ogot, ed., *Hadith*, V (1972) and Robin Palmer, 'Working Conditions and Worker Response on Nyasaland Tea Estates 1930–53', *JAH*, XXVII (1986). The settler land problem is the focus of Palmer's *Land and Racial Domination in Rhodesia* (Heinemann, 1977). There is an excellent survey of the economy of settlerdom in the Congo: Bogumil Jewsiewicki, 'Le colonat agricole européen au Congo beige 1910–60', *JAH*, XX (1979). On a large plantation system, Leroy Vail and Landeg White, *Capitalism and Colonialism in Mozambique* (Heinemann, 1980) is outstanding. For early 'development' planning, Dickson Eyoh, 'National Policy vs. Local Power: The Lafia Project in Nigeria 1916–34', *CJAS*, XXIV (1990) is instructive while the Office du Niger scheme and the failure of plans to create a second Gezira in Mali are studied in Richard Roberts, *Two Worlds of Cotton: Colonialism and the Regional Economy in the French Soudan 1800–1946* (Stanford UP 1996) and Monica van Beusekom, *Negotiating Development: African Farmers and Colonial Experts at the Office du Niger 1920–1960* (Heinemann, James Currey and David Philip, 2002).

The ecological aspect of colonial agriculture was opened up as an historical topic by the work of Heige Kjekshus, *Ecology Control and Economic Development in East Africa* (Heinemann, 1977). This is a subject where African agency looms especially large. See also Paul Richards, *Indigeous African Revolution* (Hutchinson, 1985); James Fairhead and Melissa Leach, *Reframing Deforestation: Global Analysis and Local Realities: Studies in West* Africa (Routledge, 1998); Leroy Vail, 'Ecology and Society: the Example of Eastern Zambia', *JSAS*, III (1977); Terence Ranger, 'Whose Heritage? The Case of the Matobo National Park', *JSAS*, XV (1989); Fiona Mackenzie, 'Political Economy of the Environment: Gender and Resistance under Colonialism, Murang'a

District, Kenya', *CJAS*, XXV (1991); William Beinart and Joann McGregor, eds., *Social History and African Environments* (James Currey, Ohio University Press and David Philip, 2002) and Kate Showers, 'Soil Erosion in the Kingdom of Lesotho: Origins and Colonial Response', *JSAS*, XV (1989). Scientific interventions in colonial times are the subject of William Beinart, Karen Brown and Daniel Gilfoyle, 'Experts and Expertise in Colonial Africa Reconsidered: Science and the Interpenetration of Knowledge', *AA*, 432 (2008). On colonialism and conservation, David Anderson and Richard Grove, eds, *Conservation in Africa* (Cambridge University Press, 1987), Stephen Ellis, 'Of Elephants and Men: Politics and Nature Conservation in Africa', *JSAS*, XX (1994) and Thaddeus Sunseri, *Wielding the Ax: State Forestry and Social Conflict in Tanzania 1820–2000* (Ohio UP 2009), provide a critical gaze.

Demographic thinking might begin with Dennis Cordell and Joel Gregory, eds, *African Population and Capitalism: Historical Perspectives* (University of Wisconsin Press, 2nd edition, 1994), who rejected a view based on individual choices for more structural analysis and Shane Doyle, 'Population Decline and Delayed Recovery in Bunyoro 1800–1960', *JAH*, XLI (2000). Cordell and Gregory also considered colonial perceptions of population patterns: 'Labour Reservoirs and Population: French Colonial Strategies in Koudougou, Upper Volta', *JAH*, XXIII (1982).

There has been increasing interest in research into poverty and deprivation in Africa, especially rural Africa. Some provocative studies are John Iliffe, *The African Poor: A History* (Cambridge University Press, 1987) and *Famine in Zimbabwe 1890–1960* (Mambo Press, 1990); Michael Watts, *Silent Violence: Food, Famine and Peasantry in Northern Nigeria* (University of California Press, 1983), Holger Weiss, *Babban Yunwa: Hunger und Gesellschaft in Nord-Nigeria und den Nachbarregionen in der frühen Kolonialzeit* (Suomen Historiallinen 22, Helsinki, 1997); James McCann, *From Poverty to Famine in North-east Ethiopia 1900–35* (University of Pennsylvania Press, 1987), Megan Vaughan and Henrietta Moore, *Cutting Down Trees* (James Currey & Heinemann, 1995), Diana Wylie, 'The Changing Face of Hunger in Southern African History 1890–1980', *Past and Present* 122 (1989), Gregory Maddox, 'Mtunya; Famine in Central Tanzania 1917–20', *JAH*, XXXI (1990) and Elias Mandala, *The End of Chidyerano: A History of Food and Everyday Life in Malawi, 1860–2004* (Heinemann 2005).

On mining, Charles van Onselen made a major breakthrough in placing the mines in the context of African labour and social history in *Chibaro: African Mines Labour in Southern Rhodesia* (Pluto Press, 1976). See also Carolyn Brown, '"We Were All Slaves": African Miners, Culture and Resistance at the Enugu Government Colliery* (Heinemann, James Currey and David Philip, 2003), Raymond Dumett, *El Dorado in West Africa: The Gold Mining Frontier, African Labour and Colonial Capital in the Gold Coast 1875–1900* (Ohio University Press and John Currey, 1998), Bill Freund, *Capital and Labour in the Nigerian Tin Mines* (Longman, 1981), John Higginson, *A Working Class in the Making: Belgian Colonial Labour Policy, Private Enterprise and the African Mineworker* (University of Wisconsin Press, 1989), Charles Perrings, *Black Mineworkers in Central Africa* (Heinemann, 1979) and Sean Hanretta,

'Space and Conflict in the Elisabethville Mining Camps 1923–38' in Florence Bernault, ed., *A History of Prison and Confinement in Africa* (Heinemann 2003).

The history of colonial capitalist enterprise in Africa is far better developed in French than in English as note the work of Suret-Canale and Coquery-Vidrovitch, although see A. G. Hopkins, 'Big Business in African Studies', *JAH*, XXVIII (1987). Business receives detailed attention in the special edition of the *Revue française d'histoire d'outremer*, LXIII (1976), edited by Coquery-Vidrovitch, entitled 'L'Afrique et la crise de 1930'. She has also written the important article: 'L'impact des intérêts coloniaux: SCOA et CFAO dans l'Ouest africain 1910–65', *JAH*, XVI (1975). Her two-volume edited collection, *Entreprises et entrepreneurs en Afrique Noire XIX–XX siècles* (Harmattan, 1983) continues into the post-colonial era. A standard source for Belgian Africa is P. Joye and R. Lewin, *Les trusts au Congo* (Brussels, 1961). On capitalism in Central Africa in addition to Phimister there is S. E. Katzenellenbogen, *Railways and the Copper Mines of Katanga* (Clarendon Press, 1973), Peter Slinn, 'Commercial Concessions and Politics During the Colonial Period: The Role of the British South Africa Company in Northern Rhodesia 1890–1964', *AA*, LXX (1971) and L. J. Butler, *Copper Empire: Mining and the Colonial State in Northern Rhodesia c.1930–64* (Palgrave Macmillan, 2007).

Different aspects of how the trading minorities of colonial Africa lived and worked can be studied in Dharam Ghai, ed., *Portrait of a Minority: Asians in East Africa* (Oxford University Press, 1970); John Zarwan, 'The Social and Economic Network of an Indian Family Business in Kenya 1920–70', *Kroniek van Afrika*, N.S. VI (1975); Vishnu Padayachee and Robert Morrell, 'Indian Merchants and Dukawallahs in the Natal Economy c. 1875–1914', *JSAS*, XVII (1991); Toyin Falola, 'Lebanese Traders in Southwestern Nigeria', *AA*, 89 (1990) and Hugh Macmillan, *Zion in Africa: The Jews of Zambia* (IB Tauris, 1999). Said Bumedouha, 'Adjustments to West African Realities: The Lebanese in Senegal', *Africa*, LX (1990), Christopher Bierwirth, 'The Lebanese Communities of Cote d'Ivoire', *AA* 390 (1997), David Himbara, *Kenyan Capitalists, the State and Development* (Lynne Rienner, 1994), carry the story to the present. On African merchant strata, Mahir Saul, 'Development of the Grain Market and Grain Merchants in Burkina Faso', *JMAS*, XXIV (1986), Jean-Loup Amselle, *Les négociants de la savane* (ed. Anthropos, 1977) and Jean-Pierre Warnier, *L'esprit d'entreprise au Cameroun* (Karthala, 1994) are samples of a growing literature.

Michael Crowder emphasised the importance of indirect rule as a mechanism of British domination in colonial Africa, notably in the edited collection, Crowder and Obaro Ikime, eds, *West African Chiefs* (University of Ife Press, 1970). His views have been criticised in M. Semakula Kiwanuka, 'Colonial Policies and Administrations: the Myth of Contrasts', *AHS*, III (1970). For other assessments see Hubert Deschamps, 'Et maintenant, Lord Lugard', *Africa*, XXXIII (1963) and I. F. Nicolson, *The Administration of Nigeria* (Clarendon Press, 1969). A powerful contemporary assessment of the long shadow of this kind of political structure has been made by Mahmood Mamdani, *Citizen and Subject* (Princeton University Press & James Currey, 1996). Differences in how indirect rule worked in different contexts and territories are stressed by Roger Gocking, 'The "Legal Factor" in Ghana and Lesotho', *Africa*, 67 (1) (1997), 61–85 and Holly Hanson, 'Mapping Conflict: Hierarchy and Accountability in the Ancient Capital of Buganda', *JAH*, 50, 2 (2009). There are numerous, generally narrowly administrative, case studies, especially for Nigeria. Perhaps the best are A. E. Afigbo, *The Warrant Chiefs* (Longman, 1972) and J. D. Y. Peel's dense and informative *Ijeshas and Nigerians c1890s–1970s* (Cambridge University Press, 1983). Other areas are examined in Michael Twaddle, 'The Bakungu Chiefs of Buganda under British Colonial Rule, 1900–30', *JAH*, X (1969) and Gerald Caplan, *The Elites of Barotseland* (C. Hurst, 1970). A very sympathetic portrait of a colonial chief is drawn by Francis Deng, *The Man called Deng Majok* (Yale University Press, 1986). For a parallel story of growing up in a prosperous family in Asante, see T. E. Kyei, *Our Days Dwindle: Memories of my Childhood Days in Asante* (Heinemann, 2001).

CHAPTER 7. Culture, Class and Social Change in Colonial Africa

Two novels on the same part of Nigeria that evoke the meaning of conquest from the point of view of the two sexes are Chinua Achebe, *Things Fall Apart* (Heinemann, 1967) and Buchi Emecheta, *The Joys of Motherhood* (Allison & Busby, 1979). There is a perspective on art and African history suggested by the special issue of the *CJAS*, XXII (1988).

Disparate views of social change in twentieth-century Africa can be found in Peter Lloyd, *Africa in Social Change* (Penguin, 1967) and Claudine Vidal, *Sociologie des passions* (Karthala, 1991). A feature of the more recent literature on Africa has been the Annales school-like emergence of local and regional studies covering long time periods with much to say on both material and social life, a technique which has particular power and authority when applied to rural contexts. Some examples are David Cohen and E. S. Atieno Odhiambo, *Siaya: The Historical Anthropology of an African Landscape* (James Currey, Heinemann & Ohio University Press, 1989); Landeg White, *Magomero: Portrait of an African Village* (Cambridge University Press, 1987); Elias Mandala, *Work and Control in a Peasant Economy; A History of the Lower Tchiri Valley in Malawi 1859–1960* (University of Wisconsin Press, 1990) and Steven Feiermann, *Peasant Intellectuals: Anthropology and History* (University of Wisconsin Press, 1990). Class analysis is central to Gavin Kitching's complex *Class and Economic Change in Kenya* (Yale University Press, 1980) and K. W. Post's 'Peasantization in Western Africa', in P. Gutkind and P. Waterman, eds, *African Social Studies: A Radical Reader* (Heinemann, 1977). The makings of a new bourgeoisie are the subject of Joan Vincent, 'Colonial Chiefs and the Making of a Class', *Africa*, XLVII (1977) on Uganda and Martin Chanock, 'The New Men Revisited' in R. Macdonald, ed., *From Nyasaland to Malawi*, cited previously for Chapter 4. How did Africans, elites to one side, think and speak about white colonisers? A creative approach to this fundamental question is essayed in Luise White, *Speaking with Vampires; Rumour and History in Colonial Africa* (University of California Press, 2000) which makes a fascinating contrast with Karin Barber, ed., *Africa's Hidden Histories; Everyday Literacy and Making the Self* (Indiana University Press, 2006).

The literature specifically on African women and their modern history is now highly developed. References in Chapter 2 can be consulted with profit for this period and later as well. Ester Boserup presented a debatable paradigm on female farming systems in *Women's Role in Development* (George Allen & Unwin, 1970). Amongst collections, see Nancy Hafkin and Edna Bay, eds, *Women in Africa* (Stanford University Press, 1976); the special issue on women of *CEA* XVII (1977); M. J. Hay and Marcia Wright, *African Women and the Law: Historical Perspectives* (Boston University Press, 1982); Sharon Stichter and Jane Parpart, eds, *Patriarchy and Class: African Women at Home and in the Workforce* (Westview Press, 1988) and Cherryl Walker, ed., *Women and Gender in Southern Africa* (James Currey & David Philip, 1990). Elizabeth Schmidt, *Peasants, Traders and Wives: Shona Women in the History of Zimbabwe 1890–1939* (Heinemann, 1992) touches the bases of this literature effectively.

Monographs that have bristled with ideas are Claire Robertson, *Sharing the Same Bowl: A Socioeconomic History of Women and Class in Accra, Ghana* (Indiana University Press, 1984) and Luise White, *The Comforts of Home: Prostitution in Colonial Nairobi* (University of Chicago Press, 1990). Other readings to be recommended are Mona Etienne, 'Women and Men, Cloth and Cultivation: Transformation of Production and Distribution Relations Among the Baule', *CEA*, XVII (1977); Jane Guyer, 'Food, Cocoa and Division of Labour by Sex in Two West African Societies', *CSSH*, XXII (1980); Achola Pala Okeyo, 'Daughters of the Lakes and Rivers' in Mona Etienne and Eleanor Leacock, eds, *Women and Colonization* (Praeger, 1980); Jane Parpart, 'The Household and the Mineshaft', *JSAS*, XIII (1986), Megan Vaughan, 'Household Units and Historical Process in Southern Malawi', *ROAPE*, 34 (1985); Jean Davison, 'Tenacious Women: Clinging to Banja Household Production in the Face of Changing Gender Relations in Malawi, *JSAS*, XIX (1993); Renee Pittin, *Women and Work in Northern Nigeria: Transcending Boundaries* (Palgrave Macmillan, 2002); Chantal Rondeau, *Les paysannes de Mali* (Karthala, 1994), Dorothy Hodgson, 'Pastoralism, Patriarchy and History', *JAH*, 40 (1999), Beatrice Duncan, 'Cocoa, Marriage, Labour and Land in Ghana: Some Matrilineal and Patrilineal Perspectives', *Africa*, 80 (2010), and Christine Obbo, *African Women* (Zed Press, 1980). These readings tend to be those which take an historical perspective and which consider gender relations beyond the question of women's history per se. Far less has been written on childhood but especially with reference to labour see Beverly Grier, 'Invisible Hand; The Political Economy of Child Labour in Colonial Zimbabwe', *JSAS*, XX (1994) and Karen Hansen, 'Labor Migration and Urban Child Labor during the Colonial Period in Zambia' in Bruce Fetter, ed., *Demography from Scanty Evidence: Central Africa in the Colonial Era* (Lynne Rienner, 1990).

Two collections that reveal trends in writing on religion in colonial Africa are T. O. Ranger and I. Kimambo, *The Historical Study of African Religion* (Heinemann, 1972) and Ranger and John Weller, eds, *Themes in the Christian History of Central Africa* (Heinemann, 1975), a more parochial volume. Of theoretical insight is W. van Binsbergen, *Religious Change in Zambia* (Kegan Paul International, 1981). The close relations of church and state in the Belgian colonies are discussed in Marvin Markowitz, *The Cross and the Sword:*

The Political Role of the Missions in the Congo, 1908–60 (Stanford University Press, 1973) and Ian Linden, *Church and Revolution in Rwanda* (Manchester University Press, 1977). On the mission mind, Andrew Ross, 'The Blantyre Mission and Problems of Land and Labour, 1891–1915', in R. Macdonald, ed., *From Nyasaland to Malawi*, cited above, and T. O. Beidelman, 'Social Theory and the Study of Christian Missions in Africa', *Africa*, XLIV (1974) are suggestive. On the relationship between capitalism and mission Christianity, see J. Bertin Webster, 'The Bible and the Plough' and Sara S. Berry, 'Christianity and the Rise of Cocoa-Farming in Ibadan and Ondo', *JHSN*, II (1963) and IV (1968) respectively, and J. McCracken, *Politics and Christianity in Malawi* (Cambridge University Press, 1977). A masterly study of both Christianity and ethnicity in south-western Nigeria is J. D. Y. Peel, *Religious Encounter and the Making of the Yoruba* (Indiana UP, 2003).

Studies of non-Christian African religious movements include Audrey Wipper, *Rural Rebels* (Oxford University Press, 1977) and Elizabeth Hopkins, 'The Nyabingi Cult of Southwestern Uganda' in Robert Rotberg and Ali Mazrui, eds, *Protest and Power in Black Africa*, cited under Chapter 5. The independent churches and their relationship to the colonial order have fascinated many writers on Africa. Some of the most interesting studies are Karen Fields, *Revival and Rebellion in Colonial Central Africa* (Princeton University Press, 1985); Matthew Schoffeleers, 'Ritual Healing and Political Acquiescence; The Case of the Zionist Churches in Southern Africa', *Africa*, LXI (1991); Norman Long, *Social Change and the Individual* (Manchester University Press, 1968); Wyatt MacGaffey, *Modern Kongo Prophets; Religion in a Plural Society* (Indiana University Press, 1983); Damaso Feci, 'La vie cachée et vie publique de Simon Kimbangu selon la littérature coloniale et missionaire belge', *Cahiers du CEDAF*, 9/10, 1972; Thomas Turner and Kasongo Wembolua, 'Le Vandisme (Sankuru-Zaïre) et sa signification politique', *Cahiers du CEDAF* 5 (1978), and J. D. Y. Peel, *Aladura: a Religious Movement Among the Yoruba* (Oxford University Press, 1968).

For Islam during the colonial period standard works will include Donal Cruise O'Brien, *The Mourides of Senegal* (Clarendon Press, 1971), Jean Copans, *Les marabouts de l'arachide* (Le Sycomore, 1980) and now Cheikh Anta Babou, *Fighting the Greater Jihad: Amadu Bamba and the Founding of the Muridiyya of Senegal, 1853–1913* (Ohio University Press, 2007). On other parts of West Africa, John Paden, *Religion and Political Culture in Kano* (University of California Press, 1973) and Brian Peterson, 'Slave Emancipation, Trans-Local Social Processes and the Spread of Islam', *JAH*, XLV (2004) are noteworthy. There is a *Journal of Religion in Africa* published in the Netherlands.

The social context of disease and colonial perspectives on health has become a subject of considerable academic enquiry in the African historical literature after 1980. Two interesting studies are Megan Vaughan, *Curing their Ills: Colonial Power and African Illness* (Polity Press, 1992) and Randall Packard, 'Maize, Cotton and Mosquitoes: The Political Economy of Malaria Epidemics in Colonial Swaziland', *JAH*, XXV (1984) A useful overview can be obtained from Steven Feierman and John Janzen, eds, *The Social Basis of Health and Healing in Africa* (University of California Press, 1992). On the limited success of colonial health regimes especially before World War II, Faranirina Esoavelomandroso, 'Résistance à la medicine en situation coloniale: la peste à Madagascar,' *Annales*, XXXVI (1981) is stimulating.

A good assessment of formal education in Africa exists in Kenneth Blakemore and Brian Cooksey, *Sociology of Education for Africa* (George Allen & Unwin, 1981). An early critical assessment is D. B. Abernethy, *The Political Dilemma of Popular Education in Southern Nigeria* (Stanford University Press, 1969). Other writings with a critical edge include Denise Bouche, 'Les écoles française au Soudan à l'époque de la conquête, 1884–1900', *CEA*, VI (1966) and 'Autrefois, notre pays s'appelait le Gaule', *CEA*, VIII (1968), Brendan Carmody, 'Conversion and School at Chikumi', *Africa*, LVIII (1988); Carol Summers, 'Educational Controversies: African Activism and Educational Strategies in Southern Rhodesia 1920–34', *JSAS*, XXX (1994) and T. O. Ranger, 'African Attempts to Control Education in East and Central Africa', *Past and Present*, XXXII (1965).

For analyses of legal systems in colonial Africa, there is an excellent set of readings in Kristin Mann and Richard Roberts, eds, *Law in Colonial Africa* (Heinemann & James Currey, 1991). Other topics are considered in Francis Snyder, *Capitalism and Legal Change: An African Transformation* (Academic Press, 1981); Sally Falk Moore, *Social Facts and Fabrications* (Cambridge University Press, 1986); Issa Shivji, *Law, State and the Working Class in Tanzania* (James Currey, Heinemann & Tanzania Publishing House, 1986); Omoniyi Adewoye, *The Judicial System in Southern Nigeria, 1854–1954* (Longman, 1977) and Douglas Johnson, 'Judicial Regulation and Administrative Control: Customary Law and the Nuer 1898–1954', *JAH*, XXVII (1986). The problem for colonial authorities of how to deal with killing witches as a crime is considered in Katherine Luongo, *Witchcraft and Colonial Rule in Kenya, 1900–1955* (Cambridge University Press, 2011). John McCracken, 'Coercion and Control in Nyasaland: Aspects of the History of a Colonial Police Force', *JAH*, XXVI (1986) was a pioneering contribution. Florence Bernault, ed., *A History of Prison and Confinement in Africa* (Heinemann 2003) is interesting. Prisons scarcely existed in pre-colonial Africa and, if they did, they were intended for the incarceration of the politically dangerous. Under colonial rule, floggings became commonplace punishment and prisoners sent to forced labour regimes. However, the slackness of the system and widespread corruption tended to mitigate harsh conditions.

For distinctive African performance traditions and organisation in new settings, an interested reader could begin by consulting T. O. Ranger, *Dance and Society in Eastern Africa, 1890–1940* (Heinemann, 1975), Wolfgang Werner, 'Playing Soldiers': The Truppenspieler Movement among the Herero of Namibia 1915–c.1945', *JSAS*, XVI (1990) and Bruce Fetter, 'African Associations in Elisabethville, 1910–35', *EHA* VI (1974). On African football, Nuno Domingos, 'The Malicious Football Game: Urban Interactions and Power Relations in Lourenço Marques, Capital of Mozambique', *JSAS*, XLI (2015), is excellent.

For ethnicity and tribalism in colonial society, some useful readings could include Richard Waller and Thomas Spear, eds, *Becoming Maasai* (James

Currey, 1993); Abner Cohen, *Custom and Politics in Urban Africa* (University of California Press, 1969); Obaro Ikime, *Niger Delta Rivalry: Itsekiri-Urhobo Relations and the European Presence, 1884–1936* (Longman, 1969); M. J. Hay, 'Local Trade and Ethnicity in Western Kenya', *AEHR*, III (1975); John Lonsdale, 'When did the Gusii (or Any Other Group) Become a Tribe?', *KHR*, V (1977); Aidan Southall, 'From Segmentary Lineage to Ethnic Association' in M. Owusu, ed., *Colonialism and Change* (Mouton, 1975) and the special issue on 'l'archipel peul', *CEA*, 133–5 (1993). Major collections are Leroy Vail, ed., *The Creation of Tribalism in Southern Africa* (University of California Press & James Currey, 1989) and Jean-Pierre Chrétien & Gérard Prunier, eds, *Les ethnies ont une histoire* (Karthala, 1989) An original aspect is proposed by Jeff Guy and Motlatsi Tabane in 'Technology, Ethnicity and Ideology: Basotho and Shaft Sinking on the South African Gold Mines' *JSAS*, XIV (1988). On the related subject of language use, Johannes Fabian, *Language and Colonial Power* (Cambridge University Press, 1986) and William Samarin, 'The Colonial Heritage of the Central African Republic: A Linguistic Perspective', *IJAHS*, XXII (1989) are stimulating.

Some essays in writing urban history in Africa (a much stronger French than English tradition with urban studies that look from the colonial into the post-colonial period) include: Catherine Coquery-Vidrovitch's collection, *Processus d'urbanisation en Afrique* (Harmattan, 1988, 2 volumes). Other select titles might be Marc le Pape, 'De l'espace et des races à Abidjan entre 1903 et 1934'; Odile Goerg, 'Conakry, une modèle de ville coloniale?' both in *CEA*, 99 (1985); Marc Pain, *Kinshasa; la ville et la cité* (Editions de l'ORSTOM, 1984); Guy Maïnet, *Douala: Croissances et servitudes* (Harmattan, 1985), Claude Meillassoux, *Urbanization of an African Community* (University of Washington Press, 1968); John Parker, *Making the Town: Ga State and Society in Early Colonial Accra* (Heinemann, James Currey and David Philip, 2000), Bruce Fetter, *The Creation of Elisabethville, 1910–40* (Stanford University Press, 1976); David Birmingham, 'Carnival at Luanda', *JAH*, XXIX (1988) and Bogumil Jewsiewicki, 'Histoire économique d'une ville coloniale: Kisangani', *Cahiers du CEDAF* (1978). Recent articles with an emphasis on the cultural and the emergence of unprecedented problems for the authorities are Andrew Burton, 'Urchins, Loafers and the Cult of the Cowboy: Urbanization and Delinquency in Dar es Salaam 1919–61', *JAH*, 2001, and Laurent Fourchard, 'Lagos and the Invention of Juvenile Delinquency in Nigeria 1920–60', *JAH* (2005).

There is a considerable literature on the economic and political life of the West African bourgeoisie during the colonial period. See especially: J. Ayo Langley, *Pan-Africanism and Nationalism in West Africa, 1900–45* (Clarendon Press, 1975); J. K. Obatala, 'An African Case Study in the Bourgeois Origins of Cultural Nationalism', *SS*, XXXVI (1972); Patrick Cole, *Modern and Traditional Elites in the Politics of Lagos* (Cambridge University Press, 1975); Kristin Mann, *Marrying Well: Marriage, Status and Social Change among the Educated Elite in Colonial Lagos* (Cambridge University Press, 1985); A. G. Hopkins, 'Economic Aspects of Political Movements in Nigeria and the Gold Coast, 1918–39', *JAH*, IX (1968); Felicia Ekejuiba, 'Omu Okwei, the Merchant Queen of Ossomari', *JHSN*, III (1967); G. Wesley Johnson, *The Emergence of Black Politics in*

Senegal (Stanford University Press, 1971) and Samir Amin, 'La politique coloniale française à l'egard de la bourgeoisie commerçante sénégalaise' in Claude Meillassoux, ed., *Development of Indigenous Trade and Markets in West Africa*, already cited for Chapter 4. Looking beyond the elite at the problem of class and political economy is Sam Rhodie, 'The Gold Coast Cocoa Hold-up of 1930–31', *THSG* IX (1968). A more recent assessment is Gareth Austin, 'Capitalists and Chiefs in the Cocoa Hold-Ups in Southern Asante 1927–38', *IJAH*S, XXI (1988).

Writing on African 'resistance' in eastern and south-central Africa has created something of a school and has focused primarily on post-conquest revolts. The classic studies are by Terence Ranger: *Revolt in Southern Rhodesia, 1896–7* (Heinemann, 1967) and 'Connections Between Primary Resistance Movements and Modern Mass Nationalism in East and Central Africa', *JAH*, IX (1968). Ranger is subjected to an important critique by Julian Cobbing, 'The Absent Priesthood', *JAH*, XVIII (1977). Other studies following from Ranger's analysis are numerous; among the most highly considered is John Iliffe, 'Origins of the Maji Maji Rebellion', *JAH*, VIII (1967). Women's activities are central in Audrey Wipper, 'Kikuyu Women and the Harry Thuku Disturbances: Some Uniformities of Female Militancy', *Africa*, LIX (1989). For the Women's War, see Toyin Falola and Adam Paddock, eds., *The Women's War of 1929: A History of Anti-colonial Resistance in Eastern Nigeria* (Carolina University Press, 2011). The Chilembwe rising is the subject of George Shepperson and T. Price, *Independent African* (Edinburgh University Press, 1958), a pioneering landmark generally speaking in the historiography of Africa. Also important are George Mwase, *Strike a Blow and Die* (Harvard University Press, 1967) and Shepperson's reconsideration, 'The Place of John Chilembwe in Malawi Historiography', in B. Pachai, ed., *The Early History of Malawi* (Longman, 1972). For other revolts, see Paul Lovejoy and Jan Hogendorn, 'Mahdism and Resistance to Colonial Rule in the Sokoto Caliphate 1905–6', *JAH*, XXXI (1990), J. A. Ballard, 'The Porto Novo Incident of 1923', *Odu*, N.S. 11 (1965); Sikitele Gize, 'Racines de la révolte pende de 1931', *EHA*, V (1973) and J. P. Chrétien, 'Une révolte au Burundi en 1934', *Annales*, XXV (1970).

CHAPTER 8. Industrialisation and South African Society, 1900–48

The best currently available detailed survey of modern South African history is T. R. H. Davenport and C. C. Saunders, eds, *South Africa: a Modern History* (Palgrave Macmillan, 5th edn, 2000) by liberal scholars who refer to a wider range of perspectives. The second volume of the *Cambridge History of South Africa*, edited by Robert Ross, Anne Mager and Bill Nasson (2011) covers this period also. William Beinart, *Twentieth-Century South Africa* (Oxford University Press, 1994) is an interesting interpretation giving much emphasis to social and rural themes. On the burning theme of racism, a judicious assessment is evident in Saul Dubow, *Scientific Racism in Modern South Africa* (Cambridge University Press, 1995).

For a general introduction to the fundamental features of South African development, Alf Stadler, *The Political Economy of Modern South Africa* (Croom

Helm & David Philip, 1987) and Daryl Glaser, *Politics and Society in South Africa* (Sage, 2000) are great guides. Glaser has an excellent bibliography. A classic liberal analysis of the political economy can be found in Sheila van der Horst, *Native Labour in South Africa* (Frank Cass, 1971). A number of the classic radical studies attempting to link the racial system in South Africa to industrial capitalism as a whole – by Wolpe, Legassick, Johnstone and others – can be found in Harold Wolpe, ed. *The Articulation of Modes of Production* (RKP, 1980) and William Beinart and Saul Dubow, eds, *Segregation and Apartheid in Twentieth-Century South Africa* (Routledge, 1995).

The work of a second generation of South African Marxists can be found as well in the Review of African Political Economy, 7 (1977) and subsequent debate. See too Robert Davies, *Capital, State and White Labour in South Africa, 1900–60* (Harvester Press, 1979). An interesting light is shed on the famous whites only blasting certificate in Elaine Katz, 'Revisiting the Origins of the Colour Bar in the Witwatersrand Gold Mining Industry, 1891–99', *JSAS*, XXV (1999). Merle Lipton, *Capitalism and Apartheid* (Wildwood House, 1985) partially accepts and partially rejects the 'revisionist' writers on the relationship of capitalism to apartheid. Terence Moll, 'Did the Apartheid Economy Fail?', *JSAS*, XVII (1991) reflects liberal thinking on the state of this debate.

A third phase of writers tend to be bunched together as the 'social' historians. Their concerns begin to emerge with Shula Marks and Stanley Trapido, eds, *The Politics of Race, Class and Nationalism in Twentieth Century South Africa* (Longman, 1987). One of the best collections of their work is Belinda Bozzoli, ed., *Class, Community and Conflict: South African Perspectives* (Ravan Press, 1987). Another, taking the story somewhat further than the material in this chapter, is Philip Bonner et al., *Apartheid's Genesis 1935–62* (Ravan Press, 1993). A very useful collection on economic development that exists in four volumes is D. Hobart Houghton and Jennifer Dagut, *Source Material on the South African Economy* (Oxford University Press, Cape Town, 1972–3). Nancy Clark, *Manufacturing Apartheid; State Corporations in South Africa* (Yale University Press, 1994), is convincing on the parastatals and their importance.

There is a large sociological and anthropological literature on African society in South Africa. Deserving special attention are the seminal books of Bengt Sundkler on separatist churches, *Bantu Prophets in South Africa* (Oxford University Press, 1961 revised edn) and *Zulu Zion and Some Swazi Zionists* (Gleerups, 1976) and those of Philip Mayer, *Townsmen or Tribesmen* (Oxford University Press, 1961) and his edited collection, *Black Villagers in an Industrial Society* (Oxford University Press, 1981). A look at new cultural forms emerging can be found in Veit Erlmann, *African Stars: Studies in Black South African Performance* (University of Chicago Press, 2nd edn. 2001) David Coplan, *In Township Tonight, South Africa's Black Music and Theatre* (University of Chicago Press, 2000) and Christopher Ballantine, *Marabi Nights: Jazz, Race and Society in Early Apartheid South Africa* (Ravan, 1993). On education, a stand-out in the literature is Jon Hyslop, 'State Education Policy and the Social Reproduction of the Urban African Working Class: The Case of the Southern Transvaal', *JSAS* XIV (1988) which looks ahead to the material in Chapter 11 as well. The life of one part of the urban working class is captured for a later generation (but with earlier relevance no doubt too) by Jacklyn Cock in *Maids and Madams* (Ravan Press, 1981). Outstanding accounts of community life in South Africa include Monica Wilson and Archie Mafeje, *Langa* (Oxford University Press, 1963); Pierre van den Berghe, *Caneville* (Wesleyan University Press, 1964); J. B. Loudon, *White Farmers, Black Labourers* (Afrikastudiecentrum, Leiden and Africa Studies Centre, Cambridge, 1970) and, set in South-West Africa, Rob Gordon, *Mines, Migrants and Masters* (Ravan Press, 1977). On social change in the reserves, William Beinart, 'Joyini Inkomo': The Origins of Migrancy from Pondoland', *JSAS*, V (1979) is impressive as is *The Politics of Pondoland 1860–1930* (Cambridge University Press, 1982). Colin Murray, *Families Divided* (Cambridge University Press, 1981) is a major study of labour migration.

On the residual rural areas left for blacks, valuable accounts are found in William Beinart, 'Soil Erosion, Conservationism and Ideas about Development: A Southern African Exploration 1900–60', *JSAS*, XI (1984); Pat McAllister, 'Resistance to "Betterment" in the Transkei: A Case Study from the Willowvale District', *JSAS*, XV (1989) and Fred Hendricks, 'Loose Planning and Rapid Resettlement: The Politics of Conservation and Control in Transkei 1950–70', *JSAS*, XV (1989). A complex, long-term regional study was written by the anthropologist Colin Murray: *Black Mountain: Land, Class and Power in the Eastern Orange Free State 1880s–1980s* (Witwatersrand University Press, 1986).

Murray's terrain includes 'white' farm country. On the administrative system of pre-apartheid days, see Dubow, *Racial Segregation and the Origins of Apartheid in South Africa 1919–36* (Macmillan, 1989) and Ivan Evans, *Bureaucracy and Race: Native Administration in South Africa* (University of California Press, 1997). South Africa's colony is the subject of Patricia Hayes et al., *Namibia under South African Rule: Mobility and Containment 1915–46* (James Currey, Out of Africa and Ohio University Press, 1998). For more on what has been termed agrarian history, see the important collection edited by Beinart, Delius and Trapido, *Putting a Plough to the Ground; Accumulation and Dispossession in Rural South Africa 1850–1930* (Ravan Press, 1986) and William Beinart and Colin Bundy, *Hidden Struggles in Rural South Africa: Politics and Popular Movements in the Transkei and Eastern Cape 1890–1930* (Ravan Press, 1987). A biography of a sharecropper that becomes a history of agrarian change on the Highveld already mentioned is the classic *The Seed is Mine: The Life of Kas Maine* by Charles van Onselen.

The political history of struggle is described by three moving if partisan accounts: Edward Roux, *Time Longer than Rope* (University of Wisconsin Press, 1964); H. J. and R. Simons, *Class and Colour in South Africa* (Penguin, 1969) and A. Lerumo, *Fifty Fighting Years* (Inkululeko, 1971). Peter Limb has done a remarkable job unearthing the history of forgotten early political movements and strikes in *Nation, Class and Place in South Africa Before 1940* (UNISA Press, 2010). For the first president of the ANC, there is now Heather Hughes, *The First President: A Life of John L. Dube* (Jacana, 2011). On another of the early African politicians, see Brian Willan, *The Life of Sol Plaatje; South African Nationalist 1876–1932* (University of California Press, 1982). D. D. T. Jabavu, *The Black Question in South Africa* (Negro Universities Press, reprint

1969) gives a feel for his time. Perhaps the most interesting assessment of early African politics is to be found in Shula Marks, *The Ambiguities of Dependence in South Africa* (Johns Hopkins Press, 1986). Gwendolen Carter and Thomas Karis, *From Protest to Challenge: A Documentary History of African Politics in South Africa, 1882–1964* (Hoover Institution Press, 1972–7), is an invaluable documentary collection in four volumes initially that has been continued.

A very different perspective informed by the social history phase and also post-modernism is Patrick Harries, *Work Culture and Identity: Migrant Labourers in Mozambique and South Africa c. 1860–1910* (Heinemann & Witwatersrand University Press, 1994). See also Alan Booth, 'Homestead, State and Migrant Labour', *AEH*, 14 (1985). A large study of the migrant labour regimes over time is Jonathan Crush, Alan Jeeves and David Yudelman, *South Africa's Labor Empire: A History of Black Migrancy to the Gold Mines* (Westview Press, 1991). An attractive overview using a rich weave of sources is Luli Callinicos, *Working Life 1886–1940* (Ravan, 1987).

On the war and reconstruction, Shula Marks and Stanley Trapido, 'Lord Milner and the South African State', *HWJ*, 8 (1979) is itself of great importance and also refers extensively to a large controversial literature on the period. Relevant are Donald Denoon, *A Grand Illusion* (Longman, 1973), Tim Keegan, 'Restructuring of Agrarian Class Relations in a Colonial Economy: The Orange River Colony 1902–10', *JSAS*, V (1979) and Jeremy Krikler, *Revolution from Above, Rebellion from Below: the Agrarian Transvaal at the Turn of the Century* (Oxford University Press, 1993). Peter Richardson, *Chinese Mine Labour in the Transvaal* (Macmillan, 1982) covers the migration of Chinese to the mines during this era. The political history of unification was skilfully assessed in Leonard Thompson, *The Unification of South Africa* (Clarendon Press, 1960). Shula Marks has written a history of the Bambatha Rebellion, *Reluctant Rebellion* (Clarendon Press, 1970).

For the post-World War I period, the Rand Revolt serves as the central focus of a major analysis, Frederick Johnstone, *Class, Race and Gold* (Routledge & Kegan Paul, 1976) For an excellent narrative history, see Jeremy Krikler, *White Rising: the 1922 Insurrection and Racial Killing in South Africa* (Manchester University Press, 2005). Apart from Crush et al., Randall Packard, *White Plague, Black Labour* (Witwatersrand University Press, 1990) and Elaine Katz, *The White Death* (Witwatersrand University Press, 1995) on tuberculosis and miners' phthisis add an important dimension. On the ICU, P. L. Wickins, *The Industrial and Commercial Workers' Union of Africa* (Oxford University Press, 1978) can be supplemented by Helen Bradford, *A Taste of Freedom* (Yale University Press, 1987) on the rural activities of this popular movement cum trade union. There is also Kadalie's own account, *My Life and the ICU* (Frank Cass, 1970).

Davenport and Saunders, among others, can be used as a guide to the vagaries of 'white' politics and the large literature on the subject. Saul Dubow, *Racial Segregation and the Origins of Apartheid in South Africa 1919–36* (Macmillan, 1989) looks at the way the modern South African system was debated and fought over. The imperial historian Keith Hancock wrote an authorised two-volume biography of Smuts (Cambridge University Press, 1965–8) while the novelist Alan Paton produced an engaging and attractively written biography of his chief lieutenant, *Hofmeyr* (Oxford University Press, 1964). A classic statement of the liberal capitalist outlook is R. F. A. Hoernlé, *South African Native Policy and the Liberal Spirit* (Negro Universities Press, reprint, 1969). His career has been explored by Martin Legassick, 'Race, Industrialization and Social Change: The Case of R. F. Hoernlé', *AA*, LXXV (1976). On business and race in South Africa, there is an important study: Belinda Bozzoli, *The Political Ideology of a Ruling Class* (Routledge & Kegan Paul, 1981).

Saul Dubow and Alan Jeeves, eds, *South Africa's 1940s: Worlds of Possibilities* (Double Storey, 2005) tries to capture the turbulent 1940s when much social contestation moved to the labour and urban spheres. An important addition to this literature is Gary Kynoch, *We Are Fighting the World: A History of the Marashea Gangs in South Africa 1947–99* (Ohio University Press and University of KwaZulu-Natal Press, 2005). In addition note David Hemson, 'Dock Workers, Labour Circulation and Class Struggles in Durban 1940–59', *JSAS*, IV (1977); Alf Stadler, 'Birds in the Cornfield: Squatter Movements in Johannesburg, 1944–7', *JSAS*, VI (1979); Dan O'Meara, 'The 1946 Miners' Strike and the Political Economy of South Africa', *Journal of Commonwealth & Comparative Politics*, XIII (1975); Dunbar Moodie, 'The South African State and Industrial Conflict in the 1940s', *IJAHS*, XXI (1988) and 'The Moral Economy of the Black Miners' Strike of 1946', *JSAS*, XIII (1986). On the early labour movement, Baruch Hirson, *Yours for the Union: Class and Community Struggles in South Africa* (Zed Press & Witwatersrand University Press, 1989) pioneered new approaches. Luli Callinicos captures the period for one key section of the country in *A Place in the Sun: The Rand on the Eve of Apartheid* (Ravan Press, 1993). One cannot but mention on the subject of Rand history the two-volume urban history, taken back to the nineteenth century however, by Charles van Onselen, *New Babylon, New Nineveh* (Longman, 2 volumes, 1982).

CHAPTER 9. The Decolonisation of Africa, 1940–60

Only recently has this period been treated as a historical one, deserving analytical discussion. There is a good survey in Frederick Cooper, *Africa since 1940: The Past of the Present* (Cambridge University Press, 2002), which looks ahead to the next chapter's material as well. John Hargreaves, *The End of Colonial Rule in West Africa* (Macmillan, 1979) and J. E. Flint, 'Planned Decolonization and its Failure in British Africa' *AA*, 82 (1983) are suggestive and serious. Thomas Hodgkin, *Nationalism in Colonial Africa* (New York University Press, 1956) is a classic that set the tone for later assessments and still bears re-reading. Jack Woddis, *Africa: The Lion Awakes* (Lawrence & Wishart, 1961), is journalistic but useful as an enthusiastic left-wing survey of the labour insurgency of the post-war era that liberal and nationalist writers sometimes forget. There are several relevant sections in the already cited collection of Gutkind, Cohen and Copans, *African Labour History* (Sage, 1978), that touch on this period. Frederick Cooper, 'The Dialectics of Decolonization: Nationalism and Labor Movements in Postwar French Africa', in Frederick Cooper and Ann

Stoler, *Tensions of Empire: Colonial Cultures in a Bourgeois World* (University of California Press, 1997) and in Cooper's major study which knits together labour resistance, labour reform and decolonisation, *Decolonization and African Society: The Labor Question in French and British Africa* (Cambridge University Press, 1996), Cooper points out crucial aspects of working class life in Africa that did not fit the reformist perspective coming from Europe. See also Lisa Lindsay who puts the emphasis on the gender issue: 'No Need to Think of Home? Domestic Life on the Nigerian Railways c. 1940–1961', *JAH*, XXXIX (1997).

For an introduction to the great Malagasy rising of 1947–8, Jacques Tronchon, *L'insurrection malgache de 1947* (Maspéro, 1974) is stimulating. On the UPC rebellion in Cameroun the standard work in English is Richard Joseph, *Radical Nationalism in Cameroun* (Oxford University Press, 1977); Achille Mbembe, *La naissance du maquis dans le Sud-Cameroun 1920–60* (Karthala, 1996) is imaginative and suggestive.

There is a large bibliography on Mau Mau. Two major introductions are Rosberg and Nottingham, *The Myth of Mau Mau, Nationalism in Kenya*, Frederick Praeger 1966, while Berman and Lonsdale, cited for Chapter 6, is important. Several primary accounts by participants are available: Waruhiu Itote, *Mau Mau General* (EAPH, 1971); J. M. Kariuki, *Mau Mau Detainee* (Oxford University Press, 1963) and Donald Barnett and Karari Njama, *Mau Mau From Within* (Monthly Review Press, 1966). Mau Mau was the subject of a special issue of the *Kenya Historical Review*, V (2) (1977) and the important articles of Frank Furedi, 'The African Crowd in Nairobi', *JAH*, XIV (1973) and 'The Social Composition of the Mau Mau Movement in the White Highlands', *Journal of Peasant Studies*, 1 (1974). See also Tabitha Kanogo, *Squatters and the Roots of Mau Mau* (James Currey, Ohio University Press & Heinemann, 1987), Sharon Stichter, 'Workers, Trade Unions and the Mau Mau Rebellion', *CJAS*, IX (1975), Luise White, 'Separating the Men from the Boys: Construction of Gender, Sexuality and Terrorism in Central Kenya', *IJAHS*, XXIII (1990), Daniel Branch, 'The Enemy Within: Loyalists and the War Against Mau Mau in Kenya', *JAH*, XLVIII (2007) and Furedi's *The Mau Mau War in Perspective* (James Currey, Heinemann & Ohio University Press, 1989). David Anderson, *Histories of the Hanged: Britain's Dirty War in Kenya and the End of Empire* (Weidenfeld and Nicolson, 2005), is an eloquent introduction to the form British repression took. On particular countries, the reader should look at previous lists of general histories cited earlier. However, for British West Africa, two particular studies carry special weight: Martin Kilson, *Political Change in a West African State* (Harvard University Press, 1966), which highlights the peasant struggles in rural Sierra Leone and K. Post and G. Vickers, *The Price of Liberty* (Cambridge University Press, 1973), a biography of Adegoke Adelabu that powerfully conveys the realities of nationalist politics in Nigeria.

The standard sources on Nigeria are informative and so far still to be replaced: James Coleman, *Nigeria: Background to Nationalism* (University of California Press, 1958); Richard Sklar, *Nigerian Political Parties* (Princeton University Press, 1963) and for the economic background, Gerald Helleiner, *Peasant Agriculture, Government and Economic Growth in Nigeria* (Richard

Irwin, 1966). A brief corrective is Segun Osoba, 'The Nigerian Power Élite, 1952–65' in the Gutkind and Waterman reader cited for Chapters 6 and 7. Confrontations are summarised in Toyin Falola, *Colonialism and Violence in Nigeria*, cited for Chapter 5. For a social history of the coal miners, see Carolyn Brown, *'We Were All Slaves': African Miners, Culture and Resistance in the Enugu Government Colliery* (Heinemann, James Currey and David Philip 2003). On the North, note C. S. Whitaker, *The Politics of Tradition: Continuity and Change in Northern Nigeria* (Princeton University Press, 1970), B. J. Dudley, *Parties and Politics in Northern Nigeria* (Cass, 1968), Alhaji Mahmood Yakubu, *An Aristocracy in Political Crisis: The End of Indirect Rule and the Emergence of Party Politics in the Emirates of Northern Nigeria* (Avebury, 1996) and Moses Ochonu, *Colonialism By Proxy: Hausa Imperial Agents and Middle Belt Consciousness in Nigeria* (Indiana UP, 2014).

The standard source for decolonisation in the Gold Coast has been Dennis Austin, *Politics in Ghana, 1946–60* (Oxford University Press, 1964). Most of the work on Nkrumah stresses the independence period. An illuminating exception is Richard Rathbone, 'Businessmen in Politics: Party Struggle in Ghana 1949–57', *JDS*, IX (1973). For the resistant politics in Asante, see Jean Allman, *The Quills of the Porcupine: Asante Nationalism in an Emergent Ghana* (University of Wisconsin Press, 1993) and more generally Rathbone's *Nkrumah & the Chiefs: The Politics of Chieftaincy in Ghana, 1951–1960* (Ohio University Press 2000). John Cartwright, *Politics in Sierra Leone, 1947–67* (University of Toronto Press, 1970) is a standard work.

British East Africa is treated in the third volume of the History of East Africa edited by D. A. Low and Alison Smith (Clarendon Press, 1976). Apart from Mau Mau, other aspects of Kenya are discussed in M. P. K. Sorrenson, *Land Reform in the Kikuyu Country* (Oxford University Press, 1967); David Anderson and David Throup, 'Africans and Agricultural Production in Colonial Kenya: The Myth of the War as a Watershed', *JAH*, XXVI (1985); John Spencer, The *KAU* (KPI, 1985); E. S. Atieno-Odhiambo, 'Seek Ye First the Economic Kingdom: A History of the Luo Thrift and Trading Corporation', *Hadith*, V (B. Ogot, ed. 1975). On Tanganyika, there is Cranford Pratt, *The Critical Phase in Tanzania, 1945–68* (Cambridge University Press, 1976); G. A. Maguire, *Towards 'Uhuru' in Tanganyika* (Cambridge University Press, 1969); Lionel Cliffe, 'Nationalism and the Reaction to Enforced Agricultural Improvement in Tanganyika During the Colonial Period', in the collection, Lionel Cliffe and John Saul, *Socialism in Tanzania* (Tanzania Publishing House, 1973) Dorothy Hodgson, '"Taking Stock", State Control, Ethnic Identity and Pastoralist Development in Tanganyika 1948–58', *JAH*, XLI (2000) and, on labour, W. H. Friedland, 'Co-operation, Conflict and Conscription: TANU-TFL Relations, 1895–64', in J. Butler and A. A. Castagno, eds, *Boston University Papers on Africa*, I (1967). The political salience of mainly Muslim urban women is revealed by Susan Geiger, *TANU Women: Gender and Culture in the Making of Tanganyikan Nationalism, 1955–65* (Heinemann, James Currey, EAEP and Mkuki na Nyota, 1998). For Uganda, Gardner Thompson, 'Colonialism in Crisis: The Uganda Disturbances of 1945', *AA*, 91 (1992) is interesting.

On British Central Africa, federation inspired a myriad of rather inter-changeable liberal assessments of 'race relations' for British consumption. One of the better is Patrick Keatley, *The Politics of Partnership* (Penguin, 1963). Change on the Copperbelt is studied in an anthropology classic, A. L. Epstein, *Politics in an Urban African Community* (Manchester University Press, 1958) and J. R. Hooker, 'Role of the Labour Department in the Birth of African Trade Unionism in Northern Rhodesia', *IRSH*, X (1965). Carrying the story up into the twenty-first century is Miles Larmer, *Mineworkers in Zambia: Labour and Political Change in Post-colonial Africa* (Tauris 2007). Among works already cited the reader should turn to Roberts' general history and Caplan on Barotseland for Zambia. Other works on Zambia include David Mulford, *Zambia: The Politics of Independence, 1957–64* (Oxford University Press, 1967); Ian Henderson, 'The Economic Origins of Decolonisation in Zambia, 1940–45', *RH*, V (1974); Thomas Rasmussen, 'The Popular Basis of Anti-Colonial Protest' in William Tordoff, ed., *Politics in Zambia* (Manchester University Press, 1974); Mwelwa Musambachime, 'Rural Political Protest: The 1953 Disturbances in Mweru-Luapula', *IJAHS*, XX (1987) and Mac Dixon-Fyle, 'Agricultural Improvement and Political Protest on the Tonga Plateau, Northern Rhodesia' *JAH*, XVIII (1977). A reconsideration of these years in Northern Rhodesia is gathered in the collection edited by Jan-Bart Gewald et al., *One Zambia, Many Histories: Towards a History of Post-colonial Zambia* (Brill, 2008). The spell of modernity and how it was broken is the subject of James Ferguson, *Expectations of Modernity: Myths and Meanings on the Zambian Copperbelt* (Duke University Press, 1999).

For an interesting essay on Malawi in the Roderick Macdonald collection already cited see Roger Tangri, 'From the Politics of Unionism to Mass Nationalism'. This is also the subject matter of Joey Power, 'Building Relevance: The Blantyre Congress 1953 to 56', *JSAS* XXVIII (2002), and indirectly John McCracken, 'Democracy and Nationalism in Historical Perspective: The Case of Malawi', *AA*, 387 (1998). Tony Woods covers a subject usually associated with more industrialised colonies in 'Bread with Freedom and Peace; Rail Workers in Malawi', *JSAS*, XVIII (1992). Rhodesia is considered primarily in Chapter 11 as it does not decolonise, but note also James Barber, *The Road to Rebellion* (Oxford University Press, 1967) and Peter Harris, 'Industrial Workers in Rhodesia, 1946–72', *JSAS*, I (1975).

Ruth Schachter Morgenthau, *Political Parties in French West Africa* (Clarendon Press, 1964) has long been the introduction to her subject for English language readers. It is, in reality, much stronger on French than on African politics and has little to say on social and economic history. Jean Suret-Canale, *Afrique Noire: de la colonisation à l'indépendance*, 1945–60 (Editions Sociales, 1972) is less successful than the preceding volume on the colonial era. A pathbreaking article by Fred Cooper, 'The Senegalese General Strike of 1946 and the Labour Question in Post-War French Africa', *CJAS*, XXIV (1990) captures a critical moment in the decolonisation process. On the non-co-operators, see Elizabeth Schmidt, *Cold War and Decolonization in Guinea 1946–58* (Ohio University Press, 2007) and Kees van Walvaren, 'Decolonization by Referendum: The Anomaly of Niger and the Fall of Sawaba

1958–59', *JAH*, L (2009). There is some inspired journalism in Georges Chaffard, *Les carnets secrets de la décolonisation* (Calmann-Levy, 1967). For a survey on Equatorial Africa, see Elikia M'Bokolo, 'Forces sociales et idéologies dans la décolonisation de l'AEF', *JAH*, XXII (1981).

On the Belgian Congo, Crawford Young, *Politics in the Congo* (Princeton University Press, 1965) is a mine of information. For little-known conflicts at the end of World War II, see B. Jewsiewicki, Kiloma Lema and Jean-Jacques Vellut, 'Documents pour servir à l'histoire du Zaïre: grèves dans le Bas Congo en 1945', *EHA* V (1973) and Maurice Lovens, 'La révolte de Masisi-Lubutu (Congo belge, janvier-mai 1944)', *Cahiers du CEDAF* 3/4 (1974). Jean LaFontaine, *City Politics: A Study of Leopoldville 1962–63* (Cambridge University Press, 1970) is a striking account of a place and a time that anticipates much later social historical and anthropological literature. There is an eloquent brief assessment in Gerard Althabe, *Les fleurs du Congo* (Maspéro, 1972). Thomas Kanza, *Crisis in the Congo* (Penguin, 1972) is an interesting account from the moderate Left. Also on the crisis years, see Jules Gérard-Libois, *Katanga Secession* (University of Wisconsin Press, 1966) and Conor Cruise O'Brien, *To Katanga and Back* (Simon & Schuster, 1962). The American role is revealed in Steve Weissman, *American Foreign Policy in the Congo 1960–1964* (Cornell University Press, 1974). Luc de Witte, *The Assassination of Lumumba* (Verso, 2002) tries to recapture the sad events leading to Patrice Lumumba's murder. More specialised study can be guided by the numerous volumes of annotated primary source material on the Congo and also Ruanda-Urundi published by the Brussels research centre, CRISP.

On the ferment of the 1940s in Eritrea see G. K. N. Trevaskis, *Eritrea, A Colony in Transition* (Oxford University Press, 1960) and Lloyd Ellingson, 'Emergence of Political Parties in Eritrea, 1941–50', *JAH*, XVIII (1977). Compare with Gebru Tareke, 'Peasant Resistance in Ethiopia: The Case of Weyane', *JAH*, XXV (1984). For the nationalist era in the Sudan there is a focus on this period in Gabriel Warburg, *Islam, Nationalism and Communism in a Traditional Society: The Case of the Sudan* (Frank Cass, 1978) and Peter Woodward, *Condominium and Sudanese Nationalism* (Collings, 1979).

Many African politicians of the decolonisation era have produced memoirs or political manifestos. A sampling includes: (Kenya) Jomo Kenyatta, *Facing Mount Kenya* (Secker & Warburg, 1953); Bildad Kaggia, *The Roots of Freedom* (EAPH, 1975); Tom Mboya, *Freedom and After* (Little, Brown, 1963); Oginga Odinga, *Not Yet Uhuru* (Heinemann, 1967); (Democratic Republic of Congo) Anicet Kashamura, *De Lumumba aux colonels* (Buchet-Castel, 1966); Ludo Martens, *Abo: une femme de Congo* (Harmattan, 1994); (Senegal) Mamadou Dia, *Mémoires d'un militant du Tiers-Monde* (Publisud, 1985); (Malawi) M. W. K. Chiume, *Kwacha* (EAPH, 1975); (Nigeria) Nnamdi Azikiwe, *Zik: A Selection from the Speeches* (Cambridge University Press, 1961), and Sir Ahmadu Bello, *My Life* (Cambridge University Press, 1962). There is a published collection of *Speeches and Writings of Patrice Lumumba* (Little, Brown, 1972). Apart from Post and Jenkins, useful biographies of African politicians are Jeremy Murray-Brown, *Kenyatta* (George Allen & Unwin, 1972) and Philip Short, *Banda* (Routledge & Kegan Paul, 1974).

Janet Vaillant, *Black, French and African* (Harvard University Press 1990) discusses Senghor.

African writers of fiction convey the feeling of the period well in certain novels. These include, in a short selection, James Ngugi (Ngugi wa Thiongo), *A Grain of Wheat* (Heinemann, 1967) and *Weep Not, Child* (Heinemann, 1964) which evokes Mau Mau; Sembene Ousmane's epic of the great railway workers' strike in French West Africa, *God's Bits of Wood* (Doubleday, English translation, 1962) and the tragicomic fiction of Chinua Achebe, *No Longer at Ease* (Obolensky, 1961) and *A Man of the People* (Heinemann, 1966).

French scholars were fascinated in this period already with the African city and began to focus on social and cultural change. Classic studies are Georges Balandier, *Sociologie des Brazzaville Noirs* (Armand Colin, 1955) and then Claude Meillassoux, *Urban Life of an African Community: Voluntary Associations in Bamako* (University of Washington Press, 1968). On cultural changes and the emergence of a new urban leisure and communications culture, a pioneering book was Phyllis Martin, *Leisure and Society in Colonial Brazzaville* (Cambridge University Press, 2002). The parallel issue of the *IJAHS* 35(1) (2002) that looks at popular music and dance, sport and film is important. On this period, see also Emily Collaci, 'Dancehall Politics; Mobility, Sexuality and Spectacles of Racial Respectability in Late Colonial Tanganyika 1930s–1961', *JAH*, 52 (2011). For the growing significance of personal memory through commercial photography, see Richard Vokes, *Photography in Africa; Ethnographic Perspectives* (James Currey, 2012).

CHAPTER 10. Tropical Africa 1960–80: Class, State and the Problem of Development

For the material in Chapters 10 onwards, where articles as opposed to books must play a major part as sources of more information, two important journals are the British-based *Review of African Economy* and the French *Politique Africaine*. A number of scholarly journals on contemporary Africa are also important, containing a host of articles varying both in outlook and quality. A shortlist must include *African Affairs*, the *Journal of Modern African Studies*, the *African Studies Review* (USA) and the *Revue française de politique africaine*. For some years, the American Social Science Research Council (SSRC) sponsored so-called 'state of the art' review articles on many aspects of African society which are useful and appeared in the *African Studies Review*. A number of contemporary collections were orientated towards the issues stressed in this chapter: Peter Gutkind and Peter Waterman, eds, *African Social Studies: A Radical Reader* (Heinemann, 1977); Gutkind and Immanuel Wallerstein, eds, *The Political Economy of Contemporary Africa* (Sage, 1976); Richard Sandbrook and Robin Cohen, eds, *Development of an African Working Class* (Longman, 1975) and Henry Bernstein and Bonnie Campbell, eds, *Contradictions of Accumulation in Africa* (Sage, 1985).

The underdevelopment paradigm has been developed most effectively for Africa by the Egyptian economist Samir Amin whose many works on tropical Africa include *Neo-Colonialism in West Africa* (Penguin, 1973) and *Développement du capitalisme en Côte d'Ivoire* (Editions du Minuit, 1967);

other influential writing in similar vein includes Reg Green and Ann Seidman, *Unity or Poverty? Economics of Panafricanism* (Penguin, 1969) and Tamas Szentes, *The Political Economy of Underdevelopment* (Akademiai Kiadoi, 1976). Claude Ake made a substantial contribution in his overview *A Political Economy of Africa* (Longman, 1981).

On African politics in general, Immanuel Wallerstein, *Africa: The Politics of Unity* (Random House, 1967) covered the factual developments in the early years of interstate relations. There are useful assessments in Crawford Young, *Ideology and Development in Africa* (Yale University Press, 1982) and Nelson Kasfir, ed., *State and Class in Africa* (Frank Cass, 1984). A long and detailed political history by Paul Nugent, *Africa since Independence,* Palgrave Macmillan (2nd edn, 2012) makes a very useful mine of information. At the local level so much more rarely considered, Dele Olowu, 'Local Institutes and Development: The African Experience', *CJAS,* XXIII (1989) provided a different dimension. Gisela Geisler covers the emerging position of women in African politics in *Women and the Remaking of Politics in Southern Africa: Negotiating Autonomy, Incorporation and Representation* (Nordiska Afrikainstitutet, 2004).

On the relationship of the African state to the economy, Robert Bates' influential *Markets and States in Africa* (University of California Press, 1981) is provocative. A very helpful general assessment and description of military and state power was Ruth First's *The Barrel of a Gun* (Allen Lane, 1970). An excellent article on militarism in Africa can be found in Robin Luckham, 'The Military, Militarization and Democratization in Africa: A Survey of the Literature and Issues', *African Studies Review,* XXXVII (1994). Yves Benot, *Idéologies d'indépendances africaines* (Maspéro, 1969) is a penetrating assessment of the outlook of the African ruling class in the 1960s; a useful collection along these lines in English is William Friedland and Carl Rosberg, eds, *African Socialism* (Stanford University Press, 1964). Among the better studies of the myth of educational opportunity in Africa are Pierre van den Bergh, *Power and Privilege at an African University* (Routledge & Kegan Paul, 1973) and Benoît Verhaegen, *L'enseignement universitaire au Zaire* (CEDAF, 1978). See also Abernethy on Nigeria, cited for Chapter 7.

There are many good descriptions of clientelism and how it works such as Pierre Englebert, *State Legitimacy and Development in Africa* (Lynne Rienner, 2000). A telling negative assessment of the state in Africa was written by Basil Davidson, *The Black Man's Burden: Africa and the Curse of the Nation-State* (James Currey, 1992). A creative and memorable development of the idea of clientelism and why it makes little sense to evaluate African regimes only through Western conceptions of development and democracy was Jean-François Bayart, *The State in Africa: The Politics of the Belly* (Longman, 1993) and the somewhat cynically titled *Africa Works: Disorder as Political Instrument* (Indiana UP and James Currey, 1999) by Patrick Chabal and Jean-Pacal Daloz.

For discussion of cultural changes and the emergence of a new kind of Africa, see Andrew Ivaska, *Cultured States: Youth, Gender and Modern Style in 1960s Dar es Salaam* (Duke University Press, 2011) and Bob White, *Rumba Rules: The Politics of Dance Music in Mobutu's Zaïre* (Duke University Press, 2008). Performativity, it can be argued, became extremely important in moving people to believe in change in Africa. For this see Joseph Trapido, 'The Political Economy of Migration and Reputation in Kinshasa', *Africa*, 81 (2011). Nobody has surpassed the numerous contributions of the Congolese thinker T. K. Biaya on shifts in African cultural values. Examples are 'La cuistrerie de Mbujimayi (Zaïre): organisation, fonctionnement et idéologie d'une bourgeoisie africaine', *Genève-Afrique*, XXIII (1985) and, 'Mundele Ndumbu et Ambiance; le vrai "bal blanc et noir(e)"', *Cahiers africains*, 9-10-11 (1994). A favoured subject of cultural observers of this period has become the efflorescence of the so-called *sape* culture where Congolese men dressed competitively in brightly coloured adaptations of formal Western dress, particularly in the Brazzaville republic where oil revenues created a febrile prosperity during this period. The sense of design is extraordinary but it gives one also a sense of the importance of performativity in the display of the modern. For wonderful illustrations see Daniele Tamagni, *Bacongo Elegance* (Trolley, 2009).

The new state tried to promote what it saw as healthy national culture as Kelly Askew, *Performing the Nation: Swahili Music and Cultural Politics in Tanzania* (University of Chicago Press, 2002), demonstrates. A very good view on the contradictions in the new commercialised popular culture is presented in Laura Fair, 'Drive-In Socialism: Debating Modernities and Development in Dar es Salaam, Tanzania', *American Historical Review*, CXVIII (2013). Musical forms themselves and their diverse roots outside the directions one could possibly call neo-colonial are explored by Thomas Turino, *Nationalists, Cosmopolitans and Popular Music in Zimbabwe* (University of Chicago Press, 2000).

There are some very good considerations of the politics of ethnicity, admittedly from a primarily East African angle in Hiroyuki Hino et al., *Ethnic Diversity and Economic Stability in Africa: Interdisciplinary Perspectives* (Cambridge University Press, 2012), notably by John Lonsdale, Bruce Berman and Bethwell Ogot. Berman is also the author of 'Ethnicity, Patronage and the African State: The Politics of Uncivil Nationalism', 388, *AA* 97 (1998). The classic statement by Peter Ekeh is 'Colonialism and the Two Publics in Africa: A Theoretical Statement', *Comparative Studies in Society and History*, XVII (1975). Another good collection with some of the same authors including Ekeh from a somewhat later date is Bruce Berman, Jackson Eyoh and Will Kimlycka, eds *Ethnicity and Politics in Africa* (James Currey and Ohio University Press, 2004). For contradictory consequences, Carola Lentz, 'The Chief, the Mine Captain and the Politician: Legitimating Power in Northern Ghana', *Africa*, 68 (1998), is insightful.

Apart from the Sandbrook and Cohen collection, a number of important studies have looked at the history and sociology of the emergent African industrial proletariat, including Sandbrook's *Proletarians and African Capitalism: The Kenyan Case 1960–72* (Cambridge University Press, 1975); Cohen's *Labour and Politics in Nigeria* (Heinemann, 1974); Richard Jeffries, *Class, Ideology and Power in Africa: The Railwaymen of Sekondi* (Cambridge University Press, 1978); Adrian Peace, *Choice, Class and Conflict* (Harvester, 1979); Bruce Kapferer, *Strategy and Transaction in an African Factory* (Manchester University Press, 1972); Michael Burawoy, 'The Colour of Class in the Copper Mines', *Zambian Papers*, 7 (1972) and R. D. Grillo, *Race, Class and Militancy*

(Chandler, 1974), dealing respectively with Ghana, Nigeria, Zambia in two cases and Uganda (for those books without the relevant country in their title). For an alternative approach see Carola Lentz and Veit Erlmann, 'A Working Class in Formation? Economic Crisis and Strategies of Survival among Dagara Mine Workers in Ghana', *CEA*, 113 (1989) as well as James Ferguson's work mentioned in Chapter 1.

On specific regions and countries, the literature is more substantial than for any historic period and what follows is only selective and perhaps arbitrary, excluding numerous standard sources in favour of interesting interpretations. The collections and journals mentioned above are taken as read; selections from them are not included below with few exceptions.

For West Africa in general, a useful if uneven collection at the end of the period covered here is John Dunn, ed., *West African States: Failure and Promise* (Cambridge University Press, 1978). On Nigeria, the analytical quality of the literature is not outstanding but Eghosa Osaghae, *Crippled Giant: Nigeria since Independence* (Hurst, London, 1998) is serviceable. The wisdom of mainstream Western scholarship focusing on the military, ethnicity, etc. was collected in Robert Melson and Howard Wolpe, eds, *Nigeria: Modernization and the Politics of Communalism* (Michigan State University Press, 1972). The best account of the civil war, at this point still lacking in the treatment it deserves, is journalist John de St Jorre's *The Brothers' War* (Houghton Mifflin, 1972). On the army and army rule, see Robin Luckham, *The Nigerian Military* (Cambridge University Press, 1972) and S. K. Panter-Brick, ed., *Nigerian Politics and Military Rule* (Athlone Press, 1970). A feel for local politics comes forward from Howard Wolpe, *Urban Politics in Nigeria: A Study of Port Harcourt* (University of California Press, 1975) and Sandra Barnes, *Patrons and Power: Creating a Political Community in Metropolitan Lagos* (Indiana University Press, 1986). Nigerian industry has much deeper roots than exist in most African countries. For a study of manufacturing in what is now considered to be the informal sector on a large scale, see Kate Meagher, *Identity Economics: Social Networks and the Informal Economy in Nigeria* (James Currey and HEBN, 2010) and also Paul Lubeck, *Islam and Urban Labor in Northern Nigeria, The Making of a Muslim Working Class* (Cambridge University Press, 1987). Catherine Boone, *Merchant Power and the Roots of State Power in Senegal 1930–85* (Cambridge University Press, 1992) provides a very clear answer to why industrial growth has been stifled in that country.

Not surprisingly, Ghana under Nkrumah attracted many engaged and interesting scholars during that period although there still is a lack of a magisterial assessment by a Ghanaian. Nkrumah's view of his own life is expressed in his autobiography, *Ghana, an Autobiography* (Nelson, 1957) and his downfall in *Dark Days in Ghana* (International Publishers, 1969). An apologetic biography prepared after his death in exile is Basil Davidson, *Black Star* (Allen Lane, 1973). The most coherent defence of his economic policies is Roger Genoud, *Nationalism and Economic Development in Ghana* (Praeger, 1969). The fall of Nkrumah brought about a serious reconsideration of his significance and the beginning of a materialist analysis of contemporary Africa, landmarks in which were Bob Fitch and Mary Oppenheimer, *Ghana: End of an Illusion* (Monthly

Review Press, 1967); Jitendra Mohan, 'Nkrumah and Nkrumahism', *Socialist Register* (1967) and Roger Murray, 'Second Thoughts on Ghana', *New Left Review*, 42 (1967) and particularly Bjørn Beckman's outstanding *Organizing the Farmers* (Scandinavian Institute of African Studies, 1976). A good monograph on aspects of post-independence Sierra Leone is David Fashole Luke, *Labour and Parastatal Politics in Sierra Leone* (University Press of America, 1984).

Nkrumah's contemporary Modibo Keita presided over a similarly contradictory 'socialist' regime in Mali. Among several assessments of significance are Claude Meillassoux, 'Class Analysis of the Bureaucratic Process in Mali', *Journal of Development Studies*, VI (1970); W. I. Jones, 'The Mise and Demise of Socialist Institutions in Rural Mali', *Genève-Afrique*, XI (1972) and Guy Martin, 'Socialism, Economic Development and Planning in Mali 1960–68', *CJAS*, X (1976). See also Claus Ernst, *Tradition and Progress in an African Village* (C. Hurst, 1976). The Republic of Guinea was fairly closed to research under Sékou Touré's regime and has inspired a particularly polemical literature (or a bland one, in some cases). Among available studies are B. Ameillon, *Guinée, bilan d'une indépendence* (Maspéro, 1964) and Ladipo Ademolekun, *Sékou Touré's Guinea* (Methuen, 1976). William Derman, *Serfs, Peasants and Socialists* (University of California Press, 1973) is an important study of rural social relationships. Touré himself had his speeches and writings published over many years in a multi-volume series from Conakry.

The richest literature on Francophone West Africa (especially in translation) deals with Senegal. Donal Cruise O'Brien, *Saints and Politicians* (Cambridge University Press, 1975) contains several stimulating essays. Left scholarship in English on the republic is collected by Rita Cruise O'Brien, ed., *The Political Economy of Development: Dependence in Senegal* (Sage, 1979). Robert Fatton, *The Making of a Liberal Democracy; Senegal's Passive Revolution* (Lynne Rienner, 1985), Monar Couba Diop and Mamadou Diouf, *Le Sénégal sous Abdou Diouf* (Karthala, 1990) brings the story to the post-Senghor era. There is an excellent study of the authoritarian political system of Cameroun in Jean-François Bayart, *L'Etat au Cameroun* (Presses de la fondation nationale des sciences politiques, 1979) while Roger Charlton and Roy May, 'Warlords and Militarism in Chad', *ROAPE*, 45/46 (1990) is an introduction to part of the former French Equatorial Africa. On the Ivory Coast, a good collection is Y.-A. Fauré and J.-F. Médard, *Etat et bourgeoisie en Côte d'Ivoire* (Editions Karthala, 1982). It supplements Aristide Zolberg, *One Party Government in the Ivory Coast* (Princeton University Press, 1964). For some radical Francophone regimes, see Hugues Bertrand, *Le Congo: formation sociale et mode de développement economique* (Maspéro, 1975) and Maureen Covell, *Madagascar: Politics, Economy and Society* (Frances Pinter, 1987).

The French relationship with Africa was reviewed in a special issue of *Politique africaine* commemorating the end of the Mitterrand presidency (58, 1995). For special facets see Guy Martin, 'Uranium: A Case Study in Franco-African Relations', *JMAS*, XXVII (1989), Nicholas van der Walle, 'The Decline of the Franc Zone; Monetary Politics in Francophone Africa', *AA*, 90 (1991) and also Tony Chafer, 'French African Policy in Historical Perspective', *JCAS*,

XIX (2001). This perennial subject of interest is surveyed in admirable journalistic style in a recent exhaustive summary, Patrick Pesnot et M. X, *Les dessous de la Françafrique* (Nouveau Monde, 2014).

On Zaïre and its fundamental problems under General Mobutu, readings might include Crawford Young and Thomas Turner, *The Rise and Decline of the Zaïrian State* (University of Wisconsin Press, 1985), Jean-Claude Willame, *L'automne d'un despotisme* (Karthala, 1992); Michael Schatzberg, *Politics and Class in Zaire* (Africana, 1981) and Emizet Kisangani, 'Implementation of Stabilization Policies in an Authoritarian Setting: Zaïre 1970–80', *CJAS*, XXI (1987) as well as the special issue of *CJAS* edited by Bogumil Jewsiewicki, XVIII (1984). David Gibbs, 'International Commercial Rivalries and the Zairian Copper Nationalization of 1967', *ROAPE*, 72 (1997), 171–84, considers the role of copper in the economy.

There is an excellent one-volume study of the political economy of independent Kenya: Colin Leys, *Underdevelopment in Kenya* (Heinemann, 1975) which the author corrected in favour of a greater emphasis on internal class formation in 'Capital Accumulation, Class Formation and Dependency – the Significance of the Kenyan Case', *Socialist Register* (1978). Other important contributions on class, state and dependency in books on Kenya include Alice Amsden, *International Firms and Labour in Kenya 1945–70* (Frank Cass, 1971) and Nicola Swainson, *Development of Corporate Capitalism in Kenya* (Heinemann, 1980). Himbara's book, referred to with reference to Chapter 6, is a recent contribution. There is a valuable corrective in Michael Chege, 'Introducing Race as a Variable into the Political Economy of the Kenya Debate; An Incendiary Idea' *AA*, 387 (1998).

Daniel Branch, *Kenya Between Hope and Despair, 1963–2011* (Yale University Press, 2012) is an excellent political study which continues well beyond this period. Another valuable reference is the special Kenyan issue of the *JCAS*, XXVII(3) (2009). Power and local politics are the subject of Geoff Lamb, *Peasant Politics* (Friedmann, 1974) and David Parkin, *Palms, Wine and Witnesses* (Chandler, 1972), while Gary Wasserman, *The Politics of Decolonization* (Cambridge University Press, 1976), Christopher Leo, *Land and Class in Kenya* (University of Toronto Press, 1984) and Angelique Haugerud, 'Land Tenure and Agrarian Change in Kenya' *Africa*, LIX (1989) have explored the 'Africanisation' of the once white highlands.

On the Zanzibar revolution see Michael Lofchie, *Zanzibar: Background to Revolution* (Princeton University Press, 1965), Anthony Clayton, *The Zanzibar Revolution and its Aftermath* (C. Hurst, 1981) and Jonathan Glassman, *War of Words, War of Stones* (Indiana University Press, 2011). No African state is so well-studied as unified Tanzania on which a rich literature developed during the 1970s, particularly on social change in rural society. Julius Nyerere was a very eloquent defender of his own concept of socialism, put forth in several collections, *Freedom and Unity* (Oxford University Press, 1967); *Freedom and Socialism* (Oxford University Press, 1968) and *Freedom and Development* (Oxford University Press, 1973). For a critical view by a former cabinet minister and politician of the Left, A. M. Babu, *African Socialism or Socialist Africa?* (Zed Press, 1981) is engaging. The best local writing from the late 1960s into the new decade was collected in John Saul and Lionel Cliffe, eds, *Socialism in Tanzania* (Tanzania Publishing House, 2 vols, 1973). Saul's important analyses may also be found in his volume with Giovanni Arrighi, *Essays on the Political Economy of Africa* (Monthly Review Press, 1973) and *State and Revolution in Eastern Africa* (Monthly Review Press, 1980). Cliffe edited a somewhat later collection that continues the themes of Saul and Cliffe, *Rural Co-operation in Tanzania* (Tanzania Publishing House, 1975).

A deeply critical and more coherently Marxist analysis with its roots in the Tanzanian student movement was Issa Shivji, *Class Struggles in Tanzania* (Heinemann and Tanzania Publishing House, 1976). It is a sort of signal post for two slightly later collections, Andrew Coulson, ed., *African Socialism in Practice* (Spokesman Books, 1979) and Bismarck Mwansasu and Cranford Pratt, eds, *Towards Socialism in Tanzania* (Tanzania Publishing House and University of Toronto Press, 1979). As the titles imply, the first is on the whole critical and the second defensive. The one significant defence of the workers' movement is Henry Mapolu, ed., *Workers and Management* (Tanzania Publishing House, 1976). Slightly later analyses of the state and rural development of particular merit are Michaela von Freyhold, *Ujamaa Villages in Tanzania* (Heinemann, 1979) and the searching articles of Suzanne Mueller, notably 'Retarded Capitalism in Tanzania', *Socialist Register* (1980). Dianne Bolton considers the sisal industry in *Nationalisation: A Road to Socialism* (Zed Press, 1985). I once attempted a synthesis with more citations in 'Class Conflict, Political Economy and the Struggle for Socialism in Tanzania', *AA*, LXXXI (1981).

On Zambia, perhaps the most distinctive contributions have been those that have considered the nationalisation of the copper industry: Antony Martin, *Minding their Own Business: Zambia's Struggle Against Western Control* (Hutchinson, 1972); M. Bostock and C. Harvey, eds, *Economic Independence and Zambian Copper* (Praeger, 1972) and Richard Sklar, *Corporate Power in an African State* (University of California Press, 1975). For useful introductions to Zambian politics and economy, see William Tordoff, ed., *Politics in Zambia* (Manchester University Press, 1974) and Tim Shaw, 'Zambia: Dependence and Underdevelopment', *CJAS*, X (1976). Reconsiderations with more of an edge on the early hollowing out of formal democracy are collected in Jan-Bart Gewald et al., *One Zambia, Many Histories: Towards a History of Post-colonial Zambia* (Brill 2008). An interesting case study can be found in Jotham Momba, 'The State, Rural Class Formation and Peasant Participation in Zambia: The Case of the Southern Province', *AA*, 88 (1989). For the declining character of democratic practice in neighbouring Malawi, see John McCracken, 'Democracy and Nationalism in Historical Perspective: The Case of Malawi', *AA*, 387 (1998).

Some important work on the former High Commission Territories clustered within and around South Africa are Hugh Macmillan, 'Swaziland: Decolonisation and the Triumph of Tradition', *JMAS*, XXIII (1985), Pauline Peters, 'Struggles over Meaning and Struggles over Power: Cattle, Water and the State in Botswana', *Africa*, LIV (1984), Jack Parson, *Botswana: Liberal Democracy and the Labor Reserve System in Southern Africa* (Westview &

Gower, 1984), and James Ferguson on Lesotho, *The Anti-Politics Machine* (Cambridge University Press, 1990).

For background on pre-revolutionary Ethiopia, one can consult John Markakis, *Ethiopia: Anatomy of a Traditional Polity* (Clarendon Press, 1974) and John Cohen and Dov Weintraub, *Land and Peasants in Imperial Ethiopia* (Van Gorcum, 1975). For the revolutionary regime of the Horn that emerged next door see David Laitin and Said Samatar, *Somalia: Nation in Search of a State* (Westview and Gower, 1987) and Ahmed Samatar, *Socialist Somalia* (Zed Press, 1988). Norman O'Neill and Jay O'Brien, eds, *Economy and Class in the Sudan* (Avebury, 1988) provides material on that country. I. M. Lewis, *Nationalism and Self-Determination in the Horn of Africa* (Ithaca Press, 1983) was a useful regional introduction.

Fiction is often a powerful force for comprehending social conditions. Ayi Kwei Armah's symbolic portrayal of the Nkrumah years in Ghana, *The Beautyful Ones are Not Yet Born*, Ngugi wa Thiongo's *Petals of Blood* on Kenya and Ben Okri, *Dangerous Love*, are testimony to a political and social sensibility with striking common features. Chinamanda Adichie, *Half of a Golden Sun* (Knopf, 2006), is an unforgettable novel set in the Biafran war from a critical Igbo point of view.

CHAPTER 11. Southern Africa: The Liberation Struggles

For a remarkable survey with an excellent bibliography, one must refer again to Glaser, *Politics and Society in South Africa*, op.cit. For Afrikaner nationalism, see Patrick Furlong, *Between Crown and Swastika* (Witwatersrand University Press, 1991); T. Dunbar Moodie, *The Rise of Afrikanerdom* (University of California Press, 1975); Heribert Adam and Hermann Giliomee, *Ethnic Power Mobilized* (Yale University Press, 1977) and above all Dan O'Meara's unequalled *Forty Lost Years* (Ravan Press, 1996). The last two have much to say about the changing state. This was also true of Heribert Adam, *Modernizing Racial Domination* (University of California Press, 1971). There is some historical discussion in Albie Sachs' *Justice in South Africa* (University of California Press, 1973). On the architect of separate development, Alex Hepple, *Verwoerd* (Penguin, 1967) is still interesting.

On the Bantustans see Jeffrey Butler, Robert Rotberg and John Adams, *The Black Homelands of South Africa* (University of California Press, 1977) written at a time when American policy was circumspect, Gerhard Maré and Georgina Hamilton, *An Appetite for Power: Buthelezi's Inkatha and South Africa* (Ravan Press and Indiana U Press, 1988) and D. C. Hindson, 'Orderly Urbanization and Influx Control: From Territorial Apartheid to Regional Spatial Order in South Africa' *CEA*, 99 (1985). A new look at Transkei politics and its imbrication with the liberation movement is to be found in Timothy Gibbs, 'Chris Hani's "Country Bumpkins": Regional Networks in the ANC Underground', *JSAS*, XXXVII (2011) and *Mandela's Kinsmen* (James Currey and Jacana, 2014).

For the ANC, consult the autobiography of Chief Albert Luthuli, *Let My People Go* (Collins, 1962) and the collected speeches of Nelson Mandela, *No Easy Walk to Freedom* (Heinemann, 1965). Mandela's *Long Walk to Freedom*

(Macdonald Purnell, 1995) is a remarkable testimony in some respects. Oliver Tambo, the leader in exile and equally important, is studied in a biography, Luli Callinicos, *Oliver Tambo: Beyond the Engeli Mountains* (David Philip, 2004). Thabo Mbeki is the subject of two critical book-length studies by Mark Gevisser, *A Legacy of Liberation: Thabo Mbeki and the Future of the South African Dream* (Palgrave Macmillan, 2009) and William Gumede, *Thabo Mbeki and the Battle for the Soul of the African National Congress* (Zebra, 2007). Many of the key white activists and supporters of the ANC have written testimony and autobiographies but one by a particularly important figure is Rusty Bernstein, *Memory Against Forgetting: Memoirs from a Life in South African Politics 1938–64* (Viking, 1999). Tom Lodge, *Black Politics in South Africa since 1945* (Longman, 1983) is still useful.

For the turn to armed struggle, Basil Davidson, Joe Slovo and A. R. Wilkinson, *Southern Africa: The New Politics of Revolution* (Penguin, 1976) is instructive and Ronnie Kasrils, *Armed and Dangerous: My Undercover Struggle Against Apartheid* (Heinemann, 1992) and Padraic O'Malley's *Shades of Difference: Mac Maharaj and the Struggle for South Africa* (Viking, 2007) entertaining. See also Stephen Ellis, 'The Genesis of the ANC's Armed Struggle in SA 1948–63', *JSAS*, XXXVII (4) (2011). Janet Cherry, *Umkhonto we Sizwe* (Jacana, 2011) provides a very balanced assessment. A documents-based assessment of the Soviet role is the strength of Irina Filatova and Apollon Davidson, *The Hidden Thread: Russia and South Africa in the Soviet Era* (Jonathan Ball, 2013). On the Pondoland risings Govan Mbeki's advocacy text, *South Africa: The Peasants' Revolt* (Penguin, 1964) can be coupled with Lungisile Ntsebeza and Thembela Kepe, *The Pondoland Revolts after Fifty Years* (University of Cape Town Press, 2012) and, for a comparison with Sekhukhuneland, Peter Delius, *A Lion Amongst the Cattle: Reconstruction and Resistance 1930–94* (Heinemann, Ravan and James Currey, 1996). Both Cosmas Desmond, *The Discarded People* (Penguin, 1971), and Laurine Platzky and Cherryl Walker, eds, *The Surplus People: Forced Removals in South Africa* (Ravan Press, 1985) described the dumping of Africans into the homelands, probably the cruellest aspect of apartheid policies that carried deep into the reform period.

South African journals in the struggle years that followed the changing pattern of events and contained analytical pieces include *Work in Progress*, *Africa Perspective*, the *South African Labour Bulletin*, *Agenda* and *Transformation*, the latter three still in existence. A good introduction to this era is Robert Price, *The Apartheid State in Crisis: Political Transformation in South Africa* (Oxford University Press, 1991). An excellent later assessment can be found in Martin Legassick, 'Myth and Reality in the Struggle Against Apartheid', *JSAS*, XXIV (1998). On the development of the apartheid system, Martin Legassick, 'Legislation, Ideology and Economy in Post-1948 South Africa', *JSAS*, 1 (1974) is still very valuable, but see also Doug Hindson, *Pass Controls and the Urban African Proletariat* (Ravan Press, 1987), Deborah Posel, *The Making of Apartheid 1948–61: Conflict and Compromise* (Clarendon Press, 1991) and Alan Mabin, 'Comprehensive Segregation: The Origins of the Group Areas Act and its Planning Apparatuses', *JSAS*, XVIII (1992). Some of the readings on South African society suggested for Chapter 8 are relevant here too.

Events in the 1970s started to cause considerable re-examination of the underpinnings of the South African system. Noteworthy was John Saul and Stephen Gelb, 'Crisis in South Africa: Class Defense, Class Revolution', *Monthly Review*, XXXIII (1981), also issued as a book by the review press, Alex Callinicos and John Rogers, *Southern Africa After Soweto* (Pluto Press, 1977); Baruch Hirson, *Year of Fire, Year of Ash* (Zed Press, 1979) and J. Kane-Berman, *South Africa: The Method in the Madness* (Pluto Press, 1979). For Steve Biko, the most memorable Black Consciousness figure, see his own *I Write What I Like* (Heinemann, 1987).

For the 1980s, William Cobbett and Robin Cohen, eds., *Popular Struggles in South Africa* (ROAPE & James Currey, 1988) and Colin Bundy, 'Street Sociology and Pavement Politics', *JSAS*, XIII (1987) are resonant. From 1983, the United Democratic Front was a key umbrella body for activists: Jeremy Seekings, *The UDF: A History of the United Democratic Front in South Africa 1983–1991* (David Philip, James Currey and Ohio University Press, 2000) covers its history critically. For some detailed resistance studies, Belinda Bozzoli, *Theatres of Struggle and the End of Apartheid* (Wits University Press, 2004), Charles Carter, 'We are the Progressives: Alexandra Youth Congress Activists and the Freedom Charter 1983–85', *JSAS* XVII (1991), Ineke van Kessel, 'From Confusion to Lusaka': The Youth Revolt in Sekhukhuneland', *JSAS*, XIX (1993) and Nkosikathi Gwala, 'Political Violence and the Struggle for Control in Pietermaritzburg', *JSAS*, XV (1989) are all stimulating.

On the labour movement and politics, there is much available. See Steven Friedman, *Building Tomorrow Today* (Ravan Press, 1987), Jeremy Baskin, *Striking Back: A History of COSATU* (Ravan Press, 1991) and Karl von Holdt, *Transition from Below: Forging Trade Unionism and Workplace Change in South Africa* (University of KwaZulu-Natal Press, 2006). The pioneering study of women and politics in Africa was Cherryl Walker, *Women and Gender in Southern Africa to 1945* (David Philip and James Currey, 1990) with the more recent scene explored by Shireen Hassim, *Women's Organisations and Democracy in South Africa: Contesting Authority* (University of Wisconsin Press, 2006). The interest in studying masculinity took off after the special issue of the *JSAS*, XXIV(4) (1998), edited by Robert Morrell.

On different aspects of social change at the end of apartheid in South Africa some distinctive studies are Michael de Klerk, 'Seasons that Will Never Return', *JSAS* XI (1984) on labour and the grain economy of the Highveld; Andries du Toit, 'The Micro-Politics of Paternalism: The Discourses of Management and Resistance on South African Fruit and Wine Farms', *JSAS* XIX (1993) and Mamphela Ramphele, *A Bed Called Home: Life in the Migrant Labour Hostels of Cape Town* (David Philip, Ohio University Press & Edinburgh University Press, 1993) Elsa Joubert's novel *Poppie* (Hodder & Stoughton, 1980) powerfully expressed the impact of labour control/Bantustan policy on the lives of black working-class women in particular. Striking journalistic testimony abounds in Joseph Lelyveld's *Move Your Shadow* (Michael Joseph, 1986) and Rian Malan's *My Traitor's Heart* (Vintage Books, 1991).

For the transition years consult the book of an American reporter, Patti Waldmeier: *Anatomy of a Miracle and the End of Apartheid* (W.W. Norton,

1997). Assessments of the transition include Hein Marais, *South Africa Pushed to the Limits: The Political Economy of Change* (Zed Press, 2011); Patrick Bond, *Elite Transition: From Apartheid to Neoliberalism in South Africa* (Pluto Press, 2000), Bill Freund, 'Swimming Against the Tide: The Macro-Economic Research Group in the South African Transition 1991–94', *ROAPE*, 138 (2013) and Padraic Carmody, 'Between Globalization and (Post) Apartheid; The Political Economy of Restructuring in South Africa', *JSAS*, XXVIII, 2002. Later political issues and the fate of the ANC are broached acutely by Susan Booysen, *The African National Congress and the Regeneration of Political Power* (Wits University Press, 2011) and Tom Lodge, 'Neo-patrimonial Politics in the ANC', *AA*, 450 (2011). *State of the Nation* annual volumes and *New South African Review*s look at many issues and have attempted to replace the South African Review series of the late apartheid years. They are very strong on South Africa's continental interrelationships but Patrick McGowan and Fred Ahwireng-Obeng, 'Partner or Hegemon: South Africa in Africa', *JCAS*, XVI(1) and XVI(2), 1998 is also an excellent assessment.

A guide to poverty and class in post-apartheid South Africa is Jeremy Seekings and Nicoli Nattrass, *Class, Race and Inequality in South Africa* (Yale University Press, 2005) A very accessible account flows from Sampie Terreblanche, *A History of Inequality in South Africa 1652–2002* (University of KwaZulu-Natal Press, 2003). One example of a book that puts centre stage worker experience is Dhiraj Nite and Paul Stewart, eds, *Mining Faces: An Oral History of Work in Gold and Coal Mines in South Africa 1951–2011* (Jacana 2012). The situation of workers and former workers in a major industrial area is the subject of Franco Barchiesi, *Precarious Liberation: Workers, the State and Social Citizenship in Postapartheid South Africa* (SUNY Press, 2011). Jonathan Crush et al., 'Undermining Labour; The Rise of Sub-Contracting in South African Gold Mines', *JSAS*, XXVII (2001) and Gavin Capps, 'Victim of its Own Success? The Platinum Mining Industry and the Apartheid Mineral Property System in South Africa's Political Transition,' *ROAPE*, 131 (2012) all look at mining while Simon Roberts and Grace Mohamed, 'Weak Links in the BEE Chain: Procurement, Skills and Employment Equity in the Metals and Engineering Industry', *JCAS*, XXVI(1) (2008) give a good insight into a key secondary industry. Ingrid Horwitz and John Luiz, 'Urban Working Class Credit Usage and Over-Indebtedness in South Africa, *JSAS*, XXXIII(1) (2007), reveals a key factor in economic life developed further by Deborah James, *Money from Nothing: Indebtedness and Aspiration in South Africa* (Stanford University Press, 2014). The trade unions in post-apartheid South Africa are the subject of Eddie Webster and Karl von Holdt, eds, *Beyond the Apartheid Workplace: Studies in Transformation* (University of KwaZulu-Natal Press, 2005) and Sakhela Buhlungu, *A Paradox of Victory: COSATU and the Democratic Transition in South Africa* (University of Kwa-Zulu Natal Press, 2007). Race remains a much-discussed subject. Its continued significance is considered in Jeremy Seekings, 'The Continuing Salience of Race: Discrimination and Diversity in South Africa', *JCAS*, XXVI (1) (2008), 1–26, Michael MacDonald, *Why Race Matters in South Africa* (Harvard University Press, 2005) and Gerhard Maré, *Declassified: Moving Beyond the Dead End of Race in South Africa* (University of

Kwa Zulu-Natal Press 2015). Neville Alexander, *An Ordinary Country: Issues in the Transition from Apartheid to Democracy in South Africa* (University of Natal Press, 2002) was a striking voice on the national question.

Many writers have been fascinated with local protests often centred on demands for 'delivery', of which perhaps far more is expected politically than is really plausible. However, apart from many excellent research-based standalone articles, the collection edited by Richard Ballard, Adam Habib and Imraan Valodia, *Voices of Protest: Social Movements in Post-Apartheid South Africa* (University of KwaZulu-Natal Press, 2005) could be supplemented by Elke Zuern, *The Politics of Necessity: Community Organizing and Democracy in South Africa* (University of KwaZulu-Natal Press, 2011). Numerous parallel research reports and articles discuss the foibles of local government in South Africa, notably the special issue of *Transformation* edited by Claire Bénit-Gbaffou, 67/68 (2008).

Perspectives on development issues generally are placed together in Bill Freund and Harald Witt, eds, *Development Dilemmas in Post-Apartheid South Africa* (University of KwaZulu-Natal Press, 2010). This contains a number of contributions on the land issue. However, despite the largely failed exercise in land redistribution, this question has led to several searching collections which do have rich detail on agriculture and farming in South Africa. These include Henry Bernstein, ed., *The Agrarian Question in South Africa* (Frank Cass, 1996); Fred Hendricks, Lungisile Ntsebeza and Kirk Helliker, eds, *The Promise of Land: Undoing a Century of Dispossession in South Africa* (Wits University Press, 2013); Deborah James, *Gaining Ground? 'Rights' and 'Property' in South African Land Reform* (Routledge, 2007) and Ben Cousins and Cherryl Walker, eds., *Land Divided, Land Restored: Land Reform in South Africa for the 21st Century* (Jacana, 2015). Numerous excellent shorter contributions are also to be consulted such as the special issue of the *Journal of Agrarian Change*, XIII, 1 (2013). In addition, Barbara Oomen, *Chiefs in South Africa: Law, Power and Culture in the Post-Apartheid Era* (James Currey, Palgrave and University of KwaZulu-Natal Press, 2005) takes on the obvious continuities in chiefly authority. For the living conditions, beliefs and the gender relationships that link up to poverty and provide deeper insight into the AIDS epidemic, see Peter Delius and Clive Glaser, 'The Myths of Polygamy: a History of Extramarital and Multiple Partnership Sex in South Africa', *South African Historical Journal*, L(1) (2004); Mark Hunter, *Love in a Time of AIDS* (University of KwaZulu-Natal Press, 2010), Jonny Steinberg, *Three Letter Plague: A Young Man's Journey through a Great Epidemic* (Jonathan Ball, 2008) and Sarah Mathis, 'Disobedient Daughters? Changing Women's Role in Rural Households in KwaZulu-Natal', *JSAS*, XXXVII (4) (2011). Women's lives are stressed by Sarah Mosoetsa, *Eating from One Pot: The Dynamics of Survival in Poor South African Households* (Wits University Press, 2011). On belief systems in transition, two contributions of interest are Isak Niehaus with Eliazaar Moohlala and Kally Shokane, *Witchcraft, Power and Politics: Exploring the Occult in the South African Lowveld* (David Philip and Pluto Press, 2001) and Adam Ashforth, *Madumo: A Man Bewitched* (University of Chicago Press, 2000). Crime is a burning issue in South Africa. For one useful approach see Tony Samara, *Cape*

Town after Apartheid: Crime and Governance in the Divided City (University of Minnesota Press, 2011). Beyond these somewhat arbitrary choices from many good analyses of these and other social phenomena, those interested should explore other forms of writing and even other media such as film. Writers who capture some of the new urban scene with a new imaginary South Africans like to term 'hectic' are Ivan Vladislavic, Lauren Beukes, Zakes Mda and the late Phaswane Mpe. The unequalled author of searching reportage is Jonny Steinberg, author of *Midlands, The Number* and other memorable works.

On conflicts elsewhere in southern Africa there is also a large but uneven literature. Two long if not authoritative studies of Angola are John Marcum, *The Angolan Revolution* (MIT Press, 1969–78) and René Pelissier, *La guerre du minotaure* (Orgeval, France, 1978). Basil Davidson wrote an attractive account of the MPLA in the field during their strongest phase, *In The Eye of the Storm* (Longman, 1972). For a critical survey of Angola since the MPLA victory see W. G. Clarence-Smith, 'Class Structure and Class Struggle in Angola in the 1970s', *JSAS*, VII (1980) and the contribution of Michel Cahen to *Bourgs et villes en Afrique lusophone* (Harmattan, 1989). On the war and why and how it was the pivot of regional change, see Piero Gleijeses, *Visions of Freedom: Havana, Washington and Pretoria and the Struggle for Southern Africa 1976–91* (University of North Carolina Press, 2013). Angola at the end of the century was the subject of the special issue on Angola, *ROAPE*, 90 (2001) and for a later view, Ricardo Olivieira Soares, *Magnificient and Beggar Land: Angola since the Civil War* (Hurst, 2014). The emerging society is also observed by Cristina Udelsman Rodrigues, 'From Family Solidarity to Social Classes: Urban Stratification in Angola', *JSAS*, XXXIII (2007). For the aligned revolution, outside this region of course, in Guinea-Bissau, and its consequences, see Rosemary Galli and Jocelyn Jones, *Guinea-Bissau: Politics, Economics and Society* (Frances Pinter, 1987).

Eduardo Mondlane's account of the Mozambican revolution covers up conflict but is valuable: *The Struggle for Mozambique* (Penguin Books, 1969) and see also John Saul, 'FRELIMO and the Mozambique Revolution' in Saul and Arrighi, *Essays in the Political Economy of Africa*, cited for Chapter 10. Mozambique's many intellectual supporters did not provide as effective or convincing an engaged literature as was found in Tanzania. For a sample, however, see John Saul, ed., *A Difficult Road: The Transition to Socialism in Mozambique* (Monthly Review Press, 1985). For the mortal struggle between FRELIMO and RENAMO, Alex Vines, *RENAMO: Terrorism in Mozambique* (James Currey Indiana University Press, 1991) captured the time but see as well a remarkable monograph by an anthropologist on one region, Christian Geffray, *La cause des armes au Mozambique: anthropologie d'une guerre* (Karthala, 1990). Bertil Egero provides a thoughtful assessment in *A Dream Undone: The Political Economy of Democracy 1975–84* (Nordiska Afrikainstitutet, 1987). Mozambican rural society before and after independence is considered as a whole in Bridget O'Laughlin, 'Proletarianisation, Agency and Changing Rural Livelihoods: Forced Labour and Resistance in Colonial Mozambique', *JSAS*, XXVIII, 2002. Some essays emphasising particular aspects of the Mozambican experience are Signe Arnfred, 'Women in Mozambique; Gender Struggle and Gender Politics',

ROAPE, 41 (1984); Merle Bowen, 'Peasant Agriculture in Mozambique', *CJAS*, XXIII (1989), Otto Roesch, 'Rural Mozambique since the FRELIMO 4th Party Congress: The Situation in the Baixo Limpopo', *ROAPE*, 41 (1984) and 'RENAMO and the Peasantry in Southern Mozambique', *CJAS*, XXVI (1992). Joseph Hanlon surveyed the post-revolutionary scene of the 1990s in *Mozambique: Who Calls the Shots?* (James Currey & Indiana University Press, 1991) which also comments on the weight of the so-called non-governmental organisations (NGOs) such as to have a much wider relevance. For later commentary see the work of Anne Pitcher, *Transforming Mozambique; The Politics of Privatisation 1975–2000* (Cambridge University Press, 2002). On the FRELIMO heritage, one could contrast her 'Forgetting from Above and Memory from Below: Strategies of Legitimation and Struggle in Post-Socialist Mozambique', *Africa*, 76 (2006) with Bjørn Enge Bertelsen (2014) 'Effervescence and Ephemerality: Popular Urban Uprisings in Mozambique', *Ethnos: Journal of Anthropology* (2014), which stress respectively forgetting and memory. On other current themes: Jeanne Vivet, *Deplacés de guerre dans la ville: la citadination des deslocados à Maputo (Mozambique)* (Karthala et IFAS, 2012) and Jason Sumich, 'Politics After the Time of Hunger in Mozambique: A Critique of Patrimonial Interpretations of African Elites', *JSAS*, XXXIV (2004).

Timothy Scarnecchia, *The Urban Roots of Democracy and Political Violence* (University of Rochester Press, 2008) has looked back at the declining importance of democratic discourse as Zimbabwean nationalism radicalised. On the Rhodesian war the best accounts are Kees Maxey, *The Fight for Zimbabwe* (Rex Collings, 1975) and David Martin and Phyllis Johnson's book 'authorised' by ZANU, *The Struggle for Zimbabwe* (Monthly Review Press, 1981). On the social context and impact, see Terence Ranger, *Peasant Consciousness and Guerrilla War in Zimbabwe* (James Currey, 1985); Irene Staunton, *Mothers of the Revolution* (Baobab Books, 1990); Norma Kriger, *Zimbabwe's Guerrilla War: Peasant Voices* (Cambridge University Press, 1992) and David Maxwell, 'Local Politics and the War of Liberation in North-eastern Zimbabwe', *JSAS*, XIX (1993). For the UDI regime see Larry Bowman, *Politics in Rhodesia* (Harvard University Press, 1973) and Martin Loney, *Rhodesia: White Racism and Imperial Response* (Penguin, 1975). There is a sensitive feeling for African politics in the future minister Nathan Shamuyarira's *Crisis in Rhodesia* (André Deutsch, 1965).

The post-1980 regime was evaluated in Colin Stoneman and Lionel Cliffe, *Zimbabwe: Politics, Economics and Society* (Frances Pinter, 1989) and Jeffrey Herbst, *Politics in Zimbabwe* (University Press of Zimbabwe, 1990). Some supplementary material of particular value would be Jocelyn Alexander, 'State, Peasantry and Resettlement in Zimbabwe', *ROAPE*, 61 (1994); Ben Cousins et al., 'Social Differentiation in Communal Lands in Zimbabwe', *ROAPE* 53 (1992) and Dan Wiener et al., 'Land Use and Productivity in Zimbabwe', *JMAS*, XXIII (1985). For interesting cultural takes on the struggle and after, there is David Lan, *Guns and Rain: Guerrillas and Spirit Mediums in Zimbabwe* (University of California Press, 1984) and Thomas Turino, *Nationalists, Cosmopolitans and Popular Music in Zimbabwe*, op.cit.. The *Journal of Southern African Studies* is a rich source of articles on the crisis years. See especially the following numbers: XXXII(2) (2006), *JSAS* XXXVI(2) (2010), *JSAS* XXXIX(4) (2013).

A selection of contributions from different perspectives on the controversial land invasions might include Sam Moyo, *The Land Question in Zimbabwe* (SAPES Books, 1995); JoAnn McGregor, '"The Politics of Disruption"; War Veterans and the Local State in Zimbabwe', *AA*, 402 (2002); Brian Raftopoulos, 'Crisis in Zimbabwe 1998–2008' in Raftopoulous and Alois Mlambo, (eds) *Becoming Zimbabwe* (Weaver and Jacana, 2009); Lloyd Sachikonye, *Zimbabwe's Lost Decade: Politics, Development and Society* (Weaver, 2012), and Ian Scoones et al., *Zimbabwe's Land Reform: Myths and Realities* (James Currey, Weaver and Jacana, 2010).

For the recent history of Namibia, see Reg Green, Marja-Liisa and Kimmo Kiljunen, eds, *Namibia: The Last Colony* (Longman, 1982). On the liberation war, we know more thanks to Colin Leys and John Saul, *Namibia's Liberation Struggle: The Two-Edged Sword* (James Currey & Ohio University Press, 1995). On post-war Namibia, Ingolf Diener and Olivier Graefe provided a good collection, *Contemporary Namibia: The First Landmarks of a Post-Apartheid Society* (Gamsberg Macmillan, 2001). There is a judicious summary of the achievements and limitations of the Botswana model in Ian Taylor, 'As Good As It Gets: Botswana's "Democratic Development"', *JCAS*, XXI (2003). By contrast, there are a number of rather denunciatory accounts of the conservative Swaziland 'way'. One that is handy is by Richard Levine, *When the Sleeping Grass Awakens* (Wits University Press, 1997). James Ferguson, *The Anti-Politics Machine; Development, Depoliticisation and Bureaucratic State Power in Lesotho*, op.cit. is perhaps the best book ever written on development in Africa; everyone should read it.

CHAPTER 12. Structural Adjustment Kicks In

In trying to understand current African politics and the debate about democratisation, I have been especially influenced by Mamdani and Davidson, already cited above with reference to Chapters 6 and 10; Davidson blames the colonial experience for foisting a particular kind of state-form on Africa; and, although only partially concerned with Africa, Michel Cahen's *Ethnicité politique* (Harmattan, 1994), a polemic against the attempt to erase ethnicity from the political map of the world, is provocative. Then there is Jean-François Bayart to which reference has been made earlier. He explored further in Bayart, ed., *Le politique par le bas en Afrique noire* (Karthala, 1992) and his ideas influenced the also already mentioned (for Chapter 10) Chabal and Daloz, *Africa Works*. Morris Szeftel, 'Misunderstanding African Politics: Corruption and the Governance Agenda', *ROAPE*, 76 (1998) and '"Eat with Us": Managing Corruption and Patronage under Zambia's Three Republics', *JCAS*, XVIII(2) (2000), are insightful. E. Terray, ed., *L'état contemporain en Afrique* (Harmattan, 1987) is a good collection.

For lack of a practicable alternative, chiefs, no longer so clearly defined as in colonial times, remain significant in weak rural governance systems. For contemporary examples, a few studies would include Tendai Murisa, 'Democratisation and Control: Fast Track and Local Government Reforms in Zimbabwe' *JCAS*, XXXII(1) (2014); Øyvind Eggen, 'Chiefs and Everyday Governance: Parallel State Organisations in Malawi', *JSAS*, XXXVII (2011); Francis Nyamnjoh, 'Chieftaincy and the Negotiation of Might and Right in Botswana Democracy', *JCAS*, XXI (2003), and Wazha Morapedi, 'Demise or Resilience: Customary Law and Chieftaincy in 21st century Botswana', *JCAS*, XXVIII (2010).

While this book does not place much emphasis on international relations, students should certainly be aware of the continued salience, at least through this period, of Françafrique. This is the subject of numerous books and a regular spate of articles in English. In addition to *Les dessous de la Françafrique*, a good supplement might be Tony Chafer, 'French African Policy in Historical Perspective', *JCAS*, XIX (2001). For EU relations with Africa more broadly, see *ROAPE*, 112 (2007) for articles by Paul Goodison and others and Adrian Flint, 'The End of a Special Relationship? The New EU-ACP Economic Partnership Agreements', *ROAPE*, 119 (2009).

Our major source on the peasant risings of the 1960s in the Leopoldville Congo republic is Benoît Verhaegen, *Rebellions au Congo* (CRISP, Brussels, 2 vols, 1966–9) with a rich selection of documents. See also his *Mulele et la révolution populaire à Kwilu* (L'Harmattan, 2006). Renee Fox, Willy de Craemer and Jean-Marie Ribeaucourt, 'The Second Independence: A Case Study of the Kwilu Rebellion of the Congo', *CSSH*, VIII (1965) and Herbert Weiss, *Political Protest in the Congo* (Princeton University Press, 1967) are also important. The emerging system was captured by Jean-Claude Willame, *Patrimonialism and Political Change in the Congo* (Stanford University Press, 1972) and Jean-Philippe Peemans, 'The Social and Economic Development of Zaïre since Independence', *AA*, LXXIV (1975).

On the Ethiopian revolution, see Gebru Tareke, *The Ethiopian Revolution: War in the Horn of Africa* (Yale University Press, 2009), Donald Donham, *Marxist Modern: An Ethnographic History of the Ethiopian Revolution* (University of California Press and James Currey, 1999), Christopher Clapham, *Transformation and Continuity in Revolutionary Ethiopia* (Cambridge University Press, 1988) and Dessalegn Rahmato, *Agrarian Reform in Ethiopia* (Scandinavian African Studies Institute, 1984). Other perceptions are found in John Markakis, 'Garrison Socialism: The Case of Ethiopia', *Middle East Research and Information Project (MERIP) Report* IX (1979); Addis Hiwet, 'Analysing the Ethiopian Revolution', *ROAPE*, 30 (1984) and Michael Stahl, 'Capturing the Peasants through Cooperatives: The Case of Ethiopia', *ROAPE*, 44 (1989). There is little to read on Sankara apart from the enthusiastic accounts of Ernest Harsch but see the work of another great sympathiser: Bruno Jaffre, *Biographie de Thomas Sankara; la patrie ou la mort* (L'Harmattan, revised edn, 1997).

For late twentieth-century analysis of the political context in Africa, Peter Gibbon, Y. Bangura and A. Ofstad, *Adjustment, Authoritarianism and Democracy: The Politics of Economic Liberalisation in Africa* (Scandinavian Institute of African Studies, 1992) follows well from the radical literature of the 1970s. A useful set of collections whose readings expose the African crisis and the meaning of structural adjustment are: Peter Lawrence, ed., *World Recession and the Food Crisis in Africa* (*ROAPE* & James Currey, 1986); John Ravenhill, ed., *Africa in Economic Crisis* (Macmillan, 1986) John Ravenhill and Thomas Callaghy, eds, *Hemmed In: Responses to Africa's Economic Decline* (Columbia University Press, 1993) and Giles Mohan et al., *Structural Adjustment: Theory, Practice and Impacts* (Routledge, 2000). There have been many African ripostes to structural adjustment. One of the best is Bade Onimode, *A Future for Africa: Beyond the Politics of Adjustment* (Earthscan, 1992). On the Malawi food storage story, see Andrew Mavuto Mpesi and Ragnhild Muriaas, 'Food Security as a Political Issue: The 2009 Elections in Malawi', *JCAS*, XXX (2012) and William Attwell, '"When We Have Nothing, We All Eat Grass"; Debt, Dependence and the Food Crisis in Malawi 2001 to 2003', *JCAS*, 31 (2013). A French interpretation of the whole structural adjustment phenomenon is found in G. Duruflé, *L'ajustement structurel en Afrique* (Karthala, 1988). The contradictions come to the fore in Gavin Williams, 'Why Structural Adjustment is Necessary and Why It Doesn't Work', *ROAPE*, 60 (1994), 214–25 and Bjørn Beckman, 'Empowerment or Repression? The World Bank and the Politics of African Adjustment' in P. Gibbon et al., *Authoritarianism, Democracy and Adjustment* (cited for Chapter 12). How structural adjustment policies became indigenised is the subject of Duncan Holton, 'Reconsidering the Power of the IFIs: Tanzania and the World Bank, 1978–85' *ROAPE*, 106 (2005).

This chapter has emphasised two countries in particular. For Ghana, some readings on the structural adjustment period are George Dei, 'The Renewal of a Ghanaian Rural Economy', *CJAS*, XXVI (1992); Jeffrey Haynes, 'Railway Workers and the PNDC Government in Ghana 1982–90', *JMAS*, XXIX (1991); John Loxley, 'Structural Adjustment Programmes in Africa: Reflections on Ghana and Zambia', *ROAPE* 47 (1990); Jeffrey Herbst, *The Politics of Reform in Ghana 1982–91* (University of California Press, 1993) and E. Gyimah-Boadi, ed., *Ghana under PNDC Rule* (CODESRIA, 1993). For Uganda, companion pieces might be Holger Bernt Hansen and Michael Twaddle, *Uganda Now* (Heinemann, Ohio University Press & James Currey, 1988); Emmanuel Nabuguzi, 'Peasant Responses to Crisis in Uganda: Rice Farmers in Busoga', *ROAPE*, 56 (1993); Mahmood Mamdani, 'Uganda: Contradictions of the IMF Programme and Perspective', *Development and Change* XXI (1990) and E. A. Brett, 'Rebuilding Organizational Capacity in Uganda under the National Resistance Movement' *JMAS*, XXXII (1994). Perhaps the next best studied example is Zambia. Apart from the Loxley article cited just above, Jan-Bart Gewald et al., *One Zambia, Many Histories: Towards a History of Post-colonial Zambia* (Brill, 2008); Carolyn Baylies and Morris Szeftel, 'The Fall and Rise of Multi-Party Politics in Zambia', *ROAPE*, 54 (1992); Hans-Otto Savo, 'The International Monetary Fund and Zambia: The Contradictions of Exchange Rate Auctioning and the Desubsidisation of Agriculture', *AA*, 87 (1988) and Jürgen Wolf, 'Zambia under the IMF Regime', *AA*, 88 (1989) are particularly useful.

Selected writing on less studied countries are Myriam Gervais, 'Structural Adjustment in Niger; Implementations, Effects and Determining Political Factors', *ROAPE*, 63 (1994); Lars Rudebeck, 'The Effects of Structural Adjustment on Kandjadja, Guinea-Bissau', *ROAPE*, 49 (1990) and Horace Campbell, 'Tanzania and the World Bank's Urban Shelter Project; Ideology and International Finance', *ROAPE,* 41 (1988). Some of the most important current studies of the African situation in the structural adjustment era have focused on agriculture. See especially Peter Lawrence's collection, already cited above, Philip Raikes, *Modernizing Hunger: Famine, Food Surplus and Farm Policy in the EEC and Africa* (James Currey & Heinemann, 1988); Peter Gibbon, Kjell Havnevik and Kenneth Hermele, *A Blighted Harvest: The World Bank and African Agriculture in the 1980s* (James Currey, 1993) and Hamid Ait Amara and Bernard Founou-Tchuigoua, eds, *African Agriculture: The Critical Choices* (Zed Press and United Nations University, 1990).

But what was actually happening in African agriculture? Some perceptive answers can be found in Sara Berry, *No Condition is Permanent: The Social Dynamics of Agrarian Change in Sub-Saharan Africa* (University of Wisconsin Press, 1993); Dominique Desjeux, *Stratégies paysannes en Afrique noire* (Harmattan, 1987); Christian Santoir, 'Décadence et résistance de pastoralisme; les peuls de la vallée du fleuve Senegal', *CEA,* 133 (1993); Fiona Mackenzie, 'Local Initiative and National Policy: Gender and Agricultural Change in Muranga's District, Kenya', *CJAS,* XX (1986); Maureen Mackintosh, *Gender, Class and Rural Transition: Agribusiness and the Food Crisis in Senegal* (Zed Press, 1989) and Martha Starr, 'Risk, Environmental Variability and Drought-Induced Impoverishment: The Pastoral Economy of Central Niger', *Africa,* LVII (1987). On one key aspect that continues to expand: Barbara Dinham and Colin Hines, *Agribusiness in Africa* (Earth Resources Research, 1983). The radical green perspective is portrayed by Lloyd Timberlake, *Africa in Crisis: The Causes, the Cures of Environmental Bankruptcy* (Earthscan, 1985). While the developmental literature remained largely focused on agriculture, useful surveys for the late twentieth century are found in Faysal Yachir, *Mining in Africa Today: Strategies and Prospects* (United Nations University and Zed Press, 1988) and Roger Riddell, ed., *Manufacturing Africa* (ODI & James Currey, 1990).

Some scathing attacks on the structure of aid have been written in recent years. Ferguson's *Anti-Politics Machine* is perhaps the most remarkable. On large projects and their implications, see Gunilla Andrae and Bjorn Beckman, *The Wheat Trap* (Zed Press, 1985) and Adrian Adams, *La terre et les gens du fleuve* (Harmattan, 1985). In the previous chapter, Hanlon's critique of NGOs in Mozambique was highlighted. Others in at the kill are Richard Hogg, 'Development in Kenya; Drought, Desertification and Food Scarcity', *AA,* 86 (1987), William Adams and David Anderson, 'Irrigation Before Development: Indigenous and Induced Change in Agricultural and Water Management in East Africa', *AA,* 87 (1988) and Doug Porter et al., *Development in Practice: Paved with Good Intentions* (Routledge, 1991). Other assessments of importance can be found in *ROAPE,* 71 (1997), notably Shelagh Stewart, 'Happy Ever After in the Marketplace: NGOS and Uncivil Society', with other articles in that special issue, Joe Hanlon, *Mozambique; Who Calls the Shots?,* op.cit., and Tina Wallace, 'NGO Dilemma: Trojan Horses to Global Neoliberalism', *Socialist Register* (2004).

The disarray of state intervention in the economy under the pressures of structural adjustment and other forces has not come to an end and the so-called informal sector is certainly more than still with us. The spell of modernity and how it was broken is the subject of James Ferguson, *Expectations of Modernity: Myths and Meanings on the Zambian Copperbelt* (Duke University Press, 1999) and see also Johan Pottier, *Migrants No More: Settlement and Survival in Mambwe Villages* (Manchester University Press, 1988). These new forces are explored for the late twentieth century in Janet MacGaffey, *The Real Economy in Zaire* (James Currey & University of Pennsylvania Press, 1991); Nicholas van Hear, '"By-Day Boys" and Dariga Men', *ROAPE*, 31 (1984); Lars Rudebeck, 'Kandjadja, Guinea-Bissau: 1976–86: Observations on the Political Economy of an African Family', *ROAPE*, 41 (1988) and T. L. Maliyamkomo and M. S. D. Bagachwa, *The Second Economy in Tanzania* (Heinemann, James Currey & Ohio University Press, 1990). On the urban side, one may note Emmanuel Ndione, *Dakar: une société en grappe* (Karthala, 1993); Abdou Touré, *Les petits métiers à Abidjan: l'imagination au secours de la conjoncture* (Karthala, 1985); Ph. Antoine et al., *Abidjan, 'côté cours'* (Karthala, 1987) and Aili Tripp, 'Women and the Changing Urban Household Economy in Tanzania', *JMAS*, XXVII (1989). The complexity and variety of activities in the markets of West Africa are systematically studied in Thierry Paulhais and Laurence Wilhelm, *Marchés d'Afrique* (Karthala, 2000). These studies open the door to a new literature that emerges in the new century basic to the final chapter of this book.

CHAPTER 13. Democracies, Dictatorships and Disasters: Africa into the Twenty-First Century

Readers of this edition will note the substantial increase in important writing by Africans noted in the bibliography. Indeed a growing proportion of foreign writers to the continent do not come from the former colonial powers either. This is an ongoing and healthy development that will no doubt expand further. However, most African scholars find it desirable to work in America or Europe, in part for practical reasons. An important organisation aimed at creating a different balance is CODESRIA, the Council for the Development of Social Science Research in Africa based in Dakar and able to function in four languages. CODESRIA, which is, however, dependent on aid from European countries, has been especially helpful to intellectuals from the smaller and poorer countries. Its publications are ideal for concentrating on African voices as authors and notably on the ongoing development of African politics. Two of the most interesting, Nigerian Adebayo Olukoshi and Malawian Thandeka Mkandawire, contribute to an American collection written at the height of the democracy wave, Richard Joseph, ed., *State, Conflict and Democracy in Africa* (Lynne Rienner, 1999). For a variety of Western views such as Bayart and Chabal, see the readings for Chapters 8 and 10. Bayart's sweeping, 'Africa in the World: A History of Extraversion', *AA*, 395 (2000) was provocative. For a contrast, see Rita Abrahamsen, *Disciplining Democracy: Development Discourse and Good Governance in Africa* (Zed, 2000). Newer thoughtful contributions include Crawford Young, 'The End of the Post-Colonial State in Africa; Reflections on Changing African Political Dynamics', *AA*, 410 (2004), Stephen Ellis, 'The Okiji Shrine; Death and Life in Nigerian Politics', *JAH*, IL (2008) and Ellis's *Seasons of Rain: Africa in the World* (Hurst, 2011). A dated book that nonetheless anticipates much of the analysis here is Christopher Clapham, *African Guerrillas* (James Currey, Fountain and Indiana UP, 1998).

The beginnings of democracy in one Francophone country were captured analytically in Chris Allen, 'Restructuring and the Authoritarian State: "Democratic Renewal" in Benin', *ROAPE*, 54 (1992). The tale of Chad and its oil money is considered in Ketil Fred Hansen, 'A Democratic Dictator's Success: How Chad's President Deby Defeated the Military Opposition in Three Years 2008–11' *JCAS*, 31 (2013) and Gilbert Tagem Fah, 'The War on Terror, the Chad-Cameroun Pipeline and the New Identity of the Lake Chad Basin', *JCAS*, XXV (2006). This situation in turn can be compared with the squalid one not, however, lacking in dynamism in the mini-state of Equatorial Guinea: Alicia Campos Serrano, 'Extraction Offshore, Politics Inshore and the Role of the State in Equatorial Guinea', *Africa*, 83 (2013), and the articles by Jędrzej Frynas and Geoffrey Wood on this mini-state in *AA*, 103, 413 (2004).

A compelling story highlighting Kenyan corruption is *Our Turn to Eat: The Story of a Kenyan Whistleblower* (Harper Collins, 2009) by Michaela Wrong. Modern Kenyan politics is very well-covered in Daniel Branch's sobering *Kenya Between Hope and Despair, 1963–2011* (Yale University Press, 2012). In a considerable literature on the subject, some outstanding titles are Jennifer Widner, *The Rise of a Party-State in Kenya: From Harambee to Nyayo* (University of Calfornia Press, 1992); David Throup, 'The Construction and Destruction of the State' in Michael Schatzberg, ed., *The Political Economy of Kenya* (Praeger 1987); Angelique Haugerud, *The Culture of Politics in Modern Kenya* (Cambridge UP 1995); Gabrielle Lynch, 'Negotiating Ethnicity; Identity Politics in Contemporary Kenya', *ROAPE*, 107 (2006) and her *I Say to You: Ethnic Power and the Kalenjin in Kenya* (University of Chicago Press, 2011); Susanne Mueller, 'The Political Economy of Kenya's Crisis', *Journal of Eastern African Studies*, II (2008) and Peter Kangwanja, 'Facing Mt. Kenya or Facing Mecca? The Mungiki, Ethnic Violence and the Politics of the Moi Succession in Kenya 1987–2002', *AA*, 406 (2003).

There is nothing like the quality of Branch on Kenya for Nigeria where one must search through shorter contributions to get a feel for the state and its enemies. The situation in the time of Abacha was considered in Michael Watts, ed., *State, Oil and Agriculture in Nigeria* (Institute of International Affairs, Berkeley, 1987) and Toyin Falola and Julius Ihonvbere, *The Rise and Fall of Nigeria's Second Republic 1979–84* (Zed Books, 1985). On how the system operates, Rotimi Suberu, 'The Nigerian Federal System: Performance, Problems and Prospects', *JCAS*, XXVIII (2010) is excellent. The circumstances in the Delta are summarised well by Uwafiokun Idemudia and Uwem Ite, 'Demystifying the Niger Delta Conflict: Towards an Integrated Explanation', *ROAPE*, 109 (2006), Jędrzej George Frynas, 'Corporate State Responses to Anti-Oil Protests in the Niger Delta', *AA*, 398 (2001), Michael Watts, 'Petro-Insurgency or Criminal Syndicate? Conflict and Violence in the Niger Delta', *ROAPE*, 114 (2007) and Kathryn Nwajiaku-Dahou, 'The Political Economy of Oil and "Rebellion" in the Niger Delta', *ROAPE*, 132 (2012). Recent new developments are addressed in Paul Ugor, 'Survival Strategies and Citizenship

Claims: Youth and the Underground Oil Economy in Post-Amnesty Nigeria', *Africa*, 83 (2013). For identifying the Ogoni who burst suddenly but late into Nigerian history, see V. Adefemi Isumonah, 'Making of the Ogoni Ethnic Group', *Africa*, 74(3) (2004). Scholars are only just catching up at point of publication with the sorrows of the North but a good first introduction is Adam Hijazi, 'Social Mobilization and Collective Violence: Vigilantes and Militias in the Lowlands of Plateau State, Central Nigeria', *Africa*, 78 (2008).

For the Ivory Coast, some key readings would be Richard Banégas, 'Côte d'Ivoire, Patriotism, Ethnonationalism and Other African Modes of Self-Writing', *AA*, 421 (2006); Alfred Babo, *L' Étranger en Côte d'Ivoire, crises et controverses autour d'une catégorie sociale* (L'Harmattan, 2013) and Jean-Pierre Dozon, *Les clefs de la crise ivoirienne* (Karthala, 2011). Marc le Pape and Claudine Vidal (eds), *Côte d'Ivoire; l'année terrible 1999–2000* (Karthala, Paris, 2002) was a good collection. The cultural underpinnings of the Gbagbo years are pursued by Sasha Newell, *The Modernity Bluff: Crime, Consumption and Citizenship in Côte d'Ivoire* (University of Chicago Press, 2012). A good understanding of the forces underlying ongoing Ghanaian democracy comes forth in Paul Nugent, *Big Men, Small Boys and Politics in Ghana: Power, Ideology and the Burden of History 1982–94* (Pinter, 1995) and Anja Osei, 'Political Parties in Ghana, Agents of Democracy?', *JCAS*, 31 (2013).

The troubles in Liberia have not received a great deal of scholarly attention. The best study is by Stephen Ellis, *The Mask of Anarchy: The Destruction of Liberia and the Religious Dimension of an African Civil War* (Hurst, London, 1999). See also the vivid narrative account of Mark Huband on earlier phases, *The Liberian Civil War* (Frank Cass, 1998). There is certainly a need for more Liberian voices. By contrast there are many somewhat contentious discussions of Sierra Leone: K. Peters and Paul Richards, '"Why We Fight"; Voices of Youth Combatants in Sierra Leone' *Africa*, 68 (1998); William Reno, *Corruption and State Politics in Sierra Leone* (Cambridge University Press, 1995); Ibrahim Abdullah, ed., *Between Democracy and Terror* (CODESRIA, 2004); Lansana Gberie, *A Dirty War in West Africa: The RUF and the Destruction of Sierra Leone* (Hurst, 2005), the same author's 'African Civil Society: "Blood Diamonds" and the Kimberley Process' in Stephen Ellis and Ineke van Kessel, eds., *Movers and Shakers: Social Movements in Africa* (Brill, 2009) and David Keen, *Conflict and Collusion in Sierra Leone* (James Currey and Palgrave, 2005). For a good summary of Libyan policies vis-à-vis Africa in the 1990s, see Asteris Huliaris, 'Qadhafi's Comeback: Libya and Sub-Saharan Africa; Africa in the 1990s', *AA*, 398 (2001).

For the Rwandan genocide placed in context, amongst many accounts some noteworthy ones are Mahmood Mamdani, *When Victims Become Killers: Colonialism, Nativism and the Genocide in Rwanda* (Fountain, James Currey and David Philip, 2001); Alison Des Forges, *Leave None to Tell the Tale* (Human Rights Watch, 1999) or *Aucun Témoin ne soit Survivre: le génocide à Rwanda* (Karthala) and Gérard Prunier, *The Rwanda Crisis: History of a Genocide* (Columbia UP, 1995). For the wider context, Andy Storey, 'Structural Adjustment, State Power and Genocide: The World Bank and Rwanda', *ROAPE*, 89 (2001), Filip Reyntjens, *L'Afrique des grands lacs en crise: Rwanda, Burundi*

1988–94 (Karthala, 1994), Gerard Prunier, *Africa's World War: Congo, the Rwandan Genocide and the Making of a Continental Catastrophe* (Oxford UP, 2009) and Jean-Pierre Chrétien, *The Great Lakes of Africa; Two Thousand Years of History* cited earlier are all enlightening. Reyntjens and Chrétien concern themselves with Burundi while Liisa Malkki, *Purity and Exile: Violence, Memory and National Cosmology among Hutu Refugees in Tanzania* (University of Chicago Press, 1995) takes on the world of refugee camps in interlacustrine East Africa.

For the Congo, Prunier is a good political guide through very complicated waters. Some interesting insights on the east are to be found in Klaas Vlassenroot and Timothy Raeymakers, 'The Politics of Rebellion and Intervention in Ituri; The Emergence of a New Political Complex', *AA*, 412 (2004); Ann Laudati, 'Beyond Minerals; Broadening "Economies of Violence" in Eastern DRC'; Judith Verweijen, 'Military Business and the Business of the Military in the Kivus', both in *ROAPE*, 135 (2013) and Patience Kabamba, *The Business of Civil War: New Forms of Life in the Debris of the Democratic Republic of the Congo* (CODESRIA, 2012). A poignant account of the failed state is Jean Omasombo Tshonda's portrait of late Mobutist Kisangani, once Stanleyville, third city of the Belgian Congo: 'Kisangani and the Curse of Destiny' in Okwui Enwezor et al., *Under Siege: Four African Cities* (Hatje Cantz, 2003). A number of scholars have taken forward the literature mentioned above for previous chapters on how the Congolese cope. In this regard, Theodore Trefon, ed., *Reinventing Order in the Congo: How People Respond to State Failure in Kinshasa* (Zed Books, 2004) and Kristof Titeca and Tom de Herdt, 'Real Governance Beyond the "Failed State": Negotiation Education in the DRC', *AA*, 439 (2011) are guides.

This sense of the failed state and what comes after is even more present in the literature on Somalia. See Hussein Adam, 'Somalia: Militarism, Warlordism or Democracy?', *ROAPE*, 54 (1992); Ken Menkhaus, 'State Collapse in Somalia: Second Thoughts', *ROAPE*, 97 (2003); Jon Abbink, 'The Islamic Courts Union; the Ebb and Flow of a Somali Islamist Movement' in Stephen Ellis and Ineke van Kessel, eds, op.cit.; Alice Hills, 'Somalia Works; Police Development as State Building', *AA*, 450 (2014); Anna Lindley, 'Between "Dirty Money" and "Development Capital", Somali Money Infrastructure under Global Scrutiny', *AA*, 433 (2008) and Peter Little, *Economic and Political Reform in Africa: Anthropological Perspectives* (Indiana UP, 2014) which also has interesting things to say about pastoralism generally.

On Eritrea, a succinct approach to its post-independence problems is found in a study by a former enthusiast for the Eritrean cause: Dan Connell, 'From Resistance to Governance: Eritrea's Trouble with Transition', *ROAPE*, 129 (2011). Compare with *Against All Odds: A Chronicle of the Eritrean Revolution* (Red Sea Press, 1997). The Sudan deserves far more attention than it gets in Western sources but see the standard but passionate assessment of Michel Raimbaud, *Le Soudan dans tous ses états* (Karthala, 2013) and for the Darfur crisis, Alex de Waal, '"Who are the Darfurians?" Arab and African Identities, Violence and External Engagement', *AA*, 415 (2005) and Mahmood Mamdani, *Saints and Saviours: Darfur, Politics and the War on Terror* (Verso, 2009).

Extending the analysis, Alex de Waal's ideas also are bruited in 'Sudan's Elusive Democratisation: Civic Mobilisation, Provincial Rebellion and Chameleon Dictatorships', *JCAS*, XXXI (2013) and 'When Kleptocracy Becomes Insolvent', *AA*, 452 (2011).

For perspectives on the present-day Sahara, see Janet McDougall and Judith Scheele, eds, *Saharan Frontiers* (Indiana UP, 2012); Jeremy Keenan [essentially a Tuareg proponent] *The Dying Sahara* (Pluto, 2013) and Baz Lecocq, *Disputed Desert: Decolonisation, Competing Nationalisms and Tuareg Rebellions in Northern Mali* (Brill, 2013). On the LRA and the difficulties Museveni's Uganda found in confronting an apparently religious movement, Tim Allen and Koen Vlassenroot, eds., *The Lord's Resistance Army, Myth and Reality* (Zed Press, 2010) is very helpful. The very different situation in Buganda makes an instructive contrast: J. Oloka-Onyango, 'The Question of Buganda in Contemporary Ugandan Politics', *JCAS*, XV (1997).

The heyday of illegality, smuggling, the flourishing of black markets and a counter-economics is captured in Kate Meagher, 'A Back Door to Globalisation? Structural Adjustment, Globalisation and the Transborder Trade in Africa', *ROAPE*, 95 (2003); Jean-Francois Bayart, 'Africa in the World: A History of Extraversion', *AA*, 395 (2000), Bayart and Béatrice Hibou, *The Criminalisation of the State in Africa* (James Currey, 1999) and Janet Roitman, *Fiscal Disobedience* (University of Chicago Press, 2005). The topic of borders was really opened by Paul Nugent and Antony Asiwaju, eds, *African Boundaries* (Pinter, 1996). See as well David Coplan, 'A River Runs Through It; The Meaning of the Lesotho-Free State Border', *AA*, 398 (2001) and Fredrik Söderbaum and Ian Taylor, *Afro-Regions: The Dynamics of Cross-Border Micro Regionalism in Africa* (Nordiska Afrikainstitutet, 2008). Just on the Namibian-Angolan border, compare Gregor Dobler, 'Oshikango: The Dynamics of Growth and Regulation in a Namibian Boom Town (2010)', and Wolfgang Zeller, 'Danger and Opportunity in Katima Mulilo: A Namibian Border Boomtown at Transnational Crossroads', *JSAS*, XXXV(1) (2010).

The problems that vigilantism engenders when states are weak, at least in some regards, are highlighted in Suzanne Heald, 'Mafias in Africa: The Rise of Drinking Companies and Vigilante Groups in Bugisu, Uganda', *Africa*, LVI (1986), Ray Abrahams, 'Sungusungu: Village Vigilante Groups in Tanzania', *AA*, 86 (1987), Michael Fleisher, 'Sungu-Sungu and State-Sponsored Village Vigilante Groups among the Kuria of Tanzania', *Africa*, 70 (2000), Steve Tomah, 'State Policies, Local Prejudices and Cattle Rustling along the Ghana-Burkina Faso Border', *Africa*, 70 (2000), Bruce Baker, 'When the Bakassi Boys Come: Eastern Nigeria Confronts Vigilantism', *JCAS*, XX (2002), and the special issue of *Africa* on vigilantism: 78(1) (2008).

The appeal of migration to Africans as a way out of what Marx long ago called rural idiocy is documented interestingly in works cited much earlier for the colonial era by Sylvie Bredeloup, François Manchuelle and Isaie Dougnon, who all are interested in contemporary migration as well. Here the migrants turn into actors in their own right. The stories Nigerien Hausa speakers who venture into Nigeria tell are brought out vividly by Adeline Masquelier, 'Of Headhunters and Cannibals', *Cultural Anthropology*, 15(1) (2001).

Very high levels of inequality are typical of modern Africa and not often discussed, glaring as they are in popular culture. An exception with respect to the AIDS epidemic of recent years is Janet Bujra, 'Class Relations and Socio-economic Privilege in Africa: AIDS and the Conjuncture of Middle Class and Poor Africans', *ROAPE*, 107 (2006). The developmental state hypothesis is suggested in Tim Kelsall and David Booth, *Developmental Patrimonialism? Questioning the Orthodoxy on Political Governance and Economic Progress in Africa* (University of Sussex, Africa Power and Politics Programme Working Paper 9, 2010). On the developmental states of Africa, recent political processes are assessed in a more comprehensive study of regions and spatial inequities in Ethiopia by John Markakis, *Ethiopia: The Last Two Frontiers* (James Currey, 2011). Markakis looks searchingly at the regional policy meant to satisfy different ethnic groupings in the country and form a plausible modern state. Alex de Waal tends to be more willing to support a developmentalist argument but see Rene Lefort, 'The Theory and Practice of Meles Zenawi; A Response to Alex de Waal' (and de Waal before and after), *AA*, 448 (2013) who sees Ethiopia as overly dependent on foreign investment and poor in capital.

On Rwanda, An Ansoms, 'Re-engineering Rural Society: The Visions and Ambitions of the Rwandan Elite', *AA*, 431 (2009) is perceptive. The developmental model is stressed in David Booth and Frederick Golooba-Mutebi, 'Developmental Patrimonialism: The Case of Rwanda', *AA*, 444. (2011). A collection of assessments on Madagascar can be found in Solofo Randrianja, ed., *Madagascar; le coup d'etat de mars 2009* (Karthala, 2012). For ideas about mass distribution of very basic consumption items and thus taking their production out of the equation, the issue of *JSAS* XXXVII(4) (2011), particularly Jonathan Crush and Michael Frayne, 'Supermarket Expansion and the Informal Food Economy in Southern African Cities: Implications for Urban Food Security' and Daniel Warshawsky, 'Foodbank Johannesburg, State and Civil Society in Post-Apartheid Johannesburg', are suggestive.

Many writers in the West, usually with little understanding of China, have written on the arrival of this new player on the African economic turf very much from the outside but a more convincing picture with some detail has gradually emerged with other 'emerging market' players also considered. An introduction to the subject could include Ian Taylor, 'Emerging Powers, State Capitalism and the Oil Sector in Africa', *ROAPE*, 141 (2014); Ching Kwon Lee, 'Spectre of Global China', *New Left Review*, 2nd series (2014), 89; Lucy Corkin, *Uncovering African Agency: Angola's Management of China's Credit Lines* (Farnham, 2013) and Luke Patey, *The New Kings of Crude: China, India and the Global Struggle for Oil in Sudan and South Sudan* (London, 2014).

For a radical take on famines and how to view them, Alex de Waal, *Famine Crimes in Africa; Politics and the Disaster Relief Industry in Africa* (James Currey, Indiana UP etc, 1997) and David Keen, *The Benefits of Famine: A Political Economy of Famine and Relief in Southwestern Sudan 1983–89* (Princeton University Press, 1994), are eye-opening. The deagrarianisation hypothesis is forcefully pursued by Deborah Bryceson and Vali Jamal, *Farewell to Farms: Deagrarianisation and Employment in Africa* (Ashgate, 1997). Localised insights on privatisation of land are given attention in Pauline Peters,

'Conflicts over Land and Threats to Customary Tenure in Africa', *AA*, 449 (2011), Festus Boamah, 'How and Why Chiefs Formalise Land Use in Recent Times: The Politics of Land Dispossession through Biofuels Investment in Ghana', *ROAPE*, 141 (2014), Hanan Sabea, 'Reviving the Dead; Entangled Histories in the Privatisation of the Tanzanian Sisal Industry', *Africa*, 71 (2001), Nicholas Sitko, 'Fractured Governance and Local Fictions: The Exclusionary Nature of a Clandestine Land Market in Southern Zambia', *Africa*, 80 (2010) and Kelly Askew et al., 'Of Land and Legitimacy; A Tale of Two Lawsuits', *Africa*, 83 (2013). For an unambiguous defender of private land ownership, see Jean Ensminger, *Making a Market: The Institutional Transformation of an African Society* (Cambridge University Press, 1992). What can happen when politics and privatisation meet in the urban context is signalled by Luke M Obala and Michael Mattingly, 'Ethnicity, Corruption and Violence in Urban Land Conflict in Kenya', *Urban Studies*, LI, 13 (2013).

The circumstances under which new kinds of agriculture (and industry) have taken off in certain African countries are captured by Peter Gibbon 'Present-Day Capitalism, the New International Trade Regime and Africa', *ROAPE*, 91 (2002). On changing conditions in African agriculture in recent years, a very small selection might include Michael Mortimore and William Adams, *Working the Sahel: Environment and Society in Northern Nigeria* (Routledge, 1999); K. Swindell, M. A. Iliya and A. B. Mamman, 'Making a Profit, Making a Living: Commercial Food Farming and Urban Hinterlands in North-west Nigeria', *Africa*, 69 (1999); Paul Clough, *Morality and Economic Growth in Rural West Africa: Indigenous Accumulation in Hausaland* (Berghahn, 2014); Stefano Ponte, 'The Politics of Ownership: Tanzanian Coffee Policy in the Age of Liberal Reformism', *AA*, 413 (2004), and Carlos Oya, 'Stories of Rural Accumulation in Africa: Trajectories and Transitions among Rural Capitalists in Senegal', *Journal of Agrarian Change*, 7 (2007). These all reveal more continuity and adaptation as well as rural class differentiation than a scare literature on land-grabs tends to allow for. Henry Bernstein, *Class Dynamics of Agrarian Change* (Fernwood, 2010) contains an assessment that includes African agrarian life in a global picture.

CHAPTER 14. A New Africa: Cultural and Social History Since Independence

How to treat 'modernity' in Africa is the subject of a special issue of the *American Historical Review*, 116 (3) (2011). For very different discussions, readers might explore Kwame Gyekye, *Tradition and Modernity: Philosophical Reflections on the African Experience* (Oxford UP, 1997) and John and Jean Comaroff, *Modernity and its Malcontents* (University of Chicago Press, 1993).

For guides to the rise and importance of cities in contemporary Africa, see Bill Freund, *The African City: A History* (Cambridge University Press, 2007) but also the following, principally collections: Garth Myers, *African Cities: Alternative Visions of Urban Theory and Practice* (Zed, 2011), Okwui Enwezor et al., *Under Siege: Four African Cities Freetown, Johannesburg, Kinshasa, Lagos* (Documenta 11 Platform 4, Hatje Cantz, 2002); Carole Rakodi, ed., *The*

Urban Challenge in Africa; Growth and Management of its Large Cities (United Nations Press, 1997); Abdou Maliq Simone, *For the City Yet to Come: Changing African Life in Four Cities* (Duke University Press, 2004); Filip de Boeck and Marie-Françoise Plissart, *Kinshasa: Tales of the Invisible City* (Ludion, n.d.) and Charles Didier Gondola, *Villes Miroirs: Migrations et identités urbaines à Kinshasa et Brazzaville* (L'Harmattan 1997). On the question of urban land, Jean-Luc Piermay, *Citadins et la quête de sol dans les villes d'Afrique centrale* (L'Harmattan, 1993) is a patient and illuminating monograph. These and other volumes point to the drastic shortcomings of urban services, particularly those aimed at the general population. For an example of a large literature, Herman Chitonge, 'Cities Beyond Networks: The Status of Water Services for the Urban Poor in African Cities', *African Studies*, LXXIII (2014), is straightforward. See also David McDonald and Greg Ruiters, eds, *The Age of Commodity: Water Privatization in Southern Africa* (Earthscan, 2005). Women's growing significance in the Central African economy was the subject of an excellent chapter by Karen Hansen in Jan-Bart Gewald et al., *One Zambia, Many Histories: Towards a History of Post-colonial Zambia*, op.cit. and in some cases, gender roles have evolved in a way favourable to women's initiatives in rural settings too: Amrit Heyer, 'The Gender of Wealth: Markets and Power in Central Kenya', *ROAPE*, 107 (2006). The tragic story of AIDS and its reception in much of Africa is powerfully expressed in Jonny Steinberg's *Three Letter Plague: A Young Man's Journey through a Great Epidemic* (Jonathan Ball, 2008).

On urban economies, consumerism and credit, see, apart from the above, Arne Tostensen, Inge Tvedten and Mariken Vaa, eds, *Associational Life in African Cities: Popular Responses to the Urban Crisis* (Nordiska Afrikainstitutet, 2001); Emmanuel Seyni Ndione, *L'economie urbaine en Afrique; le don et le recours* (Karthala and Enda Graf Sahel, 1994); Deborah Bryceson and Deborah Potts, eds, *African Urban Economies: Viability, Vitality or Vitiation?* (Palgrave Macmillan, 2006); Abdou Maliq Simone and Abdelghani Abouhani, eds, *Urban Africa: Changing Contours of Survival in the City* (CODESRIA, Zed and UNISA Press, 2005) and the special issue of *Africa*, 81(1) (2012). Apart from Martin Verlet, *Grandir à Nima, Ghana, Les figures de travail dans dans un faubourg populaire d'Accra* (Karthala, 2005) as discussed in this chapter, Karen Hansen, *Keeping House in Lusaka* (Columbia University Press, 1997) and Ilsa Glaser Schuster, *New Women of Lusaka* (Mayfield, 1979) are interesting in providing some parallels but with more emphasis on the lot of women. The way elites construct their homes stage by stage on the outskirts of Accra is well-told in Ian Yeboah, 'Structural Adjustment and Emerging Urban Form in Accra, Ghana', *Africa Today*, 47(2) (2000). This model is also to be found in Philippe Antoine, *Abidjan; côté cours* (ORSTOM/Karthala, 1987). A further comparison with a relatively older city that had some developed contours before the arrival of colonists may be made via Adrienne Polomack, 'Mixity and Territoriality in a Rapidly Expanding City: How Dar es Salaam was Shaped by its Suburbs' in Bernard Calas, ed., *From Dar es Salaam to Bongoland, Urban Mutations in Tanzania* (Mkuki ya Nyota, 2010). If Polomack stresses gradualism and stages, Inge Brinkman suggests the drastic impact of war and forcible migration in rapid change in 'War and Identity in Angola; Two Case-Studies',

Lusotopie (2003). The example of a Nigerian city where some industrial production has emerged out of the so-called informal sector is brought forth in rich detail by Kate Meagher, 'Social Capital, Social Liabilities and Political Capital; Social Networks and Informal Manufacturing in Nigeria', *AA*, 421 (2006).

For the idea of creolisation, see Ulf Hannerz, 'The World in Creolisation', *Africa*, 57 (1987). Leisure is taken up as a topic in the *International Journal of African Historical Studies*, 35(1) (2002), 'Leisure in African History' special issue following Martin's pioneering work and Laura Fair's conceptually bolder *Pastimes and Politics: Culture, Community and Identity in Post-Abolition Urban Zanzibar 1890–1945* (James Currey, 2001). Market literature is covered in a still insight-yielding study by the Nigerian Emmanuel Obiechina, *An African Popular Literature: A Study of Onitsha Market Pamphlets* (Cambridge UP, 1973). For an excellent study of later popular literature in Hausa, see Graham Furniss in Barber, op. cit..

The early impact of film in an African setting is discussed by James Burns, 'John Wayne on the Zambesi; Cinema, Empire and the American Western in British Central Africa', *IJAHS*, 35 (2002), Nigerian film and magazines are the subject of Bruce Larkin, *Signal and Noise: Media Infrastructure and Urban Culture in Nigeria* (Duke University Press, 2008) and 'Indian Films and Nigerian Lovers: Media and the Creation of Parallel Modernities', *Africa*, 67 (1997). Also interesting is Matthias Krings and Onookome Okomo, *Global Nollywood: The Transnational Dimensions of an African Video Film Industry* (Indiana University Press, 2013). For the limited political element, see Akin Aderonkan, 'Practising "Democracy" in Nigerian Films', *AA*, 433 (2008). Ned Bertz, 'Indian Ocean World Cinema; Viewing the History of Race, Diaspora and Nationalism in Urban Tanzania', *Africa*, 81 (2011), discusses the reception of Bollywood in another country. For parallels with that other medium, television, in the Congo, see Katrien Pype, 'Media Celebrity, Charisma and Morality in Post-Mobutu Kinshasa', *JSAS*, XXXV (2009). Affection for kung fu films comes out in Charles Ambler, 'Mass Media and Leisure in Africa,' *IJAHS*, 35 (2002).

A rich and varied introduction to the world of African music today is Eric Charry, ed., *Hip Hop Africa: New African Music in a Globalising World* (Indiana University Press, 2012) with a much broader coverage than the title suggests. Some of his contributors look, especially via drumming techniques, at links to older musical forms in Africa. The roots of commercial African popular music are explored in Nate Plageman, *High Life Saturday Night, Popular Music and Social Change in Urban Ghana* (Indiana University Press, 2013), Richard Shane, 'Roots in Reverse; Cubanismo in Twentieth Century Senegalese Music', *IJAHS*, 35, 2002, and Steven Feld, *Jazz Cosmopolitanism in Accra* (Duke University Press, 2012). For an excellent conspectus, Thomas Turino, cited above, is very readable. See also Mark Perullo, *Live from Dar es Salaam: Popular Music and Tanzania's Music Economy* (Indiana University Press, 2011). For hip hop, a selection of writers could include Koen Stroeken, 'Immunizing Strategies: Hip-Hop and Critique in Tanzania', *Africa*, 75 (2005), Andrew Eisenberg, 'Hip-Hop and Cultural Citizenship on Kenya's Swahili Coast', *Africa*, 82 (2012), Mwenda Ntarangwi, *East African Hip Hop. Youth Culture and Globalization* (University of Illinois Press, 2009) and R. Fredericks, '"The Old Man is Dead": Hip Hop and the Arts of Citizenship of Senegalese Youth', *Antipode*, 46 (2014). For a broader and politically connected analysis of the world of disconnected West African youth, Sasha Newell, already cited (for Chapter 13), is revealing and sobering.

For two modest but telling pieces of scholarship that suggest the moral crisis that many Africans less taken with consumerism feel that they are facing in an unjust world, see Ann Kaler, '"When They See Money, They Think It's Life": Money, Modernity and Morality in Two Sites in Rural Malawi', *JSAS*, XXXII (2006) and Jörg Wiegratz, 'Fake Capitalism? The Dynamics of Neoliberal Moral Restructuring and Pseudo-Development: The Case of Uganda', *ROAPE*, 124 (2010).

The political mobilisation up to a point of established churches in Africa is examined by Paul Gifford, *Christianity, Politics and Public Life in Kenya* (Hurst, 2009), Sara Rich Dorman, '"Rocking the Boat?", Church-NGOs and Democratization in Zimbabwe', *AA*, 402 (2002), Boniface Dulani, 'Nurtured from the Pulpit: The Emergence and Growth of Malawi's Democratic Movement' in Stephen Ellis and Ineke van Kessel, eds., *Movers and Shakers*, op.cit., 138–55 and Galia Sabar-Friedman, 'Church and State in Kenya 1986–92', *AA*, 382 (1997). The activities of a forerunner of Pentecostalism in Africa are traced by Adam Mohr in 'Capitalism, Chaos and Christian Healing: the Faith Tabernacle Congregation in Southern Colonial Ghana' *JAH*, 52 (2011). Mohr looks at the way Pentecostal type practices have taken over much of the Presbyterian Church in Ghana: *Enchanted Calvinism: Labor Migration, Afflicting Spirits and Christian Therapy in the Presbyterian Church of Ghana* (University of Rochester Press, 2013).

The Pentecostal invasion and the changing nature of Christianity have been addressed in Ruth Marshall, *Political Spiritualities: The Pentecostal Revolution in Nigeria* (University of Chicago Press, 2009) and less sympathetically by Paul Gifford, *Christianity, Politics and Public Life in Kenya* (Hurst, 2009) and David Maxwell, '"Catch the Cockerel Before Dawn"; Pentecostalism and Politics in Post-Colonial Zimbabwe', *Africa*, 70 (2000). In addition, other sources would include the special issue of *ROAPE*, 110 (2006); Daniel Jordan Smith, '"The Arrow of God"; Pentecostalism, Inequality and the Supernatural in South-eastern Nigeria', *Africa,* 71 (2001) and Afe Adogame, 'How God Became a Nigerian: Religious Impulse and the Unfolding of a Nation', *JCAS*, XXVIII (2010).

A collection surveying the changes in Islam discussed in this chapter is Louis Brenner, ed., *Muslim Identity and Social Change in Sub-Saharan Africa* (C. Hurst, 1993). More traditional and comprehensive is Nehemia Levtzion and Randall L. Pouwels, eds, *The History of Islam in Africa* (Ohio University Press, James Currey and David Philip, 1993). For the rise of stricter Islam in northern Nigeria, Murray Last, 'Search for Security in Muslim Northern Nigeria', *Africa*, 78 (2008) and Paul Clough, 'Gender Relations in Islamizing Hausaland', *Africa*, 78 (2008), are very instructive. The impact on the wide range of media and print material in Hausa is briefly mentioned by Graham Furniss in the Barber collection. On the other hand, Benjamin Soares, 'An

Islamic Social Movement in Contemporary West Africa: NASFAT of Nigeria', in Stephen Ellis and Ineke van Kessel, op.cit., shows the resilience of moderate tendencies amongst Yoruba Muslims in a movement clearly influenced by Pentecostal Christians. The Senegal Muridiyya continue to have a kind of flexibility and ability to speak to today's needs that is discussed in Jean-François Havard, 'La phénomène Cheik Bethio Thiounbe et le djihah migratoire des étudiants sénégalais (Thiamtakones)' in Farida Adelkhah and Jean-Francois Bayart, eds, *Voyages de développement; émigration, commerce, exil* (Karthala, 2007). Ellen Foley and Cheikh Babou, 'Diaspora, Faith and Science; Building a Mouride Hospital in Senegal', *AA*, 438 (2011) and Linda Beck, 'Reining in the Marabouts: Democratization and Local Governance in Senegal', *AA* (2001) have interesting takes on the Muridiyya. Increasingly successful Salafist activity in another country where Muslims are a minority is considered by Terje Østebrø, 'Local Reformers and the Search for Change; The Emergence of Salafism in Bale, Ethiopia', *Africa,* 81 (2011). In Mali, the change is comparable but perhaps less dramatic: see Louis Brenner, *Controlling Knowledge: Religion, Power and Schooling in a West African Muslim Society* (Indiana UP, 2001).

The use of contemporary technology by West African Muslims is highlighted in Cheikh Guèye, 'New Information and Communication Technology Use by Muslim Mourides in Senegal', *ROAPE*, 98 (2003), and Serigne Mansour Tall, 'Senegalese Emigrés: New Information and Communication Technologies', *ROAPE*, 99 (2004). This is also the theme of Dorothea Schulz, *Muslims and New Media in Africa: Pathways to God* (Indiana University Press, 2012), which looks as well at the way some Muslim women, far from being victims, embrace and use the new Islam to make an unprecedented social mark. Finally, for a way of looking at globalisation not dependent on technology, Giles Mohan and A. B. Zack-Williams, in 'Globalisation from Below: Conceptualising the Role of the African Diasporas in Africa's Development', *ROAPE*, 92 (2002), offer an interesting alternative.

Index